Ruinen

Reflexionen über Gewalt, Chaos und Vergänglichkeit

Ruins

Reflexions about Violence, Chaos and Transience

Hans Dieter Schaal

Ruinen
Reflexionen über Gewalt, Chaos und Vergänglichkeit

Ruins
Reflexions about Violence, Chaos and Transience

Edition Axel Menges

Besonders danken möchte ich meiner Frau Verena
sowie Rikola-Gunnar Lüttgenau und Torben Giese
für die Mithilfe an diesem Buch.

My special thanks go to my wife Verena as well as
to Rikola-Gunnar Lüttgenau and Torben Giese for
their help on this book.

Druck und Bindearbeiten/Printing and binding:
Graspo CZ, a. s., Zlín, Tschechische Republik/
Czech Republic

Projektleitung / Project management: Dorothea
Duwe
Übersetzung ins Englische / Translation into Eng-
lish: Ilze Müller, Michael Robinson
Lektorat / Editing: Verena Schaal, Nora Krehl-von
Mühlendahl, Jürgen Banse
Design: Axel Menges
Layout: Helga Danz

Vorwort

Denken wir über den Begriff »Ruine« nach, fallen uns Themen ein, die mit Zerstörung, Verwüstung, Zusammenbruch, Krieg, Attentat, Erdbeben, Ende, Resignation, Krise (Ölkrise, Stahlkrise, Börsenkrise, Bankenkrise), Scheitern, Bankrott und Krankheit zu tun haben … Ruine … ruinieren … Ruin … ruinös … ruinenartig … Ruinengrundstück …

Primär wird der Begriff »Ruine« im Bereich der Architektur verwendet. Ist ein Gebäude zerfallen oder zerstört und steht nur noch mit wenigen Mauern vor uns, nennen wir das Gebilde eine Ruine. In diesem Zustand ist es für den Gebrauch – das Schutzsuchen und Bewohnen – nicht mehr verwendbar. Ein wertloses Denkmal, das nur dazu in der Lage ist, Erinnerungen zu wecken.

Für einen Architekten, dessen Aufgabe es sein sollte, aufrecht und stolz dastehende Häuser zu entwerfen und zu bauen, stellt die Ruine eine Provokation dar, eine Verneinung seiner Absichten. Er, der vom Stützen und Tragen, vom Schweben und von geordneten, trockenen Innenräumen träumt, muß jetzt sehen, daß Dachbalken kreuz und quer durch Kellerdächer gestürzt sind, daß kein Fußboden mehr begehbar ist und Treppenhäuser nur noch wie sinnlose, gerippte Formen an Wandfragmenten hängen, unbetretbar für Auf- und Abstiege. Die einstigen Besitzer und Bewohner sind verschwunden, Wind und Wetter dringen bis ins Innerste vor, und die Natur erobert sich den ihr einst genommenen Raum zurück. Erste Baumtriebe sprießen aus Ziegelbergen und Betontrümmern, die sich im Keller aufgetürmt haben. Vögel und Fledermäuse fliegen, auf der Suche nach Futter und Nistplätzen, durch Fensterhöhlen. Steht eine Ruine über Jahre ungenutzt in der Landschaft oder in der Stadt, dann gewöhnt man sich an ihren Anblick, sie verliert ihren provokativen Charakter, der negative Aspekt des Sterbens, Verwesens und des Todes verschwindet langsam. Gelassen und ruhig fügt sie sich, ihrer Aufgabe als Klimahülle und Schutzraum enthoben, in den Naturkreislauf ein. Irgendwann wird sie von Gras, Efeu, wildem Wein und Brombeersträuchern überwuchert sein. Die meisten berühmten architektonischen Kulturzeugnisse der Welt ragen nur als zerfallene und zerfallende Objekte in unsere Gegenwart hinein: die Pyramiden von Gizeh, die Tempel von Karnak und Luxor, die Ruinen auf dem Machu Picchu, in Angkor Wat, Borobudur und Gandhara, in Jerusalem und Petra, in Babylon und Ur, in Troja, Pergamon und Ephesos, in Knossos, Mykene, Pompeji, Epidauros, Delphi und Karthago, die Ruinen der Akropolis in Athen und des Forum Romanum in Rom. Warum viele Kulturen, Städte und Religionen untergegangen sind, darüber rätseln Fachwissenschaftler und phantasievoll spekulierende Laien bis heute. Waren es Klimakatastrophen, selbstverursachte – etwa Raubbau an der Natur – oder fremdverschuldete Vulkanausbrüche oder Meteoriteneinschläge, waren es Hungerkatastrophen, Epidemien, Kriege und Niederlagen oder Machtkämpfe innerhalb der eigenen Herrscherfamilien? Führten zu großer Luxus, Verweichlichung, Dekadenz, mangelnde Verteidigung, übertriebene Ausbeutung unterworfener Sklaven, Geldspekulation zum Untergang?

Archäologen und Reiseführer versuchen, uns die Reste zu erklären, ihre Geschichte zu erzählen und das einstige Aussehen der Städte zu rekonstruieren. Das eigentliche Ruinensein wird dabei oft ignoriert und kaum bewertet. In Wirklichkeit gleicht jeder Besuch einer archäologischen Fundstätte dem Besuch auf einem Friedhof.

Oft sind reale Gräber, die in der Nähe der untergegangenen Städte und Tempel entdeckt werden, die Hauptfundstätten von wertvollem Kulturgut. Neben Skeletten tauchen Vasen, Schmuck, Kleidungsstücke, Waffen und manchmal auch schriftliche Nachrichten im Tageslicht auf. Der Glaube an das Jenseits und an ein Leben nach dem Tode brachte die einstigen Erdenbewohner auf die Idee, diese Zeitkapseln mit ihren Flaschenpostnachrichten anzulegen. Viele Kulturen allerdings, wie die der Indianer und der Kelten, kannten keine Schrift. So sind heutige Archäologen darauf angewiesen, die gefundenen Objekte als stumme Indizien zu betrachten und zu deuten. Restauratoren versuchen später in Labors, die ursprüngliche Zusammensetzung des Trümmer-Puzzles aufzuspüren und zu rekonstruieren. Nur widerwillig und selten lassen sie den Ruinenzustand der Objekte auf sich beruhen und geben sich mit der rätselhaften Wirkung von Zeitablagerungen und Zerstörungen zufrieden.

Jede Geschichtserzählung ist eine fiktive Rekonstruktion. Verflossene Zeit und gelebtes Leben bleiben ein für allemal verschwunden und zeichnen sich – wenn überhaupt – nur in dürftigen Spuren ab. Die Idee, aus Höhlenzeichnungen den Bewußtseinszustand einstiger Steinzeitmenschen und gar deren Lebensabläufe zu rekonstruieren, scheint illusionär. Alle einst belebten Landschaften bergen Spuren und Ruinen menschlicher Zivilisation in sich. Auch eine der evolutionären Urformen unserer Spezies fanden die Forscher im afrikanischen Savannenboden. Der Sand

Preface

When we think about the word »ruin«, the ideas that occur to us have to do with destruction, devastation, collapse, war, assassination, earthquakes, endings, resignation, crises (oil crisis, steel crisis, stock exchange crisis, bank crisis), failure, bankruptcy and illness ... Ruin ... to ruin ... ruination ... ruinous ... ruin-like ...

The expression »ruin« is used primarily in the sphere of architecture. When a building is dilapidated or destroyed and only a few walls still remain standing, we call the structure a »ruin«. In this condition it is no longer fit for use – shelter and human habitation. A worthless monument, capable only of bringing back memories.

For an architect, whose task should be the designing and building of upright, proud houses, a ruin represents a provocation, a negation of his intentions. The architect, who dreams of buttresses and pillars, of suspension and ordered, dry interiors, is now forced to see roof beams that have collapsed crisscross through basement roofs, floors you can't walk on anymore and stairwells that merely hang like meaningless ribbed shapes from fragments of wall that no one may climb up or down. The original owners and inhabitants have vanished, wind and weather are free to enter into the innermost rooms, and nature recaptures the space that was once taken from it. The first young trees sprout from bricks and concrete rubble that have piled up in the basement. Birds and bats, in search of food and nesting places, fly through unglazed windows. If a ruin stands unused in the landscape or in the city for years, people get used to the sight, it loses its provocative character; the negative aspect of dying, decay and death slowly vanishes. Calmly and peacefully, relieved of its task as protection from the climate and as shelter, it adjusts to the cycles of nature. At some point it will become overgrown with grass, ivy, Virginia creepers and blackberry vines. Most of the famous architectural cultural monuments of the world protrude into our present only as decaying or decayed objects: the pyramids of Gizeh, the temples of Karnak and Luxor, the ruins on Machu Picchu, in Angkor Wat, Borobodur and Gandhara, the ruins in Jerusalem and Petra, in Babylon and Ur, the ruins in Troy, Pergamon and Ephesus, the ruins in Knossos, Mycenae, Pompeii, Epidauros, Delphi and Carthage, the ruins of the Acropolis in Athens and the Forum Romanum in Rome. Why did many cultures, cities and religions perish? Experts and wildly speculating laymen are still puzzling over this question. Was it due to climatic disasters, caused by the people themselves – overexploitation of nature perhaps – or other reasons – volcanic eruptions or the impacts of meteorites, was it catastrophes caused by hunger or disease, wars and defeats or power struggles within local ruling families? Was the downfall caused by excessive luxury, emasculation, decadence, lack of adequate defense, overexploitation of subjugated slaves or financial speculation?

Archeologists and tour guides try to explain the remains to us, tell their story and reconstruct what the cities once looked like. The actual fact that these are ruins is often ignored in the process and hardly evaluated. In reality every visit to an archeological site is like a visit to a cemetery.

Often real graves that are excavated near the lost cities and temples are the principal places where valuable cultural treasures are found. Not only skeletons, but vases, jewelry, clothing, weapons and sometimes written documents as well are unearthed. The belief in the hereafter and in a life after death gave people in former times the idea of creating these time capsules with their messages for posterity. To be sure, many cultures, such as those of the American Indians and the Celts, had no writing. Thus archeologists today have to rely on the found objects as silent evidence. Restorers in labs later attempt to piece together the ruin fragments into the original jigsaw puzzle. Only reluctantly and rarely they leave the ruined objects alone and are satisfied with the mysterious effect of the sediments of time and the destruction it wreaks.

Every historical narrative is a fictitious reconstruction. Time, once gone, and life, once lived, are lost for ever, leaving only scanty traces – if any. The idea of reconstructing the state of consciousness, let alone the lives, of Stone Age people from cave drawings seems illusionary. All landscapes that were once inhabited contain vestiges and ruins of human civilization. One of the evolutionary prototypes of our species was also found in the earth, in the African savanna, by research scientists. The sand had buried »Lucy« beneath it. This loving name was given to her by the two men who found her, Donald Johanson and Tom Gray, when, in 1974, they came upon the skeleton of the creature that was the link between apes and human beings. So it was there, in Africa, in the Ethiopian Afar Desert, north of Addis Ababa, that the crucial evolutionary step took place; ever since, we have walked upright and looked ahead at what the future has in store for us.

But let us zoom even further back and look down from a fictitious spaceship at our planet circling freely in the cosmos. This planet, too, is really a ruin, although it is overgrown by vibrant

hatte »Lucy« unter sich begraben. Diesen liebevollen Namen gaben ihr die beiden Finder Donald Johanson und Tom Gray, als sie 1974 auf das Skelett des zwischen Affen und Menschen vermittelnden Wesens stießen. Dort also, in Afrika, in der äthiopischen Afar-Wüste, nördlich von Addis Abeba, geschah vielleicht der entscheidende, evolutionäre Schritt; seither gehen wir aufrecht und schauen, was die Zukunft für uns bereithält.

Doch zoomen wir noch weiter zurück und blicken aus einem fiktiven Raumschiff auf unsere frei im Weltall kreisende Erdkugel. Auch sie ist in Wirklichkeit eine Ruine, obwohl sie von der Natur lebendig überwuchert und von Menschen und Tieren bevölkert wird. Alle aus den Meeren herausragenden Erdmassen und Gebirge wuchsen einst bei monumentalen Verschiebe- und Eruptionsvorgängen aus dem Erdmantel hervor (in der *Bibel* als »Schöpfung« beschrieben), aber seit ihrer Erstarrung zu Fels kennen sie nur ein Ziel, und das lautet: Zerfall zu Steinbrocken, zu Kies und schließlich zu Sand. Wind und Wetter arbeiten jede Minute an dieser Zersetzung. Vielleicht wird die Erde eines Tages, nach dem Ende der menschlichen Zivilisationen und dem Verschwinden der Atmosphäre, aussehen wie die Mondruine: leer und tot, zerschossen von Meteoriten. Eine kugelförmige Kraterwüste, die einsam und schweigend durch das Weltall kreist. Gemessen an den Jahrmillionen vor und nach uns, an dem unendlich großen Raum um uns, wird die menschliche Zivilisation auf der Erdkugel nur eine Episode gewesen sein, geprägt von Evolution, Kriegen, Tod und unzähligen Ruinen.

Zunächst jedoch gibt es uns Menschen noch, und mit all den technischen Erfindungen der letzten hundert Jahre kann man sagen, daß keine Zeit besser in der Lage war, das eigene Leben und die eigene Kultur auf Dauer zu konservieren. Der uralte Menschheitstraum, Bilder der Realität und damit des gelebten Lebens als Photos und Filme dauerhaft und jederzeit abrufbar aufzuzeichnen, stellt heute kein Problem mehr dar. Nahezu jeder Mensch auf der Erde hat Zugriff auf diese Techniken. Das Archiv expandiert mit unglaublicher Geschwindigkeit und platzt aus allen Nähten. Theoretisch läßt sich heute jede Stunde eines Menschenlebens in Originalzeit dokumentieren, vorausgesetzt eine Kamera läuft immer mit. Zweite und dritte mediale Parallelwelten sind denkbar und existieren bereits. Damit scheint es eine Möglichkeit zu geben, den Tod mit seiner Endgültigkeit medial zu überlisten und der Vergänglichkeit entgegenzuarbeiten. Bei genauer Betrachtung bleibt das Projekt absurd, weil niemand in Zukunft die Datenmengen je anschauen kann. Also würden hier monumentale Medienarchive heranwachsen (oder sie wachsen bereits), die hoffentlich ihr eigenes Zerstörungsprogramm in sich tragen und so im Laufe der Zeit zu monumentalen Parallelwelt-Ruinen zerfallen.

Ich werde im folgenden näher auf verschiedene Ruinenarten, Ruinen- und Untergangsgeschichten aus der Mythologie, der Geschichte und der Gegenwart eingehen. Da jedes intakte Gebäude auch eine potentielle Ruine darstellt (oder in sich trägt, wie wir Menschen alle den Tod in uns tragen), stellt dies ein fast unendlich ausferndes Thema dar. Deshalb beschränke ich mich auf Bilder und Ruinen, die mir besonders wichtig erscheinen. Dabei werden echte Ruinen genauso berücksichtigt wie unecht-künstliche, gemalte, beschriebene, photographierte, fiktionale und mediale.

Natürlich hat jede Zeit und jede Gesellschaft ihr eigenes, sehr spezielles Verhältnis zum Phänomen »Ruine«. Romantische Zeiten interessieren sich mehr dafür als nüchtern-funktionale. Während des Zweiten Weltkriegs wurde den meisten betroffenen Menschen jede vielleicht vorhandene Liebe zu Ruinen ausgetrieben. Am Ende mußten die Ausgebombten in städtischen Ruinenlandschaften leben, die alles bisher Gekannte an Totalität und Grausamkeit übertrafen.

Nach dem Krieg begann die Zeit des Wiederaufbaus und damit der Ruinenauslöschung. Manche Historiker sprechen davon, daß in dieser Zeit noch mehr alte Gebäude durch Abriß zerstört worden seien als während des gesamten Krieges. Irgendwann in den 1970er Jahren waren fast alle Kriegsspuren verschwunden, und der architektonische Funktionalismus beherrschte die nüchtern-modern gewordenen Städte. Jetzt begannen die Bewohner, sich darüber klarzuwerden, daß diese neue, kahle Umgebung nicht ihren Vorstellungen von Romantik und Wärme entsprach. Alexander Mitscherlich nannte es *Die Unwirtlichkeit unserer Städte*.

Viele Menschen wurden von nostalgischen Gedanken befallen und sehnten sich nach alten, maroden Städten, nach dem malerischen Charme italienischer, griechischer oder spanischer Häuser und Gassen. Man begann temporär, den eigenen städtischen Umgebungen zu entfliehen und die Traumorte tatsächlich aufzusuchen. Der Tourismus lief auf Hochtouren. Erst mit der aufkommenden Postmoderne, Ende der 1970er Jahre, begannen sich zeitgenössische Architekten mit diesen Phänomenen zu beschäftigen. Malerische und historisierende Entwürfe galten nun als avantgardistisch.

Manche neu entstanden Gebäude spielten jetzt mit längst untergegangenen Motiven, wie Sockel, Giebel, Säulen oder skulpturalem Bauschmuck. Der englische Architekt James Stirling er-

1. Öffnung mit scheinbar aus der Garagenwand der Neuen Staatsgalerie in Stuttgart, 1984, von James Stirling herausgefallenen Steinquadern.

1. Öffnung mit scheinbar aus der Garagenwand der Neuen Staatsgalerie in Stuttgart, 1984, von James Stirling herausgefallenen Steinquadern.

1. Opening with stone blocks that appear to have fallen out of the garage wall of James Stirling's Neue Staatsgalerie in Stuttgart, 1984.

vegetation and populated by human beings and animals. All the masses of earth and mountain ranges that project from the oceans once rose from the mantle of the earth when monumental shifts and eruptions took place (described as »creation« in the *Bible*), but ever since they solidified to rock, they have had only one goal: to disintegrate into boulders, gravel and finally sand. Wind and weather perform this task of erosion around the clock. Perhaps one day, after human civilizations have come to an end and the atmosphere disappears, the Earth will look like the lunar ruin, empty and dead, riddled with meteorites. A spherical desert full of craters, revolving lonely and silent through the universe. Measured in terms of the millions of years before and after us, and of the boundless space around us, human civilization on Planet Earth will have been just an episode, marked by evolution, wars, death and countless ruins.

But for the time being we humans still exist, and with all the technical inventions of the past hundred years one might say that no period in history was better able to preserve its own life and culture permanently. The age-old dream of the human race – recording images of reality and of the lives we live as photographs and films, long-lasting and accessible at all times – is not a problem anymore. Almost everyone on the planet has access to these technologies. The archive keeps expanding with incredible speed and is bursting at the seams. In theory every hour of a human life can be documented in real time, provided there is a camera rolling at all times. A second and third media parallel universe is conceivable and already exists. Thus there seems to be a possibility of outwitting death and its finality by means of the media, and of counteracting transience. On closer examination the project remains absurd, because no one in the future will ever be able to look at the vast amounts of data. That means monumental media archives would be accumulated (or are already accumulating) that hopefully have their own built-in program and will thus disintegrate into monumental parallel world ruins over time.

In this book, I will discuss in more detail various types of ruins, stories of ruins and destruction taken from myths, history and the present. Since every intact building also represents a potential ruin (or carries ruin within it just as we human beings all carry death within us), this topic is almost inexhaustible. That is why I will restrict myself to images and ruins that seem especially important to me. I shall consider not only actual ruins but also artificial, painted, described, photographed, fictional, and media ruins.

Of course every period and every society has its own very special relationship to the phenomenon of ruins. Romantic periods are more interested in it than sober and practical ones. During the Second World War, most people who were affected lost whatever love for ruins they had had. At the end, those whose homes had been bombed were forced to live amid the ruins of their cities in circumstances more overwhelming and cruel than anything they had ever known.

After the war, a time of reconstruction began, and thus the erasure of ruins. Some historians speak of the fact that during this period even more old buildings were razed than had been de-

laubte sich zuweilen skurril-romantische Ruinenscherze; so ließ er in seiner berühmten Stuttgarter Staatsgalerie die Steine einer Öffnung im Sockelgeschoß aus der Fassung purzeln, ganz so, als hätte sich eben ein ganz kleines Erdbeben ereignet. Wahrscheinlich wollte er darauf verweisen, daß trotz aller Geschichtsbezüge die Zeiten klassisch-vollendeter Architekturordnungen vorüber sind.

Im Jahr 2009, nach der Eröffnung des Neuen Museums in Berlin, der allerletzten großen rekonstruierten Kriegsruine in Deutschland, flammte überraschend eine neue Ruinendiskussion auf. Nach anfänglicher Skepsis war die Begeisterung von Kritikern und Besuchern über den Stüler-Chipperfield-Bau so überwältigend positiv, daß man fast von einer neuen Ruineneuphorie sprechen konnte. Diese neu aufbrechende Nostalgie, die wahrscheinlich immer noch in einer tiefen Ablehnung vieler Menschen gegenüber der modernen Architektur wurzelt, ist vielleicht tatsächlich der Beginn einer neuen »Ruinenromantik«, wie sie der konservative Schriftsteller Martin Mosebach in einem Gespräch mit der *Süddeutschen Zeitung* am 13. Januar 2010 konstatierte.

Neben dieser konservativ gestimmten, bildungsbürgerlichen Gesellschaftsschicht hat sich in den letzten Jahrzehnten eine immer stärker werdende Bewegung von »grün« motivierten Menschen entwickelt, die ausschließlich in der ökologischen Wende das Heil der Architektur, ja der ganzen Welt zu finden glauben. Ihr Grundgefühl wird von einer tiefen Skepsis gegenüber der technischen Zivilisation, der rabiaten Ausbeutung aller Bodenschätze und der kapitalistischen Gier bestimmt. Wahrscheinlich würden Kritiker aus diesem Umfeld im Motiv der Ruine ein lächerliches Symbol der Dekadenz und des überflüssigen Gartenschmucks erkennen. Ihr Ruinenbild wird von dem Katastrophenszenario in Tschernobyl geprägt, jenem Wrack eines Atomkraftwerks, das heute mit einem dicken Betonmantel umhüllt ist, immer noch strahlt und zu einer tödlichen Gefährdung der Natur geworden ist.

stroyed during the war. At one point in the 1970s almost all traces of the war had disappeared, and architectural functionalism predominated in the cities, which had become sober and modern. Now the inhabitants began to realize that this new, bleak environment was not in keeping with their ideas of romanticism and warmth. Mitscherlich called it *Die Unwirtlichkeit unserer Städte* (*The Inhospitability of Our Cities*).

Many people were filled with nostalgia and longed for the old, ailing cities, the picturesque charm of Italian, Greek or Spanish houses and alleyways. People began to seek temporary escape from their own urban environments and to actually travel to the places they dreamed of. It was the heyday of tourism. Not until the rise of Postmodernism in the late 1970s did contemporary architects begin to consider these phenomena. Picturesque and historicist designs were considered to be avant-garde.

A number of recently constructed buildings now toyed with long-defunct motifs such as plinths, gables, columns or sculptural architectural decoration. The British architect James Stirling occasionally indulged in scurrilous romantic jokes that involved ruins; thus, in his famous Stuttgart Staatsgalerie, he had stones tumbling from an opening frame in the basement floor of the building, exactly as if there had just been a tiny earthquake. No doubt he wanted to point out that in spite of all the historical references the days of classically perfect orders of architecture are over.

In 2009, after the opening of the Neues Museum in Berlin, the very last large reconstructed wartime ruin in Germany, a new discussion of ruins surprisingly flared up. After initial skepticism, the enthusiasm of critics and visitors about the Stüler-Chipperfield building was so overpoweringly positive that one could almost speak of a new ruin craze. This new outbreak of nostalgia, which is probably rooted in the fact that many people still profoundly reject modern architecture, is perhaps in fact the beginning of a new »romanticism of ruins«, as the conservative writer Martin Mosebach observed in an interview with *Süddeutsche Zeitung* on 13 January 2010.

In addition to this conservative, educated middle-class social stratum, the last decades have seen the rise of an ever growing »green« movement that believes the salvation of architecture – indeed, of the whole world – is only possible if there is an ecological about-face. Basically, they feel deep pessimism in the face of technological civilization, the ruthless exploitation of all resources and capitalist greed. Probably critics who share these views would consider the motif of the ruin to be a ridiculous symbol of decadence, like a surfeit of garden ornaments. Their idea of a ruin has been shaped by the catastrophe of Chernobyl, that wreck of a nuclear power plant which today is sheathed with a thick sarcophagus, still emits radiation, and has come to pose a deadly risk to the natural world.

1. Ruinen … Ruinen

Seit Menschen Städte bauen, gehören Stadtuntergänge durch Erdbeben, Überschwemmungen, Stürme, Brände, Überfälle und Kriege zum Gang der Geschichte. Aber es gibt auch Gebäude, die aus anderen Ursachen – wie mangelnde statische Kenntnisse, schlechte Gründungen, überzogene Größenverhältnisse oder Sprachverwirrung – einstürzten und zu Ruinen verfielen.

Den Archetyp einer solchen Architekturkatastrophe verkörpert der »Turmbau zu Babel«. Die *Bibel* berichtet vom Hochmut der Bauherren und Handwerker. Sie wollten eine Turmstadt bauen, die bis an die Wolken reicht. Allerdings war weder der schlechte Boden noch das Baumaterial der Grund dafür, daß der Bau aufgegeben werden mußte, sondern jene berühmte »Sprachverwirrung«, die der erzürnte Gott unter die Handwerker brachte. Die *Bibel* erzählt die Geschichte in wenigen Abschnitten: »Die Menschen hatten die gleiche Sprache und gebrauchten die gleichen Worte. Als sie von Osten aufbrachen, fanden sie eine Ebene im Land Schinar und siedelten sich dort an. Sie sagten zueinander: Auf, formen wir Lehmziegel und brennen wir sie zu Backsteinen. So dienten ihnen gebrannte Ziegel als Steine und Erdpech als Mörtel. Dann sagten sie: Auf, bauen wir uns eine Stadt und einen Turm mit einer Spitze bis zum Himmel und machen uns damit einen Namen, dann werden wir uns nicht über die ganze Erde zerstreuen.

Da stieg der Herr herab, um sich Stadt und Turm anzusehen, die die Menschenkinder bauten. Er sprach: Seht nur, ein Volk sind sie und eine Sprache haben sie alle. Und das ist erst der Anfang ihres Tuns. Jetzt wird ihnen nichts mehr unerreichbar sein, was sie sich auch vornehmen. Auf, steigen wir hinab und verwirren wir dort ihre Sprache, so daß keiner mehr die Sprache des andern versteht,

Der Herr zerstreute sie von dort aus über die ganze Erde und sie hörten auf, an der Stadt zu bauen. Darum nannte man die Stadt Babel (Wirrsal), denn dort hat der Herr die Sprache aller Welt verwirrt, und von dort aus hat er die Menschen über die ganze Erde zerstreut.« (Gen. 11:5–8)

Eine merkwürdige Geschichte, die zunächst harmlos erscheint, bei genauer Betrachtung jedoch vielschichtig schillert. Da ist ein Nomadenvolk, das sich zur Seßhaftigkeit entschließt und eine Stadt aus Ziegeln bauen will. In der Mitte der Anlage soll sich ein Turm erheben, der alles bisher Gebaute in den Schatten stellt. Hier, an diesem Punkt, schreckt Gott auf, empfindet den Vorgang als überheblich. Hybris, denkt er, treibt die Menschen an, sie wollen mich, Gott, herausfordern, provozieren und mir Konkurrenz machen. Wie ein eitler Künstler-Architekt reagiert der Schöpfer beleidigt, steigt aus seinem Himmel herab und schreitet ein. Als Strafe wäre ein Erdbeben angemessen, er jedoch entscheidet sich für die Sprachverwirrung. Eine originelle Lösung mit großer Tragweite, bis heute (wenn man die Geschichte für Wahrheit hält). Anstatt das Gebäude zu zerstören, sorgt er dafür, daß sich die Menschen untereinander nicht mehr verstehen, keine Gemeinsamkeiten, keine gemeinsame Kultur mehr haben, in Streit geraten und auseinandergehen müssen. Den Turmbau überlassen sie Wind, Wetter und zukünftigen Plünderern. Am Anfang des Endes steht demnach eine Sprachen- und Wortruine, ihr folgt die Bauruine erst viel später.

Zu allen Zeiten faszinierte Künstler diese (wahre oder erfundene) Hybris-Geschichte. Am berühmtesten wurde das Gemälde von Pieter Bruegel d. Ä. aus dem Jahr 1563, das heute im Wiener Kunsthistorischen Museum hängt. Der Turm sieht darauf aus wie ein riesiger, halbfertiger Termitenbau, der an das Kolosseum denken läßt. Kein Wunder, denn der Künstler hatte zehn Jahre zuvor Rom besucht. Den möglichen, späteren Einsturzvorgang haben zwei andere Künstler, die beiden Niederländer Maerten van Heemskerck und Cornelis Anthonizoon, ebenfalls Mitte des 16. Jahrhunderts, in Kupferstichen dargestellt. Werner Hofmann schreibt darüber in *Zauber der Medusa*: »Das Urbild menschlicher Hybris und Vermessenheit ist der Turm zu Babel – sein Einsturz steht für das rechte Maß, auf das der Mensch von Gott zurückverwiesen wird. Fasziniert nicht nur vom allegorischen Tiefsinn der Genesis-Erzählung, sondern vor allem auch von den Motiven des Stürzens, der Trümmer und Ruinen, traf sich die Darstellung des frevelhaften Bauwerks mit den Grunddispositionen des Manierismus. Diese Darstellung des zerstörten (von Cornelis Anthonizoon) geht jener des (noch) intakten Turmes durch Pieter Bruegel zeitlich voraus und spricht aus, was der spätere Meister nur andeuten wird.«

Heute wissen wir, daß es diesen Turmbau tatsächlich gegeben hat. Babylon liegt 80 km südlich von Bagdad am alten Euphratlauf. Von der ehemaligen Stadt haben sich nur zahlreiche mächtige Lehmschutthügel erhalten. Einer davon beinhaltet die Reste des ehemaligen Turmes. Nur ein Teil des Ruinenfeldes ist ausgegraben.

Auch andere antike Stadt- und Gebäudezerstörungen kennen wir nur aus Erzählungen. Homer berichtet in der *Ilias* vom Untergang Trojas. Heinrich Schliemann fand den Ruinenberg im 19.

1. Ruins … Ruins

Ever since human beings began building cities, the destruction of cities by earthquakes, floods, storms, fire, invasions and wars has been part of the course of history. But there are also buildings that have collapsed and fallen into disrepair for other reasons – a lack of knowledge of statics, poor foundations, excessive proportions or a confusion of tongues.

The archetype of such an architectural catastrophe is embodied by the »Tower of Babel«. The *Bible* tells us of the arrogance of the builders and workmen. They wanted to build a tower city that would reach the clouds. To be sure, neither the poor soil nor the building materials were the reason that the building had to be abandoned. The reason was that famous »confusion of tongues« that an angry God caused among the workmen. The *Bible* tells the story in a few short chapters: »Now the whole world had one language and a common speech. As men moved eastward, they found a plain in Shinar and settled there.

They said to each other, Come, let's make bricks and bake them thoroughly. They used brick instead of stone, and tar for mortar. Then they said, Come, let us build ourselves a city, with a tower that reaches to the heavens, so that we may make a name for ourselves and not be scattered over the face of the whole earth.

But the Lord came down to see the city and the tower that the men were building. The Lord said, If as one people speaking the same language they have begun to do this, then nothing they plan to do will be impossible for them. Come, let us go down and confuse their language so they will not understand each other.

So the Lord scattered them from there over all the earth, and they stopped building the city. That is why it was called Babel – because there the Lord confused the language of the whole world. From there the Lord scattered them over the face of the whole earth.«

(Genesis 11:5–8)

A remarkable story that initially appears to be harmless, but on closer examination can be interpreted in a number of ways. Here is a nomadic tribe that decides to become sedentary and build a town out of bricks. In the center there is to be a tower that overshadows everything ever built up to then. Here, at this point, God is startled, feeling that their plan is arrogant. The men are driven by hubris, he thinks, they are trying to challenge me, God, they want to provoke me and compete with me. The Creator is insulted, reacts like a vain artist-architect, descends from his Heaven and intervenes. An earthquake would be a fit punishment, but he opts for the confusion of language. An original solution with vast implications, to this day (if we consider this story to be true). Instead of the building collapsing he makes sure that people no longer understand each other, have nothing in common, no common culture anymore, that they begin to argue and have to disperse. They abandon the tower to wind, weather and future looters. Accordingly the beginning of the end is marked by the ruin of language and words, followed only much later by the ruined building.

Artists through the ages have been fascinated by this (true or invented) story of hubris. One of its most famous depictions is the painting by Pieter Bruegel the Elder, dated 1563, which today hangs in the Kunsthistorisches Museum in Vienna. Here, the tower looks like a gigantic, half-finished termites' nest that reminds one of the Colosseum. No wonder, for the artist had visited Rome ten years previously. Two other artists, the Dutchmen Maerten van Heemskerck and Cornelis Anthonizoon, have depicted the possible later collapse of the tower in copperplate etchings, also in the middle of the 16th century. Werner Hofmann, in *Zauber der Medusa*, comments: »The archetype of human hubris and presumption is the Tower of Babel – its collapse represents the right balance of which God reminds the human race. Fascinated not only by the allegorical profundity of the story in Genesis, but also particularly by the motifs of collapse, of rubble and ruins, this depiction of the blasphemous structure coincided with the basic inclinations of mannerism … This representation of the ruined tower (by Cornelis Anthonizoon) predates that of the (still) intact tower by Pieter Bruegel and expresses what the later master will merely suggest.«

Today we know that this tower was actually built. Babylon is 80 kilometers south of Baghdad near the former course of the Euphrates River. Of the former city, only a large number of huge piles of clay rubble remain. One of them contains the remnants of the original tower. As of this date, the entire field of ruins has been only partially excavated.

There were other cities and buildings destroyed in antiquity that we know about only from stories. Homer in his *Iliad* tells of the fall of Troy. Heinrich Schliemann found the hill of ruins in the 19th century, excavated the remnants of the walls beginning in 1870 and thus proved that the mythical story was rooted in truth.

Jahrhundert, grub die Mauerreste von 1870 an aus und bewies damit, daß die mythische Geschichte wahre Wurzeln besaß.

In der *Bibel* wird im Buch »Josuah« der israelitische Angriff auf die Stadt Jericho beschrieben, wobei die Soldaten eine eigenartige Eroberungstechnik anwendeten: Sie umkreisten in stummer Prozession die stark bewachte Stadtmauer an sechs aufeinanderfolgenden Tagen, ohne sie zu berühren, am siebten Tag bliesen sie, gemäß einer göttlichen Anweisung, in ihre Hörner und brachten damit die gewaltigen Mauern zum Einsturz. Über Sodom und Gomorrha ließ der alttestamentarische strafende Gott besonders viel Unheil niedergehen. Ihm war zu Ohren gekommen, daß diese beiden am Südufer des Toten Meeres gelegenen Städte Horte der Unzucht und der menschlichen Verkommenheit geworden seien. Er schickte zwei Engel aus, um die Anschuldigungen zu überprüfen. Schnell wurde klar, daß die Realität noch viel schlimmer war als vermutet. Die Stadtbewohner schreckten nicht davor zurück, von Lot, in dessen Haus die verkleideten Engel als Gäste aufgenommen worden waren, deren Herausgabe zu fordern: Sie wollten vergewaltigend über sie herfallen. In beiden Städten herrschte hemmungslose sexuelle Zügellosigkeit. Homosexualität und Sodomie gehörten zum Alltag. Bevor Gott Sodom und Gomorrha durch einen alles zerstörenden Feuerregen auslöschte, ließ er Lot mit seiner Frau und den beiden Töchtern fliehen. Unterwegs drehte sich die Ehefrau entgegen dem Verbot um, schaute auf die brennenden Städte und erstarrte daraufhin zur Salzsäule. Lot ließ sich in einer Höhle nieder und zeugte mit seinen Töchtern zwei Söhne, Moab und Ben-Ammi.

Die legendär-berühmten Stadtauslöschungen von Ninive, Persepolis, Babylon, Jerusalem (mehrmals), später auch von Karthago sind uns aus verschiedenen antiken Texten bekannt. Kaiser Nero gab im Jahr 64 n.Chr., nachdem er seine Mutter und seine Gattin Octavia umgebracht hatte, den Befehl, die Stadt Rom anzuzünden. Um von sich als Brandstifter abzulenken, lastete er das Feuer den Christen an und ließ sie verfolgen. Vier Jahre später mußte er aus Rom fliehen und beging mit 31 Jahren Selbstmord.

Gebäudeeinstürze, die auf Erdbeben, Architektenfehler oder falsche Baugrundanalysen zurückzuführen sind, kamen in allen Jahrhunderten vor. Legendär ist der Einsturz des Leuchtturms von Alexandria bei einem Erdbeben im 14. Jahrhundert. Bis zu diesem Zeitpunkt war der Turm, den der Architekt Sostratos von Knidos entworfen hatte, neben den Pyramiden von Gizeh, mit seinen fast 140 Metern das höchste Gebäude der Welt. Er war bald nach seiner Errichtung, im 3. Jahrhundert v. Chr., in die antike Liste der Weltwunder aufgenommen worden.

Auch der teilweise Einsturz der Hagia-Sophia-Kuppel in Byzanz-Konstantinopel prägte sich tief in das Menschheitsgedächtnis ein. Die größte bis dahin errichtete christliche Kirche der Welt wurde zwischen 532 und 537 nach Christi Geburt, also in unglaublich kurzer Zeit, erbaut. Der Entwurf stammte von den beiden Architekten Anthemios von Tralleis und Isidoros von Milet. Wahrscheinlich war das zu schnelle Bauen, bei dem nicht auf gründliches Trocknen der Mörtelschichten geachtet wurde, der Grund dafür, daß die gewaltige Kuppel im Jahr 558 zum ersten Mal einstürzte. Nach dem Wiederaufbau kam es bei Erdbeben im 10. und 14. Jahrhundert zu erneuten Einstürzen. Vor allem die Kuppel war, bezogen auf die bautechnischen Möglichkeiten der Zeit, zu groß dimensioniert.

Tragisch verlief auch der Fall von Andreas Schlüter, der 1694 durch Kurfürst Friedrich III., den späteren König Friedrich I. von Preußen, als Bildhauer nach Berlin berufen wurde. Nachdem er über 100 skulpturale Schlußsteine für das Zeughaus angefertigt hatte, ernannte ihn der König

In the *Bible*, in the book of Joshua, there is a description of the Israelite attack on the city of Jericho, during which the soldiers used a peculiar conquest technique: In silent procession, they circled the heavily guarded city wall on six successive days without touching it; on the seventh day, following divine instructions, they blew their horns, causing the mighty walls to collapse. The punishing God of the Old Testament brought down an especially huge calamity on Sodom and Gomorrah. It had come to his attention that the two cities, located on the southern shore of the Dead Sea, had become breeding grounds of fornication and human depravity. He sent out two angels in order to check the truth of the suspicions. Quickly it became clear that the reality was even worse than had been thought. The townspeople had no qualms about demanding that Lot, in whose house the disguised angels had been welcomed as guests, hand them over: They wanted to rape them. In both cities sexual licentiousness ran rampant. Homosexuality and sodomy were daily practices. Before God obliterated Sodom and Gomorrah with a rain of fire that destroyed everything, he told Lot and his wife and two daughters to flee. On the way, the wife turned around, disregarding the prohibition, looked at the burning cities and turned into a pillar of salt. Lot settled in a cave and fathered two sons on his daughters – Moab and Ben-Ammi.

We are familiar, from various ancient texts, with the legendary obliteration of Nineveh, Persepolis, Babylon, Jerusalem (repeatedly) and later of Carthage. In 64 C. E., Emperor Nero, having killed his mother and his wife Octavia, gave the order to set fire to the city of Rome. In order to divert suspicion from himself as the arsonist, he blamed the fire on the Christians and instigated their persecution. Four years later, he had to flee from Rome, and committed suicide at the age of 31.

Collapsed buildings due to earthquakes, the fault of architects or mistaken analyses of the building site, have been a common occurrence in all centuries. Legendary was the collapse of the Alexandria lighthouse during an earthquake in the 14th century. Up to that time, the 140-meter tower, designed by the architect Sostratus of Cnidus, was, beside the Pyramids of Giza, the tallest building in the world. Soon after it was built in the third century B.C.E., it was included in the list of the Seven Wonders of the Ancient World.

The partial collapse of the cupola of the Hagia Sophia in Byzantium-Constantinople also left a deep impression on human memory. The largest Christian church in the world erected up to that time was built between 532 and 537 C.E., i.e., in an incredibly short time. It was designed by the two architects Anthemius of Tralles and Isidorus of Miletus. Probably the fact that it had been built too fast and that no attention was paid to making sure the mortar dried thoroughly were the reasons that the mighty cupola collapsed for the first time, in 558. After it was rebuilt, there were new

zum Schloßbaudirektor als Nachfolger von Johann Arnold Nering. Da ihm jedoch konstruktive Grundkenntnisse fehlten, stieß er mit dem 1702 entworfenen Münzturmprojekt an seine Grenzen. Der Bau stürzte teilweise ein und mußte schließlich vollständig abgerissen werden. Schlüter verlor alle seine Ämter, verließ Berlin unehrenhaft und starb 1714 in Sankt Petersburg. Einen Turm als Ruine konnte sich der König nicht vorstellen, denn dies entsprach nicht dem Stil der Zeit.

Die ersten gemalten Ruinendarstellungen der Kunstgeschichte tauchen im Zusammenhang mit Szenen der Geburt Christi auf. Warum viele Maler aus dem armseligen Stall in Bethlehem oft Palast- und Burgruinen mit Scheunenanbauten machten, bleibt rätselhaft. Eine pittoreske Mode, die mit der Realität im römisch besetzten Palästina wenig zu tun hatte. Aber wer fragt schon nach Realität im Zusammenhang mit den Traumgebilden von Religionen, außerdem war keiner der mittelalterlichen Maler selbst im Nahen Osten gewesen. Sehr gepflegt und aufge- räumt sehen sie aus, die Geburtszenen bei Rogier van der Weyden, Sandro Botticelli, Vittore Carpaccio, Domenico Ghirlandaio, Giovanni Bellini, Andrea del Sarto, Tintoretto und Albrecht Dürer.

Andere Maler in der Übergangszeit zwischen Mittelalter und Renaissance interessierten sich zunehmend für die grausamen Untergangs- und Ruinenaspekte der Bibeltexte. Die Qualen der Heiligen, der Turmbau zu Babel und die brennenden Apokalypsenreiter der Offenbarung kamen in Mode. Viele Menschen waren geradezu besessen von der Idee des bevorstehenden Weltunter- gangs (ein Zeitgefühl, das dem heutigen sehr nahe kommt!).

Einen ersten künstlerischen Höhepunkt stellt die *Versuchung des heiligen Antonius* dar, die Matthias Grünewald, der eigentlich Mathis Neithart hieß, auf dem zweiten Verwandlungsflügel des »Isenheimer Altars« zwischen 1512 und 1516 dargestellt hat.

Riesige, halbmenschliche Vogelwesen bedrohen den armen Heiligen mit Holzkeulen, ein Drachen beißt in seine rechte Hand, ein pestbeulenübersäter, nackter Mönch mit aufgebläh- tem Bauch und Schwimmhäuten zwischen den Zehen krümmt sich vor Schmerzen am vorderen linken Bildrand, Tiermenschendämonen fletschen die Zähne und fuchteln mit Knochen durch die Luft. Ein tierköpfiger Teufel zerrt den am Boden liegenden Heiligen an seinen langen, weißen Haaren, ein anderer tritt ihm mit seinem Krallenfuß auf die wehrlose, nur von einer Mönchskutte bekleidete Brust.

Im Hintergrund des Bildes ist ein Haus – Scheune oder Berghütte? – dargestellt, das gerade von kleineren Kobolden in seine Einzelteile zerlegt wird. Kein Balken ruht mehr auf seinem ange- stammten Platz, und die Trümmer des Daches türmen sich in einem wilden Haufen am Boden des Ruineninnenraums. Selbst die Natur befindet sich in Auflösung, und die Äste, die von rechts in den Bildraum eindringen, scheinen am Kampf gegen den Heiligen teilzunehmen. Die Welt ist aus den Fugen geraten. Aus ihrem tiefsten Inneren quellen unheilvolle, grausame Mächte hervor. Ein Alptraum von surrealer Gewalt.

Allerdings würde ich diese Kampf- und Ruinenszene, die der Legende nach eigentlich in der ägyptischen Wüste spielen müßte, wo der Einsiedler Antonius lebte, nicht als »Versuchung« be- zeichnen, sondern als »Bedrohung«. Quälen, Zerstören und Auslöschen aller Harmonie scheint das Ziel der teuflischen Mißgeburten zu sein. Oder empfindet der Heilige gar Lust an diesem Überfall, weil er insgeheim einer sadomasochistischen Sekte angehört? Vielleicht sind derartige Wahnvorstellungen auch nur Ausgeburten der kochend-heißen Wüstenluft? Erleidet Antonius in Wirklichkeit gerade einen Hitzschlag und brauchte nur Wasser, um wieder zu klarem Bewußtsein zurückzukehren? Warum dieser Heilige, der als Vater des Mönchtums gilt, später zum Schutz- heiligen der Haustiere erklärt wurde, bleibt unklar.

Jede Zeit produziert ihre Ruinen. Kriege, Naturkatastrophen und Unglücke sorgen für Nach- schub. Raub, Überfall, Brandschatzung und gewaltsamer Tod gehörten im Mittelalter zum Alltag, vor allem für Menschen, die außerhalb der Städte lebten. Einsame Landgüter und kleine, unge- schützte Dörfer waren beliebte Plünderungsziele für ausgehungerte, marodierende Soldaten- trupps. Vorratsspeicher wurden geleert, Frauen vergewaltigt, Kinder und Männer ermordet. Im Vollrausch zündeten die brutalen Räuber alle Gebäude an und erfreuten sich aus der Ferne an ihrem Zerstörungswerk. Da an Munition gespart wurde, es noch kein Dynamit und keine Bomben gab, diente das Feuer als häufigste Zerstörungsart von Häusern, Dörfern und Städten.

Kein anderer Künstler stellte apokalyptische Landschaften mit brennenden Gebäuden, Ruinen und aufgewühlten Menschenansammlungen, die den absurdesten Tätigkeiten nachgehen, dras- tischer und bildmächtiger dar als der niederländische Maler Hieronymus Bosch. In allen drei gro- ßen Triptychen, die er zwischen 1480 und 1516, seinem Todesjahr, gemalt hat, gleichen sich die Katastrophen und menschlichen Qualen: im *Heuwagen*, im *Garten der Lüste* (beide Madrid, Museo del Prado) und im *Weltgericht* (Wien, Gemäldegalerie der Akademie der Künste). Plötzlich

4. Albrecht Dürer, *Die Geburt Christi*, 1504, Kupfer-
stichkabinett, Berlin.
5. Matthias Grünewald, Isenheimer Altar, um 1516,
geöffneter Zustand, rechter Altarflügel: *Die Versuchung des Heiligen Antonius*, Musée d'Unterlinden,
Colmar.

4. Albrecht Dürer, *Birth of Christ*, 1504, Kupferstich-
kabinett, Berlin.
5. Matthias Grünewald, Isenheimer Altar, c. 1516,
open state, *The Temptation of Saint Anthony*, right
outer panel, Musée d'Unterlinden, Colmar.

collapses during earthquakes in the 10th and 14th century. The dimensions of the cupola in particular were too large, considering the structural engineering capabilities at the time.

Another tragic case was that of Andreas Schlüter, who was invited to come to Berlin to work
as court sculptor in 1694 by the Elector Frederick III, later King Frederick I of Prussia. After Schlüter had created over 100 sculptured keystones for the armory, the king appointed him surveyor
general of works as the successor of Johann Arnold Nering. But since he lacked a basic knowledge of construction, he reached his limits with the water tower of the Berlin Mint, which he designed in 1702. The structure partially collapsed and finally had to be razed completely. Schlüter
lost all his positions, left Berlin in disgrace and died in 1714 in Saint Petersburg. The king could
not imagine a tower as a ruin. This was not exactly in the style of the times.

The first painted representations of ruins in art history appear in connection with scenes of the
birth of Christ. It is still a mystery why many painters often turned the wretched stable of Bethlehem into the ruins of palaces and castles with attached barns. It was a painterly fashion that had
little to do with the reality that might have existed under Roman occupation in Palestine. But who
wants reality when it comes to the phantasms of religions? Besides, none of the medieval painters

schlägt die Idylle in eine bürgerkriegsähnliche Hölle um. Spielen wird zu Jagen, Reden zu Zerstören, Gehen zu Quälen, Liebe wird zu Haß, Sex zu Mord, gemütliches Kochen zu Kannibalismus, Trinken zu Folter, und die liebevolle Familie verwandelt sich in eine brutale Terrorzelle. Das allgemeine Abschlachten greift um sich wie ein Krankheitsbazillus. Alle Menschen wirken wie verhext, von grausamen Dämonen beherrscht. Ein Bauer durchschneidet dem andern die Kehle, drei Mönche sind in eine wilde, tödlich ernste Keilerei verwickelt, ein weiterer Bauer wird von einem Wagenrad überrollt, ein Paar liebt sich in aller Öffentlichkeit, Männer reiten sodomistisch auf Riesenfischen und erdolchen nebenbei ihre Kameraden. Liebespaare haben sich in Fruchtblasen zurückgezogen, andere in Muscheln oder übergroße Küchengeräte. Einzelne Gequälte versuchen sich in Wurzelhohlräumen oder Rieseneiern zu verstecken. Aber es gibt kein Entkommen. Alle Lebenslust ist in Perversion umgeschlagen.

Männer braten Frauen über dem offenen Feuer, Fischmenschen vergewaltigen madonnengleiche Mädchen auf Tischen und Bänken, Pflanzen und Blüten blähen sich zu gigantischen, fleischfressenden Ungeheuern auf, dazwischen spielen Kinder ihre kleinen, sadistischen Spiele. Kein Gebäude, das nicht längst zur Ruine verbrannt wäre, keine Wolke, die nicht Tod und Verderben in sich trüge. Selbst Regen und Sonnenstrahlen haben einen verheerenden Einfluß. Krieg ist zum Alltag geworden. Jeder fällt über jeden her. Liebe, Sexualität, Mord und Kannibalismus sind nicht

6. Hieronymus Bosch, *Das Jüngste Gericht*, zwischen 1480 und 1518, Mitteltafel des Triptychons, Gemäldegalerie der Akademie der Künste, Wien.
7. Hieronymus Bosch, *Das Jüngste Gericht*, Bildausschnitt.

6. Hieronymus Bosch, *The Last Judgement*, between 1480 and 1518, centre panel of the triptych, Gemäldegalerie der Akademie der Künste, Vienna.
7. Hieronymus Bosch, *The Last Judgement*, picture detail.

had ever been in the Middle East themselves. They look very well-kept and tidy – the birth scenes in the work of Rogier van der Weyden, Sandro Botticelli, Vittore Carpaccio, Domenico Ghirlandaio, Giovanni Bellini, Andrea del Sarto, Tintoretto and Albrecht Dürer.

Other painters during the transition period from the Middle Ages to the Renaissance were increasingly interested in the dreadful aspects of destruction and ruins found in biblical texts. The torture of saints, the »Tower of Babel« and the burning Horsemen of the Apocalypse in the Book of Revelation came into fashion. Many people were virtually obsessed with the idea of the imminent end of the world (a feeling of the times that comes very close to ours!). A first artistic high point is the *Temptation of Saint Anthony*, painted by Matthias Grünewald, whose actual name was Mathis Neithart, on the wing of the second view of the »Isenheim Altarpiece« between 1512 and 1516.

Gigantic half-human, birdlike creatures menace the poor saint with cudgels, a dragon bites his right hand, a naked monk covered with plague spots, his belly bloated and webs between his toes, writhes with pain in the left forefront of the painting, demons in human and animal shape gnash their teeth and brandish bones. An animal-headed devil drags the saint along the ground by his long white hair, another kicks his defenseless chest, clad only in a monk's habit, with his taloned foot.

In the background of the picture there is a house – a barn or a mountain hut – that is in the process of being dismantled by smaller goblins. Not one beam is still in its original place, and the debris of the roof are piled up in wild disarray on the floor of the ruined interior. Even nature is disrupted, and the branches that are thrust into the frame of the painting from the right seem to be part of the fight against the saint. The world is out of joint. From its deepest bowels, sinister, dreadful forces surge forth. A nightmare of surreal proportions.

To be sure I would not describe this scene of struggle and ruins, which according to legend should actually take place in the Egyptian desert where the hermit Anthony lived, as a »temptation«, but as »menace«. Torture, destruction and the extinction of all harmony seems to be the aim of the diabolical fiends. Or could it be that the saint feels pleasure at being attacked this way because he secretly belongs to a sadomasochistic sect? Perhaps this kind of delusions are merely monstrous creations of the burning desert air? Is Anthony in reality suffering from heat stroke, and simply needs water to return to clear consciousness? It remains unclear why this saint, who is considered to be the father of monasticism, was later declared the patron saint of domestic animals.

Every period produces its ruins. Wars, natural catastrophes and disasters bring more scenes of destruction in their wake. In the Middle Ages, robbery, attacks, arson and violent death were part of daily life, especially for people who lived outside the towns. Starved, marauding troops of soldiers preferred to plunder isolated country estates and small, unprotected villages. Storerooms were emptied, women raped, children and men murdered. In a drunken frenzy the brutal robbers set fire to all the buildings and enjoyed the destruction from afar. To save on ammunition, and since dynamite and bombs had not yet been invented, fire was the most frequent method for destroying houses, villages and towns.

No other artist has depicted apocalyptic landscapes with burning buildings, ruins and turbulent gatherings of people going about the absurdest tasks more graphically and powerfully than the Dutch painter Hieronymus Bosch. In all three of the large triptychs he painted between 1480 and 1516, the year of his death, catastrophes and human torment are similar: in the *Haywain*, in the *Garden of Earthly Delights* (both in Madrid, Museo del Prado) and in *The Last Judgment* (Vienna, Painting Gallery of the Akademie der bildenden Künste). Suddenly, the idyll turns into an inferno that resembles a civil war. Games turn into hunts, talking into destruction, walking into tormenting, love into hate, sex into murder, leisurely cooking into cannibalism, drinking into torture, and a loving family is transformed into a brutal terrorist cell. Indiscriminate butchery spread like a pathogenic bacillus. All the people seem to be bewitched, possessed by horrifying demons. A peasant slits another's throat, three monks are engaged in a wild, deadly brawl, another peasant is being crushed by a cartwheel, a couple makes love in public, men sodomize giant fish, stabbing their companions all the while. Lovers have taken refuge in fruit bubbles, others in seashells or oversized kitchen utensils. Some of those who are being tortured are trying to hide in the hollow cavities of roots or huge eggs. But there is no escape. All delight has suddenly changed to perversion.

Men are roasting women over an open fire, human fish rape Madonna-like young girls on tables and benches, plants and blossoms swell to become gigantic flesh-eating monsters, while among them children play their little sadistic games. Not a building has been left unburned to a

mehr voneinander zu unterscheiden. Erdolchte liegen neben Fressenden und Saufenden. Pfeile stecken in Aftern und Geschlechtsteilen, Schlangen treiben ihr obszönes Spiel. Kein Maß stimmt mehr. Pflanzen, Messer, Dosen und Teller sind zu hausgroßen Ungeheuern angewachsen, Menschen zu Ameisen geschrumpft. Im Hintergrund brennen alle Häuser. Ruine steht neben Ruine, schwarzgebrannt, ausgelöscht. Ein rotes Flammenmeer erhellt den nächtlichen Horizont.

Daß über der untergehenden Welt ein winziger Christus in einer Wolkengloriole schwebt, sieht fast aus wie Hohn. Niemand nimmt ihn zur Kenntnis. Man hat ihn vergessen, genauso wie die in lange Trompeten blasenden Engel. Es sind die letzten Momente der Menschheit. Man hat Kriege, Plünderung, Pest und Cholera überstanden, man hat betrogen, gestohlen, gefressen, gehurt und gemordet, und jetzt trifft die Strafe Gottes ein. Offenbarung. Jüngster Tag. Die letzten Siegel sind geöffnet. Apokalypse.

Im Gegensatz zur griechisch-römischen Mythologie, die ihre Anhänger nicht mit einem infernalischen Ende bedrohte, gehört es beim Christentum zum Prinzip, das Diesseits als Jammertal zu beschreiben und das Jenseits als Paradies. Allerdings kann nur derjenige ins himmlische Jerusalem eintreten, der gottgefällig gelebt hat, alle anderen Menschen sind zum Schmoren in der Hölle verdammt.

So gesehen, war und ist das Christentum – auch bei Hieronymus Bosch — eine erzieherische Religion, die ihre Anhänger durch Abschreckungsbilder dazu zwingen will, böse Taten zu unterlassen. Es gibt, nach Meinung der christlichen Kirche, nur diesen einen Weg, nur diese eine Religion. Wer nicht an den christlichen Gott glaubt und die Zehn Gebote nicht befolgt, wird auf dem Scheiterhaufen enden wie einst die Ketzer Savonarola oder Jan Hus. Die Inquisition übersah keinen Sünder.

Ein Grund mehr, die gesamte Menschheit zu missionieren. Somit überrascht es nicht, daß das Christentum die meisten Anhänger aller Weltreligionen besitzt und damit die anderen Weltreligionen, heute vor allem den Islam, zu terroristischen Gegenschlägen provoziert. Sahen die apokalyptischen Bilder der brennenden und einstürzenden Twin Towers in Manhattan nicht aus wie von Hieronymus Bosch gemalt? In unserer Zeit haben sich die Engel in todbringende Flugzeuge verwandelt, gefüllt mit unschuldigen Männern, Frauen und Kindern.

Unzählige Kriege und Gefährdungen mußten die Gemälde von Matthias Grünewald und Hieronymus Bosch überstehen. Heute hängen sie friedlich, unzerstört und sicher in ihren angestammten Klöstern und Museen. Ein Wunder, das nicht allen Kunstwerken beschieden war. Viele wurden selbst zu Ruinen, als Zielscheiben benutzt, verbrannten bei Luftangriffen, wurden als Kriegsbeute entführt oder als entartet zerstört. Eine Bildruine, die mich bereits als Schüler in Ulm sehr beeindruckt hat, findet sich im Ulmer Münster. Sie stammt aus der Zeit des Bildersturms, zu Beginn des 16. Jahrhunderts. Am Kopfende des rechten Seitenschiffs hatte Hans Multscher, neben Jörg Syrlin der berühmteste Ulmer Bildhauer des 15. Jahrhunderts, einen Altar aus Sandstein in die Wand eingelassen, der – wie eine Inschrift besagt – 1433 vollendet wurde. Nach seinem Stifter wurde sie *Karg-Nische* benannt. Bilderstürmende Bauern zerschlugen die Figuren – wahrscheinlich eine Marienanbetungsszene mit der Stifterfamilie im Vordergrund – mit Sensen und Äxten fast genau 100 Jahre später, am 21. Juni 1531. Heute ist nur noch die Ruine des einstigen Altars zu sehen. Bei genauer Betrachtung lassen sich die einzelnen Beilhiebe an den Flügelresten der Engel und am goldenen Hintergrundtuch erkennen. Der leere Altar wurde über die Jahrhunderte in seiner Verletzung als versteinerte Wunde belassen, niemand versuchte, die Figuren zu rekonstruieren. Ein Zustand, wie er in Kirchen nicht oft anzutreffen ist.

Auch der Hauptaltar im zentralen Chorraum des Ulmer Münsters ist jenen Bildsturmeiferern zum Opfer gefallen. Von ihm fehlt bis heute jede Spur. Wahrscheinlich wurde er als Brennholz verfeuert. Niemand hat versucht, ihn zu rekonstruieren. An seiner Stelle steht heute ein armselig kleines Ersatzobjekt. Erstaunlich bleibt, daß Jörg Syrlins Chorgestühl der Bilderzerstörungswut entgangen ist, obwohl die Figuren und Möbel bestimmt gut gebrannt hätten. Weshalb war das so? Vielleicht erkannten sich die »christlichen Vandalen« in den erstaunlich realistischen Porträts wieder, die über den seitlichen Lehnen thronen.

Seit der Neuentdeckung des antiken Rom im 16. Jahrhundert gehört die Ruine zum normalen Requisit vieler Landschaftsgemälde und Gartengestaltungen. Die Künstler strebten mit der Anwesenheit verfallener Gemäuer eine Atmosphäre der Zeitoffenheit und der Vergänglichkeit an. Geschichte hat sich ereignet und Spuren hinterlassen. Jede Landschaft ist Lebens- und Totenraum zugleich. Wir gehen auf den Gräbern der Gestorbenen.

Auch in Garten- und Parkanlagen der Renaissance begegnen wir zunehmend dem Motiv der Ruine. Eine der berühmtesten, später allerdings wieder vergessenen »künstlichen Ruinen« steht im »Sacro Bosco von Bomarzo«, den der einstige Diplomat und Kriegsherr Fürst Vicino Orsini

ruin, not a cloud that does not bear death and corruption within it. Even rain and sunshine have a devastating influence. War has become an everyday occurrence. Everyone falls upon everyone else. It is impossible to tell love, sexuality, murder and cannibalism apart. People who have been stabbed to death lie next to people who are stuffing their faces and getting blind drunk. Arrows protrude from anuses and private parts, snakes play their obscene games. Every measurement is out of kilter. Plants, knives, jars and plates have grown as tall as houses, while people have shrunk to the size of ants. In the background all the houses are burning. One ruin after another stands scorched and black, extinguished. A red ocean of flames lights up the nocturnal horizon.

The fact that above this dying world a tiny Christ figure soars in a halo of clouds almost looks like mockery. No one takes notice of him. He has been forgotten, like the angels who are blowing long trumpets. These are the last moments of the human race. People have survived wars, pillage, pestilence and cholera, they have cheated, stolen, stuffed themselves, whored and murdered, and now God's punishment is at hand. Revelation. Last Judgment. The last seals are opened. Apocalypse.

In contrast to Greco-Roman mythology, whose adherents were not threatened with an infernal end, it is a basic tenet of Christianity that the here and now is described as a vale of tears and the hereafter is portrayed as paradise. Though of course only those who have lived lives that are pleasing to God can enter the New Jerusalem, while all others are condemned to roast in hell.

Seen from this perspective Christianity has always been a pedagogical religion – and that goes for Hieronymus Bosch as well. Christianity tries to force its adherents by means of deterrent images to desist from doing evil. In the opinion of the Christian church there is only this one path, this one religion. Those who do not believe in the Christian God and do not obey the Ten Commandments will end up at the stake, as the heretics Savonarola or Jan Hus did once. The Inquisition did not overlook a single sinner.

One more reason to proselytize the entire human race. No wonder Jesus and his Christianity have more adherents than any world religion, and thus provoke the other world religions – today primarily Islam – to terrorist reprisals. Did not the apocalyptic images of the burning and collapsing Twin Towers in Manhattan look as though they had been painted by Hieronymus Bosch? In our times, the angels have been transformed into death-dealing planes, filled with innocent men, women and children.

The paintings of Matthias Grünewald and Hieronymus Bosch had to survive countless wars and dangers. Today they hang peacefully, undestroyed and secure, in their accustomed monasteries and museums. It's a miracle that was not granted to all works of art. Many became ruins themselves, were used as targets, were burned in air raids, were carried off as booty in war or destroyed as degenerate. A ruined sculpture that impressed me profoundly even as a schoolboy

zwischen 1547 und 1580 bei Viterbo anlegen ließ. Im Gegensatz zu den meisten anderen Parks seiner Zeit breitet sich Orsinis grünes Traumreich nicht in der Ebene, sondern in einem wilden Bergwald unterhalb seines Schlosses aus. Es scheint so, als hätte er folgende Verse aus Dantes *Göttlicher Komödie* zum Ausgangspunkt seiner inszenierten Naturerzählung genommen:

> »Wohl in der Mitte unseres Lebensweges
> geriet ich tief in einen dunklen Wald,
> so daß vom graden Pfade ich verirrte.
> Oh, schwer wird's mir, zu sagen, wie er war,
> der wilde Wald, so finster und so rauh;
> Angst faßt aufs neue mich, wenn ich dran denke;
> So schmerzlich, daß der Tod kaum bitter ist.
> Doch, um vom Guten, das ich fand zu reden,
> will ich von andrem, das ich sah, erzählen. «
> (I. Gesang, Vers 1 bis 7)

Und dieses »andre« bestand aus steinernen Ungeheuern, kämpfenden Riesen, Nymphen, Schlangen, verführerischen Nixen und vor allem: Ruinen. Gleich am Eingang steht jenes berühmte, ruinös-schiefe Haus, das aussieht, als hätte es gerade ein Erdbeben überstanden. Jeder Eintretende muß es durchschreiten. Er soll erschreckt und verunsichert werden. Es gibt Mächte, unsichtbare Naturkräfte, kosmische und mythologische Beziehungsnetze, die er nicht sieht und nur erahnen kann. Kein Wunder, daß sich im 20. Jahrhundert vor allem der »Metaphysiker« Giorgio de Chirico auf diesen Park berief und sogar behauptete, als erster den »Sacro Bosco von Bomarzo« entdeckt zu haben.

In den Gemälden der nachfolgenden Generationen tauchen Ruinen und antike Tempelfragmente nur noch als selbstverständliche, die Melancholie evozierende Zitate auf; bei den Franzosen Nicolas Poussin, François de Nomé (genannt Monsù Desiderio), Claude Lorrain und Hubert Robert, den Italienern Annibale Carraci, Salvatore Rosa, Giovanni Paolo Pannini, den Niederländern Joachim Patinir, Hercules Seghers, Jacob van Ruisdael und Rembrandt van Rijn. Erst die Maler des 19. und 20. Jahrhunderts knüpfen wieder an die Grausamkeiten und Brutalitäten Matthias Grünewalds und Hieronymus Boschs an. Bei Francisco Goya und Pablo Picasso lösen sich nicht nur Häuser in Ruinen auf, sondern auch Menschen. Zerfetzte Körper, zerstückelte Gesichter und abgeschlagene Gliedmaßen durchziehen ihre Bilder wie eine grausam-blutige Spur. Die kriegerischen Auseinandersetzungen waren brutaler, totaler und globaler geworden. Immer mehr unschuldige Zivilisten kamen in den Bombenhageln um,

in Ulm is located in the Ulm Cathedral. It dates back to the time of the iconoclasts at the beginning of the 16th century. At the head of the right aisle Hans Multscher, the most famous Ulm sculptor in the 15th century besides Jörg Syrlin, had let a sandstone altar into the wall, which, as an inscription states, was completed in 1433. It was called *Karg-Nische* [Karg Alcove] after its donor. Iconoclastic peasants smashed the figures – probably a Veneration of the Virgin Mary scene with the donor family in the foreground – with scythes and axes almost exactly 100 years later, on 21 June 1531. Today only the ruin of the former altar still remains. On closer scrutiny the individual hatchet marks can still be recognized on what remains of the angels' wings and the gold cloth of the background. The empty altar was left as a petrified wound through the centuries – no one tried to reconstruct the figures, a state of affairs not often found in churches.

The main altar in the central choir of Ulm Minster also fell victim to the fanatical iconoclasts. There is no trace of it to this day. It was probably burned as firewood. No one has attempted to reconstruct it. In its place today there is a pitifully small substitute object. What is amazing is that Jörg Syrlin's choir stalls escaped the rage of the iconoclasts, although the figures and furnishings would certainly have burned well. Why was this? Perhaps the »Christian vandals« recognized themselves in the amazingly realistic portraits that are enthroned above the side arm rests.

Since the rediscovery of ancient Rome in the 16th century, ruins have been part of the normal requisite of many landscape paintings and garden designs. By including dilapidated walls the artists strove for an atmosphere of openness to the times and transience. History has taken place and has left traces. Every landscape is a space of both life and death. We are walking on the graves of those who died.

In the gardens and parks of the Renaissance we increasingly encounter the motif of the »ruin«. One of the most famous »artificial ruins« (though one that was later forgotten again) stands in the »Sacro Bosco of Bomarzo«, which the former diplomat and commander Prince Vicino Orsini had laid out between 1547 and 1580 near Viterbo. In contrast to most of the other parks of the period, Orsini's green dream realm does not lie in the plain but in a wild mountain forest below his castle. It seems as if he had taken the following verses from Dante's *Divine Comedy* as the point of departure of his staged nature narrative:

»Midway upon the journey of our life
I found myself within a forest dark,
For the straightforward pathway had been lost.
Ah me! how hard a thing it is to say
What was this forest savage, rough, and stern,
Which in the very thought renews the fear.
So bitter is it, death is little more;
But of the good to treat, which there I found,
Speak will I of the other things I saw there.«
(Inferno: Canto I, verses 1 to 7, translated by Henry Wadsworth Longfellow)

And these »other things« were stone monsters, fighting giants, nymphs, serpents, seductive water sprites and above all: ruins. At the very entrance stands that famous, ruinously crooked house that looks as if it had just survived an earthquake. All those who enter must walk through it. The intention is that they should be frightened and confused. There are forces, invisible natural forces, cosmic and mythological networks of connection that they cannot see and can only surmise. No wonder that in the 20th century it was primarily the »metaphysician« Giorgio de Chirico who referred to this park and even claimed that he was the first person to have discovered the »Sacro Bosco of Bomarzo«.

In the paintings of subsequent generations, ruins and fragments of ancient temples appear only as self-evident quotations that evoke melancholy. Instances are the works of the French artists Nicolas Poussin, François de Nomé (aka Monsù Desiderio), Claude Lorrain and Hubert Robert, the Italians Annibale Carraci, Salvatore Rosa, Giovanni Paolo Pannini, the Dutchmen Joachim Patinir, Hercules Seghers, Jacob van Ruisdael and Rembrandt van Rijn. Not till the 19th and the 20th centuries do painters again go back to the atrocities and brutality of the work of Matthias Grünewald and Hieronymus Bosch. In the paintings of Francisco Goya and Pablo Picasso it is not only the houses that disintegrate into ruins, but the people as well. Bodies torn into shreds, fragments of faces and cut-off limbs run through their paintings like a dreadful trail of blood. The military conflicts had become more brutal, more total and more global. More and more innocent civilians were killed in the hail of bombs.

2. Antike Ruinen

Johann Joachim Winckelmann und Giovanni Battista Piranesi, Rom und Pompeji

Im Frühjahr 1506 wurde in den Ruinen des »Goldenen Hauses« von Nero, nordöstlich des Kolosseums (nach anderen Berichten in einem Weinberg bei Santa Maria Maggiore), die antike, marmorne Figurengruppe des *Laokoon* im Boden gefunden. Bei ihrer Ausgrabung und Bergung war Michelangelo anwesend. Auf seine Empfehlung hin kaufte Papst Julius II. das Werk für 500 Scudi und ließ es im Vatikan aufstellen. Von einem Moment zum andern stieg die *Laokoon-Gruppe* zum berühmtesten und stilbildendsten Werk der Renaissance auf. Allerdings war die Gruppe, wie alle antiken Skulpturen und Architekturen, nicht vollständig erhalten. Über 1000 Jahre hatte sie zwischen Steinen, Bauschutt und Müll in der römischen Erde gelegen. Einige Teile – Arme, Hände, Glieder, auch ein Schlangenkopf – fehlten. Den rechten Arm des Trojanischen Priesters fanden Archäologen erst bei Ausgrabungen im Jahr 1904. Die rechten, erhobenen Arme der beiden Söhne blieben verschwunden.

Da der Papst ein vollkommenes Kunstwerk sehen wollte, ließ er die fehlenden Teile von zeitgenössischen Bildhauern ergänzen. Er ertrug das Ruinöse, Fragmentarische nicht. Es widersprach seinem Schönheitsempfinden. Diese Einstellung teilten mit ihm fast alle nachfolgenden Kunstgenießer bis ins 19. Jahrhundert hinein. Überhaupt bleibt es erstaunlich, daß der Papst, das Oberhaupt aller katholischen Christen, eine derartig heidnische Figurengruppe in seiner Umgebung aufstellen ließ. Aber die Antikenbewunderung hatte inzwischen so um sich gegriffen, daß auch er nicht mehr vor eindeutig unchristlichen Kunstwerken zurückschreckte. Immerhin waren hier drei nackte Männer im Todeskampf dargestellt, ein Vater und seine beiden halbwüchsigen Söhne. Bis heute ist die Interpretation der Szene umstritten.

Es gibt auch eine moralische Interpretation: Der Priester habe die Trojaner – ähnlich wie die gleichgesinnte Kassandra – vor dem Hereinziehen des hölzernen Pferdes gewarnt, aber die Göttin, die wollte, daß Troja untergeht, habe zwei Giftschlangen (aus dem Meer?) geschickt, um die Laokoon-Sippe auszulöschen. Nach der unmoralischen Interpretation, die natürlich den aufgeklärten, das Frivole bevorzugenden Renaissancedeutern besser ins Konzept paßte, habe der Priester eine junge Frau hinter dem Altar seines Tempels verführt, und die Göttin habe ihn für seine Frevelei mit dem Tode bestrafen wollen.

Heutige Kunsthistoriker neigen übrigens zur zweiten Variante und sind sich darüber einig, daß es sich bei der *Laokoon-Gruppe*, im Gegensatz zu vielen anderen Funden aus römischer Zeit, um ein echtes griechisches Kunstwerk aus hellenistischer Zeit handelt, das Kaiser Nero wahrscheinlich persönlich bei Bildhauern aus Rhodos bestellt hatte.

Michelangelo war von dem neuen Fund restlos begeistert und fühlte sich in seiner Ästhetik und seinem Kunstwillen bestätigt. Er, der schroffe, zur Tragödie neigende Kämpfer, konnte auch mit ruinösen Werken leben. Sein Ziel war nicht immer das perfekt vollendete Kunstwerk, wie er es in jungen Jahren mit dem *David* in Florenz realisiert hatte. Später erklärte er auch seine vier lebensgroßen, ihre Carrara-Marmorblöcke nie ganz aufgebenden, für die Boboli-Gärten geplanten Sklaven für vollendet. Das »Non-finito« als Ideal und Haltung gegenüber Auftraggeber und Welt der Bewunderer erhielt bei Michelangelo eine geradezu existentielle Bedeutung (ähnlich wie bei seinem Zeitgenossen Leonardo da Vinci). Nach seiner Meinung überschreitet das Vollendete eine Grenze, hinter der eine Zone des Unmenschlichen, vielleicht Göttlichen oder auch Tödlichen beginnt.

Nicht nur die *Laokoon-Gruppe* war Fragment, sondern auch der ähnlich euphorisch bewunderte, ebenfalls in römischer Erde gefundene *Apollo von Belvedere*. Ihm, dem Gott des Lichts, der Dichtung, der Musik und der Jugend, der Heilkunde und der Weissagung, ihm, dem strafenden Bogenschützen und Helfer im Kampf, fehlen die linke Hand und der rechte Unterarm. Als besonders schöner Gott, Sohn des Zeus und der Leto, hätte er bei seinen zahlreichen Liebesabenteuern mit Frauen und Männern, handlos manches Problem gehabt. In Wirklichkeit ist uns sein Marmorbild als grausam verstümmelte Schönheit überliefert worden. Wer hat ihm wohl die beiden Hände abgeschlagen? Vielleicht ist er irgendwann vom Sockel gestürzt worden, und seine fehlenden Glieder liegen noch heute einsam irgendwo in der römischen Erde. Begeisterte Bewunderer wie Johann Joachim Winckelmann, Johann Wolfgang von Goethe oder Rainer Maria Rilke standen tief beeindruckt vor so viel (lädierter) Vollkommenheit. Goethe allerdings schreckte später zurück und fragte 1771 in einem Brief an Herder: »Apollo vom Belvedere, warum zeigst du dich uns in deiner Nacktheit, daß wir uns der unsrigen schämen müssen?«

Erst in der Zeit um 1800 änderte sich die allgemeine Einstellung gegenüber Körperruinen und Torsi. Fürst Pückler Muskau schrieb in dieser Zeit beim Anblick der kopflosen Venus von Medici:

2. The ruins of antiquity

Johann Joachim Winckelmann and Giovanni Battista Piranesi, Rome and Pompeii

In the spring of 1506 the ancient marble figure group of the »Laocoön« was discovered in the ground in the ruins of the »Golden House« of Nero, northeast of the Colosseum (according to other reports, it was in a vineyard near Santa Maria Maggiore). Michelangelo was present at the excavation and salvage. On his recommendation Pope Julius II bought the work for 500 scudi and had it placed in the Vatican. From one moment to the next, the *Laocoön Group* became the most famous and stylistically most influential work of the Renaissance. It is true that the group, like all ancient sculptures and architectural monuments, was not perfectly preserved. It had lain for over a thousand years among rocks, construction rubble and garbage in the Roman soil. Some parts – arms, hands, limbs, as well as the head of a snake – were missing. Archeologists did not excavate the Trojan priest's right arm until 1904. The two sons' raised right arms were never found.

Since the pope wanted to see a perfect work of art, he had the missing parts replaced by contemporary sculptors. He could not bear the ruinous, the fragmentary. It went against his sense of beauty. This was a view shared by almost all subsequent art lovers, until well into the 19th century. Anyway, it is still amazing that the pope, the head of all the Catholic Christians, had a pagan group of figures like this placed in his surroundings. But the admiration of antiquities had in the meantime proliferated to such an extent that even he no longer shied away from clearly non-Christian works of art. At any rate the sculpture represented the death throes of three naked men, a father and his two young sons. To this day the interpretation of the scene is controversial.

There is a moral interpretation: The priest, so the story went, had warned the Trojans – as had the like-minded Cassandra – not to bring the wooden horse inside, but the goddess, who wanted Troy to be destroyed, had sent two poisonous serpents (from the sea?) to wipe out the Laocoön clan. According to the nonmoral interpretation, which naturally fit in better with the ideas of the enlightened Renaissance interpreters, who preferred frivolous things, the priest had seduced a young woman behind the altar of his temple, and the goddess had wanted to punish him with death for his blasphemy.

Present-day art historians, by the way, tend to subscribe to the second variant and are in agreement that the *Laocoön Group*, unlike many other finds from Roman times, is a genuine Greek work of art from the Hellenistic period that Emperor Nero probably personally commissioned from sculptors from Rhodes.

Michelangelo was thrilled by the new find and felt that it confirmed his aesthetics and his artistic intentions. He, the brusque fighter who had a tendency toward tragedy, was also able to live with ruinous works. His objective was not always the perfected work of art, the kind he had created in his youth with his *David* in Florence. His four life-size slaves, intended for the Boboli Gardens, never quite emerged from their Carrara marble blocks, though later he declared that they too were completed. The »non-finito« as an ideal and stance in the face of the patron and the world of admirers was to have an almost existential meaning in Michelangelo's work (as it did in the work of his contemporary Leonardo da Vinci). According to him that which is perfect crosses a boundary behind which begins a zone of the inhuman, perhaps of the divine or even the deadly.

It was not only the *Laocoön Group* that was a fragment, but the *Apollo Belvedere* as well – also passionately admired, and also found in Roman earth. Apollo, the god of light, poetry, music and youth, of medicine and prophecy, the avenging archer and helper in battle, is missing a left hand and a right lower arm. As an especially handsome god, the son of Zeus and Leto, he would have had quite a few problems without a hand in his numerous amorous adventures with women and men. In reality his marble statue has come down to us as cruelly mutilated beauty. I wonder who knocked off both his hands? Maybe at some point he was toppled from the pedestal, and his missing limbs still lie lonely somewhere in the Roman earth. Enthusiastic admirers such as Johann Joachim Winckelmann, Johann Wolfgang von Goethe or Rainer Maria Rilke stood deeply impressed in front of so much (damaged) perfection. True, Goethe later had second thoughts, wondering in a 1771 letter to Herder: »Apollo of Belvedere, why do you show yourself to us in your nakedness, so that we have to be ashamed of ours?«

The general attitude toward ruined statues and torsos did not change until around 1800. In this period Prince Pückler-Muskau wrote at the sight of the headless Venus de Medici: »The mere body of the Venus Medici without a head, hands and feet makes more of an impression on me, as I have to confess to my shame, than the whole figure has ever been able to instill in me, at

»Ein bloßer Körper der Venus von Medici ohne Kopf, Hände und Füße macht, wie ich zu meiner Schande gestehen muß, mehr Eindruck auf mich, als je die ganze Figur mir hat einflößen können, in so fern man nämlich von Abgüssen auf das Original schließen kann. Da ich kein Kunstsach-verständiger bin, wage ich nicht den Grund erklären zu wollen, der mein Gefühl bestimmte; kam es daher, daß dieser Teil wirklich einen höheren Kunstwert hat, oder machte das einzelne Schöne, daß ich seine Vortrefflichkeit besser auffassen konnte als beim Ganzen?«

Rainer Maria Rilke, durch seinen Aufenthalt bei Rodin zum Torso-Anhänger bekehrt, trieb seine Empfindungen in dem Gedicht *Archaischer Torso Apollos* zu einem existentiellen Endpunkt, der in der berühmten ethischen Forderung endet: »Du mußt dein Leben ändern.« Die übergroße Schön-heit erschien ihm als Wand, die den Weg versperrt.

»Denn das Schöne ist nichts
als des Schrecklichen Anfang, den wir noch grade ertragen,
und wir bewundern es so, weil es gelassen verschmäht,
uns zu zerstören.
Ein jeder Engel ist schrecklich.«
So dichtet er in seinen *Duineser Elegien*.

Als Johann Joachim Winckelmann, der 1717 in Stendal geborene Schusterssohn, 1755 zum ersten Mal nach Rom kam, war er überwältigt. Natürlich verkörperten auch für ihn die *Laokoon-Gruppe* und der *Apollo von Belvedere* Höhepunkte künstlerischen Ausdrucks.

Mitte August 1757 formuliert er an Heinrich Wilhelm Muzell, genannt Baron Stosch, folgenden schwärmerischen, uns allerdings etwas lächerlich erscheinenden Bericht: »Die Statue des Apollo ist das höchste Ideal der Kunst unter allen Werken des Altertums, welche der Zerstörung dersel-ben entgangen sind … Über die Menschheit erhaben ist sein Gewächs, und sein Stand zeuget von der ihn erfüllenden Größe. Ein ewiger Frühling wie in den glücklichen Elysien bekleidet die reizende Männlichkeit vollkommener Jahre und spielet mit sanften Zärtlichkeiten auf dem stolzen Gebäude seiner Glieder … Keine Adern noch Sehnen erhitzen und regen diesen Körper, sondern ein himmlischer Geist, der sich wie ein sanfter Strom ergossen, hat gleichsam die ganze Um-schreibung dieser Figur erfüllet.«

Und im Juli 1756 schreibt Winckelmann, der davon träumt, sich ganz in Rom niederzulassen, an Hieronymus Dietrich Berendis: »Ich glaube, ich bin nach Rom gekommen, denjenigen, die Rom nach mir sehen werden, die Augen ein wenig zu öffnen: ich rede nur von Künstlern: denn alle Kavaliere kommen als Narren und gehen als Esel wieder weg; dieses Geschlecht verdient nicht, daß man sie unterrichte und lehre. Einer gewissen Nation ist Rom gar unerträglich. Ein Franzose ist unverbesserlich: das Altertum und er widersprechen einander. Es ärgert mich, daß ich aus Gefälligkeit einigen neuern Künstlern gewisse Vorzüge eingeräumt. Die Neuern sind Esel gegen die Alten, von denen wir gleichwohl das Allerschönste nicht haben, und Bernini ist der größte Esel unter den Neuern, die Franzosen ausgenommen; denen man die Ehre in dieser Art lassen muß. Ich sage Dir eine Regel: bewundere niemals die Arbeit eines neuern Bildhauers; Du würdest erstaunen, wenn Du das Beste der modernité, welches gewiß in Rom ist, gegen das Mittelmäßige von den Alten hältst.«

Im Jahr 1763 ist es dann endlich soweit. Winckelmann wird Oberaufseher der römischen Al-tertümer und verfügt jetzt über genügend finanzielle Mittel, ganz in Rom zu leben. Er ist inzwi-schen eine bekannte Persönlichkeit geworden, und viele Besucher wünschen, von ihm durch die antiken Trümmerlandschaften und die päpstlichen Sammlungen geführt zu werden. Nachdem er seine mehrbändige *Geschichte der Kunst des Altertums* geschrieben und veröffentlicht hatte, galt er als der bedeutendste Altertumskenner seiner Zeit. Heutige Archäologen und Kunstgeschichtler sehen in ihm den Begründer ihrer Fächer. Zum ersten Mal faßte ein Gelehrter die Kunst als ent-wicklungsgeschichtliches Phänomen auf, in dessen Verlauf sich ästhetische Werte und Ausdrucks-möglichkeiten von Generation zu Generation verfeinerten und verbesserten. Allerdings stellte er die griechische Kunst weit über die seiner Meinung nach epigonale römische Kunst. Das Ziel seiner Kunstbetrachtungen sah er darin, die Zeitgenossen – vor allem die Künstler und Architek-ten unter ihnen – auf klassische Ideale einzustimmen und sie von übertriebenen barocken Ideen (eben Bernini!) abzubringen. Er wollte, daß die klassische Antike mit ihren Werken zum absoluten Vorbild für alle Künstler der Welt werde. Der Klassizismus mit dem von ihm formulierten (und oft strapazierten) Ideal der »edlen Einfalt und stillen Größe« war geboren.

Später entzündeten sich am Thema »Laokoon« weiterhin heiße Diskussionen. Nicht nur Win-ckelmann, sondern auch Lessing, Goethe und Schiller verfaßten über die legendäre Figurengrup-

least in so far as it is possible to judge the original from casts. Since I am no art expert, I will not venture to explain the reason for my emotion; was it because this fragment really has a higher artistic value, or did the beauty of the separate part make it possible for me better to understand its excellence than would have been the case with the whole?«

Rainer Maria Rilke, converted by his stay with Rodin to be a Torso fan, escalated his feelings in the poem *Archaischer Torso Apollos* [*Archaic Torso of Apollo*] to an existential conclusion that ends with the famous ethical demand »You must change your life.« To Rilke, the Torso's enormous beauty seemed a wall blocking the way. In his *Duino Elegies* he writes:

»For beauty is nothing but the beginning of terror, which we are still just able to endure,
and we are so awed because it serenely disdains to annihilate us.
Every angel is terrifying.«

When Johann Joachim Winckelmann, a cobbler's son born in 1717 in Stendal, first came to Rome in 1756, he was overwhelmed. Naturally, for him, too, the *Laocoön Group* and the *Apollo Belvedere* embodied high points of artistic expression.

pe Aufsätze. Winckelmann hatte geschrieben: »Der Schmerz, welcher sich in allen Muskeln und Sehnen entdecket, und den man ganz allein, ohne das Gesicht und andere Teile zu betrachten, an dem schmerzlich eingezogenen Unterleibe beinahe selbst zu empfinden glaubet; dieser Schmerz, sage ich, äußert sich dennoch mit keiner Wut in dem Gesicht und in der ganzen Stellung. Er erhebet kein schreckliches Geschrei, wie Vergil von seinem Laokoon singet: die Öffnung des Mundes gestattet es nicht. «

Goethe und Lessing sahen in der Figurengruppe weit mehr Expression und Schmerz. Für Winckelmann gehörte die ausgeglichene Ruhe zur Grundaussage der Klassik, dabei entging ihm, daß es sich hier um eine Katastrophe handelt, schließlich werden ein Vater und seine beiden Söhne von zwei riesigen Schlangen erdrückt und vergiftet!

Winckelmanns Intimfeind Bernini glaubte, in der Figurengruppe den Moment der Erstarrung zu erkennen. Das Gift wirkt, und eine Gegenwehr ist nicht mehr möglich. Im nächsten Moment wird die Schlange den ersten, vom Gift gelähmten Knaben verschlingen! Zerstörung, Verwesung, Ruinenhaftigkeit und Emotionen interessierten Winckelmann nicht. Für ihn glänzte die Antike weiß, erhaben und in Vollkommenheit erstarrt. Jeder, der sich mit ihr befaßte, mußte ein besserer Mensch werden. Das »Schöne« und das »Gute« waren für ihn geschwisterliche Eigenschaften.

Natürlich fiel auch schon den Zeitgenossen auf, daß er – wie Michelangelo – die männlichen Körper weit höher stellte als die weiblichen. Für ihn trug die Klassik eindeutig männliche Züge. Er verlor sich in schwärmerischen Liebeserklärungen für Apoll und Laokoon. Wie wir heute wissen, neigte Winckelmann – im Gegensatz zu seinen Verehrern Goethe und Lessing – zu einer homoerotischen Weltsicht. Es wundert daher nicht, daß er ein ähnlich tragisches Ende gefunden hat wie viel später der Filmregisseur Pier Paolo Pasolini. Winckelmann starb im Alter von 50 Jahren in einem Triester Hotel durch die Messerstiche Francesco Arcangelis, eines vorbestraften und einschlägig bekannten Kleinkriminellen. Die Gründe seiner Ermordung konnten nie ganz ermittelt werden, obwohl man genau über den Tathergang Bescheid wußte. Der Täter wohnte im Zimmer neben Winckelmann und floh nach der Tat nicht. Nach gründlicher Vernehmung und einem ausführlichen Prozeß verurteilten ihn seine Richter zum Tode durch Rädern. Am Ende wurde Winckelmann fernab seiner Traumstadt Rom in Triest beerdigt. Heute kann man sich kaum vorstellen, welche unglaubliche Berühmtheit er erlangt hatte. Ihm war es gelungen, den Bildungsreisen vieler europäischer Adliger eine andere, wissenschaftlichere Richtung zu geben. Plötzlich erschloß sich die Antike auf eine ganz neue, tiefere, nicht mehr ausschließlich sentimentale Weise.

Auch Ruinen- und Zerstörungsgedanken spielten dabei eine zunehmend wichtigere Rolle. Viele Besucher betätigten sich als halbwissenschaftliche Detektive, nahmen teil an der Geschichtsrecherche und versuchten, die untergegangenen großen Zeiten zu verstehen. Rom galt als stimmungsvolle Ruinenstadt schlechthin, und die Tatsache, daß ein Großteil der Antike noch unausgegraben unter der Erde lag, regte die Phantasie der adligen und reichen Touristen zu Spekulationen an. Als gar noch die unterirdische Welt der Katakomben entdeckt wurde, nahm der schaurige Kitzel zu.

Jacob Burckhardt kommt in seinem berühmten Buch *Die Kultur der Renaissance in Italien* immer wieder auf das Thema »Ruine« zu sprechen: »Außer dem archäologischen Eifer und der feierlich-patriotischen Stimmung weckten die Ruinen als solche, in und außer Rom, auch schon eine elegisch-sentimentale. Bereits bei Petrarca und Boccaccio finden sich Anklänge dieser Art; Poggio besucht oft den Tempel der Venus und Roma, in der Meinung, es sei der des Castors und Polluxs, wo einst so oft Senat gehalten worden, und vertieft sich hier in die Erinnerung an die großen Redner Crassus, Hortensius, Cicero. Vollkommen sentimental äußert sich dann Pius II., zumal bei der Beschreibung von Tibur, und bald darauf ensteht die erste ideale Ruinenansicht nebst Schilderung bei Polifilo: Trümmer mächtiger Gewölbe und Kolonnaden, durchwachsen von alten Platanen, Lorbeeren und Zypressen nebst wildem Buschwerk. In der heiligen Geschichte wird es, man kann kaum sagen wie, gebräuchlich, die Darstellung der Geburt Christi in die möglichst prachtvollen Ruinen eines Palastes zu verlegen. Daß dann endlich die künstliche Ruine zum Requisit prächtiger Gartenanlagen wurde, ist nur die praktische Äußerung desselben Gefühls.«

Das ganze 19. Jahrhundert über wirkten Winckelmanns Gedanken fort. Akademien, Rathäuser, Parlamente, Opernhäuser und Villen entstanden nach seinen Idealvorstellungen. Aber auch die Ruinenverehrer vermehrten sich und wuchsen zu einer starken, romantischen Fraktion heran. Vor allem Nietzsche war es, der die tragischen Komponenten der griechischen Kunst betonte, auf die blutige Brutalität der griechischen Tragödien hinwies und damit am hehren, weiß rekonstruierten Klassikbild sägte.

Aber erst zu Beginn des 20. Jahrhunderts schlug das Pendel endgültig um. Als Hugo von Hofmannsthal zusammen mit Harry Graf Keßler und dem französischen Bildhauer Aristide Mail-

In mid-August 1757 he pens the following effusive report to Heinrich Wilhelm Muzell, called Baron Stosch. To us, it is true, the letter sounds somewhat laughable: »The statue of Apollo is the highest ideal of art among all the works of antiquity that have escaped destruction … His stature is elevated above the rest of humanity, and his stance bespeaks the greatness that fills him. An eternal spring, like that in happy Elysium, clothes the appealing masculinity of perfect years and plays on the majestic building of his limbs with gentle caresses … Neither blood-vessels nor sinews heat and stir this body, but a heavenly essence, diffusing itself like a gentle stream, seems to fill the whole contour of the figure …«

And in July 1756 Winckelmann, who dreams of settling in Rome for good, writes to Hieronymus Dietrich Berendis: »I believe I came to Rome to open the eyes, just a little, of those who will see Rome after me: I speak only of artists: for all the cavaliers come as fools and leave again as asses; their sort does not deserve being instructed and taught. A certain nation actually cannot bear Rome. A Frenchman is incorrigible: antiquity and he are mutually contradictory. I am annoyed that out of the kindness of my heart I conceded that a few newer artists had certain merits. The modern artists are silly asses compared to the ancients, notwithstanding the fact that we do not have their finest works, and Bernini is the biggest ass of the moderns, except for the French, whom we must allow to have that distinction. I'll tell you a rule of thumb: never admire the work of a modern sculptor; you would be amazed if you compare the best works of modernity, which are definitely in Rome, with the mediocre work of the ancients.«

In 1763 the time has finally come. Winckelmann becomes prefect of Roman antiquities and now has the financial means to live in Rome permanently. In the meantime he has become a famous personality, and many visitors want him to give them a guided tour through the ancient fields of rubble and the papal collections. After he had written and published the two-volume *Geschichte der Kunst des Altertums* (*History of the Art of Antiquity*), he was considered to be the most important expert on antiquity of his time. Present-day archeologists and art historians regard him as the founder of their disciplines. For the first time, a scholar thought of art as a developmental phenomenon, observing how aesthetic values and modes of expression were refined and improved from generation to generation. It is true that he placed Greek art far above Roman art, which in his opinion was imitative. The goal of his reflections on art, he felt, was to attune his contemporaries – particularly the artists and architects among them – to classical ideals and to persuade them to abandon exaggerated baroque ideas (Bernini, to be precise!). He wanted the works of classical antiquity to become the absolute model for all the artists in the world. It was the birth of Classicism and of the ideal – formulated by Winckelmann (and often flogged to death) – of »noble simplicity and quiet grandeur«.

Later the topic of »Laocoön« sparked off further lively discussions. Not only Winckelmann, but Lessing, Goethe and Schiller as well wrote essays about the legendary group of figures. Winckelmann had written: »The pain that is visible in every muscle and sinew of the body, which one can almost feel as one examines the horribly contorted lower body, not to speak of the face and other parts of the body; this pain, I repeat, is borne on the face without a hint of rage, as is true of the figure's whole bearing. Here there is no cry of horror, as Virgil writes of his Laocoön; the position of the mouth clearly precludes that.«

Goethe and Lessing saw far more expression and pain in the group of figures. For Winckelmann one of the basic messages of classical antiquity was balanced serenity, and he failed to notice that this was the depiction of a catastrophe: After all, a father and his two sons are being crushed to death and poisoned by two huge snakes!

Winckelmann's favorite enemy Bernini believed the group of figures showed the moment of paralysis. The poison has taken effect and resistance is no longer possible. The next moment the serpent will devour the first young boy, who has been paralyzed by the poison. Winckelmann was not interested in destruction, decay, ruins and emotions. For him, antiquity gleamed white, sublime and frozen in perfection. Those who studied it could not help becoming better human beings. For him, the »beautiful« and the »good« were related qualities.

Naturally, even his contemporaries were struck by the fact that – like Michelangelo – he valued male bodies far more than female ones. For him, classical antiquity had clearly masculine traits. He lost himself in effusive declarations of love for Apollo and Laocoön. As we know today, Winckelmann – unlike his admirers Goethe and Lessing – leaned toward a homoerotic worldview. It is therefore not surprising that he met with a similarly tragic end as the film director Pier Paolo Pasolini did much later. Winckelmann was knifed to death at the age of 50 in a Trieste hotel by Francesco Arcangeli, a previously convicted and notorious petty criminal. The reasons for his murder could never be completely determined, although the exact details of the crime were

lol 1908 zu einer längeren Griechenlandreise aufbrach, sah er schnell ein, daß dieses ruinenge-
füllte Land nichts mit der alten Vorstellung von der Antike zu tun hatte.

Bereits im Jahr 1903 hatte er sich mit Sophokles' Tragödie *Elektra* auseinandergesetzt und ein
expressionistisches Stück geschrieben, das von weiblicher Ohnmacht und Rachsucht handelt.
Ein Fall für die Couch Sigmund Freuds. Der Komponist Richard Strauss fand in seiner Vertonung
dafür die richtigen Klänge von Raserei, Wut und Ekstase. Plötzlich waren die blutigen Neurosen
und Psychosen der Elektra ganz modern und zeitgemäß geworden.

Obwohl der Gedanke naheliegt, daß die klassische Antike im 20. Jahrhundert endgültig ausgedient haben müsse, verhielt es sich in Wirklichkeit ganz anders. Sie spukte und spukt weiterhin
durch viele Künstlerköpfe, wenn auch zunehmend verfremdet und zertrümmert. Nicht nur Picasso
suchte ihr Echo (*Minotauros*, etwa), sondern auch Schriftsteller wie James Joyce, der mit seinem
Ulysses eine sprachgewaltige Banal-Parodie auf das antike Epos schrieb. Der listenreiche Odysseus war jetzt zu Leopold Bloom, einem trinkfreudigen, bei einer Dubliner Zeitung angestellten
Anzeigenverkäufer geworden und die wartende Penelope zu seiner Frau Marion, genannt Molly,
einer langschlafenden, von Sex träumenden Hausfrau, die ihn am Nachmittag des 16. Juni 1904 –
an diesem einzigen Tag spielt der Roman – mit einem Liebhaber betrügt.

Später griffen Igor Strawinsky, Jean Giraudoux, Jean Anouilh, Albert Camus, Jean-Paul Sartre,
Peter Hacks, Botho Strauß, Edward Bond, Hans Werner Henze, Christa Wolf und Heiner Müller
auf antike Themen zurück. Der Fundus lebt. Die Zeitgenossen erkennen sich wieder in den archaischen Trümmern, Ruinen und Spiegelscherben. Dissonante Gegenwelten zu Winckelmanns
(falschen) Harmonieträumen.

Aber hier eilen wir der Entwicklung voraus. Zunächst gilt es, den größten und berühmtesten
aller Ruinenverherrlicher dieser Zeit vorzustellen, Winckelmanns Zeitgenossen und Gegenspieler
Giovanni Battista Piranesi. Während wir Winckelmanns Ideen heute nur noch als historisches
Phänomen betrachten, das in den Werken des Klassizismus weiterlebt, können wir in Piranesi
und seinen Werken den visionär-modernen Zeitgenossen erkennen, der in theatralisch-romanti-
scher Weise moderne Architekturvisionen und Horrorwelten vorwegnahm.

Giovanni Battista Piranesi wurde am 4. Oktober 1720 in Mogliano (Mestre) bei Venedig als
Sohn eines Steinmetzen geboren. Von 1730 bis 1740 unterrichtete ihn zunächst sein Bruder, ein
Kartäusermönch, in Latein und begeisterte den Knaben für römische Geschichte. Anschließend
ging Giovanni Battista bei seinem Onkel, dem Architekten Matteo Lucchesi, in die Lehre und erhielt durch ihn eine fundierte architektonisch-ingenieurtechnische Ausbildung. Nach einem Streit
mit ihm setzte er seine Ausbildung bei den venezianischen Architekten Carlo Zucchi und Giovanni Scalfarotti fort. Zunehmend betrieb er in diesen Jahren auch bühnenbildnerische Studien, ein
Thema, das im theater- und opernbesessenen Venedig sehr nahelag. Ob er jemals dem berühmtesten Bühnenmaler seiner Zeit, dem Bologneser Ferdinando Bibiena, begegnete, ist umstritten.
Sicher jedoch kannte er dessen Werke und seine geniale Methode, Raumdurchblicke effektvoll
darzustellen. Bibiena hatte sich als typischer Barockkünstler von der Zentralperspektive abge-
wendet und wählte oft einen Übereckblick in mehrere – mindestens zwei – verschiedene Raum-
situationen gleichzeitig. Die schrägen Diagonalen mit zwei Fluchtpunkten stiegen damit zum Ideal
der barocken Kunst auf. Zu dieser Zeit wußte Piranesi noch nicht, ob er Maler, Graphiker, Büh-
nenbildner oder praktischer Architekt werden sollte. 1740 kam er zum ersten Mal nach Rom und
trat dort in die Werkstatt des wichtigsten römischen Vedutenstechers Giuseppe Vasi ein. Allerdings geriet er, bedingt durch seinen cholerisch-temperamentvollen Charakter, mit dem Lehrherrn
immer wieder in Streit und mußte nach wenigen Jahren die Werkstatt verlassen. 1744 kehrte er
nach Venedig zurück und lernte dort den größten Meister barocker Himmelsdarstellungen,
Giovanni Battista Tiepolo, kennen. Dessen Perspektivtaumel, man könnte auch sagen Perspek-
tivenexplosionen, regten Piranesi zu eigener fieberhafter Tätigkeit an. Er begann – als freier
Künstler – mit seinen visionär-dunklen *Carceri*-Radierungen, die ihn sein Leben lang begleiten
sollten. 1745 kehrte er nach Rom zurück, beschäftigte sich weiter mit römischer Geschichte und
studierte die Ruinenwelt der Antike. Fiebrig und erregt zeichnete er vor Ort das Forum Romanum,
oder das, was davon noch zu sehen war, abends arbeitete er weiter an seinen *Carceri*. Manche
Forscher sprechen von einer Nervenkrise, die der Künstler möglicherweise in dieser Zeit durchlebt
hat. Ob gewisse Blätter der *Carceri* unter Opiumeinfluß entstanden sind, bleibt umstritten. Auto-
biographische Äußerungen Piranesis, die durch Verwandte und Freunde überliefert wurden, legen
die Spuren für diese Vermutung.

Von 1752 an beruhigte sich das Leben Piranesis, er heiratete die Gärtnerstochter Angela
Pasquini. Drei ihrer acht Kinder werden später seine Werkstatt weiterführen. Inzwischen hatte er
damit begonnen, alle historisch wichtigen Plätze, Brunnen, Denkmäler und Paläste Roms zu

known. The perpetrator lived in a room next door to Winckelmann and did not run away after the crime. After a thorough interrogation and a comprehensive trial his judges condemned him to death by being broken on the wheel. At the end Winckelmann was buried in Trieste far from his dream city of Rome. Today it is almost impossible to imagine how incredibly famous he had become. He had succeeded in giving the educational journeys of many European aristocrats a different, more scholarly direction. Suddenly antiquity was revealed in quite a new, more profound, no longer exclusively sentimental way.

Ideas related to ruins and destruction also played an increasingly more important part here. Many visitors acted as half-scholarly detectives, took part in historical research and tried to understand the great extinct eras of the past. Rome was considered to be the atmospheric city of ruins par excellence, and the fact that a large part of antiquity still lay unexcavated below ground stimulated the fantasy of the rich and aristocratic tourists to all kinds of speculations. When, on top of it all, the subterranean world of the catacombs was discovered, the spine-chilling titillation increased.

Jacob Burckhardt, in his famous book *Die Kultur der Renaissance in Italien* (*The Culture of the Renaissance in Italy*) keeps coming back to the topic of »ruins«. »Besides archeological enthusiasm and a solemn patriotic feeling, ruins as such, within and outside Rome, awakened not only archaeological zeal and patriotic enthusiasm, but an elegiac of sentimental melancholy. In Petrarch and Boccaccio we find touches of this feeling. Poggio Bracciolini often visited the temple of Venus and Roma, in the belief that it was that of Castor and Pollux, where the senate used so often to meet, and would lose himself in memories of the great orators Crassus, Hortensius, Ciicero. The language of Pius II, especially in describing Tivoli, has a thoroughly sentimental ring, and soon afterwards (1467) appeared the first pictures of ruins, with a commentary by Polifilo. Ruins of mighty arches and colonnades, half hid in plane trees, laurels, cypresses and brushwood, figure in his pages. In the sacred legends it became the custom, we can hardly say how, to lay the scene of the birth of Christ in the ruins of a magnificent palace. That artificial ruins became afterwards a necessity of landscape gardening is only a practical consequence of this feeling.«

Winckelmann's ideas held sway throughout the entire 19th century. Academies, town halls, parliaments, opera houses and villas were built in accordance with his ideals. But the number of admirers of ruins increased as well and grew into a strong, romantic fraction. It was primarily Nietzsche who emphasized the tragic components of Greek art, drew attention to the bloody brutality of Greek tragedies and thus attacked the sublime, white, reconstructed image of classical antiquity.

Not until the beginning of the 20th century, however, did the pendulum finally swing in the other direction. When, in 1908, Hugo von Hofmannsthal together with Count Harry Kessler and the French sculptor Aristide Maillol set out on a long journey to Greece, he soon realized that this ruin-filled land had nothing in common with the old idea of antiquity. As early as 1903 he had had a good look at Sophocles' tragedy *Electra* and written an expressionist piece dealing with feminine powerlessness and vindictiveness. A case for Sigmund Freud's couch. The composer Richard Strauss, who set it to music, found the right tones for it of fury, rage and ecstasy. Suddenly the bloodstained neuroses and psychoses of Electra had become quite modern and up-to-date.

Although one would assume that classical antiquity had finally had its day by the 20th century, the reality was quite different. The art of classical Greece continued to haunt, and still haunts, many artists, though increasingly alienated and fragmented. It was not only Picasso who looked for its echo (for instance, in his »Minotaur«), but also writers such as James Joyce, who with his *Ulysses* wrote an eloquent banal parody of the ancient epic. The cunning Odysseus had now become Leopold Bloom, a bibulous seller of advertisements working for a Dublin newspaper, and the waiting Penelope had become his wife Marion, aka Molly, a late-rising housewife who dreams of sex and who, on the afternoon of 16 June 1904 – the novel takes place on this one day – cheats on him with a lover.

Later Igor Stravinsky, Jean Giraudoux, Jean Anouilh, Albert Camus, Jean-Paul Sartre, Peter Hacks, Botho Strauss, Edward Bond, Hans Werner Henze, Christa Wolf and Heiner Müller went back to themes from classical antiquity. It is a rich resource. Our contemporaries recognize themselves in the archaic rubble, ruins and shards of broken mirrors. Dissonant alternate worlds to Winckelmann's (false) dreams of harmony.

But here we are anticipating later developments. First, we need to introduce the greatest and most famous of all those who glorified ruins during this period, Winckelmann's contemporary and

zeichnen und später in Radierungen umzuarbeiten. Daraus entstand das monumentale Werk *Antichità Romane*, das 1756 erschien und sofort ein großer, europaweiter Erfolg wurde. Endlich konnte sich der Künstler einen großen Arbeitsraum (mit Angestellten) in der Via del Corso einrichten. Zur Straße hin gab es einen Laden – heute würde man von einer Kunstgalerie sprechen –, in dem seine Radierungen zum Verkauf angeboten wurden. Der Rom-Tourismus wuchs von Jahr zu Jahr, und jeder Adlige oder wohlhabende Bürgerliche wollte ein bildhaftes Andenken der Stadt Rom mit nach Hause bringen. Neben Piranesi und Vasi lebten noch viele andere Künstler in Rom, die sich mit Ruinen, Stadtbildern, Platz- und Gebäudeansichten befaßten. Aber Piranesi übertrumpfte bald alle mit seinem Erfolg. Bereits Goethes Vater hatte sich Radierungen von Piranesi gekauft und in der Frankfurter Wohnung aufgehängt. Johann Wolfgang wuchs mit ihnen auf. Piranesi selbst berief sich als architektonischer Bilderfinder auf kein italienisches Vorbild, sondern auf den Österreicher Johann Bernhard Fischer von Erlach. Dieser 1656 in Graz geborene Künstler-Architekt hatte 1721, zwei Jahre vor seinem Tod, ein Buch veröffentlicht, das damals für sensationelles Aufsehen gesorgt hatte: *Entwurf einer historischen Architektur*. Ziel seiner gezeichneten Architekturdarstellungen war, wie Norbert Miller schreibt »die Wiederherstellung der Weltwunder aus der einheitsstiftenden Phantasie des Künstlers«.

Von Johann Bernhard Fischer von Erlach, dem Erbauer der Wiener Karlskirche und der Nationalbibliothek im Hofburg-Komplex, übernahm Piranesi die monumental-grandiose Sicht auf historische Architekturen. Dabei vergaß er allerdings nicht, deren Ruinenhaftigkeit darzustellen. Ja man kann fast sagen, daß sich die Ruinen mit den Jahren zu seiner wahren Obsession auswuchsen. Gerhard Köpf schreibt in seinem Roman *Piranesis Traum* darüber: »Die Ruine war schon immer der Bereich, in dem sich Architektur und Natur am deutlichsten begegneten. ›Folge der Eule‹, sagt ein Sprichwort aus dem Maghreb, ›und sie wird dich zu einer Ruine führen‹. Die Eule ist das Symbol der Weisheit: ergo führt die Weisheit zur Ruine. Die Ruine, so sagen die Kunsthistoriker, sei ein Stimmungsträger, und Ruinenarchitektur sei auf Wirkung bedacht. Alleine schon die Dunkelheit, die bröckelnde geschundene Majestät des Gebäudes, der stumme Wiederhall fordern unseren demütigen Respekt heraus …« Und weiter: »Deshalb sind die Kunsthistoriker und Kunstkritiker die eigentlichen Kunstvernichter, wie einmal ein Bruder im Geiste gesagt hat, auch so ein Verdammter und Besessener … Seine Worte sind mir mittlerweile in Fleisch und Blut übergegangen, zumal ich als Liebhaber von Ruinen geradezu ein Zertrümmerungsverehrer bin.«

Ähnlich wie sein Zeitgenosse Winckelmann sammelte Piranesi Bewunderer aus ganz Europa um sich und behandelte sie alle – ob Fürst, Graf oder einfacher Architekt – als seine Schüler. Sie hingen an seinen Lippen und beobachteten die Bewegungen seines Zeichenstifts wie Offenbarungen. Es gibt zahlreiche Beschreibungen, die den Eindruck erwecken, Piranesi sei ein Paganini des Zeichenstifts gewesen. Allerdings bildete die Realisierbarkeit des Dargestellten immer den Hintergrund der Bewunderung. Niemand zweifelte daran, daß Piranesi alle gezeichneten Visionen auch hätte bauen können. In Wirklichkeit beschränkte sich seine praktische Tätigkeit als Architekt auf ganz wenige Um- und Anbauten. Sein Interesse in praktischen Dingen war – neben dem Florieren seiner Galerie – eher auf Ausgrabungen und archäologische Forschungen gerichtet. Er sah sich auch, ähnlich seinem Widersacher Winckelmann, als Wissenschaftler und Forscher.

Etwa um 1760 begannen die schon lange schwelenden Spannungen zwischen Piranesi und Winckelmann schärfere Formen anzunehmen. Winckelmann schwärmte bekanntlich von griechischer Kunst, stellte sie qualitativ weit über die römische. Für Piranesi hingegen gab es nur die römische Kunst, die sich, seiner (irrigen) Meinung nach, aus der etruskischen entwickelt hätte. 1761 kaufte Piranesi, dessen Geschäfte blendend liefen, den Palazzo Tomati in der Strada Felice (heute Via Sistina) und baute eine noch größere Druckerei auf. Er arbeitete an der zweiten Fassung seiner *Carceri*. Im Jahr 1765 erreichten die Auseinandersetzungen mit den Anhängern Winckelmanns ihren Höhepunkt und waren allgemeines Stadtgespräch in Rom. Seit 1769 rekonstruierte Piranesi, ganz der erfolgreiche Geschäftsmann, zusammen mit römischen Kunsthandwerkern alte, antike, jetzt sogar leicht ägyptisch angehauchte Kamine (das war damals die neueste Mode!) und verkaufte sie vor allem an englische Antikenliebhaber. Auch diese Geschäfte liefen sehr gut. Zwischen 1770 und 1775 zog er sich bei Ausgrabungen ein Nierenleiden zu, dem er am 9. November 1778 erlag. Nach seinem Tode verbreitete sich in der Stadt das Gerücht, der Sterbende habe nicht nach der Heiligen Schrift, sondern nach der *Römischen Geschichte* des Livius verlangt.

Auf Piranesis Radierung mit dem Titel *Veduta di Campo Vaccino* (Das Forum Romanum als Kuhweide) aus dem Jahr 1757 will ich nachfolgend näher eingehen. Es ist ein merkwürdiges Bild, von dem ich sogar einen Originalabzug besitze. Rom erscheint weniger als bewohnte Stadt, eher als eine hügelige, weitgehend leere Campagna-Landschaft, in die sich einige Ruinenrelikte

12. Giovanni Battista Piranesi, *Carceri*, 1761, Blatt XIV.
12. Giovanni Battista Piranesi, *Carceri*, 1761, sheet XIV.

antagonist Giovanni Battista Piranesi. While today we regard Winckelmann's ideas merely as a historical phenomenon that lives on in the works of Classicism, in Piranesi and his works we are able to recognize a visionary modern contemporary who theatrically and romantically anticipated modern architectural visions, and worlds of horror.

Giovanni Battista Piranesi was born on 4 October 1720 in Mogliano (Mestre) near Venice, the son of a stonemason. From 1730 to 1740, his brother, a Carthusian monk, taught him Latin and filled the boy with enthusiasm for Roman history. Later Giovanni Battista was an apprentice with his uncle, the architect Matteo Lucchesi, and received a sound education in architecture and technical engineering from him. After a quarrel with him, Piranesi continued his training with the Venetian architects Carlo Zucchi and Giovanni Scalfarotti. Increasingly, during these years, he also studied stage design, which made a great deal of sense in theater- and opera-obsessed Venice. It is debatable whether he ever met the most famous scene painter of his time, the Bolognese Ferdinando Bibiena. However, he certainly knew his work and his ingenious method of depicting scenes in perspective to great effect. A typical baroque artist, Bibiena had turned away from the central single-point perspective and often chose an angle perspective into several – at least two – different spatial situations simultaneously. Oblique diagonals with two vanishing points thus became the ideal of baroque art. At this point Piranesi was not yet sure whether he wanted to be a painter, graphic artist or practical architect. In 1740 he visited Rome for the first time and there joined the studio of the most important Roman engraver of vedutas, Giuseppe Vasi. However, since Piranesi was choleric and temperamental by nature, he would constantly get into arguments with his master, and had to leave the studio a few years later. In 1744 he returned to Venice and met the greatest baroque master of painted skies, Giovanni Battista Tiepolo. Tiepolo's dizzying perspectives – one might even say, his perspective explosions – prompted Piranesi to frenzied activity. As a freelance artist, he began work on his visionary, dark *Carceri* etchings, which were to accompany him for the rest of his life. In 1745 he returned to Rome, and continued to study Roman history and the ruins of antiquity. Feverishly and excitedly he sketched the local Forum Romanum, or what was still left of it. At night he continued work on his *Carceri*. Some researchers speak of a nervous breakdown the artist may have experienced at this time. It is debatable whether certain pages of the *Carceri* were created under the influence of opium. This conjecture is based on Piranesi's autobiographical statements reported by relatives and friends.

From 1752 on Piranesi's life became calmer. He married Angela Pasquini, a gardener's daughter. Three of their eight children would later continue his artist's workshop. In the meantime he

EDUTA del sotterraneo Fondamento del Mausoleo, che fu eretto da Elio... ...d Adriano Imp! In questa parte, la qual è opposta alla Facciata, gli Speroni sono tutti ... ...di di angoli Travertini. A Parte di Ricompitura... ...Opera incerta a corsi, la quale veste d'ogni interno il Fondam. B Palizzate. C Parte del Mausoleo

13. Giovanni Battista Piranesi, Radierung aus der Reihe *Antichità Romane*, 1756.

13. Giovanni Battista Piranesi, etching from the *Antichità Romane* series, 1756.

aus der römischen Vergangenheit verirrt haben. Die Wiesen überwiegen. Kühe allerdings kann ich keine entdecken.

Was war aus dem »ewigen Rom« geworden? In den Jahrhunderten nach Christus galt Rom mit über einer Million Einwohnern als größte Stadt der Welt. Eine so gewaltige Konzentration von Menschen hatte es bisher auf dem Erdball noch nicht gegeben. Doch dann begann der langsame Niedergang, und er hing mit dem Christentum zusammen. Kaiser Konstantin war als erster römischer Herrscher zur neuen Religion übergetreten und verlegte, wahrscheinlich aus strategischen Gründen, seinen Regierungssitz von Westrom nach Ostrom, das bisher Byzanz geheißen hatte und von da an Konstantinopel hieß. Westrom wurde zunehmend von barbarischen Stämmen

had begun to sketch and later turn into engravings all the historically important squares, fountains, monuments and palaces of Rome. The result was the monumental work *Antichità Romane*, which was published in 1756 and immediately became a great success throughout Europe. Finally the artist was able to set up a large workroom (with employees) in Via del Corso. Facing the street there was a shop – today we would call it an art gallery – in which his etchings were offered for sale. Tourism to Rome grew from year to year, and every aristocrat or wealthy commoner wanted to bring home a pictorial souvenir of Rome. Besides Piranesi and Vasi many other artists lived in Rome and dealt with ruins, pictures of the city, and views of squares and buildings. But Piranesi's success outshone all the rest. Even Goethe's father had bought etchings from Piranesi and hung them in his Frankfurt home. Johann Wolfgang grew up with them. Piranesi himself as a finder of architectural pictures did not refer to an Italian model but to the Austrian Johann Bernhard Fischer of Erlach. This artist and architect, born in 1656 in Graz, had published a sensational book in 1721, two years before his death: *Entwurf einer historischen Architektur* (*Outline of a Historical Architecture*). The goal of his drawings of architectural monuments was, as Norbert Miller writes, »the restoration of the wonders of the world from the unifying fantasy of the artist.«

From Johann Bernhard Fischer of Erlach, the man who built the Karlskirche [St. Charles' Church] in Vienna and the National Library in the Hofburg complex, Piranesi borrowed his monumental, grandiose view of historical pieces of architecture. At the same time, though, he did not forget to represent the fact that they were ruins. Indeed, one could almost say that as the years went by ruins became his true obsession. Gerhard Köpf writes about this in his novel *Piranesis Traum* (*Piranesi's Dream*): »The ruin has always been the realm where architecture and nature encounter each other most unmistakably. ›Follow the owl‹, says a proverb from the Maghreb, ›and it will take you to a ruin‹. The owl is the symbol of wisdom: hence wisdom leads to the ruin. The ruin, say art historians, evokes a mood, and the architecture of ruins is intent on having an effect. The mere fact of darkness, the crumbling abused majesty of the building, the mute echo invite our humble respect …« And he goes on: »That's why art historians and art critics are the actual destroyers of art, as a kindred spirit once said, another one of the damned and obsessed … His words in the meantime have become part of me, particularly since as a lover of ruins I am virtually an admirer of destruction.«

Like his contemporary Winckelmann, Piranesi gathered around him admirers from all over Europe and treated them all – whether they were princes, counts or simple architects – as his pupils. They hung on every word he said and observed the movements of his crayon as though they were revelations. Many descriptions give the impression that Piranesi was a Paganini of the crayon. Of course the fact that what he had drawn could have been realized was always implied in their admiration. No one had the least doubt that Piranesi could also have built all the visions he had drawn. In reality his practical work as an architect was limited to a very small number of conversions and additions. His interest in practical things – other than the financial success of his gallery – tended to focus on excavations and archeological research. Like his adversary Winckelmann, he too saw himself as a scholar and researcher.

Around the year 1760, the tension between Piranesi and Winckelmann, which had been smoldering for a long time, began to intensify. Winckelmann was known to be wild about Greek art and felt it was far superior to that of Rome. For Piranesi, on the other hand, there was no art but Roman art, which, in his (erroneous) opinion, had developed from Etruscan art. In 1761 Piranesi, whose financial affairs were in splendid shape, bought the Palazzo Tomati on Strada Felice (now Via Sistina) and set up an even larger printing shop. He was working on the second version of his *Carceri*. In 1765 conflicts with the supporters of Winckelmann reached their peak and were the talk of the town in Rome. Since 1769 Piranesi, successful businessman that he was, together with Roman craftsmen had been reconstructing old, antique fireplaces, including some that showed a faint Egyptian influence (this was the latest fashion!), and selling them primarily to English lovers of antiquities. This business, too, was flourishing. During excavations between 1770 and 1775 he contracted a kidney ailment to which he succumbed on 9 November 1778. After his death a rumor spread in town that the dying man had asked, not for the Holy Scriptures, but for Livy's »History of Rome«.

In the following I shall discuss in more detail Piranesi's engraving *Veduta di Campo Vaccino* (»*The Forum Romanum as a Cow Pasture*«), dated 1757. It is a remarkable picture, of which I even have an original print. Rome seems less an inhabited city than a hilly, mostly empty Campagna landscape with a few ruins, relics of the Roman past, disconsolately scattered about in it. The meadows are predominant. I can't see any cows though.

aus dem Norden Europas bedrängt und angegriffen. Ob sich Kaiser Konstantin in Ostrom mehr Sicherheit versprach oder vielleicht auch vor den Nachwirkungen seiner eigenen Untaten floh, wissen wir nicht. Aus Machthunger hatte er fast alle seine Familienangehörigen umgebracht. Zuletzt ließ er seine Ehefrau im Bade ersticken.

Mit Konstantins Emigration brach nicht nur das Wachstum Roms zusammen, sondern auch die städtische Wehrhaftigkeit und Sicherheit. Obwohl ein Papst in der Stadt residierte, gab es keine Verteidigungskraft gegenüber den immer zahlreicher werdenden Überfällen der Barbaren. Plünderungen und Zerstörungen gehörten zum Alltag der sterbenden Stadt. Schließlich verfielen fast alle Häuser zu Ruinen, auf den Straßen wuchs Gras, und die klassischen Bauten stürzten nach und nach in sich zusammen. Der Stadtzerfall zog sich über Jahrhunderte hin und erreichte im 14. Jahrhundert seinen Höhepunkt, als die Päpste ins Exil nach Avignon zogen. Zeitweise schrumpfte die Einwohnerzahl Roms auf weniger als 1000. Eine einzige gespenstische Ruinenlandschaft. Erst Mitte des 15. Jahrhunderts, nachdem die Päpste in die Stadt zurückgekehrt waren, ging es langsam wieder aufwärts. Aber mit seinen damals 50 000 Einwohnern war Rom immer noch eine arme, schlecht ausgebaute und gesicherte Stadt. Die unbenutzten ruinösen Bereiche überwogen. Als Michelangelo und Bernini hier wirkten, hatten sie mit all ihren Aktivitäten, Planungen und Bauten gegen eine übermächtige Ruinenumwelt anzukämpfen. Jetzt, zu Piranesis Zeiten, waren die Verhältnisse nicht wesentlich anders. Bewohner und Reisende mußten sich schon für Ruinen interessieren, um nicht schnell von Langeweile übermannt zu werden.

Zurück zu Piranesis Radierung: Was sich unter der Oberfläche verbirgt, darüber kann man als Betrachter nur Vermutungen anstellen. So ist anzunehmen, daß die korinthischen Säulen im rechten Vordergrund, von denen nur die Kapitelle zu sehen sind, sich unter der Erde vollständig erhalten haben. Ein Großteil der antiken Tempelarchitektur – der Vespasian-Tempel – entzieht sich also unseren Blicken und wurde, von wem auch immer, verschüttet, begraben wie ein Toter auf dem Friedhof.

Das marmorne Architravfragment über den Kapitellen sieht aus wie eine leicht verschobene Brücke. Jeden Moment droht sein Absturz, und die beiden vornehm gekleideten Touristen, die plaudernd in der Nähe stehen, würden von ihm erschlagen. Aber auch ohne Absturz wird der Weg hinunter in die Senke zwischen Kapitol, Palatin und Esquilin, in den eigentlichen Forumsbereich, für sie nicht einfach werden. Es müssen gewaltige, am Boden liegende Marmortrümmer, die an die Felsen von Capri erinnern, überwunden werden. In der linken Bildhälfte ragt der obere Teil eines schon leicht verfallenen Triumphbogens aus der Erde. Auch davor steht eine Touristengruppe mit erklärendem Führer. Im Hintergrund, zwischen Pinien, Zypressen und Platanen, ist

14. Giovanni Battista Piranesi, *Veduta di Campo Vaccino* (Forum Romanum), Radierung aus der Reihe *Antichità Romane*, 1757.
15. Das Forum Romanum (Fragmente des Trajan-Forums) im heutigen, ausgegrabenen Ruinenzustand.

14. Giovanni Battista Piranesi, *Veduta di Campo Vaccino* (Forum Romanum), etching from the *Antichità Romane* series, 1757.
15. The Forum Romanum (fragments from Trajan's Forum) in its present state as an excavated ruin.

What had become of »Eternal Rome«? In the centuries after Christ, Rome, with its over one million inhabitants, was considered to be the largest city in the world. Up to that time, there had never been such a massive concentration of people anywhere on the planet. But then began its slow decline, and it was connected with Christendom. Emperor Constantine was the first to convert to the new religion and moved his seat of government, probably for strategic reasons, from Western to Eastern Rome, previously called Byzantium and now renamed Constantinople. Western Rome was increasingly harried and attacked by barbaric tribes from northern Europe. We do not know if Emperor Constantine hoped to be safer in the Eastern Roman Empire or perhaps fled the consequences of his own atrocities. Greedy for power, he had killed almost all his family members. Finally he had his own wife suffocated in her bath.

After Constantine's emigration, Rome not only stopped growing, but the city's ability to defend itself and its security collapsed as well. Although a pope resided in the city, there was no longer a defense force to ward off the increasingly numerous attacks of the barbarians. In the dying city, plundering and destruction were part of daily life. Finally almost all the houses fell into disrepair, grass grew in the streets, and the classical buildings gradually collapsed. The decline of the city took centuries and reached its peak in the 14th century, when the popes went into exile in Avignon. At times, the number of Rome's inhabitants shrank to less than a thousand. The city was one vast ghostly expanse of ruins. It was not until the middle of the 15th century, after the return of the popes, that things slowly began to look up again. But with its then 50,000 inhabitants Rome was still an impoverished, poorly planned and protected city. Unused stretches of ruined buildings predominated. When Michelangelo and Bernini were active here, they had to battle against an overpowering environment of ruins in everything they did, planned and built. Now, in Piranesi's day and age, conditions were not substantially different. Residents and travelers alike had to take an interest in ruins unless they wanted to be quickly overcome by boredom.

But back to Piranesi's engraving: As an observer, one can only guess at what was hidden under the surface. Thus we may assume that the Corinthian columns in the right foreground, of which we can only see the capitals, have been perfectly preserved below the ground. Thus a large part of the ancient temple architecture – the Temple of Vespasian – is not visible and was buried, we don't know by whom, interred like a corpse at the cemetery.

The marble fragment of the architrave above the capitals looks like a bridge that is slightly off-center. It might collapse any minute, and the two elegantly dressed tourists standing in conversation close to it would be crushed to death. But even if it doesn't collapse, the way down into the hollow between the Capitoline Hill, the Palatine Hill and the Esquiline Hill, into the actual area of

16. Piranesis römische Ruinen haben sich bis heute erhalten. Blick in das Kolosseum.

16. Piranesi's Roman ruins have survived to this day. View into the Colosseum.

deutlich die ovale Rundung des Kolosseums zu erkennen. Die eigentlichen Wohnhäuser der Stadt Rom schieben sich nur ganz bescheiden von der linken Seite ins Bild. Neben den Ruinen der Vergangenheit wirken sie klein, schmucklos und etwas armselig. Die großen Zeiten der Stadt gehören der Vergangenheit an. Man lebt mit den antiken Ruinen wie mit versteinerten Verwandten aus untergegangenen Generationen. Wir betrachten die Stadt, die sich nach Jahrhunderten des Zerfalls ganz langsam zur modernen Touristenmetropole umformt.

Leider haben nach Winckelmanns und Piranesis Tod Archäologen aus der ganzen Welt die Stadt Rom gründlich aus- und umgegraben. Heute sind nur noch selten malerische Ruinensituationen, wie sie auf Piranesis Radierungen erscheinen, anzutreffen. Die archäologischen Grabungen haben aus den romantischen Ruinenandeutungen trostlose Ruinenwunden gemacht. Statt Ziegen und Kühen ziehen Touristen aus der ganzen Welt durch schmerzhaft aufgedeckte, nackte Gräberfelder und tun so, als seien sie beeindruckt von diesen abgenagten, bleich-häßlichen Marmor- und Ziegelskeletten. Romantische Ruinen sehen anders aus, sie sind efeubewachsen verwildert und geben sich ganz der Natur hin. Außerdem stören heute Verkehrslärm und Benzingestank die hehren Vanitas-Gefühle. Wie auch immer. Niemand, kein moderner Architekt, nimmt sich mehr das Kolosseum, die Kaiserforen oder das Pantheon zum Vorbild. Diese Zeiten sind endgültig dahin. Der heutige Tourist muß in Rom Ruinenfelder und marode Häuser lieben, ansonsten wird er enttäuscht sein. Die glorreiche, stilbewußte, machtvolle und vor Kultur strotzende Antike gab es vielleicht nie wirklich, möglicherweise existierte sie nur in den Köpfen ihrer Verehrer und Nachahmer. Und wenn es sie gab, wurde sie hervorgebracht von Hunderttausenden von Sklaven, die bis zur tödlichen Erschöpfung arbeiten mußten. Das »Gute und Schöne« ist dann in Wirklichkeit ein erzwungenes Produkt gnadenloser Eroberer, Unterdrücker und Sklaventreiber gewesen. So gesehen, beruhigt der Blick über die römischen Ruinenlandschaften: gut, daß diese Dinge zerfallen und zerstört sind. Vielleicht sollten wir sie in den nächsten Jahren wieder gänzlich mit Erde bedecken und uns endgültig von ihren falschen Idealen befreien. Wir erinnern uns: Das letzte Mal, als sich Diktatoren wie Hitler und Mussolini auf sie beriefen, endete der angestrebte Aufschwung in der blutigen Katastrophe des zweiten Weltkriegs. Krüppel, Juden, Slawen und Andersdenkende wurden vergast, weil sie den klassischen Idealen nicht entsprachen!

Wenigstens auf eine Radierung aus dem berühmten »Gefängnis«-Zyklus Giovanni Battista Piranesis will ich hier näher eingehen. Es handelt sich um das Blatt XIV der *Carceri* aus dem Jahr 1761. Während Piranesis Darstellungen der Stadt Rom vor allem seine Zeitgenossen faszinierten und für uns heute wertvolle Dokumente (vergleichbar mit Photos) dafür sind, wie Rom im 18. Jahrhundert aussah, entfalteten seine *Carceri* ihre volle Wirkung erst im 19. und 20. Jahrhundert.

the Forum, will not be easy for them. They have to clamber over huge blocks of marble that lie on the ground, reminiscent of the cliffs of Capri. On the left side of the picture, the upper part of a triumphal arch that already shows signs of dilapidation juts from the ground. Before this, too, there is a group of tourists with their guide. In the background, between pines, cypresses and plane trees, the oval curve of the Colosseum can clearly be discerned. The actual residential buildings of the city of Rome merely push their way into the picture quite unassumingly from the left. Next to the ruins of the past they appear small, plain and somewhat pitiful. The city's great periods belong to the past. People live with the ancient ruins as they would with petrified relatives of lost generations. We are looking at a city that is slowly being transformed into a modern tourist metropolis after centuries of decline.

Unfortunately, after Winckelmann's and Piranesi's death, archeologists from all over the world thoroughly excavated and dug up the soil of the city of Rome. Today it is only rarely that one encounters picturesque ruins of the kind that appear in Piranesi's etchings. Archeological digs have turned suggestions of romantic ruins into cheerless ruin wounds. Instead of goats and cows, tourists from all over the world parade through painfully uncovered, naked burial grounds, acting as if they were impressed by these abraded, pale, ugly marble and brick skeletons. Romantic ruins don't look like this, they are overgrown with ivy and have completely surrendered to nature. Besides, today the noise of traffic and the stench of gasoline interfere with lofty sentiments of vanitas. Whatever. No one, no modern architect, now takes the Colosseum, the Imperial Forums or the Pantheon as a model. Those times are gone forever. Today a tourist in Rome must love fields of ruins and broken-down houses, or else he'll be disappointed. Perhaps that glorious, style-conscious, mighty antiquity, teeming with culture, never really existed; possibly it existed only in the minds of its admirers and imitators. And if it did exist, it was created by hundreds of thousands of slaves, who had to work to the point of deadly exhaustion. The »good and the beautiful« was then in reality a forced product of pitiless conquerors, oppressors and slave drivers. From this perspective, we are relieved as we gaze at the Roman landscapes of ruins: How fortunate that these things are broken-down and destroyed. Perhaps in the years to come we ought to cover them over completely with dirt and liberate ourselves once and for all from their false ideals. We remember: The last time dictators like Hitler and Mussolini invoked them, the upturn they strived for ended in a bloody world-war catastrophe. The disabled, Jews, Slavs and dissidents were gassed because they did not conform to classical ideals!

At this point, I should like to discuss in more detail an engraving from Giovanni Battista Piranesi's famous »Prisons« cycle. It is print XIV of the *Carceri*, dated 1761. While Piranesi's portrayals of the city of Rome fascinated his contemporaries in particular and are valuable documents for us today (comparable to photographs), showing what Rome looked like in the 18th century, the full effect of his *Carceri* was not felt until the 19th and 20th century. That was when viewers recognized their visionary utopian potential. Writers and poets transfigured them into a myth: Alfred de Musset, Charles Baudelaire, Théophile Gautier, Edgar Allen Poe, Victor Hugo, Herman Melville, Aldous Huxley, Jorge Luis Borges and Marguerite Yourcenar. Perhaps Ludwig van Beethoven, too, knew the engravings and had them next to him on his desk as he composed his opera *Fidelio*? I wonder if Franz Kafka visualized Piranesi's obsessions as he was writing *The Castle*?

The most alarming thing about the representation of space is its abstruse monumentality. We have the feeling we are observers who have lost their way in an endless space, a labyrinth of ruins. In these menacing, all-engulfing space traps there are neither entrances nor exits. The only positive aspect is the fact that in here it is never completely dark and that because of the light that falls piecemeal and striped from above through the destroyed timberwork of the roof we can perceive the convolutions of space. Countless bridges and stairways turn this cavernous world into an obviously completely senseless architectural monster whose actual function remains unclear. Perhaps the pillars, arches, bridges, stairways, beams, bars and bracings of ropes were indeed at some point built as a prison, who knows? It seems more likely that a crazed tyrant in an exaggerated building frenzy that lasted all of his life had a piece of architecture built that could be used not only as a castle, church and theater but also as a prison or catacomb cemetery. Perhaps it was to be flooded some day, drowning all the wrongdoers and freedom fighters imprisoned there. At any rate, seeing this spatial web today, we are deeply troubled. Beautiful architecture, we feel, can grow, if excessively exaggerated, into an endless interior monster, a negative Tower of Babel, a labyrinthine building of the subconscious and of fear in which one is forced to wander for the rest of one's life without ever finding the way out. Architecture turns into a weapon, into the opposite of its true purpose – which is to provide shelter and express geometric beauty. These are negative utopias.

Damals entdeckten die Betrachter in ihnen das visionär-utopische Potential. Schriftsteller und Dichter verklärten sie zu einem Mythos: Alfred de Musset, Charles Baudelaire, Théophile Gautier, Edgar Allen Poe, Victor Hugo, Herman Melville, Aldous Huxley, Jorge Luis Borges und Marguerite Yourcenar. Vielleicht kannte auch Ludwig van Beethoven die Radierungen und hatte sie neben sich auf dem Tisch liegen, als er seine Oper *Fidelio* komponierte? Ob Franz Kafka beim Schreiben von *Das Schloß* auch Piranesis Obsessionen vor Augen hatte?

Das Beängstigende an der Raumdarstellung ist ihre abstruse Monumentalität. Wir haben das Gefühl, uns als Betrachter in ein unendliches Raumruinenlabyrinth zu verirren. Es gibt in diesen bedrohlichen, alles verschlingenden Raumfallen weder Ein- noch Ausgänge. Der einzig positive Aspekt besteht darin, daß hier innen keine vollständige Dunkelheit herrscht und wir wegen des Lichtes, das von oben durch ein zerstörtes Dachstuhlgebilde zerstückelt und gestreift einfällt, die Raumverschlingungen wahrnehmen können. Unzählige Brücken und Treppen machen aus der Höhlenwelt ein offensichtlich völlig sinnloses Architektur-Ungeheuer, dessen eigentliche Funktion unklar bleibt. Vielleicht wurden die Pfeiler, Bögen, Brücken, Treppen, Balken, Gitter und Seilverspannungen ja tatsächlich irgendwann einmal als Gefängnis gebaut, wer weiß. Wahrscheinlicher scheint, daß ein verwirrter Tyrann aus übertriebener Bauwut sein Leben lang eine Architektur errichten ließ, die sowohl als Schloß, Kirche, Theater wie auch als Gefängnis oder Katakombenfriedhof dienen konnte. Vielleicht sollte sie eines Tages geflutet werden und alle darin gefangenen Missetäter und Freiheitskämpfer ertränken. In jedem Fall löst das Raumgespinst in uns heutigen Betrachtern eine große Beängstigung aus. Schöne Architektur, haben wir das Gefühl, kann durch maßlose Übertreibung zu einem unendlichen Innenraum-Ungeheuer auswachsen, zu einem negativen Babylonischen Turm, zu einem Baulabyrinth des Unterbewußtseins und der Angst, in dem man sein Leben lang herumirren muß, ohne je den Ausgang zu finden. Architektur wird zur Waffe, zum Gegenteil ihrer eigentlichen Aufgabe, Schutz und Formulierung geometrischer Schönheit zu sein. Negative Utopien.

Natürlich denken wir beim Betrachten der *Carceri*-Radierung auch an die repräsentativen, ihre Benutzer und Besucher einschüchternden Staatsarchitekturen vieler Diktatoren der Welt. Wir sehen die nie verwirklichte »Große Halle« vor uns, die Albert Speer nach einer Skizze von Adolf Hitler in Berlin errichten wollte, aber auch die endlos langen, marmornen Flursäle der Berliner Reichskanzlei, die am Ende des Krieges zerstört und später abgerissen wurde.

Während die Stadt Rom, trotz ihrer Zerstörungen, das ganze Mittelalter über im Bewußtsein der Menschen anwesend war, gab es auch antike Städte, die irgendwann ganz von der Landkarte verschwanden und von niemandem vermißt wurden. Dazu gehört die einst blühende römische Provinzstadt Pompeji am Fuße des Vesuvs. Sie fand, wie heute jeder Gebildete weiß, am 24. August im Jahr 79 n. Chr. durch einen gewaltigen Ausbruch des Vesuvs ihr abruptes Ende. Eine 20 Meter hohe Schicht aus Schlamm, Lava, Asche und Steinen begrub alles Leben. Kein Bewohner der Stadt überlebte die Katastrophe, es sei denn, er war rechtzeitig geflohen. Von einem Moment zum andern erlosch alles Leben.

Jahrhundertelang lag die verschüttete Stadt unberührt in ihrem Grab. Die Bewohner der Vesuvlandschaft hatten Pompeji vergessen. Ziegenherden grasten, Kaufleute, Pilger und Soldaten zogen darüber hinweg, ohne etwas von der Existenz der einstigen Stadt zu ahnen. Erst nach 1700 Jahren entdeckten Brunnengräber zufällig Spuren und Reste, die auf einstige Bewohner in dieser Gegend hinwiesen. Aber keiner von ihnen bemühte sich um Aufklärung. Warum auch? Durch Erzählungen und Berichte wurden Jahre später professionelle Schatzgräber und Kunstobjektsucher auf die Gegend aufmerksam. Sie begannen, wahllos Löcher auszuheben. Manche Plünderer fanden Scherben und Alltagsgegenstände, was ihnen wertlos erschien, warfen sie achtlos weg.

Erst seit 1763 führte ein Schweizer Architekt namens Karl Weber (1712–1764), angeregt durch Winckelmanns und Piranesis Aktivitäten in Rom, gründlichere Grabungen durch und dokumentierte die ersten Häuser in Pompeji genauer. Mit ihm stieg Pompeji zur wichtigen Grabungsstätte auf. Andere Interessierte – Wissenschaftler, Touristen, aber auch Piranesi selbst – tauchten auf. Man erinnerte sich an die antiken Katastrophenberichte und wurde sich bewußt, daß hier ein einzigartiges Kulturdokument unter der Lava liegen könnte.

Mitte des 19. Jahrhunderts erreichten die archäologischen Aufdeckungen unter dem damaligen offiziellen Grabungsleiter Giuseppe Fiorelli (1823–1896) ihren Höhepunkt. Fiorelli war es auch, der die rätselhaften Hohlkörper in der versteinerten Asche entdeckte und mit Gipsbeton ausgoß. Dadurch entstanden jene berühmten menschlichen Figuren, die uns heute noch durch ihre konservierten Todesängste rühren und beeindrucken. Nicht nur das Wohnen in antiken römischen Städten wurde mit einem Mal sichtbar, sondern auch das alltägliche Leben. Kochgeräte, Essens-

17. Verschüttetes, Ausgegrabenes, Trümmer, Fragmente, Reste. Rätselhafte Spuren. Indizien. Steinerne Nachrichten aus der Vergangenheit.

17. Things to be entombed and excavated, wreckage, ruins, remnants. Cryptic traces. Signs. Stony messages from the past.

Naturally, as we look at the *Carceri* etching we also think of the imposing government buildings of many dictators of the world, which intimidate those who use them and visit them. We visualize the »Great Hall« based on a sketch by Adolf Hitler, which Albert Speer wanted to erect in Berlin but never actually built, but also the endlessly long marble corridors of the Reich Chancellery in Berlin, which was destroyed at the end of the war and later torn down.

While the city of Rome, in spite of its destructions, was present in human consciousness throughout the Middle Ages, there were also ancient cities that completely disappeared from the map at some point and that nobody even missed. One of them is the once flourishing Roman provincial town of Pompeii at the foot of Mount Vesuvius. It met with an abrupt end, as all educated people know today, on 24 August in the year 79 C.E. when there was a powerful eruption of Mount Vesuvius. A 20-meter-deep layer of mud, lava, ashes and rocks buried all life. None of the town's inhabitants survived the catastrophe, unless they had fled in time. From one moment to the next, all life was extinguished.

For centuries the buried town lay untouched in its grave. The inhabitants of the area around Vesuvius had forgotten Pompeii. Herds of goats grazed, merchants, pilgrims and soldiers roamed over it without suspecting that the former town even existed. Not until 1700 years later well diggers accidentally discovered traces and remains that indicated people had once lived in the region. But none of them tried to find out more. Why should they? Years later, stories and reports drew the attention of professional treasure hunters and people looking for art objects to the region. They began haphazardly digging holes. Some of the looters found potsherds and everyday objects, and carelessly threw away whatever seemed worthless.

After 1763, however, a Swiss architect called Karl Weber (1712–1764), inspired by Winckelmann's and Piranesi's activities in Rome, carried out more thorough excavations and documented the first houses of Pompeii in greater detail. Thanks to him Pompeii became an important excavation site. Other interested people – scholars, tourists, but also Piranesi himself – turned up. People remembered the ancient reports of the catastrophe and realized that a unique cultural document might be lying under the lava soil here. In the middle of the 19th century, archeological discoveries, headed by the then official director of excavations, Giuseppe Fiorelli (1823–1896), reached their peak. It was Fiorelli who discovered the mysterious cavities left by bodies in the petrified ash, and pumped them full of plaster. This process produced the famous human figures that still move and impress us by the mortal agony preserved in their features. Not only homes in an-

reste und Lagerbestände tauchten auf, außerdem Malereien und Skulpturen, die uns einen authentischen Eindruck vom Leben in jener Zeit vermitteln. Plötzlich erschien die Vulkantragödie, die Stadtruine, als Glücksfall.

Wer heute durch die erst zur Hälfte ausgegrabene Ruinenstadt geht, kann sich einen guten Eindruck von den Dimensionen der Wohnhäuser, Innenhofgärten, Gassen und Plätze verschaffen. Die Stadt war weitgehend eingeschossig gebaut. Nur in wenigen Fällen gab es ein Obergeschoß. In Rom selbst haben sich keine Wohnhäuser und Alltagsreste aus dieser Zeit erhalten. Ich selbst habe Pompeji 1976 und 1982 besucht. Beide Male beeindruckten mich die Hohlraum-Abgüsse der Verschütteten am meisten. Die Idee dazu kam mir genial vor, außerdem erinnerten die liegenden und hockenden Figuren an moderne Kunstwerke, etwa des amerikanischen Pop-Art-Bildhauers George Segal.

Im Jahr 1993 konnte ich in Stuttgart (Galerie der Stadt Stuttgart) und in Hamburg (Museum für Kunst und Gewerbe) die Ausstellung »Pompeji wiederentdeckt« inszenieren und dafür eigene Räume für die Menschenabgüsse bauen. In Vitrinen wurden zahlreiche Alltags- und Kultobjekte gezeigt. Glanzpunkt der Ausstellung war ein vollständig ausgemalter Wohnraum, der in Pompeji von den Wänden gelöst worden war. Ruinen. Zeitspuren. Erinnerungsräume.

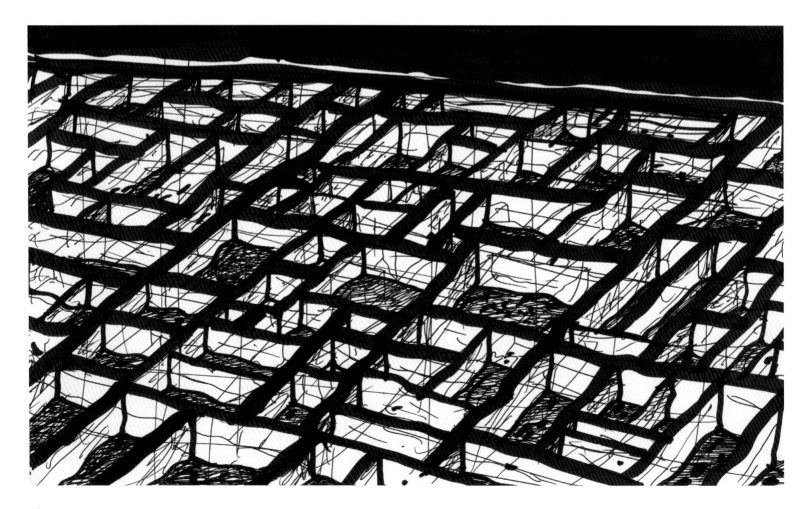

cient Roman towns suddenly became visible, but daily life as well. Cooking utensils, scraps of food and goods appeared. There were also paintings and sculptures that gave us an authentic impression of life in those days. Suddenly the tragedy of the volcanic eruption, and the ruined town, seemed a stroke of luck.

Those who walk through the only half excavated ruined town today can get a good idea of the dimensions of homes, inner courtyard gardens, streets and squares. Most of the town buildings were one story high. Only in a few cases was there a second floor. In Rome itself no residential buildings or remnants of everyday life from this period have been preserved. I myself visited Pompeii in 1976 and 1982. Both times I was most impressed by the plaster casts of those who were buried alive. The idea seemed ingenious, and also the recumbent and crouching figures reminded me of modern works of art, for instance, the American Pop Art sculptor George Segal.

In 1993 I was able to organize the exhibition »Pompeii rediscovered« in Stuttgart (Galerie der Stadt Stuttgart) and in Hamburg (Museum für Kunst und Gewerbe) and to build special rooms for the casts of human bodies as part of the exhibition. In glass cabinets, numerous everyday and religious objects were displayed. The highlight of the exhibition was a completely painted room whose frescoes had been detached from the walls of a Pompeian home. Ruins. Traces of time. Spaces of memory.

18. Hans Dieter Schaal, Pompeji-Strukturen, 2005.
19. Hans Dieter Schaal, Pompeji wiederentdeckt. Ausstellung in der Galerie der Stadt Stuttgart, 1993.

18. Hans Dieter Schaal, Pompeii structures, 2005.
19. Hans Dieter Schaal, Pompeii rediscovered. Exhibition in the Galerie der Stadt Stuttgart, 1993.

3. »Zurück zur Natur«

Jean-Jacques Rousseau, Ermenonville und die Französische Revolution

Nachdem Jean-Jacques Rousseau endlich zugestimmt hatte und im Mai 1778 nach Ermenonville, dem Schloß seines Verehrers und Gönners Marquis de Girardin, umgezogen war, lernte er dort einen Schloßpark kennen, der ganz nach seinen Ideen gestaltet worden war. Der Marquis war ein Anhänger der aus England stammenden Landschaftsparkidee und hatte im Jahr 1777 ein naturschwärmerisches Buch, ganz im Sinne Rousseaus, mit dem Titel *De la composition de la paysage* veröffentlicht.

Es gab hier weder Wegachsen noch beschnittene Hecken, die Natur durfte sich frei entfalten, allerdings nicht nach dem Prinzip Zufall, sondern nach einer festgelegten Plankomposition. Der Marquis wollte in Ermenonville eine romantisch-pittoreske Naturwelt erschaffen, wie sie damals bei vielen Adligen in Mode war. Um ein möglichst originelles Ergebnis zu erzielen, hatte er seinen Freund, den berühmten Ruinenmaler Hubert Robert, in die Planungen miteinbezogen. Robert entwarf, neben kleineren Ruinenobjekten, einen »Tempel der Philosophie«. Dieser bestand aus einem runden, ruinösen Turm aus Natursteinquadern, der von sechs Säulen umrahmt wurde. Jede Säule war einem Philosophen zugeordnet und trug Widmungen für Newton, Descartes, Voltaire, Rousseau, Penn und Montesquieu. In eine siebente, unvollendete Säule war die Frage eingemeißelt: »Wer wird alles vollenden?«

Rousseau konnte bei seiner Ankunft die anmutigen Seen, sanften Wiesen, geschwungenen Wege, Waldstücke, Haine und die schon leicht verwilderten Ruineneinbauten bewundern. Ob ihm die Naturbefreiungen und Kompositionen wirklich gefielen, wissen wir nicht. Vielleicht nahm er sie überhaupt nicht mehr wahr. Denn im Laufe der Jahre war er zu einem hypochondrischen Neurotiker geworden, der die Menschen mied und ihre Intrigen haßte. Ein krankhafter Verfolgungswahn zwang ihn dazu, sich ständig einzuschließen. Bereits am 2. Juli 1778, nur sechs Wochen nach seiner Ankunft, ist er 66jährig in Ermenonville gestorben. Da Marquis und Marquise sein zukünftiges Grab auf der eigens dafür angelegten »Ile des Peupliers«, der »Insel der Pappeln«, vorbereitet hatten, gab es nicht wenige Zeitgenossen, die von einem möglichen Mord sprachen. Bis heute sind die Umstände seines Todes nicht ganz geklärt. Allerdings tendiert die Wissenschaft zu der Annahme, daß es ein Schlaganfall gewesen sei, der den Philosophen dahingerafft habe. Wieder war Hubert Robert sofort zur Stelle, er hatte schon einen Sarkophag für den berühmten Toten entworfen. Der Bildhauer Jacques Philippe Lesueur führte ihn aus. Schnell entwickelte dieses Grab große Anziehungskraft und wurde über Jahre zu einer vielbesuchten Wallfahrtsstätte.

Mit seinen Schriften war Jean-Jacques Rousseau einer der Vorbereiter der Französischen Revolution. Er vertrat die Ansicht, jeder Mensch sei von Natur aus gut und frei, Erziehung und Zivilisation förderten in ihm nur das Böse. »Der Mensch ist frei geboren, und überall liegt er in Ketten«, mit diesem Satz beginnt das erste Kapitel seines Buches *Du contrat social ou Principes du droit politique*. Konsequent lautete seine radikale These: »Zurück zur Natur!«, die ab jetzt vor allem Adlige und Kleinfürsten verinnerlichten, ihre streng-geometrischen Gärten zerstörten oder mit freien Parkgestaltungen ergänzten. Die neue Bewegung hatte in England Vorläufer, aber keiner der englischen Philosophen oder Gartengestalter formulierte die neuen Ideen so radikal und antifeudal wie Rousseau, der dafür von der Zensur verfolgt wurde und viele Jahre seines Lebens auf der Flucht verbringen mußte.

Voller romantischer Gefühle (allerdings nicht »auf allen Vieren«, wie Voltaire spottete) wanderten jetzt die naturbewegten Kleinfürsten durch die eigenen, vom Zwang befreiten und zerstörten (ruinierten) geometrischen Gartenanlagen, verweilten in Waldstücken und Tälern, in Grotten und künstlich gebauten Ruinen. Keiner von ihnen ahnte, daß der neue, angeblich so »natürliche« Freiheitsbegriff zu ihrem baldigen Ende führen würde. Wenige Jahre später, zur Zeit der Französischen Revolution, wurden viele Kleinfürsten und Adlige von aufgebrachten Bauern gewaltsam aus ihren Schlössern und befreiten Gärten vertrieben, manchmal auch gelyncht oder der neuen Terrorjustiz ausgeliefert. Auf der Place de la Concorde in Paris rollten ihre Köpfe.

Das Wort »Freiheit« war ab jetzt kein romantisch-dekorativer Begriff mehr, der als seelenvoller, manchmal auch sentimentaler Windhauch durch Auen, Haine und künstliche Ruinen wehte, das Wort bedeutete jetzt: Aufruf zum Widerstand, zum Kampf, zur Revolution. Mit neuem Selbstbewußtsein verurteilten Bürger die maroden aristokratischen Gesellschaftszustände, die übertriebene Hofetikette und surreale Perückenseligkeit, den provozierenden, allerdings immer auch von Langeweile bedrohten Müßiggang und die ungerechte Ausbeutung von Bauern und Handwerkern. Ab jetzt sollte jeder für seinen Lebensunterhalt selbst arbeiten.

3. »Back to nature«

Jean-Jacques Rousseau, Ermenonville and the French Revolution

After Jean-Jacques Rousseau had finally agreed and, in May 1778, had moved to Ermenonville, the stately home of his admirer and patron Marquis de Girardin, he got to know a park there whose design was based entirely on his ideas. The marquis was a supporter of the concept of landscape parks, which originated in England, and in 1777 had published an effusive book about his love of nature, exactly what Rousseau himself would have written, titled *De la composition des paysages*.

Here, there were neither roadways nor trimmed hedges – nature was able to unfold freely, though this was not based on chance, but rather a predetermined plan and composition. In Ermenonville the marquis wanted to create the kind of romantic, picturesque natural world that was fashionable among many aristocrats of the period. In order to obtain as original a result as possible, he had included his friend, the famous painter of ruins Hubert Robert, in the planning process. Besides smaller groups of ruins, Robert designed a »Temple of Philosophy«. This consisted of a round, ruined tower made of blocks of natural stone and framed by six columns. Each column was assigned to a philosopher and bore dedications for Newton, Descartes, Voltaire, Rousseau, Penn and Montesquieu. A seventh, uncompleted column bore the engraved question: »Who will complete everything?«

After his arrival, Rousseau was able to admire the lovely lakes, gentle meadows, curving paths, woods, groves and, already somewhat overgrown, the specially built ruins. We do not know if he really liked the free unfolding of nature and the compositions. Perhaps he was no longer aware of them. For over the years he had become a hypochondriac neurotic who avoided people and hated their intrigues. A morbid persecution complex forced him to constantly shut himself up indoors. He died in Ermenonville, on 2 July 1778, only six weeks after his arrival. Since the marquis and marquise had prepared his future grave on an »Island of Poplars« – »Ile des Peupliers« – that had been specially designed for the purpose, quite a few contemporaries thought he might have been murdered. To this day the circumstances of his death have not been completely cleared up. However, scholars tend to assume that a stroke carried off the philosopher. Again Hubert Robert was on the spot at once. He had already designed a sarcophagus for the famous man. The sculptor Jacques-Philippe Lesueur executed the design. Quickly this grave began to attract large numbers of people and in the course of time became a much-visited place of pilgrimage. The writings of Jean-Jacques Rousseau prepared the way for the French Revolution. He believed that every human being was good and free by nature, while education and civilization only fostered evil in him. »Man was born free, and everywhere he lies in chains«, begins the first chapter of his book *Du contrat social ou Principes du droit politique*. Logically his radical thesis was »Back to nature!«, and from now on aristocrats and minor princes took to heart the precept, destroyed their strictly geometrical parks or expanded them to include free park designs. The new movement had precursors in England, but none of the English philosophers or designers of gardens expressed the new ideas as radically and anti-feudally as Rousseau, who was persecuted by censorship because of this and had to spend many years of his life on the run.

Full of romantic feelings (though not »on all fours«, as Voltaire said mockingly), the nature-loving minor princes now roamed through their own formerly geometric gardens, which had been freed from constraint and destroyed (ruined). They tarried in woods and valleys, in grottoes and artificially built ruins. None of them foresaw that the new, allegedly so »natural« concept of freedom would result in their own imminent end. Not many years later, during the French Revolution, many princes and nobles were driven out by force from their stately homes and liberated parks by irate peasants, sometimes even lynched or handed over to the new justice of the Terror. Their heads rolled on the Place de la Concorde in Paris.

The word »freedom« was from now on no longer a romantic, decorative concept that wafted as a soulful, often sentimental breeze through meadows, groves and artificial ruins; the word now meant: a call to resistance, battle, revolution. With new self-confidence, citizens condemned the rotten social conditions of the aristocrats, the exaggerated etiquette and surreal life at court, the provocative idleness of the rich (though always assailed by boredom) and the unjust exploitation of peasants and manual workers. Henceforth everyone should earn his own living.

It was Rousseau who had put his finger on the problem. He, the self-taught petty bourgeois from Geneva who had his own five children taken to an orphanage immediately after birth, was the prophet of the new era.

Rousseau also hatte die Gedanken auf den Punkt gebracht. Er, der autodidaktische Kleinbürger aus Genf, der seine eigenen fünf Kinder gleich nach der Geburt ins Waisenhaus bringen ließ, war der Prophet der neuen Zeit.

Als Ludwig XV. und seine Frau Marie Antoinette unter der Guillotine starben, wurde symbolisch die Jahrhunderte alte Feudalordnung ermordet, und die aufständischen Volksmassen übernahmen die Herrschaft. Sie stürmten das verhaßte Bastille-Gefängnis und zündeten die Tuillerien an. Zum ersten Mal in der Weltgeschichte realisierten sie ihre blutrünstigen Gedanken. Daß das folgende Terrorregime weit brutaler mit menschlichem Leben umging, als es der Adel jemals getan hatte, sollte manchem Zeitgenossen die Augen öffnen. Aber die meisten Intellektuellen und Schriftsteller, vor allem auch in deutschen Landen, berauschten sich an den neuen Ideen von »Gleichheit, Brüderlichkeit und Freiheit«. Nur Goethe schwenkte – wie Rüdiger Safranski in seinem großartigen Buch *Romantik. Eine deutsche Affäre* schreibt – nach anfänglicher Sympathie um und kehrte zu seinen alten, eher evolutionären Gedanken zurück. Er verabscheute Gewalt, der Mob war ihm suspekt. Demokratie im modernen Sinne lehnte er ab.

Jetzt also lag Rousseau als Leiche auf seiner Insel und empfing posthum die geistige Elite seiner adligen Verehrer. Kaum hatten die Revolutionäre 1789 in Paris die Macht übernommen, ließen sie die sterblichen Überreste ihres geistigen Heroen ins Pantheon überführen. Die Veranstaltung wurde mit großem Pomp durchgeführt. Eine feierliche Prozession zog mit seinen halbverwesten Überresten durch Paris. Als Monstranz trug ein Revolutionär das aufgeschlagene Exemplar des *Contrat social* an der Spitze des Zuges. Noch heute ruht Rousseaus Sarkophag in den Gewölben unter der Pariser Kirche, genau gegenüber seinem Erzfeind und Verspotter Voltaire.

Anhänger und Gegner des immer noch stark umstrittenen Philosophen fordern an jedem Jahrestag seines Todes die Rückführung auf die angestammte Pappelinsel in Ermenonville. Aber die Regierung hat dem nie zugestimmt. Viele Gegner bezweifeln bis heute seinen Einfluß auf den Ausbruch der Französischen Revolution und werfen ihm vor, wegen privater Probleme ein Gesellschaftssystem entworfen zu haben, das ihm mehr Vorteile im Leben verschaffen sollte. Mit seinen posthum veröffentlichten Memoiren – den *Les Confessions* – trug er wenig zur Aufhellung der wahren Umstände bei. Tatsache ist, daß er als junger Mann lange Zeit vergeblich versuchte, in die große Gesellschaft aufzusteigen. Als er sein Scheitern erkannte, entwickelte er einen unerbittlichen Haß auf die ihm verschlossene aristokratische Welt. Aus diesem Grundgefühl heraus entstand seine Philosophie. Diejenigen, die ihm den Weg nach oben verwehrten, wurden ab jetzt in ihrer Dekadenz denunziert und gedanklich liquidiert. Über den Natur-Umweg wollte er die bestehenden Gesetze und Zustände aushebeln. Verbal entzog er den Aristokraten das Fundament ihrer Vorrechte und entschied – wie andere zeitgenössische, vor allem englische und amerikanische Denker auch –, daß jeder Mensch vor der Natur und damit vor dem Gesetz gleich sein müsse. Warum er die eigenen Kinder ins Asyl gab, obwohl er mit *Émile* ein Hauptwerk der Erziehungsliteratur schrieb, bleibt bis heute ein Rätsel. Widerspruch auf Widerspruch. Gedankenbaustellen. Gedankenruinen.

Sein spöttisch-ironischer Widersacher Voltaire übrigens bekämpfte als überzeugter Aufklärer ebenfalls die Dummheit und Engstirnigkeit von Religionen und Menschen allgemein, blieb jedoch sein Leben lang Anhänger des Adels und damit der feudalen Ordnung. Seine Forderung nach Toleranz brachte auch ihn immer wieder in Konflikt mit dem Gesetz. 1717 saß er sogar ein Jahr lang im Bastille-Gefängnis. Wie Rousseau blieb ihm das grausam-ernüchternde Erlebnis der Französischen Revolution erspart. Voltaire starb genau zwei Monate vor Rousseau, am 30. Mai 1778 in Paris.

Der Park von Ermenonville hat sich erhalten. Auch ich habe ihn vor Jahren besucht und mich für die lauschige Pappelinsel begeistert, die heute immer noch mit dem leeren Sarkophag im See schwimmt wie eine Mischung aus Watteaus *Aufbruch nach Kythera* und Böcklins *Toteninsel*. Der Pappelkreis formt eine Art gewachsenes Stonehenge, einen Rundtempel, gebaut aus lebendigen Baumsäulen. Bei jeder Jahreszeit zeigt er ein anderes Gesicht. Die Pappelinsel wurde später in vielen Gärten und Parks nachgebaut. Man kann ihr in Wörlitz genauso begegnen wie im Berliner Tiergarten. Auch ich habe das Motiv in meinem Biberacher »Wieland-Park« aufgegriffen.

Hubert Robert stieg nach Rousseaus Tod zum Chefkonservator des Louvre auf, was ihn allerdings nicht daran hinderte, 1796 die große, jetzt mit vermauerten Seitenfenstern und Oberlichtern ausgestattete Galerie im allgemein zugänglichen Schloßmuseum als Ruine zu malen. Eine surreale Endzeitvision, die an Albert Speers »Ruinenmehrwerttheorie« denken läßt. Durch die eingebrochenen Deckengewölbe sieht man hinauf zum blauen, von weißen Wolken überzogenen Himmel. Gedämpftes Sonnenlicht fällt in die ehemaligen Ausstellungssäle. Alle Bilder sind verschwunden, nur noch eine Kopie des *Apollo von Belvedere* steht auf seinem Sockel, ansonsten

When Louis XV and his wife Marie Antoinette died on the guillotine, the centuries-old feudal order was symbolically murdered, and the rebellious masses of the people seized power. They stormed the hated Bastille prison and set fire to the Tuileries. For the first time in world history they carried out their bloodthirsty ideas. The Reign of Terror that followed was far more brutal in the way it dealt with human life than the aristocracy had ever been – an eye-opener for many contemporaries. But most intellectuals and writers, especially in the German states, were intoxicated by the new ideas of »liberty, equality and fraternity«. Only Goethe did an about-face – as Rüdiger Safranski writes in his magnificent book *Romantik. Eine deutsche Affäre* (*Romanticism. A German Affair*) – after initially sympathizing, and returned to his old ideas, which tended to be evolutionary. He despised violence, and found mobs suspect. He was against democracy in the modern sense of the word.

So now Rousseau lay buried on his isle and posthumously received the intellectual elite of his aristocratic admirers. Hardly had the revolutionaries seized power in Paris in 1789 than they had the mortal remains of their spiritual hero transferred to the Pantheon. The event was accompanied by great pomp. A solemn procession marched through Paris with his half-decayed remains. As a monstrance a revolutionary carried an open copy of the »Contrat social« at the head of the procession. To this day, Rousseau's sarcophagus lies in the vaults under the Parisian church, right across from the man who mocked him, his archenemy Voltaire.

Every time the anniversary of his death rolls around, the followers and opponents of this still extremely controversial philosopher demand that he be returned to the Isle of Poplars in Ermenonville where he belongs. But the government has never agreed to this. To this day, many opponents question his influence on the eruption of the French Revolution and accuse him of having envisioned, due to his own private problems, a social system that was supposed to provide him with more advantages in life. With his posthumously published memoir – *Les Confessions* – he did little to throw light on the true facts. What is true is that as a young man he tried in vain for a long time to make his way into high society. When he realized he had failed, he came to feel an implacable hatred for the aristocratic world that was closed to him. It was from this underlying feeling that his philosophy developed. He now denounced the decadence of those who barred his way into society, and he liquidated them in his mind. By writing about nature, he wanted in a roundabout way to eliminate the existing laws and conditions. Verbally, he took away the foundation of the aristocrats' privileges and decided – like other contemporary, primarily English and American thinkers – that every human being must be equal before nature and thus before the law. To this day it is a mystery why he sent his own children to an orphanage, even though, with *Émile,*

20. Hans Dieter Schaal, Das ehemalige Grab Jean-Jacques Rousseaus im Park von Ermenonville, 2007.
21. Hubert Robert, *Fiktive Ansicht des Louvre als Ruine*, 1796, Musée du Louvre, Paris.

20. Hans Dieter Schaal, The former tomb of Jean-Jacques Rousseau in the Ermenonville park, 2007.
21. Hubert Robert, *Imaginary view of the Louvre as a ruin*, 1796, Musée du Louvre, Paris.

Trümmer, Scherben, Michelangelos »Sterbender Sklave« (eine Kopie?) und eine große Vase. In der Mitte des Bildes sitzt ein Maler, der gerade den »Apoll« zeichnet und mit erhobenem Stift in der Hand die Proportionen der Marmorfigur mißt. Zwischen seinem Zeichenpapier und der Skulptur, die ebenfalls einen Arm erhoben hat, als wolle sie den Maler grüßen oder in seiner Geste nachahmen, kann man zwei Frauen erkennen, die über einem offenen Feuer ihre Suppe in einem großen Topf erhitzen. Rauch steigt auf. Ob es sich bei der Dreiergruppe im linken Bildvordergrund um Kunstbewunderer oder eher um Kunstdiebe handelt, läßt sich nicht genau entscheiden. Noch gibt es unter den Trümmern (der Revolution) einige Werke, die sich vielleicht verkaufen lassen. Im Hintergrund des Saales irren zwei Kinder, ganz klein und verloren, durch die Trümmerlandschaft.

Das Gemälde besitzt wegen seiner zentralperspektivischen Komposition eine große Tiefenwirkung. Winzig öffnet sich am Ende der Ruinensaalflucht ein helles Türrechteck, durch das ein helles Himmelsfragment zu sehen ist. Ameisenkleine Menschen stehen in der Nähe dieser Öffnung und scheinen die an Rom erinnernde Szene zu betrachten.

Fiktive Ruinendarstellungen wie diese geistern durch zahlreiche Gemälde jener Zeit. Robert hatte ja während seines elfjährigen Aufenthalts in Rom von 1754 bis 1765 auch Piranesi persönlich kennengelernt, genauso wie den 40 Jahre älteren Ruinenmaler Giovanni Paolo Pannini, der sich vor allem mit seinem grandiosen Gemälde *Galerie der Ansichten des antiken Rom* in das Gedächtnis kunstgeschichtlich Interessierter eingeprägt hat. Hubert Robert – ironisch-liebevoll genannt »Robert des Ruines« – wird von seinen Zeitgenossen als genußsüchtiger Lebemann geschildert, der keinesfalls von depressiver (Ruinen)-Melancholie befallen war wie etwa Caspar David Friedrich. Während der Revolution war er fast ein Jahr lang in den Gefängnissen von Sainte-Pélagie und Saint-Lazare eingekerkert. Woran sollte er glauben: an die Ideen der Revolutionäre oder an den neu aufleuchtenden Stern Napoleon? Viele Künstler pendelten verwirrt zwischen den Fronten hin und her, nicht nur Hubert Robert, sondern auch Jacques-Louis David, der thematisch in die ferne Geschichte auswich, römisch-antike Szenen malte, dabei jedoch reine Ruinendarstellungen vermied und später zum großen, malerischen Verherrlicher Napoleons aufstieg. Roberts Ruinenbild wirkt, von heute aus gesehen, wie ein geistiger Salto mortale, eine Zeitverschlingung. Das Heute wird zum Gestern, das Gestern zum Morgen, das Morgen zum Vorgestern ...

Was nützt die Öffnung der königlichen Sammlungen für das große Publikum, wenn kurz darauf marodierende Revolutionäre die Tuillerien, dicht neben dem Louvre gelegen, niederbrennen, dahinter, auf der Place de la Concorde, die aristokratischen Köpfe rollen lassen, was nützt das der Kunst? Vielleicht wird alles enden wie in Rom, als schweigende, fast menschenleere, von Erde bedeckte Ruinenlandschaft? Oder wird Napoleon das Ruder herumreißen, die Welt wieder ins Lot bringen und Frankreich zu neuem Glanz hinaufführen?

Als Hubert Robert 1808 mit 75 Jahren in Paris starb, strahlten Napoleons Siege über ganz Europa, noch lagen die Niederlagen von Leipzig und Waterloo in weiter Ferne.

he wrote a principal work on education. One contradiction after another. Construction sites of ideas. Ruins of ideas.

Incidentally, his mocking, ironic antagonist Voltaire, a dedicated Enlightenment philosopher, also fought against the stupidity and narrow-mindedness of religions and people in general, though all his life he remained a member of the nobility and thus of the feudal order. His demand for tolerance constantly brought him into conflict with the law. In 1717 he even spent a year in the Bastille prison. Like Rousseau he was spared the cruel, sobering experience of the French Revolution. Voltaire died exactly two months before Rousseau, on 30 May 1778 in Paris.

The park of Ermenonville still exists. I too visited it years ago and was thrilled by the secluded Isle of Poplars that still floats in the lake with its empty sarcophagus like a blend of Watteau's *Pilgrimage to Cythera* and Böcklin's *Isle of the Dead*. The circle of poplars forms a kind of live Stonehenge, a round temple built of living tree columns. The garden has a different face in every season. Replicas of the Isle of Poplars were later created in many gardens and parks. You can encounter them not only in Wörlitz but also in Berlin's Tiergarten Park. I too picked up on the motif in my Wieland Park in Biberach.

After Rousseau's death Hubert Robert was promoted to head curator of the Louvre, which, however, did not prevent him, in 1796, from painting the large gallery in the castle museum as a ruin. (Incidentally, the gallery now has walled-up side windows and new skylights, and the museum is open to the general public.) A surreal vision of the end-time, reminiscent of Albert Speer's »Theory of Ruin Value«. Through the broken vault of the ceiling you look up at the blue sky covered with white clouds. Subdued sunlight falls into the former exhibition halls. All the pictures have vanished, only a copy of the *Apollo Belvedere* stands on his pedestal. Nothing besides except debris, potsherds, Michelangelo's »Dying Slave« (a copy?) and a large vase. In the middle of the painting sits a painter in process of drawing the »Apollo«. His pencil raised, he is measuring the proportions of the marble figure. Between his drawing paper and the sculpture, whose arm is also raised as though it was trying to welcome the painter, you can recognize two women who are heating their soup in a big pot over an open fire. Smoke is rising. You can't tell if the group of three figures in the left foreground of the picture are admirers of art or art thieves. Among the debris (of the revolution) there are still a few artworks that can perhaps be sold. In the back of the hall two children, very small and lost, wander through the ruin landscape.

Because of its central perspective composition the painting has a strong depth effect. A tiny bright rectangle of a door opens at the end of the suite of ruined halls. A bright fragment of sky is visible through it. People the size of ants stand near this opening and seem to be observing a scene reminiscent of Rome.

Fictitious representations of ruins like this one haunt many paintings of that period. After all, Robert had also personally met Piranesi during his eleven-year stay in Rome from 1754 until 1765, just as he met the 40 years older painter of ruins Giovanni Paolo Pannini, who left his mark in the memory of those who are interested in art history primarily with his superb painting *Picture Gallery with Views of Ancient Rome*. Hubert Robert – ironically and lovingly nicknamed »Robert des Ruines« – is portrayed by his contemporaries as a pleasure-seeking roué, who did not suffer from depressive (ruin) melancholy at all, as Caspar David Friedrich had, for instance. During the revolution Robert was incarcerated for almost a year in the prisons of Sainte-Pélagie and Saint-Lazare. What was he supposed to believe in: the ideas of the revolutionaries or the rising star Napoleon? Many artists wavered in confusion back and forth between the two fronts, not only Hubert Robert, but also Jacques-Louis David, who skirted the issue by looking for his themes in the distant past, painted ancient Roman scenes though he avoided pure representations of ruins, and later glorified Napoleon in his paintings. Robert's painting of ruins, seen from today's perspective, seems like an intellectual salto mortale, time intertwined. Today becomes yesterday, yesterday becomes tomorrow, tomorrow the day before yesterday ...

What is the use of admitting the public at large to the royal collections if shortly thereafter marauding revolutionaries burn down the Tuileries, not far from the Louvre, if aristocratic heads are rolling in the back of the museum, on the Place de la Concorde? How does that benefit art? Perhaps it will all end the way it did in Rome, as a silent, almost deserted landscape of ruins covered with earth? Or will Napoleon change course, restore order again in the world and take France to new heights of splendor? When, in 1808, Hubert Robert died at the age of 75 in Paris, the light of Napoleon's victories shone across Europe. The defeats of Leipzig and Waterloo were still in the distant future.

4. Romantische Ruinen

Gartenträume und künstliche Ruinen

Fast zeitgleich mit dem Park von Ermenonville und seinen künstlichen Ruineneinbauten entstand, ebenfalls in der Nähe von Paris, am Rande des Waldes von Marly, eine Parkruine, die vor allem wegen ihrer Größe Aufsehen erregte: der monumentale, abgebrochene Säulenstumpf von Désert de Retz. Da dieser Säulenstumpf über drei Stockwerke bewohnbar und eigentlich nur im oberen Drittel ruinös abgebrochen war, mußte hier die Ruinenhaftigkeit zur Tarnung und Ablenkung von der wahren Funktion des temporären Wohnens dienen. Aus der Ferne hatten Besucher den Eindruck, dem toten Rest eines ehemals unvorstellbar großen Tempels zu begegnen. Die wenigen Fenster in den Kanneluren und die Risse im Mauerwerk, die das Tages- oder Mondlicht in die Innenräume einließen, fielen nicht wirklich auf.

Insgesamt hatte der Besitzer des Parks, Racine de Monville, zwölf ruinöse Bauten auf seinem Gelände errichten lassen, darunter ein künstliches Grabmal und eine Einsiedelei. Aber der 1780/81 von Nicolas-François Barbier erbaute, 15 Meter im Querschnitt messende dorische Säulenstumpf machte am meisten Eindruck, wahrscheinlich weil er alles bisher Dagewesene in den Schatten stellte. Neben dem Ruinenaspekt war es die Naturhaftigkeit dieses Bauwerks, das dem neuen Landschaftserleben entgegenkam. Im Säulenstumpf konnte auch der Rest eines einst gewaltig hohen Mammutbaums gesehen werden. Man wollte bewußt die Übergänge zwischen Natur, Architektur und Kunst verwischen, ganz im Sinn der Theorien des »Pittoresken« von William Gilpin, der 1789 folgende Gedanken formulierte: »Ruinen sind Heiligthümer. Sie sind seit Jahrhunderten im Boden befestigt, mit ihm eins geworden, und machen gleichsam einen Theil von ihm aus; und wir halten sie daher mehr für ein Werk der Natur als der Kunst. Die Kunst vermag sie nicht zu erreichen.«

Natürlich waren es vor allem die Surrealisten um André Breton, die im 20. Jahrhundert das merkwürdige Bauwerk neu entdeckten und als Hauptwerk des frühen Surrealismus anerkannten. Was sie über Marie Antoinettes Gartenwelt, die sie sich in der umzäunten Landschaft um das Petit Trianon in Versailles einrichten ließ, dachten, weiß ich nicht. Die Königin schwärmte für das malerische Landleben und liebte ebenfalls künstliche Ruinen. Neben Liebestempeln und ruinösen Grotten ließ sie sich einen Miniaturbauernhof mit Molkerei, Mühle und Taubenhaus erbauen. Schafherden und Hühner ergänzten das traumhaft-trügerische Bild einer landwirtschaftlichen Idylle. Man versteht, daß die verarmten französischen Bauern dafür kein Verständnis hatten und die Königin mit ihren Sicheln und Sensen aus dem vermeintlichen Paradies vertrieben.

Trotz der beschriebenen französischen Ruinenbeispiele hielt sich die Begeisterung in Frankreich für das neue Motiv in Grenzen. Im Land Le Nôtres war der Glanz geometrischer Gärten noch nicht verblaßt. Viele Fürsten, Grafen und Landadlige behielten die alte, wenn auch mit Mühe erzwungene Natur-Eleganz bei. Ganz anders in England. Hier hatte der skurrile Individualismus mit privatmythologischen Interpretationen von Architekturgeschichte und Natur eine ganz andere Tradition. Es wundert deswegen nicht, daß England als das eigentliche Erfinderland des künstlichen Ruinenmotivs gilt. Michel Makarius schreibt in seinem Buch *Ruins* (deutsch: *Ruinen. Die gegenwärtige Vergangenheit*), daß der erste, der diese imitierten Ruinen vorgeschlagen habe, Batty Langley in seiner Abhandlung *New Principles of Gardening* (1728) gewesen sei. Seine Idee wird dann von William Kent aufgegriffen. In Kents Stowe Garden wechseln sich Pagoden und Ruinen ab. Der Duke of Cumberland läßt 1746 sogar künstlich vergrößerte echte Ruinen im Park des Schlosses Windsor aufstellen. Neben dem Kent-Schüler William Chambers, der die Vorzüge des chinesischen Gartens rühmt, ist hier noch Sanderson Miller zu nennen, auf den die 1745 im Garten von Hagley Park Castle errichteten Kulissenbauten zurückgehen.

Der Ästhetikprofessor an der Universität Kiel, Christian Hirschfeld, der auch enge Verbindungen mit Dänemark pflegt, veröffentlicht 1777–1782 seine *Theorie der Gartenkunst*. Das fünfbändige Werk wird großen Einfluß auf die Verbreitung des Landschaftsgarten in Skandinavien haben. Kurz bevor William Gilpin seine Ideen über das malerische Schöne entwickelt, vertritt der deutsche Philosoph die Ansicht, daß der Garten, der zahlreiche unterschiedliche Ruinenbauten aufweist, die von in Stein gehauenen Inschriften begleitet werden, eine ganze Reihe von Gefühlen hervorrufe. Nach Gilpins Theorien sind es die unterschiedlichen Ausblicke, die Kontraste der Texturen, die Licht- und Schatteneffekte, die Unregelmäßigkeit der Formen sowie das Geheimnis der Prinzipien, die die Emotionen der Besucher ansprechen und deren Phantasie anregen sollen. Dafür wird eine Reihe von Einzelelementen aufgeboten: Felsen, Wasserfälle, einzelne Bäume und Ruinen.

4. Romantic ruins

Garden dreams and artificial ruins

Almost contemporaneous with the park of Ermenonville and its artificial ruins, another park ruin was created, also in the vicinity of Paris, at the edge of the forest of Marly. It caused a sensation primarily because of its size: the monumental, truncated column of the Désert de Retz. Since almost three floors of this truncated column were inhabitable, and actually only the top third was ruinously broken off, the fact that the building looked like a ruin here had to camouflage and distract from the fact that its true function was as a temporary residence. From the distance visitors had the impression they were seeing the dead relics of a former inconceivably large temple. The few windows in the fluting of the columns and the cracks in the walls that let daylight or moonlight into the interior rooms were not really conspicuous. Altogether the owner of the park, Racine de Monville, had had twelve ruinlike buildings erected on his land, including a faux tomb and a hermitage. But the Doric truncated column, built in 1780/81 by Nicolas-François Barbier, which had a 15-meter diameter, made the strongest impression, probably because it eclipsed everything that had come before it. There was the fact that it looked like a ruin, but the building also looked very natural, thus fitting in with the new way of experiencing the landscape. In the truncated column, it was possible to discern what was left of a once enormously tall sequoia. There was a deliberate attempt to erase the transitions between nature, architecture and art, in accordance with William Gilpin's theories of the »picturesque«. In 1789, Gilpin put it as follows: »Ruins are holy relics. They have been fixed in the ground for centuries, have become one with it, and are almost a part of it; and we therefore consider them more a work of nature than of art. Art cannot attain their grandeur.«

Naturally it was mainly the surrealists in the group around André Breton who rediscovered the remarkable building in the 20th century and proclaimed it to be the principal work of early surrealism. I do not know what they thought about Marie Antoinette's garden world, which she had had set up in the fenced landscape around the Petit Trianon in Versailles. The queen went into raptures about picturesque country life and also loved artificial ruins. Next to temples of love and ruined grottoes, she had a miniature farm built. It included a dairy, mill and dovecote. Chickens and herds of sheep completed the dreamily deceptive scene of a rural idyll. It is understandable that the impoverished French peasants had no sympathy for this and drove the queen out of this supposed paradise with their sickles and scythes.

In spite of the French ruin scenes I have described, enthusiasm for the new fashion in France was limited. In the land of Le Nôtre, the splendor of geometric gardens had not faded yet. Many princes, counts and country nobles preserved the old elegant style of keeping nature under control, though this took some effort. It was quite different in England. Here there was a tradition of quirky individualism, with private mythological interpretations of architectural history and nature. It is therefore no surprise that England is considered to be the country that actually invented the

22. Désert de Retz, eine kolossale Säule als künstliche, teilweise bewohnbare Ruine, 1781.

22. Désert de Retz, a colossal column as an artificial, partly habitable ruin, 1781.

Auch in Deutschland verbreitete sich die neue Mode schnell. Die Adligen hatten auf ihrer »Grand Tour« genügend römische Anregungen gesammelt, und die Engländer trugen mit ihrer Reisewut dazu bei, das Phänomen zu internationalisieren. Wer zur feinen, gehobenen Gesellschaft gehören wollte, mußte zu Hause eine künstliche Ruine im Garten oder Park besitzen. Von Anfang an gab es stilistisch zwei Möglichkeiten: Entweder man errichtete sie aus nachgeahmten römischen Säulen und Architraven, oder man entschied sich für die mittelalterlich-gotisierende Variante und baute eine fiktive, weitgehend zerstörte Ritterburg. Die erste Version sprach von der klassischen Bildung des Besitzers, die zweite von seiner eher national-romantischen Gesinnung. Wer sich nicht festlegen wollte, wählte beide Möglichkeiten gleichzeitig, als Baucollage oder einzeln im Garten verteilt.

Ein berühmtes Beispiel für die zweite Variante war der Schloßpark in Stuttgart-Hohenheim. Hier konnten die Besucher Herzog Carl Eugens eine ländliche Kolonie durchwandern, die sich um die Ruinen einer untergegangenen, fiktiven römischen Stadt und manche gotischen Klosterzitate angesiedelt hatte. Neben landwirtschaftlich genutzten Feldern und Wiesen gab es Haine, Wälder, Bäche, Kaskaden und Seen mit Gondeln, klassische Säulenreste von Tempeln, römische Katakomben, Einsiedeleien, mittelalterlich-gotische Turmruinen und schilfbedeckte Bauernkaten. Der Hauptnutzer der malerischen Anlagen war der Herzog selbst, der sich hier mit seiner Geliebten und späteren, unstandesgemäßen Ehefrau – sie wurde nachträglich als Franziska von Hohenheim geadelt – zu verträumten Sommernachmittagen traf. Der Park übte (gemeinsam mit seiner geliebten Frau) einen positiv-beruhigenden Einfluß auf den früheren Despoten aus, dessen einst so ausschweifendes Leben seine Gesundheit stark angegriffen hatte. Indem er sich den neuen, befreienden frühromantischen Landschaftsideen öffnete, legte er zunehmend die starre Hofetikette ab, wurde milder und nachsichtiger. Rousseau hätte seine Freude gehabt.

Herzog Carl Eugen besaß alle wichtigen Rom-Radierungen Piranesis und orientierte sich bei den antiken Parkeinbauten an diesen Abbildungen. Mitten aus einem Kornfeld wuchsen die »Drei Säulen vom Tempel des donnernden Jupiter«. Sie sahen aus wie auf Piranesis Radierung *Tempio di Giove Tonante in Roma*. Allerdings war das Original weit monumentaler als die doch etwas kümmerlichen schwäbischen Nachbildungen. Bestimmt ging auch das römische Wirtshaus, das in die Ruinen eines fiktiven Aquädukts hineingebaut worden war, auf eine Radierung Piranesis zurück.

Natürlich durften in dieses romantische Tivoli nur auserwählte Besucher eintreten. Zu ihnen gehörte merkwürdigerweise auch der einst revolutionär gesinnte Karlsschüler Friedrich Schiller, dem der Herzog die Aufführung seines dichterischen Erstlings *Die Räuber* verboten hatte, woraufhin der 20jährige nach Mannheim geflohen war und dort sein Stück 1782 mit großem Erfolg herausbrachte. Warum Schiller 1795, nach den Ereignissen der Französischen Revolution, den Park von Hohenheim und seinen einst verhaßten Landesvater in einem Artikel für Cottas *Gartenkalender* lobend besprach, ist unklar und doch etwas verwunderlich. In der Erinnerung verklären sich eben manche Dinge:

»Die meisten Reisenden, denen die Gunst widerfahren ist, die Anlage in Hohenheim zu besichtigen …, haben die Einbildungskraft nicht begreifen können, die sich erlauben durfte, so disparate Dinge in ein Ganzes zu verknüpfen. Die Vorstellung, daß wir eine ländliche Kolonie vor uns haben, die sich unter den Ruinen einer römischen Stadt niederließ, hebt auf einmal diesen Widerspruch auf und bringt eine geistvolle Einheit in diese Komposition. Ländliche Simplizität und versunkene städtische Herrlichkeit, die zwei äußersten Zustände der Gesellschaft, grenzen auf eine rührende Art aneinander, und das ernste Gefühl der Vergänglichkeit verliert sich wunderbar schön im Gefühl des siegenden Lebens.«

Vom Hohenheimer Park haben sich nur wenige Reste erhalten. Das Gelände wurde nach und nach zu einem botanischen Garten umgestaltet, das Schloß zur Universität Hohenheim umgebaut. Wer heute durch die Parkanlagen geht, begegnet nur noch Spuren einstiger Ruineneinbauten (Ruinen der Ruinen). So sind die »Säulen des Tempels des donnernden Jupiter« zu einem kläglichen Steinhaufen verfallen, auch das römische Gasthaus ist kaum noch zu erkennen.

1997 fragte der bekannte, von mir bewunderte Landschaftsarchitekt Hans Luz aus Stuttgart bei mir an, ob ich Lust hätte, innerhalb der von ihm geplanten Hohenheimer Parkerweiterung einen neuen »Monopteros« zu errichten. Wir trafen uns mehrfach vor Ort, wanderten durch das Gelände und begeisterten uns für den Dialog mit alten Zeiten. Der »Monopteros« sollte architektonisch in Kontakt treten mit dem ursprünglichen Park und seinen romantischen Ruineneinbauten. Tatsächlich konnte das Projekt realisiert werden und Ende 1998 stand der »Monopteros« wie geplant auf dem Aussichtshügel, den Hans Luz hatte aufschütten lassen. Da ich den Säulentempel ohne Dach geplant hatte, kann er getrost als künstliche Ruine bezeichnet werden.

motif of artificial ruins. Michel Makarius in his book *Ruins* reports that the first person to propose these imitated ruins was Batty Langley in his treatise *New Principles of Gardening* (1728). His idea was then adopted by William Kent. In Kent's Stowe gardens, pagodas and ruins alternate. In 1746 the Duke of Cumberland even has artificially enlarged genuine ruins in the park of Windsor Castle. In addition to Kent's student William Chambers, who praises the advantages of the Chinese garden, another landscape designer worth mentioning here is Sanderson Miller, who in 1745 built mock ruined buildings in the gardens of Hagley Park.

In 1777–1782, the aesthetics professor at the University of Kiel, Christian Hirschfeld, who also maintains close relations with Denmark, publishes his *Theorie der Gartenkunst* (*Theory of Garden Art*). The five-volume work was to have a profound influence on the spread of landscape gardens in Scandinavia. Shortly before William Gilpin develops his ideas about picturesque beauty, the German philosopher advocates the view that a garden containing a large number of various ruined buildings with inscriptions engraved in stone evokes a whole series of feelings. According to Gilpin's theories it is the different vistas, the contrasts of textures, the effects of light and shadow, the irregularity of the forms and the mystery of the principles that are meant to speak to the visitors' emotions and stimulate their imagination. To do this, a series of individual elements are summoned up: rocks, waterfalls, solitary trees and ruins. In Germany, too, the new fashion spread quickly. During their »grand tour« the aristocrats had gathered quite a few ideas in Rome, and the English with their obsessive love of traveling played a part in internationalizing the phenomenon. If you wanted to belong to refined, sophisticated society, you had to have an artificial ruin at home, in your garden or park. From the very beginning, there were two stylistic possibilities: Either you built it from reproductions of Roman columns and architraves or you decided on a medieval-Gothic variant and built a faux, largely destroyed, castle. The first version indicated the owner's classical education, while the second showed his more national, romantic views. Those who did not want to restrict themselves to either one chose both versions at the same time – in the form of an architectural collage, or of ruins scattered here and there in the garden.

A famous example of the second variant was the castle grounds in Stuttgart-Hohenheim. Here, Duke Carl Eugen's visitors could wander through a rural colony that had grown up around the ruins of a bygone, faux Roman town and a number of allusions to Gothic monasteries. Besides farmed fields and meadows there were groves, woods, brooks, cascades and lakes with gondolas, the remains of classical temple columns, Roman catacombs, hermitages, the ruins of medieval-Gothic towers and thatched peasant cottages. The main user of the picturesque grounds was the duke himself. On dreamy summer afternoons, he met his mistress, later to be his wife, here. She was below him in rank but was subsequently ennobled and given the title of Franziska von Hohenheim. The park (and his beloved wife) had a positive and calming influence on the former despot, whose once so dissipated life had badly affected his health. By opening his mind to the early Romantics' new, liberating ideas about landscape, he increasingly rid himself of rigid court etiquette, becoming milder and more lenient. Rousseau would have been pleased.

Duke Carl Eugen owned all the important Piranesi engravings of Rome and was inspired by them when he installed copies of classical ruins in his own park. In the middle of a field of wheat rose the »Three Columns from the Temple of Thundering Jove«. They looked exactly like the *Tempio di Giove Tonante in Roma* in Piranesi's etching. To be sure, the original was far more monumental than the somewhat pitiful Swabian copies. No doubt the Roman inn that had been built into the ruins of a faux aqueduct also went back to a Piranesi etching.

Naturally only select visitors were allowed to enter this romantic Tivoli. Among them, oddly enough, was the formerly revolutionary-minded Friedrich Schiller, who had once attended the duke's Karlsschule military academy in Stuttgart and whom the duke had forbidden to stage his first literary work, *Die Räuber* (*The Robbers*), whereupon the 20-year-old had fled to Mannheim and there staged his play in 1782 with great success. It is unclear, yet somewhat surprising why Schiller praised the park of Hohenheim and his once hated sovereign in an article for Cotta's *Gartenkalender*, written in 1795, after the events of the French Revolution. Funny how some things become transfigured in memory.

»Most travelers who have had the privilege of viewing the park in Hohenheim … have not been able to understand the powers of imagination that dared to take the liberty of combining such disparate things into a whole. The idea that we have before us a rural settlement that was established among the ruins of a Roman town suddenly heightens this contradiction and gives this composition a sophisticated unity. Rural simplicity and long-gone urban splendor, the two most extreme conditions of society, here adjoin each other touchingly, and a solemn feeling of mortality vanishes wonderfully as we sense that life has triumphed.«

In den Gärten des Markgrafen von Bayreuth und seiner Frau Wilhelmine, einer Tochter Friedrich Wilhelm I. von Preußen, entstanden schon sehr früh, zwischen 1735 und 1763, insgesamt neun künstliche Ruinen. Die älteste ist wahrscheinlich die »Einsiedlerhaus-Ruine«, die sich die Markgräfin in der Eremitage erbauen ließ. Nach 1743 fügte der Markgraf seine eigene »Einsiedlerhaus-Ruine« als Teil einer größeren Grottenanlage hinzu. Wir stellen uns vor, wie das Markgrafenpaar getrennt und einsam seine Sonntagnachmittage in ruinösen Höhlenhäuschen verbrachte und romantischen Naturgedanken nachhing!

Wenige Jahre danach erbaute der Bayreuther Hofbaumeister Joseph Saint-Pierre das berühmte Ruinentheater im Sanspareil, das zum Theaterspielen höchst ungeeignet war, da der Zuschauerraum beträchtlich tiefer liegt als der Bühnenboden, wie Sylvia Habermann schreibt. Die Ruine besteht aus fünf Kulissenpaaren, die von gedrückten Korbbögen überwölbt sind. Dorische Halbsäulen, ein Gesims mit Bukranien, das heißt Stierschädelreliefs, und starke Bossenquader in den Bögen verleihen dem Bau eine monumentale Ernsthaftigkeit. Er scheint von der Architektur des Manierismus angeregt zu sein. Auch an Vorbilder bei Rubens könnte man denken, etwa an die Architektur im »Liebesgarten«. Am meisten beeindruckte mich in den Gärten der Bayreuther Eremitage die zuletzt entstandene künstliche Ruine eines verfallenen Gartenhauses, dessen Innenraumwände mit zerbrochenen Spiegeln tapeziert sind. Dadurch entsteht der verwirrende Eindruck eines ruinösen Spiegellabyrinths. Imaginäre und reale Raumelemente vermischen sich. Der Begriff »Ruine« erhält eine ganz neue, surreale Dimension.

Auch im Schönbrunner Schloßpark steht heute noch eine künstliche »Römische Ruine«, die nach dem Vorbild Piranesis mit Rundbogen und Säulenstümpfen 1777/78 von Johann Ferdinand Hetzendorf errichtet worden ist. Hier sorgt ein schilfbewachsenes Wasserbecken für malerische Spiegeleffekte und einen anderen wichtigen Aspekt künstlicher Ruinen: Sie müssen halb in Wiesen- und Wasserflächen versunken sein, ganz so, wie Piranesi die Reste des antiken Roms dargestellt hatte. Künstliche Ruinen gibt es außerdem in den Parks von Dessau, Wörlitz, Potsdam, Aschaffenburg, Ludwigslust, Weimar, Wiesbaden-Biebrich, Schwetzingen, Kassel, München (Nymphenburg), Berlin (Pfaueninsel), Oranienburg, Hanau (Wilhelmsbad), Ludwigsburg (Schloßgarten).

Seit dem schockierenden Erdbeben 1755 in Lissabon steigerte sich die Ruinenlust zur allgemeinen Schauer- und Katastrophenbegeisterung. Manche adlige Bauherren gingen sogar dazu über, bestehende Gebäude künstlich zu »ruinieren« und sie in »charmante Trümmerfelder« zu verwandeln. Schon zur Entstehungszeit gab es viele Kritiker dieses skurril-romantischen, im Grunde recht überflüssigen und verspielten Rokokomotivs. Man warf den Erbauern unnütze Zeitverschwendung, Verlogenheit und Falschheit vor. Das »Theatralische« und »Bühnenbildhafte« wurde den »künstlichen Ruinen« als bewußte architektonische Formulierung der »Unwahrheit« vorgeworfen.

23. Hans Dieter Schaal, Monopteros im Schloßpark von Hohenheim. Ruinös-transparenter Tempelbau, 1998.
24. Vulkan, künstliche Bergruine im Schloßpark von Wörlitz.

23. Hans Dieter Schaal, Monopteros in the Hohenheim palace garden. A ruinous, transparent temple building, 1998.
24. Volcano, artificial mountain ruin in the Wörlitz palace garden.

Little remains of the former Hohenheim Park. The property was gradually turned into a botanical garden, and the palace became the University of Hohenheim. Walking through the park today one encounters only traces of former faux ruins (ruins of ruins). Thus the »columns of the Temple of Thundering Jove« have collapsed into a pitiable pile of rocks, and the Roman inn is also barely recognizable.

In 1997 Professor Hans Luz of Stuttgart, a famous landscape architect I admire, inquired whether I would like to erect a new »Monopteros« inside the Hohenheim park expansion he was planning. We met in Hohenheim several times and strolled through the grounds, thrilled at the dialogue with bygone days. The »Monopteros« was intended to create an architectural link with the original park and its romantic ruin installations. The project was actually implemented, and by the end of 1998 the »Monopteros« was standing as planned on the lookout hill that Professor Luz had had raised in the park. Since I had planned the temple of columns without a roof, we need have no hesitation in calling it an artificial ruin.

In the gardens of the Margrave of Bayreuth and his wife Wilhelmine, one of the daughters of Friedrich Wilhelm I of Prussia, a total of nine artificial ruins were built very early, between 1735 and 1763. The oldest is most likely the »Hermitage House Ruin« that the margravine had built in the Hermitage. After 1743 the margrave added his own »Hermitage House Ruin« as part of a larger series of grottoes. We can imagine the margrave and margravine spending their Sunday afternoons separate and lonely in ruinlike grotto habitations as they lost themselves in romantic thoughts about nature!

Not many years later the Bayreuth court architect Joseph Saint-Pierre built the famous imitation ruin theater in the Sanspareil, which was most unsuitable for theatrical performances since the auditorium is considerably lower than the floor of the stage, as Sylvia Habermann writes. The ruin consists of five pairs of backdrops vaulted by depressed three-centered arches. Doric half columns, a ledge with bucrania, i.e., reliefs of ox skulls, and massive boss stones in the arches give the building monumental gravity. It seems to have been inspired by the architecture of mannerism. One might also think of examples in the work of Rubens, for instance, the architecture in the »Garden of Love«. What most impressed me in the gardens of the Bayreuth Eremitage was the artificial ruin of a dilapidated summer house – the last to be built – the walls of whose interior are decorated with broken mirrors. The bewildering effect is of a ruined labyrinth of mirrors. Imaginary and real spatial elements are intermingled. The term *ruin* is given a completely new, surreal dimension.

In the grounds of Schönbrunn Palace, too, there is still an artificial »Roman Ruin« that was built in 1777/78 by Johann Ferdinand Hetzendorf and modeled on the work of Piranesi, with round arches and truncated columns. Here a pool overgrown with reeds provides picturesque mirror ef-

Was aber bedeutet »Wahrheit« im Zusammenhang mit Architektur? Ist eine Architektur »wahr«, die ausschließlich nützlich ist und einer praktischen Funktion dient? Mit der Natur verhält es sich einfacher. Ein Baum ist ein wahres, lebendiges Naturelement, Funktion und Form scheinen sich gegenseitig zu bedingen, ganz für einander geschaffen zu sein. Ein Baum ist ein Baum. Ein Blatt ist ein Blatt. Niemand stellt dieses komplexe Natursystem in Frage, weder in seiner Funktion noch in seinem Aussehen. Diese lebendigen Wesen verlieren ihre angeborene Wahrhaftigkeit zum Teil nur dann, wenn Gärtner sie beschneiden oder den Wuchs beeinträchtigen. Dennoch verlassen sie auch dann den Bereich der natürlichen Wahrheit nie ganz. Definiert man die »Lüge« als Vorspiegelung falscher Tatsachen (ein Objekt gibt vor, ein anderes zu sein, als es wirklich ist, eine Aussage führt bewußt in die Irre), so ist Architektur immer etwas Vortäuschendes, Unnatürliches, Künstliches und damit »Verlogenes«. Jedes Gebäude, ob benutzbar oder unbenutzbar, bedeutet eine materielle, sichtbare Setzung, eine hölzerne oder steinerne Behauptung: So könnte ein Gebäude dieser Art aussehen! Je selbstverständlicher es wirkt, um so weniger werden Fragen nach dem »Warum« und dem »Wie« auftauchen. Architektur lebt demnach, wie jedes andere Kunstwerk auch, von ihrer Überzeugungskraft.

Das Schloß Schönbrunn sieht aus wie das Schloß Schönbrunn, niemand wird an der überzeugenden Architektur zweifeln oder seine Form in Frage stellen. Genauso verhält es sich mit den Pyramiden von Gizeh, dem Parthenon, dem Kolosseum, dem Pantheon, dem Ulmer Münster, der Domkuppel von Florenz, dem Schloß von Versailles, den Houses of Parliament, dem Eiffelturm oder dem Empire State Building. Jedes Gebäude ist alles zugleich: Lüge, Fiktion und behauptete Wahrheit. Man könnte sagen, mit der Erschaffung eines Gebäudes wird auch seine neue Wahrheit in die Welt gesetzt, es ist die Wahrheit des Faktischen. Für künstliche Ruinen gelten die gleichen Kriterien und Erkenntnisse. Ihr Bedeutungsfeld ist nur komplexer, erfaßt Heutiges genauso wie Vergangenes und Zukünftiges. Wer will diese Vieldeutigkeit, diese Überlagerung der Zeitebenen als Lüge bezeichnen? Künstliche Ruinen argumentieren eben doppelbödiger und raffinierter. Und sie strahlen, bezogen auf Funktionsbauten, eine starke Prise Provokation aus. Ich, scheinen sie zu sagen, ich stehe nur da, verwandle meine Umgebung in eine diffuse Zeitcollage, vielleicht können Besucher in mir auch hochklettern oder gar in einer Raumhöhle übernachten, aber ansonsten bin ich nicht zu gebrauchen und befinde mich auf dem langsamen Weg des Verschwindens in der Erde.

Immer, wenn ich den in der Nähe von Heidelberg liegenden Schloßgarten von Schwetzingen besuche, bin ich aufs neue verzaubert von dieser Gartenwelt, die mit ihren beiden so konträr gestalteten Parkbereichen unser Gespaltensein zwischen künstlicher und natürlicher Welt bildhaft vor uns ausbreitet. Wer den dunklen Torbogen unter dem ehemaligen Jagdschloß durchschritten hat, wird von der Mittelachse des geometrisch gestalteten Parkbereichs in die Ferne gezogen wie ein startendes Flugzeug. Am Horizont wölbt sich eine blaue Hügelkette aus der Ebene, davor glänzt ein See, der den strengen Parkbereich begrenzt. Die Mittelachse wird kurz nach dem Schloß von einer großen, kreisförmigen Parterrefläche umschlossen. Am Rand des Kreises stehen elegante, eingeschossige Gebäude und Laubengänge. Sie umschließen das Parkbild wie ein kräftiger Rahmen. Die Kreisinnenfläche ist mit niedrigen Zierrabatten und Wiesensegmenten bepflanzt, Rokokomuster, verschnörkelt, selbstverliebt. Von der Seite dringen geometrisch geordnete Baumreihen zum Mittelpunkt des Kreises vor, außerdem begleitet eine Allee aus beschnittenen Bäumen die Hauptachse. Durch diese klaren Baumarchitekturen wird der Kreis fixiert und daran gehindert, sich in Bewegung zu setzen, zu rotieren. Die Geometrie ist perfekt, in sich ruhend und läßt sich in ihrer energischen Bestimmtheit kaum noch steigern. Ich denke an einen riesigen Kompaß, an die vier Himmelsrichtungen, an kosmische Formen, die Sonne, den Mond, aber auch an Stonehenge und die Blüte einer Sonnenblume.

Ich befinde mich auf der Hauptachse und lasse mich in die Ferne ziehen. Weiße, nahezu nackte Figuren auf Sockeln schweben an mir vorüber, Götter vielleicht, die es nie gegeben hat, außer in den Erzählungen der Dichter, den Vorstellungen der Bildhauer und den Phantasien mancher Menschen. Hier in diesem Park führen sie ihr fiktives Dasein fort, stellen fragmentarisch Szenen, Gesten oder Vorgänge nach, die wir nicht mehr kennen. Worum es geht, läßt sich nicht genau ermitteln, man kann die Figuren nicht befragen, da sie leblos und stumm sind. Sie scheinen alle während einer Theateraufführung mythologischer Szenen plötzlich zu Eis, Schnee oder Gips erstarrt zu sein. Niemand allerdings kann den Moment ausschließen, in dem sie zum Leben zurückkehren. Ruinen einstiger Erzählungen, traumhafter Mythologien. Ruinen fremder Träume, märchenhafter Weltanschauungen.

Unter beschnittenen Linden geht es weiter, an wasserspeienden Hirschen, an Obelisken auf Wiesen, an weißen Parkbänken vorbei bis zum See, der die Achse daran hindert, sich weiterzu-

fects and an additional important aspect of artificial ruins: They must be half drowned in meadows and bodies of water, exactly the way Piranesi represented the remnants of ancient Rome. More artificial ruins can be found in the parks of Dessau, Wörlitz, Potsdam, Aschaffenburg, Ludwigslust, Weimar, Wiesbaden-Biebrich, Schwetzingen, Kassel, Munich (Nymphenburg), Berlin (Pfaueninsel), Oranienburg, Hanau (Wilhelmsbad), Ludwigsburg (Palace Gardens).

Since the shocking 1755 earthquake in Lisbon the taste for ruins grew into a general enthusiasm for thrills and catastrophes. A number of aristocratic builders even proceeded to »ruin« existing buildings artificially and to transform them into »charming scenes of devastation«. Even among their contemporaries there were many critics of this quirkily romantic, essentially quite superfluous and whimsical rococo motif. The builders were accused of idle waste of time, mendacity and falseness. The fact that the »artificial ruins« were »theatrical« and »reminded one of stage sets«, critics felt, was a deliberate architectural formulation of »untruth«. But what does »truth« mean in relation to architecture? Is an architectural structure »true« if it is exclusively utilitarian and serves a practical function? When it comes to nature, things are much simpler. A tree is a true, living element of nature; function and form seem to be mutually dependent, to be created totally for each other. A tree is a tree. A leaf is a leaf. No one questions either the function or the appearance of this complex natural system. These living beings partially lose their innate truthfulness only when gardeners trim them or interfere with their growth. Nonetheless, even then they never entirely leave the realm of natural truth. If we define »lie« as the attempt to delude others into believing false facts (an object claims to be something other than it really is, a statement is deliberately misleading), then architecture is always something that pretends, something unnatural, artificial and thus »mendacious«. Every building, whether usable or not, indicates a material, visible assumption, a wood or stone assertion: This is what a building of this type could look like! The more natural its effect, the fewer questions are asked as to the »why« and »how«. Accordingly, what gives life to architecture, and all other works of art, is its power of persuasion.

Schönbrunn Palace looks like Schönbrunn Palace, no one will doubt its convincing architecture or question its form. The same is true of the Pyramids of Giza, the Parthenon, the Colosseum, the Pantheon, Ulm Minster, the cupola of the cathedral in Florence, the palace of Versailles, the Houses of Parliament, the Eiffel Tower or the Empire State Building. Every building is simultaneously everything at the same time: lie, fiction and an assertion of truth. One might say that with the creation of a building its new truth also sees the light of day – the truth of the actual. The same criteria and insights are true of artificial ruins. Their potential meanings are only more complex, including not only the present but also the past and the future. Why call this ambiguity, this layering of time levels a lie? The arguments of artificial ruins are simply more ambiguous and sophisticated. And, in relation to functional buildings, they emanate a good deal of provocation. I – they seem to say – I just stand there and transform my surroundings into a diffuse chronological collage, maybe visitors can climb around inside me or even spend the night in a grotto room, but otherwise I have no practical use and I am slowly in the process of disappearing in the ground.

Whenever I visit the castle grounds of Schwetzingen not far from Heidelberg, I again fall under the spell of this garden world, which with its two separate park areas, based on such antithetical design principles, graphically demonstrates the fact that we are split between an artificial and a natural world. Once a visitor walks through the dark archway below the former hunting lodge, he is drawn into the distance by the central axis of the geometrically designed park terrain, like a plane taking off. On the horizon a blue chain of hills arches from the plain. In front of them glitters a lake, which forms the boundary of what is strictly the park itself. Just after the palace the central axis is surrounded by a large, circular parterre. At the edge of the circle are elegant one-story buildings and pergolas. They form a strong frame for the vista of the park. The inner surface of the circle is planted with low ornamental borders and lawn segments – rococo patterns, ornate, narcissistic. From the side, geometrically arranged rows of trees advance up to the center of the circle. Also, an avenue of topiary trees accompanies the main axis. The clear architectural shapes of the trees fix the circle, keep it from being set in motion, from rotating. The geometry is perfect, at one with itself, and its energetic certainty can hardly be intensified. I think of a huge compass, of the four cardinal directions, of cosmic forms, the sun, the moon, but also of Stonehenge and a sunflower in bloom.

I am standing on the main axis, letting myself be drawn into the distance. White, almost naked figures on pedestals glide past me, gods perhaps, that never existed except in the tales of poets, the minds of sculptors and the fantasies of many a person. Here, in this park, they continue their fictitious existence, recreate fragmentary scenes, gestures or events with which we are no longer familiar. We cannot really tell what it is all about, we cannot question the figures, since they are

entwickeln oder gar fortzufliegen. In Wirklichkeit markiert der See auch den Beginn jener zweiten, von der Geometrie befreiten Welt, der Welt des Landschaftsparks. Während Kreisfläche und anschließende Achsenschneise noch dem italienisch-französischen Gartenstil angehören, verwandelt sich die Parklandschaft jetzt in einen »englischen Garten«.

Es war ein Glücksfall der Geschichte, daß Kurfürst Carl Theodor für jede Gestaltungsphase die richtigen Architekten und Landschaftsgestalter fand. Zunächst war es Johann Ludwig Petri, der das Kreisparterre entwarf, baute und anlegte, dann wurde 1762 der Lothringer Nicolas de Pigage als »Intendant der Gärten, Wasserkünste und Architekturen« nach Schwetzingen engagiert. 1768 unternahm Pigage eine längere Studienreise nach Italien, 1776 reiste er nach England. Dort traf er mit seinem späteren Nachfolger Friedrich Ludwig von Sckell zusammen. Bis 1796, seinem Todesjahr, bestimmte Pigage die Garten- und Architekturentwürfe in Schwetzingen. Danach übernahm von Sckell die Leitung, ein Epochenwechsel. Pigage vertrat am Anfang seiner Laufbahn noch einen klassisch strengen Architektur- und Gartenstil, später entwarf er, gemäß dem sich wandelnden Zeitgefühl, auch die romantischen Rokoko-Einbauten im Schwetzinger Schloßpark. Friedrich Ludwig von Sckell gehörte von Anfang an zur »englischen« Fraktion und zeichnete seine Entwürfe ausschließlich im freien Landschaftsstil.

Sckells Vater war bereits Hofgärtner und Hauptmitarbeiter Pigages in Schwetzingen. Der Sohn ging bei ihm in die Lehre. Danach finanzierte der Kurfürst dem begabten jungen Gärtner längere Studienaufenthalte in Frankreich und England. Italien war damals aus der Mode geraten und stand nicht mehr auf dem Ausbildungsprogramm. Obwohl der Kurfürst bereits 1778 wegen einer Erbfolge seine Residenz von Mannheim nach München verlegen mußte, wurde Schwetzingen bis 1804 weiter erhalten und ausgebaut. Dann verlor Carl Theodor langsam das Interesse an dem weit entfernten Schloßpark, holte Sckell nach München und ließ ihn dort den Nymphenburger Schloßgarten und den Englischen Garten ausbauen. Friedrich Ludwig von Sckell starb 1823 hochgeehrt und angesehen mit 73 Jahren in München.

Hinter beschnittenen Hainbuchenhecken öffnet sich eine versteckte Wiesenlichtung, die den Blick auf den höher gelegenen Tempel freigibt. Unter dem Tempel sind finstere Ruinenlöcher, Höhlenwege in eine Unterwelt zu erkennen, die nichts Gutes versprechen. Beim Eindringen glaube ich immer wieder eigenartige Zeichen an der Wand zu entdecken. Man vermutet, daß der Kurfürst den Freimaurern nahegestanden habe und hier Symbole des merkwürdigen Geheimbunds,

lifeless and silent. They all seem to have suddenly frozen into ice, snow or plaster statues during a theatrical performance of mythological scenes. No one can rule out that there will come a moment when they return to life. They are ruins of long-ago stories, dreamlike myths. Ruins of the dreams of strangers, of fairy-tale worldviews.

Under topiary linden trees the path takes us past stags that spew water, obelisks on expanses of lawn and white park benches, to the lake, which prevents the axis from developing further or even flying off into the sky. In reality the lake also marks the beginning of the second world, liberated from geometry – the world of the landscape park. While the circle and adjacent axis lane still belong to an Italian-French garden style, the park landscape now turns into an »English garden«.

It was by a lucky chance that Elector Carl Theodor found the right architects and landscape designers for every stage of planning. Initially, Johann Ludwig Petri designed, built and laid out the circular parterre. Then, in 1762, Nicolas de Pigage (from the Lorraine) was hired to be the »director of the gardens, waterworks and buildings« in Schwetzingen. In 1768 Pigage went on a lengthy study trip to Italy, and in 1776 he traveled to England. There he encountered the man who was later to be his successor, Friedrich Ludwig von Sckell. Up till 1796, the year of his death, Pigage determined the designs of the gardens and pieces of architecture in Schwetzingen. After that von Sckell took charge. It was the beginning of a new era. At the beginning of his career Pigage still advocated a classically strict style in architecture and landscape design. Later, as the spirit of the times changed, he also designed the romantic rococo installations in the castle grounds of Schwetzingen. From the very beginning, Friedrich Ludwig von Sckell belonged to the »English« faction and drafted his designs exclusively in the free landscape style.

Sckell's father, too, had been court gardener and Pigage's main collaborator in Schwetzingen. The son was trained by the father. Subsequently the Elector financed lengthy periods of study for the gifted young gardener in France and England. At the time, Italy had gone out of fashion and was no longer part of training programs. Although the Elector had to move his residence from Mannheim to Munich as early as 1778 due to hereditary succession, Schwetzingen continued to be maintained and enlarged until 1804. Then Carl Theodor slowly lost interest in the distant castle grounds, brought Sckell to Munich and had him expand the palace grounds of Nymphenburg and the Englischer Garten (English Garden) there. Friedrich Ludwig von Sckell died in Munich in 1823 at the age of 73, highly esteemed and respected.

Behind trimmed hornbeam hedges, a hidden meadow clearing is revealed, giving a view of the temple, which is higher up. Discernible below the temple are dark holes in the ruins, cavernous paths into an underworld, promising nothing good. As I enter I always believe I can see strange symbols on the wall. Presumably the Elector sympathized with the Freemasons and had symbols of that curious secret society, which also counted Mozart and Goethe among its members, engraved here. Some 100 meters from the Apollo Temple, hidden in the green thicket, are the »Bird Bath« and the »End of the World«, both also works by Nicolas de Pigage.

In the middle of the oval pool of the »Bird Bath«, which is edged by a delicate cast-iron lattice, a bronze eagle owl attacks a pheasant. Other bronze birds sit on the curved ledge of the surrounding pergola. Water streams from their beaks into the central pool. The scene is based on one of Aesop's fables in which the birds are outraged at the owl's action and give him a piece of their mind, scolding loudly and spewing water.

Since the pergolas lack roofs and are only suggested as walls with ledges, they can also be called ruins. The transparent slats can also be viewed as open-worked architectural pieces that resemble spatial drawings in the great outdoors. The »End of the World« for me is one of the greatest masterpieces of the art of horticulture. The roughly 30-meter-long arbor, the »Telescope«, ends in a ruined building whose inside is painted black, since its purpose is to darken the passage. Pigage had an irregular ruin aperture broken into the wall at the end. Through the window in the cave we see not the forest that grows in back of it, but a painted landscape showing a romantic water meadow. In the evening haze, trees, bushes and clouds are reflected in the gently gliding stream. Since there is a certain space between the room in the ruin cave and the painted panorama, daylight can illuminate the picture.

A cave, an artificial ruin, a fragmented vista, and before them a pergola telescope built of wooden slats with vine leaves twining around it – an unsurpassable composition that makes it graphically clear for us, the visitors, that a real Arcady, a paradise, can exist only as a distant panorama painting, and that no one can really ever enter it. A wonderful place for meditating on dream, reality, ruins, artificial and biological nature. From the beginning of time the history of art and architecture has involved crossing borders. Transcendence has always been part of the magic of buildings, pictures and sculptures. They were either achieved by installations of paths or

dem auch Mozart und Goethe angehörten, einmeißeln ließ. Wenige 100 Meter vom Apollotempel entfernt, befinden sich, im grünen Dickicht versteckt, das »Vogelbad« und das »Ende der Welt«, beides ebenfalls Werke von Nicolas de Pigage.

In der Mitte des ovalen, von einem zarten Gußeisengitter eingefaßten Wasserbeckens des »Vogelbads«, fällt ein bronzener Uhu über einen Fasan her. Weitere Bronzevögel sitzen auf dem gebogenen Sims der umgebenden Laubenkonstruktion. Aus ihren Schnäbeln läuft Wasser in das zentrale Becken hinein. Die Szene geht auf eine Fabel des Äsop zurück, in der sich die Vögel über die Tat des Uhus empören und sie lautstark schimpfend und wasserspeiend kommentieren.

Da die Laubenkonstruktionen nur als Wände mit Simsen ohne Raumdecken angedeutet sind, kann man auch hier von Ruinen sprechen. Die transparenten Lattungen lassen sich auch als skelettierte Architekturen lesen, die Ähnlichkeit mit räumlichen Zeichnungen in freier Natur besitzen. Das »Ende der Welt« ist für mich eines der größten Meisterwerke der Gartenbaukunst. Der etwa 30 Meter lange Laubengang, das »Perspektiv«, wird von einem innen schwarz eingefärbten Ruinengebäude abgeschlossen, das die Aufgabe hat, den Gang zu verdunkeln. In die Abschlußwand ließ Pigage eine unregelmäßige Ruinenöffnung brechen. Durch das Höhlenfenster sehen wir nicht etwa in den dahinter wachsenden Wald, sondern auf ein gemaltes Landschaftsbild mit einer romantisch gestimmten Flußaue. Abendlich dunstig spiegeln sich Bäume, Büsche und Wolken im sanft dahinziehenden Wasser. Da zwischen Höhlen-Ruinen-Raum und gemaltem Panorama ein gewisser Abstand besteht, hat das Tageslicht die Möglichkeit, das Bild zu erhellen.

open-air space, by symbolic or narrative additions, by religious excesses or by illusionistic magic tricks. This is true both of the wall paintings of Pompeii that suggested views of fictitious garden surroundings, and of almost all paintings with Christian iconography. Naturally it was the baroque and rococo periods that particularly loved it when real-life spatial boundaries burst open. Beyond them appeared painted pastoral scenes, hovering angels and naked putti, exotic parts of the world with wild, hitherto unknown animals. The nightmarish aspects of this second world were not discovered until later, after the French Revolution, in the period of radical Romanticism.

In the palace grounds there is one more masterpiece by Pigage, the »Roman Ruin«, based on models by Piranesi, that he planned and erected between 1779 and 1780. Rough natural stone masonry gives the façade a rugged appearance, familiar to us from the tomb towers along the Via Appia Antica – the grave of Cecilia Metella, for instance – and from the Colosseum. Two large open arches placed one above the other break up the façade and allow one to look into their not very deep interior. Here water runs over the stones, staining them dark and wet. Behind a bridge located inside, water collects and drops as a narrow rivulet into the lake that spreads in front of the ruin, a perfect mirroring surface. The façade abruptly ends above, roofless as a ruin ought to be. A small gable belvedere tops the building. The fact that to the left and right of the »Roman Ruin« the remains of the arches of a faux aqueduct abut it indicates that they may once have had a water-engineering function. But they might also be placed there to create an illusion or romantic camouflage. The secret endures.

In the interior of the ruin visitors can climb to the top and look into the distance from the gable structure. As they do so they will discover an additional aqueduct fragment that is detached from the back of the ruin and moves off into the faux Roman Campagna. Around it poplars sway in the wind like cypresses.

Ludwig von Sckell was also active for a time in the park of Biebrich Palace near Wiesbaden. A plaque near the entrance provides information about the history of the park and the »Moosburg« ruin. »In 1804 Prince Friedrich August, Duke of Nassau as of 1806, purchases the ›Moosburg‹ ruin. He has what remains of a medieval fortress converted into a romantic residence. Beginning in 1817, Ludwig von Sckell redesigns the entire park of Biebrich and integrates the baroque gardens in his concept. After 1846 the Wiesbaden park director Carl Friedrich Thelemann carries out many replanting operations.«

The ruin of the fortress is as small and playful as something out of Lilliput, a dream that shrank or never quite unfolded to its full size. A ruin chrysalis. Perhaps the Moosburg would make a picturesque kindergarten in a rural setting. To see real knights in armor here would feel like watching scattered Don Quixote fools at the famous carnival in Mainz. The gentle, freshly mowed grassy hollow that surrounds the walls is probably meant to suggest a dried-out castle pond. The actual lake, which was planned by Sckell, is 20 meters from the bare, ivyless fortress walls.

The ruin looks its best from the lake side. No doubt this is how Sckell imagined the romantic scene. The fortress walls now look as if they had half sunk into the ground or the lake, just as they do in the paintings of Jacob van Ruisdael that served as Sckell's models. Piranesi was no

26, 27. Blick vom »Vogelbad« zum »Ende der Welt«. Garteneinbauten von Nicolas de Pigage im Schloß-park von Schwetzingen, zwischen 1762 und 1775.
28. »Ende der Welt«. Blick von außen auf den oberen Abschluß des romantischen Panoramagemäldes.

26, 27. View from the »Vogelbad« (birdbath) to the »Ende der Welt« (end of the world). Garden installations by Nicolas de Pigage in the Schwetzingen palace garden, between 1762 and 1775.
28. »Ende der Welt« (end of the world). View from the outside on the top section of the romantic panorama painting.

Höhle, künstliche Ruine, fragmentierter Fernblick, davor ein aus Holzlatten gebautes, von Weinblättern umranktes Laubenfernrohr – eine unübertreffliche Komposition, die uns Besuchern bildhaft deutlich macht, daß ein wirkliches Arkadien, ein Paradies nur als fernes Panoramagemälde existieren und nie wirklich betreten werden kann. Ein wunderbarer Ort, um über Traum, Wirklichkeit, Ruinen, künstliche und gewachsene Natur nachzudenken. Grenzüberschreitungen begleiten die Kunst- und Architekturgeschichte von Anfang an. Transzendenz gehörte zu allen Zeiten zur Magie von Gebäuden, Bildern und Skulpturen. Entweder wurden sie durch Weg- und Rauminszenierungen, durch symbolische oder erzählerische Ergänzungen, durch religiöse Überhöhungen oder durch illusionistische Zaubertricks erreicht. Das gilt für die pompejanischen Wandmalereien, die Blicke in eine fiktive Gartenumgebung suggerierten, genauso wie für fast alle Gemälde mit christlicher Ikonographie. Natürlich liebte besonders die Barock- und Rokokozeit das Aufplatzen der realen Raumhäute. Dahinter erschienen gemalte Schäferszenen, schwebende Engel und nackte Putten, fremde Erdteile mit wilden, bisher unbekannten Tieren. Die alptraumhaften Nachtseiten dieser zweiten Welt wurden erst später, nach der Französischen Revolution, in der Zeit der radikalen Romantik, entdeckt.

Im Schloßgarten findet sich ein weiteres Meisterwerk von Pigage, die »Römische Ruine«, die er zwischen 1779 und 1780 nach Vorlagen Piranesis geplant und errichtet hat. Grobes Natursteinmauerwerk verleiht der Fassade ein wildes Aussehen, wie wir es von Grabtürmen an der Via Appia Antica – dem Grab der Cecilia Metella etwa – und vom Kolosseum her kennen. Zwei große, übereinanderstehende Bogenöffnungen reißen die Fassade auf und geben den Blick in ihre nicht allzu tiefen Innereien frei. Hier rinnt Wasser über die Steine und färbt sie dunkelnaß. Hinter einer innen liegenden Brücke sammelt sich das Wasser und fällt als schmales Rinnsal in den See, der sich als perfekte Spiegelfläche vor der Ruine ausbreitet. Die Fassade endet in der Höhe abrupt und dachlos – wie es sich für eine Ruine gehört. Ein kleines Giebel-Belvedere krönt den Bau. Daß sich links und rechts der »Römischen Ruine« die Bogenreste eines fiktiven Aquädukts anschließen, deutet auf eine ehemalige wassertechnische Funktion hin. Aber sie könnten auch Täuschung oder romantische Maskierung sein. Das Geheimnis bleibt bestehen.

Im Inneren der Ruine kann man als Besucher hochsteigen und aus dem Giebelaufbau in die Ferne schauen. Dabei wird man ein weiteres Aquäduktfragment entdecken, das sich aus dem Rücken der Ruine löst und hinaus in die falsche römische Campagna flieht. Ringsum wiegen sich Pappeln im Wind wie Zypressen.

Auch im Park von Schloß Biebrich bei Wiesbaden war Friedrich Ludwig von Sckell eine Zeitlang tätig. Eine Tafel in der Nähe des Eingangsbereichs informiert über die Parkgeschichte und die Ruine »Moosburg«. »1804 erwirbt Fürst Friedrich August, ab 1806 Herzog von Nassau, die Ruine ›Moosburg‹. Er läßt die Überreste einer mittelalterlichen Burg in eine romantische Wohnburg umbauen. Seit 1817 plant Ludwig von Sckell den gesamten Biebricher Park um und integriert dabei

29. Nicolas de Pigage, Römische Ruine, Schloßpark von Schwetzingen, zwischen 1779 und 1780.
30. Die Moosburg, künstliche Ruine, Schloßpark von Biebrich bei Wiesbaden.

29. Nicolas de Pigage, Roman Ruin, Schwetzingen palace garden, between 1779 and 1780.
30. The Moosburg, artificial ruin, Biebrich palace garden near Wiesbaden.

longer in demand as far as Sckell was concerned. An elongated grassy hollow that extends from the distant Biebrich Palace to the ruin is the last remnant of a former garden parterre axis. Sckell has modified its severity and transformed it into gentle, natural beauty with irregular planted borders. If we approach the castle by walking along the grassy hollow in the direction of the Rhine, the park loses its slightly wild appearance after a while; the meadows on both sides of the path have just been mowed and the shrubbery too becomes more sparse. In front of the castle white tents are visible through the trees on the opposite side: Elegant horse show grounds have been installed there; there seems to be a show today.

Like the palaces of Mainz and Mannheim, the palace itself cannot be called a showpiece. Actually it is only worthy of note because it is situated directly on the Rhine River. In the old days visitors could come here by boat. A fine romantic idea.

In contrast with the Biebrich palace grounds, »Peacock Island« or »Pfaueninsel«, once called »Rabbit Island«, in Berlin, is an old acquaintance of mine. I've been admiring the famous artificial ruin on the island for decades.

The special and characteristic feature of this ruin structure, which actually consists of nothing but a quadratic cube with broken-off battlements, is the two overly high round towers that rise at the south corners of the house, which are turned toward the water and thus the town of Potsdam, and look like the heads of two giraffes. While the tower on the left ends in an overhanging round balcony with battlements, the tower on the right is one story higher than the other. At the very top, above the clock, a small semicircular cupola that looks like a cap completes the soaring building. A cast-iron, filigree bridge spans the space between the two towers. Its lower structure is reminiscent of a pointed Gothic arch. Through the space between this pointed arch and the broken-off battlements lower down one can see the tops of the trees that grow behind the building. At the point where the central entrance gate should be located in the main façade, an artist has painted a view of an Arcadian landscape, just as though there was a gate here for people to pass through.

Judging by the style quoted here this is supposed to be a dilapidated Roman country house – or so the island guidebook explains –, but what I recognize looks more like an English fortress ruin, painted white, with later additions, such as an alpine lookout bridge and a small observatory. At any rate I find the cheery rococo brightness of the building confusing: It seems so remote from gloomy moonlit romanticism and black melancholy. The collage of buildings, reminiscent of stage scenery, theatrically ambiguous, is bewildering. Indeed, it gets even more bewildering when one enters the inner rooms. Here too various styles and dream journeys are quoted. One room is painted to look like a bamboo hut. It was the lure of the South Seas. Two decades before the Pfaueninsel (Peacock Island) ruin was built, the island of Tahiti had been discovered in the South Seas, and travelers who returned gave enthusiastic reports of a pristine tropic paradise.

die barocken Anlagen in sein Konzept. Ab 1846 führt der Wiesbadener Gartendirektor Carl Friedrich Thelemann zahlreiche Neupflanzungen durch.«

Die Burgruine ist so klein und verspielt wie eine Liliputanlage, geschrumpfter oder nie ganz entfalteter Traum. Ruinenverpuppung. Vielleicht wäre sie als malerischer Kindergarten im Grünen gut geeignet. Reale Ritter in Rüstungen kämen mir hier vor wie versprengte Don-Quichote-Narren der berühmten Mainzer Fastnacht. Die sanfte, frisch gemähte Wiesenmulde, die das Gemäuer umgibt, soll wohl einen ausgetrockneten Burgweiher andeuten. Der wirkliche See, den Sckell geplant hat, liegt 20 Meter von den kahlen, efeulosen Burgmauern entfernt.

Von der Seeseite aus betrachtet, wirkt die Ruine am besten. So hat sich Sckell das romantische Bild wahrscheinlich vorgestellt. Die Burgmauern sehen jetzt aus, als wären sie halb in der Erde oder in den See eingesunken, ganz wie auf den Gemälden Jakob von Ruisdaels, die Sckell als Vorbilder dienten. Piranesi war bei ihm nicht mehr gefragt. Eine langgezogene Wiesenmulde, die sich vom in der Ferne liegenden Biebricher Schloß bis zur Ruine erstreckt, ist der letzte Rest einer früheren Garten-Parterre-Achse. Sckell hat ihr die Strenge genommen und sie in eine sanfte Naturschönheit mit bewegter Randbepflanzung verwandelt. Nähert man sich dem Schloß entlang der Wiesenmulde in Richtung Rhein, verliert der Park nach einiger Zeit seine leichte Verkommenheit; die Wiesen links und rechts sind frisch gemäht, und auch die Buschvegetation wird spärlicher. Vor dem Schloß sind durch die Bäume auf der gegenüberliegenden Seite weiße Zelte zu erkennen, dort drüben wurde ein vornehmer Reitturnierplatz eingerichtet, der auch heute noch in Betrieb zu sein scheint.

Das Schloß selbst kann man, ähnlich dem Mainzer und dem Mannheimer Schloß, nicht als Prunkstück bezeichnen. Eigentlich ist es nur wegen seiner Lage direkt am Rhein bemerkenswert. Früher konnten hier Schiffe an- und ablegen. Eine schöne, romantische Vorstellung.

Im Gegensatz zum Schloßpark von Biebrich gehört die »Pfaueninsel«, früher »Kaninchenwerder« genannt, in Berlin zu meinen »alten Bekannten«. Die berühmte künstliche Ruine auf der Insel bewundere ich schon seit Jahrzehnten.

Das Besondere und Charakteristische dieses Ruinenbaus, der eigentlich nur aus einem quadratischen Kubus mit abgebrochenen Zinnen besteht, sind die beiden überhohen Rundtürme, die sich an den südlichen, dem Wasser und damit der Stadt Potsdam zugewendeten Hausecken in die Höhe recken und aussehen wie zwei Giraffenhälse. Während der linke Turm mit einem runden, ringsum auskragenden Zinnenbalkon endet, überragt ihn der rechte Turm um ein Geschoß. Ganz oben, über der Uhr, beendet eine kleine halbrunde Kuppel, die aussieht wie eine Mütze, das Aufstreben der Architektur. Zwischen den beiden Türmen spannt sich eine gusseiserne, filigrane Brücke. Ihre Unterkonstruktion ist so geformt, daß sie an einen gotischen Spitzbogen erinnert. Durch den Hohlraum zwischen diesem Spitzbogen und den tieferliegenden, abgebrochenen Zinnen sieht man auf die hinter dem Gebäude stehenden Baumkronen. Dort, wo sich in der Hauptfassade das zentrale Eingangstor befinden müßte, hat ein Künstler den Blick in eine arkadische Landschaft aufgemalt, ganz so, als befände sich hier ein Tordurchgang.

Bei dem hier zitierten Stil soll es sich – gemäß dem Erläuterungstext im Inselführer – um ein verfallenes römisches Landhaus handeln, ich erkenne darin aber eher eine weiß angestrichene englische Burgruine mit späteren Zutaten, einer hochalpinen Aussichtsbrücke etwa und einem kleinen Observatorium. In jedem Fall irritiert die heitere Rokokohelligkeit des Baus, die weit entfernt scheint von düsterer Mondromantik und schwarzer Melancholie. Die kulissenhafte, theatralische Uneindeutigkeit der Baucollage bleibt verwirrend, ja sie steigert sich noch, wenn man die Innenräume betritt. Auch hier werden verschiedene Stile und Traumreisen zitiert. Ein Raum ist als Bambushütte ausgemalt. Die Südsee lockte. Zwei Jahrzehnte vor dem Bau der Pfaueninsel-Ruine war die Insel Tahiti in der Südsee entdeckt worden, und zurückgekehrte Reisende berichteten begeistert von dem unberührten Tropenparadies.

Die schilfumgürtete Insel war einst Ausflugs- und Jagdrevier König Friedrich Wilhelms II. Hier traf er sich als junger Kronprinz heimlich mit seiner lebenslangen Geliebten und späteren Mätresse Wilhelmine Encke, der Tochter eines Hoftrompeters und Gastwirts. Die damals erst 13jährige wurde zwei Jahre später Mutter. In den Jahren danach gebar sie dem König – jetzt zur Gräfin von Lichtenau geadelt – noch vier weitere Kinder. Sie war es auch, die ab 1794 die Planungen der Pfaueninsel mit ihren Gebäuden und künstlichen Ruinen maßgeblich beeinflußte. Nachdem der König 1797 gestorben war, fiel seine Geliebte am Hof in Ungnade und wurde sogar wegen »unrechtmäßiger Bereicherung« angeklagt. Trotz Freispruchs mußte sie ihr Leben in der Verbannung beenden.

Friedrich Wilhelm III., dessen Frau – die im Volk überaus beliebte Königin Luise – früh an Typhus starb, ließ die Insel von Peter Joseph Lenné zum Mustergut umbauen. Karl Friedrich

31. Blick auf die Moosburg über einen See hinweg,
den Ludwig von Sckell in den Jahren nach 1817 geplant hat und anlegen ließ.

31. View of the Moosburg (moss castel) across a
lake planned and designed by Ludwig von Sckell
after 1817.

Girded by reeds, the island was once the hunting preserve of King Friedrich Wilhelm II, where he also went on outings. Here, as a young crown prince, he had secret assignments with his life-long sweetheart and later mistress Wilhelmine Encke, the daughter of a court trumpeter and innkeeper. Thirteen years old at the time, she became a mother two years later. In the years that followed – now raised to the nobility as the Countess of Lichtenau – she bore the king four more children. As of 1794 it was also she who substantially influenced the planning of the Pfaueninsel with its buildings and artificial ruins. After the king died in 1797, his mistress fell out of favor at court and was even accused of »unlawful enrichment«. Although she was acquitted, she had to live the rest of her life in banishment.

Friedrich Wilhelm III, whose wife – Queen Luise, who was extremely well liked by the people – died early of typhoid, had the island converted to a model estate by Joseph Peter Lenné. Karl Friedrich Schinkel expanded the Kavaliershaus (or gentleman's house) and designed a glass palm house, which was burned to the ground in May 1880.

It was this king who, inspired by a visit to the »Jardin des Plantes« in Paris, began to get interested in unusual plants and animals. He introduced peacocks, kangaroos, buffaloes, monkeys, llamas, lions, bears, reindeer and exotic birds, and had Lenné set up a menagerie on the island. In 1832 the menagerie administration listed 847 animals. A special attraction for visitors were a couple of South Seas natives who were settled on the island and lived there for years. Toward the middle of the 19th century, under the heir to the throne Friedrich Wilhelm IV, the royal house lost interest in this private zoo, and in 1842 all the animals were presented to the newly founded first public zoo of Germany in Berlin. This marked the beginning of hard times for the island. No one was interested in it anymore, but at the same time people did not want to let it fall into total disrepair. Thanks to minimal upkeep, the responsible authorities saved the former paradise over the years. A bed of reeds that became thicker and wider made access to the island, even for yachtsmen and fishermen, almost impossible.

During fighting in World War II the Pfaueninsel was never hit by bombs. In the last days of the war, however, there was danger of devastation again. Though the situation was hopeless – the Red Army had already penetrated into the inner city – Adolf Hitler sent two small squads of soldiers from the Führer's bunker to the Pfaueninsel with his testament. There, it was to be given to the crew of a plane that was supposed to land by night on the Havel River. Of course, the action

Schinkel erweiterte das Kavaliershaus und entwarf ein gläsernes Palmenhaus, das im Mai 1880 durch einen Brand völlig zerstört wurde. Dieser König war es auch, der sich, angeregt durch einen Besuch des Jardin des Plantes in Paris, begann, für fremdartige Pflanzen und Tiere zu interessieren. Er führte Pfauen, Känguruhs, Büffel, Affen, Lamas, Löwen, Bären, Rentiere und exotische Vögel ein und ließ von Lenné auf der Insel eine Menagerie einrichten. 1832 zählte eine Liste der Menagerieverwaltung 847 Tiere auf. Eine besondere Attraktion für die Besucher stellte das Eingeborenenpaar aus der Südsee dar, das auf der Pfaueninsel angesiedelt worden war und dort über Jahre wohnte.

Gegen Mitte des 19. Jahrhunderts, unter dem Thronfolger Friedrich Wilhelm IV., erlosch das Interesse des Königshauses an diesem Privatzoo, und 1842 wurden alle Tiere dem neu gegründeten, ersten öffentlichen Zoo Deutschlands in Berlin übergeben. Danach begann eine schwierige Zeit für die Insel. Niemand interessierte sich mehr für sie, aber ganz verfallen lassen wollte man sie auch nicht. Mit minimaler Pflege retteten die zuständigen Behörden das einstige Paradies über die Jahre. Ein immer dichter und breiter werdender Schilfgürtel machte das Betreten, selbst für Segler und Angler, nahezu unmöglich.

Während der Kampfhandlungen im Zweiten Weltkrieg blieb die Pfaueninsel von Bombentreffern verschont. In den letzten Kriegstagen jedoch drohte die Gefahr der Verwüstung ein weiteres Mal. Trotz der aussichtslosen Lage, die Rote Armee war schon bis in die Innenstadt vorgedrungen, schickte Adolf Hitler zwei kleine Soldatentrupps aus dem Führerbunker mit seinem Testament auf die Pfaueninsel, wo es von einer Flugzeugbesatzung entgegezunehmen war, die nachts auf der Havel landen sollte. Natürlich mißglückte die Aktion, weil das zur Landung ansetzende Flugzeug so stark beschossen wurde, daß es durchstarten mußte. So blieb es still auf der Insel, während ringsum die letzten Stadtverteidigungskämpfe geführt wurden. Nach dem Krieg wurde die Pfaueninsel, die zum Westsektor der Stadt gehörte, langsam wieder belebt und als Wochenendausflugsziel von den Berlinern neu entdeckt. Wenige Meter vom Ufer entfernt, zog sich die schwerbewachte und bewaffnete Grenze der DDR hin. Unweit südlich, direkt bei den königlichen Bauten Schinkels, überspannte die legendäre Glienicker Brücke die Havel. Für die meisten Westbürger war an dieser Stelle die Berliner Stadtwelt zu Ende, finstere Volkspolizisten beobachteten die Ankommenden mißtrauisch und ängstlich. Mehrmals im Jahr fanden hier gespenstische Gefangenenaustausche zwischen West- und Ostbehörden statt. Es war die Zeit der Freikäufe: Westpolitiker konnten Gefangene, die wegen politischer Vergehen (oft Fluchtversuche) in DDR-Gefängnissen einsaßen, mit viel Geld freikaufen. Der kommunistische Staat verhielt sich wie ein mafiöser Piratenstaat und erpreßte mit diesen Gefangenen den in seinen Augen zu Unrecht steinreichen Westen. Das Geschäft florierte, und oft berichtete die Tagesschau in Live-Übertragungen von den Austauschaktionen.

Dazu passend, fanden in den 1960er Jahren auf der Insel Dreharbeiten zu einigen Edgar-Wallace-Filmen statt: *Die Tür mit den sieben Schlössern* (1961), *Neues vom Hexer* (1965), *Der Hund von Blackwood Castle* (1967/68) und *Im Banne des Unheimlichen* (1968).

Heute gehört die Pfaueninsel, ebenso wie die Bauten von Schinkel in Glienicke und Sanssouci, die Parkanlagen von Lenné und Fürst Pückler-Muskau zum Weltkulturerbe der Unesco. Die Hauptbedrohung des einmaligen Bau- und Parkbestands geht jetzt nicht mehr von Besuchern aus, sondern von der übermächtig angewachsenen Berliner Population der Wildschweine. Inzwischen wurde sogar ein versteckter Elektrozaun rings um die Pfaueninsel angelegt, um die nächtlichen Angriffe der erstaunlich gut schwimmenden Borstentiere vom Wasser aus abzuwehren. Einmal auf der Insel angekommen, würden die Wildschweine in wenigen Nachtschichten den gesamten, gut gepflegten Parkbestand umpflügen und vernichten.

32. Die berühmte künstliche, malerisch-romantische Ruine auf der Berliner Pfaueninsel, errichtet als Liebesnest für König Wilhelm II. um das Jahr 1794.

32. The well-known artificial picturesque and romantic ruin on the Pfaueninsel in Berlin, erected as a love-nest for King Wilhelm II c. 1794.

failed, because as it started to land the plane was shelled so badly that it had to pull up again. Thus the island remained quiet as the last battles in defense of the city were fought all around it. After the war the Pfaueninsel, which was part of the Western sector of the city, slowly came to life again and Berliners rediscovered it as a weekend excursion destination once more. A few meters from the riverbank was the heavily guarded and armed border of the GDR. A short distance south, right by Schinkel's royal buildings, the legendary Glienicke Bridge spanned the Havel River. For most Westerners the city of Berlin ended at this point; somber People's Police observed the arrivals full of mistrust and apprehension. Several times a year ghostly exchanges of prisoners took place here between West and East German authorities. It was a time when, for a great deal of money, West German politicians were able to buy the freedom of prisoners who sat in GDR jails because of political offenses (often attempts to escape). The Communist state acted like a Mafia-like pirate state and with these prisoners extorted the West, which in their eyes was stinking rich for all the wrong reasons. Business was booming, and often the TV newscast broadcasted reports of the exchanges live.

Along the same lines, a number of Edgar Wallace films were shot on the island in the 1960s: *The Door with Seven Locks* (1961), *Again the Ringer* (1965), *The Monster of Blackwood Castle* (1967/68) and *The Hands of Power* (1968).

Today the Pfaueninsel as well as the buildings of Schinkel in Glienicke and Sanssouci, and the parks of Lenné and Prince Pückler-Muskau are part of the World Cultural Heritage of the UNESCO. Now the main danger that threatens the unique buildings and park no longer comes from the visitors, but from the Berlin population of wild pigs, which has grown extremely numerous. In the meantime authorities have even installed a hidden electric fence around the Pfaueninsel, to ward off the nocturnal sallies of the pigs, which are amazingly good swimmers. Once on the island, the wild pigs would plow up and destroy the entire well-kept park in a few night shifts.

5. Ruinen und Untergänge in der romantischen Malerei, Dichtung und Musik

Caspar David Friedrich, Carl Gustav Carus, Karl Friedrich Schinkel, Novalis. Deutsche Rhein-Romantik. Robert Schumann

Seit Anfang des 18. Jahrhunderts orientierten sich Parkgestalter bei ihren Entwürfen nicht mehr nur an den Radierungen von Giovanni Battista Piranesi, sondern auch an den Gemälden der berühmten Landschafts- und Ruinenmaler Claude Lorrain, Nicolas Poussin, Hubert Robert, Claude Joseph Vernet und Jacob van Ruisdael. Das Hauptinteresse lag jetzt auf der malerischen Gesamtkomposition, Einzelmotive wie Ruinen, Gräber, Tempel, Steine und Bäume spielten nur noch eine untergeordnete Rolle. In den neuen, naturhaft angelegten Parks sollten, nach Vorstellung ihrer Gestalter, immer wieder Landschaftsbilder entstehen, die an diese Gemälde erinnern.

Obwohl man zunehmend auf gerade, oft von Alleen begleitete Wegachsen verzichtete, weil sie die Blicke der Wandernden zu sehr bevormundeten und kanalisierten, liebten auch die neuen Gartenplaner Blickachsen, allerdings sollten sie sich über weglose Wiesenschneisen oder Seen hinweg ergeben. Die Wege selbst wurden geschwungen und mäandernd angelegt, in der Annahme, daß derartige Formen der Natur und ihrem Wuchs mehr entsprächen. Insgesamt strebte man eine mehr zufällige, zwanglos-fragmentarische und romantisch-pittoreske Bildfolge an, die mit Vorder-, Mittel- und Hintergründen arbeitete. Die Perspektiven verschoben sich permanent beim Durchgehen in überraschender Weise. Während im italienischen und französischen Garten fast alle Bilder von einer Aussichtsterrasse herab überblickbar waren, der Weg durch den Garten manchmal überhaupt nicht nötig war, wußte in den neuen Parks kein Besucher, was genau ihn erwartete. Die Abfolge der Bilder-Blicke war nicht vorhersehbar und barg permanent Überraschungen in sich. Plötzlich tauchte eine gotische Ruine in der Ferne auf, dann versank sie wieder hinter einem Hügel oder einer Baumgruppe, später stand man direkt vor ihr und erschrak über die Nähe. Das dramaturgische Konzept war unübersichtlicher, labyrinthischer, psychologisch spannender, dynamisch-fließender, vielleicht auch unterhaltsamer geworden. Man arbeitete mit bekannten Zitaten (aus Gemälden) und mit unbekannten, überraschenden Effekten. Hirschfeld schreibt dazu: »Die Composition giebt einen neuen Standpunkt an, wo er – der Gartenkünstler – neben den Landschaftsmaler hintritt. Sie verstattet zuvörderst beyden eine vollkommene Freyheit in ihren Zusammensetzungen, in der Ausdehnung der Flächen und Fernen, in der Mischung und Bildung der Bäume, der Rasen, des Wassers, in der Bepflanzung und Verzierung, in offenen oder eingeschränkten, hügeligen oder ebenen, heiteren oder öden Lagen – der unendlichen Mannigfaltigkeit zu folgen, wodurch die Natur mit einer unerschöpflichen Kunst Ergötzung wirkt.«

Die neue Dramaturgie entsprach mehr literarischen (heute würden wir sagen: filmischen) Vorgängen. Etymologisch leitet sich der Begriff »Romantik« von »Roman« ab. »Romantische Bilder« bedeuten somit im Grunde nichts anderes als »romanhafte Bilder«. Und die beliebten Romane der Zeit befaßten sich mit mittelalterlichen Themen, schauerlichen Schloßgeschichten, mit Märchen, Gespenstern und Feen. Man liebte die Emotionen Werthers und die archaische Wildheit des neu entdeckten William Shakespeare. Merkwürdigerweise war es der mehr dem antikisierenden Rokoko zuneigende Dichter Christoph Martin Wieland, der als erster das Theaterstück *Der Sturm* übersetzte und mit einer Laienspieltruppe in einem Saal über dem damaligen Schlachthaus von Biberach an der Riss aufführen ließ.

Nach der Französischen Revolution reisten viele Adlige und reich gewordene Bürger – unter ihnen auch der exzentrische, schreibfreudige Fürst Pückler-Muskau – auf die britische Insel und schauten sich dort um. Sie entdeckten nicht nur die Manufakturen der beginnenden Industrialisierung und den schon seit langem praktizierten freien Landschaftsstil, sondern auch die Vorliebe der Engländer zum Gotischen. Das »gothic revival« paßte genauso in die Zeitströmung wie die skurrile Vorliebe der Engländer für Ruinen. Gotik und Ruinen gehörten zusammen.

Schon der junge Goethe hatte mit seiner Schrift *Von deutscher Baukunst* vom Straßburger Münster und der organisch-unvollendeten Naturgewalt der Gotik geschwärmt. Allerdings schwenkte er später um und bekannte sich zur griechisch-römischen Klassik. Aber die neue Blickrichtung arbeitete in vielen Zeitgenossen weiter. Die Romantiker sahen in der Gotik den eigentlichen architektonischen Nationalstil des ersehnten Deutschen Reiches, das die verhaßte Kleinstaaterei ablösen sollte. Zu Unrecht hielten sie diesen Stil für eine echt deutsche Erfindung. In Wirklichkeit liegen die Anfänge der Gotik bekanntlich in Frankreich. Den jüngeren, radikal-romantischen Künstlern erschien die klassische Antike viel zu ausgewogen und emotionslos. Sie suchten die Tiefe der Gefühle, das Extreme, Fragmentarisch-Ruinöse, Exzentrische, auch in der Religion. Verständlich, daß der alternde Goethe der neuen Denkrichtung mehr als skeptisch gegenüberstand.

5. Ruins and scenes of destruction in Romantic painting, literature and music

Caspar David Friedrich, Carl Gustav Carus, Karl Friedrich Schinkel, Novalis. German Rhine Romanticism. Schumann

Since the beginning of the 18th century landscape architects had been modeling their designs not only on the engravings of Giovanni Battista Piranesi, but also on the paintings of the famous landscape and ruin painters Claude Lorrain, Nicolas Poussin, Hubert Robert, Claude Joseph Vernet and Jacob van Ruisdael. The main focus of interest was now on a picturesque overall composition; individual motifs such as ruins, graves, temples, rocks and trees now had only a subordinate role. The designers intended that in the new, naturally laid out parks visitors would constantly encounter panoramas that reminded them of these paintings.

Although landscape architects increasingly stopped designing straight axes, often accompanied by tree- or shrub-lined walkways because they dominated and channeled the gaze of park visitors, the new park designers also loved visual axes, though these were supposed to direct the eye over pathless meadow clearings or lakes. The paths themselves curved or meandered, the assumption being that these kinds of forms were more in accordance with nature and natural growth. All in all, the goal was to create a more accidental, informally fragmentary and romantically picturesque series of vistas that worked with foreground, middle distance and background. Perspectives constantly shifted, to the surprise of those who walked through these parks. While in the Italian and French garden almost all the panoramic views could be seen from an overlook terrace, and a walk through the garden was sometimes not necessary at all, in the new parks none of the visitors knew exactly what to expect. The sequence of panoramic views was not predictable and was full of surprises. Suddenly, a Gothic ruin would appear in the distance, then vanish again behind a hill or a group of trees. Later, one would be standing directly in front of it, startled at how near it was. The dramatic concept had become more complex, more labyrinthine, psychologically more exciting, dynamically more fluid and perhaps more entertaining. The designs included well-known quotations (from paintings) and unfamiliar, surprising effects. Hirschfeld comments: »The composition shows a new viewpoint where the landscape designer takes his place next to the landscape painter. First and foremost it allows both of them complete freedom, in the way elements are combined, in the expanse of surfaces and distances, in the mixture and formation of the trees, the lawns, the water, in the plants and ornaments used, in open or cramped, hilly or flat, cheery or desolate locations – following the infinite diversity by which Nature delights us with inexhaustible art.«

The new dramaturgy was in keeping with more literary (or, as we would say today, cinematic) processes. Etymologically the term »Romanticism« comes from the French word »roman« or »novel«. »Romantic pictures« thus basically means simply »novel-like pictures«. And the popular novels of the period dealt with medieval themes, spine-chilling stories of castles, with fairy tales, ghosts and fairies. Readers loved Werther's emotions and the archaic wildness of a newly discovered William Shakespeare. Oddly enough, the first to translate *The Tempest* was the writer Christoph Martin Wieland, whose sympathies lay more with the faux antique style of the rococo. He had the play performed by a group of amateur actors in a hall above the then slaughterhouse of Biberach an der Riss.

After the French Revolution many aristocrats and nouveaux riches – including the eccentric, prolific writer Prince Pückler-Muskau – traveled to the British Isles and toured the countryside. They discovered not only the factories of the early industrial age and the free landscape style that had been practiced here for a long time, but also the predilection of the English for the Gothic style. The »Gothic Revival« was just as much part of the times as the quirky British preference for ruins. Strictly speaking the Gothic style and ruins went together.

Early on, young Goethe, in his essay *Von deutscher Baukunst* [»On German architecture«] had fallen into raptures about Straßbourg Cathedral and the organically uncompleted force of nature represented by Gothic style. It is true that later he did an about-face and declared his support for Greek and Roman classicism. But the new outlook was still prevalent among many of his contemporaries. In Gothic style the Romantics saw the true architectonic national style of the longed-for German Empire, which was to take the place of the hated proliferation of small states. Erroneously they considered this style to be a truly German invention. In reality it is common knowledge that the beginnings of Gothic style can be traced to France. The younger, radically romantic artists felt that classical antiquity was much too balanced and unemotional. They looked for depth of feeling, for the extreme, for fragments and ruins, for the eccentric, even in religion. It is under-

Die echte, alte Ruine kam den romantischen Gefühlen sehr nahe. Sie verband Vergangenheit und Zukunft, sie sprach vom Scheitern und von der Vergänglichkeit, sie erinnerte an Friedhof und Tod. Die künstlichen Rokokoruinen in den aristokratischen Parks verachteten die romantischen Dichter allerdings, manche bezeichneten sie sogar als lächerliche Fälschungen. Wer Großes anstrebt, läuft Gefahr zu scheitern. Nur im Fragment konnte die Wahrheit liegen. Auch viele große gotische Dome waren nicht zu Ende gebaut worden, das Straßburger Münster besaß nur einen Turm, der Kölner Dom und das Ulmer Münster ragten als monumentale, unfertige Bauwerke (Bauruinen) in den Himmel. Das Fragment verweigert die letztgültige Antwort, es sträubt sich gegen Abrundung, Vollkommenheit und Happy-End. Bei einem echten Ruinenfragment fehlt immer der Schluß, es bricht mitten im Leben ab – Schweigen, Himmel, Wolken und Pflanzen ergänzen den offenen Rest. Die (gotische) Ruine ist da und gleichzeitig abwesend. Im Kern ist sie unbenutzbar und unbewohnbar.

Vor allem Friedrich Schlegel und Novalis hielten das Fragment für die ideale literarische Form. Zu keiner Zeit der Literaturgeschichte wurden so viele Roman- und Gedichtfragmente veröffentlicht wie zwischen 1800 und 1830. »Ein Fragment muß gleich einem kleinen Kunstwerke von der umgebenden Welt ganz abgesondert und in sich vollendet sein wie ein Igel.« So definiert Friedrich Schlegel diese literarische Form. Novalis nennt sie »Blütenstaub«. Im Gegensatz zu Goethe, der Zeit seines Lebens in der Natur eine harmonischvollendete Schöpfung sah, die es zu entschlüsseln und nachzuahmen gilt, glaubten die Romantiker an das Prinzip des ewigen Rätsels, des für immer Verschlüsselten, des Zufalls und des Chaos. Den Offenbarungen der angeblichen Wahrheit – auch in der Religion und der *Bibel* – trauten sie nicht.

Die Schönheit der Welt schloß jetzt auch das Häßliche, die wuchernde Phantasie und den Alptraum mit ein. Phantasmagorien und Grotesken wurden mehr bewundert als harmoniesüchtige Gedichte und griechisch-römische Tempel.

Manche Dichter, wie Victor Hugo und Justinus Kerner, experimentierten mit dem Zufall, Farbtropfen, Tuscheflecken und ihre gespiegelten Abdruckbilder berichten vielleicht aus einer bisher unsichtbaren Gegenwelt. Flecken gebären Ungeheuer, man muß die Nachrichten nur lesen können. Surrealistisches klingt an.

Jean Louis Théodore Géricault beschäftigte sich mit frisch Hingerichteten und malte das Gesicht eines Geköpften. Ihn interessierte, was in diesem Gehirn vor sich geht, kurz vor der endgültigen Auslöschung, der ewigen Nacht.

Justinus Kerner schrieb ein Buch über die schizophrene *Seherin von Prevorst*. Friedrich Hölderlin verbrachte die zweite Hälfte seines Lebens, geistig verwirrt in einem engen Wohnturm am Neckar. Manchmal trat er in seinen kleinen Garten hinaus, riß Grasbüschel aus der Erde und murmelte Worte wie: »Palaksch … palaksch …« Wortruinen aus einem geistigen Jenseits, das hinter Hyperions Griechenland und unter der Vulkanglut liegt, in die sich einst Empedokles hineinstürzte.

Johann Heinrich Füssli malte Alpträume, die aus ähnlichen Sphären gespeist wurden. Auch Francisco Goya verstrickte sich zunehmend in Kämpfe mit den Geistern, die er rief oder die ihn in den Nächten der Verstummung heimsuchten. E. T. A. Hoffmann tauchte in Alkoholmeeren unter und ließ sich zu Angstszenarien inspirieren, die uns heute ganz vertraut erscheinen.

Zwischen 1816 und 1818 reisten Lord Byron, sein Freund Percy Shelley und dessen Geliebte und spätere Ehefrau Mary quer durch Deutschland in die Schweiz. Mit von der Partie war auch Marys Stiefschwester Claire, die unterwegs das Herz von Lord Byron eroberte. Vor allem die Shelleys waren auf der Flucht vor Gläubigern und bösartigen Familienangehörigen. Gemeinsam verbrachte die Gruppe einige Monate in Lord Byrons Haus am Genfer See. Er genoß zu dieser Zeit schon europäischen Ruhm, außerdem verfügte er über ein stattliches Vermögen. Da es ständig regnete, waren die Freunde gezwungen, viele Tage in den Zimmern zu verbringen. Lord Byron regte aus Langeweile an, daß jeder von ihnen einen Schauerroman erfinden sollte. Zunächst fiel Mary nichts Spannendes ein. Aber eines Nachts hatte sie eine Vision, und in den folgenden Wochen brachte die schwangere, nicht einmal 19jährige Mary jenen visionären Roman zu Papier, der alle damaligen Labor- und Ruinenalpträume in schauerlicher Weise zusammenfaßte: *Frankenstein*. Einem Arzt gelingt es, aus Leichenteilen mit Hilfe von Elektrizität einen künstlichen Menschen zum Leben zu erwecken. Die gotischen Ruinen hatten einen neuen Inhalt erhalten: Aus dem ehemaligen Schloß- und Burggespenst war ein realer, wenn auch künstlicher Mensch geworden, geheimnisvoll und rätselhaft. Erst die Surrealisten und Expressionisten, später auch die Skriptschreiber und Regisseure einschlägiger Horrorfilme in Hollywood werden sich erneut mit diesen dunkel-romantischen Themen beschäftigen.

Mary waren nur wenige Jahre des Glückes beschieden. Ihr Mann Percy Shelley ertrank 30jährig 1822 bei einem Segeltörn mit einem Verlegerfreund im Golf von Livorno. Auch Lord

standable that the aging Goethe had a more than skeptical attitude toward this new school of thought.

Genuine ancient ruins came very close to romantic feelings. They were a link between past and future, they spoke of breakdown and mortality, they reminded one of cemeteries and death. However, the romantic poets despised the artificial rococo ruins in the parks of the aristocrats. Some even referred to them as ludicrous forgeries. Those who strive for greatness are in danger of failing. Truth could be found only in the fragmentary. Many great Gothic cathedrals had also never been completed: Straßbourg Cathedral had only one tower, Cologne Cathedral and Ulm Minster loomed in the sky as monumental, unfinished structures (architectural ruins). The fragment refuses to give the ultimate answer, it resists being rounded off, perfected, provided with a happy ending. With a genuine ruin fragment the conclusion is always missing, it breaks off in the midst of life – silence, sky, clouds and plants complete the open-ended remainder. The (Gothic) ruin is both present and absent. It is essentially unusable and uninhabitable.

It was primarily Friedrich Schlegel and Novalis who considered the fragment to be the ideal literary form. At no time in literary history were so many novel and poem fragments published as between 1800 and 1830. »A fragment, like a small work of art, has to be entirely isolated from the surrounding world and be complete in itself like a hedgehog,« is how Friedrich Schlegel defines this literary form. Novalis calls it »Blütenstaub« (»Pollen«). Unlike Goethe, who all his life saw Nature as a harmoniously perfect creation that must be deciphered and imitated, the Romantics believed in the principle of the eternal mystery, of the ever encrypted, of chance and chaos. They did not trust revelations of so-called truth – including truth in religion and in the *Bible*. The beauty of the world now included the ugly, proliferating fantasy and nightmare as well. Phantasmagoria and grotesques were admired more than Greco-Roman temples and poems that craved harmony.

Some writers, such as Victor Hugo and Justinus Kerner, experimented with chance, drops of paint, blots of Indian ink, and perhaps their reflected impressions give reports of a hitherto invisible alternate world. Blots engender monsters, one must simply know how to read the news. There is a hint of the surreal.

Jean Louis Théodore Géricault studied the bodies of the recently executed and painted the face of a man who had been beheaded. He was interested in what is taking place in the brain just before final extinction, eternal night.

Justinus Kerner wrote a book about the schizophrenic *Seeress of Prevorst*. Friedrich Hölderlin spent the second half of his life mentally ill in a cramped tower by the Neckar River. Sometimes he would go outside into his little garden, tear tufts of grass from the ground and murmur words that sounded like »Palaksh … palaksh …« Word ruins from a mental hereafter located beyond Hyperion's Greece and below the glowing lava of the volcano into which Empedocles once threw himself.

Johann Heinrich Füssli painted nightmares that were fed by similar sources. Francisco Goya, too, became more and more enmeshed in struggles with the spirits he conjured or who haunted him in the nights of his silence. E. T. A. Hoffmann dived into oceans of alcohol, and imagined scenarios of dread that seem quite familiar to us today.

Between 1816 and 1818 Lord Byron, his friend Percy Shelley, and Shelley's lover and wife-to-be Mary traveled across Germany to Switzerland. Mary's stepsister Claire was also one of the party. She captured Lord Byron's heart en route. The Shelleys above all were on the run from creditors and from malicious family members. The group spent a few months together in Lord Byron's house on Lake Geneva. He was already famous throughout Europe at this point. Also, he had a sizable fortune. Since it was constantly raining, the friends were forced to spend many days indoors. Bored, Lord Byron suggested that each of them should make up a Gothic novel. At first, Mary could think of nothing exciting. But one night she had a vision, and during the weeks that followed Mary, pregnant and not yet 19 years old, wrote the visionary novel that summarized all the nightmares about laboratories and ruins that were current at the time in a spine-chilling tale: *Frankenstein*. A physician succeeds in creating an artificial human being from body parts and in bringing him to life by means of electricity. The Gothic ruins had been given new contents: The onetime ghost that haunted a castle or fortress had become a real, though artificial, human being, mysterious and enigmatic. It was not until the surrealists and expressionists, and later the scriptwriters and film directors of Hollywood horror movies came along that anyone again dealt with these dark, romantic topics.

Mary was to have only a few years of happiness. Her husband, Percy Shelley, was drowned at 30 years of age in 1822 during a cruise with his publisher friend in the Gulf of Livorno. Lord

Byron lebte nicht mehr lange. 1824 erlag er der Malaria in Mesolongion, wohin ihn der griechische Freiheitskampf gezogen hatte. Romantische Lebensruinen, emotionsgeladen, stürmisch und früh vollendet. Mary selbst allerdings lebte noch bis 1851 als zurückgezogene Schriftstellerin in London. Sie hat nie mehr geheiratet. Von ihren vier Kindern überlebte nur ein Sohn, der sich später hingebungsvoll um seine Mutter kümmerte.

Bevor ich mich mit der Ruinenbegeisterung weiterer romantischer Dichter und Komponisten befasse, möchte ich näher auf den wichtigsten aller Ruinenmaler, Caspar David Friedrich, eingehen. Ob seine Gemälde jemals als Vorlage für künstliche Parkruinen gedient haben, ist ungewiß. Sein Einfluß auf das allgemeine Landschafts- und Naturgefühl der Zeitgenossen jedenfalls läßt sich nicht hoch genug einschätzen.

Er war es, der das Drama der radikalen, mythologiefreien Landschaftsstimmungen entdeckte. Obwohl manchmal noch religiöse Motive zitiert werden, steht der ergriffene Betrachter hier oft einsam einer verzauberten, aber auch herzlos schweigenden Naturwelt gegenüber. Daß Friedrich in seinen Gemälden Dämmerungs- und Nebelphasen bevorzugte und die helle Mittagszeit ausblendete, ist verständlich. Auch seine Vorliebe für dunkle Vollmondnächte ist durchaus konsequent. Schließlich interessiert sich ein echter Romantiker nicht für den banalen Alltag, sondern nur für die gefühlvollen, dunklen Momente der eigenen Seele, die er im Landschaftsraum gespiegelt sieht, der zu einem dunklen Seelen-Innenraum wird, und im Nachtbild verschmelzen Innen- und Außenwelt endgültig.

Novalis dichtete in den *Hymnen an die Nacht* die passenden Verse zu diesem Vorgang:

»Abwärts wend ich mich
Zu der heiligen, unaussprechlichen
Geheimnisvollen Nacht –
Fernab liegt die Welt
Wie versenkt in eine tiefe Gruft,
Wie wüst und einsam
Ihre Stelle!
Tiefe Wehmut
Weht in den Saiten der Brust.
Fernen der Erinnerung,
Wünsche der Jugend,
Der Kindheit Träume …
Wie Abendnebel
Nach der Sonne
Untergang.
Fernab liegt die Welt,
Mit ihren bunten Genüssen.
In andern Räumen
Schlug das Licht auf
Die lustigen Gezelte.«

Caspar David Friedrich, der am 5. September 1774 in der kleinen, damals unter schwedischer Herrschaft stehenden Universitäts- und Hafenstadt Greifswald an der Ostsee geboren wurde, bevorzugte sein Leben lang den Norden und verachtete die Italien- und Englandsehnsüchte seiner künstlerischen Zeitgenossen. (Besonders haßerfüllt verurteilte er die Bemühungen der katholischen »Nazarener«). Daher lag es für ihn nahe, zum Studium der Malerei an die damals berühmte Kunstakademie nach Kopenhagen zu gehen. Mit seinen Freunden träumte er jahrelang von einer Schiffsreise nach Island, jenem legendären Eis-Land, das immer wieder durch seine Gemälde spukt. Allerdings fand diese Reise nie statt. Man begnügte sich mit Ausflügen nach Rügen, ins Riesengebirge und später in die Sächsische Schweiz. Nach einem äußerlich wenig aufregenden Leben, das er weitgehend im meist eisfreien Dresden verbrachte, starb Friedrich am 7. Mai 1840 im Alter von 66 Jahren.

Obgleich er anfänglich sehr erfolgreich gewesen war und seine Gemälde sich einer wachsenden Beliebtheit erfreut hatten, kam er in späteren Jahren zunehmend aus der Mode. Erst zu Beginn des 20. Jahrhunderts entdeckte man sein Werk aufs neue. Sein Credo formulierte er in den folgenden Sätzen, die eine Innenschau verherrlichen, wie sie von einem Blinden stammen könnten: »Schließe dein leibliches Auge, damit du mit dem geistigen Auge zuerst siehst dein Bild. Dann fördere zutage, was du im Dunkeln gesehen, daß es zurückwirke auf andere von

Byron also did not live long. In 1824 he succumbed to malaria in Mesolongion, to which he had been drawn by the struggle for Greek freedom. Ruined Romantic lives, full of emotion, stormy and precocious. Mary herself, however, lived until 1851 as a secluded writer in London. She did not marry again. Of her four children, only one son survived. Later, he devotedly looked after his mother.

Before I deal with other Romantic writers and composers who were fascinated by ruins, I should like to go into more detail regarding the most important of all ruin painters, Caspar David Friedrich. It is not certain whether his paintings ever served as models for artificial park ruins. But his influence on his contemporaries' general feeling for landscapes and nature cannot be underestimated.

It was he who discovered the drama of radical landscape moods, free of mythology. Although religious motifs are still quoted at times in his works, the solitary viewer, deeply moved, often faces an enchanted but also heartlessly silent world here. It is understandable that in his paintings Friedrich preferred twilight and fog, and faded out bright noonday lighting. His predilection for dark, full-moon nights makes perfect sense. After all, a true Romantic is not interested in banal everyday life, but in the emotional, dark aspects of his own soul, which he sees mirrored in the landscape that becomes the dark interior of the psyche as inner and outer world ultimately merge.

In *Hymnen an die Nacht* Novalis wrote the verses that reflected this process:

»I turn aside
To the holy, ineffable,
Mysterious night –
Far away lies the world
As if sunk in a deep grave,
How waste and lonely
Is its place!
In the chords of my breast
Blows a deep sadness.
Distances of memory,
Wishes of youth,
The dreams of childhood …
Like evening mists
After the sun
Goes down.
Far away lies the world,
With its bright pleasures.
In other regions
The light has pitched
Its joyous tents …«

Caspar David Friedrich was born on 5 September 1774 in the small university town and seaport of Greifswald on the Baltic Sea, which at the time was under Swedish rule. All his life he preferred the north, despising his artist contemporaries' longings for Italy and England (he condemned the efforts of the Catholic »Nazarenes« with particular virulence). That is why it was only natural that he went to the then famous college of art in Copenhagen to study painting. Together with his friends he dreamed for years of traveling by boat to Iceland, the legendary land of ice that keeps haunting his paintings. The journey never took place, however. The friends had to be content with excursions to Rügen, to the Sudeten Mountains and later to Saxon Switzerland (part of the Elbe Sandstone Mountains). After a life that outwardly had little excitement, spent largely in a mostly ice-free Dresden, Friedrich died on 7 May 1840 at the age of 66.

Although he had initially been very successful and his paintings had grown in popularity, he gradually went out of fashion in his later years. His work was not rediscovered until the early 20th century. He formulated his credo in the following sentences, which celebrate an inner vision that could have come from a blind man: »Close your physical eyes, so that you may first see your picture with your mental eyes. Then bring to light what you have seen in the dark, that it may react upon others from the outside to the inside … The painter must not merely paint what he sees before him, but also what he sees within himself. But if he sees nothing within, he must also desist from painting what he sees before him.«

außen nach innen … Der Maler soll nicht bloß malen, was er vor sich sieht, sondern auch, was er in sich sieht. Sieht er aber nichts in sich, so unterlasse er auch zu malen, was er vor sich sieht.«

Caspar David Friedrich liebte nicht nur den kalten, unwirtlichen Norden, das Eismeer und den Nordpol, sondern auch die Ruinen. Jedes Gebäude, jeder Baum, jedes Schiff, jeder Berg, jeder Fels und jedes Kloster zerfällt vor seinen ins Metaphysische ausgerichteten Augen zu einem Gerippe und sehnt sich in einen verwesenden Naturzustand zurück. Selbst religiöse Darstellungen und Altäre geraten ihm bei aller Schönheit zu dämonischen Opfer- oder Hinrichtungsstätten. Jedes mögliche Glück wird überschattet von Krankheit, Scheitern und Tod. Über eines seiner radikalsten Gemälde – der *Mönch am Meer* (1808–1810) –, das erstaunlicherweise die königliche Familie in Berlin erwarb, schreibt Heinrich von Kleist den berühmten Satz, der in jeder Friedrich-Monographie zitiert wird: »So ist es, wenn man es betrachtet, als ob einem die Augenlider weggeschnitten wären.« Natürlich denke ich bei diesem Text sofort an das von einer Rasierklinge aufgeschnittene Auge in Bunuels surrealistischem Film *Ein andalusischer Hund*.

Zum ersten Mal in der Kunstgeschichte wird Landschaft in ihrer unerbittlichen Leere und Menschenfeindlichkeit dargestellt. Da gibt es keine versöhnlichen Schiffe, Segel und Möwen mehr, auch keine Seeleute, Schäfer, Nymphen oder Meerjungfrauen. Drei waagerecht gestaffelte Zonen müssen genügen: der Sandstrand (vielleicht einst ein stolzes Gebirge), das fast schwarze Meer und der grau verhangene Himmel. Wie eine Störung hat sich eine einzige Figur in die öde Monotonie verirrt. Einsam und winzig steht jener Mönch am Meer, der dem Bild seinen Titel gibt. »Ich ward selbst der Kapuziner«, schreibt Kleist weiter. Und dieser Kapuziner ist gefährdet. Die übermächtige Natur bedroht ihn. Ein Windstoß könnte die menschliche Ameise ins Meer fegen.

Plötzlich wird ein Postkartenmeerblick zum apokalyptischen Endzeitbild, kurz vor dem Verschwinden der Menschen von der Erde. Kein Gott (er wird bald von Nietzsche für tot erklärt werden) rettet den Mönch, er ist vielleicht der letzte Überlebende nach einer finalen (atomaren) Katastrophe.

In dem Gemälde *Das Eismeer* von 1823/24, das manchmal »Die verunglückte Nordpolexpedition« oder auch »Die gescheiterte Hoffnung« genannt wird, steht keine Rückenfigur mehr im Vordergrund. Die Szene ist vollkommen menschenleer, die Natur scheint endgültig gesiegt zu haben.

Friedrich wurde am Ufer der Ostsee geboren und wuchs dort auf. Ein- und auslaufende Schiffe gehörten zu seinen Kindheitsimpressionen. Seine Meer- und Eis-Motive wurden jedoch schon früh von Unglück und Tod überschattet, da er mit 13 Jahren hilflos zuschauen mußte, wie sein Bruder, der kurz vorher ihn selbst rettete, im Eis einbrach und ertrank. Carl Gustav Carus berichtet darüber in seinen Memoiren. Als die Elbe vor seinem Dresdner Atelierfenster im Winter 1821/22 zufror und sich die mächtigen Eisschollen zu Bergen auftürmten, erinnerte er sich schmerzhaft an seine traumatischen Jugenderlebnisse.

Caspar David Friedrich loved not only the cold, inhospitable north, the sea of ice and the North Pole, but also ruins. Before his eyes, which focus on the metaphysical, every building, every tree, ship, mountain, rock and monastery disintegrates into a skeleton and longs to return to a decaying state of nature. Even his religious scenes and altars, though beautiful, turn into demonic places of sacrifice or execution. Every possible happiness is overshadowed by illness, failure and death. About one of his most radical paintings – Monk by the Sea (1808–1810) –, which was astonishingly purchased by the royal family in Berlin, Heinrich von Kleist writes the famous sentence that is quoted in every Friedrich monograph: »… and so, when you look at it, it feels as though your eyelids had been cut away.« Naturally, reading this text, I immediately think of the eye sliced open by a razor in Bunuel's surrealistic film An Andalusian Dog.

For the first time in art history landscape is portrayed as mercilessly empty and hostile to mankind. There are no longer any conciliatory ships, sails and gulls, or sailors, shepherds and mermaids. Three horizontally layered zones must suffice: the sandy beach (perhaps once a proud mountain range), the almost black sea and the overcast gray sky. A single figure, like a disruption, has strayed into the desolate monotony. Lonely and infinitesimal, the monk for whom the picture is named stands by the sea. »I myself became the Capuchin«, Kleist continues. And this Capuchin is in danger. Overpowering Nature menaces him. A gust of wind could sweep this human ant into the sea.

Suddenly a picture-postcard seascape becomes the image of an apocalyptic end-time, shortly before human beings vanish from the face of the earth. No god (Nietzsche will soon declare he is dead) saves the monk; he is perhaps the sole survivor after a final (nuclear) catastrophe.

In the 1823/24 painting The Sea of Ice, sometimes called »The Wreck of the North Pole Expedition« or also »The Wreck of Hope«, no figure stands in the foreground with its back to the viewer anymore. The scene is completely deserted. Nature seems to have been ultimately victorious.

Friedrich was born and grew up on the Baltic coast. Arriving and departing ships were among the impressions of his childhood. However, his sea and ice motifs were overshadowed early on by misfortune and death. At 13, he had to watch helplessly as his brother, who had saved his life shortly beforehand, broke through the ice and drowned. Carl Gustav Carus reports the event in his memoirs. When the Elbe River froze in front of Friedrich's Dresden studio window in the winter of 1821/22 and the huge ice floes piled up into mountains, he painfully remembered the traumatic experiences of his youth.

33. Caspar David Friedrich, *Mönch am Meer*, 1809, Staatliche Museen Berlin.
34. Caspar David Friedrich, *Das Eismeer oder Die gescheiterte Hoffnung*, 1824, Hamburger Kunsthalle.

33. Caspar David Friedrich, *The Monk by the Sea*, 1809, Staatliche Museen Berlin.
34. Caspar David Friedrich, *The Sea of Ice or The Wreck of Hope*, 1824, Hamburger Kunsthalle.

Außerdem fügte es sich, daß der Kunstsammler Johann Gottlieb von Quandt die Idee hatte, sich von zwei verschiedenen Malern den Norden und den Süden Europas darstellen zu lassen. »Die südliche Natur in ihrer üppigen und majestätischen Pracht« sollte Martin von Rohden malen, die »Natur des Nordens in ihrer ganzen Schönheit und ihrem Schrecken« Caspar David Friedrich.

Hinzu kam, daß damals in den Zeitungen häufig von der Nordpolexpedition William Edward Parrys berichtet wurde, der 1819/20 mit zwei Schiffen versuchte, eine Nordwestpassage vom Atlantik zum Pazifik zu finden. Bestimmt hat auch Caspar David Friedrich darüber gelesen. Allerdings kehrten beide Schiffe Parrys – auch die hier dargestellte »Gripper« – heil, aber erfolglos, in ihre Heimathäfen zurück. Caspar David Friedrich erfand das dargestellte Schiffsunglück in aller künstlerischen Freiheit eigenständig dazu.

Vielleicht kannte der Maler auch Abbildungen des damals berühmten, monumentalen *Floß der Medusa* (1818/19) von Jean Louis Théodore Géricault, das heute im Louvre hängt. Französische Schiffbrüchige hatten sich vor der afrikanischen Küste auf ein Floß gerettet. Zwölf Tage lang trieben sie hilflos im Meer. Es kam zu Brutalitäten und Kannibalismus. Nur wenige überlebten. Géricault kannte die Geschichte aus Erzählungen. Im Gegensatz zu Friedrich dramatisierte er das vielfigurige Geschehen in michelangelohafter Manier. Körper winden sich in unerbittlicher Sonnenhitze, fallen übereinander her, liegen erschöpft am Floßrand, verstümmeln einander, starren in die Ferne und winken dem am Horizont auftauchenden, noch stecknadel-kleinen Schiff zu, das vielleicht die Rettung bringen wird, ein Moment der Hoffnung, der bei Caspar David Friedrich nicht existiert. Sein Eisschollengemälde verherrlicht die Natur in ihrer ganzen teilnahmslosen Schrecklichkeit. Sie benötigt uns Menschen nicht, wir sind für sie nur lästige Schmarotzer. Die ins Eismeer eingedrungenen Schiffsleute werden im nächsten Moment endgültig in der Tiefe des Ozeans versinken wie später, zu Beginn des 20. Jahrhunderts, die Passagiere der *Titanic*.

Die aufgetürmten Eisschollen wirken einerseits wie eine Reminiszenz an die vulkanische Entstehung der Erdlandschaften, an Kontinentaldriften, eruptive Gebirgsgeburten und Eiszeit, andererseits stellen sie die Ruinen eines in sich zusammengebrochenen, zerstörten Gebäudes, vielleicht eines gotischen Eisdoms, dar. Ganz klein erkennen wir unter den Schollen das zerdrückte Schiff. Es scheint keine Hoffnung mehr zu geben. Das Ende der Besatzung ist unvermeidlich. Und doch ist nicht zu übersehen, daß sich die Eisränder braun färben und daß aus dem Bildvordergrund merkwürdiges Grün in die Eiswüste hineinwuchert, ganz so, als sei hier ein unerwarteter Frühling ausgebrochen, bemoost und veralgt, von neuem Leben durchtränkt. Also besteht doch ein Funken Hoffnung?

Vielleicht schaut der Maler und mit ihm der heutige Betrachter aus einer warmen Wohnkapsel – sein karges, wohltemperiertes Atelier oder die Hamburger Kunsthalle, wo das Gemälde heute hängt – hinaus in ein konserviert-erstarrtes Geschehen der fernen Vergangenheit. Eine unsichtbare Glaswand trennt die beiden Temperaturzustände. So mag die Welt einmal untergegangen sein, inzwischen ist sie in einem zweiten Anlauf aufs neue entstanden, und wir blicken in ein bizarres Museumsdiorama, in dem wie verpuppt gotische Dome, gebaut aus Eiskristallen, am blaudunstigen Horizont auftauchen. Es war einmal …

»Das Bild, könnte man sagen, ist ein fixierter Blick …«, schrieb Carl Gustav Carus. Und plötzlich stellen wir die Abwesenheit von Bewegung und Zeit fest. Es herrscht der Stillstand einer Schrecksekunde, eines mit Blitzlicht beleuchteten Photos. Vielleicht wird der Film im nächsten Moment rückwärts laufen, das Schiff taucht wieder auf, jetzt als elegantes Kreuzfahrtschiff, die Eisschollen ziehen sich zurück in ihren arktischen Gletscherkörper, Pinguine und Eisbären bevölkern die Szene, und fröhliche Touristen beginnen, das neu belebte Bild zu filmen und zu photographieren …

Manche Interpreten wollten in diesem Bild auch ein Denkmal für die gescheiterte Französische Revolution sehen. *Die gescheiterte Hoffnung* als symbolisch-politisches Statement des Malers? Gewiß, wie viele Künstler seiner Zeit war auch Friedrich verwirrt, erst der hoffnungsvolle, revolutionäre Aufschwung, dann das nachrevolutionäre Chaos und schließlich Napoleon. Seine Begeisterung für den Korsen schlug schnell in Haß um, als dieser versuchte, ganz Europa zu unterwerfen. Während Dresden unter französischer Regentschaft stand, zog sich Friedrich ganz zurück. Die nachfolgenden Befreiungskriege stärkten bei ihm den Wunsch nach einem eigenständigen Nationalstaat.

Auch Caspar David Friedrichs zeitweiliger Freund, der Arzt und Maler Carl Gustav Carus, liebte Ruinen. In eifriger Verehrung malte er oft die gleichen Motive, die gleichen Ruinen, machte die gleichen Wanderungen und schwärmte für die gleichen nächtlichen Stimmungen. Da Carus jedoch kein akademisch ausgebildeter und nur mittelmäßig begabter Freizeitmaler war, erreichte er selten ähnlich dichte Bildatmosphären wie sein Vorbild Friedrich. Vor allem in seinen späteren

Besides, it so happened that the art collector Johann Gottlieb von Quandt had the idea of asking two different painters to portray the north and the south of Europe. Martin von Rohden was to paint »southern nature in its lush and majestic glory«, while Caspar David Friedrich would paint »the nature of the north in all its beauty and terror«.

Added to this there were frequent newspaper reports about William Edward Parry's North Pole expedition. In 1819/20 Parry tried with two ships to find a northwest passage from the Atlantic to the Pacific. No doubt Caspar David Friedrich, too, read about it. Of course, both of Parry's ships – including the »Gripper«, which is depicted here – returned to their home ports safe and sound, but unsuccessful. Using artistic license Caspar David Friedrich independently invented the shipwreck portrayed in the painting.

Perhaps the painter was also familiar with depictions of the then famous, monumental *Raft of the Médusa* (1818/19) by Jean Louis Théodore Géricault, which today hangs in the Louvre. A group of French shipwrecked people had saved themselves on a raft near the coast of Africa. There was brutality and cannibalism. Only a few survived. Géricault had heard tales of the shipwreck. In contrast to Friedrich he dramatized the event, which involved many protagonists, in the manner of Michelangelo. Bodies are contorted in the relentless heat, fall upon each other, lie exhausted at the edge of the raft, mutilate each other, stare into the distance and wave to the pin-sized ship that has appeared on the horizon and will perhaps come to the rescue, a moment of hope that does not exist in Caspar David Friedrich. His painting of the ice floes glorifies nature in all its impassive grimness. It does not need us humans, we are merely annoying parasites as far as nature is concerned. The sailors who have penetrated into the sea of ice will be drowned in the depths of the ocean the next moment, as the passengers of the *Titanic* were later, at the beginning of the 20th century.

On the one hand, the piled-up ice floes have the effect of a reminiscence of the volcanic origins of the earth's landscapes, continental drift, eruptions that give birth to mountain chains and the Ice Age; on the other hand they represent the ruins of a collapsed, demolished building, perhaps a Gothic ice cathedral. Quite small, under the ice floes, we recognize the crushed ship. There no longer seems to be any hope. The end of the crew is inevitable. And yet we must not overlook the fact that the rims of the ice floes have a brown tinge and that from the foreground of the painting a strange green spreads rankly into the icy waste, just as if an unexpected spring had erupted here, with mosses and algae, imbued with new life. Is there a spark of hope then, in spite of everything?

Perhaps the painter and with him the present-day observer looks out of a warm residential capsule – his sparsely furnished, well-tempered studio or the Hamburger Kunsthalle, where the painting hangs today – into a preserved, frozen event in the distant past. An invisible glass wall separates the two temperature zones. That is how the world may have perished once, but in the meantime it has come into being again, a second attempt, and we are looking into a bizarre museum diorama, in which Gothic cathedrals, built of ice crystals, appear like insects undergoing metamorphosis on the hazy, blue horizon. Once upon a time …

»The picture, one might say, is a fixed gaze …«, wrote Carl Gustav Carus. And suddenly we realize the absence of movement and of time. A second of terror, a snapshot lit by a flashbulb, has been arrested in time. Perhaps in the next moment the film will reverse, the ship will reappear, now as an elegant cruise ship, the ice floes will reconnect to their arctic glaciers, penguins and polar bears will fill the scene and cheerful tourists will start filming a picture that has come to life again …

Some interpreters also wanted to see a monument to the failed French Revolution in this picture. *The Wreck of Hope* as the painter's symbolic, political statement? No doubt, like many artists of his time, Friedrich too was confused: first the hopeful revolutionary upturn, then postrevolutionary chaos and finally Napoleon. His enthusiasm for the Corsican was quickly transformed to hatred when Napoleon tried to subjugate all of Europe. While Dresden was under French regency, Friedrich totally withdrew into himself. The subsequent Wars of Liberation strengthened his desire for an independent national state.

Caspar David Friedrich's onetime friend, the physician and painter Carl Gustav Carus, also loved ruins. In eager admiration he often painted the same motifs, the same ruins, went on the same walks and went into raptures over the same nocturnal moods. However, since Carus was not academically trained and an only moderately talented Sunday painter, he rarely managed to create anything like the dense atmospheres in the paintings of his model Friedrich. Especially in his later works, which he painted after Friedrich's death, a sentimental, kitschy note that affects today's viewers unpleasantly would creep in.

Werken, die er nach Friedrichs Tod malte, schlich sich ein sentimentaler Kitschton ein, der heute unangenehm berührt.

Dennoch ist Carus eine interessante Persönlichkeit. Als Naturwissenschaftler und Arzt befaßte er sich mehr mit der Entstehung des Lebens und tendierte so innerlich eher zu Goethes Evolutionsgedanken als zu Friedrichs depressiver Sterbe- und Todessehnsucht. Vielleicht war der Bruch zwischen den beiden deshalb vorprogrammiert. In die radikale Hermetik der Gefühlswelt Caspar David Friedrichs paßte keine Urpflanze, keine Geburtshilfe und keine natürliche Entfaltung des Lebens.

Aber nicht nur die Maler begeisterten sich für Landschaften, Eisschollen und mittelalterliche Kirchenruinen, sondern auch die Dichter. Die beiden eng befreundeten Dichter Ludwig Tieck und Wilhelm Heinrich Wackenroder wanderten zu Fuß von Erlangen nach Nürnberg und berauschten sich auf ihrem Weg am düsteren Raunen der alten Wälder, die für sie die undurchschaubare, menschenleere, vielleicht von Feen und Geistern belebte Gegenwelt zur Stadt verkörperten. Im wilden Wald überwogen die Weglosigkeit, das ruinenhaft Gefährliche; die damals modernen Städte galten ihnen als aufgeklärt, militarisiert und modisch verseucht. Es gab nur vorgefertigte Gassen, Straßen und Plätze. Im Wald konnte man sich leicht verirren und begegnete frei lebenden wilden Tieren, möglicherweise auch Räubern (wie dem Schinderhannes etwa). Der Wald war der Bereich der Ausgestoßenen, der Geflohenen, der Hexen, der Freiheitskämpfer, der Mönche und Einsiedler, der Verbrecher und Mörder (wir erinnern uns auch an Schillers *Räuber*). Der Wald hatte mythologische Wurzeln, hier konnte man am ehesten zurückkehren zum nebulösen Anfang. Zwischen schleierhaften Ursuppen, verfallenden Baumruinen, Efeuteppichen, giftigen Beerensträuchern und versteckten Bächen zeigte sich der romantisch verklärte Beginn. Ein paradiesisches Labyrinth, Freischütz-Welten, Wolfsschluchten um Mitternacht. Joseph Freiherr von Eichendorff dichtete:

»O Täler weit, o Höhen,
O schöner, grüner Wald,
Du meiner Lust und Wehen
Andächt'ger Aufenthalt!
Da draußen, stets betrogen,
Saust die geschäft'ge Welt,
Schlag noch einmal die Bogen
Um mich, du grünes Zelt!«

Je wilder die Felsschluchten und Steinbrocken über den Wanderern drohten, um so begeisterter waren die romantischen Dichter. Ludwig Tieck schreibt in seiner Erzählung *Der Runenberg* darüber: »Seine Angst nahm zu, indem er sich dem Gebirge näherte, die fernen Ruinen wurden schon sichtbar und traten nach und nach kenntlicher hervor, viele Bergspitzen hoben sich abgeründet aus dem blauen Nebel. Sein Schritt wurde zaghaft, er blieb oft stehen und verwunderte sich über seine Furcht, über die Schauer, die ihm mit jedem Schritte gedrängter nahe kamen. ›Ich kenne dich Wahnsinn wohl‹, rief er aus, ›und dein gefährliches Locken, aber ich will dir männlich widerstehen!‹«

Andere romantische Dichter entdeckten bei Wanderungen entlang der großen Flüsse alte, bisher nicht beachtete Burgen und Burgruinen, die einst von Raubrittern erbaut wurden. In ihren Raumresten, Kellern und Zinnen verbargen sich dunkle Geschichten von Burggespenstern, edlen Rittern und deren angebeteten Damen. Hier verschmolzen Architektur, Natur und historische Ereignisse zu einer abenteuerlichen Einheit. Als die ersten Romantiker auf Schiffen den Rhein hinunterfuhren und die Burgruinen zu beiden Seiten bewunderten, waren englische Reisende schon vor ihnen hier gewesen. Der mythenumwaberte, deutsche Strom, der seine Wasser aus den alpinen Felsmassen heraus, quer durch den Bodensee, vorbei an den romanischen und gotischen Domen bis in die Nordsee spült, hatte sie angezogen. Eine rätselhafte, für sie so fremde Welt, die gut zu ihrem skurrilen, immer noch lebendigen »Gothic Revival« paßte.

Achim von Arnim und Clemens Brentano sammelten, am Rheinufer entlangwandernd, Gedichte für ihre später berühmt gewordene Anthologie *Des Knaben Wunderhorn*. In den Jahren danach sorgte die neu eingerichtete Dampfschiffahrt für den allgemein einsetzenden, bürgerlichen, bis heute anhaltenden Rheintourismus. Schon bald gab es täglich zehn Schiffsverbindungen zwischen Mainz und Köln.

In den ersten Jahrzehnten des 19. Jahrhunderts hatten die nationalistischen Töne zugenommen, und die sich langsam formierenden »Deutschen« betrachteten den Rhein als ihren National-

And yet Carus is an interesting person. As a natural scientist and physician, he was more concerned with how life began, inwardly leaning more towards Goethe's ideas about evolution than Friedrich's depressive yearning for death and dying. Perhaps that was why the break between the two was inevitable. The *ur-plant*, obstetrics and the natural unfolding of life had no place in the radical hermetism of Caspar David Friedrich's emotional world.

But not only painters, poets too were enthusiastic about landscapes, ice floes and the ruins of medieval churches. The two close friends, poets Ludwig Tieck and Wilhelm Heinrich Wackenroder traveled on foot from Erlangen to Nürnberg enraptured as they walked by the gloomy murmuring of the ancient forests, which for them embodied the counter-world to the city: inscrutable, deserted, perhaps inhabited by fairies and spirits. In the wild forest, there were generally no paths, and dangers abounded; the modern towns of the period, they felt, were enlightened, militarized and modishly contaminated. There were only predetermined lanes, streets and squares. In the forest one could easily get lost. One would encounter feral wild animals, and possibly robbers (such as the outlaw Schinderhannes). The forest was the realm of outcasts, fugitives, witches, freedom fighters, monks, hermits, criminals and murderers (we are reminded of Schiller's *Robbers*). The forest had mythological roots; here you could have the easiest access to a nebulous origin. Amid mysterious primordial soups, decaying tree stumps, carpets of ivy, bushes with poisonous berries and hidden streams, romantically transfigured beginnings were revealed. A paradisiacal labyrinth, worlds that call up the opera *Freischütz*, wolves' glens at midnight. Joseph von Eichendorff wrote:

»O broad valleys, O hills, O beautiful green forest, you pensive refuge of my joys and sorrows! Outside there, ever deluded, the busy world rushes; raise your arches round me once more, you green tent! «
[*The Penguin Book of German Verse*, introd., ed. and trans. by Leonard Forster (Baltimore, Md.: Penguin Books, 1957)]

The wilder the rocky gorges and boulders that loomed menacingly over the wanderers, the more enthusiastic the Romantic poets were. Ludwig Tieck writes about this in his story *Der Runenberg*: »His terror grew as he approached the mountains, the distant ruins were already becoming visible, gradually emerging more and more distinctly, and many mountaintops rose rounded from the blue mist. He walked more hesitantly, stopping often and astonished by his fear, by the shudders of horror that came crowding in on him at every step. ›Madness, I know you well‹, he exclaimed, ›you and your perilous temptations, but I intend to resist you manfully!‹«

Journeying along the great rivers, other Romantic poets discovered old, hitherto ignored fortresses and fortress ruins once built by robber barons. Concealed in what was left of their halls, cellars and battlements were dark stories of ghosts, noble knights and the ladies they worshipped. Here architecture, nature and historical events fused into an adventurous whole. When the first Romantics sailed down the Rhine River in ships and admired the fortress ruins on both sides, English travelers had already been there before them. Surrounded by myths, the German river whose waters stream from the massive rocks of the Alps, across Lake Constance, past Romanesque and Gothic cathedrals up to the North Sea had attracted them. This was an enigmatic, alien world that was in keeping with their whimsical, still vibrant »Gothic Revival«.

Achim von Arnim and Clemens Brentano, wandering along the banks of the Rhine, collected poems for their anthology *Des Knaben Wunderhorn* (*The Youth's Magic Horn*), which later became famous. In the years that followed, newly established steamboat companies made tourism on the Rhine possible for the general public, a trend that has continued to this day. Very soon there were ten daily steamboat connections between Mainz and Cologne.

In the first decades of the 19th century nationalist feelings had intensified, and those who slowly joined the ranks of the »Germans« regarded the Rhine as their national river, symbolizing awareness and memory of their common history. Since Napoleon's invasion of the territories across the Rhine, the French were considered »archenemies« who must at some point be militarily defeated.

A composer who directly dealt with the theme of the Rhine – other than Richard Wagner – was Robert Schumann, born in Zwickau in 1810. When he composed his *Third Symphony,* the »Rhenish«, (Opus 97) in 1850, he had just moved to Düsseldorf from Dresden as a newly appointed music director and spent a relatively happy time there with his wife, the pianist Clara Wieck, famous in her day, and their six children. The lighthearted Rhenish lifestyle was able to brighten his melancholy soul for a short time.

fluß, als Bewußtseins- und Erinnerungsstrom ihrer Geschichte. Seit der Eroberungspolitik Napoleons über den Rhein hinweg galten die Franzosen als »Erbfeinde«, die irgendwann militärisch vernichtend zu schlagen seien.

Direkt mit dem Thema »Rhein« befaßte sich – außer Richard Wagner – auch der 1810 in Zwickau geborene Robert Schumann. Als er 1850 seine *Dritte Symphonie*, die »Rheinische«, (Opus 97) komponierte, war er gerade als neu ernannter Musikdirektor von Dresden nach Düsseldorf umgezogen und verbrachte dort eine relativ glückliche Zeit mit seiner Frau, der damals berühmten Pianistin Clara Wieck, und seinen sechs Kindern. Die leichte rheinische Lebensart vermochte sein melancholisches Gemüt für kurze Zeit aufzuheitern.

Wenige Jahre später verdüsterte sich sein Zustand, er begann unter Halluzinationen zu leiden, hörte fremdartige Töne und notierte das aus unbekannten Welten Empfangene auf seinen Notenblättern. Hatte der Rhein mit seinen dunklen Mächten, seinen Nibelungenalpträumen von Schumanns Gehirn Besitz ergriffen? War die locker-leichte Lebensart nur Tarnung? Verbargen sich hinter Katholizismus und wildem Fastnachtstreiben in Wirklichkeit die Dämonen und Ungeheuer aus den Untiefen des Wassers?

Als sich die empfangenen Klänge in seinem Kopf zu einem Höllenlärm steigerten, ihn unablässig verfolgten, es kein Entrinnen mehr gab, stürzte er sich am 27. Februar 1854 von einer Düsseldorfer Brücke in den eiskalten Rhein. Sie hatten ihn gerufen, und er war ihnen, in der Hoffnung auf Stille und Erlösung von der lärmenden Musik in die Falle gegangen. Passanten retteten den Verwirrten, und er wurde in das Sanatorium von Dr. Richarz in Enderich bei Bonn eingeliefert. Dort verbrachte er die letzten Monate seines Lebens, in denen er sich nur noch mühsam mitteilen und nichts mehr komponieren konnte. Offensichtlich schwiegen die Rheingeister tatsächlich. Um die Stille und den Bewegungsmangel zu bekämpfen, unternahm er jetzt imaginäre Reisen, schrieb aus Atlanten Städte- und Ländernamen ab und brachte sie in eine alphabetische Reihenfolge. Beim Schreiben besuchte er in Gedanken die Orte, sah sich in ihnen um und erfreute sich an den schönen, romantischen Bildern.

Am 29. Juli 1856 wurde er mit 46 Jahren von seinem Leiden erlöst. Das einst so romantisch gestimmte Leben endete in progressiver Paralyse, wahrscheinlich infolge einer Neurosyphilis. Andere Lebensmüde wurden nach dem Sturz in den Rhein nicht gerettet, wie etwa die arme Selbstmörderin Karoline von Günderode, die in einem Anfall tiefer Depression – verursacht durch ihre unglückliche Liebe zu dem Heidelberger Sprachforscher Friedrich Creuzer – am 26. Juli 1806 in Winkel am Rhein den Wassertod gesucht und gefunden hat. Lebensfragmente, Lebenstragödien, Lebensruinen.

Richard Wagners monumentales Werk *Der Ring des Nibelungen* beginnt in diesem Flußwasser, tief unten, am märchenhaften Boden des germanischen Stroms. Der Rhein ist bei Wagner kein männliches Wesen, kein »Vater Rhein«, er träumt sich in weibliches Fruchtwasser hinein, in eine mythische Gebärmutter, durchflossen vom Blut zukünftiger Kämpfe. In *Rheingold*, der ersten, 1869 am Münchner Hof- und Nationaltheater uraufgeführten Oper dieser Tetralogie, beschreibt er den rätselhaft-romantischen Handlungsort mit folgenden Sätzen: »Auf dem Grund des Rheins. Grünliche Dämmerung, nach oben zu lichter, nach unten zu dunkler. Die Höhe ist von wogendem Gewässer erfüllt, das rastlos von rechts nach links zu strömt. Nach der Tiefe zu lösen sich die Fluten in einem immer feineren feuchten Nebel auf, so daß der Raum der Manneshöhe vom Boden auf gänzlich frei vom Wasser zu sein scheint, welches wie in Wolkenzügen über den nächtlichen Grund dahinfließt. Überall ragen schroffe Felsenriffe aus der Tiefe auf und grenzen den Raum der Bühne ab; der ganze Boden ist in ein wildes Zackengewirr gespalten, so daß er nirgends vollkommen eben ist und nach allen Seiten hin in dichtester Finsternis tiefere Schluchten annehmen läßt.

Um ein Riff in der Mitte der Bühne, welches mit einer schlanken Spitze bis in die dichtere, heller dämmernde Wasserflut hinaufragt, kreist in anmutig schwimmender Bewegung eine der Rheintöchter.

»Woglinde:
Weia! Waga!
Woge, du Welle!
Walle du Wiege!
Wagalaweia!
Wallala weiala weia!«

35. Burg Kaub im Rhein und Burg Gutenfels hoch über dem rechten Rheinufer.

35. Burg Kaub in the Rhine und Burg Gutenfels high above the right bank of the Rhine.

A few years later his condition darkened. He began to suffer from hallucinations, heard strange sounds and wrote down what he had received from unknown worlds on his sheets of music. Had the Rhine with its dark forces, its Nibelungen nightmares taken possession of Schumann's brain? Was the relaxed, lighthearted lifestyle mere camouflage? Were demons and monsters from the water's depths actually concealed behind Catholicism and the wild carryings-on of the carnival?

When the sounds in his head that he was receiving climaxed into an infernal noise, hounded him incessantly, and there was no escape anymore, he threw himself into the icy-cold Rhine from a Düsseldorf bridge on 27 February 1854. They had called him, and he had walked into their trap, hoping for silence and deliverance from the blaring music. Passersby saved the sick man, and he was taken to the sanitarium of Dr. Richarz in Enderich near Bonn. There he spent the last months of his life, barely able to speak and no longer able to compose. Apparently the spirits of the Rhine were actually silenced. In order to fight the silence and lack of exercise, he now went on imaginary journeys, copied the names of cities and countries from atlases and arranged them in alphabetical order. As he wrote he visited the places in thought, looked around in them and enjoyed the beautiful romantic scenes.

On 29 July 1856, at the age of 46, he was delivered from his suffering. His life, once so romantically tempered, ended in progressive paralysis, probably as a result of neurosyphilis. Other individuals who were weary of life were not rescued after throwing themselves into the Rhine: for instance, the wretched suicide Caroline von Günderode, who in a fit of deep depression – caused by her unhappy love for the Heidelberg linguist Friedrich Creuzer – drowned herself in Winkel am Rhein on 26 July 1806. Fragments, tragedies and ruins of lives.

Richard Wagner's monumental work *The Ring of the Nibelung* begins in the water, deep below the surface, on the legendary riverbed of the Germanic stream. In Wagner's work the Rhine is not male, not »Father Rhine«. Wagner dreams he is in female amniotic fluid, in a mythical womb through which flows the blood of future battles. In *Rheingold*, the first opera of this tetralogy, which premiered at the Munich Hof- und Nationaltheater in 1869, he describes the mysterious romantic setting in the following sentences: »At the bottom of the Rhine. Greenish dusk, lighter to-

Mit lautmalerischen, nahezu dadaistischen Urlauten führt uns Wagner zurück zum Anfang, kurz vor die Geburt der Menschheit und der deutschen Nation (oder wenige Stunden danach). Wo genau sich die Rheintöchter aufhalten, darüber läßt sich nur spekulieren. Auf jeden Fall blickt der Komponist von der linken – französischen? – Rheinseite hinüber zur rechten, da sich das Wasser in seiner Szenenanweisung von rechts nach links bewegt. Viel ist über diesen Standpunkt gerätselt worden, vielleicht hing er auch nur mit einem Rheinaufenthalt Wagners zusammen, als dieser die ersten Noten seines Monumentalwerks niederschrieb. Naheliegend wäre die Gegend bei Worms oder die Rheinschleife am Loreleyfelsen.

Beides nibelungen-kontaminierte Orte, die auch heute noch romantisch wirken, obwohl Eisenbahnschienen, Asphaltstraßen, befestigte Uferböschungen und motorisierte, container- oder kohlebeladene Rheinschiffe die gefühlvolle Idylle bedrängen.

Wer heute am sagenumwobenen, burgruinenfreien Loreleyfelsen vorbeifährt, kann die Stelle kaum übersehen, da an Stromkilometer 554 mit weißer Ölfarbe deutlich der Name des Ortes auf den Schieferfelsen gepinselt worden ist. Davor strömt der Fluß graugrün vorbei und ist, trotz Trübung, dazu in der Lage, den Himmel und auch den schroffen Felsen zu spiegeln. Natürlich denkt jeder einigermaßen gebildete Reisende sofort an Heinrich Heines berühmtes Gedicht, das allerdings den Sachverhalt nur eingeschränkt korrekt wiedergibt. Die Loreleysage ist in Wirklichkeit kein »uraltes Märchen«, sondern eine Erfindung von Clemens Brentano. Seine Zauberin »Lureley«, die an dieser Stelle den Nibelungenschatz bewachte (war sie vielleicht eine der Rheintöchter?), hatte sich aus Rache vorgenommen, alle vorbeiziehenden Männer mit ihren weiblichen Reizen zu vernichten, nur weil der Mann, den sie einmal wirklich liebte, weitergezogen ist und sie verlassen hat. Am Ende der Geschichte wird sie verhaftet und in ein Kloster gebracht. Doch auch ihren letzten Bewacher umgarnt sie und bittet ihn, sie auf den Felsen zu begleiten. Von dort stürzt sie sich in einem unbemerkten Moment hinunter in den Rhein, und der Fluch nimmt seinen Lauf.

Heinrich Heine formulierte die Geschichte so:

»Ich weiß nicht, was soll es bedeuten,
Daß ich so traurig bin;
Ein Märchen aus alten Zeiten,
Das kommt mir nicht aus dem Sinn.

Die Luft ist kühl und es dunkelt,
Und ruhig fließt der Rhein;
Der Gipfel des Berges funkelt
Im Abendsonnenschein.

Die schönste Jungfrau sitzet
Dort oben wunderbar,
Ihr gold'nes Geschmeide blitzet,
Sie kämmt ihr goldenes Haar.

Sie kämmt es mit goldenem Kamme,
Und singt ein Lied dabei,
Das hat eine wundersame,
Gewaltige Melodei.

Den Schiffer im kleinen Schiffe
Ergreift es mit wildem Weh,
Er schaut nicht die Felsenriffe,
Er schaut nur hinauf in die Höh`.

Ich glaube, die Wellen verschlingen
Am Ende Schiffer und Kahn;
Und das hat mit ihrem Singen
Die Loreley getan.«

Das Gegengedicht dazu hat sich der leicht zynische Spötter Erich Kästner im 20. Jahrhundert ausgedacht.

ward the top, darker lower down. The space above is filled with surging water streaming cease-lessly from right to left. Deeper down the floods disintegrate into an ever finer damp mist, so that from the ground up to a man's height the space seems to be entirely free of water, which flows like drifting clouds over the nocturnal ground. Everywhere steep cliffs jut from the depths, forming the boundaries of the stage; the whole floor is split into a wild confusion of jagged rocks, so that it is never completely level and leads us to assume that in all directions, in the densest darkness, there are deeper ravines.«

Around a reef in the center of the stage whose slender tip projects into the denser, brighter waters, one of the Rhine-daughters circles with graceful, swimming motion.

»Woglinde:
Weia! Waga!
Surge, O wave!
Flow, O cradle!
Wagalaweia!
Wallala weiala weia!«

With onomatopoeic, almost dadaistic primeval sounds Wagner takes us back to the beginning, shortly before the birth of the human race and of the German nation (or a few hours after it). We can only speculate where exactly the Rhine-daughters are. At any rate, the composer looks from the left – French? – side of the Rhine to the right side, since the water in his stage directions moves from right to left. People have often racked their brains about this standpoint. Perhaps it merely had to do with Wagner's stay near the Rhine when he wrote down the first notes of his monumental work. An obvious suggestion would be the region near Worms or the bow of the Rhine near the Loreley Rock.

Both are places contaminated by the Nibelungs that still feel romantic today, although railroad lines, asphalted roads, reinforced embankments and motorized barges carrying containers or coal disturb the sentimental idyll.

Those who travel past the legendary Loreley Rock today, even though it has no castle ruins, can hardly fail to notice the place, since at the 554-kilometer mark the name of the place has been clearly painted with white oil paint on the slate rock. The gray-green river streams past it and, though turbid, is able to reflect the sky as well as the steep rock. Naturally any even mildly well-read traveler immediately thinks of Heinrich Heine's famous poem, which, however, gives only a partially correct account of the facts. The Loreley legend is in reality not an »ancient fairy tale«, but was invented by Clemens Brentano. His enchantress »Lureley«, who guarded the trea-sure of the Nibelungs here (was she perhaps one of the Rhine-daughters?), had resolved in re-venge to destroy with her feminine charms all men who passed this spot, simply because the man she had once truly loved had moved on and abandoned her. At the end of the story she is arrested and is to be taken to a convent. Yet she beguiles even one of her guards, and begs him to accompany her to the rock. From there she leaps into the Rhine at an unobserved moment, and the curse is fulfilled. Heinrich Heine told the story as follows:

»I do not know why it should be, but I am so sad: there is an old-time fairy tale that I can't put out of my mind.
The air is cool and twilight is falling and the Rhine is flowing calmly by; the top of the mountain is glittering in the evening sun.
Up there sits the most beautiful maiden; her golden jewelry sparkles and she is combing her golden hair.
She combs it with a golden comb and sings a song as she does so; it has a wonderful compelling melody.
It makes a wild nostalgia possess the boatman in his boat; he pays no attention to the submerged rocks, he can only look up and up.
In the end, if I remember rightly, the waves swallow up the boatman and his boat. And it was Loreley who did this with her singing.«
[*The Penguin Book of German Verse*, introd., ed. and trans. by Leonard Forster (Baltimore, Md.: Penguin Books, 1957)]

The counter-poem to Heine's poem was thought up by the somewhat cynical satirist Erich Käst-ner in the 20th century:

»Die Loreley, bekannt als Fee und Felsen,
ist jener Fleck am Rhein, nicht weit von Bingen,
wo früher Schiffer mit verdrehten Hälsen,
von blonden Haaren schwärmend, untergingen.

Wir wandeln uns. Die Schiffer inbegriffen.
Der Rhein ist reguliert und eingedämmt.
Die Zeit vergeht. Man stirbt nicht mehr beim Schiffen,
bloß weil ein blondes Weib sich dauernd kämmt.

Nichtsdestotrotz geschieht auch heutzutage
noch manches, was der Steinzeit ähnlich sieht.
So alt ist keine deutsche Heldensage,
daß sie nicht doch noch Helden nach sich zieht.

Erst neulich machte auf der Loreley
hoch überm Rhein ein Turner einen Handstand!
Von allen Dampfern tönte Angstgeschrei,
als er kopfüber oben auf der Wand stand.

Er stand, als ob er auf dem Barren stünde.
Mit hohlem Kreuz. Und lustbetonten Zügen.
Man frage nicht: Was hatte er für Gründe?
Er war ein Held. Das dürfte wohl genügen.

Er stand, verkehrt, im Abendsonnenscheine.
Da trübte Wehmut seinen Turnerblick.
Er dachte an die Loreley von Heine.

Und stürzte ab. Und brach sich das Genick.
Er starb als Held. Man muß ihn nicht beweinen.
Sein Handstand war vom Schicksal überstrahlt.
Ein Augenblick mit zwei gehobnen Beinen
ist nicht zu teuer mit dem Tod bezahlt!

P.S. Eins wäre allerdings noch nachzutragen:
Der Turner hinterließ uns Frau und Kind.
Hinwiederum, man soll sie nicht beklagen,
weil im Bezirk der Helden und der Sagen
die Überlebenden nicht wichtig sind.«

Die Rheinbegeisterung hielt das ganze 19. Jahrhundert über an. Nachdem Preußen ab 1814
die Macht am Rhein – als Rheinprovinz – übernommen hatte, wurde es in Berlin Mode, Burgruinen am größten, ehrwürdigsten Fluß Deutschlands zu erwerben. Der Rhein wurde weiter
zum Symbol des neu erwachenden Nationalbewußtseins ausgebaut. Zur Legitimierung eigener
Herrschaftsansprüche setzten Adel und Monarchie verstärkt auf Tradition. Eine ruhmreiche
Vergangenheit, die mit einer mittelalterlichen Burg bewiesen werden konnte, paßte gut in ein
solches Konzept. Außerdem galt es »Die Wacht am Rhein« gegenüber den Franzosen zu halten.
    Wer eine Rheinruine erworben oder geschenkt bekommen hatte, bemühte sich allerdings schnell
darum, sie aus ihrem Ruinendasein zu befreien und ein schmuckes, wohnliches Burgschloß daraus
zu machen. Prinz Friedrich Ludwig Wilhelm war der erste, der mit Burg Rheinstein begann. Wenige
Jahre später erhielt der Kronprinz von der Stadt Koblenz die Ruine Stolzenfels als Geschenk. Nachdem Friedrich Wilhelm IV. zum König ernannt worden war, beauftragte er Karl Friedrich Schinkel mit
der Renovierung und dem Ausbau. Auch der preußische König wollte seine symbolische Anwesenheit am Rhein gegenüber den Franzosen demonstrieren. Militärisch ergänzten die modernen Fes-
tungsstädte Koblenz, Köln und Wesel seinen Machtanspruch. Hier am Rhein war es Schinkel, der
bisher nur klassizistische Bauten errichten konnte, endlich möglich, seine neugotischen Jugend-
träume, die nur auf Gemälden und Zeichnungen existierten, zu verwirklichen.

36. Schloß Stolzenfels bei Koblenz, nach Plänen von Karl Friedrich Schinkel zwischen 1825 und 1839 für den preußischen Kronprinzen und späteren König Friedrich Wilhelm IV. unter weitgehender Beibehaltung der mittelalterlichen Bausubstanz im romantischen Zeitgeschmack errichet.

36. Schloß Stolzenfels (Stolzenfels castle) near Koblenz, built to plans by Karl Friedrich Schinkel from 1825 to 1839 for the Prussian crown prince and later king Friedrich Wilhelm IV in the romantic style fashionable at the time, leaving the medieval building largely untouched.

»The Loreley, known as a fairy and a rock, is that place on the Rhine, not far from Bingen, where in the old days boatmen craned their necks, then perished raving about blonde hair.

We've changed. Including boatmen. The Rhine's been regulated and dammed up. The years go by. Men no longer die while boating just 'cause a blonde keeps combing her hair.

Still even in our days a lot is happening that could have happened in the Stone Age. No German saga is so old that it no longer drags heroes in its wake.

Just recently a gymnast did a handstand on the Loreley, high above the Rhine! Screams of terrror were heard from all the steamboats as he stood on his head there on the rock.

He stood as if he were standing on the parallel bars. With hollow back. A pleased expression on his face. Don't ask: What were his reasons? He was a hero. That ought to suffice.

He stood there upside down in the evening sun. Then melancholy troubled his gymnast's gaze. He thought of Heine's Loreley. And fell. And broke his neck.

He died a hero's death. We mustn't weep for him. His handstand was illuminated by fate. Death is not too high a price for a moment with both legs in the air.

P.S. One detail should be added here: The gymnast was survived by wife and child. On the other hand, we mustn't bemoan their fate, for in the realm of heroes and of legends survivors aren't important.«

Als die Deutschen den Franzosen 1870/71 zeigen konnten, wer von beiden der stärkere war, mußte anschließend ein monumentales Denkmal am Rhein der ganzen Welt für alle Zeiten vom preußisch-deutschen Triumph künden. Man wählte einen Ort in der Nähe von Bingen und türmte dort auf, was an nationalistischen Symbolen zur Verfügung stand. Als krönende Figur blickte eine monumentale »Germania« in Richtung Frankreich. Sie sollte die feindliche, jedoch stärkere und erfindungsreichere Gegenfigur zur französischen »Marianne« bilden. Kriegerische Friese und Inschriften zierten den gewaltigen Sockel der Figur. Als das Denkmal vollendet war, stellte sich heraus, daß niemand das wagnerhafte Bronze- und Steinungeheuer wirklich mochte, am wenigsten Bismarck, der hochverehrte, jeden Abend französischen Champagner trinkende Reichsgründer. Ihm war die »Germania« zu revolutionsbelastet, schließlich hing sie als Gemälde bereits 1848 in der Frankfurter Paulskirche. Wegen der einsamen Lage überstand das Niederwalddenkmal beide Weltkriege unbeschadet. Ein anderes Nationaldenkmal, das zu Ehren von Wilhelm I. auf dem Deutschen Eck in Koblenz errichtet worden war, zerstörten Bomben im Zweiten Weltkrieg. Bis 1989 diente es in Ruinenform als »Denkmal für die deutsche Einheit«. Nach der Wende erinnerten sich die Politiker an die alte nationale Bedeutung und gaben die Restaurierung in Auftrag. Heute steht Wilhelm I. wieder neu und frisch poliert auf seinem angestammten Monumentalsockel und erinnert an die zweifache Entstehung des gesamtdeutschen Staates. In Wilhelm I. steckt jetzt unsichtbar, aber dennoch deutlich zu spüren auch der ehemalige, für die Wiedervereinigung verantwortliche Bundeskanzler Helmut Kohl.

Die größte und berühmteste Schloßruine Deutschlands steht erstaunlicherweise nicht am Rhein, sondern am Neckar, unweit der Mündung des Neckars in den Rhein. Natürlich entging diese malerische Ruine nicht der Aufmerksamkeit der Romantiker. In Scharen reisten sie zu Beginn des 19. Jahrhunderts nach Heidelberg, einige studierten an der dortigen Universität, andere unterrichteten als Professoren. Zwar kam es hier nicht zu vergleichbaren geistigen Gipfeltreffen wie in Tübingen, wo Hölderlin, Schelling und Schlegel sogar eine Kammer im Stift miteinander teilten, aber Arndt und Görres regten die Gemüter genauso an. Joseph Görres wurde mit seinem epochalen Werk über *Die Mythengeschichte der asiatischen Welt* zur bewunderten Zentralgestalt der Heidelberger Romantik. Richard Wagner und Friedrich Nietzsche nutzten später seine Erkenntnisse für die eigenen Werke. Görres erforschte die mythische Herkunft der Menschheit und suchte nach den Ursprüngen der verschiedenen Weltkulturen. Zum ersten Mal öffnete er dabei den Blick in den Fernen Osten und kam damit der romantischen Abneigung gegen die griechisch-römische Klassik entgegen. Der Orient mit seinen exotischen Städten und Bauruinen, mit seinen fremdartigen Religionen und seiner ornamental-üppigen Kunst trat ins Blickfeld.

Jedesmal, wenn ich nach Heidelberg komme, frage ich mich, warum hier einst an der engsten Stelle des Odenwalds, kurz vor Öffnung des Neckartals zum Rhein hin, eine Stadt gegründet worden war. Vielleicht versprachen sich die früheren Bewohner durch die Hügel im Norden und die Burg im Süden Schutz vor Feinden. Für eine kleine Ansiedlung mag die Lage günstig sein,

Fascination with the Rhine continued throughout the 19th century. After Prussia had taken over the Rhine province on the left bank of the Rhine beginning in 1814, it became the fashion in Berlin to purchase castle ruins along Germany's biggest, most venerable river. The Rhine was turned into the symbol of reawakening national consciousness. To legitimize their own claims to power, the nobility and monarchy backed tradition. A glorious past that could be proved with a medieval castle suited their plans perfectly. Also, it was necessary to »keep watch on the Rhine« where the French were concerned, as the song said.

Of course, those who had purchased a Rhine ruin or received it as a gift would quickly make every effort to liberate it from its ruined existence and turn it into a handsome, comfortable fortified castle. Prince Friedrich Ludwig Wilhelm was the first to begin, with Burg Rheinstein. A few years later the crown prince received the Stolzenfels ruin as a present from the town of Koblenz. After Friedrich Wilhelm IV had been elected king, he commissioned Karl Friedrich Schinkel to renovate and remodel it. The Prussian king also wanted to demonstrate his symbolic presence on the Rhine to the French. The modern fortress towns of Koblenz, Cologne and Wesel completed his claim to power militarily. Here on the Rhine it was finally possible for Schinkel, who had only been able to build classicistic buildings up to that point, to turn the neo-Gothic dreams of his youth, which existed only in paintings and sketches, into a reality.

When the time had come and the Germans were able to show the French, in 1870/71, which of the two was stronger, a monumental memorial by the Rhine subsequently had to proclaim the Prussian-German triumph to the entire world for all time. A place was selected near Bingen. Every possible nationalist symbol that was available was piled up on the memorial. The crowning figure was a monumental »Germania«, facing in the direction of France. She was supposed to represent a hostile, yet stronger and more ingenious, counter-figure to the French »Marianne«. Warlike friezes and inscriptions adorned the figure's mighty pedestal. When the monument was finished, it turned out that no one really liked the Wagnerian bronze and stone monster, least of all Bismarck, the highly esteemed founder of the Reich, who drank French champagne every night. He felt »Germania« was too tainted by the revolution: After all, her picture had been hanging in the Paulskirche in Frankfurt since 1848. Because of its isolated location the Niederwald monument survived both world wars intact. Another national monument, erected in honor of Wilhelm I on the Deutsches Eck in Koblenz, was destroyed by bombs in World War II. Until 1989 its ruin served as a »memorial for German unity«. After unification, politicians remembered the old national meaning and commissioned its restoration. Today Wilhelm I again stands new and freshly polished on his original monumental pedestal, reminding visitors of the double genesis of the all-German state. Hidden inside Wilhelm I now, invisible yet clearly noticeable, is former Chancellor Helmut Kohl, who is responsible for the reunification.

Surprisingly, the biggest and most famous castle ruin in Germany is not on the Rhine but on the Neckar River, not far from the confluence of the Neckar and the Rhine. Naturally this picturesque ruin did not escape the attention of the Romantics. In the early 19th century they traveled to Heidelberg in droves. Some studied at the local university, others taught there as professors. True, there were no intellectual summit meetings here as there were in Tübingen, where Hölderlin, Schelling and Schlegel even shared a room in the seminary, but Arndt and Görres had the same stimulating effect on the minds of contemporaries. Joseph Görres, who wrote the momentous work *Die Mythengeschichte der asiatischen Welt,* became an admired central figure of Heidelberg Romanticism. Richard Wagner and Friedrich Nietzsche later used his insights for their own works. Görres studied the mythical origins of the human race and searched for the beginnings of various world cultures. In the process, for the first time, he provided a view of the Far East, which fit in with the Romantics' dislike for Greco-Roman classicism. The Orient with its exotic cities and ruins, with its strange religions and its ornamental, voluptuous art became the focus of attention.

Every time I come to Heidelberg I wonder why a town was once founded here at the narrowest part of the Odenwald mountain range, just before the opening of the Neckar Valley toward the Rhine. Perhaps the former inhabitants hoped that the hills in the north and the fortress in the south would provide protection from enemies. For a small settlement the situation may be favorable, but for a modern town with 135,000 inhabitants there is too little room. The result is that the town is cramped and lacks light. Squeezed together, the townspeople's houses stand along the main street, which runs parallel to the Neckar River and was redeveloped a few years ago into the inevitable, traffic-free, two-kilometer-long pedestrian zone. From here one can hardly see the castle ruin high above the city; only now and then fragments of its red sandstone masonry appear between the gables, distant, unreal and as high as a massif.

aber für eine heutige Stadt mit 135 000 Einwohnern ist zu wenig Platz vorhanden. Die Folge davon sind Enge und Lichtmangel. Zusammengepreßt stehen die bürgerlichen Häuser entlang der neckar-parallelen Hauptstraße, die vor wenigen Jahren zur verkehrsfreien, zwei Kilometer langen Fußgängerzone umgestaltet worden ist. Von hier aus kann man die über der Stadt thronende Schloßruine kaum sehen, nur hin und wieder tauchen Fragmente ihrer roten Sandsteinmauern zwischen den Giebeln auf, fern, unwirklich und felsenhaft hoch wie ein Gebirgsmassiv.

Heidelberg blieb während des Zweiten Weltkriegs als einzige große historische Stadt im Rhein-Neckartal von Luftangriffen verschont. Wahrscheinlich weil die Alliierten hier – wie in Wiesbaden auch – ihre Nachkriegsverwaltung aufbauen wollten. Außerdem gab es vielleicht auch sentimentale Gründe, denn nicht nur in romantischen Zeiten, sondern auch zu Beginn des 20. Jahrhunderts leuchtete die uralte Universitätsstadt mit ihren schlagenden Verbindungen und ihren verwunschenen Gasthäusern manchem Touristen aus Amerika oder England wie ein städtisches Juwel entgegen. Operetten und Filme verbreiteten den romantisch-sentimentalen Stadtmythos unermüdlich und verklärend weiter: »Ich hab mein Herz in Heidelberg verloren …« Selbst ein so hartgesottener Spötter wie Mark Twain geriet beim Anblick von Heidelberg ins Schwärmen. In seinem *Bummel durch Europa* schrieb er 1880: »Man glaubt, Heidelberg – mit seiner Umgebung – bei Tage sei das Höchstmögliche an Schönheit; aber wenn man Heidelberg bei Nacht sieht, eine herabstürzende Milchstraße, an deren Rand jenes glitzernde Sternbild der Eisenbahn geheftet ist, dann braucht man Zeit, um sich das Urteil noch einmal zu überlegen.«

Nur drei Bögen der ältesten Neckarbrücke wurden am 29. März 1945 gesprengt. Alle übrigen Bauten und Häuser, auch die entlang der Hauptstraße, sind wirklich alt. Die meisten wurden allerdings inzwischen modernisiert und mit großflächig verglasten Schaufenstern in zeitgemäße Geschäftshäuser umgebaut. Ich kann nicht sagen, daß ich die Umwandlung gelungen finde. Der Fluch aller Fußgängerzonen liegt auch auf dieser Straße. Ich spüre keinen romantischen Hauch mehr und kein wirklich modernes Flair. Die Stimmung hat etwas touristisch Verlogenes. Besonders unangenehm wirken auf mich die nostalgisch kostümierten Gasthäuser. Ob sie Mark Twain gefallen hätten? Heutige japanische Touristengruppen bleiben begeistert stehen und photographieren sich davor gegenseitig. Auch amerikanische Pärchen, laut redend und lachend, gehören zu den Besuchern. Heidelberg ist nicht weit vom Frankfurter Flughafen entfernt und gehört als wichtiger Besichtigungsort zum Europa-in-drei-Tagen-Programm.

Wieder denke ich an die Romantiker und erinnere mich an ein Gedicht über die Schloßruine von Ludwig Uhland, das Gustav Schwab in seinen *Wanderungen durch Schwaben* zitiert:

»Es scheint ein Schloß – doch ist es keines.
Du siehst vom hohen Bergesrücken
Es stolz im Sonnenstrahle blicken,
Mit Türmen und mit Zinnen prangen,
Mit tiefem Graben rings umfangen,
Voll Heldenbilder aller Orte,
Zween Marmorlöwen an der Pforte;
Doch drinnen ist es öd' und stille,
Im Hofe hohes Gras die Fülle,
Im Graben quillt das Wasser nimmer,
Im Haus ist Treppe nicht noch Zimmer;
Ringsum die Efeuranken schleichen,
Zugvögel durch die Fenster streichen.«

Auch Mark Twain beteiligt sich, wenn auch Jahrzehnte später, an der Ruineneuphorie und schreibt über das Schloß: »Um gut zu wirken, muß eine Ruine den richtigen Standort haben. Diese hier hätte nicht günstiger gelegen sein können. Sie steht auf einer die Umgebung beherrschenden Höhe, sie ist in grünen Wäldern verborgen, um sie herum gibt es keinen ebenen Grund, sondern im Gegenteil bewaldete Terrassen, man blickt durch glänzende Blätter in tiefe Klüfte und Abgründe hinab, wo Dämmer herrscht und die Sonne nicht eindringen kann. Die Natur versteht es, eine Ruine zu schmücken, um die beste Wirkung zu erzielen.«

Hier oben gab es früher eine berühmte Gartenanlage von Salomon de Caus. Ich besitze mehrere Bücher darüber. Hätte der Gartenkünstler nicht Stiche seines Werkes anfertigen lassen, würden wir heute wahrscheinlich wenig darüber wissen. Da dieser Garten einmal ähnlich über der Stadt schwebte wie die Terrasse, auf der ich stehe, beeindruckte er die Zeitgenossen besonders stark. Berggärten waren in unseren Breiten eher selten.

Heidelberg was the only large historic town in the Rhine-Neckar Valley to be spared air raids during World War II. This was probably because the Allies wanted to build up their postwar administration here – as was the case in Wiesbaden as well. Besides there may also have been sentimental reasons, for not only in Romantic times but even at the beginning of the 20th century the ancient university town with its dueling fraternities and enchanted inns shone like an urban jewel welcoming many a tourist from America or England. Operettas and movies indefatigably disseminated the myth of a romantic, sentimental, transfigured town: »Ich hab mein Herz in Heidelberg verloren …« (»I lost my heart in Heidelberg …«) Even as hardboiled a cynic as Mark Twain fell into raptures at the sight of Heidelberg. In his *A Tramp Abroad* in 1880 he wrote: »One thinks Heidelberg by day – with its surroundings – is the last possibility of the beautiful; but when he sees Heidelberg by night, a fallen Milky Way, with that glittering railway constellation pinned to the border, he requires time to consider upon the verdict …«

Only three arches of the oldest Neckar bridge were blown up on 29 March 1945. All the rest of the buildings, even those along the main street, are really old. To be sure, most have been modernized in the meantime and turned into contemporary businesses with large glass display windows. I can't say that I find the transformation a success. The curse of all pedestrian zones lies upon this street as well. I no longer feel even a tinge of romanticism, and no really modern atmosphere, either. There is something touristically hypocritical about the ambience. I find that the nostalgically costumed inns have an especially unpleasant effect on me. I wonder if Mark Twain would have liked them? Modern-day Japanese tourist groups stop enthusiastically and take pictures of each other in front of them. The visitors also include young American couples, talking loudly and laughing. Heidelberg is not far from the Frankfurt airport and as an important tourist attraction is part of the Europe-in-three-days program.

Again I think of the Romantics and remember a poem about the castle ruin by Ludwig Uhland that Gustav Schwab quotes in his »Wanderungen durch Schwaben (Walks through Swabia)«:

»It seems to be a castle – but it isn't one.
In the sun's bright rays you see it proudly looking
Down from the tall mountain's crest,
Resplendent with battlements and towers,
Encircled by a deep moat,
With heroes' statues everywhere,
Two marble lions at the gate;
But inside it is desolate and silent.
Tall grass grows in the courtyard,
The moat is dry, and in the house
There are no stairs or rooms;
The walls are ivy-covered, and birds
Of passage streak through the windows …«

Mark Twain, too, feels the euphoria of the ruins, and writes about the castle, though decades later: »A ruin must be rightly situated, to be effective. This one could not have been better placed. It stands upon a commanding elevation, it is buried in green woods, there is no level ground about it, but, on the contrary, there are wooded terraces upon terraces, and one looks down through shining leaves into profound chasms and abysses where twilight reigns and the sun cannot intrude. Nature knows how to garnish a ruin to the best effect.«

There used to be a famous garden designed by Salomon de Caus up here. I have several books about it. If the garden designer had not had etchings made of his work, we would probably know little about it today. Since this garden once soared above the town like the terrace I am standing on, it made an especially strong impression on contemporaries. Mountain gardens were rather rare in our area.

6. Untergangsphantasien

Richard Wagner und König Ludwig von Bayern. Bayreuth und Neuschwanstein, Arnold Böcklins *Toteninsel*, Korngolds *Die Tote Stadt*, Thomas Manns *Buddenbrooks* und *Tod in Venedig*. Der Untergang der *Titanic* im April 1912

Als Karl Friedrich Schinkels monumentales, klassizistisches Schauspielhaus am Berliner Gendarmenmarkt 1821 mit dem *Freischütz* von Carl Maria von Weber eingeweiht wurde, waren die Zuschauer begeistert. Endlich hatten die romantischen, wenn auch schon etwas biedermeierlich gestimmten Bürgerseelen ein musikalisches Spiegelbild erhalten. Alle volkstümlichen und antistädtischen Motive, die hinaus in die Natur drängten, tauchen in dieser Oper auf: der geheimnisvoll rauschende Wald, felsige Schluchten um Mitternacht, wilde Tiere und Vögel, Naturgeister und Samiel, ein schauerlicher schwarzer Jäger, der sein nächtliches Unwesen treibt, die treubrave Braut und Ehefrau, der fürstliche Erbförster mit Namen Kuno, Max, der junge, ängstliche, sich dem Teufel verschreibende Mann und die Gesellschaft als ordentlicher Gesangverein. Zugegeben, das Libretto von Johann Friedrich Kind entbehrt nicht einer gewissen unfreiwilligen Komik und formuliert schon manches Ganghofer-Klischee voraus, aber die Musik ist so schön, daß sie auch heute noch ans Herz geht.

Richard Wagner war damals acht Jahre alt. Später, im Jahr 1841, wird er über diese Oper gerührt schreiben: »O mein herrliches deutsches Vaterland, wie muß ich dich lieben, wie muß ich für dich schwärmen, wäre es nur, weil auf deinem Boden der *Freischütz* entstand!« An diese Musik wollte er als Komponist anknüpfen und in die gleichen deutschen Waldgefühle, gemischt mit germanischen Mythen, eintauchen. Nicht mehr die Griechen und Römer sollten ihm die Erzählstoffe liefern, sondern die nordischen Vorfahren mit ihren mythischen Erzählungen. Zeus, Apollon, Dionysos und Aphrodite hatten ausgedient. Wotan, Tyr, Donar und Fricka traten nun an ihre Stelle. Übermenschen auch sie, mit rätselhaften Kräften ausgestattet, die sie durch Ringe, Getränke und Gifte steigerten. Aus den antiken Tempeln wurden Naturheiligtümer, Haine, Wolkenpaläste, märchenhafte Unterwasserwelten und dunkle Höhlenlabyrinthe mit glühenden Bergwerken und Fabriken.

Da sich aus germanischer Frühzeit nur wenig schriftliche Nachrichten und Gedichtfragmente erhalten hatten – die *Edda*, die *Völsunga-Saga*, die *Wilkina- und Niflunga-Saga*, das *Nibelungenlied* – war Richard Wagner dazu gezwungen, alle seine Libretti selbst zu schreiben. Dazu erfand er eine stabreimverliebte, archaische Sprache. Als musiklose Theaterstücke wären die Texte wahrscheinlich nicht aufführbar, zu lächerlich sind die Reime, zu simpel die Satzkonstruktionen. Es wundert daher nicht, dass Wagners Dichtungen ein gefundenes Fressen für Kabarettisten waren, ähnlich den absurden Wort-Tautologien Martin Heideggers im 20. Jahrhundert.

Als Komponist erfand Richard Wagner jedoch so grandios-verführerische Klänge, daß ihm alle Hörer und Zuschauer seine dilettantische Sprachakrobatik verziehen. Die Musik zielt, und das ist wahrscheinlich ihr Geheimnis, direkt ins erotische Sinnenzentrum. Sie schmeichelt sich ein, liebkost, verführt und streichelt, sie wabert und nebelt, sie flüstert und donnert, sie ahmt in jedem Moment das Liebesspiel der Menschen (und der Tiere) nach. Richard Wagner ging aufs Ganze und siegte. Das Opernpublikum Europas, später der Welt, wurde geradezu süchtig nach seinen Werken.

Er selbst sah sich als Heilsbringer, Mythenschöpfer, Offenbarer und unwiderstehlichen Guru. Bereits in einer 1841, mit 28 Jahren geschriebenen Novelle *Ein Ende in Paris* faßte er seine Bestrebungen so zusammen: »Ich glaube an Gott, Mozart und Beethoven, in gleichem an ihre Jünger und Apostel – ich glaube an den heiligen Geist und an die Wahrheit der einen unteilbaren Kunst … ich glaube, daß alle durch diese Kunst selig werden und daß es daher jedem erlaubt sei, für sie Hungers zu sterben … ich glaube, daß ich auf Erden ein dissonierender Akkord war, der sogleich durch den Tod herrlich und rein aufgelöst werden wird.«

Natürlich schwiegen seine Feinde und Neider nicht. Besonders vehement griff ihn der einstige Freund und Verehrer Friedrich Nietzsche an, der ihm vorwarf, den dekadenten Massengeschmack seiner Zeit zu bedienen. Es bleibt erstaunlich, daß weder der *Ring des Nibelungen*, noch *Tristan und Isolde* oder *Parsifal* unvollendete Fragmente sind. Selbst das Festspielprojekt »Bayreuth« fand statt, wenn auch mit einigen Umwegen und Schwierigkeiten. Wahrscheinlich lag es einfach an der unglaublichen Berühmtheit des Komponisten und an der Bereitschaft seiner Förderer, allen voran des exzentrischen Bayernkönigs Ludwig II., nicht aufzugeben. Selbst nach Wagners Tod brach das Unternehmen nicht zusammen: ein Verdienst seiner selbstbewußten und herrschsüchtigen Witwe Cosima, der Tochter von Franz Liszt. Viele andere Komponisten versuchten ähnliches

6. Fantasies of destruction

Freischütz, Richard Wagner and King Ludwig of Bavaria. Bayreuth and the Castle of Neuschwanstein. Arnold Böcklin's *Isle of the Dead*. Korngold's *The Dead City*. Thomas Mann's *Buddenbrooks* and *Death in Venice*. The sinking of the *Titanic* in April 1912

When Karl Friedrich Schinkel's monumental, classicistic theater on the Gendarmenmarkt in Berlin had its official opening in 1821 with Carl Maria von Weber's *Freischütz*, the audience was thrilled. Finally the romantic, though somewhat Philistine bourgeois souls had been given a musical mirror image. All the traditional folk and anti-urban motifs that called one out into the countryside and nature appear in this opera: the forest, rustling mysteriously, rocky ravines at midnight, wild beasts and birds, the spirits of nature and Samiel, a frightening dark hunter who does his dastardly deeds at night, the faithful, good bride and wife, the prince's head gamekeeper, named Kuno, Max, the young, timid gamekeeper, who signs away his soul to the devil, and society as a regular glee club. Admittedly the libretto by Johann Friedrich Kind is not lacking in certain involuntary comic elements and foreshadows a number of Ganghofer clichés, but the music is so beautiful that it still touches the heart.

Richard Wagner was eight at the time. Later, in 1841, he would write about this opera in moving terms: »O my wonderful German fatherland, how I must love you, how I must sing your praises, if only because *Freischütz* was created on your soil!« It was this music he wished to emulate as a composer, immersing himself in the same German feelings about the forest, commingled with Germanic myths. No longer would the Greeks and Romans provide him with narrative material; instead, it would be his Nordic forebears and their myths. He had no more use for Zeus, Apollo, Dionysus and Aphrodite. Wodan, Tyr, Donar and Frija took their place. They too were superhuman, possessing mysterious powers that they intensified by means of rings, potions and poisons. Instead of the temples of classical antiquity, Wagner would have natural sanctuaries, groves, cloud palaces, legendary underwater worlds and dark cave labyrinths, with glowing mines and factories.

Since few written documents and fragments of poems had been preserved from Germanic antiquity – the Edda, the Völsunga Saga, the Wilkina and Niflunga Saga, the Nibelungenlied [Song of the Nibelungs] – Richard Wagner was forced to write all his librettos himself. For this purpose he invented an archaic language enamored of alliteration. As plays without music the texts would probably not be performable: The rhymes are too laughable, the sentence construction too simplistic. It is therefore no surprise that Wagner's literary creations were grist to the mill for cabaret artists, as would be the absurd word tautologies of Martin Heidegger in the 20th century.

As a composer, however, Richard Wagner created such grandiose, seductive sounds that his audiences forgave him for his amateurish linguistic acrobatics. The music aims – and that is probably its secret – directly for the erotic sensual center. It insinuates itself, fondles, seduces and caresses, it undulates and wafts, whispers and thunders, imitates the loveplay of humans (and animals) at all times. Richard Wagner went all out and triumphed. The opera-going public of Europe, and later the world, became virtually addicted to his works.

He saw himself as the bringer of salvation, creator of myths and revelations, and irresistible guru. As early as in a novella he wrote in 1841 at the age of 28, *Ein Ende in Paris,* he summed up his endeavors as follows: »I believe in God, Mozart and Beethoven, and also in their disciples and apostles – I believe in the holy spirit and in the truth of the one indivisible art … I believe that everyone will be saved by this art, and that therefore everyone must be permitted to starve for its sake … I believe that I've been a dissonant chord here on earth that will forthwith be gloriously and purely resolved by death.«

Naturally those who hated and envied him did not keep silent. He was especially vehemently attacked by his former friend and admirer Friedrich Nietzsche, who accused him of catering to the decadent taste of the masses of his time. It is still amazing that neither the *Ring of the Nibelung* nor *Tristan and Isolde* nor *Parsifal* are incomplete fragments. Even the Bayreuth festival project did take place, though there were a few detours and problems. Probably this was simply due to the composer's incredible fame and the refusal of his sponsors, particularly the eccentric king of Bavaria, Ludwig II, to give up. Even after Wagner's death the enterprise did not collapse, thanks to his self-important and domineering widow Cosima, the daughter of Franz Liszt. Many other composers tried similar things, only to fail sooner or later. The list begins with George Frideric Handel in London and continues with Jacques Offenbach in Paris. The only success

und scheiterten früher oder später. Die Reihe beginnt mit Georg Friedrich Händel in London und setzt sich fort mit Jacques Offenbach in Paris. Einzig im Bereich des Musicals gibt es im 20. Jahrhundert eine ähnliche Erfolgsgeschichte: die von Sir Andrew Lloyd Webber.

Richard Wagner, der zwischen Restauration und Revolution, zwischen Historismus und aufkommender Moderne, zwischen reaktionärer Mythenwiederbelebung und utopischem Freiheitsdenken hin- und herschwankte, träumte bekanntlich vom »Gesamtkunstwerk«. Er strebte eine Synthese aus Tonkunst, Dichtung, Tanz, Bildhauerei, Malerei und Architektur an. In seinem *Ring des Nibelungen* beschreibt er als Negativ-Utopie ausführlich – 15 Stunden lang – den Untergang der germanischen Helden und Götter.

Der titelgebende Ring existiert tatsächlich, als Motiv aller Gier und Begehrlichkeiten durchzieht er das gesamte monumentale Werk. Am Anfang liegt er noch ungestaltet in Form eines Goldklumpens auf dem Grund des Rheins, bewacht von den verführerisch schönen Rheintöchtern. Als der Nibelungenzwerg Alberich erfährt, welche Macht in dem Goldklumpen-Ring steckt, verzichtet er auf die Befriedigung seiner erotischen Wünsche und richtet seine ganze Lust auf das wertvolle Erz. Damit nimmt das Unheil seinen Lauf. Auch die Götter, allen voran ihr Chef Wotan und seine Frau Fricka, beteiligen sich an dieser Jagd. Im Verlauf der Tetralogie wechselt der Ring mehrmals den Besitzer. Niemandem bringt er Glück, denn in Wirklichkeit haftet ihm ein Fluch an. Neid, Haß, Mißgunst und übersteigerte Gier sind die Folge. Die archaische Menschengesellschaft ist von nun an vergiftet, goldvergiftet. Im Goldrauschfieber wird überfallen, erpreßt und gemordet, ganz wie in der Wirklichkeit.

Durch den Raub wurde die ursprüngliche Weltharmonie aus dem Gleichgewicht gebracht und zerstört. Sieht man den »Ring« als Schöpfungsmythos, besteht der Sündenfall im Goldraub und nicht im Pflücken eines Apfels der Erkenntnis.

Am Ende, nach vier langen Festspieltagen, wird der bösartige Hagen, ein Sohn Alberichs, dem Helden Siegfried seinen Speer in die einzig verletzbare Stelle am Rücken stoßen und ihn damit töten. Während der feierlichen Verbrennungsszene seiner Leiche vor der Gibichungenhalle am Rhein singt Brünnhilde ihren ergreifenden Abschiedsgesang:

> »Starke Scheite schichtet mir dort
> Am Rande des Rheines zuhauf!
> hoch und hell lodre die Glut,
> Die den edlen Leib
> Des hehrsten Helden verzehrt.
> Sein Roß führet daher,
> Daß mit mir dem Recken es folge;
> Denn des Helden heiligste
> Ehre zu teilen, verlangt mein eigener Leib.
> Vollbringt Brünnhildes Wunsch!«

Brünnhilde opfert sich selbst wie eine indische Witwe den Flammen. Der Rhein tritt über seine Ufer, und die herbeischwimmenden Rheintöchter greifen nach dem unglückbringenden Ring. Die Geschichte kehrt zu ihrem Ausgangsort zurück, schließt sich selbst zum Ring und beendet den Machtkampf unter Menschen und Göttern. Die Ereignisse werden sich in ewiger Wiederkehr – ganz nach Wagners, von Schopenhauer beeinflußtem Weltbild – immer aufs neue wiederholen.

Wie genial-grandios die Visionen Wagners die Wirklichkeit spiegeln, erleben wir im Augenblick im globalen, kapitalistischen Finanzbereich. Die Gier führt viele Manager zu immer gewagteren Geldmanipulationen. In der Folge brechen Bankimperien zusammen und reißen Millionen von Sparern mit in den Abgrund. Auch sie hatten sich fiebrig und goldverblendet beteiligt am Poker um immer höhere Renditen.

Die Anweisung für die Schlußszene in Richard Wagners *Götterdämmerung* lautet: »Sie (Brünnhilde) hat sich stürmisch auf das Roß geschwungen, und sprengt es mit einem Satze in den brennenden Scheiterhaufen. Sogleich steigt prasselnd der Brand hoch auf, so daß das Feuer den ganzen Raum vor der Halle erfüllt und diese selbst schon zu ergreifen scheint. Entsetzt drängen sich die Frauen nach dem Vordergrunde. Plötzlich bricht das Feuer zusammen, so daß nur noch eine düstere Glutwolke über der Stätte schwebt; diese steigt auf und zerteilt sich ganz: der Rhein ist vom Ufer her mächtig angeschwollen, und wälzt seine Flut über die Brandstätte bis an die Schwelle der Halle. Auf den Wogen sind die drei Rheintöchter herbeigeschwommen … Flosshilde, ihnen voran, hält jubelnd den gewonnenen Ring in die Höhe. Am Himmel bricht zugleich von fern her eine, dem Nordlicht ähnliche, rötliche Glut aus, die sich immer weiter und stärker verbreitet. –

story similar to Wagner's is recorded in the realm of the musical in the 20th century: that of Sir Andrew Lloyd Webber.

As we know, Richard Wagner, who vacillated between restoration and revolution, between historicism and an incipient modern age, between the reactionary revival of myths and utopian thoughts of freedom, dreamed of the »Gesamtkunstwerk«. He strived for a synthesis of music, poetry, dance, sculpture, painting and architecture. In his *Ring of the Nibelung* – for 15 hours – he describes, in detail, the downfall of the Germanic heroes and gods as a negative utopia.

The titular ring actually exists. As a motive for all greed and covetousness it runs through the entire monumental work. In the beginning it still lies unformed as a nugget of gold at the bottom of the Rhine, guarded by the seductively beautiful Rhine-daughters. When the Nibelung dwarf Alberich finds out what power is concealed in the ring, he gives up all thought of satisfying his erotic longings and focuses all his desire on the valuable metal. The disaster takes its course. The gods, too, led by their chief Wotan and his wife Fricka, take part in this hunt. In the course of the tetralogy, the ring changes owners several times. It brings no one good fortune, for in reality there is a curse on it. The result is jealousy, hatred, envy and exaggerated greed. From now on archaic human society is poisoned – poisoned by gold. In the fever of the gold rush there are attacks, blackmail and murder, just as in real life.

The theft of the ring destroys the original harmony of the world. If we look at the »Ring« as a creation myth, then the Fall of Man is the theft of gold, not the picking of an apple from the Tree of Knowledge.

At the end, after four long festival days, wicked Hagen, a son of Alberich, stabs and kills the hero Siegfried by plunging his spear in the only vulnerable place in his back. As his body is solemnly cremated in front of the hall of the Gibichungs by the Rhine, Brünnhilde sings her moving song of farewell:

»Heap heavy logs
for me by the Rhine:
let the flames rise
high and bright
that consumed
the noble hero's
precious body! –
Bring me his horse,
let it follow the rider
with me:
for my own body
longs to share
the hero's holiest
honor. – Fulfill
Brünnhilde's wish!«

Brünnhilde immolates herself in the flames like a Hindu widow. The Rhine overflows its banks and the Rhine-daughters come swimming, reaching for the disastrous ring. The story returns to its starting point, it has come full circle, ending the mortals' and the gods' struggle for power. In accordance with Wagner's worldview, which was influenced by Schopenhauer, these events will recur over and over again, through all eternity.

At present, in the global capitalist economy, we are experiencing how ingeniously and superbly Wagner's visions mirror reality. Greed causes many managers to engage in ever more risky financial manipulations. As a result bank empires collapse, sweeping millions of savers into the abyss with them. They, too, had taken part in the poker game, feverish, blinded by gold, hoping for ever higher returns on their capital.

The stage direction for the final scene of Richard Wagner's *Götterdämmerung* is as follows: »She (Brünnhilde) has impetuously leapt on the horse, and rides it at full speed into the burning pyre. At once the crackling flames rise so high that the fire fills the entire space in front of the hall and seems about to engulf it as well. Horrified, the women crowd into the foreground. Suddenly the pyre caves in, so that now only a murky glowing cloud hangs overhead; it rises and disperses completely: the swollen Rhine has overflowed its banks, and the floodwaters roll over the funeral pyre to the very threshold of the hall. On the waves, the three Rhine-daughters come swimming … Flosshilde, who is in front, jubilantly holds up the regained ring. At the same time, a red-

Die Männer und Frauen schauen in sprachloser Erschütterung dem Vorgange und der Erscheinung zu. Der Vorhang fällt.«

Es scheint so, als habe der einstige Revolutionär Wagner in der Geldwirtschaft und in der modernen Gier, mit Hilfe industrieller Techniken die Welt auszubeuten, das Unheil über die Menschheit hereinbrechen sehen, ganz so, wie es Karl Marx vorhergesagt hatte. Sein Fazit ist pessimistisch. Als deutscher Spätromantiker liebte er den tragischen Untergang, allerdings inszeniert im eigenen Festspielhaus, mit einem Riesenorchester und den besten Sängern der Welt. Außerdem sollte dieser Untergang nicht einmal stattfinden, sondern mehrmals hintereinander… wochenlang…jahrelang…jahrzehntelang…im nächsten Jahr kommen wir wieder…weil es so schön war…leider gibt es längst keine Karten mehr…der Andrang ist zu groß…

Bayreuthbesucher betrachten den Ort immer noch wie eine Wallfahrtsstätte, ein Lourdes der Musik. Aufführungen dort mitzuerleben, gleicht Gottesdiensten. Wagner, ahnen sie, hat den Untergangsweltgeist gesehen, ihm wurden Ruinen-Wahrheiten offenbart, die dem Rest der Welt ohne seine Werke verborgen geblieben wären.

Weil er, der so berühmte Komponist, immer in Geldnöten war, mußte er in ganz Europa nach reichen Gönnern suchen. Zuerst war es der reiche Züricher Geschäftsmann Wesendonck, mit dessen Frau Mathilde er umgehend ein Liebesverhältnis einging, in der Mitte seines Lebens erlag er der schwärmerischen Verehrung König Ludwigs II. von Bayern und machte sich finanziell vollständig von ihm abhängig.

Blicken wir zurück: Als der König am 25. August 1845 in Münchner Schloß Nymphenburg das Licht der Welt erblickte, war Richard Wagner schon 32 Jahre alt. Während das königliche Baby, von Ammen verwöhnt, seine ersten Schritte wagte, wurde Wagner, nach dem Scheitern der Revolution 1848/49 von der Dresdner Polizei als Revolutionär gesucht. Sein damaliger Steckbrief, der an öffentlichen Wänden und allen Zollstationen aushing, lautete:

»Der unten etwas näher bezeichnete Königliche Capellmeister Richard Wagner von hier ist wegen wesentlicher Theilnahme an der in hiesiger Stadt stattgefundenen aufrührerischen Bewegung zur Untersuchung zu ziehen, zur Zeit aber nicht zu erlangen gewesen. Es werden daher alle Polizeibehörden auf denselben aufmerksam gemacht und ersucht, Wagnern im Betretungsfalle zu verhaften und uns davon schleunigst Nachricht zu erteilen.

Dresden, den 16. Mai 1849. Die Stadt-Polizei-Deputation, von Oppell.

Wagner ist 37–38 Jahre alt, mittlerer Statur, hat braunes Haar und trägt eine Brille.«

Zwei Welten, zwei Leben. Ludwig, inzwischen nach Schloß Hohenschwangau umgezogen und von Privatlehrern betreut, wurde bereits mit 18 Jahren, am 11. März 1864, zum König von Bayern, Franken und Schwaben ernannt. Wenige Tage danach treffen sich die beiden – der berühmte Komponist und der König – zum ersten Mal. Ludwig, ein schüchterner, fast zwei Meter großer, bayerischer junger Mann, und Wagner, ein kleiner, aber sehr selbstbewußter Sachse mit starkem Akzent. Träumer, jeder auf seine Art. Der König hatte als 16jähriger Aufführungen von *Tannhäuser* und *Lohengrin* in München gesehen und in diesen fiktiven Märchenwelten seine eigenen Träume wiederentdeckt. Er identifizierte sich schwärmerisch mit den Hauptfiguren und begann schon damals, gedanklich in einem märchenhaften Opern-Mittelalter zu leben.

Bei der Unterredung erzählte ihm Wagner von seinem gewaltigen Opernprojekt, dem *Ring des Nibelungen,* und von seinen Geldproblemen. Der König händigte dem Komponisten die enorme Summe von 170 000 Gulden aus. Aber das war noch nicht alles. Er versprach ihm außerdem, ein eigenes Festspielhaus nur für seine Werke in München zu errichten. Das allerdings wird in den Jahren danach von den unmusischen, meist militaristisch gesinnten, bayrischen Politikern verhindert. Auch Wagner selbst war nicht sicher, ob er das Gebäude, das Gottfried Semper inzwischen entworfen hatte, wirklich wollte. Er bevorzugte einen abgelegenen Ort – eben Bayreuth –, dort seien die späteren Besucher, sagte er, durch keinerlei Großstadttrubel abgelenkt und könnten sich ganz auf seine Musik konzentrieren.

Bevor das Festspielhaus in Bayreuth fertig war, wurden die neuen Opernwerke Wagners am Münchner Nationaltheater uraufgeführt: *Tristan und Isolde* (1865), *Die Meistersinger von Nürnberg* (1868), *Das Rheingold* (1869) und *Die Walküre* (1870).

Nach dem Scheitern seiner Verlobung mit Sophie, der jüngeren Schwester der Kaiserin Sissi, konzentrierte sich König Ludwig II. ganz auf seine Schloßbauprojekte. Neben Herrenchiemsee und Linderhof war es vor allem das Schloß Neuschwanstein, welches seine Phantasie fesselte. 1869 erfolgte die Grundsteinlegung, aber erst 1884, zwei Jahre vor seinem Tod, wurde es fertiggestellt.

Ein mittelalterliches Gralsprojekt, »das erst nach vielen Vorentwürfen zu seiner landschaftsbeherrschenden Monumentalität herangewachsen ist. Bei diesem allmählichen Formfindungsprozeß

dish glow resembling the northern lights dawns from afar in the sky. The glow spreads farther and farther, growing more intense all the while. – The men and women watch the events unfolding and gaze at the apparition, shaken and speechless. The curtain falls.«

It seems as if the former revolutionary Wagner foresaw the disaster that would descend upon mankind due to the collapse of the money economy and to the modern greed to exploit the world by means of industrial technologies, exactly the way Karl Marx had predicted. The conclusions he draws are pessimistic. As a German late Romantic he loved the tragic end of the world, though staged in his own festival hall, with a huge orchestra and the finest singers in the world. Besides, this end was to take place not once but several times in a row …for weeks…years…decades… we'll be back next year…because it was so beautiful…too bad that the tickets are all sold out…the crowd was too big…

Visitors to Bayreuth still regard the town as a place of pilgrimage, a Lourdes for music lovers. Being present at a performance there is like being at a church service. Wagner, they sense, saw the world spirit foretelling destruction, revelations of ruin truths that would have remained hidden from the rest of the world if it had not been for his works.

Because he, the famous composer, was always in financial difficulties, he was forced to look for rich patrons all over Europe. One of the first was the rich Zurich businessman Wesendonck, with whose wife Mathilde he immediately began a liaison. In midlife, he succumbed to the infatuated adoration of King Ludwig II of Bavaria and became completely financially dependent on him.

Let's take a look back: When the king first saw the light of day on 25 August 1845 in Nymphenburg Palace in Munich, Richard Wagner was already 32 years old. While the royal baby, spoiled by his nurses, took his first hesitant steps, the revolutionary Wagner was wanted by the Dresden police after the failure of the 1848/49 revolution. Posted on public walls and in all customs posts, his description read:

»Royal Director of Music Richard Wagner, described below in more detail, of this city, is to be brought in for questioning because of his considerable participation in the rebellious movement that has been active in the city. At this time, it has not been possible to apprehend him. Therefore all police authorities are being alerted and requested to arrest Wagner should he enter [a customs office] and to inform us of the arrest forthwith.

Dresden, 16th May, 1849. Deputy of the Municipal Police, von Oppell.

Wagner is 37–38 years old, of average height, has brown hair and wears glasses.«

Two worlds, two lives. Ludwig, who had meanwhile moved to the Castle of Hohenschwangau and was being taught by private tutors, was elected to be the king of Bavaria, Franconia and Saxony at the early age of 18, on 11 March 1864. A few days later, the famous composer and the king meet for the first time. Ludwig, a shy young Bavarian, almost 6 feet 7 inches tall and Wagner, a short but very self-assured Saxon with a heavy accent. Both of them dreamers, each in his own way. At 16 the king had seen performances of *Tannhäuser* and *Lohengrin* in Munich and had rediscovered his own dreams in these fictitious fairy-tale worlds. He rapturously identified with the leading protagonists and began even at that time to live, in his imagination, in the medieval fantasy world of operas.

At their first meeting Wagner told him about his vast operatic project, *The Ring of the Nibelung,* and about his financial problems. The king handed the composer the enormous sum of 170,000 Bavarian guldens. But that was not all. He also promised him to build a special festival hall in Munich solely for his works. This plan, however, would be stopped in the years that followed by largely militarily minded Bavarian politicians who did not appreciate the fine arts. Wagner himself was also not sure whether he really wanted the building that Gottfried Semper had designed in the meantime. He preferred a remote town – Bayreuth, to be precise. There, future visitors would not be distracted by the hurly-burly of a large city, he said, and could concentrate completely on his music.

Before the Festival Hall in Bayreuth was completed, Wagner's new operatic works premiered at the Munich National Theater: *Tristan and Isolde* (1865), *The Mastersingers of Nuremberg* (1868), *The Rhine Gold* (1869) and *The Valkyrie* (1870).

After his engagement to Sophie, the younger sister of Sissi, fell through, King Ludwig II focused entirely on his castle building projects. In addition to Herrenchiemsee and Linderhof, Neuschwanstein Castle in particular captivated his imagination. The foundation stone was laid in 1869, but the castle was not completed until 1884, two years before his death.

It was a medieval Grail project »that did not grow to its monumental size, which would dominate the landscape, until many preliminary designs had been discarded. In the gradual process of evolving a final design, the scene painter Christian Jank with his sketches and alternative visions

hat der Bühnenmaler Christian Jank mit seinen Entwürfen und Alternativvisionen eine wichtige Rolle gespielt. Die Architekten Eduard Riedel, Georg Dollmann und Julius Hofmann, die nacheinander als Bauleiter abgelöst wurden, waren dazu verdammt, die gemalten Bühnenbildvisionen bautechnisch umzusetzen. Sie bekamen für ihre fundamentalistische Arbeit nur Tadel vom König zu hören; doch ohne ihre konstruktiven Pioniertaten, ihre technischen Erfindungen und ihre stilistischen Korrekturen hätte der Traum von der Gralsburg auf dem Felsen nie den Status der aquarellierten Vision überwunden«, schreibt Gottfried Knapp in seinem schönen und informativen Buch über das berühmteste Bauwerk Bayerns.

Da Neuschwanstein heute noch in voller Pracht auf den alpinen Felszinnen in der Nähe von Füssen steht, gehört das Schloß nur bedingt in dieses Ruinenbuch. Ihm wurde das Schicksal Walhalls erspart, ähnlich der Wartburg, die als Vorbild diente. Während die Zeitgenossen dem weltfremden König übel mitspielten – er wurde entmündigt und starb einen bis heute unaufgeklärten Tod durch Ertrinken im Starnberger See –, stieg sein Schloß zur Weltberühmtheit auf. Für viele Amerikaner und Japaner verkörpert Neuschwanstein bis heute die deutsche Märchenseele. Selbst Walt Disney war bei einem Besuch einst so begeistert, daß er Neuschwanstein – amerikanisch verkitscht – als Vorbild für seine Märchenschlösser in den Disney Worlds verwendete.

Damals, beim Bau, ahnte niemand, daß Neuschwanstein eine gewaltige Zukunftsinvestition darstellte, die sich für den Bayerischen Staat und die Tourismusindustrie einmal auszahlen würde. Das gleiche gilt für Ludwigs Investition in das Werk *Der Ring des Nibelungen*. Er wird an allen großen Opernhäusern der Welt aufgeführt und trägt den Namen Wagners, aber auch seines Mäzens bis heute rund um den Erdball.

Dem bayerischen Träumer Ludwig, der Militär und Kriege haßte, blieb nur wenig Zeit, sein Märchenschloß zu genießen. Kein fremder Staatsgast wurde je dorthin eingeladen. Er wollte die Räume ganz für sich allein haben. Nachts geisterte er, angespornt durch Unmengen von Champagner, einsam durch die Säle und verwandelte sich in Lohengrin, Tannhäuser oder Tristan. Manchmal ließ er sich mit einer Gondel durch seine kerzenbeleuchtete Grotte fahren, ringsum weiße Schwäne, seine einzigen Verbündeten. Die Musik Richard Wagners, die der scheue König auch allein auf dem Klavier spielte, diente als ideale Filmmusik für ein Leben, das nur aus Traumstunden bestehen sollte.

Inzwischen war mit seiner finanziellen Hilfe auch das Festspielhaus in Bayreuth fertig geworden. 1876 fand die feierliche Eröffnung statt. Da der König öffentliche Auftritte haßte, besuchte er nur die Generalproben des *Rings*. Dafür war er in aller Heimlichkeit nachts mit einem Spezialzug aus München angereist.

In seinem Testament hatte er verfügt, daß Schloß Neuschwanstein nach seinem Tod gesprengt werden solle. Zugegeben, dann erst, in diesem zerstörten Zustand hätte es wirklich in dieses Ruinenbuch hineingehört. Aber seien wir froh, daß sein letzter Wille nicht erfüllt worden ist. Im Gegenteil: Sieben Wochen nach seinem Tod wurden die Schloßräume für das Publikum geöffnet. Heute besuchen jedes Jahr 1,5 Millionen Touristen die »Burg des Märchenkönigs«.

Eine tragische Ironie des Schicksals sei an dieser Stelle noch erwähnt: Während München nach 1940 zunehmend von britischen Bombern heimgesucht wurde und die Museumsdirektoren Auslagerungsorte für ihre wertvollen Gemälde suchten, diente Neuschwanstein – neben Herrenchiemsee – als sicheres Depot. Und tatsächlich verirrte sich nie ein englischer Bomber in diese abgelegenen Landschaften. Sicher und heil konnten die Altdorfers, Grünewalds und Dürers die Kriegszeit überstehen und Ende 1945 zurück nach München gebracht werden. Bereits am 17. Januar 1946 wurde im Westflügel des ehemaligen »Hauses der deutschen Kunst« eine große Ausstellung unter dem Titel »Bayerische Gemälde des 15. und 16. Jahrhunderts« mit Dürer- und Altdorfer-Gemälden eröffnet.

Richard Wagner ist am 13. Februar 1883, drei Jahre vor dem rätselhaften Tod seines königlichen Gönners, im Venezianer Palazzo Vendramin eines ganz natürlichen Todes gestorben. Starnberger See und Canal Grande, beide Tode hatten mit Wasser zu tun, nicht mit dem Rhein, der mythischen Ursuppe, aber immerhin mit Wasser. Die Friedhofsinsel von Venedig – Isola di San Michele – wäre ein idealer Ort für die Gräber beider Männer gewesen (wie für Strawinsky und Diaghilew), aber Wagner wurde nach Bayreuth überführt und im Garten seiner Villa Wahnfried beerdigt. Wo aber liegt das Grab König Ludwigs?

Etwa zur gleichen Zeit malte ein Schweizer Künstler, der meist in Florenz lebte und arbeitete, eine fiktive Friedhofsinsel, die – wie Neuschwanstein und der *Ring* in das kollektive Bewußtsein vieler Zeitgenossen einging. Es ist das Gemälde von Arnold Böcklin *Die Toteninsel*. Die erste Version entstand 1880 im Auftrag der jungen Witwe Marie Berna aus Frankfurt am Main. Aber sie gefiel Böcklin nicht, und er hielt das Gemälde zurück. Erst 1883 gelang ihm die endgültige Fassung.

played an important part. The architects Eduard Riedel, Georg Dollmann and Julius Hofmann, who succeeded each other as on-site managers, had the thankless task of turning the painted stage-set visions into architectural structures. In return for their fundamental work the king offered them nothing but criticism; yet without their pioneering constructional feats, their technical inventions and their stylistic corrections, the dream of the Castle of the Holy Grail on the rock would never have been developed beyond a water-color vision …«, writes Gottfried Knapp in his beautiful and informative book about the most famous building in Bavaria.

Since to this day Neuschwanstein stands in its full glory on the Alpine cliffs near Füssen, the castle only partially belongs in this book about ruins. It was spared the fate of Valhalla, as was Wartburg Castle, on which it was modeled. While his contemporaries treated the unwordly king badly – he was certified and died by drowning in Lake Starnberg, a death that has not been explained to this day – his castle became world famous. For many Americans and Japanese Neuschwanstein still embodies the German fairy-tale soul. Even Walt Disney was once so thrilled during a visit that he used Neuschwanstein – or a kitschy American version of it – as a model for his fairy-tale castles in the Disney Worlds.

At the time it was built no one imagined that Neuschwanstein represented a huge future investment that would one day pay off for the Bavarian state and the tourism industry. The same thing is true of Ludwig's investment in the work *The Ring of the Nibelung*. It is performed in all the great opera houses of the world and still carries Wagner's name, but also that of his patron, around the globe.

The Bavarian dreamer Ludwig, who hated the military and war, was to have little time to enjoy his fairy-tale castle. No foreign official visitors were ever invited to the castle. He wanted to have the space all to himself. At night he would haunt the castle, spurred on by vast amounts of champagne, wandering lonely through the halls, transformed into Lohengrin, Tannhäuser or Tristan. Sometimes he would have a gondola take him through his candle-lit grotto, surrounded by white swans, his only allies. The music of Richard Wagner, which the shy king would also play alone on the piano, served as the ideal background music for a life that was to consist only of hours filled with daydreams.

In the meantime, with his financial help, the Festival Hall in Bayreuth had been completed. It officially opened in 1876. Since the king hated public appearances, he only visited the dress rehearsals of the *Ring*. In order to do so, he secretly traveled by special train from Munich.

In his testament he had decreed that Neuschwanstein Castle should be blown up after his death. Admittedly, the castle would really have belonged in this book about ruins if it had been destroyed. But we can be glad that his last will was not fulfilled. On the contrary: Seven weeks after his death the rooms of the castle were opened to the public. Now 1.5 million tourists per year visit the »castle of the fairy-tale king«.

By an irony of fate, while Munich was increasingly attacked by British bombers after 1940 and museum directors tried to find places to which they could evacuate their valuable paintings, Neuschwanstein – as well as Herrenchiemsee – served as a safe depository. And sure enough, no British bomber ever strayed into these remote regions. Safe and sound, the Altdorfers, Grüne-walds and Dürers survived the war and could be returned to Munich in late 1945. As early as 17 January 1946, a large exhibition titled »Bavarian paintings of the 15th and 16th centuries« was opened in the west wing of the former »Haus der deutschen Kunst« with paintings by Dürer and Altdorfer.

Richard Wagner died a completely natural death on 13 February 1883, three years before the mysterious death of his royal patron, in Palazzo Vendramin, Venice. Lake Starnberg and Canal Grande – both deaths had something to do with water, not with the Rhine, the mythical primeval soup, but still with water. The cemetery island of Venice – Isola di San Michele – would have been an ideal place for the graves of both men (as it was for Stravinsky and Diaghilev), but Wagner was transported to Bayreuth and buried in the garden of his Villa Wahnfried. But where is King Ludwig's grave?

At about the same time a Swiss artist who mostly lived and worked in Florence painted a fictitious cemetery island, which – like Neuschwanstein and the *Ring* – influenced the collective consciousness of many contemporaries. It is Arnold Böcklin's painting *The Isle of the Dead*. The first version was painted in 1880, commissioned by the young widow Marie Berna, of Frankfurt am Main. But Böcklin did not like it, and kept the painting himself. It was not until 1883 that he successfully completed the definitive version.

When I take a closer look at the picture, I think not only of Capri and the Isola di San Michele but once again of Rousseau's Isle of Poplars and his burial in Ermenonville by night. The poplars

Ich denke beim genauen Betrachten des Bildes – außer an Capri und die Isola di San Michele – wieder einmal an Rousseaus Pappelinsel und an seine nächtliche Beerdigung in Ermenonville. Die Pappeln sind zu Zypressen geworden, dunkler, drohender, immergrün. Wie zum Schutz dieser Pappel-Zypressen-Insel hat Böcklin eine halbkreisförmige, ruinöse Felsenfestung um sie herumgebaut. Man könnte darin auch ein halbzerfallenes Amphitheater, ein Natur-Kolosseum sehen, an dessen Innenwänden für uns unsichtbare Stufen und Ränge eingemeißelt worden sind. Hier sitzen keine Zuschauer, hier führen Tore ins dunkle Felseninnere, in Höhlengräber hinein. Aus dem Bildvordergrund und damit aus unserer Betrachterperspektive nähert sich ein Totenschiff mit Fährmann, weißgekleideter Witwe und quergelegtem Sarg der Treppe, die aus dem Wasser heraus zur Insel führt. Symbolische Assoziationen an Charon und Styx sind unvermeidlich und wirken, von heute aus gesehen, weniger mythisch als vielmehr etwas aufdringlich, gespenstisch, horrorfilmartig.

Es herrscht eine düster-stürmische Atmosphäre, der Himmel ist von bedrohlichen Wolken überzogen, und die Zypressenspitzen biegen sich im Wind. Merkwürdigerweise zeigt das Wasser keinerlei Windspuren, es ist wellenlos und kann so eine optimale Spiegelfläche für die gespenstische Totenüberfahrt bilden.

Die laute, lebendige, bunte Welt liegt hinter uns, wir schauen mit dem Boot hinüber in ein malerisch-theatralisches Jenseits, das, durchaus einladend, touristische Qualitäten besitzt. Böcklin versuchte, ein Bild des Todes zu malen, das der neuen, götterlosen Zeit entspricht. Kein Altar, kein Kreuz. Die Bildtotale läßt Platz und Raum zum Träumen und Spekulieren. Jeder Betrachter mag in in diesem Toten-Capri etwas anderes sehen: einen Naturtempel, ein Hotel … Niemand weiß, was sich hinter den Felsenmauern, den Zypressen und den Toren wirklich verbirgt. Vielleicht ist die Insel auch nur ein ganz banaler Friedhof, eine Cimitero-Insel wie in Venedig. In den Höhlen liegen möglicherweise nur Särge mit verwesenden und vertrocknenden Leichen. Die Wolken ziehen teilnahmslos darüber hinweg, und die Spiegelung im Wasser ist ausschließlich ein schönes, optisches Phänomen.

Wir allerdings, die wir Bilder von Stalingrad, von den Leichenbergen der befreiten Lager in Bergen-Belsen und Auschwitz kennen, wir, die wir die zerfetzten Körper der Selbstmordattentate im Fernsehen gesehen haben, können über die harmlose Romantik, die ruhige, verführerische Gemütlichkeit dieser Darstellung des Jenseits nur gelinde lächeln. Dennoch ist Böcklin mit diesem Ruinenbild eine Ikone des Todes gelungen, die – ähnlich dem *Eismeer* von Caspar David Friedrich – die Jenseitsgedanken der Betrachter romantisch beruhigt und auf eine Postkartengröße hinunterverkleinert. Beim Anblick dieses Bildes verflüchtigen sich Todesängste, ja, fast könnte man sagen, daß dieses Bild zum Sterben geradezu einlädt.

Das Gemälde *Die Toteninsel* gehörte zu den populärsten Bildern Deutschlands um 1900. Im Ersten Weltkrieg diente es als beliebte Feldpostkarte. Wer weiß, wie viele Soldaten ihren Heldentod mit diesem Bild im Rucksack gestorben sind?!

Auch die Surrealisten Max Ernst und Salvador Dalí schätzten das Motiv und variierten es in den eigenen Werken immer wieder.

Als ich gelesen habe, daß Adolf Hitler eine *Toteninsel*-Version 1933 für seine Sammlung erworben hatte, wunderte ich mich nicht, schließlich paßte das Motiv genau in seine romantisch-todessüchtige, untergangsverliebte Weltsicht. Es wird berichtet, daß er in das Gemälde eine germanische Mythenwelt hineininterpretiert hat, schließlich zog es ihn – wie Richard Wagner und Caspar David Friedrich – mehr in den Norden, in die Eismeere von Skandinavien und Rußland. Der Süden lockte ihn weniger, dort hatte sich ja bereits sein Kollege Benito Mussolini festgesetzt. Außerdem verlief seine Hilfe für den »Blutsbruder« in Nordafrika – unter der Führung des »Wüstenfuchses Rommel« – auch nicht gerade sehr erfolgreich. Nach dem Krieg blieb das Bild aus Hitlers Sammlung verschwunden und tauchte erst im Jahr 1980 wieder im Kunsthandel auf. Heute hängt es in der Berliner Nationalgalerie. Rätselhafte Bildwanderungen!

Die zweite Hälfte des 19. Jahrhunderts ist angefüllt mit Widersprüchen. Während Gustave Eiffel seinen umstrittenen, später weltberühmten Pariser Weltausstellungsturm entwarf und bauen ließ, vollendeten rückwärts gewandte Architekten in Deutschland die gotischen Türme des Kölner Doms und des Ulmer Münsters. Sie zerstörten damit die über Jahrhunderte gewachsene, markante Ruinenhaftigkeit der Stadtbilder. Stahl gegen Stein, Eisenbahnschienen gegen Neuschwansteinromantik. Schlösser gegen Barrikaden. Fürstenfamilien, die um ihre Existenz bangten, unterhielten nicht nur Burgruinen-Wochenendhäuser am Rhein, sondern errichteten riesige neugotische Schlösser, wie etwa in Hechingen-Hohenzollern und Schwerin. Der Rückgriff auf historische Vorbilder sollte ihre uralte, gottgegebene Regierungsberechtigung untermauern, wenn nicht sogar beweisen. Aber die demokratischen Kräfte wurden immer lauter und erhielten zunehmend die

have become cypresses, darker, more menacing, evergreen. As though to protect this poplar-cypress island Böcklin has built a semicircular, ruinous rocky fortress around it. One might also see it as a half-ruined amphitheater, a natural Colosseum, chiseled into whose interior walls are steps and stands we cannot see. There are no spectators here. Doors lead into the dark mouth of rock, into cave sepulchers. From the foreground of the picture and thus from our perspective as observers, a ship of the dead with a ferryman, a widow dressed in white and a coffin placed across the ship approaches the steps that lead from the water up to the island. Symbolic associations with Charon and Styx are inevitable and, seen from today's perspective, their effect is not so much mythic as somewhat obtrusive, eerie, like something in a horror movie.

The atmosphere is gloomy, stormy, the sky is covered with threatening clouds and the tops of the cypresses bend in the wind. Oddly enough, the water shows no traces of a wind. There are no waves, and thus a perfectly smooth mirror surface to reflect the eerie crossing of the dead.

The loud, colorful world of the living lies behind us, we are looking with the boat into a picturesque theatrical hereafter that looks quite inviting and has touristic characteristics. Böcklin has tried to paint a picture of death that corresponds to the new, godless era. There is no altar, no cross. The picture as a whole leaves room for dreams and speculation. Every observer may see something different in this Capri of the dead: a natural temple, a hotel … No one knows what is really concealed behind the rocky walls, the cypresses and the gates. And perhaps the island is merely a perfectly commonplace cemetery, a cemetery island like the one in Venice. It is possible that there are only coffins with decaying and desiccated bodies in the caves. Clouds drift indifferently overhead, and the reflection in the water is just a beautiful optical phenomenon…

We, however, familiar with images of Stalingrad and Auschwitz, of the mountains of corpses in the liberated camps of Bergen-Belsen and Auschwitz, we who have seen the torn bodies of suicide bombers on TV, can only smile mildly about the harmless romanticism, the peaceful, seductive coziness of this representation of the hereafter. And yet with this picture of ruins Böcklin has succeeded in creating an icon of death, which – like Caspar David Friedrich's *Sea of Ice* – romantically reassures the viewers' thoughts about the next world and reduces them to the size of a postcard. At the sight of this painting, fears of death are dispelled. Indeed, one might almost say that this picture practically invites one to die.

The painting *Isle of the Dead* was one of the most popular pictures in Germany around 1900. In World War I it was used as a favorite postcard. Who knows how many soldiers died their hero's death with this picture in their backpack?!

The surrealists Max Ernst and Salvador Dalí also thought highly of the motif and kept including variations on the theme in their own works.

When I heard that Adolf Hitler purchased a version of the *Isle of the Dead* for his collection in 1933, I was not surprised. After all, the motif exactly fits into his romantic worldview – addicted to

Unterstützung breiter Volksmassen. Seit der Französischen Revolution flackerten überall in Europa immer wieder Unruhen durch die Befreiungsbewegungen auf.

Die ersten, noch burschenschaftlich bewegten Demokraten in Deutschland versammelten sich am 27. Mai 1832 in der Hambacher Schloßruine. Ein bemerkenswerter Vorgang, der wahrscheinlich weniger mit dem Ruinencharakter des Versammlungsorts zu tun hatte als vielmehr mit dem relativ liberalen Umfeld. Allerdings bekamen die Behörden Angst, als sie die unerwartet große Menschenmenge sahen, die auf den bisher völlig unbedeutenden Schloßberg strömte. Selbst den Veranstaltern des Treffens wuchs das Ereignis über den Kopf. Beim Einsturz einer maroden Schloßwand, auf die begeisterte Aktivisten hinaufgestiegen waren, gab es sogar Verletzte und Tote. Danach nahmen die Repressionen eher zu. Erst 1848 trat in der Frankfurter Paulskirche das erste frei gewählte deutsche Parlament zusammen.

In der zweiten Hälfte des 19. Jahrhunderts formulierte eine neue Generation von Dichtern und Schriftstellern ihre depressiven, ruinengeschwängerten Zukunftsängste. Während Jules Verne noch hoffnungsvoll von utopischen Reisen zum Mond, zum Mittelpunkt der Erde und 20 000 Meilen unter den Meeresspiegel träumte und Karl May seine Wildwestabenteuer zusammenflunkerte, saß Gustave Flaubert in düsterer Stimmung an seinem Schreibtisch und brütete melancholisch über den vergifteten gesellschaftlichen Zuständen. Madame Bovary mußte sterben, weil sie das kleine Eheleben nicht aushielt und ihre romantischen Gefühle ausleben wollte, auch Theodor Fontanes Effi Briest (1895 erschienen) war es nicht vergönnt, ein ruhiges bürgerliches Leben zu führen.

Tragische Untergangsvisionen überwogen. Maurice Maeterlinck, Georges Rodenbach, Oscar Wilde, Hugo von Hofmannsthal, Rainer Maria Rilke, Thomas Mann, Joseph Roth und Marcel Proust: Allen gemeinsam war das Bewußtsein, einer zum Tode verurteilten Gesellschaft anzugehören. Der Machtergreifung durch die Bevölkerungsmassen standen diese Dichter skeptisch gegenüber. Sie hatten Angst vor drohenden Ich-Verletzungen, Anonymität und kriegerischen Katastrophen.

Ein Hauptwerk dieser krisenbewußten Untergangsliteratur schrieb der junge Thomas Mann mit seinem im Jahr 1900 – damals war er erst 25 Jahre alt – veröffentlichten Roman *Die Buddenbrooks*, der zunächst den Titel »Abwärts – Verfall einer Familie« tragen sollte und weitaus kürzer geplant war. Die Handlung spannt einen Bogen von 1835 bis 1877. Am Ende stirbt Hanno, der letzte dekadente Erbe des einst so erfolgreichen Lübecker Handelshauses, mit 15 Jahren an Typhus, und nur noch die zum zweiten Mal geschiedene Tochter des Patriarchen, Frau Permaneder, bleibt übrig. Am Schluß sitzen Frau Permaneder und ihre einstige Erzieherin Sesemi Weichbrodt am Tisch und sinnieren über den Familienuntergang: »Da aber kam Sesemi Weichbrodt am

100

death, in love with annihilation. There are reports that he saw a Germanic mythical world in the painting; when all is said and done he was more drawn to the north – like Richard Wagner and Caspar David Friedrich – to the icy seas of Scandinavia and Russia. He found the south less appealing – after all, his colleague Benito Mussolini had already entrenched himself there. Besides, his campaign to help his »blood brother« in North Africa – led by Rommel, »the Desert Fox« – was also not exactly successful. After the war the picture had disappeared from Hitler's collection and did not surface again in the art trade until 1980. Today it hangs in the Berlin National Gallery. The migrations of paintings are mysterious.

The second half of the 19th century is filled with contradictions. While Gustave Eiffel designed and built his controversial, later world-famous tower for the Paris World's Fair, backward-looking architects in Germany completed the Gothic towers of Cologne Cathedral and Ulm Minster. They thus destroyed the ruinlike aspects of cityscapes, which had been growing more pronounced through the centuries. Steel against stone, railroad tracks against Neuschwanstein romanticism. Castles against barricades. Royal houses that feared for their existence maintained not only castle ruins on the Rhine serving as weekend houses, but also built gigantic neo-Gothic castles, for instance in Hechingen-Hohenzollern and Schwerin. Falling back on historical models was supposed to substantiate, or even prove, their ancient God-given right to rule. But democratic forces were becoming more and more insistent and were increasingly supported by the public at large. Since the French Revolution, everywhere in Europe, there had been sporadic riots as liberation movements grew in popularity.

The first Democrats in Germany, still part of the student organization movement, gathered on 27 May 1832 in the ruin of Hambach Castle. A remarkable event that probably had less to do with the fact that the gathering place was a ruin than with the relatively liberal region. However, the authorities became scared when they saw the unexpectedly large crowd streaming toward the hitherto completely insignificant castle hill. Even the organizers found that the event was more than they could handle. When a ramshackle wall that enthusiastic activists had climbed collapsed, several people were even injured and some were killed. After this, repression actually increased. It was not until 1848 that the first freely elected German Parliament assembled in the Paulskirche in Frankfurt.

In the second half of the 19th century a new generation of poets and writers described their despondent fears of the future, which were permeated with ruins. While Jules Vernes still hopefully dreamed of utopian journeys to the moon, to the center of the earth and 20,000 leagues under the sea, and Karl May told tall tales in his Wild West adventure books, Gustave Flaubert sat somberly at his desk in melancholy reflection about the toxic state of society. Madame Bovary had to die because she could not bear her petty married life and wanted to live her romantic feelings to the full, and the protagonist of Theodor Fontane's *Effi Briest* (published in 1895) was also not granted the privilege of leading a peaceful bourgeois existence.

Tragic visions of doom predominated. Maurice Maeterlinck, Georges Rodenbach, Oscar Wilde, Hugo von Hofmannsthal, Rainer Maria Rilke, Thomas Mann, Joseph Roth and Marcel Proust: What all of them had in common was the awareness of belonging to a society that was condemned to death. These writers viewed the fact that the masses had seized power skeptically. They were afraid their ego would be traumatized, and feared anonymity, war and catastrophes.

A seminal work of this crisis-conscious literature of doom was written by the young Thomas Mann. It was the novel *Buddenbrooks*, published in 1900 – he was only 25 at the time – initially to be titled »Downhill – Decline of a Family« and planned as a much shorter work. The action spans a period between 1835 and 1877. At the end Hanno, the last, decadent heir of the once so successful Lübeck firm, dies of typhoid fever at the age of 15, and only the patriarch's twice-divorced daughter, Frau Permaneder, is left. As the novel concludes, Frau Permaneder and her former governess Sesemi Weichbrodt sit at table and ruminate about the downfall of the family: »But then Sesemi Weichbrodt raised herself up to the table, as high as she could. She stood on her tiptoes, craned her neck, rapped on the tabletop – and her bonnet quivered on her head. ›It is so!‹ she said with all her strength and dared them with her eyes. There she stood, victorious in the good fight that she had waged all her life against the onslaughts of reason. There she stood, hunchbacked and tiny, trembling with certainty – an inspired, scolding little prophet.« [Thomas Mann, *Buddenbrooks. The Decline of a Family*, trans. John E. Wood (New York: Alfred A. Knopf, 1993)]

Architecture was of less interest to Thomas Mann. In his novel the façades and spaces of the town of Lübeck are merely suggested. It was the air raids of World War II that saw to the destruction of the »Buddenbrook House«, reducing its original – the house of Thomas Mann's own parents – to rubble.

Tisch in die Höhe, so hoch sie nur irgend konnte. Sie stellte sich auf die Zehenspitzen, reckte den Hals, pochte auf die Platte, und die Haube zitterte auf ihrem Kopfe. ›Es ist so!‹ sagte sie mit ihrer ganzen Kraft und blickte alle herausfordernd an. Sie stand da, eine Siegerin in dem guten Streite, den sie während der Zeit ihres Lebens gegen die Anfechtungen von seiten ihrer Lehrerinnenvernunft geführt hatte, bucklig, winzig und bebend vor Überzeugung, eine kleine, strafende, begeisterte Prophetin.«

Die Architektur interessierte Thomas Mann weniger. In seinem Roman erscheinen die Fassaden und Räume der Stadt Lübeck nur angedeutet. Für den Untergang des »Buddenbrook-Hauses« sorgten erst die Bombenangriffe des Zweiten Weltkriegs, die dessen Vorbild – Thomas Manns eigenes Elternhaus – in Schutt und Asche legten.

In seinen frühen Erzählungen berichtete Thomas Mann oft von Menschen, die sich zu sehr mit Figuren aus Richard Wagners Opern identifizieren und dadurch in der Realität weltfremd wirken oder gar scheitern. Ein schönes Beispiel dafür ist *Tristan*. Hier wird die Geschichte eines fragwürdigen, jungen Romanciers erzählt, der lungenkrank im Sanatorium »Einfried« weilt. Spinell ist sein Name. Im Laufe der Handlung lernt er die Gattin des erfolgreichen Großkaufmanns Klöterjahn kennen, die ebenfalls hier einsitzt und sich ziemlich langweilt. Aus der Schwärmerei für diese Frau heraus entwickelt Spinell einen abgrundtiefen Haß auf ihren Ehemann und deren gemeinsames Kind. In völliger Verkennung der Lage schreibt er einen langen Brief an Herrn Klöterjahn, in dem er wütend mit ihm, seiner Tätigkeit und seinem Lebensstil abrechnet. Der Großkaufmann, im Augenblick zu Besuch in »Einfried«, stellt den unverschämten, weit über das Ziel hinausgeschossenen jungen Mann zur Rede und beschimpft ihn, wie es einem lebensprühenden und machtvollen Realitätsteufel zusteht. Spinell, der romantische Träumer – der »Tristan« –, ist gegen die Wand gelaufen. Kleingeschrumpft zur Maus schleicht er am Ende der Geschichte hinaus in den Sanatoriumsgarten und begegnet dort einer schwarzen Gestalt, die den kleinen Klöterjahn im Kinderwagen vor sich herschiebt. Die Wirklichkeit schlägt erneut in Form dieses kleinen Ungeheuers auf den armen Weltfremdling ein: »In diesem Wägelchen aber saß das Kind, saß Anton Klöterjahn der Jüngere, saß Gabriele Eckhofs dicker Sohn!

Er saß, bekleidet mit einer weißen Flausjacke und einem großen weißen Hut, pausbäckig, prächtig und wohlgeraten in den Kissen, und sein Blick begegnete lustig und unbeirrbar demjenigen Herrn Spinells … Da aber geschah das Gräßliche, daß Anton Klöterjahn zu lachen und zu jubeln begann, er kreischte vor unerklärlicher Lust, es konnte einem unheimlich zu Sinne werden.

Gott weiß, was ihn anfocht, ob die schwarze Gestalt ihm gegenüber ihn in diese wilde Heiterkeit versetzte oder was für ein Anfall von animalischem Wohlbefinden ihn packte. Er hielt in der einen Hand einen knöchernen Beißring und in der andern eine blecherne Klapperbüchse. Diese beiden Gegenstände reckte er jauchzend in den Sonnenschein empor, schüttelte sie und schlug sie zusammen, als wollte er jemand spottend verscheuchen …

Da machte Herr Spinell kehrt und ging von dannen. Er ging, gefolgt von dem Jubilieren des kleinen Klöterjahn, mit einer gewissen behutsamen und steif-graziösen Armhaltung über den Kies, mit den gewaltsam zögernden Schritten jemandes, der verbergen will, daß er innerlich davonläuft.«

Kurz vor dem Ersten Weltkrieg umkreiste Thomas Mann erneut seine Lieblingsthemen »Weltfremdheit, Dekadenz, Untergang und Tod« in seiner Novelle *Tod in Venedig*. Jetzt ist es der alleinstehende, alternde Schriftsteller, »Gustav Aschenbach, oder von Aschenbach«, der durch eine Schreibkrise aus München, seinem eigentlichen Lebensmittelpunkt, vertrieben wird und ausgerechnet das sommerlich heiße Venedig zum Fluchtort wählt. Da er allein unterwegs ist, hat er kaum Möglichkeiten, sich mit jemandem auszutauschen. Einsam, mißgelaunt und skeptisch begegnet er der fremdartigen Gästewelt des Grandhotels auf dem Lido ausschließlich als Voyeur. Eigentlich besteht Aschenbach nur aus Blicken. Als jener Knabe, dem seine letzte Sehnsucht gilt, in sein Blickfeld gerät, weiß er noch nicht, daß dieser Tadzio sein Todesengel sein wird: »Es war eine Gruppe halb und kaum Erwachsener, unter der Obhut einer Erzieherin oder Gesellschafterin um ein Rohrtischchen versammelt: Drei junge Mädchen, 15- bis 17jährig, wie es schien, und ein langhaariger Knabe von vielleicht vierzehn Jahren. Mit Erstaunen bemerkte Aschenbach, daß der Knabe vollkommen schön war.«

Im Laufe der Erzählung beschränkt sich der Kontakt zwischen dem Dichter und dem Knaben weiterhin nur auf Blicke. Am Ende, als Aschenbach am Strand stirbt, sieht er in dem Knaben einen Gott aus dem Jenseits, der ihn erlöst: »Am Rande der Flut verweilte er sich, gesenkten Hauptes mit einer Fußspitze Figuren im feuchten Sand zeichnend, und ging dann in die seichte Vorsee, die an ihrer tiefsten Stelle noch nicht seine Knie benetzte, durchschritt sie, lässig vordringend, und gelangte zur Sandbank. Dort stand er einen Augenblick, das Gesicht der Weite zuge-

In his early stories Thomas Mann often told of people who overidentify with figures from Richard Wagner's operas and therefore seem inexperienced in the ways of the world, or even fail. A fine example of this is »Tristan«. It is the story of a questionable young novelist, Spinell, a patient at the tuberculosis sanatorium »Einfried«. As the story unfolds he meets the wife of the successful merchant Klöterjahn, also a patient here, and rather bored. Out of Spinell's infatuation for this woman grows a profound hatred for her husband and the couple's child. Totally misinterpreting the situation, Spinell writes a long, incensed letter to Herr Klöterjahn in which he settles accounts with him, his work and his lifestyle. The merchant, who is currently visiting »Einfried«, takes the impudent young man to task for overshooting the mark, as one would expect of a stolid pragmatist who is bursting with life and powerful. Spinell, the romantic dreamer – »Tristan« – has come up against a brick wall. At the end of the story, mortified, he steals out into the sanatorium garden and meets a black figure pushing Klöterjahn Junior in a baby carriage. Reality strikes the unworldly wretch in the shape of this little monster: »… in this perambulator sat the child – sat Anton Klöterjahn, Jr., Gabriele Eckhof's fat son!

There he sat among his cushions, in a white wooly jacket and a big white hat – chubby, magnificent and robust; and his eyes, unabashed and alive with merriment, looked straight into Herr Spinell's … But at that very moment the appalling thing happened: Anton Klöterjahn began to laugh – he screamed with laughter, he squealed, he crowed: it was inexplicable. It was positively uncanny.

God knows what had come over him, what had set him off into this wild hilarity: the sight of the black-clad figure in front of him perhaps, or some sudden spasm of sheer animal high spirits. He had a bone teething ring in one hand and a tin rattle in the other, and he held up these two objects triumphantly into the sunshine, brandishing them and banging them together, as if he were mockingly trying to scare someone off. …

And Herr Spinell turned on his heel and walked back the way he had come. Pursued by the infant Klöterjahn's jubilant shrieks, he walked along the gravel path, holding his arms in a careful, prim posture; and something in his gait suggested that it cost him an effort to walk slowly – the effort of a man intent upon concealing the fact that he is inwardly running away.« [Thomas Mann, *Death in Venice and Other Stories,* translated and with an introduction by David Luke (New York: Random House, 1988)]

Shortly before World War I, Thomas Mann again addresses his favorite themes, »unworldliness, decadence, downfall and death« in his novella *Death in Venice*. Now it is the aging writer Gustav Aschenbach, or von Aschenbach, who is driven by a writer's block from Munich, the actual center of his life, and chooses to escape to a sweltering Venice. Since he is traveling alone, he has few opportunities to talk to anybody. Lonely, ill-tempered and skeptical, he encounters the exotic world of guests at the Grand Hotel on the Lido solely as a voyeur. Actually Aschenbach consists only of what he sees. When the young boy who is the object of his last yearning enters his field of vision, he is as yet unaware that this Tadzio will be his angel of death: »It was a group of adolescent and barely adult young people, sitting round a cane table under the supervision of a governess or companion: three young girls, of fifteen to seventeen as it seemed, and a long-haired boy of perhaps fourteen. With astonishment Aschenbach noticed that the boy was entirely beautiful.«

As the story continues, the interaction between the writer and the boy continues to be limited only to visual contact. At the end, when Aschenbach dies on the beachfront, he sees the boy as a god from the hereafter who delivers him: »At the edge of the sea he lingered, head bowed, drawing figures in the sand with the point of one foot, then walked into the shallow high water, which at its deepest point did not even wet his knees; he waded through it, advancing easily, and reached the sandbar. There he stood for a moment looking out into the distance. … Divided from the shore by a width of water, divided from his companions by proud caprice, he walked, a quite isolated and unrelated apparition, walked with floating hair out there in the sea, in the wind, in front of the nebulous vastness. …«

Aschenbach dies in his deck chair. His last, fading vision is of the boy, his angel of death: »But to him it was as if the pale and lovely soul-summoner out there were smiling to him, beckoning to him; as if he loosed his hand from his hip and pointed outwards, hovering ahead and onwards, into an immensity rich with unutterable expectation. And as so often, he set out to follow him …« [Thomas Mann, *Death in Venice and Other Stories,* translated and with an introduction by David Luke (New York: Random House, 1988)]

Like seismographs these artists predicted future world tremors. The question remains open whether any of them really foresaw how tremendous the approaching military eruptions and fate-

kehrt … Vom Festlande geschieden durch breite Wasser, geschieden von den Genossen durch stolze Laune, wandelte er, eine höchst abgesonderte und verbindungslose Erscheinung, mit flatterndem Haar dort draußen im Meere, im Winde, vorm Nebelhaft-Grenzenlosen.«

Aschenbach stirbt in seinem Liegestuhl. Seine letzten, verlöschenden Blicke gelten dem Todesengel-Knaben: »Ihm war aber, als ob der bleiche und liebliche Psychagog dort draußen ihm lächle, ihm winke; als ob er, die Hand aus der Hüfte lösend, hinausdeute, vorausschwebe ins Verheißungsvoll-Ungeheure. Und, wie so oft, machte er sich auf, ihm zu folgen …«

Wie Seismographen sagten diese Künstler die zukünftigen Weltbeben voraus. Ob einer von ihnen wirklich ahnte, wie gewaltig die bevorstehenden militärischen Eruptionen und Untergangskatastrophen sein würden, bleibt offen. Tatsächlich ließen sich die Massen – aber auch viele Intellektuelle, Schriftsteller, Dichter, Philosophen, Maler und Komponisten – verführen, aufrühren und in sinnlose Schlachten schicken. Die Saat der Französischen Revolution war endgültig aufgegangen. Im Namen der demokratischen Vernunft überfielen und vernichteten militarisierte Massen, betrunken gemacht von nationalistischen Parolen, fremde Länder und Völker. Die Erbfeinde mußten bluten, die nationale Ehre wiederhergestellt werden.

Das Ziel Hitlers im Zweiten Weltkrieg bestand nicht nur in der Erringung der Weltherrschaft, sondern auch darin, die vermeintlich Schuldigen am bisherigen, dekadenten Zustand der Gesellschaften – die Juden, Andersdenkenden und Krüppel – auszurotten. Noch nie wurden in Kriegen so viele Menschen – vor allem unbeteiligte Zivilisten – getötet wie während der beiden Weltkriege. Noch nie zuvor wurden so viele Gebäude und Städte zerstört.

Warum Adolf Hitler Richard Wagners Opern verehrte und die Schriften von Thomas Mann auf den Index setzte, ja sogar öffentlich verbrennen ließ (oder den Vorgang nicht verhinderte), gehört zu den rätselhaften Irrationalitäten dieses so banalen Ungeheuers. War er in Wirklichkeit ein fehlgeleiteter Romantiker (wie Rüdiger Safranski in seinem *Romantik*-Buch schreibt), der Untergänge und Ruinen herbeisehnte (dann hätte er auch *Die Buddenbrooks* durchgehen lassen können!), oder war er nur ein dummdreister Politiker, der zynisch-grandios und pathetisch mit den Sehnsüchten seiner Zeitgenossen spielte?

Auch in den Kompositionen, die nach Wagners *Ring* entstanden, brodelt es. Man grub, angeregt von den Schriften Sigmund Freuds, tief im ruinösen Unterbewußtsein, führte archäologische Schächte bis in das archaische Höhlensystem, in dem auch C. G. Jungs kollektive Archetypen vermutet wurden. Die Sexualität, der Urtrieb und Motor aller Evolution, wurde enttabuisiert, in Experimenten untersucht und in der Kunst expressionistisch oder nüchtern-sachlich dargestellt. *Salome* und *Elektra* von Richard Strauss begeisterten das Opernpublikum. In der Gefühlswelt beider Frauen lagen Liebe, Lust, Haß, Rache und Mord nah beieinander. Blutrünstig phantasieren sie sich singend, gurrend, tobend, schreiend in erotische Todes- und Ruinenwelten hinein. Mit der Figur der Salome konnte das bürgerliche Opernpublikum zum ersten Mal die Ekstasen einer wilden, hexenhaft-ungehemmten Frau studieren. Ihre sexuelle Lust steigert sich so weit, daß es ihr am Ende egal ist, ob sie einen lebendigen oder toten Männermund küßt. Noch nie in der Musikgeschichte wurde obszöne Perversität so eindeutig und unverhüllt dargestellt wie bei Richard Strauss.

Hier ist sie also wieder, die Ruine eines Körpers in Form des blutig-abgeschlagenen Kopfes von Jochanaan (Johannes der Täufer), der die überzüchtet-dekadente Verkommenheit im Palast des Herodes anprangerte, wie später der mönchische Hetzprediger Savonarola die Zustände in Florenz der aufblühenden Renaissance. Aber außer Herodes, der seine Stieftochter Salome liebt und begehrt, nimmt keiner die christlichen Prophezeiungen und Weltuntergangsdrohungen ernst. Am Ende ist er es, der das Blutbad dieser Nacht vollendet, indem er ausruft: »Man töte dieses Weib!« Wie Beilhiebe fällt die Musik über die erotisch verzückte Salome her: »Ich habe deinen Mund geküßt, Jochanaan …«, singt sie immer wieder. Es waren die Lippen eines abgeschlagenen Kopfes. Rausch, Ekstase, entfesselte Sinnlichkeit und Untergangsruinen – diese Mischung traf den Nerv der Zeit genau.

Auch Erich Wolfgang Korngolds Oper *Die tote Stadt* aus dem Jahr 1920 gräbt in der Vergangenheit und in Abgründen der erotischen Wünsche, wenn auch nicht mehr so expressionistisch steil wie bei Richard Strauss. Der Roman *Das tote Brügge* von Georges Rodenbach (1892), der dem Libretto zugrunde liegt, beginnt mit folgenden Worten: »Der Abend sank herab. Es dunkelte bereits in den Gängen der großen, stillen Wohnung, und die Scheiben umflorten sich.

Hugo Viane machte sich zum Ausgehen fertig, wie stets gegen Ende des Nachmittags. Beschäftigungslos und einsam, wie er war, verbrachte er den ganzen Tag in seinem Zimmer, einer großen Stube im ersten Stock, deren Fenster auf den Quai du Rosaire gingen. Das Haus lag mit der Front am Quai und spiegelte sich in seinem Wasser.«

ful catastrophes would be. The masses – but also many intellectuals, writers, poets, philosophers, painters and composers – actually did allow themselves to be seduced, stirred up and sent into senseless battles. The seed of the French Revolution had finally germinated. In the name of democratic reason militarized masses, intoxicated by nationalist slogans, attacked and destroyed other countries and peoples. The blood of hereditary enemies had to be shed and national honor restored.

Hitler's objective in World War II was not only to achieve world domination, but also to eradicate those he considered to be responsible for the hitherto decadent state of society – the Jews, the dissidents and the cripples. Never before were so many people – and especially uninvolved civilians – killed as during the two world wars. Never before were so many buildings and cities destroyed.

The question as to why Adolf Hitler admired Richard Wagner's operas and placed the writings of Thomas Mann on the index, and even had them publicly burned (or did not prevent the process), is one of the puzzling irrationalities about this banal monster. Was he really – as Rüdiger Safranski writes in his book about Romanticism – a misguided romantic who longed for scenes of destruction and ruins (in which case he could also have allowed *Buddenbrooks* to go unchallenged!) or was he merely an impertinent politician who played cynically, grandiosely and histrionically with the longings of his contemporaries?

The compositions that were created after Wagner's *Ring* also seethe with turmoil. Inspired by the writings of Sigmund Freud, people dug deep in the ruins of the subconscious, excavated archeological shafts into the archaic system of caves in which, it was suspected, C. G. Jung's collective archetypes were hidden. Sexuality, the ur-instinct and driving force of all evolution, was freed from its taboos, studied in experiments and represented in art expressionistically or soberly and objectively. Richard Strauss' *Salome* and *Electra* thrilled the opera-going public. In the emotional world of both women, love, desire, hatred, revenge and murder exist side by side. Bloodthirsty, singing, cooing, raging, screaming, they fantasize their way into erotic worlds of death and ruins. In the character of Salome the middle-class opera-going public was able for the first time to study the ecstasies of a wild, witchlike, uninhibited woman. Her sexual desire becomes so intense that in the end she does not care if she kisses the mouth of a living or a dead man. Never before in the history of music had obscene perversity been represented as explicitly and nakedly as in the work of Richard Strauss.

So here it is again, the ruin of a body: the bloody, severed head of Jochanaan (John the Baptist), who denounced the overbred, decadent depravity in the palace of Herod, just as the inflammatory monkish preacher Savonarola later indicted conditions in Florence during the peak of the Renaissance. But except for Herod, who loves and desires his stepdaughter Salome, no one takes Jochanaan's prophecies and threats of the approaching end of the world seriously. At the end it is he who ends the bloodbath of this night by exclaiming: »Let this woman be killed!« Like blows from an axe the music comes down on an erotically enraptured Salome: »I have kissed your mouth, Jochanaan …«, she keeps singing. They were the lips of a severed head. Intoxication, ecstasy, unleashed sensuality and the ruins of doom – a mixture that reflected the spirit of the times perfectly.

Erich Wolfgang Korngold's opera *The Dead City,* dated 1920, digs in the past and in precipices of erotic desires, though they are no longer as expressionistically extreme as in the work of Richard Strauss. The novel *Bruges-la-Morte* by Georges Rodenbach (1892), on which the libretto is based, begins with the following words: »The declining day darkened the corridors of the large, quiet apartment, and the windowpanes had misted over.

Hugues Viane made his preparations for the walk he always took toward the end of the afternoon. Solitary and unoccupied as he was, it was his custom to spend the day in his spacious second-floor room, whose windows looked out on the Quai du Rosaire. The house faced the quay and was reflected in its water.«

In the opera the main character is called Paul. As in the novel, his still very young, beautiful wife has recently died. Ever since, the widower has been mourning the past. One day, during one of his walks, he meets a woman who resembles his wife to a T. He invites her home and begins a relationship with her. Soon he realizes that the similarity is only skin-deep. His late wife was angelic, charming and good-natured, while his mistress is malicious and deceitful. Besides, she is leading a very frivolous life as a singer and adventuress. The relationship becomes more tense. In the end Paul strangles his false mistress with the cut-off hair of his dead wife. It remains open whether the plot actually ended like this, since just before the curtain finally falls the mistress again appears in the doorway. Did Paul merely dream it all?

In der Oper heißt die Hauptfigur Paul. Wie in dem Roman auch, ist vor kurzem seine noch sehr junge, natürlich wunderschöne Ehefrau gestorben. Seitdem trauert der Witwer der Vergangenheit nach. Eines Tages lernt er bei seinen Spaziergängen eine Frau kennen, die seiner Ehefrau aufs Haar gleicht. Er lädt sie zu sich nach Hause ein und beginnt mit ihr ein Verhältnis. Bald stellt sich heraus, daß die Ähnlichkeit nur äußerlich ist. Seine verstorbene Frau war engelgleich, liebenswürdig und gutmütig, die Geliebte dagegen ist bösartig und hinterlistig, außerdem führt sie ein sehr leichtfertiges Leben als Sängerin und Lebedame. Das Verhältnis nimmt an Spannung zu. Am Ende erdrosselt Paul die falsche Geliebte mit den abgeschnittenen Haaren seiner toten Ehefrau. Ob die Handlung tatsächlich so stattgefunden hat, bleibt offen, da kurz bevor sich der Vorhang endgültig schließt, die Geliebte wieder in der Tür erscheint. Hat Paul alles nur geträumt?

In der Erzählung wird Brügge als tote, ruinenhafte Stadt beschrieben: »Oh, stets dieses Grau der Brügger Straßen!

Hugo fühlte seine Seele diesem Grau mehr und mehr unterliegen. Diese rings verbreitete Stille, diese menschenleere Öde wirkte ansteckend auf ihn … Oh, diese Winterabende in Brügge! … Und während er die große mystische Stadt durchquerte, erhob er die Augen zu den barmherzigen Türmen mit ihren Trost spendenden Glocken, zu den Heiligen Jungfrauen, die an jeder Straßenecke ihre Arme dem reuigen Sünder öffnen, sie selbst von Wachslichtern und Rosen umgeben, die unter einer Glasglocke stehen, wie tote Blumen in einem gläsernen Sarge … Jede Stadt ist ein Seelenzustand, und kaum hat man sie betreten, so teilt sich dieser Zustand mit und geht in uns über…«

Bei Korngold ist wenig vom sentimentalen Kitsch der Erzählung zu spüren. Die Musik klingt wie eine Collage aus Wagner, Strauss und Puccini. Der Komponist war ein Könner. Es wundert daher nicht, daß er in Hollywood – dorthin mußte er als Jude zu Beginn der Nazizeit fliehen – eine erfolgreiche Karriere als Filmkomponist machte.

Auch über die Malerei brachen die Zerstückelungskatastrophen herein. Archaische Vereinfachung und psychologische Ausleuchtung der menschlichen Seele brachten vollkommen neue Ausdrucksräume und Bildkompositionen hervor. Pablo Picasso erfand mit seinen *Demoiselles d'Avignon* (1907) den Kubismus, die Brücke-Maler zerfetzten mit wilden Pinselstrichen Körper, Landschaften und Städte, die Futuristen entdeckten die Dynamik von Großstädten, Flugzeugen und Kriegen, Kandinsky kreuzte russische Mystik mit »Blauem Reiter«, Oskar Kokoschka sezierte menschliche Gesichter und Gefühle. Ludwig Meidner, Max Beckmann und Otto Dix stellten die Verletzungen, die sie im Ersten Weltkrieg erlitten hatten, zur Schau.

Ruinen überall, allerdings nicht mehr vom Sonnenuntergangslicht romantisch verklärt, sondern grell, gezackt und wild zerfurcht. Die Zeiten waren härter geworden, und das Sterben vollzog sich im Granatenlicht, schnell, rücksichtslos und mit einer bisher nicht gekannten Brutalität.

Wer heute Strawinskys *Sacre du Printemps* hört, ist erstaunt, wie der Komponist 1913 die Zeitstimmung auf den Punkt brachte und musikalisch den Ersten Weltkrieg visionär antizipierte. Man hat das Gefühl, daß in dieser Komposition nicht mehr uralte russische Bräuche zum Ausdruck kommen, sondern daß moderne Menschen von maschinenartigen Rhythmen, die wie Gewehrsalven klingen, zerfetzt werden. In der »Frühlingsweihe« stirbt keine einzelne »Jungfrau«, sie tanzt sich auch nicht zu Tode, sondern Tausende junger Männer erschießen sich gegenseitig. Der uralte Brauch, Naturgötter durch einen Opfertanz um Fruchtbarkeit zu bitten, wird hier in den orgiastischen Exzess getrieben. Am Ende sind die zerfurchten Landschaften übersät mit blutenden Gliedmaßen, abgeschlagenen und zerfetzten Schädeln.

Bevor die Kriegskatastrophe des Ersten Weltkriegs über Europa hereinbrach, wurden die Menschen von einer Meldung aufgeschreckt, die sie in ihren Zukunftshoffnungen elementar erschütterte: der Untergang der *Titanic*! Mit spektakulärem Reklameaufwand war der bisher größte Schnelldampfer der Welt auf der Belfaster Werft Harland & Wolff vom Stapel gelaufen. Das neue Passagierschiff sollte für die britische Reederei White Star Line die Strecke Southhampton–New York–Southhampton befahren. 270 Meter lang und 30 Meter breit war das neue Schmuckstück! Die Passagiere wurden, wie damals üblich, in drei Klassen untergebracht. Vor allem in der ersten Klasse herrschte eleganter Luxus. Es gab vornehme Speise- und Ballsäle, Restaurants, Bars, Rauchsalons, Schwimmbäder, Gymnastikräume, Theater und Kinos. Eine schwimmende Luxusstadt.

Bei seiner Jungfernfahrt von England nach Amerika war das Schiff nur zur Hälfte besetzt. Warum es in der Nacht vom 14. auf den 15. April 1912 zur Kollision mit einem Eisberg kam, darüber streiten sich Historiker und Ingenieure bis heute. Die meisten Fachleute sind sich darüber einig, daß dem Kapitän Edward John Smith, der kurz vor seiner Pensionierung stand, die Hauptschuld anzulasten sei. Er fuhr mit voller Geschwindigkeit in die Eisbergzone ein. Stunden vorher

40. Titanic: das stolze Ankündigungsplakat, 1912.
41. Hans Dieter Schaal, der traurige Untergang, Collage mit Zeichnung, 2010.

40. Titanic: the proud introductory poster, 1912.
41. Hans Dieter Schaal, the tragic sinking, collage with drawing, 2010.

In the story Brügge is described as a dead, ruined town: »Oh, the constant gray of the streets of Brügge!

Hugues felt his soul succumbing more and more to this gray. This silence all around him, the dreariness of these deserted streets felt infectious … Oh, these winter evenings in Brügge! … And as he crossed the big, mystical town, he raised his eyes to the merciful towers with their comforting bells, to the Blessed Virgins who open their arms to the repenting sinner at every street corner, surrounded by wax candles and roses standing under a bell jar like dead flowers in a glass coffin … Every city is a psychological state, and no sooner have we entered it than this state communicates itself to us and becomes part of us…«

In Korngold's opera the sentimental kitsch of the story is less noticeable. The music sounds like a collage of Wagner, Strauss and Puccini. The composer was an expert in his field. It is therefore no surprise that he had a successful career as a composer of film music in Hollywood, where he had been forced to flee as a Jew at the beginning of the Nazi period.

Painting, too, experienced catastrophes of dismemberment. Archaic simplification and the psychological illumination of the human soul produced completely new forms of expression and pictorial compositions. Pablo Picasso, with his *Demoiselles d'Avignon* (1907), invented Cubism, the painters of the Brücke (the Bridge) ripped to shreds bodies, landscapes and towns with wild brushstrokes, the Futurists discovered the dynamics of cities, planes and wars, Kandinsky crossed Russian mysticism with »der Blaue Reiter« (»the Blue Rider«), Oskar Kokoschka dissected human faces and emotions. Ludwig Meidner, Max Beckmann and Otto Dix displayed the traumas they had experienced in World War I.

Ruins everywhere, though no longer romantically transfigured by the light of the setting sun, but garish, jagged and wildly furrowed. Times had become rougher, and dying took place by the light of shellfire, quick, ruthless and characterized by a hitherto unknown brutality.

Those who hear Stravinsky's *Sacre du Printemps* today are astonished how, in 1913, the composer got to the heart of the mood of the times and musically anticipated World War I in his vision. One has the feeling that this composition no longer expresses ancient Russian traditions, but rather that modern men are torn to shreds by machinelike rhythms that sound like volleys of gunfire. In »The Rite of Spring« not a single »virgin« dies, nor does she dance herself to death. Rather, thousands of young men shoot each other. The ancient tradition of imploring the gods of nature for fertility by a sacrificial dance is here driven to orgiastic excess. At the end the furrowed landscapes are strewn with bleeding limbs, and severed and shattered skulls.

Before the catastrophe of World War I descended upon Europe, people were startled by an announcement that deeply shook their hopes for the future: the sinking of the *Titanic*! The hitherto largest express liner in the world, built in Belfast by Harland & Wolff, had been launched after a spectacularly costly advertising campaign. The new passenger steamer was to sail the South-

waren bei ihm per Funk Meldungen anderer Schiffe eingetroffen, die vor den gefährlichen Hindernissen warnten. Aber der Kapitän drosselte weder die Maschinen, noch änderte er seinen Kurs; wahrscheinlich wollte er einen neuen Geschwindigkeitsrekord aufstellen. Als ihm schließlich vom Beobachterposten der riesige Eisberg gemeldet wurde, war es zu spät für ein Ausweichmanöver. Das Schiff schrammte an dem steinharten Hindernis entlang und wurde dabei fast der ganzen Länge nach aufgerissen. Über zwei Stunden zog sich der Untergang hin, genügend Zeit, um Notrufsignale zu versenden und das Schiff zu evakuieren. Aber es waren nicht genügend Rettungsboote an Bord. 63 Boote wären notwendig gewesen. Es gab jedoch nur 20. Das ist der Grund dafür, daß 1490 bis 1517 der 2200 an Bord befindlichen Personen den Tod fanden. Unter den Opfern waren viele damals prominente und reiche Persönlichkeiten. Die meisten Frauen und Kinder wurden gerettet.

Plötzlich hatte der bisher euphorische Fortschrittsglaube einen Riß bekommen. Das Schiff galt als unsinkbar. Niemand hatte sich wirklich vorstellen können, daß ein ganz banaler Eisberg, der weithin sichtbar im vollkommen wellenlosen Meer schwamm, einem Schnelldampfer dieser Größenordnung und dieses technischen Standards zum Verhängnis werden könnte. Der Kapitän ging mit seinem Schiff unter. Niemand konnte ihn mehr befragen. Spekulationen über Spekulationen wurden angestellt. Überlebende meldeten sich zu Wort, Berichte und Romane erschienen. Nach dem Zweiten Weltkrieg versuchten Forschungsboote, das Wrack zu orten. Schließlich wurde eine amerikanische Firma unter der Leitung von Jean-Louis Michel und Robert Ballard am 1. September 1985 fündig, und Tauchroboter filmten die veralgten Schiffsreste am Meeresgrund in 3803 Meter Tiefe.

Es wundert nicht, daß auch Hollywood aufmerksam wurde. 1997 kam der grandiose Monumentalfilm *Titanic* von James Cameron mit Leonardo di Caprio und Kate Winslet in die Kinos und brach alle Rekorde. Über eine Milliarde Besucher sahen den Film. Am Ende übertrumpfte er den bisherigen Rekordhalter *Jurassic Parc* um einige Millionen. Der Film beginnt mit einer langen Tauchfahrt. Wir sehen die berühmteste, legendärste aller Schiffsruinen auf dem Grund des Atlantiks liegen. Suchscheinwerfer beleuchten den Bug, dann die Reling, an deren Nachbildung sich später das ungleiche Liebespaar im Film treffen wird. Die Frau hat überlebt und erzählt die Geschichte des Untergangs, bei dem ihr Geliebter den Tod findet. Das künstliche Licht hellt für Momente die ewige Nacht am Grund des Meeres auf. Gespenstischer Blick in ein Jenseits, das uns bisher verborgen war. Hier unten also verwest diese Vergangenheit. Längst sind die einst so stolzen Technikoberflächen zu einem Teil des Meeresbodens geworden. Die Natur hat sich das Schiff einverleibt wie ein Muschelriff, eine abgesunkene Walleiche. Von den Menschen allerdings fehlt jede Spur. Ihre Körper haben sich längst aufgelöst.

hampton–New York– Southhampton route for the British shipping company White Star Line. The new gem was 270 meters long and 30 meters wide! As was customary at the time, there were three classes of passengers. Especially in the first-class sections, there was an atmosphere of elegant luxury. There were tasteful dining rooms and ballrooms, restaurants, bars, smoking rooms, swimming pools, gyms, theaters and cinemas. A floating luxury city.

During its maiden voyage from England to America the ship was only half booked. Even now historians and engineers are still arguing why, in the night from the 14th to the 15th of April 1912, there was a collision with an iceberg. Most experts agree that the main blame must be laid on Captain Edward John Smith, who was close to retirement. He came into the iceberg zone at full speed. Hours earlier, he had received radio messages from other ships warning of dangerous obstacles. But the captain neither throttled the engines nor changed his course; probably he wanted to establish a new speed record. When the observation post finally reported the giant iceberg, it was too late for evasive action. The ship sideswiped the rock-hard obstacle and its entire length was ripped open. The sinking of the ship took over two hours, time enough to send emergency signals and to evacuate the ship. But there were not enough lifeboats onboard. Sixty-three boats would have been necessary. However, there were only 20. That is the reason why between 1,490 and 1,517 of the 2,200 persons on board drowned. Among the victims were many then prominent and wealthy public figures. Most of the women and children were saved.

Suddenly a rift had developed in a hitherto euphoric belief in progress. The ship was considered unsinkable. Nobody had really been able to imagine that an ordinary iceberg, floating in a completely smooth ocean and visible from a great distance, could prove to be the undoing of an express liner of this size and this technical standard. The captain went down with his ship. No one could question him anymore. There were all kinds of speculations. Survivors came forward, reports and novels were published. After World War II research vessels tried to locate the wreck. Finally, on 1 September 1985, an American company headed by Jean-Louis Michel and Robert Ballard struck it lucky, and underwater robots filmed the algae-covered remains of the ship on the ocean floor at a depth of 3,803 meters.

No wonder Hollywood sat up and took notice. In 1997 James Cameron's grandiose, monumental film *Titanic* with Leonardo di Caprio and Kate Winslet was first screened, breaking all records. Over a billion viewers saw the film. In the end it trumped the former record holder, *Jurassic Park,* by several millions. The film begins with a long dive. We see the most famous, most legendary of all ship's ruins lying at the bottom of the Atlantic Ocean. Searchlights light the bow, then the railing near whose reconstructed version the unequal pair of lovers is to meet later in the movie. The woman has survived and tells the story of the shipwreck in which her lover was drowned. For moments the artificial light illuminates the eternal night at the bottom of the ocean. It is a ghostly look into another world that has hitherto been hidden from us. So that is where this past is decomposing. The once so impressive surfaces of the mechanical parts have long since become part of the ocean floor. Nature has swallowed up the ship like a reef covered with mussels, or an oak submerged in an embankment. There is no trace of the people, however. Their bodies disintegrated long ago.

7. Katastrophenzeiten

Das 20. Jahrhundert, die beiden Weltkriege

Nie gab es ein größeres Ruinenfeld in Europa als nach dem Zweiten Weltkrieg. Wer jetzt noch von Romantik, Wagner oder Neuschwanstein sprach, mußte verrückt sein. Alle Gedanken, die literarisch oder musikalisch mit Untergangsphantasien spielten, konnten den Vergleich mit der brutalen Realität nicht aushalten. Fast alle deutschen Städte waren 1945 zerstört und ausgelöscht. Deutschland, ein einziges Trümmermeer, unbenutzbar, abweisend, tödlich. Es gab keinen Schutz mehr vor Kälte und Nässe. Not und Hunger gehörten zum Alltag. Viele Männer waren gefallen, abgestürzt, erfroren oder kamen als Krüppel aus dem Krieg zurück. Hunderttausende litten in Gefangenenlagern. Stunde 0. *Draußen vor der Tür.*

Es war die Zeit der Trümmerfrauen, sie krempelten ihre Ärmel hoch und begannen damit, die Schuttberge wegzuräumen. Kaum jemand konnte sich damals vorstellen, daß es in Deutschland einmal wieder ein normales Leben geben würde.

1940 hatte die deutsche Luftwaffe begonnen, englische Städte – darunter London und Coventry – zu bombardieren. Kurz darauf erwiderte die Royal Air Force die Angriffe und bombardierte deutsche Städte aus der Luft. Dabei verfolgte die britische Regierung unter Churchill zwei Ziele, zum einen die Zerstörung waffenproduzierender Industrie und wichtiger Verkehrsverbindungen, zum anderen die Auslöschung kulturell wertvoller, historisch geprägter Altstädte, die von den Engländern als Biotop des Nazigedankenguts (Beispiel: Nürnberg!) angesehen wurden. Warum in all dem aggressiven Chaos die wertvollsten und unersetzlichsten Architekturzeugnisse wie der Kölner und der Mainzer Dom, das Ulmer und das Freiburger Münster unzerstört blieben, stellt sich heute immer noch als Rätsel dar und grenzt an ein Wunder. Alle einsam in der Landschaft verteilten Architekturkunstwerke – wie Neuschwanstein, Herrenchiemsee, die Wieskirche, Neresheim, Zwiefalten, Schussenried – hatten, strategisch gesehen, größere Überlebenschancen als Kulturgüter, die inmitten von Städten standen – wie etwa Stadtschlösser. Es grenzt ebenfalls an ein Wunder, daß der Mittelteil der Würzburger Residenz mit den unersetzlich wertvollen Deckengemälden Tiepolos die britischen Luftangriffe weitgehend heil überstand. Die Seitenflügel der Residenz erlitten dagegen schwere Schäden, ebenso wie die gesamte Innenstadt.

Generell lautete die Devise der Engländer: Alle deutschen Städte mit mehr als 100 000 Einwohnern müssen ausgelöscht werden, später senkte man die Zahl auf 80 000, dann auf 50 000. Negative Höhepunkte der alliierten Vernichtungsorgien waren die Stadtzerstörungen von Hamburg und Dresden. Bei den apokalyptischen Feuerstürmen kamen unzählige Zivilisten – meist Frauen, Kinder und Greise – ums Leben. Wer heute Photos und Filmaufnahmen der verkohlten und verstümmelten Leichen sieht, kann sich dem Entsetzen, der Wut und der Trauer nicht entziehen. Erst am 24. März 1945 befahl Churchill das Ende der Luftangriffe. Die Bilanz lautete: 593 000 Tote (meist Zivilisten), 13 Millionen Obdachlose (meist Zivilisten) und 400 Millionen Kubikmeter Trümmer.

Inzwischen sind zahlreiche Bücher und Dokumentationen zum Thema »Luftangriffe auf deutsche Städte« veröffentlicht worden. Im Fernsehen vergeht keine Woche ohne einen Film über das untergegangene Hamburg oder die einstige Schönheit Dresdens. Überlebende wurden befragt, Bomberpiloten, verantwortliche Generäle und Politiker. Die weltgeschichtliche Katastrophe hat an Transparenz zugenommen, aber nichts von ihrem tragischen Charakter verloren. Nachfolgend zähle ich einige der wichtigsten deutschen Städte auf, die zwischen 1940 und 1945 Luftangriffe erleiden mußten und dabei mehr oder weniger zerstört wurden. Eine Liste, eine Karteikarte, ein nüchternes Dokument …

Lübeck: Es gab nur einen einzigen Angriff auf die Stadt in der Nacht vom 28. auf den 29. März 1942. 11 % der historischen Altstadt wurden dabei zerstört. / Hamburg: Der erste Angriff auf den Hafenbereich fand am 18. Mai 1940 statt. Bei den schlimmsten Luftangriffen britischer Bomber am 24./25. Juli und am 2./3. August 1943 wurde fast die gesamte Innenstadt zerstört. Dabei kamen 37 000 Menschen ums Leben. / Bremen: Zwischen 1940 und 1945 erlitt die Stadt 181 Luftangriffe. Insgesamt wurden 58 % der Bausubstanz zerstört. / Bremerhaven: 52 Luftangriffe. 97 % der Innenstadt waren zu Kriegsende zerstört. / Berlin: Zwischen dem 7. Juni 1940 und dem 21. April 1945 erlitt die Stadt 310 Fliegerangriffe. 30 000 Wohnhäuser, das waren zwei Drittel der gesamten Bausubstanz, fielen in Schutt und Asche. / Braunschweig: 40 Luftangriffe. Am Ende des Krieges betrug die Zerstörung der Stadt 90 %. / Emden: Erst am 6. September 1944 wurde die bis dahin verschonte Stadt durch einen einzigen Luftangriff fast völlig zerstört. / Hannover: 88

7. Times of catastrophe

The 20th century, the two world wars

There has never been a more terrible field of ruins in Europe than after the Second World War. Those who now still spoke of romanticism, Wagner or Neuschwanstein must be insane. None of the ideas that played with fantasies of doom in literary or musical form could bear comparison with reality. In 1945 almost all German cities were in ruins and obliterated. Germany was one huge ocean of ruins, unusable, chilly, deadly. There was no longer any protection against the cold and humidity. Poverty and hunger were part of daily existence. Many men had been killed, had crashed or frozen to death, or returned from the war as invalids. Hundreds of thousands suffered in POW camps. Zero hour, described in Borchert's play *Draußen vor der Tür* (*Out Yonder*).

It was the era when women rolled up their sleeves and began to clear away the mountains of rubble. Hardly anyone at the time could imagine that there would ever be a normal life in Germany again.

In 1940 the German Luftwaffe had started bombing British towns – including London and Coventry. Shortly thereafter the Royal Air Force reciprocated the attacks and bombed German cities. The Churchill government had two objectives – one, to destroy the German weapons industry and important road and rail connections, and two, to obliterate culturally valuable, historical old cities that the British considered to be the habitat of Nazi ideology (for instance, Nuremberg!). It is still puzzling, and almost a miracle, why in all the aggressive chaos the most valuable and irreplaceable architectural testimonials – such as the Cologne and Mainz cathedrals, and the Ulm and Freiburg minsters – were left intact. From a strategic point of view all isolated architectural works of art that were scattered in the landscape – such as Neuschwanstein, Herrenchiemsee, the Wieskirche Pilgrimage Church, Neresheim, Zwiefalten, Schussenried – had greater chances of survival than did cultural assets that were located within cities – for instance, city palaces. It is also a quasi-miracle that the central part of the Würzburg Residence with the irreplaceable, valuable ceiling frescoes of Tiepolo survived the British air raids comparatively undamaged. The side wings of the Residence on the other hand were severely damaged, as was the entire inner city.

In general the motto of the British was: All German cities with more than 100,000 Inhabitants must be obliterated. Later the number was lowered to 80,000, then to 50,000. Low points of the Allied orgies of destruction were the destruction of Hamburg and Dresden. In the apocalyptic firestorms, countless civilians – largely women, children and old people – were killed. Seeing photographs and films of the charred and mutilated bodies today, it is hard not to feel horror, rage and grief. Churchill did not order the end of air raids until 24 March 1945. This meant a total of 593,000 dead (mostly civilians), 13 million homeless (mostly civilians) and 400 million cubic meters of rubble.

In the meantime a great deal of documentation and numerous books have been published on the topic »Air raids against German cities«. On TV not a week goes by without a movie about Hamburg before it was destroyed or the former beauty of Dresden. Survivors have been interviewed, bomber pilots, generals and politicians who were in charge. The world-scale catastrophe has become more transparent but has lost none of its tragic character. Below, I give the names of some of the most important German cities that sustained damage in air raids between 1940 and 1945 and were more or less destroyed. A list, a file card, a sober document …

Lübeck: There was only a single attack on the city in the night from 28 to 29 March 1942. 11 percent of the historic old part of the town was destroyed. / Hamburg: The first air raid on the harbor area took place on 18 May 1940. In the worst air raids by British bombers on 24 / 25 July and 2 / 3 August 1943, almost the entire inner city was destroyed. A total of 37,000 people were killed. / Bremen: Between 1940 and 1945 the city was bombed 181 times. In toto, 58 percent of the buildings were destroyed. / Bremerhaven: 52 air raids. By the end of the war, 97 percent of the inner city had been destroyed. / Berlin: Between 7 June 1940 and 21 April 1945 there were 310 air raids against the city. Two-thirds of all the houses, or 30,000 residential buildings, were reduced to rubble and ashes. / Braunschweig: 40 air raids. At the end of the war, 90 percent of the city had been destroyed. / Emden: The city, which had been spared up till then, was almost completely destroyed on 6 September 1944 in a single air raid. / Hanover: 88 air raids. 85 percent of the inner city was destroyed. / Hildesheim: After several smaller attacks, the city was almost completely destroyed during a day air raid on 22 March 1944. 85 percent of the old buildings were in ruins. / Osnabrück: 300 air raids. But only on 13 September 1944 was the inner city completely destroyed. 85 percent of the buildings were reduced to rubble. / Wilhelmshaven: 100 major air

Luftangriffe. 85 % der Innenstadt wurden zerstört. / Hildesheim: Nach mehreren kleineren Angriffen wurde die Stadt bei einem Tagesangriff am 22. März 1944 fast völlig zerstört. 85 % der alten Bausubstanz lagen in Schutt und Asche. / Osnabrück: 300 Luftangriffe. Doch erst am 13. September 1944 wurde die Innenstadt fast völlig zerstört. 85 % der Gebäude lagen in Trümmern. / Wilhelmshaven: 100 Großangriffe. Im Oktober 1944 die schwersten. Dabei wurde die Stadt fast völlig zerstört. / Wolfsburg: Mehrere Luftangriffe. Aber erst Ende 1944 wurde die Stadt durch Fliegerbomben zu zwei Dritteln zerstört. / Aachen: Zwischen 1940 und 1945 insgesamt 70 Luftangriffe. Aber erst der Angriff am 11. April 1944 zerstörte die Stadt zu zwei Dritteln. / Bochum: 12 Großangriffe, der schwerste am 4. November 1944. Dabei wurde die Stadt zu 90 % zerstört. / Bonn: Insgesamt 80 Luftangriffe. Der schwerste am 18. Oktober 1944. Dabei wurden 30 % der Stadt zerstört. / Dortmund: Bei 137 Großangriffen wurde die Stadt zu 95 % zerstört. / Dülmen: Durch einen einzigen Angriff am 22. März 1945 zu 95 % zerstört. / Düren: Durch einen einzigen Luftangriff am 16. November 1944 zu 90 % zerstört. / Düsseldorf: Insgesamt 243 Luftangriffe, davon 9 schwere. Die Hälfte der Stadt wurde zerstört. / Duisburg: 299 Luftangriffe. Weitgehende Stadtzerstörung. / Essen: 272 Luftangriffe. Der schwerste im März 1945. Die gesamte Altstadt wurde vollständig zerstört. / Hagen: 52 Luftangriffe. 100 % Zerstörung. / Hamm: 55 Luftangriffe. 60 % Zerstörung. / Köln: 262 Luftangriffe. Zu 95 % zerstört. Nur der Dom blieb weitgehend verschont. / Münster: 102 Luftangriffe, der letzte eine Woche vor Einmarsch der amerikanischen und englischen Truppen. 91 % der Stadt wurden zerstört. / Soest: 30 Bombenangriffe. 62 % der Stadt wurden zerstört. / Solingen: 68 Luftangriffe. Die Innenstadt wurde nahezu vollständig zerstört. / Wesel: Durch 4 Bombenangriffe, der letzte am 20. März 1945, wurde die Stadt zu 97 % zerstört. / Xanten: Durch vier Bombenangriffe, der letzte am 8. März 1945, zu 85 % zerstört. / Rostock: Zahlreiche Bombenangriffe. Die schlimmsten in den Nächten vom 23. bis zum 28. April 1942. 40 % der Innenstadt wurden zerstört. / Neustrelitz: Ende April 1945 zu 85 % zerstört. Das Schloß allerdings wurde erst nach dem Krieg auf Veranlassung der russischen Besatzung geschleift. / Potsdam: Am 14. April 1945 zu 47 % zerstört. / Halberstadt: Am 8. April 1945 zu 75 % zerstört. / Magdeburg: Zahlreiche alliierte Bombenangriffe. Beim schwersten am 16. Januar 1945 wurde die Stadt zu 90 % zerstört. / Darmstadt: Bei 35 Luftangriffen wurde die Innenstadt nahezu vollständig zerstört. / Frankfurt am Main: Seit 1943 insgesamt 8 Luftangriffe. Am 29. Januar und am 25. September 1944 wurde die gesamte Innenstadt fast vollständig zerstört. / Fulda: Die Stadt wurde durch Luftangriffe zu 10 % zerstört. / Giessen: Insgesamt 27 Luftangriffe. Dabei wurden 67 % der Innenstadt zerstört. / Hanau: Erst kurz vor Kriegsende, vier Wochen vor Einmarsch der Amerikaner, erfolgte ein schwerer Luftangriff, der fast die gesamte Innenstadt zerstörte. / Kassel: Zahlreiche Luftangriffe. Insgesamt 78 % der Stadt wurden zerstört. / Wiesbaden: Insgesamt 66 Luftangriffe, davon 28 schwere. Ein besonders verheerender am 2. Februar 1945. / Koblenz: Insgesamt 25 Luftangriffe zwischen dem 22. April 1944 und dem 29. Januar 1945. 85 % der Stadt wurden zerstört. / Mainz: Der erste Luftangriff erfolgte am 12. / 13. August 1942, der letzte und schwerste am 27. Februar 1945. Nahezu die gesamte Innenstadt (mit Ausnahme des Domes) wurde zerstört. 80 % . / Trier: Insgesamt 20 Luftangriffe zwischen dem 14. August und dem 24. Dezember 1944. Die Innenstadt wurde dabei weitgehend zerstört. / Worms: Luftangriffe am 21. Februar und 18. März 1945 zerstörten 65 % der Stadt. / Saarbrücken: Insgesamt 30 Luftangriffe. Das Zentrum der Stadt wurde zu 90 % , die Randgebiete zu 60 % zerstört. / Breisach: Am Ende des Krieges zu 80 % zerstört. / Bruchsal: Ein großer Fliegerangriff zerstörte am 1. März 1945 die Stadt zu 80 % . / Freiburg im Breisgau: Ein einziger Bombenangriff am Abend des 27. November 1944 zerstörte die Innenstadt – mit Ausnahme des Münsters – fast vollständig. / Freudenstadt: Diese Stadt blieb während des Krieges von Luftangriffen verschont. / Friedrichshafen: 11 Tag- und Nacht-Luftangriffe. Der schlimmste am 28. April 1944 vernichtete die Altstadt vollständig. / Heilbronn: Zahlreiche Bombenangriffe, der schlimmste in der Nacht vom 4. auf den 5. Dezember 1944. Dabei wurde die Altstadt zu 84 % zerstört. / Karlsruhe: Insgesamt 57 Luftangriffe. 21 % der Stadt wurden zerstört und 51 % schwer beschädigt. / Mannheim: Die Stadt wurde als eine der ersten, am 16. Dezember 1940 aus der Luft angegriffen. 80 % der Innenstadt und 57 % des gesamten Stadtgebiets wurden zerstört. / Pforzheim: Erster Luftangriff am 1. April 1944. Der letzte am 23. Februar 1945. Dabei wurde der historische Stadtkern von britischen Bombern völlig zerstört. 17 000 Menschen fanden dabei den Tod. / Reutlingen: Bei drei Luftangriffen 1945 wurden 20 % der Innenstadt zerstört. / Stuttgart: Erster Luftangriff am 25. August 1940. Zahlreiche weitere Angriffe folgten. Die schlimmsten im Juli 1944, dabei wurden 68 % der Bebauung zerstört. / Ulm: 22 Luftangriffe. Ein Großangriff am 17. Dezember 1944 zerstörte 80 % der Innenstadt. / Aschaffenburg: 7 Luftangriffe 1944 / 45. 23 % Zerstörung. / Augsburg: Insgesamt 21 Luftangriffe. Beim schwersten in der Nacht vom 25./26. Februar 1944 wurden 90 % der Stadt zerstört. /

42. »The Blitz«. Deutsche Fliegerangriffe auf London. Das Photo zeigt Löscharbeiten in der Queen Victoria Street am 11. 5. 1941. Die Folge: Nahezu alle deutschen Städte wurden zwischen 1940 und 1945 von alliierten Bombern zerstört.

42. »The Blitz«. German air raids on London. The photograph shows firemen at work in Queen Victoria Street at 11. 5. 1941. The consequence: nearly all German cities were destroyed by Allied bombers between 1940 and 1945.

raids. The severest took place in October 1944. The city was almost completely destroyed. / Wolfsburg: Several air raids. But it was not until the end of 1944 that two-thirds of the city was destroyed by bombs. / Aachen: Between 1940 and 1945, a total of 70 air raids. It was the attack on 11 April 1944, however, that destroyed two-thirds of the city. / Bochum: 12 major air raids, the worst on 4 November 1944. 90 percent of the city was destroyed. / Bonn: A total of 80 air raids. The heaviest on 18 October 1944. 30 percent of the city was destroyed. / Dortmund: During 137 major attacks up to 95 percent of the city was destroyed. / Dülmen: 95 percent destroyed by a single attack on 22 March 1945. / Düren: 90 percent destroyed by a single air raid on 16 November 1944. / Düsseldorf: A total of 243 air raids, nine of them severe. Half of the city is destroyed. / Duisburg: 299 air raids. Extensive destruction of the city. / Essen: 272 air raids. The heaviest in March 1945. The entire old part of the town is completely destroyed. / Hagen: 52 air raids. Destruction: 100 percent. / Hamm: 55 air raids. Destruction: 60 percent. / Cologne: 262 air raids.

43. Das brennende Lübeck, am Morgen nach dem verheerenden Luftangriff in der Nacht vom 28. auf 29. März 1942.

43. Lübeck burning, the morning after the devastating air raid on the night of 28 March 1942.

Donauwörth: Am 11. und 19. April 1945 wurden durch Luftangriffe 75 % des Stadtzentrums zerstört. / Ingolstadt: Insgesamt 12 Luftangriffe. 10 % der Stadt wurden zerstört. / Konstanz: Blieb verschont, wahrscheinlich wegen der Nähe zur Schweizer Grenze. / München: Die Stadt mußte 66 Luftangriffe ertragen. Am Ende des Krieges waren 60 % der Altstadt, 74 % im Bahnhofsviertel und 70 % in den Außenbereichen vernichtet. / Nürnberg: Insgesamt 28 Luftangriffe zwischen 1942 und 1945. 50 % der Wohnbauten und 75 % der öffentlichen Bauten sind am Ende des Krieges zerstört. / Rothenburg ob der Tauber: Am 31. März 1945 trifft es auch diese romantische Stadt. 28 % der Gebäude wurden dabei zerstört. / Schweinfurt: 22 Luftangriffe vor allem auf die Industrieanlagen der Stadt. 80 % davon waren am Ende des Krieges zerstört. / Schwerin: Weitgehend unzerstört. / Würzburg: Nach 5 kleineren Luftangriffen wurde die Stadt von britischen Bombern am 16. März 1945 zu 75 % zerstört.

So endete Hitlers Wahntraum von der Weltherrschaft und dem Sieg der nordisch-germanischen Rasse in einem apokalyptischen Inferno, das die schlimmsten Visionen Matthias Grünewalds und Hieronymus Boschs noch weit übertraf. 1944 herrschte wirklich ein »Totaler Krieg«, wie Hitler ihn befohlen hatte. Der Führer selbst hat bei näher rückenden Fronten, wie Joachim Fest in seinem Buch über Albert Speer schreibt: »…die Absicht verfolgt, das Reich in eine Zivilisationswüste zu verwandeln: Fabriken und Kanalisationssysteme sollten zerstört werden, die Lebensmittellager und die Telephonzentralen, die Unterlagen der Banken und die Grundbuchämter vernichtet werden. Zugleich verlangte Hitler, die vom Feind bedrohten Gebiete zu evakuieren, bis schließlich – dem Goebbels-Tagebuch zufolge – 17 Millionen Menschen auf den Straßen herumirrten.«

Es gab keine Fronten mehr, und die Zivilbevölkerung war genauso von Bomben, Feuer und Zerstörung betroffen wie die Soldaten in Stalingrad, Afrika oder an der Westfront. Tiefflieger jagten Flüchtlinge und versprengte Soldaten. Die Alliierten wollten das Ende erzwingen. Von heute aus gesehen, bleibt es völlig unverständlich, warum diese wahnwitzige Kriegsmaschinerie nicht von innen heraus zerstört werden konnte. Aber selbst ein Graf Stauffenberg scheiterte an banalen Zufällen. So mußte sich der Diktator am 30. April 1945 mit Zyankali und einem Revolverschuß im Führerbunker selbst töten, nachdem er noch seine langjährige Geliebte Eva Braun geheiratet hatte. Die letzten Vertrauten waren angewiesen, die beiden Leichen mit Benzin zu übergießen und zu verbrennen, damit der Verursacher der Apokalypse spurlos aus der Welt verschwände und nicht als Mumie in irgendeinem Wachsfigurenkabinett lande.

Am 9. Mai 1945 unterschrieben Feldmarschall Keitel und Marschall Schukow im sowjetischen Hauptquartier die Gesamtkapitulation der Deutschen Streitkräfte. Am Tag vorher hatten bereits

Destruction: 95 percent. Only the cathedral was largely spared. / Münster: 102 air raids, the last of them one week before the invasion of the American and British troops. 91 percent of the city is destroyed. / Soest: 30 bomb attacks. 62 percent of the city is destroyed. / Solingen: 68 air raids. The inner city was almost completely destroyed. / Wesel: In four bomb raids, the last on 20 March 1945, 97 percent of the city was destroyed. / Xanten: 85 percent destroyed by four bomb raids, the last on 8 March 1945. / Rostock: Numerous bomb raids. The worst in the nights between 23 and 28 April 1942. 40 percent of the inner city was destroyed. / Neustrelitz: 85 percent destroyed at the end of April 1945. The castle, however, was not razed until after the war at the instigation of the Russian occupying army. / Potsdam: On 14 April 1945, 47 percent destroyed. / Halberstadt: On 8 April 1945, 75 percent destroyed. / Magdeburg: Numerous Allied bomb raids. During the heaviest on 16 January 1945, 90 percent of the city was destroyed. / Darmstadt: In 35 air raids, the inner city was almost completely destroyed. / Frankfurt am Main: A total of eight air raids beginning in 1943. On 29 January and on 25 September 1944, the entire inner city was almost completely destroyed. / Fulda: 10 percent of the city was destroyed by air raids. / Giessen: A total of 27 air raids. 67 percent of the inner city was destroyed. / Hanau: Just briefly before the end of the war, four weeks before the American invasion, there was a major air raid that destroyed almost the entire inner city. / Kassel: Numerous air raids. In toto, 78 percent of the city was destroyed. / Wiesbaden: A total of 66 air raids, 28 of them major. An especially devastating attack on 2 February 1945. / Koblenz: A total of 25 air raids between 22 April 1944 and 29 January 1945. The city was 85 percent destroyed. / Mainz: The first air raid took place 12 / 13 August 1942, the last and heaviest on 27 February 1945. Almost the entire inner city (except for the cathedral) was 80 percent destroyed. / Trier: A total of 20 air raids between 14 August and 24 December 1944. Most of the inner city was destroyed. / Worms: air raids on 21 February and 18 March 1945 destroyed 65 percent of the city. / Saarbrücken: A total of 30 air raids. 90 percent of the center of the city and 60 percent of outlying areas are destroyed. / Breisach: 80 percent destroyed at the end of the war. / Bruchsal: A big air raid destroyed 80 percent of the city on 1 March 1945. / Freiburg im Breisgau: A single bomb raid on the evening of 27 November 1944 almost completely destroyed the inner city – with the exception of the minster. / Freudenstadt: This city was spared during the war. / Friedrichshafen: Eleven day and night attacks. The worst, on 28 April 1944, completely destroys the old part of town. / Heilbronn: Numerous bomb raids, the worst in the night of 4 to 5 December 1944. 84 percent of the old part of town was destroyed. / Karlsruhe: A total of 57 air raids. 21 percent of the town is destroyed and 51 percent is badly damaged. / Mannheim: The city was one of the first to be attacked from the air on 16 December 1940. 80 percent of the inner city and 57 percent of the entire urban area was destroyed. / Pforzheim: First air raid on 1 April 1944. The last on 23 February 1945. British bombers completely destroy the historic town center. A total of 17,000 people are killed. / Reutlingen: In three air raids in 1945, 20 percent of the inner city is destroyed. / Stuttgart: First air raid on 25 August 1940. Numerous additional attacks followed. The worst, in July 1944, destroyed 68 percent of the buildings. / Ulm: 22 air raids. A major attack on 17 December 1944 destroys 80 percent of the inner city. / Aschaffenburg: Seven air raids in 1944/45. 23 percent destruction. / Augsburg: A total of 21 air raids. During the heaviest, in the night from 25 / 26 February 1944, 90 percent of the city was destroyed. / Donauwörth: On 11 April and 19 April 1945, 75 percent of the city center is destroyed. / Ingolstadt: A total of 12 air raids. 10 percent of the city is destroyed. / Constance: Was spared, probably because it is close to the Swiss border. / Munich: The city had to endure 66 air raids. By the end of the war 60 percent of the old town, 74 percent of the area around the railroad station and 70 percent of the outlying areas were destroyed. / Nuremberg: A total of 28 air raids between 1942 and 1945. 50 percent of all residential buildings and 75 percent of the public buildings are destroyed by the end of the war. / Rothenburg ob der Tauber: On 31 March 1945 this romantic town is also attacked. 28 percent of the buildings are destroyed. / Schweinfurt: 22 air raids, primarily on the city's industrial plants. 80 percent of them are destroyed by the end of the war. / Schwerin: Intact for the most part. / Würzburg: After five smaller air raids, 75 percent of the city is destroyed by British bombers on 16 March 1945.

Thus Hitler's delusional dream of world domination and of the victory of the Nordic-Germanic race ended in an apocalyptic inferno that far exceeded the worst visions of Matthias Grünewald and Hieronymus Bosch. In 1944 there really was the »Total War« Hitler had ordered. As the front lines moved closer – Joachim Fest writes in his book about Albert Speer – the Führer himself »… had the intention of turning the Reich into a wasteland: Factories and sewer systems, stocks of food and telephone switchboards, bank records and land registry offices were to be destroyed. At the same time Hitler demanded that the regions threatened by the enemy be evacuated, until

Generaloberst Jodl und General Eisenhower in Reims ein gleichlautendes Dokument unterschrieben. Ab jetzt herrschte endgültig Waffenruhe an den europäischen Fronten.

Hat sich seit diesen Ereignissen unser Verhältnis zu Ruinen grundsätzlich geändert? Gewiß liegen heute längere und schwärzere Schatten über ihnen als zur Zeit der Romantik, aber ihre ursprüngliche Funktion, melancholische Mahnmale der »Vanitas« zu sein, haben sie im Grunde nicht verloren. Die vergangenen Ereignisse und Verirrungen gehören nach wie vor zu unserem kollektiven Gedächtnis. Es scheint geradezu falsch zu sein, das einmal Geschehene und Gewesene zu verdrängen oder gar zu vergessen, denn ohne die permanente Erinnerung etwa durch Ruinen oder Gedenkstätten bestünde die Gefahr einer Wiederholung mancher Irrwege und Katastrophen.

Am Ende dieses Kapitels will ich noch einen Blick auf die andere Seite des Globus, nach Japan, werfen. Auch dort tobte der Zweite Weltkrieg. Die Japaner führten sich im fernen Osten ähnlich brutal und elitebewußt auf wie die deutschen Nazis, sie überfielen China, Hongkong und Singapur. Nachdem sie 1941 sogar – ohne Kriegserklärung – die amerikanische Flotte in Pearl Harbor angegriffen hatten, entschloß sich Amerika dazu, in Japan die ersten Atombomben der Menschheitsgeschichte einzusetzen.

Am frühen Morgen des 6. August 1945 erreichte das amerikanische Bomberflugzeug seinen Zielort über Hiroshima, und genau um 8:15 Uhr wurde die erste Atombombe der Menschheitsgeschichte – zynisch »Little Boy« genannt – ausgelöst. Sekunden später lag die bisher völlig unzerstörte japanische Stadt in Schutt und Asche. Von den über 500 000 Bewohnern starben 260 000 sofort, 160 000 wurden verletzt und verseucht. Überlebende litten über Jahre an Strahlenschäden und Krebs. Mißgeburten häuften sich jahrzehntelang. Drei Tage später, am 9. August 1945, erfolgte über der Stadt Nagasaki ein zweiter Atombombenabwurf. Wegen schlechter Sicht verfehlte die Bombe ihr eigentliches Ziel, die Mitsubishi-Waffenfabrik, und explodierte über der Innenstadt. Andere topographische Verhältnisse als in Hiroshima führten dazu, daß hier »nur« etwa die Hälfte der Stadt zerstört und 36 000 der 200 000 Einwohner unmittelbar nach der Explosion starben. Die Folgen jedoch waren genauso verheerend wie in Hiroshima: Vier Monate nach der Explosion starben weitere 75 000 Menschen, ein Jahr später noch einmal 75 000. Die Strahlenverletzungen waren derartig heimtückisch und schleichend, daß sie auch Jahre später noch zum Tode führen konnten.

Der Schock, den diese Ereignisse auslösten, führte dazu. daß Japan am 2. September 1945 kapitulierte und die Amerikaner das Land besetzten. Beide Städte wurden in den Nachkriegsjahren im modernen Stil wiederaufgebaut. Nur die wichtigsten historischen Bauten – Tempel und Burgen – rekonstruierte man originalgetreu. Natürlich gibt es heute in beiden Städten Gedenk-Orte, Tempel und Friedhöfe, die an die Katastrophen erinnern. Am eindrucksvollsten ist der weitgehend leere »Friedenspark« in Hiroshima, in dem nur ein einziges original erhaltenes Ruinengebäude – die »Atombombenruine« – als Mahnmal an die grausamen Ereignisse erinnert.

finally, according to Goebbels' diary, seventeen million people were wandering along the highways.«

There were no front lines anymore, and the civilian population was just as much affected by bombs, fire and destruction as the soldiers in Stalingrad, Africa or on the western front. Low-flying aircraft went after refugees and scattered soldiers. The Allies wanted to force the end. From today's perspective it is completely incomprehensible why this lunatic war machinery could not be destroyed from within. But even someone like Count von Stauffenberg failed due to trivial coincidences. Thus the dictator had to kill himself on 30 April 1945 in the Führerbunker with potassium cyanide and a revolver shot after first marrying his mistress of many years, Eva Braun. His last intimates were instructed to pour gasoline over the bodies and to burn them so that the man who had caused the apocalypse would vanish from the world without a trace and not land in some wax museum as a mummy.

On 9 May 1945 Field Marshal von Keitel and Marshal Zhukov signed the act of unconditional surrender of the German armed forces at the Soviet headquarters. On the day before Chief of Staff Jodl and General Eisenhower had already signed an identical document in Reims. From now on there was finally a cease-fire on the European fronts.

Has our attitude toward ruins fundamentally changed since these events? Certainly longer and darker shadows loom over them than in the era of Romanticism, but basically they have not lost their original function – to be melancholy reminders of »vanitas«. The events and aberrations of the past are still part of our collective memory. It seems to be absolutely wrong to repress or even to forget what took place or existed once, for if we did not have ruins or memorials as a permanent reminder, there would be the risk of repeating many mistakes and catastrophes.

As this chapter ends I want to take a look at the other side of the globe, Japan. World War II raged there as well. The conduct of the Japanese in the Far East was as brutal and as elitist as that of the German Nazis. They invaded China, Hong Kong and Singapore. In 1941, after they had even – without declaring war – attacked the American fleet in Pearl Harbor, America decided to use the first atomic bombs in human history in Japan.

In the early morning hours of 6 August 1945 the American bomber reached its destination over Hiroshima, and exactly at 8:15 a.m. it released the bomb – cynically named »Little Boy«. Seconds later the hitherto completely intact Japanese city was in ruins. Of its more than 500,000 inhabitants 260,000 died immediately, while 160,000 were injured and contaminated. Survivors suffered from radiation damage and cancer for years. Babies were born deformed for decades. Three days later, on 9 August 1945, a second atomic bomb was dropped over the city of Nagasaki. Because of poor visibility the bomb missed its actual target, the Mitsubishi arms factory, and exploded over the inner city. Because topographical conditions were different than in Hiroshima, »only« about half of the city was destroyed here and 36,000 of the city's 200,000 inhabitants died directly after the explosion. Yet the consequences were as devastating as in Hiroshima: Four months after the explosion an additional 74,000 people died, and so did another 75,000 a year later. The injuries from radiation were so insidious and delayed that they could cause death even years later.

The shock produced by these events led to Japanese capitulation on 2 September 1945. The Americans occupied the country. In the postwar years both cities were rebuilt in modern style. Only the most important historic buildings – temples and castles – were reconstructed true to the originals. Naturally there are memorial sites, temples and cemeteries in both cities today that remind people of the catastrophes. The most impressive is the largely empty »Peace Memorial Park« in Hiroshima, in which only a single original ruined building – the »A-Bomb Dome« – reminds visitors of the cruel events of the past.

8. Ruinen des Todes und des Grauens

Auschwitz und Erfurt, die Firma Topf & Söhne, Opfergedenkstätten

Die beiden Stahlprofile der Eisenbahnschienen in Auschwitz-Birkenau, die durch das dunkle Tor hindurchführen, sind zum bildlichen Synonym des gesamten Holocaust geworden. Hier fuhren die Züge aus ganz Europa ein, hier kam es zu den Selektionen, links diejenigen, die sofort in die Gaskammern geführt wurden und rechts die Arbeitsfähigen, die man in eine der niedrigen Holzbaracken brachte.

Zwischen dünnen, winterkahlen Pappeln sind die halbeingebrochenen Schornsteine der Vergasungskammern zu erkennen. Der weite Rest des Gebietes wird rhythmisiert von Betonpfosten, die in regelmäßigen Abständen Auflager für dünne Stacheldrahtlinien bilden. Wie steinerne Zeigefinger weisen die Schornsteine der ehemaligen Baracken zum Himmel. Ohne sie fiele es schwer, sich die tödliche Grausamkeit dieser Landschaftszone zu vergegenwärtigen. Hier hat man sich dazu entschlossen, Ruinen zu erhalten.

An der Stelle, wo sich das Denkmal befindet, endete der Weg für Hunderttausende von Juden. Vor allem alte Frauen und alte Männer, Schwangere, Kranke und Kinder hatten keine Überlebenschance. Ihr Tod war eine beschlossene Sache. Sie wurden zu den Gaskammern geführt, mußten sich ausziehen, alle Wertsachen und Gepäckstücke abgeben, danach in die als Duschräume deklarierten Gaskammern hinuntersteigen. SS-Aufseher verschlossen die Türen und warfen durch Öffnungen in der Decke die todbringenden Zyklon-B Gaskapseln ein.

Aus Angst vor den anrückenden Russen und Amerikanern hatten SS-Leute die Gebäude Ende 1944 selbst gesprengt, um die Spuren ihrer Schandtaten zu verwischen.

Erinnern wir uns: Die Eroberung Polens und die Vernichtung der dort ansässigen Bevölkerung, vor allem der drei Millionen Juden, war ein erklärtes Ziel der Politik Hitlers. Das »gereinigte Land« sollte Teil eines geplanten »germanisch-deutschen Siedlungsgebiet im Osten« sein. Am 20. Januar 1942 fand in Berlin die berühmt-berüchtigte, geheime »Wannseekonferenz« unter der Leitung des SS-Obergruppenführers und Generals der Polizei und gleichzeitigen Leiters des Reichssicherheitshauptamts, Reinhard Heydrich, statt. Hier wurden die letzten Maßnahmen zur »Endlösung der Judenfrage« besprochen und beschlossen. Da die meisten Juden in den osteuropäischen Ländern lebten, lag es – für die NS-Regierung – nahe, ein Gebiet in der Nähe von Krakau als Hauptvernichtungsort zu wählen.

Wie viele Juden letztlich in Auschwitz den Gastod fanden, wird nie genau zu ermitteln sein, da die SS keine Protokolle über die sofort Ermordeten anlegte. Anhand von anderen Dokumenten gehen Historiker heute von mindestens 1 100 000 Opfern aus. In den Archiven der Gedenkstätte haben sich Tausende von Kleidern, Koffern, Töpfen, Schuhen, Brillen, Prothesen und abgeschnittenen Haarbüscheln erhalten. Ferne Abgeschiedene.

Mir fällt das berühmte Gedicht *Todesfuge* von Paul Celan ein. »Der Tod ist ein Meister aus Deutschland ... Der Tod ist ein Meister aus Deutschland ... « Dann wieder denke ich an das Gedicht von Nelly Sachs über Auschwitz:

44. Auschwitz-Birkenau im Februar 2009. Von den ehemaligen Häftlingsbaracken stehen nur noch Grundmauern und Schornsteine.
45. Auschwitz-Birkenau. Im Vordergrund die Eisenbahnschienen, auf denen die Züge mit den Deportierten aus ganz Europa ankamen. Hier wurden die berüchtigten Selektionen durchgeführt.

44. Auschwitz-Birkenau in February 2009. Only the foundation walls and chimneys of the former prisoners' huts remain.
45. Auschwitz-Birkenau. In the foreground the railway lines which carried trains with deportees from all over Europe. This is where the infamous selection process took place.

8. Ruins of death and horror

Auschwitz and the company Topf & Söhne, builders of the furnaces of Auschwitz, Erfurt. Memorials for the victims

The two steel profiles of the railway tracks in Auschwitz-Birkenau that lead through the dark gate have become the graphic symbol of the entire Holocaust. This is where trains from all over Europe arrived, this is where selections were held: to the left, those who were immediately taken to the gas chambers, and to the right, those who were capable of working and were taken to one of the low wooden barracks. Visible between scrawny, winter-bare poplars are the half-collapsed chimneys of the gas chambers. The vast remainder of the area is rhythmically articulated by concrete posts that form supports for thin lines of barbed wire at regular intervals. The chimneys of the former barracks point skyward like stone forefingers. Without them it would be difficult to imagine the deadly cruelty of this landscape. Here the decision was made to preserve ruins.

The place where the memorial is located was the end of the road for hundreds of thousands of Jews. In particular, old women and old men, pregnant women, sick people and children had no chance of survival. Their death was a done deal. They were taken to the gas chambers, told to undress, hand over all valuables and luggage and then go down the stairs to the gas chambers, which were declared to be shower rooms. SS guards locked the doors and threw the deadly capsules of Cyclone B gas through openings in the ceiling.

Afraid of the approaching Russians and Americans, SS-men themselves blew up the buildings at the end of 1944 in order to eliminate the traces of their crimes.

Let us remember: The conquest of Poland and the annihilation of the local population, and particularly the 3 million Jews, was one of the stated objectives of Hitler's policy. The »cleansed land« was to be part of a planned »Germanic-German settlement area in the East«. On 20 January 1942 the infamous, secret »Wannsee Conference« took place in Berlin under the leadership of SS Obergruppenführer and General of the Police and simultaneous head of the Reichssicherheitshauptamt, Reinhard Heydrich. Here the last measures for the »Final solution of the Jewish question« were discussed and decided. Since most of the Jews lived in the Eastern European countries, the choice of a region near Kraków as the main extermination site – for the National Socialist government – was obvious.

It will never be possible to determine exactly how many Jews were ultimately gassed in Auschwitz, since the SS kept no protocols about those who were murdered immediately. Judging by other documents historians assume there were at least 1,100,000 victims. In the archives of the memorial site, thousands of clothes, suitcases, pots, shoes, glasses, prostheses and cut-off tufts of hair have been preserved. Distant departed ones.

Paul Celan's famous poem *Todesfuge* occurs to me. » ... Death is a master from Germany ... Death is a master from Germany ... « Then again I think of the poem by Nelly Sachs about Auschwitz:

»O die Schornsteine
Auf den sinnreich erdachten Wohnungen des Todes,
Als Israels Leib zog aufgelöst in Rauch
Durch die Luft –
Als Essenkehrer ihn ein Stern empfing
Der schwarz wurde
Oder war es ein Sonnenstrahl?

O die Schornsteine
Freiheitswege für Jeremias und Hiobs Staub –
Wer erdachte euch und baute Stein auf Stein
Den Weg für Flüchtlinge aus Rauch?

O die Wohnungen des Todes,
Einladend hergerichtet
Für den Wirt des Hauses, der sonst Gast war –
O ihr Finger,
Die Eingangsschwelle legend
Wie ein Messer zwischen Leben und Tod –
O ihr Schornsteine,
O ihr Finger,
Und Israels Leib im Rauch durch die Luft!«

Nachdem sie qualvoll erstickt waren, kamen SS-Leute und brachen den Toten die Goldzähne
aus den Mündern, danach wurden die Leichen in eigens dafür errichtete Krematorien geschafft.
Ausgedacht, geplant und erbaut wurden die typisch-deutschen, sehr effektiven Verbrennungsöfen in der Stadt Erfurt.
	Hier, in der Nähe des Bahnhofs, standen damals die Büros und Fabrikationshallen der Firma
Topf & Söhne. Ein Familienbetrieb in der zweiten Generation. Man hatte sich auf Brauereibedarf
und Krematorien spezialisiert. Einer der beiden Brüder trat früh der NSDAP bei und erhielt den
Auftrag, moderne Leichenverbrennungsöfen zu entwickeln. Die Ausführung überließ er einem bei
ihm angestellten, besonders findigen Ingenieur mit dem Namen Prüfer und konnte wenige Monate später den ersten Versuchsofen nach Auschwitz liefern. Herr Prüfer berichtete später seinem

46. Auschwitz-Birkenau. Die eingeschneiten Ruinen der Gaskammern, Februar 2009.
47. Auschwitz-Birkenau. Stacheldrahtzaun und Baracken.

46. Auschwitz-Birkenau. The snowbound ruins of the gas chambers, February 2009.
47. Auschwitz-Birkenau. Barbed-wire fence and huts.

»O the chimneys
On the ingeniously devised habitations of death,
When Israel's body drifted as smoke
Through the air—
Was welcomed by a star, a chimney sweep,
A star that turned black
Or was it a ray of sun?

O the chimneys!
Freedomway for Jeremiah and Job's dust—
Who devised you and laid stone upon stone
The road for refugees of smoke?

O the habitations of death,
Invitingly appointed
For the host who used to be a guest—
O you fingers,
Laying the threshold
Like a knife between life and death—

O you chimneys,
O you fingers,
And Israel's body as smoke through the air!«

[Nelly Sachs, *O the Chimneys: Selected Poems,* trans. Michael Hamburger, Christopher Holme, Ruth and Matthew Mead, and Michael Roloff (New York: Farrar Straus Giroux, 1968)]

After their victims had died an agonizing death by suffocation, SS men broke the golden teeth from their mouths. Then the bodies were taken to crematoria built especially for this purpose. The typically German, very effective furnaces were devised, planned and built in the city of Erfurt.

Here, near the railway station, once stood the offices and manufacturing plant of the company »Topf & Söhne«. A second-generation family business. They specialized in brewery requirements and crematoria. One of the two brothers joined the NSDAP early on and was commissioned to

Chef ganz begeistert vom erfolgreichen Einsatz. Das neue Krematorium war in der Lage, pro Tag mehr als 1000 Leichen zu verbrennen – ein Rekord. Dennoch reichte dies nicht aus. Man wollte mehr, viel mehr. Herr Prüfer arbeitete fieberhaft weiter, aber seine neuesten Kreationen – Krematorien mit permanent laufenden Leichen-Fließbändern – kamen wegen des Kriegsendes nicht mehr zum Einsatz. Nachdem sowjetische Soldaten 1945 Erfurt besetzt hatten und den Gebrüdern Topf ein Prozeß bevorstand, floh der eine Bruder in den Westen, der andere nahm sich im Garten seiner Villa in der Nacht vor dem Prozeßbeginn das Leben. Herr Prüfer wurde deportiert und starb wahrscheinlich Anfang der 1950er Jahre in einem sowjetischen Arbeitslager.

48–51. Ruinen der Firma Topf und Söhne in Erfurt kurz vor ihrem Abriß im April 2009. Hier wurden während der NS-Zeit die Verbrennungsöfen für die Konzentrationslager geplant und produziert.

48–51. Ruins of the Topf und Söhne factory in Erfurt, shortly before they were demolished in April 2009. During the NS era the furnaces for the concentration camps were planned and produced here.

develop modern furnaces for cremating corpses. He left the implementation to an especially resourceful engineer by the name of Prüfer, who was working for him, and was able to deliver the first experimental furnaces to Auschwitz a few months later. Herr Prüfer enthusiastically told his boss of the successful use of the furnaces. The new crematorium was capable of burning more than 1,000 bodies a day – a record. Nevertheless it was inadequate. They wanted more, much more. Herr Prüfer continued working feverishly, but his newest creations – crematoria with permanently running conveyor belts for corpses – could no longer be used because the war ended. After Soviet soldiers occupied Erfurt in 1945 and the Topf brothers were faced with a trial, one brother fled to the West, while the other took his life in the garden of his villa the night before the beginning of the trial. Herr Prüfer was deported and died, probably in the early 1950s, in a Soviet slave labor camp.

9. Ruinen der Täterbauten

West- und Atlantikwall, Nürnberger Reichsparteitagsgelände, Spuren der Berliner Speer-Bauten, Obersalzberg

Als Paul Virilio zwischen 1958 und 1965 die Westwall- und Atlantik-Bunker aus dem Zweiten Weltkrieg studierte und photographierte war er zunehmend fasziniert von ihrer unverschämten, schmucklosen Beton-Brutalität und ihrer passiven Aggressivität. Sie erschienen ihm wie Relikte einer Kriegsreligion, nahe den frühen, ruppigen Ritterburgen. Damals schrieb er: »Man gewahre in ihnen das Spiegelbild unserer eigenen Todesmacht, unserer eigenen Destruktivität, das Spiegelbild der Kriegsindustrie.«

Die Ausstellung der Photos 1976 im Centre Pompidou und sein gleichzeitig veröffentlichtes Buch über *Bunker-Archäologie* machten ihn schlagartig berühmt. Plötzlich verlor diese inzwischen lästig gewordene und teilweise ins Vergessen verdrängte Bunkerwelt ihren ausschließlich negativ besetzten Ausdruckswert und wurde als das erkannt, was sie eigentlich ist: eine obsessive Bauverwirklichung menschlicher Angst. Im Gegensatz zu Panzern etwa, die mobil gegen den Feind eingesetzt werden können, sind Bunker und Bunkerstellungen fest in den Boden eingegraben, getarnte Schußbastionen und bewohnbare Schutzräume in einem. Allerdings blieb in den Bunkern des West- und Atlantikwalls nur wenig Platz zum Wohnen und Schlafen übrig. Das Raumvolumen glich dem eines Panzers.

Die Zahlen der errichteten Bunker sind so erschreckend hoch, daß man sich noch heute darüber wundert: Am 630 Kilometer langen Westwall, der von der Schweizer Grenze bis in die Niederlande reichte, wurden insgesamt 18 000 Bunker erbaut, am späteren Atlantikwall waren es 8119, es wären noch wesentlich mehr geworden, wenn nicht die Invasion der Alliierten dem Bauwahn ein Ende bereitet hätte. (Den Bunker-Rekord hält übrigens bis heute – neben Israel – Albanien. Dort ließ Enver Hoxha etwa 600 000 Bunker an allen strategisch wichtigen Punkten des Landes errichten. Sie stehen dort noch heute.)

Beide militärische Verteidigungslinien – der West- und der Atlantikwall – nützten wenig, sie hielten die Invasionstruppen nur wenige Stunden auf. Da die Flak- und MG-Schützen in den Bunkern bis zu ihrem Tod wild schossen, war die Anzahl der Opfer, die sie forderten, zwar strategisch »unwichtig«, dennoch aber unverhältnismäßig hoch.

Nach dem Krieg versuchte man, viele dieser Bauten zu sprengen oder mit Erde zu überdecken. Die Sprengung gelang nur bei Bunkern mit dünneren Wänden und Decken. Vor allem bei den Atlantikbunkern scheiterten die Entsorgungsversuche an den enormen Beton- und Stahlmassen. So stehen viele von ihnen noch heute, manche sind in Schräglage gerutscht, teilweise im Sand eingesunken oder von Wanderdünen überdeckt. Andere werden von Tieren oder Wanderern als Unterkünfte benutzt. Ich selbst habe am Atlantikstrand einen Maler getroffen, der in einem Bunker wohnte und an schönen Tagen seine Kunstprodukte nach draußen stellte, um sie den vorbeiziehenden Touristen zum Kauf anzubieten.

Nachdem die örtlichen Gemeinde- und Stadtverwaltungen in den Bunkern und Bunkerruinen jahrzehntelang häßlich-lästige, manchmal auch gefährliche Kriegsreste sahen, schwenkte in letzter Zeit die Stimmung um, nicht zuletzt auch deswegen, weil sich zunehmend Naturschützer für ihren Erhalt einsetzen: im Schutz der Betonmauern haben sich im Lauf der Jahre seltene Pflanzen und Tiere angesiedelt. Seltsame Umkehrung der Bedeutung: Aus Aggressions- und Angsthüllen werden Schutzhüllen für bedrohte Naturwesen!

Damals, im Jahr 1976, war Virilio noch ein Pionier. Seine Photos machten deutlich, daß viele Atlantikbunker einen visuellen Reiz besitzen und in ihrer klar-brutalen Formensprache Festungsanlagen aus dem 19. Jahrhundert – etwa den Stadtbefestigungen von Ulm, die General von Prittwitz entworfen hat – gleichgestellt werden können. Wer die Betonklötze heute besucht, kann sie als Ruinen einstigen Größen- und Verteidigungswahns erleben, als künstliche Felsmassive oder als perverse Kunstwerke. Ihre steinerne Aufgeblasenheit und sperrige Unbenutzbarkeit wirken in Friedenszeiten lächerlich, absurd. Wie konnten Militärs im Zeitalter von Flugzeugen, Raketen und Atombomben der Meinung sein, daß diese steinzeitlichen Blöcke einen wirklichen Schutz bieten?

Skepsis beschlich auch Generalfeldmarschall Erwin Rommel, als er 1943 die Leitung des Atlantikwall-Ausbaus vom tödlich verunglückten Fritz Todt übernommen hatte. 1944 formulierte er seine Bedenken – gekoppelt mit heftigen Zweifeln am Endsieg – in einem Brief an Hitler. Ein Vorgang, den er bekanntlich mit seinem Leben bezahlen mußte. Wenige Monate, nachdem er den Brief abgeschickt hatte, wurde er während eines Krankenaufenthalts in seinem Heimatort Herrlingen bei Ulm von einer Regierungsdelegation aus Berlin besucht und zum Selbstmord gezwun-

9. Ruins of perpetrator buildings

The Siegfried Line and the Atlantic Wall, the Nuremberg Nazi Party Rally Grounds, Albert Speer, Obersalzberg

When Paul Virilio studied and photographed the World War II bunkers of the Siegfried Line and the Atlantic Wall between 1958 and 1965, he became increasingly fascinated by their shamelessly unadorned concrete brutality and their passive aggression. They seemed to him to be relics of a war religion, similar to the early, rough-looking medieval castles. At the time he wrote: »In them we perceive the mirror image of our own deadly power, our own destructiveness, the mirror image of the war industry.«

The 1976 exhibition of the photos in the Centre Pompidou and the book about »bunker archeology« he published at the same time made him famous overnight. Suddenly this bunker world, which had in the meantime become a nuisance and had been partially repressed from memory, lost its exclusively negative significance and was recognized as what it actually is: an obsessive expression, in the form of buildings, of human fear. Unlike tanks, for instance, which can be used against the enemy in mobile form, bunkers and bunker positions are firmly dug into the ground, a combination of camouflaged shooting bastions and inhabitable shelters. To be sure, there was little room for living and sleeping in the bunkers of the Siegfried Line and the Atlantic Wall. The space was as cramped as that inside a tank.

The number of bunkers built is so startlingly high that it still causes surprise today: Along the 630-kilometer-long West Wall, which stretched from the Swiss border as far as the Netherlands, a total of 18,000 bunkers were built. Along the later Atlantic Wall, there were 8,119, and the number would have been considerably higher if the Allied invasion had not put a stop to the delusional construction. (Incidentally, to this day – besides Israel – Albania holds the record for bunkers. This is where Enver Hoxha had about 600,000 bunkers built at all strategically important points of the country. They are still standing there today.)

Both military lines of defense – the Siegfried Line and the Atlantic Wall – were of little use; they stopped the invading troops for mere hours, hardly more. Since the anti-aircraft and MG gunners in the bunkers shot wildly up to their death, the number of victims they claimed, though strategically »of no importance«, was still disproportionately high.

After the war there were attempts to blow up many of these buildings or to cover them with dirt. Explosions only worked with bunkers that had thinner walls and ceilings. In the case of the Atlantic bunkers especially, attempts to dispose of them failed because of the enormous masses of concrete and steel. Thus many of them are still standing today. Some have slid till they sit at a tilt, partially sunk in the sand or covered by shifting dunes. Others are being used as shelters by animals or hikers. I myself met a painter on an Atlantic beach who lived in a bunker and, on fine days, displayed his artwork outside, offering it for sale to passing tourists.

After the local communal and municipal administrations had for decades regarded the bunkers and bunker ruins as ugly, annoying, and sometimes dangerous remnants of the war, their attitude has been changing in recent times. One reason for this is that increasingly environmentalists have expressed their commitment to their preservation: In the shelter of the concrete walls, rare plants and animals have established themselves as the years go by. A strange reversal: Bunkers built out of aggression and fear now protect endangered plant and animal life!

Back then, in 1976, Virilio was still a pioneer. His photographs clearly showed that many Atlantic bunkers have visual appeal. In their bold, brutal use of forms they are on a par with 19th century fortifications – for instance, the town fortifications of Ulm designed by General von Prittwitz. Those who visit the concrete blocks today can experience them as ruins of former megalomania, and a mania for defense, as artificial massifs or as perverse artworks. Their stony self-importance and unwieldly uselessness seems ludicrous, absurd in times of peace. In the age of airplanes, rockets and atomic bombs, how could the military believe that these Stone Age blocks would offer real shelter?

General Field Marshal Rommel, too, felt skepticism when, in 1943, he took over the expansion of the Atlantic Wall from Fritz Todt, who had died in an accident. In 1944 he expressed his reservations – coupled with violent doubts about a final victory – in a letter to Hitler. As we know, he had to pay for this with his life. A few months after he had sent the letter, a government delegation from Berlin visited him while he was on sick leave in his hometown of Herrlingen near Ulm, and forced him to commit suicide. On pain of death, it was forbidden to doubt the Germans' defense capability and final victory!

gen. Es war unter Androhung der Todesstrafe verboten, die Verteidigungsfähigkeit und den Endsieg der Deutschen anzuzweifeln!

Das heutige Deutschland ist zwar übersät mit Opfergedenkstätten und Museen, aber echte
Ruinen einstiger Täter-Architekturen aus der Zeit des Faschismus sind selten. Eine der größten
ruinösen NS-Erinnerungslandschaften hat sich in Nürnberg erhalten: das Reichsparteitagsgelände von Albert Speer.

Für Albert Speer, der 1905 in Mannheim geboren wurde und bei Heinrich Tessenow in Berlin
Architektur studiert hatte, war es eine Sternstunde seines Lebens, als er am 4. Dezember 1930
im überfüllten Festsaal auf der Berliner Hasenheide zum ersten Mal seinem zukünftigen Idol Adolf
Hitler begegnete. Die Rede begeisterte den jungen angehenden Architekten so stark, daß er im
März 1931 der NSDAP beitrat. Schnell bekam er einige Innenausbau-Aufträge von der Berliner
Gauleitung. Goebbels wurde auf ihn aufmerksam und ließ seine neue Stadtvilla am Wilhelmsplatz
von Speer um- und ausbauen. Nach der zügigen Fertigstellung war Goebbels begeistert, selbst
von den Kunstwerken, die Speer von der Nationalgalerie ausgeliehen hatte. Erst als Hitler sich
über die Aquarelle von Emil Nolde empörte, merkte Goebbels, daß mit dieser Kunstrichtung in
Zukunft vorsichtiger umzugehen sei.

Goebbels ernannte Speer zum »Amtsleiter für künstlerische Gestaltung der Großkundgebun-
gen«. In dieser Funktion entwarf der 28jährige 1933 den Neubau des Reichsparteitagsgeländes
auf dem Nürnberger Zeppelinfeld. Hitler hatte Speer persönlich den Auftrag erteilt, die bisherige
Holztribüne durch eine 390 Meter lange und 23 Meter hohe Steinarchitektur zu ersetzen. Hitler
verlangte: »Es muß hier in gewaltigstem Ausmaß ein Dokument stilbildender Art geschaffen werden.«

Speer schaute sich um. Der Pergamonaltar im Berliner Antikenmuseum schien ihm als Vorbild
geeignet. Er zeichnete und plante. Zwischen 1934 und 1937 wurde gebaut. Hitler war begeistert.
Als er dann noch die abendliche Inszenierung des seither berühmten »Lichtdoms« von Albert
Speer sah, war ihm klar, daß er »seinen Architekten« gefunden hatte. Speer hatte 130 Flakschein-
werfer aufstellen lassen, die ihre Lichtstrahlen nach Einbruch der Dunkelheit hinauf in den schwarz-
blauen deutschen Himmel richteten. Eine wirklich geniale Idee, die imaginäre architektonische
Schönheit, Verteidigungswillen und zukünftige militärische Aggressionen in einem grausamen Bild
vereinigte. Der germanisch-gotische Stilwille hatte seine modern-mediale Vollendung erfahren. In
den Wolken hoch oben am Himmel leuchtete plötzlich so etwas wie ein traumhaftes Wallhalla auf.
Wer wollte, konnte darin eine Widerspiegelung Neuschwansteins, aber auch einer germanischen
Heldengedenkhalle sehen. Ehrenvoll und pathetisch würde der zukünftigen Gefallenen gedacht
werden. Jetzt allerdings standen sie noch jung und stark in geometrischen Blöcken geordnet vor
ihrem Führer, bereit, in den Krieg zu ziehen, den Feind zu schlagen und an den Fronten Europas
zu sterben. Noch ragten die Architekturen stolz in den Himmel, noch marschierten die Massen,
aber bald, nur wenige Jahre später, wird sich hier ein banales Steinfeld ausbreiten, die Rufe, Befehle und pathetischen Versprechungen werden verhallt sein. Kein Volk der Welt verirrt sich straf-
los in Hybris und Größenwahn. Die Geschichte des »Babylonischen Turmbaus« wiederholt sich
immer wieder aufs neue.

Zu den Großveranstaltungen hatte einst Leni Riefenstahl ihre Kameras aufgebaut und die
Aufmärsche wie grandiose Religionsveranstaltungen mit Balletteinlagen gefilmt. Später montierte
sie aus ihren Aufnahmen den Film Triumph des Willens, der 1935 in die Kinos kam und die Zuschauer begeisterte. Eine derartig bombastische Inszenierung von 250 000 kampfbereiten Men-
schenkörpern hatte die Welt bisher noch nicht gesehen. Man faßte nach den Depressionen der
Weltwirtschaftskrise wieder Mut und berauschte sich an der Vorstellung zukünftiger Siege und
Eroberungen. Am deutschen Wesen sollte die Welt genesen. Nur der starke, rassisch vollkommene Mann und die hingebungsvolle, blonde und fruchtbare deutsche Frau konnten die Lösung
aller Probleme darstellen. Die restliche Weltbevölkerung würde in Zukunft das Leben in Sklaverei
verbringen müssen.

Fritz Lang hatte die Bilder visionär in seinem legendären Metropolis-Film vorweggenommen.
Leni Riefenstahl wurde beim Internationalen Filmfestival in Venedig 1935 für ihr Werk ausgezeich-
net (bester »ausländischer Dokumentarfilm«) und erhielt 1937 auf der Weltausstellung in Paris dafür eine Goldmedaille.

1936 gipfelten die Masseninszenierungen bei den Veranstaltungen der Berliner Olympiade.
Wieder war Leni Riefenstahl dabei und montierte aus den Dokumentarbildern ihre beiden Filme:
Olympia – Fest der Völker und Olympia – Fest der Schönheit. In einer legendären Sequenz sehen
die Zuschauer fliegende Turmspringer. Leni Riefenstahl zeigte nur die Schwebephasen der Körper, das Abspringen und Auftreffen im Wasser schnitt sie heraus. Damit verherrlichte sie die per-

52. Ruinenspuren im Bereich Topographie des Terrors, Berlin 2009. Im Hintergrund Ernst Sagebiels ehemaliges Luftfahrtministerium, davor Reste der Berliner Mauer, darunter Kellerfragmente der einstigen Gestapo-Zentrale in der Niederkirchnerstraße.

52. Traces of ruins on the Topography of Terror site, Berlin, as in 2009. In the background Ernst Sagebiel's former air ministry, in front remnants of the Berlin Wall, under it fragments from the cellar for the former Niederkirchnerstrasse Gestapo headquarters.

While modern Germany has a large number of victims' memorials and museums, genuine ruins of former perpetrator buildings from the fascist era are rare. One of the largest ruin landscapes that serve as a reminder of the Nazi period has been preserved in Nuremberg: Albert Speer's Nazi Party Rally Grounds.

For Albert Speer, who was born in Mannheim in 1905 and had studied architecture with Heinrich Tessenow in Berlin, the 4th of December 1930, the day he first met his future idol Adolf Hitler in the crowded festival hall in Berlin's Hasenheide Park, was one of the greatest moments of his life. Hitler's speech filled the young up-and-coming architect with such enthusiasm that he joined the NSDAP in March 1931. Very soon he received a few interior design commissions from the Berlin Gauleitung. Goebbels became aware of Speer and had him renovate and expand his new city villa on Wilhelmsplatz. After the speedy completion of the work, Goebbels was thrilled, even by the works of art that Speer had borrowed from the National Gallery. It was not until Hitler expressed his indignation about the watercolors of Emil Nolde that Goebbels realized he would have to be more cautious in dealing with this art trend in future.

Goebbels appointed Speer to be the »director of the artistic design of mass rallies«. In this capacity, in 1933, the 28-year-old designed the new Nazi Party Rally Grounds on the Zeppelinfeld in Nuremberg. Hitler had personally commissioned Speer to replace the existing wooden grandstand with a 390-meter-long and 23-meter-high piece of stone architecture. Hitler demanded: »A style-setting document of the most massive scope is to be created here.«

Speer had a look around. The Pergamon Altar in the Antikenmuseum Berlin seemed to be a suitable model. He sketched and planned. The construction took place between 1934 and 1937. Hitler was thrilled. When he also saw the nighttime production of Albert Speer's »Cathedral of Light«, which has since become famous, he realized he had found »his architect«. Speer had had 130 anti-aircraft searchlights installed, which after dark pointed their beams of light up into the blue-black, German sky. A truly ingenious idea, uniting imaginary architectonic beauty, the will to defend the native land, and future military acts of aggression in one cruel image. The Germanic-Gothic conception of style had attained modern media perfection. In the clouds, high above in the sky, something like a dreamlike Valhalla suddenly lit up. If you liked, you could see it as a reflection of Neuschwanstein, but also of a memorial hall for Germanic heroes. The future fallen soldiers would be remembered with honor and pathos. Now, however, they still stood there young and strong, lined up in geometric ranks in front of their »Führer«, ready to go to war, to beat the enemy and to die on the front lines of Europe. The architectural structures still towered proudly, the masses were still marching, but soon, only a few years later, this would be an ordinary field strewn with stones. The shouts and commands and dramatic promises would have died away.

fekt durchtrainierten Athleten, als seien sie von der Erde losgelöste Vögel oder Engel und knüpfte ästhetisch bewußt – wie die Bildhauer Josef Thorak und Arno Breker – an die griechisch-römische Antike an. Wenn man sich vergegenwärtigt, daß zeitgleich Vernichtungskampagnen gegen Behinderte, geistig Zurückgebliebene, Homosexuelle, Andersdenkende, Kommunisten, »entartete« Künstler, Slawen, Sinti, Roma und Juden liefen, ein gespenstischer Vorgang.

Albert Speer war am Ziel angekommen und wurde zu Hitlers engstem Vertrauten. Zahlreiche Filmdokumentationen und Bücher befassen sich seither mit der Beziehung zwischen den beiden Männern. Hitler sah in Speer sein Alter ego, den Erfüller seiner künstlerisch-architektonischen Träume. 1937 wurde Speer zum »Generalbauinspekteur für die Neugestaltung der Reichshauptstadt Berlin und anderer deutscher Städte« ernannt. Im gleichen Jahr entwarf und baute er den Deutschen Pavillon auf der Pariser Weltausstellung am Trocadero. Dafür erhielt er eine Goldmedaille, außerdem einen »Grand Prix« für das Nürnberger Reichsparteitagsgelände. Speers Entwürfe lagen demnach im allgemeinen architektonischen Zeittrend und standen nicht isoliert in Europa da.

Bis 1942 beschäftigte sich Albert Speer vor allem mit dem Ausbau der Stadt Berlin zur Regierungshauptstadt. Hitler wollte, daß die Schönheit von Paris übertroffen werde. Als sich Speer 1942 zum Rüstungsminister ernennen ließ, wechselte er allerdings die Fronten und wurde ein Anführer der Zerstörungs- und Mordmaschinerie des »Dritten Reiches«. Ab jetzt mußte er nicht mehr aufbauen, sondern nur noch vernichten. Seine Schuld nahm damit zu und führte schließlich zu seiner Verurteilung bei den Nürnberger Prozessen.

Zurück zum Reichsparteitagsgelände. Wie sieht es heute aus? Das leicht vermüllte Zeppelinfeld besitzt keinerlei Aura mehr, es wirkt wie ein banaler, vernachlässigter Hinterhof. Gras wächst zwischen Kalksteinplatten und Asphaltflecken. Absperrungen verhindern das problemlose Herumwandern. Funktionen überlagern einander in merkwürdiger Unentschiedenheit. Parkende Autos, langsam vorbeifahrender Verkehr, Maschendrahtzäune. Ein Ruinengelände, das nicht entsorgt wurde. Teilweise anwesend, teilweise verschwunden. Nur die ehemalige Treppenanlage, auf der während der Nazizeit die Parteiprominenz saß, hat noch eine gewisse Ausstrahlung. Aber dadurch, daß die Amerikaner nach ihrer pompösen Siegesparade am 22. April 1945 in Nürnberg das zentrale Hakenkreuz – ein Gipfelkreuz – gesprengt haben, fehlt der Architektur heute die Bedeutungsmitte. 1967 wurde außerdem die Pfeilergalerie über den Treppen wegen angeblicher Baufälligkeit abgerissen, ein Vorgang, der in der Öffentlichkeit kontroverse Debatten auslöste.

Bis jetzt ist die Nutzung des Geländes und der Treppenruine unklar und damit bedeutungsdiffus. Kein erklärtes Freilichtmuseum, keine Disney-World der einstigen politischen Verirrungen, kein Andachtsraum für Neonazis und kein wirkliches Touristenziel mit Erklärungstafeln, Postkartenkiosken und Gartencafés. 1947 saßen hier noch die Zuschauer des »Norisring-Rennens«, einer lärmigen Veranstaltung mit PS-starken Motorrädern, 1963 versammelten sich Tausende von Gläubigen, um dem amerikanischen Wanderprediger Billy Graham zu lauschen. 1978 fand ein Rockkonzert mit Bob Dylan und Eric Clapton statt. Danach versank das Gelände in unentschiedenes Schweigen.

Der Umgang mit Täterbauten bleibt für bundesrepublikanische Politiker, aber auch für aufrechte Demokraten ein Problem. Was wohl die Initiatoren und Erbauer der Tribüne dazu gesagt hätten?

1960 drehte Alexander Kluge zusammen mit Peter Schamoni seinen ersten zwölf Minuten langen Schwarzweißdokumentarfilm mit dem Titel *Brutalität in Stein*. Als ich diesen Film – damals war ich noch Schüler in Ulm – in einem Kino sah, war ich tief beeindruckt. Kluge ging mit seinem Kameramann Wolf Wirth langsam über das Nürnberger Parteitagsgelände, filmte an den abgebrochenen Stufen, an Ritzen und Spalten entlang, zeigte immer wieder Blicke nach oben auf die jetzt ruinösen Steinschichtungen der einstigen Monumentalarchitektur. Dazu ließ er Texte von Nazi-Politikern und Nazi-Opfern verlesen. Aus dem Drehbuch: »Sprecher: Alle Bauwerke, die uns die Geschichte hinterlassen hat, zeugen vom Geiste ihrer Erbauer und ihrer Zeit, auch dann noch, wenn sie längst nicht mehr ihren ursprünglichen Zwecken dienen. Die verlassenen Bauwerke der Nationalsozialistischen Partei lassen als steinerne Zeugen die Erinnerung an jene Epoche lebendig werden, die in die furchtbarste Katastrophe deutscher Geschichte mündete. Bilder vom leeren Parteitagsgelände in Nürnberg, Ruinen …« Zum Schluß: »Traum eines wegen Widerstandes zum Tode Verurteilten. Sprecher: Wir werden auf einen Platz geführt, auf dem eine Fallmaschine aufgestellt ist. Es heißt, es solle nur erst ein Versuch gemacht werden … wir werden in einer Reihe aufgestellt. Ich traue der ganzen Sache nicht, vermute, daß man unversehens das Farbband mit einem Beil auswechselt. Ich traue der ganzen Sache nicht. Ich bin gerade festgeschnallt, als mein Blick sich nach oben richtet. Dort sehe ich nun tatsächlich ein Beil aufblitzen. Ich schreie – da …!

There is no nation on earth that has strayed into hubris and megalomania with impunity. The story of the Tower of Babylon constantly repeats itself.

Once, Leni Riefenstahl set up her cameras for the mass rallies and filmed the parades like grandiose religious events with ballet interludes. Later she assembled her takes into a montage, the film *Triumph des Willens* (*Triumph of the Will*), which was screened in 1935 and filled spectators with enthusiasm. The world had never before seen so bombastic a mise-en-scène of 250,000 combat-ready human bodies. After the depressions of the global economic crisis Germans plucked up courage again and became intoxicated with the idea of future victories and conquests. The world was to be healed by Germanhood (*deutsches Wesen*), to quote the poet Emanuel Geibel. Only a strong, racially perfect man and a devoted, blond and fertile German woman could represent the solution to all problems. In future the rest of the world's population would have to spend their lives in slavery.

The visionary Fritz Lang had anticipated these images in his legendary film *Metropolis*. Leni Riefenstahl was given an award for her work at the 1935 International Film Festival in Venice (best »foreign documentary«), and received a gold medal for it at the 1937 Paris World Fair.

In 1936 the mass productions culminated in the events of the Berlin Olympics. Again Leni Riefenstahl was present and from the documentary shots assembled her two films: *Olympia – Fest der Völker* (*Olympia – Festival of Nations*) and *Olympia – Fest der Schönheit* (*Olympia – Festival of Beauty*). In a fabulous sequence spectators watch flying high divers. Leni Riefenstahl showed only the phases when the bodies were in the air, and cut the parts when the dive began and when the diver hit the water. Thus she glorified the perfectly trained athletes as though they were birds or angels detached from the earth, and deliberately continued the aesthetic traditions of Greco-Roman antiquity – as did the sculptors Josef Thorak and Arno Breker. It was eerie, if we remember that at the same time there were liquidation campaigns against the disabled, the mentally retarded, homosexuals, dissidents, Communists, degenerate artists, Slavs, Sinti, Roma and Jews.

Albert Speer had reached his goal, and became Hitler's closest confidant. Many documentary films and books have since dealt with the relationship between the two men. In Speer, Hitler saw his alter ego, the man who would make his artistic and architectonic dreams come true. In 1937 Speer was appointed »general building inspector to redesign the Reich Capital Berlin and other German cities«. That same year he designed and built the German Pavilion of the Paris World Fair in the Trocadero. He received a gold medal for his work, as well as a »Grand Prix« for the Nuremberg Reich Party Rally Grounds. Thus Speer's designs were part of a general architectonic trend of the times and were not an isolated phenomenon in Europe.

Until 1942 Albert Speer was primarily busy developing the city of Berlin into the administrative capital of Germany. Hitler wanted a city whose beauty would outshine that of Paris. When, in 1942, Speer had himself appointed minister of armaments, however, he changed sides and became a leader of the Third Reich's machinery of destruction and murder. From now on his task was no longer to build, but only to destroy. His guilt thus increased and finally led to his being sentenced in the Nuremberg Trials.

But back to the Nazi Party Rally Grounds. What do they look like today? The Zeppelin Field, which today is somewhat garbage-strewn, no longer has an aura today. It feels like an ordinary, neglected backyard. Grass grows between limestone slabs and patches of asphalt. Barriers keep people from easily wandering around. Functions overlie each other in curious indecision. Parked cars, slow-moving traffic, chain-link fences. A landscape of ruins that was never cleaned up. The ruins are partially there, partially gone. Only the former risers where prominent Party members used to sit during the Nazi era still have a certain distinctive atmosphere about them. But because the Americans after their pompous victory parade on 22 April 1945 in Nuremberg blew up the central swastika – something like a cross on the summit of a mountain – the architecture today lacks its significant center. Moreover, in 1967 the gallery of pillars above the stairs was demolished, allegedly because it was unsafe, triggering public controversy and debates.

To date the use of the terrain and of the ruined staircase is unclear and thus its significance is vague. It has not been declared to be an open-air museum or a Disney World of former political aberrations. It is not a place of reverent contemplation for neo-Nazis or a real tourist destination with explanatory signs, kiosks selling postcards and garden cafés. As late as 1947 this is where people sat watching the »Norisring Race«, a noisy event with high-powered motorcycles. In 1963 the faithful gathered here by the thousands to listen to the itinerant American preacher Billy Graham. In 1978 there was a rock concert with Bob Dylan and Eric Clapton. After this the terrain sank into undecided silence.

Musikeinsatz. Die Musik geht über in die Fanfare der Sonderberichte des Oberkommandos der Wehrmacht, da bricht der Ton ab, trudelt aus. Schluß.«

Zum ehemaligen Reichsparteitagsgelände gehören neben dem Zeppelinfeld noch zahlreiche andere Bauten: die Luitpoldarena, das Deutsche Stadion, die Kongreßhalle, das Märzfeld und die große Straße.

Am Ende des Krieges blieb die monumentale Kongreßhalle als Torso stehen. Sie war einst als ehrgeiziges Projekt von Ludwig Ruff geplant worden. Nachdem er 1934 gestorben war, übernahm sein Sohn Franz Ruff zusammen mit Georg Finkler die Bauleitung. Als Vorbild diente den Architekten das römische Kolosseum (!). 1935 begannen die Bauarbeiten mit komplizierten und aufwendigen Fundamentierungen. Tausende von Bauarbeitern, nach Kriegsbeginn auch Zwangsarbeiter und Kriegsgefangene, waren an dem gewaltigen Bau, der einmal 50 000 Zuhörer fassen sollte, beschäftigt. Heute ist die Ruine »das größte erhaltene Relikt der Herrschaftsarchitektur des ›Dritten Reiches‹ « (Eckart Dietzfelbinger und Gerhard Liedtke in ihrem Buch *Nürnberg – Ort der Massen* über diesen Bau).

Nach Jahrzehnten reiner kommerzieller Nutzung der »Ruinenräume« wurde in den 1990er Jahren in einem Teil der Anlage vom Grazer Architekten Günther Domenig ein Dokumentationszentrum eingerichtet. Mit seiner dekonstruktivistischen, wilden Architektursprache richtet sich dessen Ästhetik vehement gegen die größenwahnsinnige, pseudoklassizistische Monumentalität der Nazizeit, stellt sie in Frage, zerstört sie an manchen Stellen und erschafft dadurch einen neuartigen Architekturdialog quer durch die Zeiten. Ob das Theatralische der Domenig-Gesten über das gesteckte Ziel, »Information und Aufklärung« anzubieten, weit hinausschießt, darüber läßt sich trefflich streiten.

In Gedanken sehe ich die Photos der Nürnberger Prozesse vor mir. Die Angeklagten auf ihren Bänken. Der in sich zusammengefallen Ex-Junkie Hermann Göring, welcher vor Ende des Prozesses Selbstmord begehen wird, sieht besonders fahl aus. Albert Speer dagegen blieb auch hier ganz Gentleman, gefaßt und charmant. Natürlich »wußte er von nichts«. Als einziger des inneren Führungskreises wurde er nicht zum Tode verurteilt. Selbst in seinen *Spandauer Tagebüchern* bestreitet er eine tiefere Mitschuld, stets mit Distanziertheit gegenüber den politischen Vorgängen begründet. Inzwischen sind Dokumente aufgetaucht, die eindeutig beweisen, daß Speer mehr wußte, als er zugab. Auch von der legendären »Theorie vom Ruinenwert« seiner Gebäude ist nicht viel übriggeblieben. In seinen *Erinnerungen* schrieb er darüber: »Modern konstruierte Bauwerke … waren zweifellos wenig geeignet, die von Hitler verlangte ›Traditionsbrücke‹ zu künftigen Generationen zu bilden: undenkbar, daß rostende Trümmerhaufen jene heroischen Inspirationen vermittelten, die Hitler an den Monumenten der Vergangenheit bewunderte. Diesem Dilemma sollte meine ›Theorie‹ entgegenwirken: die Verwendung besonderer Materialien sowie die Berücksichtigung besonderer statischer Überlegungen sollten Bauten ermöglichen, die im Verfallszustand, nach Hunderten oder (so rechneten wir) Tausenden von Jahren etwa den römischen Vorbildern gleichen würden.«

1937 wurde Speer von Hitler aufgefordert, seinen Hauptwohnsitz auf den Obersalzberg, die geliebte »Alpenfestung« des Führers, zu verlegen. Allerdings hatte er als Architekt dort nicht viel zu tun, schließlich war er mit seinen Berlin-Projekten genügend beschäftigt.

Als die Alliierten 1945 in Berchtesgaden eintrafen, waren vom Obersalzberg nur noch Ruinen übrig. Flugzeugpiloten hatten dort ihre Bombenlasten abgeworfen, in der irrigen Annahme, daß sich in dem Berg eine gewaltige Nazi-Festung befände. Bekanntlich gehörte der Mythos einer uneinnehmbaren »Alpenfestung« zum damaligen allgemeinen Bewußtsein von Freund und Feind. Ähnlich verhielt es sich mit den Gerüchten um die V2-Raketen und eine mögliche deutsche Atombombe.

Von 1946 an setzte ein regelrechter Obersalzberg-Tourismus ein. Viele Deutsche, aber auch Amerikaner, wollten sehen, wie Adolf Hitler mit Eva Braun, die er hier versteckt hielt, privat gewohnt hatte. Schließlich wurde den amerikanischen Besatzern das Treiben der Touristen lästig, vielleicht auch zu gefährlich, und sie entschlossen sich am 30. April 1952, genau sieben Jahre nach Hitlers Selbstmord, zu einer Sprengung. Seither wachsen die verbliebenen Stützmauerreste jedes Jahr mehr ein und versinken allmählich im Dickicht des Waldes. Neugierige Touristen suchen meist vergeblich nach den Spuren der Ruinen. Nur noch in Photobüchern können sie das riesige, versenkbare Panoramafenster bewundern, durch das der Führer einst auf seine Terrasse und den gegenüberliegenden sagenumwobenen Untersberg blicken konnte. Wer mehr wissen will, muß das neue Dokumentationszentrum nebenan besuchen. Vielleicht nimmt er auch an einer Führung durch die erhaltenen Gänge des unterirdischen Bunkersystems teil und betrachtet gruselnd die kalt-feuchten Truppenfluchten mit den plötzlichen Abknickungen. Hier stehen Schutz-

Dealing with perpetrator buildings continues to be a problem not only for the Federal Republic's politicians but also for upright democrats. Wonder what the initiators and builders of the grandstand would have said about that?

In 1960 Alexander Kluge together with Peter Schamoni shot his first 12-minute-long black-and-white documentary, titled *Brutalität in Stein* (*Brutality in Stone*). When I saw this film in a movie theater – I was still a schoolboy in Ulm – I was deeply impressed. Kluge and his cameraman, Wolf Wirth, slowly walked across the Nuremberg rally grounds, filmed as they went past the broken steps, the cracks and crevices, kept showing glimpses of the now ruined stone stratifications of the once monumental architecture overhead. Texts by Nazi politicians and Nazi victims were read out as the camera rolled. From the script: »Speaker: All buildings left us by history are evidence of the spirit of their builders and their time, even when they have long since stopped serving their original purposes. The abandoned buildings of the National Socialist Party are stone witnesses that reawaken the memory of an epoch which ended in the most horrifying catastrophe in German history. Images of the vacant Party Rally Grounds in Nuremberg, ruins …« And finally: »Dream of a man condemned to death because of resistence. Speaker: We are led to a square on which an Atwood machine has been installed. They are saying that at first only an experiment will be performed … we are told to line up. I don't trust this whole business, I suspect they'll unexpectedly replace the colored ribbon with a blade. I don't trust this whole business. I've just been strapped down when I look up. Overhead I now actually do see the flash of a blade. I scream – and then …!

Music begins. The music changes to the fanfare that introduces the special reports of the Supreme Command of the Wehrmacht, then the sound breaks off, goes into a tailspin. The end.«

In addition to the Zeppelin Field, numerous other buildings are part of the Party Rally Grounds: the Luitpold Arena, the German Stadium, the Congress Hall, the Märzfeld (March Field) and the Great Road.

At the end of the war, the monumental Congress Hall was left as a torso. It had once been the ambitious project of Ludwig Ruff. After his death in 1934 his son Franz Ruff together with Georg Finkler took over the construction supervision. The architects modeled the hall on the Roman Colosseum (!). Construction began in 1935 with complicated and extravagant foundations. Thousands of construction workers, including forced laborers and prisoners of war after the beginning of the war, were busy on the massive building, which was intended one day to hold an audience of 50,000. Today the ruin is »the largest still extant relic of the ›Third Reich‹'s architecture of dominion« (Eckart Dietzfelbinger and Gerhard Liedtke in their book *Nürnberg – Ort der Massen* concerning this building).

After decades when the »ruin spaces« were used for purely commercial purposes, a documentation center was installed in one part of the building, designed by the Graz architect Günther Domenig. With his deconstructivist, wild architectonic idiom, his aesthetic is vehemently directed against the megalomanic, pseudoclassicistic monumentality of the Nazi era, calls it into question, destroys it in places and thus creates a novel architectural dialogue across the eras. It is open to dispute – and what a dispute! – whether the theatrical aspect of Domenig's gestures goes far beyond the stated goal: to offer »information and clarification«.

In my mind I see the photos of the Nuremberg Trials before me. The accused on their benches. The broken-down ex-junkie Hermann Göring, who will commit suicide before the end of the trial, looks particularly wan. Albert Speer on the other hand remains quite the gentleman even here, composed and charming. Naturally he »knew nothing about it«. He was the only one of the Nazi inner circle who was not condemned to death. Even in his Spandau diaries he denies that a share of the deeper blame falls on him, always claiming he had distanced himself from political events. In the meantime documents have surfaced that clearly prove that Speer knew more than he admitted. Not much is left of the legendary »theory of ruin value« of his buildings, either. In his *Memoirs* he wrote about this: »Buildings constructed by modern methods … were undoubtedly hardly suitable for forming the ›bridge of tradition‹ to future generations that Hitler demanded: It is inconceivable that rusting heaps of rubble conveyed the kind of heroic inspiration that Hitler admired in the monuments of the past. My ›theory‹ was meant to counteract this dilemma: The use of special materials and the fact that we took into account special structural considerations were intended to make possible buildings that, after hundreds or (as we expected) thousands of years would resemble their (let's say) Roman models when they were in a state of dilapidation.«

In 1937 Hitler asked Speer to move his main residence to Obersalzberg, the Führer's beloved »Alpine fortress«. True, he had no business there as an architect – after all, he was busy enough with his Berlin projects.

wände mit Schlitzen, durch die im Ernstfall MG-Schützen auf die Verfolger hätten schießen können. Natürlich sind auch diese Angstbauten nie wirklich zum Einsatz gekommen. Dieses nutzlose Schicksal teilen sie mit zahlreichen Festungen anderer Zeiten. Je stärker eine Stadt oder eine Burg befestigt worden ist, um so größer war die Chance, nie angegriffen zu werden. Das galt für die Stadt Ulm genauso wie etwa für die monumentale Festung Königstein in der sächsischen Schweiz, die Napoleon nur für wenige Minuten besuchte, um anschließend mit seinen Truppen weiter gen Osten zu ziehen.

Da sich Hitler während der Endkämpfe des Zweiten Weltkriegs nicht auf dem Obersalzberg, sondern in seinem Berliner Führerbunker versteckt hielt, also tief in die Erde eingegraben wie ein gefangenes Tier, konnte er sich nicht herrschaftlich verteidigen. Vielleicht hätte er sich auf dem Berg dazu entschlossen, sein geliebtes alpines Wohnhaus, in dem er »alle großen Ideen entwickelte«, wie er selbst sagte, mit dem ganzen Inventar in die Luft zu jagen.

Ganz anders der Abgang Hermann Görings. Er verließ sein Jagdschloss Carinhall, das in der Schorfheide nördlich von Berlin lag, am Abend des 20. April 1945, um vor der anrückenden Sowjetarmee nach Berchtesgaden zu fliehen. Die zurückgebliebenen Wachsoldaten hatte er angewiesen, das gesamte Anwesen mit 400 Zentnern Sprengstoff zu bestücken. Nachdem Göring endgültig in der Nacht verschwunden war, plünderte seine Wachmannschaft zunächst einmal den Weinkeller und feierte ein Gelage mit großem Besäufnis. Als am 28. April die ersten Spähtrupps der Roten Armee in Görings Wald auftauchten, zündeten die Wachsoldaten den Sprengstoff, und eine gewaltige Explosion zerstörte das gesamte Anwesen. Sie selbst flohen Richtung Berlin.

Heute sind nicht einmal mehr die Grundmauern von Carinhall zu sehen. Neugierige Neonazis suchen meist vergeblich nach Spuren ihres Idols. Auch illegale Tauchgänge in den beiden nahegelegenen Seen verlaufen erfolglos. Lange hielten sich Gerüchte, am schlammigen Seegrund lägen märchenhafte Nazischätze, wertvolle Kunstwerke oder gar die Reste des legendären Bernsteinzimmers.

Das ähnlich komfortable Landhaus von Joseph Goebbels am nicht weit von Görings Anwesen entfernten Bogensee überstand den Krieg nahezu unbeschädigt. Es diente den Sowjets als Militärlazarett und wurde von der DDR-Regierung bis 1990 als »Zentraljugendschule der Freien Deutschen Jugend, Waldhof am Bogensee« genutzt. Im Gegensatz zum Obersalzberg existiert in dieser Gegend kein Dokumentationszentrum, das genauer über die Täter informiert. Selbst in Berlin informiert keine Stelle – außer in engem Rahmen das Deutsche Historische Museum – ausführlich über Speers große Achse, seine Monumentalbauten oder die Wohnhäuser von Göring und Goebbels. Die Originalmodelle aus dem Atelier Speers sind alle spurlos verschwunden. Außerdem fehlt ein Museum, das Nazi-Kunst ausstellt, Gemälde und Skulpturen. Ignorieren kann gefährlich werden. Man sollte den Mut haben, auch falsche kulturelle Entwicklungen genau zu betrachten und zu studieren. Jeder Museums- und Gedenkstättendirektor befaßt sich lieber mit den Opfern als mit den Tätern (dabei sind Bösewichter oft lehrreicher als Märtyrer).

When the Allies arrived in Berchtesgaden in 1945, ruins were all that was left of Obersalzberg. Airplane pilots had dropped their loads of bombs there, erroneously assuming that there was a mighty Nazi fortress in the mountain. It is common knowledge that the myth of an impregnable »Alpine fortress« was part of the general awareness of friends and foes at the time. The same was true of the rumors about the V-2 rockets and a potential German atomic bomb.

From 1946 on, a regular Obersalzberg tourism began. Many Germans, but also Americans, wanted to see what the private home of Adolf Hitler and Eva Braun, whom he kept hidden here, had been like. Finally the coming and going of the tourists became too annoying, and perhaps too dangerous, for the American occupying forces, and on 30 April 1952, exactly seven years after Hitler's suicide, they decided to blow up the retreat. Since then the remains of the retaining walls have become more overgrown year by year and gradually disappear in the dense forest. Curious tourists for the most part look for traces of the ruins in vain. Only in books of photographs are they able to admire the huge picture window which could be lowered and through which the Führer was once able to look down on his terrace and on the legendary Untersberg across the valley. Those who want to know more must visit the new documentation center next door. Perhaps they will also go on a guided tour through the still existing corridors of the underground bunker system and look with a shiver of fear at the cold, damp flights of stairs, which suddenly break off in places. Here there are protective walls with slits through which machine gunners could have shot at pursuers in case of emergency. Naturally these buildings of fear never really came to be used. They shared this useless fate with numerous fortresses of other eras. The stronger the fortifications of a town or castle, the greater was the chance that it would never be attacked. That was just as true of the city of Ulm as, say, of the monumental Königstein Fortress in Saxon Switzerland, which Napoleon visited for just a few minutes, only to continue his march eastward with his troops.

Since during the final battles of World War II Hitler hid not on Obersalzberg, but in his Berlin Führer Bunker, i.e., buried deep in the ground like a captured wild beast, he could not defend himself in a grand manner. Had he been on the mountain, he might have decided to blow up his beloved alpine residence, in which he »developed all his great ideas«, as he said himself, together with everything that was in it.

Hermann Göring's exit was quite different. He left his hunting lodge Carinhall, located in Schorfheide north of Berlin, on the evening of 20 April 1945, in order to flee to Berchtesgaden from the approaching Soviet army. He had instructed the sentries who remained behind to stock the entire estate with 400 metric hundredweights of explosives. After Göring had finally disappeared into the night, the men on guard first plundered the wine cellar and had a big spree where everybody got drunk as a lord. On 28 April, when the first Red Army reconnaissance patrols appeared in Göring's woods, the sentries ignited the explosives, and an enormous explosion destroyed the entire estate. They themselves fled in the direction of Berlin.

Today not even the foundation walls of Carinhall are visible. Curious neo-Nazis look for traces of their idol, mostly in vain. Illegal dives in the two neighboring lakes have been unsuccessful. For a long time there were rumors that fabulous Nazi treasures, valuable artworks or even the remains of the legendary Amber Room lay on the muddy bottom of the lake.

The equally comfortable country house of Joseph Goebbels by Lake Bogensee, not far from Göring's estate, survived the war almost intact. It served the Soviets as a military hospital and was used until 1990 by the GDR government as the »Central Young People's School of the Free German Youth, Waldhof am Bogensee«. In contrast to Obersalzberg, there is no documentation center in this region to give you more detailed information about the perpetrators. Even in Berlin there is no place – except, on a small scale, the Deutsches Historisches Museum – that provides specific information about Speer's great axis and his monumental buidings, or the residences of Göring and Goebbels. The original models from Speer's studio have all disappeared without a trace. There is also no museum that exhibits Nazi art, paintings and sculptures. To ignore them and not to pay attention to them may prove dangerous. One should have the courage to observe even mistaken cultural developments closely and to study them. Directors of museums and memorials would rather deal with victims than with perpetrators (and yet villains are often more instructive than martyrs).

10. Vom Verschwinden der Ruinen

Gedächtniskirche in Berlin, Alte Pinakothek und Glyptothek in München und Neues Museum in Berlin

Bereits nach der Zerstörung der ersten historisch einmaligen Stadt in Deutschland – Lübeck in der Nacht vom 28. auf den 29. März 1942 – begannen Städteplaner und Architekten mit den Neuplanungen. Manche sahen in der Auslöschung eine Katastrophe, die für alle Zeiten Gültigkeit haben würde, andere – unter ihnen Albert Speer – erkannten darin eine Chance. Endlich war der Weg frei, störungsfrei mit dem Bau monumentaler Achsen und Architekturen zu beginnen.

Rudolf Hillebrecht – er war als Architekt zuständig für die Neuplanungen in Hamburg und erlebte die Luftangriffe auf Lübeck persönlich – schrieb im Juni 1942 in einem Feldpostbrief:

»Liebe Kameraden, liebe Freunde,

Lübeck liegt zu einem großen Teil, seinem schönsten Teil, in Trümmern; Lübeck, die Krone der Hanse, Lübeck, die Stadt, die für alle Deutschen ein Vermächtnis großer deutscher Vergangenheit, für die Architekten unter uns über das historische Zeugnis hinaus ein lebendiges, ewig gültiges Vorbild ist für Sauberkeit und Gradheit, Haltung und Gesinnung des Bauens. In der Nacht zum Palmsonntag griff der Engländer Lübeck an, zunächst mit Brandbomben, die in dieser so eng bebauten Stadt mit ihren Fachwerkbauten und Giebeldächern, ohne jede Trennung durch Brandmauern, verheerende Auswirkungen haben mußten … Ihr müßt wissen: das alte Lübeck ist dahin! …

Gedanken über das, was aus dieser Stadt nun einmal werden soll, sind gestattet, aber verfrüht. Vorläufig kann es nur eines für uns alle geben: Kampf gegen diese Barbarei und Unkultur, gleichgültig ob sie von Osten oder Westen kommt, Sieg der Waffen. Der Bau eines machtvollen und starken Reiches, für das Lübeck Jahrhunderte hindurch Vorkämpfer gewesen, nun Opfer geworden ist, steht uns als Ziel und Frucht allen Mühens vor Augen. Mag Lübeck uns dann Vorbild bleiben für die Haltung und Gesinnung, mit der nur man Städte für tausend Jahre errichten kann.«

Die Zerstörung weiterer deutscher Städte regte die Phantasie der Architekten an, sie erstellten Plan um Plan, bauten Modelle und phantasierten sich in eine bessere Zukunft hinein (sofern sie nicht an den Fronten um ihr Leben bangen mußten). Auch in den Schützengräben des Ersten Weltkriegs wurden schon Pläne geschmiedet. Da saß Erich Mendelsohn und zeichnete auf kleinen Skizzierblättern seine dynamischen Hausvisionen, die er in den 1920er Jahren tatsächlich realisieren konnte. Otto Dix, Max Beckmann und George Grosz hielten auf Zeichnungen das Grauen fest, das sie erleben mußten. Später wurden daraus große Gemälde. Ludwig Wittgenstein schrieb (oder diktierte), während ringsum geschossen wurde, seinen epochalen *Tractatus Logico-philosophicus*, dessen provozierende Thesen er in einer späteren Lebensphase allerdings widerrief.

Manche Schriftsteller – Ernst Jünger etwa – berichteten in arroganter Weise von ihren Taxifahrten zur Front, wo sie kurz darauf Befehle erteilten, auf den Feind – die Franzosen – zu schießen. Andere, wie der Maler Franz Marc, überlebten das kriegerische Chaos nicht und mußten in jungen Jahren durch eine feindliche Kugel sterben. Wieder andere flüchteten sich nach den schlimmen Erlebnissen in Drogenexzesse und starben daran wie Georg Trakl, dessen Gedicht *Grodek* die düster-verzweifelte Stimmung wiedergibt:

»Am Abend tönen die herbstlichen Wälder
Von tödlichen Waffen, die goldnen Ebenen
Und blauen Seen, darüber die Sonne
Düstrer hinrollt; umfängt die Nacht
Sterbende Krieger, die wilde Klage
hrer zerbrochenen Münder.
Doch stille sammelt im Weidengrund
Rotes Gewölk, darin ein zürnender Gott wohnt
Das vergoßne Blut sich, mondne Kühle;
Alle Straßen münden in schwarze Verwesung.«

Im Zweiten Weltkrieg blieb nicht mehr soviel Zeit zum Zeichnen, Malen und Schreiben. Es entstanden nur schnelle Photos, manche Filme und später die Berichte der Überlebenden. Kriegsmaler wie in England gab es nur wenige. Lothar-Günther Buchheim, der mit seinem Roman *Das*

10. How ruins vanish

Gedächtniskirche (Kaiser Wilhelm Memorial Church) Berlin, Alte Pinakothek and Glyptothek in Munich and Neues Museum in Berlin

Immediately after the destruction of the first historically unique city in Germany – Lübeck in the night of 28 to 29 March 1942 – urban designers and architects began with new planning. Some felt the obliteration was a catastrophe that would have permanent effects, while others – including Albert Speer – recognized an opportunity. This finally opened the way toward beginning the unhampered construction of monumental axes and architectural monuments. Rudolph Hillebrecht – an architect who was in charge of new urban development in Hamburg and had personally witnessed the air raids on Lübeck – wrote the following in a letter to the front in June 1942:

»Dear comrades, dear friends,

A large part of Lübeck – its most beautiful part – is in ruins; Lübeck, the pride of the Hansa, Lübeck, the city that for all Germans is a legacy of the great German past, while for those among us who are architects it is not only historical testimony but also a living, eternally valid model for clean and straight architecture, right attitude and ethos. In the night before Palm Sunday the British attacked Lübeck, at first with incendiary bombs, which in such a densely built-up city with its half-timbered houses and gabled roofs, not separated by any fire walls, could not help having disastrous consequences … I want you to know: the old Lübeck is gone! …

Thoughts about what is to become of this city now are in order, but they are premature. For the present all of us have only one duty: to fight this barbarism and lack of culture, regardless of whether it comes from the East or the West, and to achieve a military victory. The building of a powerful and strong empire, whose champion Lübeck has been through the centuries, and for which it has now been sacrificed, is the goal we envision, and the fruit of all our efforts. May Lübeck then remain our model for right attitude and ethos – the only foundation needed to build cities that will endure for a thousand years.«

The destruction of additional German cities stimulated the architects' imagination. They drew up plan after plan, built models and fantasized about a better future (as long as they did not have to fear for their lives in the front lines). Such plans were concocted even in the trenches of the First World War. That was when Erich Mendelsohn sat sketching his dynamic visions of houses on small sheets of sketch paper, houses he was actually able to build in the 1920s. In their drawings Otto Dix, Max Beckmann and Georg Grosz recorded the horror they had to experience. While there was shooting all around him, Ludwig Wittgenstein wrote (or dictated) his epochal *Tractatus Logico-Philosophicus*, whose provocative theses he retracted, however, at a later stage of his life.

Some writers – Ernst Jünger, for instance – arrogantly described taking a taxi to the front, where they gave curt orders to shoot at the enemy – the French. Others, such as the painter Franz Marc, did not survive the chaos of war and were killed by an enemy bullet while they were still young. And there were others who after their dreadful experiences took refuge in drugs and died as a result, people like Georg Trakl, whose poem *Grodek* conveys the bleak, desperate mood:

»At evening the autumn woods resound
With deadly weapons, the golden plains
And blue lakes, over which the sun
Rolls more darkly; night embraces
Dying warriors, the wild lament
Of their broken mouths.
Yet silently red clouds, in which a wrathful god lives,
Gather, down there among willows
The blood that was shed, the moon's coolness;
All roads flow into black decay. …«

In the Second World War there was not as much time for drawing, painting and writing anymore. There were only quick snapshots, a few films and later the reports of the survivors. Unlike in England, there were few painters of the war. Lothar Günther Buchheim, who became world-famous with his novel *Das Boot* (*The Boat*), was one of them. We do not know how many artists, composers, painters, sculptors and architects, who would later have been able to accomplish

Boot weltberühmt wurde, war einer von ihnen. Wie viele Künstler, Komponisten, Maler, Bildhauer und Architekten, die später große Werke hätten vollbringen können, in jungen Jahren an den Fronten gefallen sind, wissen wir nicht. Die wenigen Überlebenden erhielten die Chance ihres Lebens.

Die Zeit der geschmückten Fassaden war nun endgültig vorbei. Jetzt herrschte – schon aus Not – schlichte Einfachheit vor. Dennoch bekämpften sich zwei Fraktionen: die Anhänger der einen wollten die zerstörten Häuser und Städte wieder in ihrem alten Erscheinungsbild aufbauen, die andern plädierten für einen Neuanfang und damit für eine harte Moderne ohne historische Bezüge. Für sie war die Vergangenheit ein gescheitertes, jetzt endgültig zu beendendes Projekt.

Aber die nicht wirklich eingestandene Orientierungslosigkeit, der Verlust an bisherigen Werten, die Demütigung durch die Niederlage, die Entbehrungen, der Geld- und Baustoffmangel – das alles zehrte am Selbstbewußtsein. Wofür man bisher sein Leben aufs Spiel gesetzt hatte und vielleicht zum Krüppel geschossen worden war, zählte nichts mehr. Im Gegenteil: Wer in der Partei gewesen war, durfte nicht arbeiten, mußte lange warten, bis er von den alliierten Behörden entnazifiziert wurde. Widerstandskämpfer hatten es leichter.

Der Psychosomatiker Alexander Mitscherlich schildert die Situation in seinem immer noch spannenden Buch *Die Unwirtlichkeit unserer Städte*, das er 1965 geschrieben hat: »1945: Ruinen, wohin man blickte, wohin man kam. Endergebnis, nachdem man ausgezogen war, die ganze Welt das Fürchten zu lehren. Hinter dieser prahlerischen Demonstration der Potenz war ein tiefer Zweifel am Selbstwert, an der Männlichkeit verborgen – nach untergegangener Reichsglorie, bei großer Arbeitslosigkeit … Ruinen waren ringsum: aber die Erde trug sie weiter, diese zahllosen Jubler, die sich von der Beutegier hatten verführen lassen, die da bereit gewesen waren, den andern ihren Platz wegzunehmen. Die Welle der Vernichtung war zu ihnen zurückgekehrt und über ihnen zusammengeschlagen. Ihre Häuser waren zerstört, nun krallten sie sich im Boden um so fester, Regression auf eine mutterähnliche Sicherheit, nachdem die Kumpanei mit dem falschen Propheten mißglückt war.«

Die wenigen älteren, überlebenden Architekten erinnerten sich zwar an die Aufbrüche der Moderne, an den Expressionismus und das Bauhaus, aber jetzt, im Anblick dieses gespenstischen Scherbenhaufens wußte niemand wirklich, in welchem Stil zu bauen sei. Das Schicksal zwang zum Handeln. Also wurde begonnen, in Lübeck, Hamburg, Kiel, Hannover, Berlin, Essen, Köln, Nürnberg, Augsburg, Heilbronn, Karlsruhe, Stuttgart, Frankfurt, Mainz, Wiesbaden, Ulm und München.

Die Besatzungsmächte achteten auf einen geordneten Ablauf der Arbeiten, manchmal nahmen sie auch Einfluß, vor allem wenn es darum ging, demokratische Vorgänge durchzusetzen. Es gab auch Fraktionen unter ihnen, die dafür plädierten, Deutschland in seinem Ruinenzustand zu konservieren. Werner Durth und Niels Gutschow berichten in ihrem informativen Buch *Deutschland in Trümmern – Stadtplanung 1940–1950* über den ehemaligen Nürnberger Baudezernenten Heinz Schmeisser, der sich 1981 erinnert: »Wir hatten in den ersten Nachkriegswochen von Seiten der Amerikaner merkwürdige Vorstellungen gehört: Vielleicht als Auswirkung des Morgenthauplans sollte die ›Stadt der Reichsparteitage‹ ausgelöscht bleiben wie einst Karthago, das einfach eliminiert wurde. Die zweite, etwas harmlosere Lösung war, dieses Ruinenfeld Altstadt so liegen und stehen zu lassen, wie es war: ›als ewiges Mahnmal gegen den Wahnsinn des Krieges‹.«

Im Rückblick bleibt die Leistung von Architekten, Handwerkern und Bauherren dennoch phänomenal. Wer heute die Photos der Zerstörungen betrachtet, wird es immer noch kaum glauben können, daß dieses nahezu ausgelöschte Land in wenigen Jahren wieder zu einem lebendigen Staat aufblühte, in dem es ganz normale Häuser und Menschen gab. Will man die Aufbauleistungen ästhetisch, vielleicht auch psychologisch beurteilen, scheinen Städte, die versucht haben, historische Konzepte zu verfolgen, die gelungeneren zu sein, sie kamen dem ursprünglichen, durch den Krieg verlorenen »städtischen und damit heimatlichen Biotop-Gefühl« (Alexander Mitscherlich) näher als die anderen, die ihre historischen Wurzeln zur Disposition stellten. Dazu gehören für mich Nürnberg, München, Lübeck, Wiesbaden, Görlitz, vielleicht auch Hamburg und Frankfurt am Main. Aber alle anderen Städte, wie Ulm, Stuttgart, Mannheim, Heilbronn, Karlsruhe, Mainz, Bonn, Köln, Essen, Gelsenkirchen, Hannover, Bremen, Kiel, Dresden, Leipzig, Cottbus und Rostock, bleiben für mich problematische Neukreationen, die nur mit wenig städtischem Charme und Eleganz aufwarten können.

Die Stadt Ulm, in der ich aufwuchs und die Vorgänge genau beobachten konnte, mag als Beispiel dienen. Die Innenstadt wurde, mit Ausnahme des gotischen Münsters, fast vollständig zerstört. In den Nachkriegsjahren beschlossen Bürgermeister und Gemeinderat, die Häuser auf ihren alten Parzellen, in ihren ursprünglichen Größen und Umrissen wiederaufzubauen. Auch die

great works, were killed on the front lines. The few survivors were given the opportunity of a lifetime.

The time of ornamental façades was over for good. Plain and simple styles prevailed – if only from necessity. And yet there were two factions fighting against each other: the followers of one wanted to rebuild the ruined houses and cities as they had looked before the war, while the others pleaded for a new beginning and thus for a hard modernity without references to history. For them the past was a failed project that must now be ended for good.

But there was a disorientation no one would really admit to, the loss of former values, the humiliation of defeat, the lack of daily necessities, money and building materials – and all of this sapped people's self-confidence. The things for which people had risked their lives and had sometimes been crippled in combat no longer counted. On the contrary: Those who had been in the Party were not allowed to work, had to wait for a long time until they had been denazified by the Allied authorities. Resistance fighters had an easier time of it. The physician and psychoanalyst Alexander Mitscherlich describes the situation in his still-exciting book *Die Unwirtlichkeit unserer Städte* (*The Inhospitability of Our Cities*), which he wrote in 1965: »1945: ruins wherever one looked, wherever one went. The end result, after they had gone out to teach the whole world the meaning of fear. Hidden behind this boastful demonstration of potency there was profound doubt of their own worth, of masculinity – now that the glory of the Reich had perished, in a time of high unemployment … Ruins were all around them: But they were still on the face of the earth, these cheering millions who had allowed themselves to be seduced, eager for booty, who had been ready to rob others of their land. The wave of destruction had returned and engulfed them. Their houses were destroyed, now they clutched the ground all the more desperately – regression to security as though to a mother's arms, after getting chummy with the false prophet had proved to be a disaster.«

The few older, surviving architects did remember such new departures as modernity, expressionism and the Bauhaus, but now, in the face of this ghostlike pile of debris, no one really knew in what style they should build. Fate forced them to act. So they made a start, in Lübeck, Hamburg, Kiel, Hannover, Berlin, Essen, Cologne, Nuremberg, Augsburg, Heilbronn, Karlsruhe, Stuttgart, Frankfurt, Mainz, Wiesbaden, Ulm and Munich.

The occupation forces made sure the work was done in an orderly fashion. Sometimes they also brought their influence to bear, particularly when it came to pushing through democratic processes. There were also factions among them who pleaded that Germany should be preserved in its ruined state. In their informative book *Deutschland in Trümmern – Stadtplanung 1940–1950* (*Germany in ruins – urban planning 1940–1950*), Werner Durth and Niels Gutschow tell about the former head of the Nuremberg department of buildings, Heinz Schmeisser, who remembers in 1981: »… In the first postwar weeks we had heard some strange ideas on the part of the Americans: Perhaps in consequence of the Morgenthau Plan the ›City of the Party Rallies‹

Gassen- und Straßenverläufe blieben weitgehend erhalten. Man wollte jetzt allerdings keine Fachwerkhäuser mit Giebeln, Erkern, Vorfenstern und Sprossungen mehr, sondern reduzierte die Gebäude auf das »Wesentliche«. Dadurch jedoch entstand eine sparsam-dürftige Ästhetik, die viele Bürger und Bewohner erschreckte und abstieß. Man bewunderte Häuser, die hartnäckig im alten Formenkanon rekonstruiert worden waren. Aber auch wirklich moderne Lösungen wurden heftig diskutiert. Immer standen die schnelle Nutzbarkeit und das Funktionieren der neuen Stadt im Vordergrund. Nicht nur die überlebenden Bürger wollten mit Wohnraum versorgt sein, sondern auch Tausende von Flüchtlingen und Vertriebenen.

Was in den 1960er Jahren noch mißmutig toleriert wurde, war in den Zeiten danach zunehmend heftiger Kritik ausgesetzt. Den wenigsten Unzufriedenen kam zu Bewußtsein, daß sie im Grunde Opfer einer langandauernden Rache Winston Churchills, seines Fliegerkommandanten Harris und General Eisenhowers, des späteren amerikanischen Präsidenten, waren. Diese englisch sprechenden Herren wollten – wie ich schon an anderer Stelle beschrieb – das deutsche Übel, den aggressiven und hochmütigen Faschismus, radikal, also von den Wurzeln her, bekämpfen und endgültig ausrotten. In den Städten und Häusern saßen, ihrer Meinung nach, die Mikroben des Bösen genauso fest wie in den Gehirnen der Bewohner. Aber nicht nur die neu-alten Gebäude der deutschen Städte sahen jetzt trostlos, leer und aller Geschichte beraubt aus, sondern auch die Gassen, Straßen und Plätze. Dazu kam einige Jahre später das Unglück des Verkehrs, der lawinenartig über sie hereinbrach. Jetzt rissen die Verantwortlichen freiwillig, ohne kriegerischen Hintergrund, Häuser ab und schufen Platz für autogerechte Durchgangsschneisen. Geschwindigkeit wurde zum modernen Zauberwort. Aber man benötigte auch Platz für den ruhenden Verkehr der Pendler und Einkaufswilligen, die täglich aus den neu entstandenen Vororten, dem ganzen Stolz der zu Geld gekommenen Neureichen, in die »Cities«, wie ab jetzt die Stadtkerne genannt wurden, ein- und ausfuhren. Riesige innerstädtische Parkplätze wucherten zwischen Häusern wie alles zerstörende Pilzgeschwüre, später schossen Parkhäuser in die Höhe, die dem temporären Verweilen der Autos in der Stadt dienten. Wie Perlenketten aus Blech säumten ab jetzt parkende Autos die Innenstadtstraßen.

Das Unheil nahm weiter seinen Lauf. Manche Kritiker rechneten aus, daß dieser Umbauphase der Städte mehr Häuser (mit historischen Resten) zum Opfer fielen als den Bomben des Zweiten Weltkriegs. Diese Theorie muß allerdings angezweifelt werden, weil gar nicht genügend überlebende Häuser zum Vergleich übriggeblieben waren. Sie kann nur bei nahezu unzerstörten Städten wie etwa Konstanz, Schwerin oder Heidelberg zutreffen.

Aus schlechtem Gewissen heraus veranstalteten Baudirektoren immer wieder Wettbewerbe mit dem Ziel, das ästhetische Niveau der Stadtarchitekturen zu erhöhen und besondere Bauten zu kreieren, was allerdings nur selten gelang. In Ulm gehört die Gestaltung des Münsterplatzes durch den New Yorker Stararchitekten Richard Meier in den 1990er Jahren dazu. Sein »Stadthaus« brachte die Stadt wieder in die Schlagzeilen. Allerdings rächte sich der architektonische Quantensprung insofern, da die übrige Stadt noch mickriger aussieht als vorher. Es fragt sich, und die Frage müssen sich fast alle wiederaufgebauten deutschen Städte stellen: Wie geht es weiter? Soll man die Nachkriegsarchitekturen alle abreißen und durch neue Bauten ersetzen, soll man sie ummanteln und maskieren, oder soll man sich mit dem jetzigen Zustand abfinden? Da sich fast alle Häuser in Privatbesitz befinden, im Grunde ein unlösbares Problem. Nur mit enormen staatlichen und städtischen Zuschüssen wären die Besitzer vielleicht zu einer Qualitätsverbesserung zu motivieren.

Bei öffentlichen Gebäuden sind die Bedingungen etwas einfacher. Deswegen ist es nicht verwunderlich, daß die Stadtbaudirektoren in Köln, Bonn, Hannover und Ulm seit einigen Jahren den ernsthaften Abriß und Neubau mancher Konzert- oder Theatergebäude aus den 1950er und 1960er Jahren diskutieren oder sogar realisieren. In Köln werden bald das Schauspielhaus und die Beethovenhalle daran glauben müssen, beide 1960er-Jahre-Bauten, die nicht zu den schlechtesten ihrer Zeit gehören. Vielleicht löst sich hier manches auch von allein. Zeit und Wetter arbeiten, wie es ihr Wesen ist, am Zerfall der Häuser, irgendwann werden sie zu Ruinen zerfallen und damit in die Kreisläufe der Natur zurückkehren.

In vielen Großstädten lebten und arbeiteten auch sensible Architekten, die noch mit den Vorkriegstraditionen vertraut waren. Sie schlugen teilweise interessante restaurierende und reparierende Neubauten vor, die jedoch oft von den Gemeinderäten abgelehnt wurden. Manches allerdings fand auch Zustimmung. So die Kölner Gürzenichbauten in den Ruinen von St. Alban und das Wallraf-Richartz-Museum von Rudolf Schwarz, St. Maria Königin von Gottfried Böhm, die Bank für Gemeinwirtschaft von Fritz Schaller und die Renovierung der Alten Pinakothek in München durch Hans Döllgast, auf die ich später genauer eingehen werde,

was to remain obliterated as Carthage had been once, which was simply eliminated. The second, somewhat more harmless solution was to leave the old part of town, this sea of debris, as it was: ›as an eternal admonition against the insanity of war‹.«

In retrospect the achievement of architects, craftsmen and building owners is nonetheless phenomenal. Today, looking at the photos of the destruction, it is still hardly believable that this almost obliterated country became a flourishing, living state again within a few years, a country in which there were quite normal houses and people. If we try to evaluate the reconstruction achievements aesthetically, and perhaps psychologically as well, then towns that attempted to follow historical plans seem to be the more successful ones. They came closer to the original »sense of an urban and thus regional native biotope« (Alexander Mitscherlich) that had been lost in the war than did other towns that questioned their historic roots. Among the former, for me, are Nuremberg, Munich, Lübeck, Wiesbaden, Görlitz, perhaps Hamburg and Frankfurt am Main as well. But all the other towns, such as Ulm, Stuttgart, Mannheim, Heilbronn, Karlsruhe, Mainz, Bonn, Cologne, Essen, Gelsenkirchen, Hannover, Bremen, Kiel, Dresden, Leipzig, Cottbus and Rostock continue to be, for me, problematic new creations that have only minimal urban charm and elegance to offer.

Let me use the city of Ulm, where I grew up and was able to closely observe what was happening, as an example. Except for the Gothic minster the inner city was almost completely destroyed. In the postwar years the mayor and the district council decided to rebuild the houses on their old lots, in their original sizes and outlines. The course of the streets and lanes remained unchanged to a large extent. Now, however, people no longer wanted half-timbered houses with gables, bay windows, storm windows and mullions, but reduced the buildings to the »essentials«. This gave rise to a skimpy, parsimonious aesthetics that many citizens and residents found shocking and repulsive. People admired houses that had been stubbornly reconstructed to reflect the old formal canon. But really modern solutions were also the subject of vehement discussions. A priority at all times was speedy availability and the functioning of the new city. It was not only the surviving citizens who wanted to be provided with housing. There were also thousands of refugees and people who had been driven out of areas where they had lived before the war.

Things that were still sullenly tolerated in the 1960s were violently criticized in the years that followed. Only a tiny minority of those who were dissatisfied realized that they were basically victims of the long-term vengeance of Winston Churchill, the marshal of the Royal Air Force, Harris, and General Eisenhower, who later became the American president. As I have said elsewhere, these anglophone gentlemen wanted to fight and definitively extirpate the German evil – aggressive and arrogant fascism – radically, that is, to pull it up by the roots. According to them the microbes of evil were just as firmly entrenched in the cities and houses as in the minds of the inhabitants. But it was not only the new-old buildings in German cities that now looked dismal, empty and bereft of all history – so did the alleyways, streets and squares as well. There was an added disaster, traffic, which descended on them like an avalanche. Now the powers that be voluntarily, without the backdrop of war, demolished houses and created space for car-friendly passages. Speed became the modern magic formula. But there also had to be room for the slow-moving traffic of commuters and shoppers driving in and out of the cities every day from recently built suburbs, the pride and joy of the nouveaux riches, into the »cities«, as the town centers were called as of now. Huge inner-city parking lots proliferated between houses like fungal growths, destroying everything. Later parking ramps shot up, making it possible for cars to be kept in town temporarily. From now on, like metal beads, parked cars lined the streets in the inner cities.

The disaster took its course. Some critics estimated that more houses (with historic remnants) fell victim to this urban renewal phase than were destroyed by the bombs of the Second World War. There is reason to question this theory, however, because not enough houses had survived for comparison. The theory may be true of cities that were virtually undamaged, such as Constance, Schwerin or Heidelberg.

Motivated by bad conscience, directors of construction kept organizing contests, the objective being to raise the aesthetic standard of urban architecture and to create exceptional buildings, which they hardly ever succeeded in doing, however. In Ulm the design of the square in front of the minster by New York star architect Richard Meier in the '90s was one such success. Because of his »Stadthaus« the town made the headlines again. However the architectonic quantum leap had its shadow side, for ever since the rest of the town has looked even more pathetic than before. The question – one that almost all rebuilt German cities must ask themselves – is: What next? Should all postwar buildings be torn down again and replaced by new buildings, should they be encased and masked, or should one come to terms with the present state of affairs?

In Ostberlin sind die Gebäude an der ehemaligen Stalinallee, die von einem Architektenkollektiv unter der Leitung von Hermann Henselmann entworfen wurden, bemerkenswert. Allerdings sahen die ersten Entwürfe Henselmanns ganz anders aus, er plante eine Reihe parallel stehender, moderner Scheibenhochhäuser. Sie entsprachen mehr Henselmanns eigentlicher Herkunft, dem Bauhaus in Weimar. Nach dem Zweiten Weltkrieg versuchte er ein neues DDR-Bauhaus zu reaktivieren, das leider viel zu wenig bekannt wurde. Erst Ende der 1950er Jahre fand er zu jenem pseudo-klassizistischen Zuckerbäckerstil, der durch die Stalinbauten in Moskau angeregt wurde und seither zum formalen Kanon aller sozialistischen Repräsentationsarchitekturen gehörte.

Von den radikal modernen Stadtentwürfen in Westdeutschland, die in der Tradition Le Corbusiers standen, wurden glücklicherweise nur wenige realisiert. Ein erschreckendes Beispiel findet sich in dem oben erwähnten Buch von Durth und Gutschow: Ein gewisser Marcel Lods schlug im Jahr 1947 vor, die Stadt Mainz – bis auf den kleinen Altstadtkern – ganz abzutragen und ausschließlich durch Scheibenhochhäuser, eingebettet in ein parkartiges Gelände, zu ersetzen.

Auch die Ernst-May-Planungen für Wiesbaden gehen mit der alten Bausubstanz ähnlich rücksichtslos um. Sie sahen vor, alle Gründerzeitvillen aus dem 19. Jahrhundert östlich der Wilhelmstraße, die den Krieg heil überstanden hatten, abreißen und ebenfalls durch Scheibenhochhäuser ersetzen zu lassen. Gott sei Dank stimmte der Gemeinderat gegen diesen Unsinn. Heute sind es genau diese Villen, die der Stadt ihren Charme bewahrt haben. Interessant ist ein Vergleich zwischen Nürnberg und Dresden. In Nürnberg entschieden sich die Politiker gleich nach 1945, während in der Stadt die Kriegsverbrecherprozesse stattfanden, dafür, die alte Bebauung, soweit es ging, zu rekonstruieren. Diese Einstellung gegenüber historischer Bausubstanz hatte hier Tradition. Im 19. Jahrhundert wurde die mittelalterliche Stadtmauer nicht abgerissen, obwohl sie – wie in vielen anderen europäischen Großstädten – ein Hindernis für die weitere Stadtentwicklung darstellte. Bis heute prägt die Mauer mit ihrem markant-eigensinnigen Verlauf das Stadtbild. Man behielt die ursprünglichen, gewachsenen Wege, Gassen und Straßenstrukturen bei, so gut es ging. Manche Trassen mußten verbreitert werden. Alle Kirchen und die Burg wurden originalgetreu rekonstruiert.

Ganz anders in Dresden. Walter Ulbricht entschied, daß aus Dresden eine moderne sozialistische Stadt werden müsse. Er kümmerte sich – entgegen massivem Bürgerprotest – wenig um alte Bausubstanzen. Nur widerwillig stimmte er schließlich zu, daß Semperoper und Schloß rekonstruiert werden. Derartige Feudalgebäude paßten nicht in die Weltanschauung eines zukunftsorientierten, antifaschistischen Staates. Aber die überlebenden Dresdner hingen an ihrer einst so berühmten Stadt mit ihren legendären Bauten, Plätzen und Kirchen. Im Gegensatz zu Nürnberg, der alten freien Reichstadt, prägten in Dresden Hof und Schloß das Stadtbild. Ohne Schloß, ohne Oper, ohne Schloßkirche und ohne Zwinger kein Dresden. Erst in der Ära Honecker lockerte sich der Geschichtshaß mancher DDR-Politiker, und allmählich setzte sich ein gewißes Verständnis für die historischen Sehnsüchte der Bürger durch. Nach und nach verschwanden die Trümmer aus dem Stadtbild. Nur die Ruine der Frauenkirche blieb übrig.

In der Nacht vom 13. zum 14. Februar 1945 warfen britische und amerikanische Flugzeuge ihre Bombenlast über Dresden ab. In kurzer Zeit brannte die gesamte Innenstadt. Ein verheerender Feuersturm brach aus, dem Tausende von Gebäuden und Menschen zum Opfer fielen. Auch die Frauenkirche wurde getroffen und brannte noch bis zum Morgen des 15. Februar. Dann hielten die geschwächten Sandsteinpfeiler die Last der schwerbeschädigten Steinkuppel nicht mehr und brachen in sich zusammen. Von der einst stadtbildbestimmenden Kirche, die zwischen 1726 und 1743 nach Plänen von George Bähr errichtet worden war, blieb nur noch ein rauchender Steinhaufen übrig. 40 Jahre lang diente der Ruinenberg mit den zwei aufragenden Wandresten als »Mahnmal gegen den Krieg«. Dann kam die Wende, und kurz danach tauchte unter den Dresdnern der Gedanke auf, die Kirche in ihrer ganzen barocken Pracht wiederaufzubauen. Mit einer beispiellosen Spendenaktion, die erfolgreich Gelder aus der ganzen Welt einbrachte, gelang es einer Bürgerinitiative tatsächlich, den Wiederaufbau anzustoßen. Die Aktion bekam schnell Symbolcharakter und wuchs zur nationalen Identitätsfindungsbewegung heran. Im späten Wiederaufbau sahen viele Menschen eine Belohnung für die erlittenen Verlustqualen. Erst mit diesem Bau sollte das neu-alte Dresden wieder ein Herz und eine Seele bekommen. Die Zeiten des Mangels und des Entzugs hatten ein Ende. So kam es, daß die Frauenkirche zwischen 1994 und 2005 neu errichtet wurde. Dabei gelang es den Restauratoren, alle vorgefundenen Steine an ihre ursprünglichen Standorte zurückzubringen. Die Folge davon ist eine sehr gewöhnungsbedürftige Patchwork-Fassade aus hellbeigen, modern rekonstruierten und alten, schwarzgefärbten Sandsteinen. Die Narben der einstigen Verletzungen bleiben sichtbar.

Since almost all the houses are privately owned, it is basically an insoluble problem. Probably only enormous state and municipal subsidies could convince the owners to improve the quality of the buildings.

In the case of public buildings circumstances are somewhat simpler. That is why it is not surprising that for a number of years the municipal directors of construction in Cologne, Bonn, Hanover and Ulm have been seriously discussing demolishing and rebuilding quite a few concert halls or theaters from the 1950s and '60s or have even done so. In Cologne it will soon be the turn of the Kölner Schauspielhaus and the Beethovenhalle, both of them '60s buildings that are by no means among the worst of their era. And perhaps some solutions will come by themselves. Time and weather work on the disintegration of the houses – that is their nature. At some point the buildings will collapse into ruins and thus become part of the natural cycle again.

Living and working in many large cities, there were also sensitive architects who were still familiar with prewar traditions. They proposed partly interesting new construction that restored and repaired existing buildings. Often these were rejected by municipal councils, however. Some things did get approved, though. Examples are the Gürzenich buildings in Cologne in the ruins of the church of St. Alban and the Wallraf Richartz Museum by Rudolf Schwarz, St. Maria Königin by Gottfried Böhm, the Bank für Gemeinwirtschaft by Fritz Schaller and the renovation of the Alte Pinakothek in Munich by Hans Döllgast, which I will discuss later in more depth.

In East Berlin the buildings on the former Stalinallee, designed by an architect collective headed by Hermann Henselmann, are remarkable. It is true that Henselmann's first plans looked quite different: He had been planning a row of parallel, modern slab high-rises. They were more in keeping with Henselmann's actual origins, the Bauhaus in Weimar. After the Second World War he tried to reactivate a new GDR Bauhaus, which, unfortunately, did not become widely known. It was not until the end of the 1950s that he adopted the pseudo-classicistic wedding-cake style inspired by Stalin's buildings in Moscow that has ever since been part of the formal canon of all representative socialist architecture.

Luckily only few of the radically modern urban designs in West Germany that were rooted in the tradition of Le Corbusier were ever implemented. An alarming example can be found in the above-mentioned book by Durth and Gutschow: A certain Marcel Lods proposed in 1947 to raze the city of Mainz completely – except for the small old-town center – and to replace it exclusively with slab high-rises embedded in a parklike tract of land. Wide highways were to provide access to the new development.

The development planned by Ernst May for Wiesbaden treats the old buildings just as ruthlessly. The plans provided for the demolition of all the 1870s villas east of Wilhelmstraße that had survived the war intact, also to be replaced by slab high-rises. Thank God the municipal council voted against this nonsense. Today it is precisely these villas that have preserved the city's charm. It is interesting to compare Nuremberg and Dresden. In Nuremberg, right after 1945, while the war crime trials were taking place in the city, the politicians decided to reconstruct the old buildings as far as possible. This attitude toward historic buildings was traditional here. In the 19th century the medieval city wall was not torn down although – as in many other European cities – it represented an obstacle to further city development. The striking, stubborn wall is still a characteristic feature of the city's profile. The city planners preserved the original historically evolved roads, lanes, and street structures wherever possible. Some routes had to be widened. All the churches and the castle were reconstructed true to the originals.

Dresden was a vastly different story. Walter Ulbricht decided that Dresden must become a modern socialist city. In spite of massive protests by the citizens, he showed little concern for old buildings. Reluctantly he finally agreed that the Semper Opera House and the castle were to be reconstructed. Such feudal buildings did not fit the ideology of a future-oriented, anti-fascist state. But the surviving Dresdeners loved their once so famous city, with its legendary buildings, squares, and churches. Unlike Nuremberg, an ancient, free city of the Holy Roman Empire, the characteristic features of Dresden were the court and the castle. Dresden without the castle, without the Opera House, without the Schlosskirche and without the Zwinger is not Dresden. Not until the Honecker era did the hatred of GDR politicians for history relax. Gradually a certain understanding for the historical nostalgia of the citizens reasserted itself. Slowly the rubble disappeared from the cityscape. Only the ruin of the Frauenkirche remained.

In the night of 13 to 14 February 1945 British and American planes repeatedly dropped their loads of bombs on Dresden. Within a short time the entire inner city was burning. A devastating firestorm broke out, claiming thousands of buildings and people as its victims. The Frauenkirche was hit and was still burning on the morning of February 15th. Then the weakened sandstone pil-

55. Ruine der Frauenkirche in Dresden. Das berühmte, stadtbildprägende Gebäude Georg Bährs war in der Nacht vom 13. auf den 14. Februar 1945 von alliierten Bombern zerstört worden. 40 Jahre lang diente die Kirchenruine der DDR als Mahnmal gegen den Krieg. Nach der Wende sorgte der Wiederaufbau symbolträchtig für weltweites Aufsehen.

55. Ruin of the Frauenkirche in Dresden. This famous and distinctive building by Georg Bähr was destroyed by Allied bombers in the night of 13 February 1945. For 40 years the ruins of the church served as an anti-war memorial. After the fall of the Berlin Wall, the reconstruction was seen as a significant symbol all over the world.

Es versteht sich, daß ich als Verehrer von Ruinen zu den Gegnern des Wiederaufbaus gehöre, zumal die jetzige Kirche mit ihren Aufzügen, kilometerlangen Elektroleitungen und ihrer Klimaanlage im Grunde als völliger Neubau – man könnte auch sagen als eine Fälschung! – bezeichnet werden muß. Vielleicht wäre es besser gewesen, dem Vorbild der Berliner Kaiser-Wilhelm-Gedächtniskirche zu folgen und die originale Ruine mit einem modernen Architekturelement zu verbinden.

Keiner der berühmten modernen Architekten tat sich in Wirklichkeit leicht mit Ruinen. Sie alle betrachteten alte Gemäuer als ihre natürlichen Feinde und propagierten ausschließlich das Neue. Radikale Rücksichtslosigkeit gehörte zum Prinzip des »Internationalen Stils«, der in der Nachfolge des Bauhauses von fast allen großen Architekten der Moderne vertreten wurde. Ihnen war es vollkommen gleichgültig, ob sie ein Gebäude für Rio de Janeiro, New York, San Francisco, London, Paris oder Berlin zu entwerfen hatten. Klarheit, Einfachheit und funktionaler Stil hatten überall gleich auszusehen. Jederzeit wäre es möglich, das Dessauer Bauhaus von Walter Gropius, den Barcelona-Pavillon oder die Berliner Nationalgalerie von Mies van der Rohe in eine andere Stadt, an eine andere Stelle auf der Welt zu transponieren. Die Zeit des regional unverwechselbaren

lars, no longer able to support the load of the severely damaged stone cupola, collapsed. Only a smoking heap of rubble remained of the church, built between 1726 and 1743 based on plans by Georg Bähr, which had once been a characteristic feature of the city. For 40 years the mountain of ruins and its two remaining looming walls served as a »memorial against the war«. Then came the collapse of the Communist system, and soon thereafter it occurred to the Dresdeners that the church should be rebuilt in all its baroque glory. With an unequalled fund-raising campaign that collected donations from all over the world, a citizens' action group succeeded in initiating the church's reconstruction. The action soon came to have a symbolic character and grew into a movement of people who were looking for a national identity. Many people saw such late reconstruction as a reward for the torments of loss they had suffered. Not until the church was rebuilt did a new-old Dresden finally get back its heart and soul. The days of shortages and deprivation were over. This is how it happened, between 1994 and 2005, that the Frauenkirche was rebuilt. In the process, the restorers managed to put back in their original positions all the building blocks that had been found. As a result there is now a patchwork façade of light beige, modern, reconstructed sandstone blocks interspersed with old black stone blocks, which takes some getting used to. The scars of the former wounds remain visible.

It goes without saying that as an admirer of ruins I am among the opponents of reconstruction, particularly as the present church with its elevators, miles of electric lines, and its air conditioning must basically be described as a completely new building – a forgery if you will. Perhaps it would have been better to follow the model of the Kaiser-Wilhelm-Gedächtnis-Kirche (Kaiser Wilhelm Memorial Church) in Berlin and to combine the original ruin with a modern architectural element.

In reality none of the famous modern architects had an easy time of it when it came to ruins. They all regarded old walls as their natural enemies and promoted what was new to the exclusion of everything else. Radical ruthlessness was one of the principles of the »International Style« that was advocated by almost all the great architects of the modern age who emulated the Bauhaus. It was a matter of complete indifference to them whether they had to design a building for Rio de Janeiro, New York, San Francisco, London, Paris, or Berlin. Clarity, simplicity and functional style had to look the same everywhere. At any time it would have been possible to transpose Walter Gropius' Dessau Bauhaus or Mies van der Rohe's Barcelona Pavilion or his New National Gallery in Berlin into another city, another part of the world. The time of regionally distinctive building was definitely over. Part of this attitude was a complete scorn for history and for all historical buildings. Here, ruins could only get in the way; they were superfluous and absurd.

The Kaiser Wilhelm Memorial Church was so badly damaged by Allied bombs in the night of 23 – 24 November 1943 that it had to be considered almost a total loss. Only sections of the tower above the entrance portal and parts of the chancel had survived the catastrophe. While in the years after the war a new West Berlin grew up around it, no one really knew just what was to be done about the tiresome ruin. Some groups of citizens pleaded that the church be rebuilt, but the Allies did not provide any funds for this. They feared that such a reconstruction might reactivate old ways of thinking in the consciousness of the German population.

If one considers what a reactionary building program the original architect of this church, Franz Heinrich Schwechten, had devised for the edifice one can understand the skepticism. Schwechten had won the competition in 1890 with a neo-Romanesque church design. The foundation stone was laid as early as the following year, and on 1 September 1895 – the commemoration of the Prussian victory in the battle of Sedan, which was celebrated with much pomp in those days – the new Lutheran church was consecrated in the presence of Kaiser Wilhelm II. He had wished that the venue be used not only as a church but also as a site of remembrance for Kaiser Wilhelm I. and his 1870/71 military victory. This is how Jesus, Mary and the disciples came to stand facing field marshals Roon and Moltke in the pompous mosaics of the entrance hall, resplendent with gold, which had survived the war almost intact. From the background even old Imperial Chancellor Bismarck looks down on the scene.

From today's perspective the effect of the mixture of monarchic, nationalist politics, war and religion is embarrassing and ridiculous. It is like an unintentional cartoon. This is why we should actually be glad that this church projects into our time as a ruin fragment.

Since damaged buildings in the '50s could be only inadequately secured because of a lack of funds, they became an ever greater hazard for passersby and traffic. Parts of the chancel had to be demolished because they were too unsafe. From that point on, the stump of a tower stood alone above the former main entrance in the busy intersection like an erratic boulder, a reminder of dark times. Finally, in 1956/57, an architects' competition was held. On 20 March 1957 the jury decided on the design of Egon Eiermann, one of the most famous German postwar architects.

Bauens war endgültig vorbei. Zu dieser Einstellung gehörte auch eine gründliche Verachtung der Geschichte und aller historischen Bauten. Ruinen können dabei nur stören, sind überflüssig und unsinnig.

Die Kaiser-Wilhelm-Gedächtniskirche wurde in der Nacht vom 23. auf den 24. November 1943 von alliierten Bomben so schwer getroffen, daß man sie fast zu den Totalverlusten rechnen mußte. Nur Turmreste über dem Eingangsportal und Teile des Chors hatten die Katastrophe überlebt. Während in den Jahren nach dem Krieg ringsum das neue Westberlin in die Höhe wuchs, wußte niemand so richtig, was mit der lästigen Ruine zu tun sei. Manche Bürgergruppen plädierten für einen Wiederaufbau, aber die Alliierten stellten dafür kein Geld zur Verfügung. Sie befürchteten, daß auf diese Weise altes Gedankengut im Bewußtsein der deutschen Bevölkerung reaktiviert werden könne.

Wenn man bedenkt, welch reaktionäres Bauprogramm der einstige Architekt dieser Kirche, Franz Heinrich Schwechten, dem Bau mit auf den Weg gegeben hat, kann man die Skepsis verstehen. Schwechten hatte 1890 den Wettbewerb mit einem neoromanischen Kirchenentwurf gewonnen. Bereits im Jahr danach erfolgte die Grundsteinlegung, und am 1. September 1895 – dem damals mit viel Pomp gefeierten Sedanstag – wurde die neue evangelische Kirche in Anwesenheit von Kaiser Wilhelm II. eingeweiht. Er hatte sich gewünscht, daß die Räume, neben ihrer kirchlichen Nutzung, auch zu einem Gedächtnisort für Kaiser Wilhelm I. und seinen militärischen Sieg von 1870/71 werden sollten. So kam es, daß in den pompösen, goldprunkenden Mosaiken der Eingangshalle, die den Krieg nahezu unversehrt überstanden haben, Jesus, Maria und die Jünger den Feldmarschällen Roon und Moltke gegenüberstehen. Aus dem Hintergrund blickt sogar der alte Reichskanzler Bismarck auf das Geschehen.

Die Vermischung von monarchisch-nationalistischer Politik, Krieg und Religion wirkt in ihrem ungebrochenen Pathos, von heute aus gesehen, peinlich und lächerlich. Eine unfreiwillige *Simplicissimus*-Karikatur. Deshalb muß man eigentlich froh darüber sein, daß diese Kirche als Ruinenfragment in unsere Gegenwart hineinragt.

Da die Baureste aus Geldmangel in den 50er Jahren nur notdürftig gesichert werden konnten, wurden sie immer mehr zu einer Gefahr für Passanten und Verkehr. Teile des Chors mußten wegen zu großer Baufälligkeit abgerissen werden. Ab jetzt stand der Turmstumpf über dem einstigen Haupteingang allein auf der verkehrsreichen Kreuzung und mahnte wie ein Irrläufer an finstere Zeiten. 1956/57 endlich wurde ein Architektenwettbewerb ausgeschrieben, und am 20. März 1957 entschied sich die Jury für den Entwurf von Egon Eiermann, der damals zu den berühmtesten deutschen Nachkriegsarchitekten gehörte. Als seine Pläne anschließend in den Zeitungen veröffentlicht wurden, brach ein Sturm der Entrüstung los. Eiermann hatte die Ruine weggelassen, abgerissen, einfach ausradiert. Sie kam in seinem Entwurf überhaupt nicht vor. In der Ausschreibung war es den Architekten freigestellt, die Turmruine zu erhalten oder abzureißen. Sechs der neun Wettbewerbsteilnehmer hatten sie stehenlassen, bei den restlichen drei tauchte sie nicht mehr auf. Und ausgerechnet einer dieser drei Architekten gewann nun die Ausschreibung.

Den Berlinern war die Ruine der Kaiser-Wilhelm-Gedächtniskirche mit den Jahren ans Herz gewachsen. Nachdem jetzt überall die neuen Gebäude in die Höhe schossen und damit die Erinnerung an die Kriegskatastrophen zu verschwinden drohte, kam der Kirchenruine eine ganz neue Bedeutung zu. Eingekreist von zunehmend optimistisch brodelndem Aufbruch, mahnte sie an die finsteren Stunden der Bedrohung, der Angst, des Schmerzes und des Todes. 47 000 Berliner und Berlinerinnen schrieben damals an eine Berliner Tageszeitung und setzten sich für den Erhalt der Ruine ein. Das Votum war so überwältigend, daß Eiermann nicht einfach darüber hinweggehen konnte. Widerwillig änderte er seine Pläne. Dieses Beispiel zeigt einmal wieder, daß man der Radikalität moderner Architekten durchaus mißtrauen sollte. Ohne das Volksbegehren hätte Eiermann die Ruine abreißen lassen und seine an sich unbedeutende Kirchenarchitektur mitten in die Stadt gesetzt. Erst in Korrespondenz mit der alten Ruine erhielt das Ensemble seine einmalige Wirkung. Und diese Einmaligkeit war so groß, daß die Kaiser-Wilhelm-Gedächtniskirche als Ruine in Kombination mit dem modernen Bau zur Stadtikone und zum wichtigsten Bauensemble der gesamten Nachkriegszeit in Deutschland aufstieg. Fast jeder Bundesbürger kannte und kennt das Bild. Es war zum Symbol der Verschmelzung von (verletzter) alter und (hoffnungsvoll-optimistischer) neuer Zeit geworden, außerdem zu einem Denkmal gegen den Krieg.

Am 17. Dezember 1961 fand die Einweihung des Neubaus statt, und seither ist die Beliebtheit des Ortes, trotz Wiedervereinigung und der daraus resultierenden City-Verlagerung Richtung Osten, ungebrochen. Täglich versammeln sich hier im Sommer Tausende von Touristen, photographieren sich gegenseitig vor dem weltberühmten, jetzt allerdings schon in die Jahre gekommenen Denkmal. Kein einziger Bau der Stadt hat danach die gleiche Symbolkraft erreicht wie

56. Gedächtniskirche in Berlin. Die leere Fenster-Rosette der Kirchen-Hauptfassade schaut auf die Stadt wie die hohle Augenhöhle eines Totenschädels.
57. Gedächtniskirche in Berlin. Beispiel einer bis heute erhaltenen Kriegsruine. Blick auf Ruine und Turmneubau von Egon Eiermann, erbaut zwischen 1957 und 1961.

56. Gedächtniskirche in Berlin. The empty rose window in the church's main façade looking at the city like a hollow eye socket in a skull.
57. Gedächtniskirche in Berlin. Example of a surviving war ruin. View of the ruin and Egon Eiermann's new tower, built between 1957 and 1961.

When his plans were subsequently published in the newspapers, there was a public outcry. Eiermann had left out the ruin, had demolished it, simply erased it. It did not even appear in his design. In the call for designs it was left up to the architects whether the tower ruin would be preserved or torn down. Six of the nine contestants had left it standing. In the remaining three it was absent. And it was one of the latter three architects of all people who was now selected as the winner.

Berliners had come to love the ruin of the Kaiser Wilhelm Memorial Church over the years. Now that the new buildings were shooting up everywhere and thus the memory of the catastrophes of war was in danger of vanishing, the ruin of the church had a completely new significance. Encircled by the increasingly optimistic signs of a new era, it reminded people of the grim hours of menacing danger, fear, pain and death. At the time 47,000 Berliners wrote to a Berlin daily paper in support of preserving the ruin. The vote was so overwhelming that Eiermann could not simply ignore it. Reluctantly he altered his plans. This example again goes to show that one should definitely mistrust the radicality of modern architects. Had it not been for the popular referendum, Eiermann would have had the ruin demolished and would have placed his intrinsically insignificant church right in the middle of the city. The ensemble only attained its full, unique impact in conjunction with the old ruin. And its originality was so great that the ruin of the Kaiser Wilhelm Memorial Church in combination with the modern building became the crowning glory of the city and the most important building ensemble of the entire postwar period in Germany. Almost every citizen of the Federal Republic knew and knows it. It had become the symbol of the fusion of a (wounded) past and a (hopeful and optimistic) new era, and it was also a memorial against the war.

On 17 December 1961 the new building was officially opened, and since then the popularity of the place, in spite of German reunification and the resulting eastward shift of the city center, has continued unabated. Daily, thousands of tourists gather here in summer and take pictures of each other in front of the world-famous building, which is now getting on in years, however. No other

diese architektonische Komposition, nicht einmal der Reichstag mit seiner neuen gläsernen Kuppel von Norman Foster, auch nicht das Jüdische Museum von Daniel Libeskind (dessen Lage in der Stadt dafür zu ungünstig ist). Daher ist es nicht verwunderlich, daß die terroristische Gruppe um Andreas Baader auch einen Blick auf das symbolträchtige Bauensemble richtete und 1967 als erste Aktion einen Brandanschlag auf die Gedächtniskirche plante. Nach langwierigen, subversiven Diskussionen beschränkte man sich später allerdings auf eine Flugblattaktion vor der Ruine. Als nächstes war ein Brandanschlag auf das berühmteste Kaufhaus Westberlins, das KDW, geplant. Weil die damalige Freundin Baaders dagegen protestierte – sie wollte sich im Durchführungsfall mit ihrem gemeinsamen Kleinkind den ganzen Tag im Kaufhaus aufhalten –, wich die Gruppe nach Frankfurt aus und zündete in einem dortigen Kaufhaus ihre erste Brandbombe. Damit hatte die 68er-Bewegung, die ja von Westberlin ausging, ihren kriminellen Nebenweg eingeschlagen, der in den folgenden Monaten und Jahren zu über 40 Morden an Politikern und Managern führte.

Leo von Klenze entwarf und baute die Alte Pinakothek in München, das damals größte Museumsgebäude der Welt, zwischen 1826 und 1836. Wegen seiner optimalen Funktionslösungen, den gläsernen Dächern, den Nordlichtkabinetten, den klima- und wassertechnischen Erfindungen galt das Museum als sehr fortschrittlich und modern. Die blockartige Außenform erinnert in ihrer klassizistisch-radikalen Formensprache an römisch-florentinische Renaissancebauten, gleichzeitig auch an den Funktionalismus des 19. Jahrhunderts, wie er bei Kasernen und später bei größeren, repräsentativen Verwaltungsbauten – etwa Finanzämtern – Anwendung fand.

Um die gleichförmige, strenge Reihung der Rundbogenfenster in den beiden Ausstellungsgeschossen nicht beliebig fortsetzen zu müssen, schloß Klenze deren Verlauf mit zwei mächtigen, querliegenden Eckbauten ab. Den Museumseingang legte er an die östliche Schmalseite und markierte ihn mit zwei Steinlöwen, die auch heute noch auf ihren Sockeln ruhen. Die übrigen unverputzten Klinkerfassaden blieben völlig skulpturenlos. Das für die Öffentlichkeit bestimmte Museum war stilbildend und diente vielen Museen der Welt als Vorbild. Klenze selbst wurde in den Jahren danach beauftragt, ein ähnliches Gebäude – die Ermitage – in Sankt Petersburg zu errichten. Von 1836 bis 1939 gehörte die Alte Pinakothek zu den berühmtesten Gemäldegalerien der Welt. Erst mit Beginn des Zweiten Weltkriegs endete die bisherige Ruhe und Gelassenheit. Von der Auslagerung der wertvollen Kunstgegenstände wegen drohender Luftangriffe war schon die Rede, auch von den schweren Zerstörungen durch britische Bomber seit 1942.

Ende des Krieges bot die Alte Pinakothek einen trostlosen Anblick, sie war zur völlig unbenutzbaren Ruine erniedrigt worden. Über Wiederaufbau und Renovierung diskutierten die Verantwortlichen von Stadt und Land jahrelang. Erst 1952 erhielt der damals 61jährige Münchner Architekturprofessor Hans Döllgast den Auftrag, das Gebäude in seiner alten Funktion wieder benutzbar zu machen. Seine Planungsarbeiten zogen sich bis 1957 hin, dann erst begann er, die Ruine zu räumen. Er verlegte den Haupteingang in die Mittelachse der Längsfront, auf die Nordseite, schuf eine großzügige Eingangshalle, entfernte die Reste der ehemaligen Kolonnaden auf der Südseite und erfand hier jenes spektakuläre Treppen-Raumtal, das die klassizistische Pseudo-Antike Klenzes mit der modernen Zeit verbindet. Ein merkwürdiger Sog geht auch heute noch von den beiden, sich spiegelnden, 68 Stufen hohen Treppenbergen aus, so als hätte Döllgast die Ruinenwunde wie einen Befreiungsschlag aus finsterer Zeit empfunden. Jeder Besucher schwebt gleichsam durch eine alpine Klamm hinauf zu den großen Werken der Kunst. Beidseitig begleiten ihn Klinkerpfeiler, die in fast gotischer Manier an die geistigen Welten der großen Dome erinnern. Durch die leeren Südfenster strömt Tageslicht, klar und hell zugleich. Keine falschen Bilder, keine Malereien und keine Skulpturen ornamentieren den Aufstieg. Man kann sich in Ruhe auf den bevorstehenden Gang durch die hehren Oberlichtsäle, gefüllt mit Gemälden von Dürer, Tizian, Raffael, Rembrandt und Rubens, vorbereiten.

Die andere gewagte, aber letztlich gelungene Entscheidung Döllgasts bestand darin, die beiden großen, zentralen Zerstörungswunden im mittleren Bereich der Hauptfassaden sichtbar zu lassen und sie mit neuen, groben Ziegeln auszufüllen. Vor allem auf der Südseite kann jeder Interessierte auch heute noch erkennen, wo die Abbruchkanten verliefen, welcher Wandteil den Krieg heil überstand und welcher ihm zum Opfer fiel. Der normalerweise so perfekte, in sich ruhende, störungsfreie Klassizismus trägt seine Ruinennarben stolz wie eine Mahnung. Dieses Haus war verletzt, hatte Schmerzen ertragen, ist jetzt wieder gesund und wird benutzt wie zu Klenzes Zeiten.

Für mich stellt diese Renovierung eine der ganz großen architektonischen Nachkriegsleistungen dar. Döllgast hat mit der Alten Pinakothek bewiesen, daß ein ehrlicher, funktionstüchtiger und ästhetisch erfreulicher Dialog zwischen den Zeiten möglich ist, ohne das Alte zu zerstören und das Neue übermächtig werden zu lassen.

building in the city built subsequently has attained the same symbolic power as this architectonic composition, not even the Reichstag with its new glass cupola by Norman Foster, or the Jewish Museum by Daniel Libeskind (whose location in the city is too unfavorable). That is why it is no surprise that the terrorist group around Andreas Baader also focused on the heavily symbolic ensemble of buildings and in 1967 planned that its first action would be an arson attack on the Memorial Church. After lengthy, subversive discussions the group finally agreed to limit themselves to a leafleting campaign in front of the ruin. They next planned an arson attack on the most famous West Berlin department store, the KDW (Kaufhaus des Westens). Because Baader's then-girlfriend protested – she was going to spend all day in the store with the couple's small child if the plan was carried out – the group switched the action to Frankfurt and ignited its first firebomb in a department store there. Thus the Movement of 1968, which originated in West Berlin, had entered upon a criminal career which in the months and years that followed led to the murders of over 40 politicians and managers.

Between 1826 and 1836, Leo von Klenze designed and built the Alte Pinakothek in Munich, the largest museum building in the world at the time. Because of its optimum functional solutions, glass roofs, cabinet galleries with a northern exposure, and air-conditioning and water technology inventions, the museum was considered to be very progressive and modern. The classicistic-radical stylistic idiom of the blocklike exterior form is reminiscent of Roman and Florentine Renaissance buildings and at the same time of the kind of 19th-century functionalism used in army barracks and later in larger, imposing administration buildings, such as internal revenue office buildings.

In order not to have to continue the uniform, austere sequence of round arched windows in both exhibition floors indefinitely, Klenze closed their progression with two massive transverse corner buildings. He placed the museum entrance on the narrow, eastern side and marked it with two stone lions, which still rest on their pedestals today. The rest of the unplastered clinker brick façades remained completely without sculptures. The museum, which was intended to be open to the public, set a style, serving as a model for many museums worldwide. In subsequent years Klenze himself was commissioned to erect a similar building – the Hermitage – in Saint Petersburg. From 1836 till 1939 the Alte Pinakothek was one of the most famous art galleries in the world. Its peace and calm came to an end at the beginning of World War II. There was talk of evacuating the valuable artworks because of imminent air raids, and of the severe damage caused by British bombers beginning in 1942.

At the end of the war the Alte Pinakothek looked bleak. It had become a completely unusable ruin. For years, the powers that be in the city and region debated how to rebuild and renovate the museum. It was not until 1952 that the then 61-year-old Munich architecture professor Hans Döllgast was commissioned with the task of making the building usable once more in its former function. The work of planning took until 1957, when he finally began to clear out the ruin. He moved the main entrance to the central axis of the longitudinal front, to the north side, created a spacious entrance hall, removed the remains of the former colonnades on the south side and here devised that spectacular canyon of a staircase that links Klenze's classicistic pseudo-antiquity with the modern era. The two mountainous 68-step-high staircases, a mirror image of each other, still emanate a strange magnetism, as though Döllgast had experienced the ruin wound as a liberating lightning stroke from a dark time. Visitors seemingly soar through an alpine gorge up to the great works of art. On both sides they are accompanied by clinker brick pillars, almost Gothic in style, reminiscent of the spiritual worlds of the great cathedrals. Clear and bright, daylight streams through the empty south windows. No faux pictures, no paintings or sculptures ornament the stairwell. Visitors can prepare at leisure for the coming walk through sublime skylit halls filled with the paintings of Dürer, Tizian, Raphael, Rembrandt and Rubens.

Döllgast's other daring but ultimately successful decision was to leave the two large, central wounds caused by destruction visible in the middle of the main façades and to fill them in with new, rough bricks. Especially on the south side anyone who is interested can still recognize the edges where demolition began, which section of the wall survived the war intact and which one was destroyed. Normally so perfect, at peace with itself, undisturbed, this classicism bears its ruin scars proudly, like an admonishing reminder. This house was wounded, has felt pain, is whole once more and is used as it was in Klenze's times.

For me this renovation represents one of the very great architectonic achievements of the postwar period. With the Alte Pinakothek Döllgast proved that an honest, functional and aesthetically pleasing dialogue between different periods is possible without destroying the old and allowing the new to become overpowering.

Auch ein anderer Klenzebau in München überstand die Bombenangriffe nicht: die Glyptothek am Königsplatz, errichtet zwischen 1816 und 1830. Im Gegensatz zur Alten Pinakothek zogen sich die Wiederaufbau- und Rekonstruktionsarbeiten bis zum 28. April 1972 hin. An diesem Tag wurde die Glyptothek wieder so der Öffentlichkeit übergeben, wie wir sie heute kennen. Davor liegen Jahre, angefüllt mit heftigen Fachdiskussionen zwischen Kultusministerium, Sammlungs-direktion, Staatlicher Bauverwaltung, Landesdenkmalamt und Landesbaukunstausschuß.

Schon kurz nach Kriegsbeginn hatte man damit begonnen, die antiken Skulpturen auszula-gern oder mit Sandsäcken und Holzkonstruktionen vor möglichen Luftangriffen zu schützen. Zwi-schen dem 11. und 16. Juli 1944 beschädigten Spreng- und Brandbomben bei mehreren Treffern das klassizistische Gebäude schwer. Die antiken Kunstwerke blieben weitgehend unbeschädigt. Zwei Jahre lang war die Ruine ohne Notdach und Sicherungszaun Wind, Wetter und Plünderun-gen ausgesetzt. Erst danach begannen die Aufräumarbeiten, die allerdings nicht verhindern konn-ten, daß weiterhin Wasser in die gemauerten Wände eindrang und die fragmentarisch erhaltenen Cornelius-Fresken nahezu vollständig zerstört wurden. Wie auch bei der Alten Pinakothek lagen hier die Meinungen über den Wiederaufbau unter Fachleuten weit auseinander. Nach Jahren der Diskussion einigte man sich darauf, die Fassaden originalgetreu zu rekonstruieren. Bei den Innenräumen wurde der Meinungskrieg jahrelang weitergeführt, man experimentierte mit ver-schiedenen Putzen, Steinböden und Farben. Rekonstruierte und modernisierte Musterräume er-regten die Gemüter, aber ein allgemeiner Konsens konnte nicht herbeigeführt werden.

Erst 1962, mit der Ernennung von Dieter Ohly zum neuen Direktor der Glyptothek, klärten sich die Fronten. Er bezog klar Stellung und plädierte für das Konzept des Architekten Josef Wiedemann, einem Schüler von Hans Döllgast. Wiedemann, der 1910 in München geboren wurde, war beteiligt an Nazi-Bauprojekten auf dem Obersalzberg (Hotel Platterhof) und in Linz (Donauhotel). Nach seiner Entnazifizierung, 1948, gründete er ein eigenes Architekturbüro in München und war maßgeblich am Wiederaufbau der Alten Akademie in der Neuhauserstraße, der Hofgartenarkaden und des Sieges-tors in der Leopoldstraße beteiligt. Sein Konzept für die Rekonstruktion der Glyptothek gehört be-stimmt zum Besten, was er gebaut hat – ganz im Geist seines Lehrers Hans Döllgast.

Josef Wiedemann schlug vor, die Ziegel des Rohbaus sichtbar zu lassen und sie mit einer dünnen, hellgrauen Mörtelschlemme zu überziehen. Da sich die Ziegel als porös herausstellten, mußten erst einige Zentimeter ihrer Oberfläche abgetragen werden, bevor die Schlemme darü-bergestrichen werden konnte. Alle Wände und Decken wurden in gleicher Weise, mit der gleichen Schlemme und der gleichen Farbe behandelt. Für den Fußboden schlug Wiedemann grauen Mu-schelkalk vor. Außerdem ließ er Fenster zum Innenhof hin einbauen und hob das Hofniveau um 80 Zentimeter an. Wer heute durch die wunderbar belichteten, schlichten Räume geht und sieht,

Another Klenze building in Munich also did not survive the air raids: the Glyptothek on Königsplatz, built between 1816 and 1830. In contrast to the Alte Pinakothek, rebuilding and reconstruction work dragged on until 28 April 1972. On that date the Glyptothek was handed over to the public in the form we know today, after years of violent technical discussions between the Ministry of Culture, the head of collections, the State Department of Building Administration, the Bavarian Office for the Protection of Historical Monuments and the Bavarian Committee for Architecture.

A short time after the beginning of the war the museum had begun to evacuate Greek and Roman sculptures or to protect them with sandbags and wood frames against possible air raids. Between 11 and 16 July 1944 explosive and incendiary bombs struck the museum several times, severely damaging the neoclassical building. The artworks of antiquity remained undamaged for the most part. For two years the ruin, which had no makeshift roof or security fence, was exposed to wind, weather and plundering. Clearing-up operations did not begin until that point, but they could not prevent water from seeping into the masonry walls and almost completely destroying the preserved fragments of the Cornelius frescoes. As in the case of the Alte Pinakothek, experts' views about the building's reconstruction were extremely diverse. After years of discussion, agreement was reached to reconstruct the façades true to the originals. The controversy regarding the interior continued for many more years. There was experimentation with different kinds of plaster, stone floors and colors. Feelings ran high regarding reconstructed and modernized model rooms, but it was difficult to achieve general consensus.

The opposing factions did not resolve their differences until 1962, when Dieter Ohly was appointed as the new director of the Glyptothek. He took a stand and pleaded for the design of the architect Josef Wiedemann, a student of Hans Döllgast. Born in Munich in 1910, Wiedemann was involved in Nazi construction projects on the Obersalzberg (Hotel Platterhof) and in Linz (Donauhotel). After his denazification in 1948, he founded his own architecture firm in Munich and played a substantial role in the reconstruction of the Alte Akademie on Neuhauserstraße, the Hofgarten colonnade and the Siegestor (Victory Gate) on Leopoldstraße. His concept for the reconstruction of the Glyptothek is definitely one of his best works – very much in the spirit of his teacher Hans Döllgast.

Josef Wiedemann proposed that the bricks of the building's shell should be left visible and coated with a thin, light gray mortar whitewash. Since the bricks turned out to be porous, a few centimeters of their surface had to be removed before the whitewash could be applied. All the walls and ceilings were treated in the same way, with the same whitewash and the same color. For the floor Wiedemann proposed gray limestone. Also he built windows looking out onto the in-

58, 59. Gelungenes Beispiel des Wiederaufbaus einer Kriegsruine: Alte Pinakothek in München von Hans Döllgast.
60. Die Wunden am klassizistischen Bau Leo von Klenzes bleiben als Verletzung bis heute sichtbar.

58, 59. Successful example of a reconstructed war ruin. The Alte Pinakothek in Munich, by Hans Döllgast.
60. The wounds in Leo von Klenze's neo-classical building can still be seen today.

wie klar, ruhig und edel die antiken Skulpturen darin wirken, kann sich nur darüber wundern, daß Josef Wiedemann für sein Werk nach der Eröffnung von Publikum und Kritikern heftig angegriffen wurde. Manche sprachen von »Purismus, archäologischem Rigorismus und von einer fragwürdigen Ästhetik der 60er Jahre des 20. Jahrhunderts«, wie Raimund Wünsche, der heutige Direktor der Glyptothek schreibt.

Wenn man die Photos der Räume aus der Entstehungszeit anschaut, möchte man sagen, jetzt erst, in der Fassung von Josef Wiedemann, haben sie ihre klassische Würde wirklich erhalten. Vorher, mit all den bunten Fresken von Cornelius, kann man eher von fragwürdig dekorierten, völlig überladenen Räumen sprechen. Vielleicht hätte sogar Leo von Klenze, der ja viel nüchterner und weniger romantisch veranlagt war als sein preußischer Kollege Schinkel, Freude an der heutigen Gebäudefassung gehabt.

In Berlin dauerte es bis zum Oktober 2009, dann war es endlich soweit: Das einst so berühmte Neue Museum von Friedrich August Stüler, das im Krieg zerstört worden war und seither sein Dasein als vernachlässigte Ruine fristete, neben dem Anhalter Bahnhof die letzte große in ganz Berlin, wurde neu eröffnet. Der englische Architekt David Chipperfield hatte zusammen mit Restauratoren, Archäologen und den Museumsdirektoren über zehn Jahre am Wiederaufbau gearbeitet.

Das Neue Museum gilt als Hauptwerk des Schinkel-Schülers Friedrich August Stüler und wurde zwischen 1843 und 1855 errichtet. Der Architekt arbeitete mit damals avantgardistischen Bautechniken und verwendete für die Raumdecken und den Dachstuhl Eisenfachwerkkonstruktionen, vor allem um die Brandgefahren zu mindern und das Gewicht der Decken zu verringern. Während die Fassaden relativ schlicht gestaltet wurden, erhielten die Innenräume prunkvolle, illustrative Wanddekorationen mit stimmungsvollen Bühnenbildeffekten. Die ägyptischen Säle waren mit stark farbigen Motiven der ägytischen Kunst ausgemalt, die Vorgeschichtsräume zeigten mythologische Figuren und Szenen aus der *Edda*.

Einem dramaturgischen Höhepunkt, der nur mit einer bombastischen Oper Richard Wagners verglichen werden kann, begegnete der Besucher im Haupttreppenhaus des Neuen Museums. Hier hatte der mit viel Geld nach Berlin abgeworbene Münchner Hofmaler Wilhelm von Kaulbach einen Zyklus von Riesenfresken gemalt, die vom Erfolg der menschlichen Kulturentwicklung auf der Erde kündete. Die Themen sparten nicht an bedeutungsvollem Pathos: »Der Babylonische Turm«, »Homer und die Griechen oder die Blüte Griechenlands«, »Die Zerstörung von Jerusalem«, »Die Hunnenschlacht«, »Die Kreuzfahrer vor Jerusalem« und »Das Zeitalter der Reformation« lauteten sie.

61. Auch die Glyptothek Leo von Klenzes am Münchner Königsplatz wurde von alliierten Bomben getroffen. Hier gelang dem Architekten Joseph Wiedemann ebenfalls eine meisterhafte Renovierung.
62, 63. Wiedemann verzichtete auf die Wiederherstellung der historischen Raumzustände und schuf mit kargen Mitteln Ausstellungsräume, die den antiken Skulpturen genügend Raum lassen, um ihre Wirkung zu entfalten.

61. Leo von Klenze's Glyptothek on Munich's Königsplatz was also hit by Alliied bombs. The building was reconstructed in a masterly fashion by Joseph Wiedemann.
62, 63. Wiedemann decided not to reconstruct the historic rooms, but used austerely limited resources to create conditions that allowed the ancient sculptures sufficient space to make an impact.

ner courtyard and raised the level of the courtyard by 80 centimeters. Visitors who walk through the wonderfully lit, simple rooms today can see how clear, peaceful and noble the classical sculptures appear in this space. It may come as a surprise that Josef Wiedemann was violently attacked for his work by both public and critics once the museum opened. Some spoke of »purism, archaeological rigor and the doubtful aesthetics of the 1960s«, to quote Raimund Wünsche, the present director of the Glyptothek.

Looking at photos of the interior taken during the time the museum was built you feel like saying that only now, in the Josef Wiedemann version, the rooms have really been given their classical dignity. Earlier, with all the many-colored Cornelius frescoes, one might rather say that the rooms were decorated in questionable taste, totally cluttered. Perhaps even Leo von Klenze, who as we know was much more sober and less romantic than his Prussian colleague Schinkel, would have been pleased by the present-day version of the building.

In Berlin, it took until October 2009 for a momentous event to arrive: The once so famous Neues Museum of Friedrich August Stüler, which had been destroyed in the war and had since languished neglected – the last large-scale ruin in all of Berlin other than the Anhalter Bahnhof railroad station – was reopened. The British architect David Chipperfield had worked on its reconstruction together with restorers, archaeologists and the directors of the museum for over ten years.

The Neues Museum is considered to be the major work of Schinkel student Friedrich August Stüler and was built between 1843 and 1855. The architect worked with structural engineering techniques that were avant-garde at the time, and used iron framework structures for the ceilings of the rooms and the roof truss, primarily to reduce the risk of fire and to decrease the weight of the ceilings. While the design of the façades was relatively simple, the interior rooms had magnificent, illustrative wall decorations – full of atmosphere, suggesting stage sets. The Egyptian halls were painted with very colorful motifs of Egyptian art, the prehistory rooms showed mythological figures and scenes from the *Edda*.

In the main stairwell of the Neues Museum visitors encountered a dramatic high point that can only be compared with a bombastic opera by Richard Wagner. Here the Munich court painter Wilhelm von Kaulbach, who had been wooed away to Berlin with a large sum of money, had painted a cycle of gigantic frescoes that told of the successful rise of human civilization on earth. The themes they touched on were filled with eloquent pathos: »The Tower of Babylon«, »Homer and the Greeks or The golden age of Greece«, »The destruction of Jerusalem«, »The Battle of the Huns«, »The crusaders at the gates of Jerusalem« and »The age of the Reformation« were their names.

All these lovely visions, which many scientifically inclined critics, soon after the opening of the Neues Museum, felt were too »romanticizing«, had fallen victim to the air raids and to decades of the building's existence as a ruin. When, in the '80s, the GDR government finally decided to rebuild the museum, the reconstruction of these frescoes and room decorations was part of the plans. After German reunification attitudes changed here as well. The museum directors and cultural authorities who were in charge chose David Chipperfield's sober designs for the interior in a contest. He wanted above all to make the large stairwell into a room that employed the methods of Döllgast and Wiedemann. The clinker brick walls of the walls of the upper rooms were to remain visible, without plaster, completely exposed, and he wanted to place the stairway itself, a modern, massive concrete structure, in the former ruin space.

When I see the outcome, which is now open to the public, the resulting collage, while interesting, does not seem to me quite as successful as the Munich solutions, because it is so monumental. At any rate, Chipperfield's and his restorers' cult of ruins has produced amazing results. Wherever he finds a crumbling, serrated fragment of the room paintings, he leaves it standing like a picture. Unfortunately this gives these random forms an obtrusive quality that I find annoying. I am almost tempted to call this a trendy ruin design. Naturally these fragments show the building's and its interior's tangible state of decay – the condition in which they were found – but this raises a question: What is predominant here? Isn't it pure chance, interchangeable and arbitrary? Isn't the aesthetics of this space dictated by a completely unimportant factor, never intended to be like this by anyone? Dilapidation as ornament? A ruin as decoration?

The melancholy of a true ruin fails to materialize among the display cases in these air-conditioned rooms and halls. The museum aspect is too predominant – idly showing off far too many wounds. I think of a contaminated hospital, walls being corroded by metastases, pockmarked, eking out an unhealthy existence. I almost want to hold my breath so as not to inhale the ancient, possibly toxic, microbes. Instead of disinfectants, the rooms smell of humidifiers and air-condi-

All diese schönen Traumbilder, die schon kurz nach der Eröffnung des Neuen Museums von vielen wissenschaftsgläubigen Kritikern als zu »romantisierend« empfunden worden sind, waren Opfer der Luftangriffe und des jahrzehntelangen Ruinendaseins des Gebäudes geworden. Als die DDR-Regierung in den 1980er Jahren den Wiederaufbau des Museums endlich beschloß, gehörte die Rekonstruktion dieser Fresken und Raumausmalungen zum Konzept. Nach der Wende änderten sich auch hier die Vorzeichen. Die maßgeblichen Museumsdirektoren und Kulturverantwortlichen entschieden sich bei einem Wettbewerb für David Chipperfields nüchterne Raumfassungen. Er wollte vor allem aus dem großen Treppenhaus einen Raum schaffen, der mit den Methoden Döllgasts und Wiedemanns arbeitete. Die Klinkerwände der oberen Raumwände sollten unverputzt, in voller Nacktheit sichtbar bleiben, und die Treppe selbst wollte er als moderne, massive Betonkonstruktion in den einstigen Ruinenraum hineinstellen.

Beim Anblick des jetzt allgemein zugänglichen Ergebnisses kommt mir die entstandene Collage zwar interessant, aber wegen ihrer Monumentalität nicht ganz so gelungen vor wie die Münchner Lösungen. Überhaupt treibt der Ruinenkult Chipperfields und seiner Restauratoren erstaunliche Blüten. Überall, wo sich ein brüchiges, ausgezacktes Fragment der Raummalereien gefunden hat, läßt er es stehen wie ein Bild. Leider erhalten diese Zufallsformen eine Aufdringlichkeit, die ich als störend empfinde. Fast möchte ich von einem schicken Ruinendesign sprechen. Natürlich zeigen diese Fragmente einen konkreten Zerfallszustand des Gebäudes und der Räume, nämlich den des Auffindens, aber es stellt sich die Frage: Überwiegt hier nicht der pure Zufall, die austauschbare Beliebigkeit? Diktiert hier nicht ein völlig unwichtiger, so von niemand gewollter Moment die Raum-Ästhetik? Verfall als Ornament? Ruine als Dekoration?

Die Melancholie einer wahren Ruine will sich in diesen klimatisierten, vitrinenbestückten Räumen und Sälen nicht einstellen. Zu sehr überwiegt der Museumsaspekt, das eitle Zeigen der viel zu vielen Wunden. Ich denke an ein verseuchtes Krankenhaus, an Mauern, die von Metastasen zerfressen werden, pockennarbig ein ungesundes Dasein fristen. Fast möchte man den Atem anhalten, um nicht die uralten, möglicherweise giftigen Mikroben in sich einzusaugen. Statt nach Desinfektionsmittel riecht es in den Räumen nach Luftbefeuchtern und Klimageräten. Ich hätte mir dort mehr Ruhe und Gelassenheit gewünscht, damit die ausgestellten Kunstwerke besser zur Wirkung kommen. Die »Wahrheit«, von der Chipperfield immer wieder gesprochen hat, »die Wahrheit der Architektur«, ist in Wirklichkeit die Wahrheit eines konkreten Moments des Zerfalls, also eines flüchtigen, jetzt konservierten Übergangs. Hier wird ein Zustand fixiert, der morgen schon wieder ganz anders aussehen könnte.

Merkwürdigerweise verstummten die meisten Kritiker nach der Eröffnung des Museums 2009. Fast alle Fernsehberichte und Zeitungsartikel überschlugen sich in euphorischen Hymnen. Am 13. Januar 2010 erschien ein interessantes Gespräch zwischen Jens Bisky und Stephan Speicher, Adrian von Buttlar und Martin Mosebach in der *Süddeutschen Zeitung*. Der konservative Schriftsteller Mosebach sagt zu Beginn: »Ich kannte die Geschichte des Neuen Museums, das als volksbildendes Museum geplant war. Es sollte die Geschichte der Menschheit in beispielhaften Epochen zeigen, in Schauräumen, die auf die Ausstellungsstücke hin ausgemalt und dekoriert waren und einen Gang durch die Weltgeschichte ermöglichten: Volksaufklärung, in Opulenz durchaus, aber mit einem klaren Unterrichtsziel. Der erste große Augenblick jetzt beim Eintritt war von denkbar anderen Empfindungen begleitet, nämlich Verblüffung, Bezauberung, Eintreten in ein überwältigendes, unendlich viele divergierende Signale sendendes Wunderland. Der erste Gesamteindruck: genau das Gegenteil von dem, was einmal gewesen ist und bezweckt war. Das Geschichtskonzept des Neuen Museums, als es neu war, war für unsere Erfahrungen ein gewiß naives Konzept. Diese Linie war nicht aufrecht zu erhalten. Jetzt ist es ein Eintreten in ein Pompeji, eine Entrückung. Ich habe in einem Museum noch nie etwas Ähnliches gesehen.«

Adrian von Buttlar entgegnet: »Wie darf man sich das vorstellen, was die Verzauberung ausgemacht hat? Orientierungslosigkeit? Fanden Sie es nicht durchsichtig?« Mosebach antwortet: »Die Anordnung der Exponate schien mir von untergeordneter Bedeutung, das gesamte Gehäuse ist die eigentliche Attraktion. Der Ruinenraum mit seiner Patina, in seiner Zerstörtheit, die einen kostbaren neuen Schönheitseffekt erzeugt, auch einen theatralischen Effekt. Es war ein sich Bewegen wie durch eine Kulissenlandschaft – deswegen Verzauberung. Verblüffend ist das Konzept, die Räume in ihrer Ruinenhaftigkeit zu belassen.«

Und tatsächlich unterscheidet sich die Wandbehandlung Döllgasts und Wiedemanns von der Chipperfields und seiner Restauratoren dadurch, daß weder in der Alten Pinakothek noch in der Glyptothek Putzreste an den Wänden belassen worden sind. Diese Idee ist neu und entstammt dem wissenschaftlichen Vorgehen von Archäologen, die dankbar für jeden aufgefundenen Rest sind.

64. Chipperfields Wiederaufbau von Friedrich August Stülers ebenfalls im Zweiten Weltkrieg zerstörtem Neuen Museum in Berlin sorgte nach der Eröffnung im Oktober 2009 für großes Aufsehen. Das Photo zeigt einen Blick in das gewaltige Treppenhaus. Hier mischen sich Ruinenmotive mit monumentalen modernen Einbauten in gewagter Konfrontation.

64. Chipperfield's reconstruction of Friedrich August Stüler's Neues Museum in Berlin, which had also been destroyed in the Second World War, caused a world-wide stir when it opened in October 2009. The photograph shows a view in the enormous stairs. Here ruin motifs riskily confront monumental modern insertions.

tioning units. I would have wished for more calm and relaxation here so that the exhibited artworks can show to better advantage. The »truth« of which Chipperfield spoke again and again, »the truth of architecture«, is in reality the truth of a specific moment of decay, i.e., of a fleeting, now preserved, transition. Here, the architect records a condition that would have looked altogether different tomorrow.

Curiously enough most of the critics fell silent after the museum opened in 2009. Almost all the TV reports and newspaper articles fell over themselves in euphoric paeans of praise. On 13 January 2010 an interesting conversation between Jens Bisky and Stephan Speicher, Adrian von Buttlar and Martin Mosebach appeared in the *Süddeutsche Zeitung*. The conservative writer Mosebach begins the conversation: »I knew the history of the Neues Museum, which was planned as a museum that would provide national education. It was to show the history of the human race in exemplary epochs, in exhibition rooms that were painted and decorated to match the exhibits and made it possible for visitors to walk through world history: enlightenment of the people, definitely opulent, but with a clear educational objective. The first great moment upon entering now was accompanied by rather different emotions – amazement, enchantment, entering into an overpowering wonderland that sends an infinite number of contradictory signals. The first

Interessant an dem Statement Mosebachs ist die Tatsache, daß er nur bereit ist, die Räume zu betrachten und die Exponate völlig ausblendet. Daran merkt man, daß etwas an seiner Argumentation nicht stimmt. Schließlich bestand die Gestaltungsidee Stülers genau in dem Einklang zwischen Exponat und Raumgestaltung. Natürlich kann man sagen, daß dieser Einklang heute nicht mehr existieren kann. Mosebach spricht zu Recht vom Gegenteil der ursprünglichen Idee. Im Grunde hätte die letzte Konsequenz darin bestanden, das Neue Museum gänzlich leer auszustellen, als halbzerstörtes Phänomen des 19. Jahrhunderts. Ähnlichen Wünschen und Sehnsüchten war auch der Neubau des Jüdischen Museums von Daniel Libeskind ausgesetzt. Die Gesprächsteilnehmer umkreisen im Verlauf der Diskussion immer wieder den Ruinenzustand des Neuen Museums, und Mosebach stellt schließlich die These auf, daß Stülers Räume mit dem Zerfall immer schöner geworden seien. Mosebach: »Ich wollte noch eine andere Frage erörtern: Das Entstehen einer neuen Ruinenromantik fasziniert mich. Wo fängt das an, das Gefühl, daß man die Schönheit nicht herstellen kann, sondern, daß viel Zeit dazu kommen muß, daß Schönheit unwillkürlich, nicht planbar entsteht. Im 19. Jahrhundert entdeckten Dichter wie Baudelaire die Schönheit des Verfalls.«

Dann holt er gegen die Moderne aus und sagt: »Aber es hat sich in unserer Empfindung etwas geändert. Es gibt ein Generalmißtrauen gegen unsere Zeit, noch humane, habitable, timbrefähige Räume herzustellen. Bis in die Mitte des 20. Jahrhunderts galt der Ruinenblick einer versunkenen Epoche, die man imitierte. Inzwischen wird aber alles, was dreißig Jahre alt ist, als Antiquität angesehen, sowie nur Gebrauchsspuren da sind … Weil die neuen Sachen nur noch im kaputten Zustand erträglich sind. Als unversehrter Gegenstand haben sie keinen ästhetisch befriedigenden Ausdruck. Das hat es meines Erachtens in der Geschichte noch nie gegeben. In Renaissance und Barock hat man die antiken Statuen, die man aus der Erde holte, ergänzt. In unserem Jahrhundert entfernte man die Ergänzungen und setzte auf das reine, authentische Stück. Und jetzt werfen wir diesen Blick schon auf die nächste Vergangenheit, jetzt wird schon die Großelternzeit behandelt wie die Antike, als Zeit der Ausgrabungen.«

Kann es sein, daß im Augenblick, aus Unmut über die Hervorbringungen der Moderne, so etwas wie eine neue Ruinenromantik entsteht? Ich bin skeptisch. Konservative und nostalgische Menschen gab es zu allen Zeiten. Sie machen auch heute einen bestimmten Prozentsatz unserer Gesellschaft aus. Viele von ihnen besuchen mit großer Begeisterung alte Burgen und Schlösser. Neuschwanstein ist und bleibt ein Traumziel, auch ohne ruinösen Verfall. Bestimmte Menschen umgeben sich im privaten Umfeld mit barocken Möbeln oder Gebrauchsgegenständen aus der Empire-Zeit – vielleicht auch nur mit Imitaten, wenn sie sich die Originale nicht leisten können. Das Neue Museum kommt dieser Klientel ein Stück weit entgegen, bleibt jedoch gleichzeitig ein Störelement, denn alle ruinösen Zonen und fragmentarischen Putzreste geben dem Gebäude etwas von einem Unfallopfer. Die Wunden sind nicht verheilt, und stolz zeigt der Verletzte jetzt seine Narben. Als Arzt könnte man sagen: Hier wurde gepfuscht, denn nur eine unsichtbare Narbe ist eine gute Narbe. Böswillig formuliert: Das Neue Museum sieht aus wie ein spätes Kriegsopfer, eine ramponierte Mumie. Insgesamt zeigt sich in der Begeisterung für diese Art von Rekonstruktion doch ein bedenklicher Manierismus des Urteils, den es nur als Luxus-Phänomen in einer reichen Gesellschaft geben kann.

general impression: exactly the opposite of what used to be there and was intended at one time. The concept of history represented by the Neues Museum when it was new was certainly naïve in terms of our own experiences. That line was unsustainable. Now it's like walking into a kind of Pompeii, being transported to a different era. I have never seen anything like it in a museum.«

Adrian von Buttlar responds: »How is one to imagine that, what made it feel like enchantment? Was it being disoriented? Didn't you find it transparent?« Mosebach answers: »To me the arrangement of the exhibits seemed to be of secondary importance. The entire building is the actual attraction. The ruin room with its hallowed air of tradition, in its state of destruction that produces a precious new effect of beauty, as well as a theatrical effect. It felt like moving through a stage-set landscape – hence enchantment. What is amazing is the concept of leaving the rooms in their ruined state.«

And indeed Döllgast's and Wiedemann's wall treatment differs from that of Chipperfield and his restorers in that neither in the Alte Pinakothek nor in the Glyptothek were remains of plaster left on the walls. This idea is new and is based on the scientific procedures of archaeologists, who are grateful for every fragment that is found.

What is interesting about Mosebach's statement is the fact that he is prepared to view only the rooms and completely fades out the exhibits. We realize that there is something wrong with his argumentation. After all, Stüler's design idea was precisely about harmony between the exhibit and the design of the exhibit space. Of course we may say that this harmony can no longer exist today. Mosebach rightly speaks of the opposite of the original idea. Basically, the last consequence would have consisted in exhibiting a completely empty Neues Museum, as a half-destroyed phenomenon of the 19th century. Daniel Libeskind's new Jüdisches Museum (Jewish Museum) building was subject to similar wishes and longings. In the course of the discussion the panel keeps circling around the ruined condition of the Neues Museum, and Mosebach finally puts forward the thesis that Stüler's interiors have become more beautiful as they have become dilapidated. Mosebach: »I had another question: I am fascinated by the fact that there is an emerging new romanticism of ruins. Where does it start – the feeling that beauty cannot be manufactured, but that a lot of time has to pass as well, that beauty comes into being spontaneously, and is unplanned. In the 19th century poets like Baudelaire discovered the beauty of decay.«

Then he takes a swing at the modern age and says: »But something has changed in our perception. There is a general mistrust whether our era can still produce spaces that are humane, habitable, and capable of timbre. Until the middle of the 20th century, a view of ruins was aimed at a vanished era that one would imitate. But in the meantime anything that is 30 years old is regarded as an antique as soon as there are signs of wear and tear … Because new things are bearable only when they are damaged. As an intact object they do not have an aesthetically satisfactory expression. As far as I know that has never happened before. In the Renaissance and Baroque they added the missing parts of statues that were unearthed. In our century they've removed the added parts and want the pure, authentic piece. And now we've started turning our attention to the recent past. Already our grandparents' days are being treated like antiquity, the period of excavations.«

Can it be that at this very moment, out of dissatisfaction about the achievements of the modern age, something like a new romanticism of ruins is coming into being? I am skeptical. There have been conservative and nostalgic people throughout history. They still account for a certain percentage of our society. Many of them enthusiastically visit old fortresses and castles. Neuschwanstein continues to be a favorite destination, even though it is not ruined. In their private space certain people surround themselves with baroque furniture or Empire-style utensils – perhaps mere copies if they cannot afford the originals. The Neues Museum meets this clientèle partway, yet at the same time continues to be a disturbing element, for all the zones that contain ruins and fragmentary remnants of plaster give the building the appearance of an accident victim. The wounds have not healed, and proudly the wounded man now shows off his scars. A doctor might say: This was a botched job, for the only good scar is an invisible scar. To put it maliciously: The Neues Museum looks like a belated war victim, a battered mummy. On the whole, enthusiasm for this kind of reconstruction reflects an alarming mannerism of judgment that can only exist as a luxury phenomenon in a wealthy society.

11. DDR-Ruinen

Berliner Stadtschloß, Palast der Republik, Mauer, Treuhand

Ob sich das Verhältnis zu den Ruinen, dem bestimmenden Stadtmotiv der Nachkriegszeit, mit den Jahren verändert hätte, wenn sie noch länger erhalten worden wären, weiß ich nicht. Entweder wären sie als Haßobjekte bekämpft oder, liebevoll renoviert, zu Exponaten surrealer Freizeitparks umgebaut worden. Bann-Städte wie Bann-Wälder, die niemand mehr betreten darf, waren und sind schwer vorstellbar.

In Deutschland gibt es heute kaum noch Orte, die Zerstörungsspuren zeigen, fast alle Kriegsruinen sind verschwunden. Nach 1945 wurde gründlich aufgeräumt und Ordnung geschaffen. Jedenfalls im Westen, im Osten verzögerten sich die Aufräumaktionen bis in die Nachwendezeit, so lange verfielen zahlreiche Gebäude, ja halbe Städte zu maroden Halbruinen; im Grunde war die DDR ein Eldorado für jeden Ruinenverehrer!

Auch in Berlin finden sich bis heute in vielen Fassaden noch Einschußlöcher der ehemaligen Straßenkämpfe am Ende des Zweiten Weltkriegs.

Bis zur Wende war auch das Tiergartenviertel zwischen Philharmonie und Siegessäule eine Fundgrube für diejenigen Touristen, die sich für Ruinen interessierten. In den 70er Jahren streifte ich tagelang durch das ehemalige Diplomatenviertel. In völlig verwilderten Gartengrundstücken, mit Wäldern aus Robinien und dichtem Unterholz, stieß man nach kurzer Suche auf die Ruinen der inzwischen halb zerfallenen Botschaftsgebäude aus der Nazizeit. Sie standen in verwunschenen Urwäldern wie geheimnisvolle Märchenschlösser. Wenn man Glück hatte und keinem Hausmeister mit Schäferhund begegnete, konnte man sogar in einzelne Gebäude eindringen,

65. Ruinöses Fragment der Berliner Mauer in der Nähe des Martin-Gropius-Baus, 2010.

65. Ruined fragment from the Berlin Wall near the Martin-Gropius-Bau, 2010.

11. GDR ruins

The Berliner Stadtschloß (City Palace), the Palast der Republik (Palace of the Republic), privatization

I do not know if people's relationship to ruins, the most important urban motif of the postwar period, would have changed over the years if the ruins had been preserved longer. They would either have been fought as objects of hatred or lovingly renovated, transformed into exhibits in surreal amusement parks. Urban preserves, like protected forests that no one may enter anymore, have always been and are still hard to imagine.

In modern-day Germany there are hardly any places that still show traces of destruction. Almost all war ruins have vanished. After 1945 the ruins were painstakingly cleared away and order was restored. At least they were in the West – in the East the clearing away of ruins was delayed until after German reunification; in the meantime many buildings, even large parts of towns, fell into disrepair until they were ramshackle half-ruins; basically the GDR was an Eldorado for all those who love ruins!

In Berlin, too, bullet holes from former street battles at the end of World War II are still found in many façades to this day.

Until German reunification, the Tiergarten District between the Philharmonie concert hall and the Siegessäule (Victory Column) was also a treasure trove for those tourists who were interested in ruins. In the '70s I roamed for days through the former diplomats' quarter. In completely overgrown gardens, with locust tree jungles and dense undergrowth, a short search would uncover the ruins of embassy buildings from the Nazi period that had in the meantime half disintegrated. They stood in enchanted primeval forests like mysterious fairy-tale palaces. If you were lucky and did not encounter a janitor with a German shepherd, you could even find your way into individual buildings, though always with the queasy feeling that you might at some point run into a dangerous criminal who might be hiding there. In reality, now and then, you would merely find the campsite of a tramp, consisting of a sleeping bag, plastic bags and a couple of empty beer and wine bottles. The windows and doors had been nailed shut; only in a few places loose boards rattled in the wind. An eerie, lost world that – had it been preserved – would no doubt be a great (tourist) attraction today. In reality everything changed after reunification. The individual countries renovated their embassy buildings or built completely new houses. The properties are protected by heavy, video-monitored gates and fences and deter all potential intruders. Today no one has the slightest inkling of the romantic ruin past of this area anymore.

The remnants of the façade of the former town palace (Stadtschloss) of the Prussian kings and German emperors might be Berlin's most grandiose ruin ensemble today. It would look splendid on the Museum Island, across from Schinkel's Altes Museum and in the shadow of the Deutscher Dom (German Cathedral). Tourists from all over the world would be thrilled by this unique photo motif.

In reality the magnificent ruin came to a sudden end on 7 September 1950, blown up on orders from the general secretary of the central committee of the SED (Socialist Unity Party of Germany), Walter Ulbricht. All protests from West Berlin and the Federal Republic of Germany were in vain. In socialist East Berlin the only people whose word counted would have been a leading GDR politician or a Soviet politician. But not one of the powers-that-be wanted to put in a good word for the architectonic »symbol of Prussian absolutism and militarism«. The principles of the socialist state of workers and peasants left no room for this. Four months later there was nothing left of Schlüter's onetime splendid building.

Andreas Schlüter had designed the most significant secular building of the Protestant Baroque in Berlin in 1699 for the Elector Frederick III, who called himself King Frederick I of Prussia after 1701. An important project, since Prussia was not exactly blessed with extraordinary pieces of architecture. I have already mentioned elsewhere that in 1706 Schlüter was dishonorably dismissed from his position as court architect because of a structural error on the northwest corner of the castle, in the Münzturm (Royal Mint Tower). Many architects, including Schinkel and Stüler, had expanded the castle, which had become more and more magnificent.

After the last German emperor had gone into exile, the castle became a museum. It was not until the final battles between German and Soviet soldiers at the end of World War II that the castle caught fire and was partially destroyed. Its ruinous condition would have made reconstruction easily possible, however. Charlottenburg Castle was in far worse condition and is today, after being lovingly rebuilt, in dazzling historic shape. Nobody would even think of opposing a postwar re-

allerdings immer mit dem mulmigen Gefühl, irgendwann auf einen gefährlichen Verbrecher zu stoßen, der sich hier vielleicht versteckt hielt. In Wirklichkeit begegnete man hin und wieder lediglich dem Lager eines Penners, bestehend aus Schlafsack, Plastiktüten und einigen leeren Bier- und Weinflaschen. Fenster und Türen waren vernagelt, nur an manchen Stellen klapperten lose Bretter im Wind. Eine gespenstische, untergegangene Welt, die – hätte man sie erhalten – heute bestimmt eine große Touristenattraktion wäre. In Wirklichkeit hat sich nach der Wende alles geändert. Die einzelnen Länder renovierten ihre Botschaftsgebäude oder errichteten völlig neue Häuser. Die Anwesen sind durch schwere, videoüberwachte Tore und Zäune gesichert und schrecken jeden potentiellen Eindringling ab. Niemand ahnt mehr etwas von der romantischen Ruinenvergangenheit dieses Gebiets.

Die Fassadenreste des ehemaligen Stadtschlosses der preußischen Könige und deutschen Kaiser könnten heute das grandioseste Ruinenensemble Berlins sein. Es würde sich auf der Museumsinsel, gegenüber des Alten Museums von Schinkel und im Schatten des Deutschen Doms, prächtig ausnehmen. Touristen aus der ganzen Welt hätten ihre Freude an diesem einmaligen Photomotiv.

In Wirklichkeit fand die großartige Ruine am 7. September 1950 auf Befehl des Generalsekretärs des ZK der SED, Walter Ulbricht, ihr plötzliches Ende durch eine Sprengung. Alle Proteste aus Westberlin und der Bundesrepublik waren vergeblich. Im sozialistischen Ostteil Berlins galt nur das Wort eines führenden DDR-Politikers oder eines sowjetischen Politikers. Aber keiner dieser Machthaber wollte ein gutes Wort für das architektonische »Symbol des preußischen Absolutismus und Militarismus« einlegen. Die Grundsätze des sozialistischen Arbeiter- und Bauernstaats ließen dafür keinen Spielraum. Vier Monate später war nichts mehr zu sehen von Schlüters einstigem Prachtbau.

Andreas Schlüter hatte den bedeutendsten Profanbau des protestantischen Barocks in Berlin 1699 für den Kurfürsten Friedrich III. entworfen, der sich ab 1701 König Friedrich I. von Preußen nannte. Ein wichtiges Projekt, da Preußen nicht gerade mit außergewöhnlichen Architekturen gesegnet war. Daß Schlüter 1706 wegen eines statischen Fehlers an der Nordwestecke des Schlosses, beim Münzturm, als Hofbaumeister unehrenhaft entlassen wurde, erwähnte ich bereits an anderer Stelle. Viele Architekten, unter ihnen Schinkel und Stüler, erweiterten den Schloßbau und ließen ihn immer prächtiger werden.

Nachdem der letzte deutsche Kaiser ins Exil gegangen war, wurde aus dem Schloß ein Museum. Erst bei den Schlußkämpfen zwischen deutschen und sowjetischen Soldaten am Ende des Zweiten Weltkriegs geriet das Schloß in Brand und wurde teilweise zerstört. Sein ruinöser Zustand hätte jedoch eine Rekonstruktion ohne weiteres zugelassen. Das Charlottenburger Schloß war viel schlechter erhalten und zeigt sich heute, nach liebevollem Wiederaufbau, in glanzvoller historischer Form. Niemand käme auf die Idee, vor einer Nachkriegsrekonstruktion zu stehen. Wie auch immer: Die Ruine des Stadtschlosses existiert nur noch auf Photos. Seit einigen Jahren geistert allerdings die unglückliche Idee durch die Köpfe mancher Verantwortlicher, das Schloß wiederaufzubauen. Tatsächlich fand inzwischen ein Wettbewerb statt, aus dem ein bisher völlig unbekannter italienischer Architekt namens Franco Stella als Sieger hervorging. Er rekonstruiert in seinem Entwurf die historischen Außenfassaden, möglicherweise auch die Schloßkuppel, die Rückseite und die Innenhöfe dagegen sprechen eine bürokratische Architektursprache, wie wir sie von modernen Finanzämtern kennen.

Ob wir einer Ruine des »Palastes der Republik« nachtrauern müssen, wage ich zu bezweifeln. Der einfache, monumentale Bau von Heinz Graffunder und seinen Leuten hätte genauso als Flughafen- oder Bahnhofsgebäude durchgehen können. Ähnliche architektonische Kreationen stehen überall auf der Welt. Während des langsamen Abbaus zwischen 1998 und 2008 konnten wir alle sehen, daß sein »Ruinenmehrwert« gegen Null tendierte. Zu keinem Moment seines Slow-motion-Verschwindens gewannen die Reste an Charme, Grazie, Eleganz oder Romantik. Möge der Bau im architektonischen Jenseits friedlich ruhen!

Ganz anders verhielt es sich mit der Mauer, diesem häßlichsten aller DDR-Bauwerke. Kaum zu glauben, wie schnell das inzwischen zum kollektiven Kunstwerk herangewachsene Gegenstück zur Chinesischen Mauer aus unserer sichtbaren Welt verschwand. Nur noch einzelne Stücke künden heute von ihr. Niemand hätte gedacht, daß ein derart kümmerlicher Betongartenzaun wirklich eine Grenze für lebendige Menschen darstellen könnte. Selbst Karnickeln gelang es innerhalb eines Tages, den Ostwall, der zu keiner Sekunde mit dem West- oder gar Atlantikwall zu vergleichen war, zu untergraben. Immer, wenn man vor der Betonwand stand, hatte man das Gefühl, ein Schubs würde genügen, sie umzuwerfen. Aber dahinter drohte der Todesstreifen, patrouillierten bewaffnete DDR-Soldaten mit ihren bissigen Schäferhunden. Von heute aus gesehen, wun-

66. Während im Westen Deutschlands fast alle Kriegsruinen verschwunden sind, kann man im Osten, in der ehemaligen DDR – etwa in Berlin, Cottbus, Frankfurt an der Oder, Görlitz oder Rostock – noch zahlreiche marode Gebäude finden, die Kriegsspuren zeigen.

66. While in West Germany nearly all the war damage has disappeared, in the East, in the former GDR – for example in Berlin, Cottbus, and Frankfurt an der Oder, Görlitz or Rostock – it is still possible to find numbers of dilapidated buildings still showing traces of the war.

construction. Be that as it may: The ruin of the Stadtschloss now exists only in photographs. For a few years, to be sure, a number of those responsible have been toying with the unfortunate idea of rebuilding the castle. There was actually a competition, from which a hitherto completely unknown Italian architect, Franco Stella, emerged as the winner. In his design he reconstructs the historic exterior façades, possibly the castle's cupola as well; on the other hand the bureaucratic architecture of the building's rear and inner courtyards is reminiscent of modern internal revenue offices.

I am inclined to doubt whether we ought to mourn a ruin of the »Palace of the Republic«. The simple monumental building by Heinz Graffunder and his team could just as easily have passed for an airport building or railroad station. There are architectural creations like this one all over the world. During its slow dismantling between 1998 and 2008 we were all aware that its »added value as a ruin« was close to zero. At no time in its slow-motion disappearance did the remnants gain charm, gracefulness, elegance or romanticism. May the building rest in peace in the architectural hereafter!

The Wall – the ugliest of all GDR structures – was quite a different story. It was hard to believe how quickly this counterpart of the Great Wall of China, which had in the meantime grown into a collective artwork, disappeared from our visible world. Only isolated pieces still bear witness to it today. No one would have imagined that so wretched a concrete garden fence could really represent a border for living human beings. It didn't take more than a day even for rabbits to undermine the East Wall, which could at no time be compared to the Westwall (Siegfried Line) or the Atlantic Wall. Whenever one stood in front of the concrete wall, one would have the feeling that it would take no more than a push to overturn it. But behind it was the menace of the death strip, patrolled by armed GDR soldiers with their vicious German shepherds. Looking at it from today's perspective I am surprised that such a ridiculous structure was meant to be taken seriously. Still, I would have been glad if longer sections of the Wall had been preserved – as a memorial to the dark night of human aberrations.

In contrast to a spick-and-span West Germany, the unloved, run-down and impoverished other half of the nation, the neglected, almost forgotten sister, turned out to be an Eldorado for Western building contractors. They could now make a killing with the subsidies intended for reconstruction in the East. Within a few years most of the ruins and dilapidated houses disap-

dert es mich, daß ein so lächerliches Bauwerk ernstgemeint war. Trotzdem hätte ich es gern gesehen, wenn längere Abschnitte der Mauer erhalten worden wären – als Denkmal an die Nacht menschlicher Verirrungen.

Im Gegensatz zu Westdeutschland, das blitzblank glänzte, entpuppte sich die ungeliebte, abgewirtschaftete und arme andere Hälfte der Nation, die vernachlässigte, fast vergessene Schwester, als Eldorado für westliche Baufirmen. Sie konnten sich jetzt mit den Fördermitteln, die für den Aufbau Ost gedacht waren, eine goldene Nase verdienen. Innerhalb weniger Jahre verschwanden die meisten Ruinen und zerfallenden Häuser. Heute muß man schon in sehr abgelegene Landstriche reisen, um noch wirklich romantische Exemplare der Spezies »ruino perfetto« zu sehen.

In den Jahren von 1991 bis 1994 war die Berliner Treuhandanstalt, untergebracht in einem monumentalen, von Ernst Sagebiel 1935/36 geplanten und errichteten Gebäude, Wilhelmstraße 97, dafür zuständig, die DDR und damit alle sozialistischen Firmen- und Fabrikruinen zu verkaufen. Mit einem unglaublichen Tempo wurde ein ganzes Land privatisiert. Alles stand zum Verkauf; jedes Kombinat wurde zerschlagen. Im Westen zählte nur Privateigentum. Der Staat besitzt nur wenig: Gold, Grundstücke, Gebäude und vor allem jede Menge Schulden. Die genaue Bezeichnung der temporären Behörde lautete: »Anstalt zur treuhänderischen Verwaltung des Volkseigentums«.

Schon der Begriff »Verwaltung« klingt in diesem Zusammenhang zynisch. Es wundert nicht, daß der Unmut des »Volkes« bald hochkochte und der zweite Chef der »Treuhand«, der ehemalige Stahlmanager Detlev Karsten Rohwedder, von Terroristen erschossen wurde, eine bis heute unaufgeklärte Tat. Seine Nachfolgerin, die ehemalige niedersächsische Wirtschaftsministerin Birgit Breuel, befehligte ihre 5 000 Mitarbeiter mit eiserner Hand. Über 42 000 Verträge wurden zu ihrer Zeit abgeschlossen. Dennoch blieb das Unternehmen nach viereinhalb Jahren auf einem Defizit von 204 Milliarden Euro sitzen. Wofür wurde das Geld ausgegeben?

Viele ehemalige DDR-Bürger sind seither ruiniert. Eine gute Einübung auf die Finanzkrise im Jahr 2009 mit ihren Banken-Zusammenbrüchen. Das Bild der Ruine erweist sich als zeitlos gültig. In unsichtbarer und sichtbarer Form.

67. Ruineninnenseite. Blicke in die Untergänge, Bankrotte und Finanzdesaster von außen oder Blicke von innen nach draußen. Mit den Trümmern untergehen oder mit ihnen auferstehen wie neugeboren.

67. Inside the ruin. Views of the failures, bankruptcies and financial disasters from the outside or views from the inside to the outside. Go down with ruins or rise up with them as if newborn.

peared. Today you would have to travel to very remote areas to see truly romantic exemplars of the species »ruino-perfetto«.

From 1991 to 1994 the Berlin Privatization Office (Treuhandanstalt), housed in a monumental building planned and built by Ernst Sagebiel in 1935/36 at Wilhelmstraße 97, was in charge of selling the GDR and thus the ruins of all socialist firms and factories. With incredible speed a whole country was privatized. Everything was for sale; every combine was broken up. In the West only private property counted. The state owns very little: gold, properties, buildings and above all plenty of debts. The exact designation of the temporary agency was »Anstalt zur treuhänderischen Verwaltung des Volkseigentums (Agency for the fiduciary management of nationally owned property)«.

Even the term »management« sounds cynical in this context. No wonder the displeasure of the »Volk« (nation) soon began to ran high and the second head of the »Treuhand« (privatization), former steel manager Detlev Karsten Rohwedder, was shot by terrorists, a crime that is still unsolved. His successor, former minister of trade and commerce of Lower Saxony Birgit Breuel, maintained an iron grip on her staff of 5,000. More than 42,000 contracts were concluded during her term of office. And yet, after four and a half years the enterprise was left with a deficit of 204 billion euros. What had the money been spent on? Many former citizens of the GDR have been ruined ever since. Good practice for the 2009 financial crisis with its bank crashes. The image of the ruin proves to be timeless. In invisible and visible form.

12. Ruinen und Untergänge im Film

Hollywood, deutsche Nachkriegs- und James-Bond-Filme

Vielleicht war der Franzose Georges Méliès der erste Filmemacher, der mit Zaubertricks in *Le Voyage à travers l'impossible* 1904 einen chaotisch-malerischen Eisenbahnunfall in Szene setzte. Unfälle, Katastrophen und Ruinen gehören seither zum gängigen Repertoire erfolgreicher Unterhaltungsfilme. Später gingen in den Pariser Studios von Méliès Schiffe unter, Häuser brannten, und Erdbeben erschütterten bürgerliche Salons. Auch Jahre nach der Erfindung des neuen Mediums sah das Publikum – abgesehen von Liebesfilmen – auf der Leinwand am liebsten Katastrophen, Unfälle, Verbrechen, abenteuerliche Verfolgungsjagden und Polizeiautos, die gegen Wände krachten oder durch die Luft flogen. Mit Dick und Doof, Harold Lloyd und den Marx Brothers griff Hollywood in das frivole Zerstörungsgeschehen ein. Slapstick-Ruinen, Slapstick-Untergänge. Bei Buster Keaton zerfielen Holzhäuser wie Papierkonstruktionen und trieben, verwandelt in leichte Flöße, den Fluß hinunter, bei Charly Chaplin neigten sich Goldrausch-Hütten über die Klippen und drohten, ins Meer hinabzustürzen. Bei Dick und Doof flogen die Sahnetorten, und Gesichter erhielten schlagartig das Aussehen von weißen Mondlandschaften. Bei Harold Lloyd mußten Bahnhofsuhren als letzte Rettungsanker herhalten. Natürlich waren sie anschließend ruiniert.

Was einmal fast spielerisch leicht begonnen hatte, konnte nicht so bleiben. Berufsschauspieler betraten die Szene und versuchten, den Katastrophen einen seriösen Kunstaspekt zu geben. *Das Kabinett des Doktor Caligari* (1920 von Robert Wiene) mit den gemalten Häusern, die aussahen, als würden sie gerade einstürzen, erschreckte nicht nur Arbeiter, Handwerker, Kellner und Dienstmädchen, sondern auch Angestellte, Lehrer und Direktoren samt Gattinnen. Das war die Stunde des Fritz Lang, eines ehemaligen Wiener Architekturstudenten, der in Berlin sein Glück beim Film suchte. Nachdem er zunächst im deutschen Mythensumpf gewühlt hatte, reiste er nach New York, war überwältigt und verfaßte 1925 zusammen mit seiner damaligen Frau Thea von Harbou, das Skript zum berühmtesten aller Stummfilme: *Metropolis*. Lang verband in seinen Bildern den deutschen Expressionismus mit der neuen, amerikanisch geprägten Sachlichkeit der 1920er Jahre. Er schwankte zwischen science-fictionhafter New-York-Faszination – in seinem Film durch die Trickkiste rekonstruiert – und bedeutungsschwangeren und kathedralschweren deutschen Untergangsängsten. Die unberechenbaren Arbeitermassen waren das große politische Thema der Zeit. Kommunisten und Nationalsozialisten versuchten, diese Massen für sich zu gewinnen und zu aktivieren. In den Wolkenkratzern von Metropolis wohnen die »Herrenmenschen«, in der Unterwelt die Arbeiter. Fritz Lang zeigt einen absolut überwachten Stadtstaat, wie ihn wenige Jahre später, 1932, Aldous Huxley in seinem Roman *Schöne neue Welt* beschreibt. Bei Fritz Lang sympathisiert der Sohn des tyrannischen Generaldirektors mit den Arbeitern, seitdem er Maria, die »Heilige der Unterdrückten«, kennengelernt hat. Ein Erfinder baut im Auftrag des Diktators eine falsche »Maschinen-Maria«, um die Arbeitermassen wieder auf den richtigen Weg zu bringen. Aber aufgestachelt, mutieren diese zu Maschinenstürmern, zerstören riesige Kraftwerke und Schleusenmauern. Die Stadt wird überflutet und droht unterzugehen. Im letzten Moment gelingt es Freder, dem Sohn des Führers, und der richtigen Maria, den Zusammenbruch des modernen »Babylonischen Turms« zu stoppen und die finale Katastrophe abzuwenden.

Von heute aus gesehen, ist dies ein immer noch erstaunlich hellsichtiger Film, der visonär die Entwicklungen hin zum terroristischen Hitlerstaat vorweggenommen hat. Thea von Harbou entschied sich übrigens schon kurz nach den Dreharbeiten für eine Mitgliedschaft in der NSDAP, Fritz Lang ließ sich von seiner Frau scheiden und floh 1933 über Frankreich nach Amerika. In Hollywood arbeitete er während des Zweiten Weltkriegs mehr oder weniger erfolgreich als Filmregisseur. Seine Rückkehr nach Deutschland in den 1950er Jahren mißlang künstlerisch, seine damals produzierten Filme fanden kein Publikum mehr.

Mit der Zeit wuchsen die technischen Möglichkeiten, und damit wurden auch die Katastrophen- und Ruinenbilder der großen Spielfilme immer raffinierter. In einem der erfolgreichsten Hollywoodfilme aller Zeiten *Vom Winde verweht* aus dem Jahr 1939 sahen die Zuschauer zum ersten Mal ganze Dörfer und Städte in Farbe verbrennen und untergehen. Das Südstaatendrama nach dem Roman von Margaret Mitchell gipfelt in der Schlacht um Atlanta. Rhett Butler, der Abenteurer, kämpft mit den Flammen. Erst zum Schluß kommen er und die schöne, hochmütige Scarlett O'Hara, die im Verlauf der Geschichte zur zweifachen Witwe wurde, zusammen, ein bitteres Happy-End. Wegen der Kriegsereignisse kam dieser Film übrigens erst im Januar 1953 in die deutschen Kinos.

12. Ruins and scenes of destruction in film

Hollywood, James Bond and German postwar films

Perhaps the Frenchman Georges Méliès was the first filmmaker to stage, by means of magic tricks, a chaotic, picturesque train crash in *Le Voyage à travers l'impossible* in 1904. Accidents, catastrophes and ruins have ever since been part of the popular repertoire of successful feature films. Later, in the Paris studios of Méliès, ships sank, houses burned and earthquakes shook bourgeois drawing rooms. Even years after the invention of the new medium the cinema-going public preferred to watch – apart from love stories – catastrophes, accidents, crimes, adventurous chases and police cars that crashed into walls or flew through the air. With Laurel and Hardy, Harold Lloyd and the Marx Brothers Hollywood began to depict frivolous destruction. Slapstick ruins, slapstick scenes of destruction. In Buster Keaton's movies wooden houses fell apart like paper constructions and floated down the river, transformed into light rafts; in Charlie Chaplin films, gold rush cabins leaned over cliffs and were in danger of tumbling into the ocean. In Laurel and Hardy movies cream pies flew back and forth, and faces suddenly changed into white lunar landscapes. In a Harold Lloyd movie a station clock had to serve as the last anchor. Of course it was ruined as a result.

What had once started almost playfully could not remain so for long. Professional actors stepped onto the stage and tried to make the catastrophes look like serious art. *The Cabinet of Dr. Caligari* (1920, by Robert Wiene) with the painted houses that appeared to be on the verge of collapse frightened not only workingmen, craftsmen, waiters and servant girls, but also white-collar employees, teachers and directors, as well as their spouses. This was Fritz Lang's finest hour. A former Viennese student of architecture, he sought his fortune in Berlin in the movie industry. After initially wallowing in the mire of German myths, he traveled to New York, was overwhelmed and in 1925 together with his then wife Thea von Harbou wrote the script for the most famous of all silent films: *Metropolis*. In his images Lang combined German expressionism with the new, typically American objectivity of the 1920s. He vacillated between a science-fiction-like fascination with New York – reconstructed in his film thanks to his bag of tricks – and German fears of doom, pregnant with meaning and grave as cathedrals. The unpredictable working masses were the hot political issue of the times. Communists and National Socialists tried to win over these masses and to make them politically active. In the skyscrapers of Metropolis lives the »master race«, while the workers live in the underworld. Fritz Lang shows a city-state under absolute surveillance, the kind described by Aldous Huxley a few years later, in 1932, in his novel *Brave New World*. In Fritz Lang's film the son of the tyrannical general manager has sympathized with the workers ever since he met Maria, the »saint of the oppressed«. The dictator commissions an inventor to build a faux »Machine Maria« in order to get the laboring masses back on the right track. But now that they have been goaded into action, they mutate, attack the machines, demolish a gigantic power plant and open floodgates. The city is inundated and is on the verge of being destroyed. At the last minute Freder, the son of the leader, and the real Maria manage to stop the collapse of the modern »Tower of Babylon« and to avert the final catastrophe.

From today's perspective this is still an amazingly clear-sighted, visionary film that anticipated developments leading to the terrorist regime of Hitler. Incidentally, shortly after the shooting of *Metropolis* Thea von Harbou decided to join the National Socialist Party, and Fritz Lang divorced his wife and fled to America by way of France in 1933. In Hollywood he worked more or less successfully as a movie director during World War II. His return to Germany in the 1950s was not an artistic success; the films he produced at the time held no appeal for the public.

Over time technical possibilities increased and as a result the catastrophe and ruin scenes of the great feature films became more and more sophisticated. In one of the most successful Hollywood movies of all time, *Gone with the Wind,* made in 1939, viewers saw for the first time whole villages and towns going up in flames and being destroyed in technicolor. Set in the South, the drama, which is based on a novel by Margaret Mitchelll, culminates in the battle for Atlanta. Rhett Butler, the adventurer, fights the flames. He and the beautiful, arrogant Scarlett O'Hara, who in the course of the story has been widowed twice, do not come together until the end, a bitter happy ending. Incidentally, because of the war this film was not screened in German cinemas until January 1953.

The horror aspect of old mansions and ruined houses always played an important part in Hollywood movies, in connection with human tragedies. This is true of Alfred Hitchcock's *Rebecca* and *Psycho* just as much as of Orson Welles' *Citizen Kane* and Billy Wilder's *Sunset*

Der Gruselaspekt von alten Herrenhäusern und Hausruinen spielte in Hollywoodfilmen, in Verbindung mit menschlichen Tragödien, immer eine große Rolle. Das gilt für *Rebecca* und *Psycho* von Alfred Hitchcock genauso wie für *Citizen Kane* von Orson Welles und *Sunset Boulevard* von Billy Wilder. Die Architekturen bilden gemauerte, unveränderbare, atmosphärisch dichte Klammern um das Geschehen. Manchmal beschränken sie sich auf passives Dastehen, dann wieder greifen sie in das Leben der Protagonisten ein, verwandeln sich in wahre Horrorlabyrinthe, düstere Vergangenheitsruinen, Fallen des Verfolgungswahns oder Gefängnisse der eigenen Angst. In diesem Zusammenhang sind natürlich Horror-, Katastrophen- und Kriegsfilme besonders interessant.

Der Film *Der dritte Mann* des englischen Regisseurs Carol Reed entstand in der Zeit von 1948/49. Nachdem Reed beschlossen hatte, im kriegszerstörten Wien einen Film zu drehen, reiste er zusammen mit Graham Greene, der das Drehbuch schreiben sollte, 1948 in die besetzte österreichische Hauptstadt. Da sie Engländer waren, konnten sich die beiden problemlos im vornehmen, unzerstörten Hotel Sacher einquartieren, das ausschließlich britischen Staatsangehörigen und Militärs vorbehalten war. Gemeinsam durchstreiften sie wochenlang die in Sektoren aufgeteilte, halbzerstörte Stadt, studierten kaputte Straßen, Gassen und marode Gebäude, besuchten dunkle Kneipen und versteckte Schwarzmärkte. Noch wußten sie nicht, wovon der Film genau handeln sollte. Eines Tages entdeckten sie einen Zugang in das unterirdische Kanalsystem. Hier glaubte Graham Greene, das ideale Szenario für eine spannende Schlußsequenz gefunden zu haben. In den Tagen danach dachte er sich die Geschichte eines skrupellosen Penicillinschiebers aus, der in Kauf nahm, daß sein verdünntes Medikament Kinder verstümmeln und töten würde. Carol Reed war begeistert. Gemeinsam suchten sie die geeigneten Locations, kein Problem in der riesigen Ruinenstadt Wien.

Ein halbes Jahr später kam Reed mit seiner Film-Crew wieder und begann im harten Schwarzweiß des amerikanisch-französischen Film noir, gemischt mit expressionistischen Anklängen, die Handlung an Originalschauplätzen zu inszenieren.

Im Zentrum steht eine alte Männerfreundschaft. Holly Martins, ein ziemlich ungebildeter amerikanischer Trivialschriftsteller (Joseph Cotten) will seinen alten Kumpel Harry Lime (Orson Welles) in Wien besuchen. Als er ankommt, wird ihm mitgeteilt, daß Lime am Tag zuvor bei einem Autounfall ums Leben gekommen sei. Martins kommt die Geschichte so unglaubwürdig vor, daß er alle Zeugen des angeblichen Unfalls nach und nach aufsucht und befragt. So begegnet er auch der ehemaligen Geliebten seines Freundes. Zwischen den beiden entsteht eine Beinahe-Liebesge-

68. Szenenbild aus dem Film *Metropolis*, 1926, von Fritz Lang. Tanz der Arbeiter vor der zerstörten großen Maschine. In Thea von Harbous Drehbuch lautet die Szenenanweisung:
»Alle Maschinen stillgelegt,
zerstört,
tot.
Die Masse
von Männern und Weibern,
mit improvisierten Fackeln ausgestattet,
tanzt einen wüsten Tanz
um die toten Maschinen,
sich an den Händen haltend,
in durcheinanderwirbelnden Kettenkreisen.«
69. Szenenbild aus Carol Reeds Film *Der dritte Mann*, 1949. Der Film wurde in der kriegszerstörten, von den Siegermächten besetzten Stadt Wien gedreht.

68. Scene from Fritz Lang's film *Metropolis*, 1926. Workers dance around the wrecked big machine. The stage direction in Thea von Harbou's screenplay says:
»Every machine shut down,
wrecked,
dead.
The mass
of men and women
equipped with improvised torches,
dances desolately
around the dead machines,
holding hands,
in a confusion of linked circles.«
69. Scene from Carol Reed's film *The Third Man*, 1949. The film was shot in Vienna, which had been badly damaged during the war and was occupied by the Allies.

Boulevard. The buildings form brick-and-mortar, unchangeable, atmospherically dense brackets around events. Sometimes they merely stand there passively, and then again they intervene in the lives of the protagonists, are transformed into true labyrinths of horror, gloomy ruins of the past, traps of paranoia or prisons of their own fear. In this context, of course, horror, catastrophe and war movies are of particular interest.

The film *The Third Man* by British film director Carol Reed was made in 1948/49. In 1948, after Reed had decided to shoot a film in Vienna, a city devastated by the war, he traveled to the occupied Austrian capital together with Graham Greene, who was to write the script. Since they were British, the two were easily able to find accommodation in the elegant, still intact Hotel Sacher, which was reserved exclusively for British nationals and military. Together they roamed for weeks through the half-destroyed city, which was divided into sectors, studied damaged streets, lanes and ramshackle buildings, visited dark pubs and hidden black markets. At this point they did not know exactly what the film would be about. One day they discovered an entrance to the subterranean canal system. Here Graham Greene believed he had found the ideal setting for an exciting final sequence. In the days that followed he made up the story of an unscrupulous profiteer who sold penicillin while realizing that his diluted medication would maim and kill children. Carol Reed was thrilled. Together they looked for the appropriate locations – not a problem in the huge ruined city of Vienna.

Half a year later Reed returned with his film crew and, in the harsh black-and-white of the American-French film noir, with echoes of expressionism, began to direct the action at original locations.

Central to the film is an old friendship between two men. Holly Martins, a rather uncultured American pulp Western writer (Joseph Cotten) wants to visit his old buddy Harry Lime (Orson Welles) in Vienna. Upon arrival he is told that Lime was killed by a truck the day before. The story seems so implausible to Martins that, one by one, he finds and questions all the witnesses of the alleged accident. Thus he also meets his friend's former girlfriend. A quasi love affair develops between the two. Roughly halfway through the film Martins realizes that his suspicions are correct and his friend is actually still alive. In order to go underground and to continue his cynical black marketeer activity, Harry Lime simply had his own funeral staged. The meeting between the two culminates in a Ferris wheel ride in the Prater amusement park. Lime, who turns out to be a vicious criminal, would be happy to push his old friend out of the cabin to his death. But the murder does not take place. Through his stubborn investigation Holly Martins has betrayed his old friend, and the chief of the British military police, Calloway (Trevor Howard), can now hunt him di-

schichte. Etwa in der Mitte des Films erkennt Martins, daß seine Vermutungen stimmen und sein Freund tatsächlich noch lebt. Um abzutauchen und im Untergrund weiter seine zynische Schiebertätigkeit ausüben zu können, hat Harry Lime die eigene Beerdigung inszenieren lassen. Die Begegnung zwischen den beiden gipfelt in einer Riesenradfahrt im Prater. Am liebsten würde Lime, der sich als bösartiger Verbrecher entpuppt, seinen alten Freund aus der Kabine in den Tod stoßen. Aber der Mord findet nicht statt. Durch seine hartnäckige Recherche hat Holly Martins seinen alten Freund verraten, und der Chef der britischen Militärpolizei Calloway (Trevor Howard) kann ihn ab jetzt gezielt jagen. Der Schluß-Countdown spielt – wie von Graham Greene geplant – im Wiener Kanalsystem. Am Ende wird Harry Lime von einer Polizeikugel getroffen und stirbt beim Versuch, einen verschlossenen Kanaldeckel zu öffnen.

Während des ganzen Films lernen wir Wien von einer Seite kennen, wie wir sie bisher nicht einmal erahnten. Eine düstere, bedrohliche, vom Krieg verwüstete Stadt. Daß in diesen Hausresten auch noch die Gespenster aus alten Vorkriegszeiten leben – die korrupten, geldgierigen und verlogen-charmanten Mitkämpfer Harry Limes, großartig dargestellt von Ernst Deutsch, Erich Ponto, Siegfried Breuer und Paul Hörbiger – erhöht die Gefährlichkeit dieser so walzerseligen Metropole. Und dann ist da noch jene geniale Musik, die Anton Karas für den Film komponiert hat. Eine Zithermelodie, die leitmotivisch immer wieder zu hören ist. In ihrer verspielten Harmlosig-

rectly. The final countdown takes place – as Graham Greene had planned – in Vienna's sewer system. In the end Harry Lime is hit by a police bullet and dies trying to open a closed sewer grating.

Throughout the film we see a side of Vienna that we had not even suspected existed: a gloomy, menacing city, devastated by war. The perilousness of this metropolis, blissed-out on waltzes though it is, is heightened by the fact that these building remnants also still house the ghosts of the prewar period – Harry Lime's corrupt, greedy and hypocritically charming accomplices, magnificently portrayed by Ernst Deutsch, Erich Ponto, Siegfried Breuer and Paul Hörbiger. And then there is the inspired music that Anton Karas composed for the film: a zither melody that provides a recurrent leitmotif. Playfully harmless, it undermines the gloomy plot like the gentle, enticing echo of chirping cicadas, turning more and more perfidious and sometimes cynically malicious – the euphoria of a Viennese tavern as a danse macabre. Only the unforgettable, catchy theme of *Doctor Zhivago* came even close to this.

In his 1946 film *Die Mörder sind unter uns* (*The Murderers Are among Us*) Wolfgang Staudte shows Berlin's postwar ruins. People lead makeshift lives, they emerge behind mountains of bricks, descend into the valleys between what is left of the houses and walk around as though they were in a completely normal, everyday city. The film tells the stories of several people brought together by chance. One is a physician, Dr. Mertens, living on the verge of insanity. He cannot deal with the memories of his war experiences, keeps having violent nightmares and has turned into a cynical, emotionally cold alcoholic. And there is a woman (Hildegard Knef) who returns from a concentration camp where she suffered for years as a prisoner, only to find this physician in her former, half devastated apartment. At first the two fight each other. But she is gentle and maternal, and finally succeeds in bringing calm and hope into the life of a man who has almost foundered.

Particularly moving is the secondary plot, the story of an old optician who lives in the ground floor apartment of the same house and longs for his son's return from the war, but dies before the first sign of life arrives in the form of a letter from America. And there is also the story of the physician's former captain, who, during the war, cold-bloodedly ordered a massacre of Polish civilians. Now, soon after the capitulation, he is once more successful as a manufacturer. At the end the physician wants to shoot him: In his opinion the man, because of his unscrupulous opportunism, shares the blame for the disaster of war. However, Hildegard Knef's character prevents the act and saves the doctor from despair and hopelessness. His hard shell of cynicism breaks down as he bursts into tears, and he confesses his love to her.

Originally Staudte actually wanted the film to end with the manufacturer's murder, but the Soviet cultural officer – the film was made in the DEFA studios of Babelsberg – demanded a different ending. Vigilante justice was not in demand. Now the film ends with a vehement accusation

70. Berliner Ruinenlandschaften in Wolfgang Staudtes Film *Die Mörder sind unter uns*, 1946.
71. Hildegard Knef am zersplitterten Fenster in *Die Mörder sind unter uns*.

70. A ruined Berlin landscape in the film *The Murderers are Among Us*, 1946, by Wolfgang Staudte.
71. Hildegard Knef by the shattered window in *The Murderers are Among Us*.

keit untergräbt sie die düstere Handlung wie ein sanftes, einschmeichelndes Zirpenecho, wird zunehmend perfide und manchmal auch zynisch-bösartig. Heurigenseligkeit als Totentanz. Das hat erst wieder der unvergeßliche *Doktor-Schiwago*-Ohrwurm geschafft.

Wolfgang Staudte zeigt in seinem Film *Die Mörder sind unter uns* von 1946 Berlins Ruinen der Nachkriegszeit. Menschen haben sich darin notdürftig eingerichtet, sie tauchen hinter Ziegel-bergen auf, steigen hinunter in die Täler zwischen den Hausresten und bewegen sich dort vor-wärts, als seien sie in einer ganz normalen, alltäglichen Stadt unterwegs. Erzählt werden die Ge-schichten mehrerer Menschen, die der Zufall zusammenführt. Da ist zunächst ein am Rande des Wahnsinns lebender Arzt, Dr. Mertens, der mit den Erinnerungen an seine Kriegserlebnisse nicht fertig wird, immer wieder unter heftigen Alpträumen leidet und zum zynisch-gefühlskalten Alko-holiker geworden ist. Und da ist eine Frau (Hildegard Knef), die aus einem KZ zurückkehrt, in dem sie jahrelang als Gefangene gelitten hatte, und auf diesen Arzt in ihrer ehemaligen, halbzerstörten Wohnung trifft. Zunächst bekämpfen sich die beiden. Aber mit ihrer sanften, mütterlichen Art gelingt es ihr schließlich, Ruhe und Hoffnung in das Leben des beinahe Gescheiterten zu bringen.

Die Nebengeschichte eines alten Optikers, der in der Erdgeschoßwohnung des gleichen Hauses wohnt und sehnsüchtig auf die Rückkehr seines Sohnes aus dem Krieg wartet, jedoch stirbt, bevor das erste Lebenszeichen in Form eines Briefes aus Amerika eintrifft, ist besonders anrührend. Und da gibt es auch noch die Geschichte vom ehemaligen Hauptmann des Arztes, der während des Krieges kaltblütig ein Massaker unter der polnischen Zivilbevölkerung anrichten ließ. Jetzt, kurz nach der Kapitulation, ist er bereits wieder als Fabrikant erfolgreich. Am Ende will der Arzt ihn, der seiner Ansicht nach durch seinen skrupellosen Opportunismus Mitschuld am Unglück des Krieges trägt, erschießen, aber Hildegard Knef verhindert die Tat und rettet den bisher Verzweifelten und Hoffnungslosen endgültig. Seine harte Schale des Zynismus zerbricht unter Tränen, und er gesteht ihr seine Liebe.

Ursprünglich wollte Staudte den Film tatsächlich mit dem Mord an dem Fabrikanten enden lassen, aber der sowjetische Kulturoffizier – der Film wurde in den DEFA-Studios von Babelsberg gedreht – verlangte ein anderes Ende. Selbstjustiz war nicht gefragt. Jetzt steht am Schluß eine heftige Anklage gegen alle Kriegsverbrecher. Sie dürfen nicht untertauchen und müssen zur Rechenschaft gezogen werden, so lautet die politisch eindeutige Forderung. Wie *Der dritte Mann* für Wien bleibt auch der Film *Die Mörder sind unter uns* ein unersetzliches Bilddokument für die Ruinenwelt im Berlin der Nachkriegszeit. Manchmal hat man den Eindruck, nicht die Menschen seien die Hauptdarsteller des Films, sondern die zerstörten Häuser und Straßen.

Auf den ersten Blick gehört das Werk Federico Fellinis *8 1/2, (Otto e mezzo)* von 1961/62 nicht in die Kategorie der Ruinenfilme. Bei genauem Hinsehen jedoch enthält der Film zahlreiche ge-dankliche Ruinenfragmente. Das Schlußbild reflektiert sogar – als Kritik des Hollywood-Monu-mentalismus – den »Turmbau zu Babel«, allerdings hier nur dargestellt als transparentes Bau-gerüst, das zur Raketenabschußrampe deklariert wird. Er handelt von dem offenbar sehr be-rühmten, krisengeschüttelten Regisseur Guido Anselmi, der ursprünglich einen Science-Fiction-Film drehen wollte, aber ihm fällt einfach nichts mehr ein. Alles ist gesagt, er fühlt sich leer und ausgelaugt, eine menschliche Ruine im besten Künstleralter. Raffinierter kann man einen Film kaum aufbauen: Die Hauptgeschichte erzählt vom Scheitern dieses umschwärmten italienischen Filmregisseurs. Er hat alle Hauptdarsteller, Produzenten, Autoren, Set- und Kostümdesigner um sich versammelt, die Dreharbeiten könnten beginnen. Aber Guido zögert, er hat das Gefühl, daß sich nichts mehr fügt und die Setaufbauten – außer der Raketenbasis ein mondänes Sanatoriums-bad, dazu ein Grandhotel, mit Halle, Treppenhäusern, Fluren und Zimmern für die Crew, sowie ein kleines Hotel für seine Geliebte (oder existieren die Architekturen außerhalb des Films, in Wirk-lichkeit?) –, daß all diese Aufbauten umsonst errichtet worden seien. Am Schluß des Films, bei einer chaotischen Pressekonferenz vor dem Stahlgestänge, sagt Guido das Projekt endgültig ab. Er ist gescheitert und reißt die Beteiligten, vor allem den Produzenten, mit in den (finanziellen) Ab-grund.

Auf der zweiten Ebene, die wir als Zuschauer parallel sehen, entsteht der Film trotzdem, indem eine zweite Crew, die für uns unsichtbar arbeitet, den scheiternden Regisseur und die ständig nach ihren Rollen fragenden Schauspieler und Schauspielerinnen beobachtet. Und diese Film-im-Film-Inszenierung, die sich vor unseren Augen wie im Spiegel entfaltet, gehört zu den spannend-sten und aufregendsten Filmereignissen, die je gedreht worden sind. Schauspieler suchen ihre Rollen, werden auf sich selbst zurückgeworfen, der Produzent ringt um die Reduzierung der es-kalierenden Kosten – jeder ist an seinem Punkt der Wahrheit und Wahrhaftigkeit angekommen. Dahinter lauern nur noch die eigenen Erinnerungen, Sehnsüchte, Leere, Ängste und Abgründe: »Was ich machen wollte, kam mir ganz einfach vor: einen Film, der jedem einzelnen gestatten

of all war criminals. They must not be allowed to go underground and must be made accountable, is the politically unambiguous demand. Like *The Third Man* for Vienna, the film *The Murderers Are among Us* still provides irreplaceable photographic documentation of the ruin world of postwar Berlin. Sometimes one has the impression that it is not the people, but the devastated houses and streets that are the main characters of the film.

At first glance Federico Fellini's 1961/62 work *8 1/2* (*Otto e mezzo*) does not belong in the category of ruin films. On closer inspection, however, the film contains many intellectual ruin fragments. The final scene even reflects – as a critique of Hollywood monumentalism – the »building of the Tower of Babel«, though here it is only represented as transparent scaffolding that is declared to be a rocket launch pad. It is about the obviously very famous, crisis-ridden film director Guido Anselmi, who was originally planning to make a science fiction movie, but simply cannot come up with any more ideas. Everything has already been said, he feels empty and exhausted, a human ruin in the prime of his (artistic) life. There is hardly a more ingenious way of structuring a movie: The main story portrays the failure of this idolized Italian movie director. He has gathered all the main actors, producers, authors, and set and costume designers around him; the shooting could begin. But Guido hesitates, he has the feeling that nothing fits together anymore and that the sets – beside the rocket base there is a trendy sanatorium spa, plus a grand hotel, with a lobby, stairwells, corridors and rooms for the crew, as well as a small hotel for his mistress (or do the buildings exist outside the film, in the real world?) –, that all these structures were built in vain. At the end of the film, during a chaotic press conference in front of the steel scaffolding, Guido calls off the project for good. He has failed, and he drags all those involved, particularly the producer, into the (financial) abyss with him.

On a second level, which we spectators see in parallel, the film is being made all the same, since a second crew, invisible to us, is observing the failing director and the actors and actresses, who keep inquiring about their roles. And this movie-within-a-movie production, unfolding before us as though in a mirror, is among the most exciting and thrilling film events that have ever been shot. Actors look for their roles, are thrown back on their own resources, the producer struggles to have the escalating costs reduced … they have all arrived at their moment of truth and veracity. Lurking in the background are only their own memories, longings, emptiness, fears and hidden depths. »What I wanted to do seemed quite simple to me: a film that would allow each single one of us finally to bury what is dead within us. However, I myself am the first who does not have the heart to bury something« … Federico Fellini summed up his intentions. We are glad that he did not bury what was dead within him, but translated it into film images – here primarily scenes from his childhood – that we will never forget. They too are ruins, but reanimated ruins that have become images. Failure has never been portrayed as fascinatingly.

We are all transformed into Marcello Mastroiannis, spiritually paralyzed film and life directors, we all gaze at the world and at people with his alert, and at the same time terribly weary, bored eyes. A Vanity Fair, a striving for information and perspective. Yet Guido Marcello, who declared that as a director he is a godlike puppeteer pulling strings, just doesn't get it anymore – like the rest of us. He no longer understands the world, his own feelings, or the feelings of the other persons. And it is precisely in this ruinous condition, lacking perspective, that the human characters really blossom in all their despair. All of them carry within them the longing for a person or an authority that will tell them where to go. Freedom of thought leads to paralyzing chaos, standstill and melancholy. Suddenly the forest in which pretty young women distribute mineral water to the patients turns into the »Sacro Bosco« of Bomarzo, a mysterious grove. The fashionable ladies with their huge hats the size of parasols appear as sphinxes and nymphs, the men as lascivious fauns. The resort's orchestra accompanies them by playing the »Ride of the Valkyries«, and later the »Thieving Magpie«. On the Italian »Magic Mountain« everyone is a puzzle to himself, and the sole alleged intellectual, the extra script writer hired by the producer, turns out to be a windbag and a pain in the neck who wears thick glasses and has a bad posture. His opinions no longer function in this inferno, which may be a paradise. The sentences sound like flatulence or belching, cynical comments by a critic who looks for links and explanations where there can be none. Allegedly »the one who understands«, he has understood nothing at all.

The director of the second level – Federico Fellini – believes the truth is found in leaving things as they are and accepting the characters – in »suchness«. One must take people as they are, with their limitations or potentials, watch them as they talk, accept their quirkiness, perhaps even love it. Then failure turns to victory. Basically both come down to the same thing.

Naturally, Hollywood saw the topic of ruins quite differently than Federico Fellini. After the dark series of the '30s and '40s, with all the bullet-riddled Al Capones, after all the burning buildings

sollte, endlich zu begraben, was wir alle an Abgestorbenem in uns tragen. Ich bin indessen selber der erste, der nicht das Herz hat, irgend etwas zu begraben«, formulierte Federico Fellini seine Absichten. Wir sind froh darüber, daß er das Abgestorbene in sich nicht begraben hat, sondern in Filmbilder – hier vor allem aus seiner Kindheit – übersetzt hat, die wir nie vergessen werden. Ruinen auch sie, aber wiederbelebte, Bild gewordene. Das Scheitern wurde nie fesselnder dargestellt.

Wir alle verwandeln uns in Marcello Mastroiannis, in geistig gelähmte Film- und Lebensregisseure, wir alle betrachten die Welt und die Menschen mit seinen wachen, gleichzeitig auch so müden, gelangweilten Augen. Ein Jahrmarkt der Eitelkeiten, ein Buhlen um Informationen und Überblick. Doch Guido Marcello, der sich selbst als Regisseur zum gottähnlichen Strippenzieher erklärt hat, blickt – zusammen mit uns – nicht mehr durch, versteht weder die Welt, seine eigenen Gefühle, noch die Gefühle der anderen Personen. Und genau in diesem ruinenhaften Zustand des mangelnden Überblicks blühen die menschlichen Charaktere in ihrer ganzen Verzweiflung erst richtig auf. Jeder trägt die Sehnsucht nach einer Person oder einer Instanz in sich, die sagt, wohin er oder sie gehen solle. Die Freiheit des Denkens führt in lähmendes Chaos, in Stillstand und Melancholie. Plötzlich wird der Wald, in dem hübsche, junge Frauen Heilwasser an die Patienten verteilen, zum »Sacro Bosco« von Bomarzo, zum rätselhaften Hain. Die mondänen Damen mit ihren sonnenschirmgroßen Hüten erscheinen als Sphinxe und Nymphen, die Männer als lüsterne Faune. Dazu spielt das Kurorchester den »Walkürenritt«, später die »Diebische Elster«. Auf dem italienischen »Zauberberg« ist sich jeder ein Rätsel, und der angeblich einzige Intellektuelle, der vom Produzenten neu dazu engagierte Drehbuchautor, entpuppt sich als phrasendreschende Nervensäge mit dicker Brille und schlechter Haltung. Seine Meinungen funktionieren in dieser Hölle, die vielleicht ein Paradies ist, nicht mehr. Die Sätze klingen wie Blähungen oder Rülpser, zynische Kommentare eines Kritikers, der überall Verknüpfungen und Erklärungen sucht, wo es keine geben kann. Er, der angebliche »Versteher«, hat überhaupt nichts verstanden.

Im Belassen der Zustände und dem Akzeptieren der Charaktere, im »Sosein, wie es ist«, glaubt der Regisseur der zweiten Ebene – Federico Fellini – die Wahrheit zu finden. Man muß die Menschen in ihrer Enge oder Weite belassen, ihnen beim Reden zuschauen, ihre Verrücktheiten akzeptieren, vielleicht sogar lieben. Dann wird das Scheitern zum Siegen. Beides ist im Grunde das gleiche.

Natürlich hat Hollywood das Ruinenthema ganz anders gesehen als Federico Fellini. Nach der schwarzen Serie der 1930er und 1940er Jahre, mit all den maschinengewehrzersiebten Al Capones, nach all den brennenden Häusern und zerschossenen Städten, blickte Alfred Hitchcock in die Abgründe der menschlichen Seele. Auch er entdeckte dort Ruinen und Raumfallen. Niemand wird je die Duschzelle im lausigen »Bates Motel« vergessen, niemand die Turmtreppen in *Vertigo*, niemand das Glas Milch in *Verdacht*, niemand die Krawattennadel in *Frenzy*. Einzelne Elemente – Duschvorhang, Treppe, Glas, Nadel – erhalten die Bedeutung von (ruinösen?) Todesboten. Es gibt kein Entrinnen mehr, der Würgegriff schließt sich unerbittlich.

Hitchcocks Filme wirkten besonders in den sauberen 1950er Jahren verstörend und beunruhigend. Die Kriegs- und Ruinenzonen müssen nicht nur in Korea oder später in Vietnam gesucht werden, sie verlaufen genauso mitten durch die gemütlichsten Wohn- und Hotelzimmer.

Ein Ruinenfilm, der als Bindeglied zwischen Europa und Hollywood angesehen werden kann, ist *A Foreign Affair* (*Eine auswärtige Affäre*) von Billy Wilder, entstanden 1948. Der Film spielt – wie *Die Mörder sind unter uns* – im zerstörten Nachkriegsberlin. Erika von Schlütow, dargestellt von Marlene Dietrich, die zum persönlichen Kreis um Hitler gehört hatte, fristet ihr Leben als Sängerin im Nachtclub »Lorelei«. Ihr Liebhaber, der amerikanische Captain »Johnnie«, schützt sie und besorgt ihr auf dem Schwarzmarkt alles, was sie braucht. Wilder, der bis zu seiner Emigration 1933 in Berlin gelebt hatte, drehte die Dokumentarsequenzen direkt nach Kriegsende in den realen Ruinenlandschaften. Alle Innenraumszenen entstanden von Dezember 1947 bis Februar 1948 in den Paramount Studios Hollywoods. Raffiniert und witzig spielt Wilder mit Marlenes Vergangenheit. Selbst ihr alter Liedertexter und Komponist Friedrich Holländer, von dem das berühmte Lied *Von Kopf bis Fuß* aus dem Film *Der Blaue Engel stammt*, war mit von der Partie. Er hat für diesen Film drei neue Songs für sie komponiert, die sie in den nächsten Jahren auch oft bei ihren Konzerten darbieten wird: »Black market«, »Illusions« und »The ruins of Berlin«. Mit rauchiger Stimme und verhangenem Blick singt sie: »..In den Ruinen von Berlin // Fangen die Blumen an zu blüh'n // In den Ruinen von Berlin ...«

Eines Tages taucht die amerikanische Kongreßabgeordnete Phoebe Frost in Berlin auf. Sie soll dort die Moral der Soldaten überprüfen. Natürlich verliebt sie sich in Marlenes Captain. Nach einigen dramatischen Komplikationen erreicht sie schließlich ihr Ziel und kann den leicht überforder-

and devastated cities, Alfred Hitchcock looked into the abysmal depths of the human psyche. He too discovered ruins and space traps there. No one will ever forget the shower scene in the lousy »Bates Motel«, the bell tower stairs in *Vertigo*, the glass of milk in *Suspicion* or the tie pin in *Frenzy*. Individual elements – shower curtain, staircase, glass, tie pin – come to signify (ruinous?) messengers of death. There is no escape, the stranglehold tightens without mercy.

The effect of Hitchcock's films was disturbing and disquieting, particularly in the respectable 1950s. The zones of war and ruins can be found not only in Korea or later in Vietnam, they are just as likely to appear in the coziest living rooms and hotel rooms.

A ruin film that may be regarded as a link between Europe and Hollywood is Billy Wilder's *A Foreign Affair*, which he made in 1948. Like *Die Mörder sind unter uns* (*The Murderers Are among Us*), the film takes place in a devastated postwar Berlin. Erika von Schlütow, played by Marlene Dietrich, who had been one of Hitler's intimates, ekes out a living as a singer in the nightclub »Lorelei«. Her lover, the American captain Johnnie, is her protector and gets her everything she needs on the black market. Wilder, who had lived in Berlin until his emigration in 1933, shot the documentary sequences directly after the end of the war in the actual ruin landscapes. All interior scenes were shot from December 1947 through February 1948 in Hollywood's Paramount Studios. Cleverly and wittily Wilder plays with Marlene's past. Even her former songwriter and composer, Friedrich Holländer, who wrote the famous song »Falling in Love Again« for the film *The Blue Angel*, was one of the team. For *A Foreign Affair,* he composed three new songs for her, which she would often perform in her concerts in the years to come: »Black Market«, »Illusions« and »The Ruins of Berlin«. With a smoky voice and languidly lidded eyes she sings: »..In den Ruinen von Berlin // Fangen die Blumen an zu blüh'n // In den Ruinen von Berlin … (Amid the ruins of Berlin // Trees are in bloom as they have never been // Amid the ruins of Berlin …)«

One day Phoebe Frost, a member of a U.S. congressional committee, appears in Berlin. She is supposed to look into the morale of the troops. Naturally she falls in love with Marlene's captain. After a few dramatic complications she finally reaches her goal and is able to hold the slightly overwhelmed captain in her arms. Erika von Schlütow, on the other hand, is arrested and led away, though she is again up to her Circean tricks, bewitching her guards. The American officer sends several soldiers one after the other to keep a watch on the guards, a truly very funny, typical Billy Wilder scene. His sarcastic humor is all the more astonishing if we consider that Wilder's mother and grandmother were murdered in Auschwitz.

In addition to all these films Hollywood still also upholds the tradition of pure gothic and horror movies. There bloodthirsty female vampires strike terror into people's hearts, there zombies – the eerie undead – terrify harmless spectators. »Frankenstein« haunts labs, castle ruins and lovely villages. Ray Harryhausen awakens eight-headed hydras, King Kongs, man-beasts, and one-eyed saurians that feed exclusively on human flesh to cinematic life in ancient, ruin-strewn landscapes. Roman Polanski invents the *Dance of the Vampires,* and no one who has ever seen the lonely, sometimes ruinously snowed-in Carpatian castle with its blood-sucking inhabitants will ever be able to drive it out of his nightmares again. The isolated mountain hotel in Stanley Kubrick's *The Shining* is also impossible to delete.

However, the ruin-addicted repertoire of horror is far from exhausted. The ghostly creatures of Stephen King, who himself made film versions of many of his own books, conclude the danse macabre and tickle our terrified nerves. At night, and sometimes during the day, the werewolves, the crazed cats and Saint Bernards, the sleepwalkers, fire devils, the black women and lawnmower men, the witches and the quite normal ghosts come out of hiding in their living rooms to attack us.

Carrie was the first novel of author Stephen King, who was completely unknown at the time. It was published in 1974. The 30,000-copy printing was sold out within a few weeks, an insiders' tip. Overnight, Stephen King became so famous that Hollywood showed an interest. After the enormous success of William Friedkin's film *The Exorcist*, producers were looking for suitable follow-up material for the director Brian di Palma. And here it was. The story is about a girl who is ridiculed by her fellow students. After they pour a bucket of pig's blood over her, she cracks up completely, discovers her psychokinetic powers, mutates into a fury and – in the novel – reduces her whole hometown to rubble. However, for the sake of economy, only her high school gym goes up in flames in the movie version. In the end she is fatally stabbed with a huge kitchen knife by her fanatically religious mother. »The nightmarish concluding sequence, even 20 years later, is still one of the most effective shock scenes in cinematic history. Carrie's only friend, Sue Snell, who has survived the massacre in the high school gym as though by a miracle, approaches the former site of the Whites' home, which apparently sank into the ground during the showdown.

ten Captain in ihre Arme schließen. Erika von Schlütow dagegen wird verhaftet und abgeführt, allerdings ist sie schon wieder dabei, ihre Bewacher zu becircen. Zur Überwachung der Überwacher schickt der amerikanische Offizier gleich mehrere Soldaten hinterher, eine wirklich sehr witzige, typische Billy-Wilder-Szene. Sein sarkastischer Humor ist um so erstaunlicher, wenn man bedenkt, daß Wilders Mutter und Großmutter in Auschwitz ermordet wurden.

Neben all diesen Filmen wird in Hollywood immer auch die Disziplin der reinen Grusel- und Horrorfilme hochgehalten. Da treiben blutrünstige weibliche Vampire ihr Unwesen, da erschrecken Zombies – gespenstische Untote – harmlose Zuschauer. »Frankenstein« geistert durch Labore, Burgruinen und liebliche Dörfer. Ray Harryhausen erweckt achtköpfige Hydren, King Kongs, Tiermenschen und einäugige Saurierwesen, die sich ausschließlich von Menschenfleisch ernähren, zum filmischen Leben in antiken, ruinenübersäten Landschaften. Roman Polanski erfindet den *Tanz der Vampire,* und niemand, der das einsame, teilweise ruinöse eingeschneite Karpatenschloß mit seinen blutsaugenden Bewohnern je gesehen hat, wird es wieder aus seinen Alpträumen verdrängen können. Auch das einsame Berghotel in Stanley Kubricks *Shining* läßt sich nicht löschen.

Das ruinensüchtige Horror-Repertoire ist jedoch noch lange nicht erschöpft. Die gespenstischen Geschöpfe Stephen Kings, der viele seiner eigenen Bücher selbst verfilmt hat, ergänzen den Reigen und kitzeln unsere verängstigten Nerven. Nachts, manchmal auch tagsüber, kommen die Werwölfe, die verrückten Katzen und Bernhardiner, die Schlafwandlerinnen, Feuerteufel, die schwarzen Frauen und Rasenmähermänner, die Hexen und die ganz normalen Gespenster aus ihren Wohnzimmerverstecken, um über uns herzufallen.

Carrie war der erste Roman des damals noch völlig unbekannten Autors Stephen King. Er erschien 1974. Die gedruckten 30000 Exemplare waren nach wenigen Wochen ausverkauft, ein Geheimtip. Stephen King wurde über Nacht so berühmt, daß Hollywood Interesse zeigte. Nach William Friedkins enorm erfolgreichem Film *Der Exorzist* suchten die Produzenten für den Regisseur Brian di Palma einen geeigneten Nachfolgestoff. Und hier war er. Die Geschichte handelt von einem Mädchen, das von ihren Mitschülern gehänselt wird. Nachdem sie von ihnen mit einem Eimer Schweineblut überschüttet worden ist, dreht sie völlig durch, entdeckt ihre psychokinetischen Kräfte, mutiert zur Furie und legt – im Roman – ihre gesamte Heimatstadt in Schutt und Asche. Aus Gründen der Sparsamkeit geht im Film jedoch nur die Turnhalle ihrer High School in Flammen auf. Zum Schluß wird sie von ihrer fanatisch religiösen Mutter mit einem riesigen Messer erdolcht. »Die alptraumhafte Schlußsequenz ist selbst nach zwanzig Jahren noch immer eine der wirkungsvollsten Schockszenen der Kinogeschichte. Carries einzige Freundin Sue Snell, die das Massaker im Ballsaal der High School wie durch ein Wunder überlebt hat, nähert sich dem Grundstück, auf dem das Haus der Whites stand, bevor es während des Showdowns sozusagen im Erdboden versank, um einen Strauß Blumen an einem ›Zu Verkaufen‹-Schild niederzulegen, auf das jemand ›Carrie White schmort in der Hölle‹ geschmiert hat, wobei unvermittelt und für den Zuschauer völlig unerwartet eine blutige Hand aus den Trümmern schießt und Sue am Arm packt.« (Andreas Kasprzak in seinem Buch über Stephen King)

Der beklemmende Film kam 1976 in die Kinos und entwickelte sich zu einem weltweiten Erfolg. Stephen King löste eine regelrechte Horrorfilmwelle aus. Nach seinen Geschichten und Drehbüchern wurden noch viele weitere Hollywoodfilme gedreht, so *Der Friedhof der Kuscheltiere*, *Cujo*, *Christine* und *Kinder des Zorns*. Die Realität hatte Risse und Löcher bekommen. Zweite und dritte Welten wurden sichtbar und arbeiteten mit geheimnisvollen Kräften an der Zerstörung des normalen, langweiligen Alltags.

Das Horror-Repertoire schien und scheint unerschöpflich. Gruselameisen, Killerviren und unsichtbare, aber tödliche Strahlen bedrohen harmlos-beschauliche Dörfer, Vögel greifen ganze Schulklassen an, Außerirdische nahen, sie landen mit ihren Ufos auf Waldlichtungen und schleichen sich nachts unbemerkt in friedliche Vorortsiedlungen ein, die im Mondlicht plötzlich aussehen wie Friedhöfe.

Erdbeben erschüttern Los Angeles und Manhattan. Wolkenkratzer und Brücken stürzen ein wie Kartenhäuser. Ruinenlandschaften wachsen und wachsen, breiten sich aus, zunächst in Modellnachbauten, später durch Computer-Animationen erzeugt – Special-Effekt-Weltuntergänge. Superman, Spiderman und Aliens bevölkern bald unsere Bilderwelt und unsere Phantasien. Was früher ausschließlich den Malern christlicher Erzählstoffe vorbehalten war – Himmelfahrt, Höllensturz und apokalyptischer Weltuntergang –, hat jetzt ein neues massenwirksames Ausdrucksmedium gefunden. Religiöse Verirrungen, Sektenabspaltungen und esoterische Gedankenblasen spielen zwar in die modernen Horrorfilme mit hinein, lassen sich aber weltanschaulich nicht konkret festlegen (christlich, judisch, animistisch, muslimisch, hinduistisch, maoistisch, kommu-

She is about to place a bouquet of flowers by a ›For Sale‹ sign on which somebody has scrawled ›Carrie White is roasting in hell‹ when suddenly and quite unexpectedly for the audience a bloody hand shoots from the rubble and grabs Sue by the arm.« (Andreas Kasprzak in his book about Stephen King.)

The oppressive film was screened in 1976 and became a worldwide success. Stephen King set off a regular flood of horror movies. Many more Hollywood movies were based on his stories and scripts, including *Pet Sematary*, *Cujo*, *Christine* and *Children of the Corn. Reality has developed cracks and holes. A second and third world have become visible, working with mysterious powers on destroying a normal, boring everyday life.

The repertoire of horror seems inexhaustible. Horrifying ants, killer viruses and invisible but deadly rays threaten harmless, quiet villages, birds attack whole classes of schoolchildren, extraterrestrials approach, they land their UFOs in forest clearings and creep unnoticed by night into peaceful suburbs, which in the moonlight suddenly look like cemeteries.

Earthquakes shake Los Angeles and Manhattan. Skyscrapers and bridges collapse like houses of cards. Ruin landscapes grow apace, spread, initially in model replicas, later produced by computer animation – a special effects staging of the end of the world. Superman, Spiderman and aliens will soon populate our world of images and our fantasies. What was once reserved exclusively for the painters of Christian narratives – ascension, descent to hell and the apocalyptic end of the world – has now found a new medium of expression with mass appeal. While religious aberrations, the formation of new sects and esoteric thought balloons do have a part to play in the modern horror movies, it is not possible to identify what specific ideology they represent (Christian, Jewish, animist, Muslim, Hindu, Maoist, Communist, capitalist, democratic …?) Horror worlds are often in contact with irrational, supernatural phenomena and forces that are vehemently rejected by natural scientists. In films it is no problem at all to make time run backwards, to leap across millennia, to beam bodies into spaceships or to other planets, to bring the dead back to life, to turn old people young again or to live forever. Ruins can turn themselves back into magnificent villas and mansions, but ruins can also lift off from the ground like Oriental carpets and fly over seas and mountain ranges with the clouds. Reading the stories in the *Bible*, you might think it would be no problem for present-day film directors, cameramen and animators to stage the former miracles as though they really happened. Even the Apocalypse of John would look good in a movie.

Besides horror and action movies, besides science fiction and catastrophe movies, movies about war are also produced, war movies that for the most part are wrongly called »antiwar films«. At their center are weapons and tough, adventurous men: Lewis Milestone's *All Quiet on the Western Front* (1930), William Wyler's *The Best Years of Our Lives* (1946) and Stanley Kubrick's *Paths of Glory* (1957).

In 1975 Kubrick again dealt with the issue of war. The film *Full Metal Jacket* was supposed to overshadow all the war movies ever made before, especially Francis Ford Coppola's *Apocalypse Now* (1976) and Oliver Stone's *Platoon* (1986). It describes a group of young men who are first trained by a malignant, bellowing U.S. Marine Corps sergeant to become soulless killing machines, and end up fighting in Vietnam. Some of them are killed, while others survive the hell that is war.

Particularly in the second half of the film we see landscapes of ruins that gradually become wilder, more and more riddled with holes, more devastated and finally are consumed in a huge sea of flames. As in all war movies, these ruins too basically look much too romantic and picturesque. We sense how much the director enjoys explosions, shooting, fire and smoke. In reality it is impossible to produce a real antiwar movie unless it is a montage patched together from authentic documentary film images, with actual wounded and dead people.

As far as brutality in war and action movies is concerned, James Cameron with his *Terminator* series surpasses all previous films of this type. Arnold Schwarzenegger is a good-natured robot fighting the almost immortal killer robot T-1000, who flattens everything in his path, rises again every time he is destroyed and emerges from pools of blood, exploded machines and cars, road surfaces and expanses of rubble as though he was Prometheus in person. An interesting thing about this film is the idea of the universal artificiality of his life; as a robot he needs neither flesh nor blood, and no metal or motor oil; he'll welcome any kind of matter, he is an idea that is capable of crystallizing out of anything and everything. His transformations tolerate hardly any destruction, he is a principle, the principle of evil that constantly dogs our footsteps. There is a suggestion of the ancient struggle between good and evil, between Faustus and Mephistopheles. Naturally good wins out in the end against all odds, as befits a successful Hollywood movie.

nistisch, kapitalistisch, demokratisch …?). Horrorwelten stehen oft in Kontakt mit irrationalen, übersinnlichen Phänomenen und Kräften, die von Naturwissenschaftlern vehement abgelehnt werden. In Filmen ist es kein Problem, Zeiten rückwärts laufen zu lassen, Sprünge über Jahrtausende durchzuführen, Körper in Raumschiffe oder auf andere Planeten zu beamen, Tote lebendig zu machen, alte Menschen in junge zu verwandeln oder ewig zu leben. Ruinen können sich in glanzvolle Villen und Herrenhäuser zurückentwickeln, Ruinen können jedoch auch vom Boden abheben wie orientalische Teppiche und mit den Wolken über Meere und Gebirge davonfliegen.

Wer die Geschichten der *Bibel* liest, könnte denken, es wäre kein Problem für heutige Regisseure, Kameramänner und Animationskünstler, die einstigen Wunder wie Realgeschehen ins Bild zu setzen. Selbst die Apokalypse des Johannes würde sich im Film gut machen.

Neben Horror- und Actionfilmen, neben Science-Fiction- und Katastrophen-Filmen, entstehen auch Filme über den Krieg, Kriegsfilme, die sich meist zu Unrecht »Antikriegsfilme« nennen: *Im Westen nichts Neues* von Lewis Milestone (1930), William Wylers *Die besten Jahre ihres Lebens* (1946) und Stanley Kubricks *Wege des Ruhms* (1957).

1975 befaßte sich Kubrick erneut mit dem Thema Krieg. Der Film *Full Metal Jacket* sollte alle bisherigen Kriegsfilme, vor allem *Apokalypse Now* von Francis Ford Coppola (1976) und *Platoon* von Oliver Stone (1986), übertrumpfen und in den Schatten stellen. Eine Gruppe junger Männer wird geschildert, die zunächst von einem bösartigen, nur brüllenden Ausbilder im US Marine Corps zu seelenlosen Killermaschinen gedrillt werden, um anschließend in Vietnam als Soldaten zu kämpfen. Einige von ihnen finden den Tod, andere überleben die Kriegshölle.

Besonders in der zweiten Hälfte des Films sehen wir Ruinenlandschaften, die immer wilder, löchriger, zerstörter werden und schließlich in einem riesigen Flammenmeer verglühen. Wie in allen Kriegsfilmen sehen auch diese Ruinen im Grunde viel zu romantisch und malerisch aus. Man spürt die Lust des Regisseurs an Explosionen, Schießereien, Feuer und Rauch. In Wirklichkeit läßt sich kein wirklicher Antikriegsfilm herstellen, es sei denn, er wird aus authentischdokumentarischen Filmbildern, mit realen Verletzten und Toten, zusammenmontiert.

Was die Brutalität in Kriegsfilmen und Action-Filmen angeht, übertrifft James Cameron mit seiner *Terminator*-Reihe alle bisher dagewesenen Bilderfindungen. Arnold Schwarzenegger kämpft als gutmütiger Roboter gegen den beinahe unsterblichen, alles niederwalzenden Killer-Roboter T-1000, der nach jeder Zerstörung neu aufersteht, sich aus Blutlachen, explodierten Maschinen und Autos, Straßenbelägen und Trümmerlandschaften herausformt, als sei er Prometheus persönlich. Interessant dabei ist der Gedanke der universalen Künstlichkeit seines Lebens; er benötigt als Roboter kein Fleisch und Blut, auch kein Metall oder Motoröl, ihm ist jede Materie willkommen, er ist ein Gedanke, der sich aus allem und jedem herauszukristallisieren vermag. Seine Transformationen dulden fast keine Zerstörung, er ist ein Prinzip, das Prinzip des Bösen, das uns ständig verfolgt. Der uralte Kampf zwischen Gut und Böse, zwischen Faust und Mephisto klingt an. Natürlich siegt am Ende dennoch das Gute, wie es sich für einen erfolgreichen Hollywoodfilm gehört.

Eine andere Filmdisziplin befaßt sich mit weltweit drohenden Umweltgefahren und Klimakatastrophen. Eiskappen schmelzen an den Polen, Meeresspiegel steigen, und Wassermassen begraben alle zivilisierten Länder, Städte und Menschen unter sich. New York mit den Wolkenkratzern von Manhattan liegt am Meeresgrund, tot und ausgestorben wie eine verlassene Korallenkolonie. Tsunamis brechen über Küstenstädte herein, neue Eiszeiten entstehen, die ganze Welt geht unter.

1995 schipperte Kevin Costner in seinem Film *Waterworld* auf einem selbstgebauten Katamaran über die Meere, die jetzt fast die gesamte Erdoberfläche bedecken. Eine mörderische Piratenwelt hat sich entwickelt, in der – wie vor Beginn der Zivilisationen – nur noch das Gesetz des Stärkeren gilt. Kevin Costners Gegner, der ein künstliches Atoll beherrscht, das aussieht wie ein Schrottplatz, wird von Dennis Hopper gespielt. Endzeitruinenbilder, die zugleich auch Anfangsbilder einer neuen Kultur darstellen könnten, einer Kultur, die sich ausschließlich auf dem Wasser entfaltet.

Roland Emmerich läßt in seinem Hollywoodfilm *The Day After Tomorrow* aus dem Jahr 2004 die Welt in einer neuen Eiszeit erstarren. Ganz New York wird von Schneemassen begraben. Nur die höchsten Wolkenkratzer Manhattans ragen über die Eislandschaft hinaus. Faszinierende Endzeitbilder entstehen, die bestimmt auch Hieronymus Bosch oder Caspar David Friedrich gefallen hätten.

Die erstaunlichsten und hartnäckigsten aller Produzenten von Ruinenbildern kommen allerdings nicht aus Hollywood, sondern aus London. Ich denke an die James-Bond-Serie, die seit den

174

72. Szenenbild aus Stanley Kubricks *Full Metal Jacket*, 1975.

72. Set for Stanley Kubrick's *Full Metal Jacket*, 1975.

Another film discipline deals with environmental dangers and climate catastrophes that threaten us worldwide. The polar ice caps are melting, sea levels are rising, and masses of water bury all civilized countries, cities and people under them. New York and the skyscrapers of Manhattan lie at the bottom of the ocean, dead and extinct like an abandoned colony of corals. Tsunamis come gushing over coastal cities, new ice ages come into being, the entire world comes to an end.

In 1995, in his film *Waterworld,* Kevin Costner sailed across the oceans that now cover almost the entire surface of our planet on a catamaran he had built himself. A murderous world of pirates has developed, in which – as before the rise of civilizations – might makes right. Kevin Costner's opponent, who rules over an artificial atoll that looks like a scrap yard, is played by Dennis Hopper. Images of ruins from an end-time that might at the same time also represent the first images of a new culture, one that unfolds exclusively on the water.

Roland Emmerich, in his 2004 Hollywood film *The Day After Tomorrow,* has the world freeze in a new ice age. All of New York is buried under masses of snow. Only the highest skyscrapers of Manhattan tower above the icy landscape. The fascinating end-time images that are created would surely have appealed to Hieronymus Bosch or Caspar David Friedrich.

However, the most astonishing and stubborn of all producers of ruin images come not from Hollywood, but from London. I am thinking of the James Bond series that has had a steady, constantly growing worldwide community of fans since the '60s. Every one of these films ends with a super-explosion of the mansion of the villain du jour, plus his labs and rocket depots. The architect who designed the classic James Bond super-buildings was Ken Adam. He devised the hideaway in *Dr. No*, the underground rocket station in *You Only Live Twice*, the Fort Knox bunkers in *Goldfinger*, the satellite lab in *Diamonds Are Forever*, the hidden submarine station in *The Spy Who Loved Me* and the space station in *Moonrakers*.

The brilliant secret agent »007«, James Bond, invented on the Caribbean island of Jamaica by former British high-class spy Ian Fleming, has the royal license to kill. In every film he uses the latest weapons and the most modern, technically sophisticated means of transportation developed in the labs of the British secret service. James Bond, who is always dressed to the nines, never tires in the struggle against the greatest and most despicable villain in the world. Actually he is always on the move, never in the same place for long in any of his movies. Probably, unlike his creator Ian Fleming, who lived in a fantastic luxury villa near Oracabessa in Jamaica, he has neither an apartment nor a house of his own. Naturally he himself is completely invulnerable and thus immortal. Also he loves women. Like all hero comic figures (Batman, Superman) he has

1960er Jahren ihre feste, sich ständig erneuernde Fangemeide in der ganzen Welt hat. Jeder dieser Filme endet mit einer Superexplosion der Villa des jeweiligen Bösewichts, samt Labors und Raketendepots. Entwurfsarchitekt der klassischen James-Bond-Superbauten war Ken Adam. Er dachte sich das Versteck von Dr. No aus, die unterirdische Raketenstation in *Man lebt nur zweimal*, die Fort-Knox-Bunker in *Goldfinger*, das Satellitenlabor in *Diamantenfieber*, den versteckten U-Boot-Bahnhof in *Der Spion, der mich liebte* und die Weltraumstation in *Moonrakers*.

Der smarte Geheimagent »007«, James Bond, erfunden auf der Karibikinsel Jamaika vom einstigen britischen Edelspion Ian Fleming, besitzt die königliche Lizenz zum Töten. Er benutzt in jedem Film die neuesten Waffen und die modernsten, technisch raffiniertesten Fortbewegungsmittel, die in den Labors des britischen Geheimdienstes entwickelt worden sind. James Bond, der immer sorgfältig wie ein Gentleman gekleidet ist, wird nie müde im Kampf gegen den größten und niederträchtigsten Bösewicht der Welt. Eigentlich ist er immer unterwegs, bleibt in allen Filmen ort- und raumlos. Wahrscheinlich besitzt er, im Gegensatz zu seinem Erfinder Ian Fleming, der eine traumhafte Luxusvilla in der Nähe von Oracabessa auf Jamaika bewohnte, weder eine eigene Wohnung noch ein eigenes Haus. Natürlich ist er selbst völlig unverletzbar und somit unsterblich. Außerdem liebt er die Frauen. Wie allen Helden-Comic-Figuren (Batman, Superman) werden ihm übermenschliche Fähigkeiten zugeordnet, die ihn sogar in eine göttergleiche Aura hüllen. Jeder (jugendliche) Filmbesucher kann sich mit ihm und seinem archaischen Kampf gegen das Böse identifizieren. Stellvertretend für ihn, der bequem in seinem Kinosessel liegt, erledigt James Bond die notwendige Arbeit.

Die Gleichsetzung von Superarchitekturen und Bösewichten hat Tradition. Nur die wirklich Reichen und Mächtigen konnten und können sich architektonisch austoben. Wir denken an Kaiser Nero und seine »Domus aurea«, an die Zaren und den Kreml in Moskau, die Schlösser Ludwigs XIV., an den Escorial, den Vatikan, den Tower in London, König Ludwigs Neuschwanstein, an die Stahlproduktionshallen Alfried Krupps und ihre Kanonen, an die V2-Raketen in den Bergwerkstollen von Mittelbau Dora, an das Niederwalddenkmal, die Befreiungshalle an der Donau, an die *Titanic*, an die Berliner und Nürnberger Monumentalbauten Adolf Hitlers, an den Obersalzberg. Und wir denken an Doktor No, Gert Fröbe, Curd Jürgens, Stromberg, General Gogo, sowie an die unterirdischen Fabrikhallen des Zwerges Alberich und an Walhalla bei Richard Wagner.

73. Szenenbild aus einem James-Bond-Film. Jeder dieser Filme endet mit einer grandiosen Zerstörung der Bösewicht-Villa.

73. Stage set for a James Bond film. Each of these films ends with the spectacular destruction of the villain's home.

been given superhuman capabilities that even envelop him in a godlike aura. Every (teenage) film-goer can identify with him and his archaic struggle against evil. James Bond, acting as his surrogate as the teenager reclines in his seat at the movies, takes care of what needs to be done.

There's a tradition that equates super-architectural structures and villains. Only those who were truly wealthy and powerful could (and still can) indulge to the hilt in their architectural passions. We immediately think of Emperor Nero and his »domus aurea«, of the czars and the Kremlin in Moscow, the castles of Louis XIV, of the Escorial, the Vatican, the Tower of London, King Ludwig's Neuschwanstein, of the steel production halls of Afried Krupp and his cannons, of the V2 rockets in the mine tunnels of the Mittelbau-Dora concentration camp, of the Niederwald Monument, the Befreiungshalle by the Danube, of the Titanic, of Adolf Hitler's monumental buildings in Berlin and Nuremberg, of the Obersalzberg. And we think of Doktor No, Gert Fröbe, Curd Jürgens, Stromberg, General Gogo, and of the underground factory halls of the dwarf Alberich and Valhalla in the works of Richard Wagner.

13. Zur Psychologie der Ruinen

Erinnerungsruinen, Erinnerungsneurosen

»Unser Unterbewußtsein ist wie unser Körper ein Lagerhaus von Relikten und Erinnerungen aus der Vergangenheit.« (C. G. Jung)

»Der Augenblick ist unbewohnbar wie die Zukunft.« (Octavio Paz)

»Wenn nämlich die Ruine das ist, was vom früher Gewesenen übrig bleibt, ist sie heute vor allem das, was vom ex abrupto Geschehenen übrig bleibt, dieses ›wichtigste Vorkommnis‹, das heute allerorten das Geschehen der zeitgenössischen Welt verdrängt. Ein Unbehagen, das nicht mehr ›in der Zivilisation‹, sondern in den Kulturnachrichten zu finden ist.« (Paul Virilio)

»Erinnerungsruinen: Ich versuche mich an Einzelheiten von Häusern, Gesichtern zu erinnern, und es kommen immer nur Ruinen zustande.« (Peter Handke)

»Ich habe das merkwürdige Haus später nie wieder gesehen, das, als mein Großvater starb, in fremde Hände kam. So wie ich es in meiner kindlich gearbeiteten Erinnerung wiederfinde, ist es kein Gebäude; es ist ganz aufgeteilt in mir; da ein Raum, dort ein Raum und hier ein Stück Gang, das diese beiden Räume nicht verbindet, sondern für sich, als Fragment, aufbewahrt ist. In dieser Weise ist alles in mir verstreut, die Zimmer, die Treppen, die mit so großer Umständlichkeit sich niederließen, und andere enge, rundgebaute Stiegen, in deren Dunkel man ging wie das Blut in den Adern; die Turmzimmer, die hochaufgehängten Balkone, die unerwarteten Altane, auf die man von einer kleinen Tür hinausgedrängt wurde: – alles das ist noch in mir und wird nie aufhören, in mir zu sein. Es ist, als wäre das Bild dieses Hauses aus unendlicher Höhe in mich hineingestürzt und auf meinem Grunde zerschlagen.« (Rainer Maria Rilke)

Eines der merkwürdigsten Haus-Fragmente, das ich je gesehen habe und das auf den ersten Blick nicht wie eine Ruine, eher wie ein viktorianisches Hotel aussieht, steht in San José, südlich von San Francisco. Es ist möglich, im Unvollendetsein dieses Bauprojekts eine Weltanschauung zu erkennen, die den Intentionen künstlicher Ruinen in der Zeit der Romantik sehr nahekommt. Allerdings wurde die amerikanische Bauherrin nicht von einem sentimental-melancholischen Traum angetrieben, sondern von einem Alptraum. Ihr Gebäudekomplex ist der gebaute Ausdruck einer Paranoia, und Angst war die Triebfeder ihrer lebenslangen Obsession.

Ich besuchte dieses verrückte Fragment-Anwesen im Oktober 2003. Bestimmt ist das »Lady-Winchester-Mystery-House« die berühmteste Touristenattraktion in San José. Der Weg dorthin ist so gut ausgeschildert, daß man ihn problemlos finden kann. Wie bei allen Einrichtungen dieser Art in Amerika, ist der Funktionsablauf gut organisiert. Es beginnt mit einem üppig-großen und bewachten Parkplatz, mit Zubringerbussen, mit freundlich lächelnden Guides, die an jeder Wegbiegung stehen und Fragen beantworten. Der Kassenraum hat die Anmutung eines Supermarkts, mit Andenkenshops, Büchertresen, Restaurants, Cafés und Toiletten.

Mister Winchester hatte in Boston ein Vermögen mit der Erfindung und Produktion des nach ihm benannten Winchester Gewehrs gemacht. Durch die Kugeln, die während der Eroberung des amerikanischen Westens daraus abgefeuert worden waren, starben erst Hunderttausende von Büffeln, später Hunderttausende von Indianern. Am Vermögen von Lady Winchester klebte also Blut, viel Blut!

Nachdem ihr Mann und ihre einzige Tochter früh gestorben waren, verkaufte die Dame ihre Fabrik und konsultierte in Boston einen Spiritisten, der ihr riet, den Ort, an dem das Geschehen seinen Ausgang nahm, zu verlassen, andernfalls würden die Geister aller getöteten Indianer zurückkehren und sie auf grausame Weise foltern, skalpieren und töten. Sie nahm die Worte ernst, zog 1884 aus dem Osten der Vereinigten Saaten in den Westen und erwarb ein Haus mit neun Zimmern und einem riesigen Grundstück in San José.

Der fluchtartige Umzug erwies sich jedoch als vergeblich, denn die Dämonen reisten mit, sie hausten in ihrem Gehirn, erschienen jeden Tag aufs neue und vermehrten sich in der Nacht. Vor ihrem geistigen Auge sah Lady Winchester Heerscharen von erschossenen Indianern, die sich zusammenrotteten, um sich nach San José aufzumachen. Nachts umstanden sie dann ihre Fluchtburg und starrten tausendäugig durch Fenster, Türen, Schornsteine, Bodenöffnungen und Ritzen. Es war nur eine Frage der Zeit, bis sie angreifen, sich hereindrängen und ihr langsam die

13. On the psychology of ruins

Memorial ruins, memory neuroses

»Our subconscious, like our body, is a storehouse of relics and memories of the past.« (C. G. Jung)

»The moment is uninhabitable just like the future.« (Octavio Paz)

»If a ruin is what is left over from things that once existed, then today it is primarily something that is left over from what happened abruptly, this ›most important of events‹ that today everywhere supersedes the happenings of the contemporary world. An uneasy feeling that is no longer to be found ›in civilization‹, but in cultural news broadcasts.« (Paul Virilio)

»Memory ruins: I try to remember details of houses, faces, and the only thing that ever materializes is ruins.« (Peter Handke)

»I never again saw that remarkable house, which passed into strangers' hands after my grandfather's death. As I find it in the memories of my childhood, it isn't a complete building; it has been broken into pieces inside me; a room here, a room there, and then a piece of a hallway that doesn't connect these two rooms, but is preserved as a fragment, by itself. In this way it is all dispersed inside me – the rooms, the staircases that descended so gracefully and ceremoniously, and other narrow, spiral stairs, where you moved through the darkness as blood moves in the veins; the tower rooms, the high, suspended balconies, the unexpected galleries you were thrust onto by a little door – all this is still inside me and will never cease to be there. It is as if the image of this house had fallen into me from an infinite height and shattered upon my ground.« [Rainer Maria Rilke, *The Notebooks of Malte Laurids Brigge*, trans. Stephen Mitchell (New York 1983)]

One of the most remarkable house fragments I have ever seen and which at first glance does not look like a ruin but like a Victorian hotel is located in San Jose, south of San Francisco. It is possible to recognize, in the unfinished condition of this construction project, a Weltanschauung that comes very close to the properties ascribed to artificial ruins during the Romantic period. However, the American woman who had it built was not driven by a sentimental melancholy dream, but by a nightmare. Her complex of buildings is the built expression of paranoia, and fear was the force behind her lifelong obsession.

I visited this crazy fragment of an estate in October of 2003. I am sure that the »Winchester Mystery House« is the most famous tourist attraction in San Jose. This is why the road to it is so thoroughly signposted that it can easily be found. As with all facilities of this kind in America the tour of the estate is well organized. It begins with an opulently large parking lot, with shuttle

74. Hans Dieter Schaal, Erinnerungsruinen, Collage mit Zeichnung, 2009.

74. Hans Dieter Schaal, Ruins of memory, collage with drawing, 2009.

Haut abziehen und glühende Messer ins Fleisch bohren würden. Hatte es sich bei dem Rat des Spiritisten um eine Falle gehandelt? Sie hätte skeptisch sein müssen! Warum beschloß sie, trotz der Gefahren und Bedrohungen, Indianergebiete zu durchqueren und sich sogar in einem ehemaligen Indianergebiet niederzulassen, war sie doch dort den Dämonen weit mehr ausgesetzt als in Boston? Problemlos hätte sie sich mit ihrem Vermögen in London oder Paris niederlassen können, weit entfernt von haßerfüllten, rachsüchtigen Dämonen! Wollte sie vielleicht sogar die reale Konfrontation, den harten Kampf mit ihren Feinden wie eine echte Wildwest-Lady herbeiführen, oder wollte sie mit ihrem Leiden nur für die (indirekten) Schandtaten ihres Mannes büßen, dessen Schuld sie mit dem Vermögen geerbt hatte?

Schon am ersten Tag nach ihrer Ankunft beschloß sie, das Haus zu einer Festung und labyrinthischen Falle auszubauen. Jeder Mensch, auch jeder Geist, der sich dem Gebäude zukünftig näherte, sollte es für ein freundliches Gasthaus halten, das mit seinen Balkonen, Loggien, Vordächern, Arkaden und Wintergärten so sympathisch altmodisch aussah wie ein verschlafenes englisches Landschloß. In der Realität wurden alle diese Merkmale von ihr nur als Lockmittel und Tarnung eingesetzt. Sollte sich tatsächlich einmal ein Mensch oder Geist zur Eingangstür oder an ein Fenster verirren, würde er abgewiesen werden oder, falls er dennoch ins Haus eindränge, sofort in ein Fallenloch stürzen, das sich unmittelbar hinter der Tür befand. Würde es ihm, trotz all dieser Hindernisse, wider Erwarten gelingen, die Flure oder Treppen zu betreten, wäre er nach kurzer Zeit so verwirrt, daß er wie eine Fliege gegen unsichtbare Scheiben knallen, daran seinen Schädel einschlagen und, davor liegend, hilflos zugrunde ginge. Zahllose Türen führen ins Leere, tiefe Abgründe lauern dahinter. Wege und Gänge enden vor Wänden, Treppen laufen gegen Decken, hinter Schränken stehen weitere Schränke, darin verstecken sich Spiegel oder Glasscheiben. Fenster sind im Fußboden eingelassen, Türen in der Decke.

Lady Winchester beobachtete jede Bewegung durch Luken und Schlitze. Ihr entging nichts. Sie war die Spinne im Netz, der Minotauros im Zentrum des Labyrinths und die Hexenmeisterin in einer Person. 40 Jahre lang beschäftigte sie 30 Maurer, Verputzer, Zimmerleute, Schreiner und Maler, die jeden Tag ohne Unterbrechung – auch sonntags, selbst über Weihnachten – für sie arbeiten mußten. Als sie 1922 mit 85 Jahren starb, war das Winchester-House auf 160 Zimmer angewachsen. In ihren Schubladen fanden sich Pläne für weitere hundert Zimmer. Das Projekt war unvollendet … Die erstaunten Zeitgenossen erkannten nach ihrem Tod schnell das sensationelle Potential dieses fantastischen Hausgeschwürs, der kalifornische Staat übernahm die Regie und baute das Anwesen – ähnlich wie »Hearst Castle« – bald zu einer touristischen Attraktion aus. König Ludwig II. hatte eine amerikanische, wenn auch bürgerliche Schwester bekommen. Allerdings fehlte Lady Winchester ein passender Komponist, ihre Haus-Alpträume blieben stumm und unvertont.

75, 77. Lady Winchester-Mystery-House in San José bei San Francisco. Was von außen wie ein freundliches Victorianisches Hotel aussieht, entpuppt sich innen als Alptraum-Architektur.
76. Ruinen-Spuren des berühmten San-Francisco-Erdbebens im Jahr 1906.

75, 77. Lady Winchester Mystery House in San José near San Francisco. This house, which looks like a friendly Victorian Hotel from the outside, turns out to be a nightmare architecture.
76. Traces of damage by the famous 1906 San Francisco earthquake.

buses, with friendly smiling guides who stand at every corner and answer questions. The entrance lobby feels like a supermarket, with souvenir shops, displays of books, restaurants, cafés and bathrooms.

Mr. Winchester had made a fortune in Boston with the invention and production of the Winchester rifle, which was named after him. The bullets that were fired from these guns during the conquest of the American West first killed hundreds of thousands of buffaloes, and later hundreds of thousands of Indians. Lady Winchester's fortune is steeped in blood, a lot of blood!

After the early deaths of her husband and her only daughter, the lady sold her factory and consulted a Boston psychic, who advised her to leave the place where the events had started, otherwise the spirits of all the Indians who had been killed would return and torture, scalp and kill her in a cruel fashion. She took him seriously, moved west from the East Coast in 1884 and purchased a nine-room house on a huge plot of land in San Jose.

The hasty move proved to be in vain, however, for the demons accompanied her on her journey, wreaked havoc in her brain, reappeared every day and multiplied at night. In her mind's eye Lady Winchester saw armies of the Indians who had been shot and had banded together to set out for San Jose. At night they stood around the fortress where she had found refuge and stared with thousand eyes through windows, doors, chimneys, openings in the ground and cracks. It was only a question of time before they would attack, push their way inside and slowly skin her and pierce her flesh with red-hot knives. Had the psychic's advice been a trap? She should have been skeptical! Why had she decided, in spite of the dangers and risks, to cross Indian territory and even settle in a former Indian region, seeing that she was far more exposed to the demons there than in Boston? She could easily have settled down in London or Paris with her fortune, far away from hostile and vengeful demons! Perhaps she even wanted to provoke a real confrontation, a hard struggle against her enemies like a real lady of the Wild West, or was she merely with her own suffering trying to atone for the (indirect) shameful deeds of her husband, whose guilt she had inherited along with the fortune?

The very first day after her arrival she decided to turn the house into a fortress and labyrinthine trap. Every person, and every ghost as well, who would approach the building in future would think it was a friendly inn, which with its balconies, open porches, canopies, arcades and winter gardens looked so pleasantly old-fashioned, like a sleepy English country mansion. In reality she installed all these features merely as lures and camouflage. Should a person or spirit actually stray to the front door or one of the windows, he would be turned away or if he did manage to enter he would immediately fall into a pit located right behind the door. If, in spite of all these obstacles and contrary to expectation, he managed to get into the hall or the stairs, he would be so confused within a short time that he would slam into invisible windowpanes like a fly, crack his skull and

Durch Türen und Flure dringen wir langsam in das Gebäude ein. Zunächst lassen wir uns von liebevollen Details und puppenstubenhaften Schränken verzaubern. Erst allmählich, nach der ersten Geisterfalle – ein im Boden falsch eingebautes Fenster –, beschleicht uns ein mulmiges Gefühl. Ich denke an *Psycho* und »Bates Motel«, an die Zeichnungen und Holzschnitte von Escher, an die Surrealisten, an Salvador Dalí, Louis Buñuel und Max Ernst. Es wundert mich, daß sich keiner von ihnen mit dieser Dame und ihren architektonischen Wahnwelten beschäftigt hat. Ob einer von ihnen jemals hier war? Falsche Türen, Klappen und Fenster werden geöffnet. Langsam umgreift uns das gebaute Wahngespinst, und wir werden zunehmend Mitspieler des Alptraums. Lady Winchester, das wird mir jetzt klar, hat sich während ihrer Lebensjahre in Kalifornien in dieses Gebäude verwandelt. Am Ende, mit ihrem Tod, ging ihre Seele endgültig in die Wände,

perish helplessly as he lay on the ground in front of them. Countless doors lead into empty space with deep holes yawning on the other side. Pathways and corridors end in front of walls, staircases run into ceilings, there are closets behind closets, with mirrors or glass panes concealed inside. There are windows in the floor, doors in the ceiling.

Lady Winchester observed every movement through skylights and slits. She did not miss a thing. She was the spider in the web, the Minotaur in the center of the labyrinth and the sorceress rolled into one. For 40 years she employed 30 masons, plasterers, carpenters, cabinetmakers and painters, who had to work for her daily without interruption – even on Sundays, even on Christmas Day. When she died in 1922 at the age of 85, Winchester House had grown to 160 rooms. In her dresser drawers plans for another hundred rooms were found. The project was un-

Decken, Fußböden und Raumfallen ein. In Wirklichkeit sind alle Hauselemente Teile ihres Körpers.

Verständlicherweise hatte die Dame nachts am meisten Angst. Es gab zwar Hausangestellte, aber die Handwerker waren abwesend. Jede Nacht verbrachte Lady Winchester in einem anderen Schlafzimmer. Sie hatte sich insgesamt hundert davon einrichten lassen. Die meisten lagen an Innenhöfen, besaßen nur winzige Fenster und kugelsichere Wände. Keiner der Hausangestellten wußte, wo Lady Winchester am Morgen zu finden war. Sie mußte jeden Tag aufs neue in ihrem eigenen Haus gesucht werden.

Ein Zeitdokument besonderer Art stellt die Raumflucht dar, in der Lady Winchester das legendäre Erdbeben in San Francisco von 1906 erlebt hat. Als es einsetzte, war sie sofort davon überzeugt, die alleinige Schuld daran zu tragen. Jetzt rächte sich also auch noch die Natur an ihr! Sie schwor, die Räume, die sie in diesem Moment betreten hatte, nie wieder aufzusuchen und ließ die Türen vermauern. Inzwischen hat man die Türen wieder geöffnet, und wir können die Räume besichtigen. Wahrscheinlich sind die Zerstörungsspuren an Wänden und Decken heute die einzigen authentischen Zeugnisse des katastrophalen Erdbebens, das vor allem die Stadt San Francisco zerstörte, aber auch große Schäden in der ganzen Bay-Region anrichtete. Ich betrachte die zersplitterten Wandplatten, die Risse im Holzboden und die herabhängenden Deckenfetzen.

In dem holzvertäfelten viktorianischen Speisesaal soll Lady Winchester einmal in der Woche zu einem großen, fiktiven Dinner eingeladen haben. Angeblich habe sie dann am Kopfende des langen, zentral aufgestellten Tisches gesessen, auf dem zwanzig Gedecke – wertvolle Teller mit schwerem Silberbesteck – und seidene Servietten bereitlagen. Während des Essens soll sie sich stets mit den Unsichtbaren unterhalten haben. Von den Dienern habe sie sich Speisen servieren und Wein in die Kristallgläser füllen lassen. Sie selbst sei zu diesem Anlaß immer festlich gekleidet gewesen und habe hin und wieder einen Toast auf ihren verstorbenen Mann und ihre verstorbene Tochter ausgebracht.

finished … After her death amazed contemporaries quickly recognized the sensational potential of this fantastic malignant growth of a house. The state of California took charge and soon turned the estate – just like »Hearst Castle« – into a tourist attraction. King Ludwig II now had an American sister, even though she was a commoner. Lady Winchester, however, did not have a suitable composer. Her house nightmares remained mute and had no soundtrack.

Through doors and corridors we slowly find our way into the building. At first we allow ourselves to be charmed by loving details and dollhouse cabinets. Only gradually, after the first ghost trap – a fake window installed in the floor – a creepy feeling comes over us. I think of *Psycho* and »Bates Motel«, of the drawings and woodcuts of Escher, of the surrealists, of Salvador Dalí, Louis Buñuel and Max Ernst. I am surprised that none of them devoted any time to this lady and her delusional architectural worlds. I wonder if any of them was ever here? False doors, trapdoors and windows are opened. Slowly the built web of illusion seizes hold of us, and we become actors in the nightmare. Lady Winchester, I realize now, was transformed into this building during her life in California. At the end, after her death, her soul passed into the walls, ceilings, floors and booby traps. In reality all the elements of the house are parts of her body.

Understandably the lady was most frightened at night. There was a house staff, of course, but the crew of workmen was not there. Lady Winchester spent every night in a different bedroom. She had had a total of a hundred of them furnished. Most of them faced inner courtyards, and had only tiny windows and bulletproof walls. None of the staff knew where Lady Winchester could be found in the morning. They had to have a new search for her every day in her own house.

An unusual contemporary document depicts the suite of rooms in which Lady Winchester went through the legendary 1906 San Francisco earthquake. When the quake began, she was immediately convinced that she alone was responsible for it. Now nature, too, was taking revenge on her! She swore she would never again enter the rooms she had gone into at that moment, and had the doors bricked up. In the meantime the doors have been opened again, and we are able to view the rooms. Probably the signs of destruction on the walls and ceilings are the only authentic evidence today of the catastrophic earthquake that devastated primarily the city of San Francisco but also caused great damage all over the Bay Area. I look at the splintered wall panels, the cracks in the wooden floor and shreds dangling from the ceiling.

It is said that in the wood-paneled Victorian dining room, once a week, Lady Winchester invited imaginary guests to a big dinner. She is said to have sat at the head of the long table set up in the middle of the room and laid with 20 place settings – expensive plates with heavy silverware, and silk napkins. During the meal she is said to have kept up a conversation with the invisible diners. Supposedly she had the servants put food on the plates and pour wine in the crystal glasses. She herself is said to have always been formally dressed on these occasions and to have toasted her late husband and daughter every now and then.

14. Mediale Ruinen

Katastrophen und Untergänge in den TV-Nachrichten

Während das Lady-Winchester-Haus – wie Neuschwanstein, der Obersalzberg oder Carinhall – genau auf der Grenze zwischen Traum, Alptraum und Wirklichkeit errichtet wurde und damit zu einem großen Teil in unsere sichtbare Welt hineinreicht, können wir von den nachfolgend beschriebenen Häusern und ihrem gewaltsamen Verschwinden bei Explosionen, Erdbeben, Kriegen, Attentaten oder sonstigen Katastrophen nicht mehr genau sagen, wo – in welcher Welt – sie anzusiedeln sind. Ich spreche von Vorgängen, die wir ausschließlich aus Filmen, dem Fernsehen und dem Internet kennen.

Stellen wir uns als erstes die minutenlange Slow-Motion-Hausexplosion vor, mit der Michelangelo Antonionis *Zabriskie Point* aus dem Jahr 1969 endet. Genüßlich verfolgt die Kamera fliegende Schränke, Sofas, Fernsehgeräte, Stehlampen, Kühlschränke und Hausfragmente. Wie befreit aus ihrem harten Los, jahrelang fest auf dem Boden einer Wohnung stehen zu müssen, schweben die Gebrauchsgegenstände durch Feuerwände und Rauchwolken. Im Film findet diese Explosion nicht wirklich statt, Daria, die weibliche Hauptfigur, träumt davon, nachdem sie im Radio gehört hat, daß ihr Freund Mark bei der Rückgabe eines gestohlenen Flugzeugs von der Polizei erschossen worden ist. Sie will sich gedanklich an ihrem superreichen Arbeitgeber rächen, der einen Luxusbungalow dieser Art besitzt. So endet diese Traumvilla in einer ästhetisch wunderbar gefilmten Katastrophe, die manche Kritiker damals als Werbefilm für malerische Haus-Explosionen bezeichnet haben. Als Zuschauer sind wir zudem Zeugen einer Explosion, die nicht wirklich in diesem Moment stattfindet, sondern uns – wie im uralten »Höhlengleichnis« von Platon – in Projektionen aus Licht, Farben, Schatten und Umrissen vorgegaukelt wird. Sie ereignete sich irgendwann, inszeniert im Studio oder in der freien Landschaft, in jedem Fall nicht jetzt, in diesem Moment. Vielleicht fand sie auch nie wirklich statt und ist das Produkt einer künstlichen Animation.

Das bewegte Bild und damit auch die Zeit wurden in einer Konserve gespeichert, die eine unendlich häufige Wiederholung zuläßt. So waren die Verhältnisse im Film. Seit es das weltweite Fernsehen (und das Internet) gibt, haben sich die Möglichkeiten vollkommen geändert. Jetzt lassen sich – sofern Kameras vor Ort aufgebaut wurden – reale Ereignisse, Olympiaden, königliche Hochzeiten oder Beerdigungen, Katastrophen, Unglücke und Explosionen in Echtzeit weltweit übertragen und beliebig oft – in alle eingeschalteten TV-Geräte und Computer – vervielfältigen. Wir Teilnehmer an der medialen Revolution werden zu gierigen Echtzeit-Voyeuren.

Ob man es wahrhaben will oder nicht: Die moderne Medienwelt des Fernsehens liebt Katastrophen, spektakuläre Untergänge und Ruinen. Sie haßt nichts so sehr wie den normalen, ereignislos dahinfließenden Alltag, wie ihn eine ständig eingeschaltete Überwachungskamera zeigt. Erst wenn etwas Außergewöhnliches und Beängstigendes passiert, entwickeln sich die Fernsehsender – und die Aufzeichnungen einer Überwachungskamera – zum interessanten Vermittlungsmedium. Die Katastrophe wird in weltweit verbreitete Fernsehbilder übersetzt, und alle Blicke wenden sich in eine Richtung. Das bisher diffus-chaotische Bewußtsein der sieben Milliarden Erdenbewohner fokussiert sich auf einen Punkt, und jeder Mensch wird zum Zuschauer.

Natürlich setzt dieses zynische Sensationsinteresse auch eine gewisse Größenordnung der Katastrophe voraus. Niemand wird sich um regionale Unglücke, bei denen drei bis zehn Tote zu beklagen sind, kümmern, es müssen schon 1000, 10 000, 100 000 oder Millionen von Toten verschüttet worden sein, dann erst schrecken die Zuschauer weltweit auf. Auch der Mord an einer global berühmten Persönlichkeit, wie etwa dem Präsidenten der Vereinigten Staaten von Amerika, würde genügen.

Bevor das Fernsehen seinen weltweiten Siegeszug antrat, leistete der Rundfunk Pionierarbeit auf dem Gebiet der Informationsverbreitung. So prägte sich der 6. Mai 1937 den damaligen Weltbewohnern unvergeßlich ins Gedächtnis ein. Ein junger Journalist namens Orson Welles kommentierte live im Radio die Landung des deutschen Luftschiffs *Hindenburg* in Lakehurst bei New York, zunächst nur ein ungewöhnliches, weil neuartiges Ereignis, das die Massen faszinierte (Paul Virilio berichtet darüber).

Plötzlich jedoch geschah das Unfaßbare, die Katastrophe. Beim Andocken an den Landemasten explodierte der Zeppelin und riß mit einer gewaltigen Stichflamme 34 Menschen in den Tod. Die Stimme des Kommentators überschlug sich, stockte, versuchte das Unbegreifliche in Worte zu fassen. Die Katastrophe schreckte auf, wuchs zur Sensation an, weltweit. Ein Attentat, ein Unfall, ein Racheakt, eine Verschwörung? Die Untersuchungskommission stellte später fest,

14. Media ruins

Catastrophes and scenes of destruction in TV news

While the Winchester House – like Neuschwanstein, the Obersalzberg or Carinhall – was built right on the borderline between dream, nightmare and reality, and thus for a large part extends into our visible world, we can no longer say, of the houses described below and their violent disappearance in explosions, earthquakes, wars, assassinations or other catastrophes, precisely where – in which world – they belong. I am speaking of events we know exclusively from films, television and the Internet.

Let us first imagine the minutelong slow-motion house explosion that ends Michelangelo Antonioni's 1969 film *Zabriskie Point*. With obvious enjoyment the camera follows flying cabinets, sofas, TV sets, standing lamps, refrigerators and house fragments. As though liberated from the tough fate of having to stay put for years on the floor of an apartment, the consumer goods soar through walls of fire and clouds of smoke. In the movie this explosion does not really take place. Daria, the female protagonist, dreams about it after hearing on the radio that her friend Mark was shot by the police while returning a stolen plane. Mentally she wants to avenge herself on her super-rich boss, who has the same type of luxury home. Thus this dream villa ends in an aesthetically beautiful, wonderfully filmed catastrophe that some critics called a commercial for picturesque house explosions. Moreover, as spectators we are the witnesses of an explosion that does not really take place at this moment, but – as in the ancient »Allegory of the Cave« of Plato – is an illusion, projections of light, colors, shadows and outlines. It took place at some point, staged in the studio or in the open landscape, at any rate not now, at this moment in time. Maybe it never really took place at all and is the product of artificial computer animation.

The moving image and thus time as well have been prerecorded, and this makes it possible to repeat them an infinite number of times. This used to be true of films. Since the coming of worldwide television (and the Internet), the possibilities have changed completely. Now – as long as there are cameras on location – real events, Olympic Games, royal weddings or funerals, catastrophes, accidents and explosions can be broadcast in real time worldwide and duplicated any number of times – to be viewed on all TV sets and computers that are tuned into them. We, the participants in the media revolution, all turn into avid real-time voyeurs.

Whether we want to admit it or not: The modern media world of television loves catastrophes, spectacular scenes of destruction and ruins. It hates nothing so much as normal, uneventful everyday life, the kind shown by a surveillance camera that is constantly switched on. Not until something extraordinary and frightening happens do TV stations – and the tapes of a surveillance camera – become an interesting communication medium. The catastrophe is translated into TV images that are disseminated worldwide, and all eyes look in the same direction. The previously diffuse, chaotic consciousness of seven billion earthlings focuses on one point, and every human being becomes a spectator.

Naturally this cynical interest in the sensational also demands that the catastrophe have a certain magnitude. No one is going to care about regional accidents involving three to ten fatalities. At least 1,000, 10,000, 100,000 or millions of people have to be buried alive before spectators worldwide are jolted out of their indifference. The murder of a globally famous personality, such as the president of the United States, would be sufficient.

Before television went on its worldwide triumphal march, radio did pioneering work in disseminating information. For instance, May 6, 1937 made an unforgettable impression on the people of the world living at the time. A young journalist by the name of Orson Welles was doing a live radio report on the landing of the German dirigible Hindenburg in Lakehurst not far from New York. Initially, because it was novel, it was merely an unusual event that fascinated the masses (Paul Virilio has written about it).

Suddenly, however, the incomprehensible happened – the catastrophe. While docking at the mooring masts the zeppelin exploded. A powerful burst of flame killed 34 people. The voice of the commentator cracked, faltered, tried to find words for the inconceivable. The catastrophe jolted listeners worldwide, became a sensation. Was this an assassination, an accident, an act of vengeance, a conspiracy? The investigating commision later found out that this was not an act of sabotage, but an accident. As a result, every kind of transportation of persons by means of such airships was prohibited in the future.

Without the direct radio broadcast the event would have had far fewer consequences. No one could do a live report on the catastrophe of the Titanic in 1912, since at that point there was no

daß es sich nicht um einen Sabotageakt, sondern um einen Unfall handelte. Die Folge davon war, daß in Zukunft jede Art von Personentransport mit derartigen Fluggeräten untersagt wurde.

Ohne die Radiodirektübertragung hätte das Ereignis weit weniger Folgen gehabt. Über die Katastrophe der *Titanic* im Jahr 1912 konnte niemand live berichten, da es zu diesem Zeitpunkt noch kein öffentliches Rundfunksystem gab. Die Weltöffentlichkeit erfuhr erst in den darauffolgenden Tagen davon. Es existieren keine Filmaufnahmen und Photos des spektakulären Untergangs, Reporter und Journalisten mußten die Ereignisse mühsam aus Funksprüchen, Passagierlisten und Berichten von Überlebenden rekonstruieren.

Inzwischen steigerten sich die Möglichkeiten der TV-Medien in unvorstellbar zeitnahe Szenarien. 1991 zeigten die Fernsehstationen der Welt während des Golfkriegs zum ersten Mal Bilder von Raketenangriffen auf konkrete Bodenziele. Wie in einem Computerspiel sahen wir den Abschuß, die Annäherung und schließlich die Explosion im Fadenkreuz. Das Zielobjekt explodierte, der Angriff war gelungen. Von Menschen, lebendigen oder getöteten, war nichts zu sehen. Wurden doch Zivilisten getroffen, sprach der Militärbeauftragte bei der anschließenden Pressekonferenz im Hauptquartier von »Kollateralschäden«. Wir Fernsehzuschauer sollten uns mit den erfolgreichen Schützen identifizieren, wie wir es bei Fußballübertragungen gelernt hatten.

Auch die Ereignisse des 11. September 2001 wurden nahezu in »Echtzeit« rund um den Globus gesendet. So konnten fast alle Erdbewohner am Einstürzen der Twin Towers teilhaben, als wären sie live dabei gewesen. Die ganze Welt ein einziger Circus maximus und alle Zuschauer ein Heer von Todes-Voyeuren. Man sah die Flugzeuge in die Fassaden krachen, Feuer und Rauch ausbrechen, Verzweifelte aus den Hochhausfenstern springen. Wahrscheinlich gehörte diese global-mediale Vervielfältigung zum Kalkül der Al-Qaida-Terroristen.

Andere Unglücke, die sich ohne Journalistenpräsenz ereigneten, schlichen sich erst allmählich ins Bewußtsein der Zeitgenossen. So etwa der Supergau des Atomkraftwerks in Tschernobyl, der zunächst in alter Sowjetmanier geheimgehalten wurde und erst nach tagelangem Schweigen an die Weltöffentlichkeit drang.

Wie lange mögen die Nachrichten vom verheerenden Erdbeben in Lissabon im 18. Jahrhundert unterwegs gewesen sein, bis sie Johann Wolfgang von Goethe und Heinrich von Kleist erreichten? Waren es Tage, Wochen oder gar Monate? Und wie verhielt es sich mit den Ereignissen der Französischen Revolution? Tatsache ist, daß die Nachrichtenübermittlung jahrhundertelang in ihrer Geschwindigkeit etwa gleichblieb, da immer nur reitende Boten und Eilkutschen dafür zur Verfügung standen. Ein galoppierendes Pferd gab das Tempo vor. Zu Beginn des 19. Jahrhunderts versuchten findige Taubenzüchter, die Geschwindigkeit zu beschleunigen. Berühmt waren die Taubenzuchten der Familie Rothschild in Paris und London. Brieftauben überbrachten die aktuellen Börsendaten so schnell, daß die Banken der Rothschilds Vorteile gegenüber ihren Konkurrenten hatten. Eine Brieftaube war es auch, die der Familie Rothschild die Nachricht von der Niederlage Napoleons auf dem Schlachtfeld von Waterloo übermittelte.

Niemand war schneller, niemand konnte geschäftlich zügiger reagieren. 1840 verschickte der amerikanische Kunstmaler Samuel Morse das erste Telegramm nach seinem System über Kabel von New York nach Baltimore. Wenige Jahre später hatte sich dieses Telegraphensystem weltweit durchgesetzt, aber jede Nachricht mußte nach 50 Kilometern neu versendet werden. Am 1. Januar 1847 wurde zwischen Bremen und Bremerhaven die erste längere Telegraphenstrecke Europas in Betrieb genommen. 1851 richtete Paul Julius Reuter (Pseudonym für Israel Beer Josaphat) die erste Nachrichtenagentur der Welt in London ein.

Schon während des Deutsch-Französischen Krieges 1870/71 waren die Kommunikationsmöglichkeiten so vortrefflich, daß sich Generalfeldmarschall Moltke mit seinem Führungsstab nicht an der Front, sondern weit dahinter, in Mainz, aufhalten konnte.

Mit kabellosen Funkverbindungen wurde von 1890 an experimentiert. Während des Ersten Weltkriegs arbeitete das Militär intensiv an der Entwicklung des Telephons. Alle Schützengräben wurden nach und nach durch Kabeltelephone miteinander verbunden. Es dauerte jedoch Jahre, bis sich das nicht ganz so leicht verletzbare, kabellose Funktelefon durchsetzte. Aus dieser Technik entwickelte sich nach dem Krieg das allgemeine Rundfunksystem. 1920 wurden die ersten Sender mit regelmäßigen Programmen in Pittsburgh/USA und 1922 in Königswusterhausen bei Berlin eingerichtet. Früh stellte sich die Frage, wem denn das neue Medium gehöre? Dem Staat? Der Wirtschaft? Den Bürgern? Politiker erkannten schnell, daß – neben der Unterhaltung und der Verbreitung von Kultur – hier ein großartiges Mittel zur Verfügung stand, die Massen in ihrem Sinne zu beeinflussen.

Parallel zur Rundfunkentwicklung arbeiteten Ingenieure in den 1930er Jahren an einer neuen Technik, mit der es möglich werden sollte, bewegte Bilder zu versenden. Das erste große Fern

public radio system yet. The world did not find out about it until the following days. There are no films or photos of the spectacular shipwreck. Reporters and journalists had to painstakingly reconstruct events from radio signals, passenger lists and the reports of survivors.

In the meantime the possibilities of TV media increased to unimaginably realtime scenarios. In 1991, during the Gulf War, TV stations all over the world showed, for the first time, images (live broadcasts) of rocket attacks on ground targets. As if in a computer game we saw the launch, the approach and finally the explosion in the crosshairs. The targeted object exploded, the attack had been successful. There was no sign of people, alive or dead. If civilians did get killed, the representative of the military during the subsequent press conference at headquarters spoke of »collateral damage«. We TV viewers were meant to identify with the successful men who had fired the rockets, as we had learned in watching football coverage.

The events of 11 September 2001 were also broadcast close to »realtime« around the globe. As a result almost everyone on the planet could watch the collapse of the Twin Towers as if they had been there live. The whole world was a veritable Circus Maximus and all viewers an army of voyeurs of death. The viewers saw the planes crashing into the façades, the eruption of fire and smoke, desperate people jumping from the windows of the skyscrapers. Probably this global media coverage was something the Al-Qaida terrorists had counted on.

Other disasters, which took place without the presence of journalists, entered the consciousness of contemporaries only gradually – for instance, the meltdown of the nuclear power plant in Chernobyl, which was initially kept secret in typical Soviet fashion and was only disclosed to the general public after days of silence.

I wonder how long the news of the devastating 18th century earthquake in Lisbon took to reach Johann Wolfgang von Goethe and Heinrich von Kleist. Was it days, weeks or even months? And what about the events of the French Revolution? The fact is that the speed of the dissemination of news remained roughly the same for centuries, since messengers on horseback and express coaches were the only means available. The pace was set by a galloping horse. At the beginning of the 19th century resourceful pigeon breeders tried to increase the speed. The Rothschild family in Paris and London had famous breeds of pigeons. Carrier pigeons brought the latest stock market reports so quickly that the banks of the Rothschilds had advantages over their competitors. It was also a carrier pigeon that brought the Rothschild family the news of Napoleon's defeat on the battlefield of Waterloo.

No one was faster, no one was able to react with more resourceful business acumen. In 1840 the American painter Samuel Morse cabled the first telegram based on his system from New York to Baltimore. A few years later this telegraph system had become established worldwide, but every news item had to be resent after 50 kilometers. On 1 January 1847 the first longer telegraph line in Europe was put into service between Bremen and Bremerhaven. In 1851 Paul Julius Reuter (a pseudonym for Israel Beer Josaphat) started the first news agency in the world in London.

As early as during the Franco-Prussian War in 1870/71 communication possibilities were so outstanding that General Moltke and his general staff were able to stay not at the front, but far behind it, in Mainz.

There were experiments with wireless radio conections starting in 1890. During World War I the military made an all-out effort to develop the telephone. All the trenches were gradually connected by cable telephones. However, it took years for the wireless telephone, which was not quite as vulnerable, to become established. After the war this technology developed into the general radio system. In 1920 the first radio stations with regular programs were set up in Pittsburgh and in 1922 in Königswusterhausen near Berlin. Early on, the question was raised to whom the new medium belonged. The state? The economy? The citizens? Politicians soon realized that – besides providing entertainment and disseminating culture – this was an excellent medium for influencing the masses as they wished.

Parallel to developing the radio, engineers in the 1930s were working on a new technology that would make it possible to transmit moving images. The first great TV spectacle of the modern age was the 1936 Olympic Games. For 16 days or 96 hours all the important sports events were broadcast to special viewing rooms. A total of over 160,000 people watched the coverage. The Second World War prevented a continued peaceful development of the spectacular and promising medium. In 1957 television had finally arrived – the first two TV stations in West and East Germany broadcast a short daily news and entertainment program. Anyhow, at the time 160,000 households (this seems to be a magic number!) already owned a TV set. The age of a daily flood of images had begun! The newspapers and radio, as well as the »newsreels« before feature films

sehspektakel der Neuzeit war die Olympiade 1936. An 16 Tagen wurden 96 Stunden lang alle wichtigen Sportereignisse in öffentliche Fernsehstuben übertragen. Insgesamt schauten dabei über 160 000 Menschen zu. Der Zweite Weltkrieg verhinderte eine friedliche Weiterentwicklung des spektakulären und zukunftträchtigen Mediums. 1957 war es dann soweit, und die ersten beiden Fernsehstationen in West- und Ostdeutschland sendeten täglich ein kurzes Informations- und Unterhaltungsprogramm. Immerhin besaßen damals schon 160 000 Haushalte (diese Zahl scheint magisch zu sein!) ein eigenes TV-Gerät. Das Zeitalter der täglichen Bilderflut hatte begonnen! Die Zeitungen, der Rundfunk, auch die »Wochenschauen« vor den Spielfilmen in den Kinos traten als Hauptinformationsmedium langsam in den Hintergrund.

Tragbare Kameras ermöglichten es, wichtige Ereignisse und Katastrophen unmittelbar zu filmen und die bewegten Bilder direkt an die Fernsehsender zu übertragen. Das Attentat auf John F. Kennedy war schon ein großes Fernsehspektakel. Kameraleute waren live dabei, als der amerikanische Präsident von den Kugeln getroffen wurde. Aus lesenden, später hörenden Bürgern waren bilder- und informationssüchtige Zeitgenossen geworden. Bewegte und starre Bilddokumente hatten damals noch mehr Beweiskraft als erläuternd-beschreibende Texte. Ihre Botschaften erreichten die Sinne direkt, unübersetzt in ein zweites, mühsam erlerntes Medium. Aus Alphabeten wurden zunehmend wieder Analphabeten gemacht. Es gab natürlich immer auch Menschen, die den flimmernden Bildern mißtrauten. So verstummten die Stimmen nie ganz, die behaupteten, die Mondlandung sei in den Studios von Cape Canaveral inszeniert worden. Wer wollte die Wahrheit wirklich überprüfen?

Bei den Ermordungen von Martin Luther King und John Lennon waren weder Kameramänner noch Photographen dabei. Deswegen fehlen die eigentlichen Tatbilder. Journalisten versuchten später, die Vorgänge an den Tatorten genau zu rekonstruieren, manchmal genauer – mit nachgespielten Szenen – als die Kriminalpolizei. Aber es blieb immer ein Defizit. Genauso wie bei dem Unfall von Lady Diana in einem Pariser Autotunnel. In den Wochen danach wurden nur Photos des zertrümmerten Autos veröffentlicht, Bildaufnahmen des eigentlichen Unfalls gab es nicht. Damit fehlte das Zentrum der Katastrophe. Man fühlte sich als trauernd betroffener Zuschauer um das Wesentliche geprellt. Ein blinder Fleck feuerte die Vermutungs- und Verschwörungsphantasien an. Wenigstens das Unglücksfahrzeug hätte zu einem allgemein zugänglichen Ruinendenkmal aufgebaut werden können, in Paris oder in London. Aber die Polizei nahm es mit, versteckte die Trümmer in irgendwelchen Werkstattlabors, zerlegte sie in Einzelstücke, immer auf der Suche nach Sendern, Empfängern oder sonstigen Manipulationsgeräten. Etwas Verdächtiges wurde nicht gefunden, jedenfalls lauteten so die Nachrichten. Damit blieb das geheimnisvolle Rätsel bestehen, das wir alle so lieben. Warum hier, warum sie, warum zu diesem Zeitpunkt?

Vorgänge, die sich länger hinziehen, wie etwa kriegerische Auseinandersetzungen, werden von TV-Berichterstattern an Ort und Stelle beobachtet. Schon im Ersten Weltkrieg begleiteten Journalisten, Photographen und Kameramänner die Soldaten bei ihren Fronteinsätzen und lieferten mehr oder weniger objektive Berichte in ihre Heimatländer. Adolf Hitler benutzte die Wochenschauberichte über seine Redenauftritte und später die Kriegsbilder von den Fronten zu Propagandazwecken. Hier wurden die Siege der deutschen Armee geradezu herbeiinszeniert. Leni Riefenstahl mit ihren Olympia- und Reichsparteitagsfilmen setzte die entsprechenden ästhetischen Maßstäbe. Das Ziel bestand darin, die Zuschauer für die neuen Ideale des Herrenmenschentums zu begeistern. Jede deutsche Familie erhielt ein Rundfunkgerät – den »Volksempfänger« – und konnte live die Reden des Führers mithören. Eine bisher noch nicht gekannte Beeinflussung der Bevölkerung durch mediale Mittel fand statt. Gegenstimmen wurden unterdrückt. Die neuen Medien dienten ausschließlich zur diktatorisch einseitigen Information der Massen.

Es gab ein eigenes »Propagandaministerium« mit dem besonders redegewandten und demagogisch begabten Joseph Goebbels an der Spitze. Wie ferngesteuert werden die ideologisch beeinflußten Männermassen wenige Monate später als schwerbewaffnete Soldaten über Polen und die übrigen europäischen Länder herfallen. Adolf Hitler beschrieb den Vorgang in *Mein Kampf*: »Krieg ist das Natürlichste, Alltäglichste, Krieg ist immer und überall … Krieg ist Leben.«

Wahrscheinlich hatten die wenigsten Deutschen das Buch wirklich gelesen, sonst wäre ihnen die Ruinenzukunft Deutschlands schon früher zu Bewußtsein gekommen. Zu Kriegszeiten war es unter Strafe verboten, Feindsender – etwa BBC London – zu hören. Die Machthabenden hatten Angst vor kritischen Gegenstimmen und der Wahrheit, die vielleicht nicht mit ihren Propagandainhalten übereinstimmte. Die Ergebnisse dieser einhämmernden Gehirnwäsche eines ganzen Volkes sind bekannt: Halb Europa war zerstört, es gab Millionen von Toten. Deutschland war eine einzige Ruinenlandschaft.

in the cinemas slowly began to fade into the background – they were no longer the main information media.

Portable cameras made it possible to film important events and catastrophes directly and to transmit the moving images directly to the TV stations. The assassination of John F. Kennedy was a great television spectacle. Camera crews were present live when the American president was hit by the bullets. A population of reading, and later listening, citizens had become contemporaries who were avid for images and information. At the time documentary images, moving or not, had much more value as evidence than explanatory or descriptive texts. Their messages reached the senses directly: They had not been translated into a second, painfully learned medium. Literate people were gradually turned back into illiterates. Naturally there were also still people who mistrusted the flickering images. Thus the voices which claimed that the moon landing had been staged in the studios of Cape Canaveral never quite fell silent. Who really wanted to check the truth?

When Martin Luther King and John Lennon were murdered neither camera crews nor photographers were present. That is why there are no actual images of the crimes. Journalists later tried to reconstruct exactly what had happened at the scenes of the crimes, sometimes more exactly – with reenacted scenes – than the criminal investigation department. But something was always missing, just as it had been when Lady Diana was in an accident in a Parisian tunnel. In the weeks that followed only photos of the wrecked car were published. There were no photos of the actual accident. That meant the center of the catastrophe was missing. As mourning, sad spectators, people felt they had been cheated out of the essential part. A blind spot gave rise to conjectures and conspiracy fantasies. The fateful car at least could have been made into a ruin monument that would have been generally accessible, in Paris or in London. But the police took it with them, hid the wreckage in some kind of workshop or labs, took it apart into pieces, always looking for transmitters, receivers or other types of remote manipulation devices. Nothing suspicious was found, or at least that was what it said in the news. Thus the mysterious enigma we all love so much has still not been solved. Why here, why her, why at that point in time?

Events that go on for a long time, such as military conflicts, are observed by TV reporters on the front lines. Even in the First World War journalists, photographers and cameramen accompanied the soldiers who were deployed, and sent home more or less objective reports. Adolf Hitler used the newsreel reports about his speaking engagements and later the images of war from the fronts for propaganda purposes. Here the victories of the German army were virtually produced. Leni Riefenstahl with her films on the Olympic Games and the Nuremberg Rally set the appropriate aesthetic standards. The objective was to fill the spectators with enthusiasm for the fascist revolution and the new ideals of the master race. Every German family was given a radio – the »people's receiver« – and was able to hear the Führer's speeches live. To an unprecedented degree the population was influenced by means of the media. Opposing voices were suppressed. The new media exclusively served the dictatorial, one-sided information of the masses.

There was a special »Propaganda Ministry« headed by the particularly eloquent and demagogically gifted Joseph Goebbels. As though remotely controlled, the ideologically influenced masses of men, heavily armed, would attack Poland and the rest of Europe a few months later. Adolf Hitler described the process in *Mein Kampf*: »War is the most natural, the most everyday thing, war is always and everywhere … war is life.«

Probably very few Germans had really read the book, or else they would have realized much earlier that Germany was facing a future filled with ruins. During the war it was a punishable crime to listen to enemy radio stations – such as BBC London. The powers that be were afraid of voices of critical opposition and of a truth that might not agree with their propaganda. The results of the constant brainwashing of an entire nation are common knowledge: Half of Europe was destroyed, there were millions of dead. Germany was one vast landscape of ruins.

Without the *Gleichschaltung* – the National Socialists' totalitarian control over all aspects of German society – and without the multiple reproduction of a single ideology – that of the Führer and his party – there would never have been such a catastrophe. The case of General Field Marshal Rommel shows how the truth was dealt with in this kind of propaganda world. Since Hitler needed great war heroes as models for his soldiers, Rommel was built up into such a hero. During his Africa campaign the newsreels showed his overpowering successes. In reality the supposed war hero kept losing one battle after another against the British. By the end of the campaign he had sent 100,000 soldiers to die a hero's death, exactly half of his military contingent. Years later, when Rommel was appointed inspector of the Atlantic Wall project, he criticized the overall military strategy and questioned the possibility of a final German victory. After this – as

Ohne die Gleichschaltung und ohne die Vervielfältigung einer einzigen Meinung – die des Führers und seiner Partei – wäre es niemals zu einer solchen Katastrophe gekommen. Wie in einer derartigen Propagandawelt mit der Wahrheit umgegangen wurde, zeigt der Fall von Generalfeldmarschall Erwin Rommel. Da Hitler große Kriegshelden brauchte, um seinen Soldaten Vorbilder zu verschaffen, wurde Rommel dafür aufgebaut. Während seines Afrikafeldzugs zeigten Wochenschauberichte seine überwältigenden Erfolge. In Wahrheit verlor der angebliche Kriegsheld eine Schlacht nach der andern gegen die Engländer. Am Ende hatte er 100 000 Soldaten in den Heldentod geschickt, genau die Hälfte seines gesamten militärischen Aufgebots. Jahre danach, als Rommel die Oberaufsicht über das Atlantikwallprojekt hatte, kritisierte er die militärische Gesamtstrategie und bezweifelte die Möglichkeit eines deutschen Endsiegs. Daraufhin wurde er, ich schrieb schon darüber, von Hitler zum Selbstmord gezwungen. Offiziell hieß es in Zeitungsmeldungen und Wochenschauberichten: »Generalfeldmarschall Rommel ist seinen Verletzungen, die er bei einem Tieffliegerangriff in Frankreich erlitten hatte, erlegen. Er starb als Held.«

Natürlich sollte die pompöse Beerdigungsveranstaltung im Ulmer Rathaus auch die Bevölkerung täuschen. Sie erfuhr die Wahrheit erst nach dem Krieg. Lügen gehören zum System der Propaganda, auch allgemein zur Arbeit von Berichterstattern. Wer weiß schon, ob der Palästinenser, der heute Steine auf israelische Soldaten wirft, nicht vielleicht von einem Kameramann dafür bezahlt wurde? Wer weiß, wie viele Bilder von der afghanischen Front für die Weltöffentlichkeit inszeniert wurden? Die Grenzen sind fließend, schließlich muß der Korrespondent gutes Filmmaterial an seinen Sender übermitteln, und wir wollen spannende Bilder von Dorfsäuberungen, Talibanüberfällen, Katastrophen und Ruinen sehen. Niemand von uns wird je das Land wirklich bereisen und anschauen. Wir lassen reisen, wir lassen andere für uns Gefahren bestehen und die fremden, kriegerischen Realitäten beobachten. Anschließend glauben wir, informiert zu sein.

Gleiches gilt auch für die großen Naturkatastrophen, die in Wirklichkeit keine Katastrophen sind, sondern normale Naturvorgänge. Erst durch die Menschen, die leichtsinnigerweise ihre Hütten und Zelte am Strand aufgebaut hatten und so von der Tsunamiwelle ins Meer gespült wurden, sind die Vorgänge zu tragischen Katastrophen erklärt worden. Die Tiere hingegen hatten die Vorzeichen erkannt und waren rechtzeitig ins Landesinnere und auf Berge geflohen.

Wie dunkle, bedrohliche Blöcke ragen Katastrophen aus der Vergangenheit heraus und bestimmten über Jahre unser Denken und unser Weltgefühl. Jeder hat die Vorgänge auf sich selbst bezogen, als Mitleidempfindender oder zynisch Distanzierter. Wir sind dank der Nachrichten und Fernsehbilder Zeugen von Todeseruptionen, strahlenden und feurigen Demonstrationen der bösen Gegenwelt geworden, und wir haben überlebt. Plötzlich, beim Anblick der tödlichen Ruinen, fühlt sich dieses Leben ganz neu an, wie ein wertvolles, allerdings ständig gefährdetes und bedrohtes Geschenk.

Die Katastrophe von Tschernobyl, die zunächst geheimgehalten wurde, blieb lange ein bilderloses Ereignis. Keine Fernsehkamera scheint die Vorgänge wirklich beobachtet zu haben. Jedenfalls wurden keine markanten Bilder übertragen. Die erste Nachricht kam aus Schweden. Am 28. April 1986, drei Tage nach Beginn des Supergaus, wurde im Kernkraftwerk Forsmark aufgrund erhöhter Radioaktivität automatischer Alarm ausgelöst. Binnen Stunden konnte der Verursacher der Strahlenwolke ermittelt werden, und die Weltöffentlichkeit erfuhr von der Katastrophe in der Ukraine, die damals noch zur Sowjetunion gehörte.

Das Atomkraftwerk von Tschernobyl, das in der Nähe der ukrainischen Stadt Pripyat, nur wenige hundert Kilometer von Kiew entfernt liegt, war als nicht besonders sicher bekannt, größere Zwischenfälle jedoch hatten sich bisher nicht ereignet. Die Vorgänge zogen sich vom 25. April bis zum 6. Mai 1986 hin. Wären die verantwortlichen Ingenieure damals nicht auf die Idee gekommen, einen totalen Stromausfall und damit die Abschaltung eines Reaktorblocks zu simulieren, hätte der Supergau, der schlimmste aller möglichen Atomkraftwerksunfälle, nie stattgefunden. Ein ähnlicher Versuch am Block 3 war im Jahr zuvor fehlgeschlagen, jetzt wollte man ihn am Block 4 wiederholen.

Um mit der eigentlichen Testphase zu beginnen, mußte am Nachmittag des 25. April 1986 das Notkühlsytem abgeschaltet werden. Zunächst lief alles planmäßig, erst in der Nacht vom 26. auf den 27. April gerieten die Vorgänge außer Kontrolle. Eine Kettenreaktion unglücklicher Umstände führte zu mehreren aufeinanderfolgenden nuklearen Explosionen. Der 1000 Tonnen schwere Deckel des Reaktorkerns flog in die Luft, und ein unkontrollierbares Feuer brach aus. Statt das Unglück nach Kiew und Moskau weiterzumelden, verschwiegen die verantwortlichen Ingenieure den Vorgang und versuchten weiter, selbst Herr der Lage zu werden. Mit örtlichen Hubschraubern wurden 40 Tonnen Borcarbid in das Deckelloch abgeworfen, um den Brand zu löschen und

I wrote above – he was forced by Hitler to commit suicide. The official version in newspaper and newsreel reports read as follows: »General Field Marshal Rommel succumbed to wounds sustained during an attack by low-flying planes in France. He died a hero's death.«

Naturally the pompous funeral staged in the city hall of Ulm was also intended to deceive the population. They did not find out the truth until after the war. Lies are part of the propaganda system, and generally also part of the work of news reporters. Who knows whether the Palestinian throwing rocks at Israeli soldiers today was not paid to do so by a cameraman perhaps, who knows how many pictures from the Afghan front were staged for the general public? The borderlines are fluid: After all, the correspondent needs to send good film material to his station, and we want to see exciting pictures of villages being cleared, Taliban attacks, catastrophes and ruins. None of us will ever take a real trip and get to see that country. We let others travel, have them survive dangers for us and observe the reality of war in foreign parts. After watching we think we know all about it …

The same is true for the great natural catastrophes – not catastrophes in reality, but normal natural events. It was only the people who had thoughtlessly built their huts and tents on the beachfront and were therefore swept into the ocean by the wave of the tsunami who declared that what happened was a tragic catastrophe. The animals, on the other hand, had recognized the early signs and had fled in time into the interior and to the mountains.

Like dark, menacing blocks catastrophes project from the past and have influenced our thinking and our view of the world over the years. Each of us has has taken the events personally, as one who feels compassion or else has cynically distanced himself. Thanks to the news and TV images we have become the witnesses of fatal eruptions, radiant, fiery demonstrations of the evil alternate world, and we have survived. Suddenly, at the sight of the deadly ruins, this life feels quite new, like a valuable gift, though one that is constantly at risk and vulnerable.

The catastrophe of Chernobyl, which was initially kept secret, remained undocumented by pictures for a long time. No TV camera seemed actually to have observed what was going on. At any rate no striking photographs were broadcast. The first news arrived from Sweden. On 28 April 1986, three days after the meltdown began, an automatic alarm was set off at the Forsmark nuclear power station because of increased radioactivity. Within hours it was possible to determine the cause of the radioactive cloud, and the world learned of the catastrophe in the Ukraine, which at the time was still part of the Soviet Union.

The nuclear power station of Chernobyl, located near the Ukrainian town of Pripyat, only a few hundred kilometers from Kiev, was known to be not particularly safe, though until that time no serious incidents had occurred there. The series of events dragged on from 25 April to 6 May 1986. If the engineers in charge had not hit on the idea of simulating a total power failure and thus the switching off of a reactor block, the meltdown, the worst of all possible nuclear power plant accidents, would never have happened. A similar attempt involving Block 3 had failed the year before, and now they wanted to repeat it on Block 4.

In order to begin the actual test phase, the emergency cooling system had to be turned off on the afternoon of 25 April 1986. At first everything went according to plan; it was not until the night of 26 to 27 April that things got out of control. A chain reaction of unfortunate circumstances led to several successive nuclear explosions. The 1,000-ton cover of the reactor's core blew up, and an uncontrollable fire erupted. Instead of reporting the accident to Kiev and Moscow, the engineers in charge kept silent about what had happened and continued trying to keep the situation under control themselves. With local helicopters, 40 metric tons of boron carbide were dropped into the hole in the roof in order to extinguish the fire and thus stop the chain reactions of the meltdown. It was not until the following day, when events at the power plant took on ever more catastrophic proportions, that authorities in Kiev and Moscow were informed, but there was still no announcement to international press agencies.

After the alarm in Sweden and persistent inquiries by governments and by journalists in Moscow, the Soviet government admitted to the catastrophe. Perhaps it would have continued concealing the meltdown had it not been for the alarming Swedish measurements. When the radioactively contaminated clouds drifted across the whole of Europe, it was too late to take precautions. Precipitation contaminated the forests, farmland, people and animals. No one knew exactly what to expect. Television stations and newspaper editors raised the alarm and warned the population. People were advised to stay in their apartments and houses. This applied especially to children and pregnant women.

But there were still no television images. Only fuzzy helicopter shots were shown on the news. This was one of those invisible, mysterious, dangerous events. To this day, no one knows exactly

damit die Kettenreaktionen des Supergaus zu unterbinden. Erst am nächsten Tag, als die Vorgänge im Kraftwerk immer katastrophalere Ausmaße annahmen, wurden die Behörden in Kiew und Moskau unterrichtet, aber zu einer Meldung an die Agenturen der Weltpresse kam es immer noch nicht.

Nach dem Alarm in Schweden und den hartnäckigen Fragen von Regierungen und Journalisten in Moskau gestand die sowjetische Regierung die Katastrophe ein. Vielleicht hätte sie ohne die alarmierenden schwedischen Messungen weiterhin geschwiegen. Als die radioaktiv verseuchten Wolken über ganz Europa zogen, war jede Vorsichtsmaßnahme zu spät. Niederschläge kontaminierten Wälder, landwirtschaftliche Flächen, Menschen und Tiere. Niemand wußte genau, welche Folgen zu erwarten seien. Fernsehsender und Zeitungsredaktionen schlugen Alarm, warnten die Bevölkerung. Man riet dazu, in den Wohnungen und Häusern zu bleiben. Das galt besonders für Kinder und Schwangere.

Aber an Fernsehbildern mangelte es weiterhin. Nur unscharfe Hubschrauberaufnahmen wurden in den Nachrichten gezeigt. Das Ereignis gehörte zur unsichtbaren, geheimnisvoll-gefährlichen Sorte. Man weiß bis heute weder genau, wie viele Menschen bei dem Unglück direkt umkamen, die Behörden sprachen von zwei Opfern, noch wie viele bei den nachfolgenden Versiegelungsmaßnahmen tödlich verseucht worden sind. Nur die Tatsache, daß alle Bewohner der näheren Umgebung und der Stadt Pripyat evakuiert wurden, ist bekannt.

Inzwischen werden immer wieder Filme gesendet, die waghalsige Touristen beim Gang durch das heutige Gelände zeigen. Die Landschaft um die endgültig abgeschaltete und von einem Betonmantel umgebene Reaktoranlage hat sich in einen nahezu menschenleeren Urwald verwandelt, durch den Bären und Wölfe streifen. Niemand weiß, wie man die radioaktive Ruine endgültig versiegeln kann. Eine 10–20 Meter dicke Beton-Stahlschicht würde soviel kosten, daß die ukrainischen Behörden überfordert wären. Bis heute strahlt der Block immer noch so stark, daß von ihm weiterhin tödliche Gefahren ausgehen.

Manchmal verirren sich Photographen in die Gegend und dokumentieren die Ruinen der leeren Häuser. Besonders eindrucksvoll ist der Photoband von Robert Polidori, der 2004 unter dem Titel *Sperrzonen – Pripyat und Tschernobyl* erschien. Er zeigt verlassene, ruinöse Schul- und Krankenhausräume, aber auch Wohn- und Schlafzimmer mit zerstörten Möbeln und abgeplatzten Tapeten. Elizabeth Culbert berichtet in ihrem Vorwort von einem Text auf einer Tafel im Kindergarten von Pripyat, die dort heute noch zu sehen ist: »Eine Rückkehr gibt es nicht. Lebt wohl! Pripyat, 28. April 1986.«

Im Gegensatz zum bildarmen Tschernobyl kann man bei der Katastrophe vom 11. September 2001 von einem regelrechten Medienspektakel sprechen. Kaum ein Unglück der letzten Jahrzehnte wurde ausführlicher mit Filmen, Photos und Zeugenberichten dokumentiert. Wahrscheinlich lebt heute kein erwachsener Mensch auf diesem Globus, der nicht wenigstens einmal in seinem Leben die Fernsehbilder der brennenden und einstürzenden Twin Towers in Manhattan gesehen hat. Da die meisten amerikanischen Fernsehanstalten auf New Yorker Wolkenkratzern permanent eingeschaltete Kameras installiert haben, war es für sie kein Problem, sofort nach Bekanntwerden der Terror-Ereignisse auf Sendung zu gehen. »America under attac … America under attac …«

Das Unvorstellbare war eingetreten, jemand hatte gewagt, Amerika anzugreifen. Bisher hatten sich die Bewohner von New Yorks absolut sicher gefühlt, obwohl es am 26. Februar 1993 schon einmal einen islamistischen Terroranschlag auf das World Trade Center gegeben hatte. Mit sechs Toten jedoch besaß er nicht das Ausmaß der Katastrophe vom 11. September, als Terroristen zwei voll besetzte Passagiermaschinen auf die beiden berühmt-berüchtigten Türme zusteuerten, die nicht nur jahrzehntelang die höchsten Gebäude der Welt waren, sondern auch als Symbole des unersättlichen Kapitalismus galten. Die »Babylonischen Türme« des Geldes, entworfen und 1972 errichtet vom japanisch-amerikanischen Architekten Minoru Yamasaki, sollten dem Erdboden gleichgemacht werden. Das hatte bisher noch niemand gewagt. Allen Amerikanern, ja allen Menschen der Welt stockte der Atem. Nach den Einschlägen und Explosionen begann eine ebenfalls von CNN live übertragene, beispiellose Rettungsaktion, aber für viele Menschen, die in den beiden Türmen arbeiteten, kam jegliche Hilfe zu spät. Etwa 18 000 Menschen konnten sich auch ohne funktionierende Aufzüge retten, 2 602 fanden den Tod, außerdem 343 Feuerwehrleute und Polizisten. Eine wirkliche Katastrophe von Hollywood-Ausmaßen, reich bebildert und TV-dokumentiert.

Terroranschläge haben keine sichtbare Vorgeschichte, sie werden im dunklen Untergrund ausgebrütet und geplant, brechen dann völlig unvermittelt über unschuldige, unvorbereitete Menschen und Gebäude herein. Es herrschte weder Krieg noch Streit, nichts deutete auf die Tat hin.

how many people were directly killed in the accident – the authorities spoke of two victims – nor how many were fatally irradiated during subsequent measures to seal off the reactor. All we know is the fact that all inhabitants in the immediate vicinity and the town of Pripyat were evacuated.

In the meantime more and more films are being broadcast, showing daredevil tourists walking through the area today. The landscape around the reactor, which is shut down for good and surrounded by a concrete sarcophagus, has turned into an almost deserted primeval forest where bears and wolves roam. No one knows how the radioactive ruin can be definitively sealed off. A 10–20-meters-thick reinforced concrete layer would be too expensive for the Ukrainian authorities. To this day the reactor is so radioactive that it continues to pose mortal danger.

Sometimes photographers stray into the region and document the ruins of the empty houses. Particularly impressive is a volume of photos by Robert Polidori, published in 2003 under the title *Zones of Exclusion: Pripyat and Chernobyl*. It shows abandoned, ruined classrooms and hospital rooms, but also living rooms and bedrooms with destroyed furniture and tattered wallpaper. In her preface Elisabeth Culbert speaks about an inscription still legible on a blackboard in the kindergarten of Pripyat: »There will be no return. Farewell! Pripyat, 28 April 1986.«

In contrast to Chernobyl with its dearth of pictures, the catastrophe of 11 September 2001 is a regular media spectacle. Hardly any other disaster during recent decades has been documented in greater detail with films, photographs and eyewitness reports. There is probably not a single adult alive on the planet today who hasn't seen the TV images of the burning and collapsing Twin Towers in Manhattan at least once in his or her lifetime. Since most American TV companies have installed permanently switched-on cameras on New York skyscrapers, it was no problem for them to go on the air as soon as the terror events became known. »America under attack … America under attack …«

The unimaginable had happened: Someone had dared to attack the United States. Up to that time the population of New York had felt absolutely safe, although on 26 February 1993 there had already been one attack by Islamist terrorists on the World Trade Center. With only six fatalities, however, it did not have the magnitude of the 9/11 catastrophe, when terrorists steered two fully occupied passenger planes into the two famous/notorious towers, which were not only the tallest buildings in the world for decades, but were also considered to be symbols of insatiable capitalism. The »Towers of Babylon« of money, designed and built in 1972 by the Japanese American architect Minoru Yamasaki, were to be razed to the ground. Up till then, no one had dared to do such a thing. All Americans – indeed, everyone on the planet – gasped with horror. After the impacts and explosions, an unprecedented rescue operation began, also broadcast live by CNN. But for many people who had been working in the two towers, help came too late. About 18,000 people were able to save themselves even without functioning elevators; 2,602 were killed, as well as 343 firefighters and police. It was a true catastrophe of Hollywood proportions, recorded in myriad images and documented on television.

Terrorist attacks have no visible prehistory. They are hatched and planned deep underground, and descend completely unexpectedly on innocent people and on buildings. There was no war or conflict, nothing to point to what was going to happen. The 9/11 terrorists saw themselves in the role of the powers of Nemesis (had they been Christians, they might have been called self-designated »Horsemen of the Apocalypse«); according to them as many infidels as possible had to die. They alone had power over life and death during their deadly flights. Intoxicated by Muhammad, they broke into a power metropolis obsessed by the devil of capitalism. With the collapse of the two tallest skyscrapers in Manhattan they wanted to send gigantic signals.

In the meantime, thanks to the media, we know almost every detail of the catastrophe: In the early morning hours of 11 September, a peaceful early fall day in 2001, a total of 19 Islamist terrorists hijacked four American commercial aircraft. They diverted two of them to New York. At 8:46 a.m. the first plane hit the north tower of the World Trade Center. At this point the authorities still assumed there had been an accident. At 9:03 a.m. the second plane hit the south tower. This made it clear to everyone that a terrorist attack was involved. The south tower collapsed at 9:59 a.m., the north tower at 10:28 a.m. The attack was covered live on worldwide television. Because of the different time zones, however, there were delays in the flow of information elsewhere in the world. And yet we can assume that ten hours after the catastrophe there was hardly anyone left in the world who had not heard about it. In constant repetitive loops the epochal images that showed the collapse of the skyscrapers were shown on TV screens worldwide. They quickly became apocalyptic icons of the new millennium, taking the place of the images of mushroom clouds.

Die Terroristen des 11. September sahen sich in der Rolle strafender Mächte (wären sie Christen gewesen, könnte man von selbsternannten »apokalytischen Reitern« sprechen), ihrer Meinung nach mußten möglichst viele Ungläubige sterben. Sie allein hatten während ihrer todbringenden Flüge die Macht über Leben und Tod. Von Mohammed berauscht, brachen sie in die vom kapitalistischen Teufel besessene Machtmetropole ein. Mit dem Zusammensturz der beiden höchsten Wolkenkratzer Manhattans wollten sie gigantische Zeichen setzen.

Inzwischen kennen wir durch die Vermittlung der Medien fast jedes Detail der Katastrophe: Am frühen Morgen des 11. September, eines ruhigen Frühherbsttages im Jahr 2001, entführten insgesamt 19 islamistische Terroristen vier amerikanische Verkehrsflugzeuge. Zwei davon lenkten sie nach New York um. Um 8:46 Uhr traf das erste Flugzeug den Nordturm des World Trade Centers. Zu diesem Zeitpunkt gingen die Behörden noch von einem Unfall aus. Um 9:03 Uhr traf das zweite Flugzeug den Südturm. Damit war allen klar, daß es sich hier um einen Terroranschlag handelte. Der Südturm stürzte um 9:59 Uhr ein, der Nordturm um 10:28 Uhr. Das Fernsehen war live auf Sendung, weltweit. Allerdings kam es durch die verschiedenen Zeitzonen zu Verzögerungen im Weltinformationsfluß. Dennoch kann man davon ausgehen, daß zehn Stunden nach der Katastrophe kaum noch ein Mensch auf der Welt nichts davon erfahren hatte. Spätestens jetzt liefen in permanenten Wiederholungsschleifen die epochalen Bilder der Wolkenkratzereinstürze weltweit über die Bildschirme. Sie entwickelten sich schnell zu apokalyptischen Ikonen des neuen Jahrtausends und lösten damit die Bilder der Atombombenpilze ab.

Niemand wußte bisher, daß sich ein Wolkenkratzer beim Einsturz in Staubwolken verwandeln kann. Nur wenige Teile des Stahlskeletts und der Fassade ragten am Abend des 11. September noch aus dem gewaltigen Krater, der bald »Ground Zero« genannt wurde. Staub erfüllte stunden- und tagelang die Luft von Manhattan. Man sah immer neue Bilder der staubbedeckten, fliehenden Menschen, der grauen Autos, Bäume und Straßen. Insgesamt waren 40 000 Personen an den Rettungs- und Aufräumarbeiten beteiligt. Ein gigantisches Szenario. Halbstündig wurden neue Interviews mit Überlebenden gesendet. Und man sah verzweifelte Menschen, die über Mobiltelephone nach Lebenszeichen ihrer vermißten Angehörigen suchten.

Mehrere Monate lang wurden die Trümmer eingesammelt und auf eine Deponie in Staten Island gebracht. Von der Fassade blieben nur bizarre Reste übrig. Eine Jahrhundert-, vielleicht sogar Jahrtausendruine, die bald danach ganz aus der zukünftigen Baugrube verschwand.

Inzwischen fand ein Architekturwettbewerb statt, den Daniel Libeskind gewann. Er durfte seinen Entwurf bei einer Pressekonferenz erläutern, die von CNN weltweit übertragen wurde. Ein ganz besonderes Medienspektakel. Träumerisch formulierte er sein Ideal: »Im Gegensatz zur landläufigen Meinung sind Bauwerke keineswegs leblose Objekte. Sie leben und atmen und besitzen genau wie wir Menschen ein Inneres und ein Äußeres, einen Körper und eine Seele. Wie schafft man es also, ein Gebäude zu entwerfen, das singen kann? Ein Gebäude, das Charakter, Menschlichkeit und Schönheit ausstrahlt?«

Daß er in den Jahren danach von seinem Hauptkonkurrenten David Childs verdrängt wurde, ist allgemein bekannt. Childs wird zwei der fünf neuen Türme bauen, die anderen werden von Norman Foster, Richard Rogers und Fumihiko Maki entworfen. Libeskind ging am Ende leer aus. Dafür hat er das Buch *Entwürfe meines Lebens* (*Breaking Ground*) über seine Ground-Zero-Erlebnisse geschrieben.

Wie die Tsunamikatastrophe vom 26. Dezember 2004 ist das Erdbeben von Haiti im Januar 2010 ein gutes Beispiel für eine leicht verzögerte Fernsehberichterstattung. Relativ zeitnah erfuhren wir zwar in den Nachrichten von den Ereignissen; richtige Ruinenbilder und -filme sahen wir jedoch erst Tage später, da Journalisten und Reporter Zeit brauchten, um nach Phuket, Jakarta, Kuala Lumpur oder Port-au-Prince zu fliegen. Genau wie bei dem Katastrophenereignis in Asien waren die Berichterstatter zunächst auf private Live-Filme von Überlebenden, aufgenommen mit Mobiltelephonen und kleinen Digitalkameras, angewiesen. Immer wieder sahen wir im Dezember 2004 verwackelte und unscharfe Filme der herannahenden Tsunami-Welle und der Menschen, die sich verzweifelt an Baumstämmen und Hausruinen festhielten.

Aus Haiti trafen zunächst nicht einmal derartige Filme ein, Telephonberichte mußten genügen. Man sah das Photo eines Reporters, daneben eine Karte von Haiti. Kaum ein Zuschauer war jemals selbst auf der Insel gewesen, die bisher vor allem mit Negativmeldungen über Armut, Korruption und Kriminalität in das Blickfeld der Öffentlichkeit geraten war. Jetzt hörte man von Zerstörungen und von verzweifelten Menschen. Offensichtlich lag das Zentrum des Bebens unmittelbar in der Nähe der Hauptstadt Port-au-Prince. Kein Haus stehe mehr aufrecht, wurde berichtet, selbst der Präsidentenpalast, die meisten Schulen und Krankenhäuser lägen in Schutt und Asche – eine große, totale Ruinenlandschaft.

80. Die islamistischen Terror-Anschläge am 11. September 2001 auf das New Yorker World Trade Center haben die ganze Welt erschüttert.

80. The Islamic terror attacks on the New York World Trade Center on 11 September 2001 shocked the whole world.

Up to that time, no one had known that a skyscraper can turn into clouds of dust when it collapses. On the evening of 11 September only a few sections of the steel skeleton and the façade still jutted from the huge crater that soon came to be called »Ground Zero«. For hours, then days, dust filled the air of Manhattan. More and more images of dust-covered, fleeing people, gray cars, trees and streets were shown. A total of 40,000 persons took part in rescue and cleanup work. It was a gigantic scenario. Every half-hour, new interviews with survivors were aired. Viewers saw desperate people using their cell phones to look for signs of life from missing relatives.

It took several months to collect the rubble and take it to a dump on Staten Island. Only bizarre fragments were left of the façade. The ruin of the century, perhaps of the millennium, completely vanished from the future excavation.

In the meantime an architectural competition took place, won by Daniel Libeskind. He was asked to explain his design at a press conference, broadcast internationally by CNN. It was a very special media spectacle. Dreamily, he described his ideal: »In contrast to current views, buildings are by no means inanimate objects. They live and breathe, and just like human beings they have an interior and an exterior, a body and a soul. How, then, do you manage to design a building that can sing? A building that radiates character, humanity and beauty?«

The fact that in subsequent years he was replaced by his chief competitor David Childs is common knowledge. Childs will build two of the five new towers. The others are being designed by Norman Foster, Richard Rogers and Fumihiko Maki. In the end Libeskind came away empty-handed. But he did write the book *Breaking Ground* about his Ground Zero experiences.

Like the tsunami catastrophe of 26 December 2004, the earthquake in Haiti in January 2010 is a good example of slightly delayed TV coverage. It is true that we heard about the events in relatively real time. However, we did not see any real pictures and films of ruins until days later, since journalists and reporters needed time to fly to Phuket, Jakarta, Kuala Lumpur or Port-au-Prince. Just as in the case of the Asian catastrophe, reporters initially had to rely on the private live films of survivors, shot with cell phones and small digital cameras. Again and again, in December 2004, we watched blurred, out-of-focus films of the approaching tsunami wave and the people who clung desperately to tree trunks and the ruins of buildings.

Not even amateur videos arrived from Haiti at first. People had to make do with phone reports. They would see the picture of a reporter, with a map of Haiti next to it. Hardly any of the viewers had ever been on the island themselves. Until that time the general public had focused primarily on negative news about poverty, corruption and crime. Now they heard about destruction and desperate people. Evidently the center of the quake was in the immediate vicinity of the capital Port-au-Prince. Reports indicated that not a single house was left standing. Even the president's palace, most schools and hospitals were in ruins – a vast, total sea of debris.

Dann, Tage später, sahen wir die ersten Filmbilder. Reporter fahren mit Landrovern durch ein Gebirge aus Schutt, Scherben und Ruinen. Verzweifelte Menschen kampieren zu Tausenden auf der Straße, betteln um Wasser und Lebensmittel. Sie haben Angst vor Nachbeben, erfahren wir. Voller Mitleid blicken wir in die Gesichter verletzter und elternloser Kinder, dann sind wir dabei, wenn nach Tagen noch ein nahezu unverletzter Mensch aus den Trümmern gezogen wird. Alle Bewohner erzählen, daß sie unter Durst und Hunger litten und daß marodierende Jugendbanden ihnen nachts die letzten Habseligkeiten nahmen. Wir erfahren, daß 20 000 amerikanische Soldaten auf der Insel gelandet seien und für Ordnung sorgen sollen. Doch wo sind sie?

Immerhin ist das Fernsehen bemüht, aktive Zuschauer aus uns zu machen. Das ist der neue Trend aller Medien, wir sollen herausgeholt werden aus unserer Voyeurshaltung und direkt eingreifen, jedenfalls mit einer Geldspende. Der Stadtaufbau wird viel Geld kosten. Millionen, Milliarden. Die Ruinen müssen entsorgt werden. Bulldozer tauchen auf. Mit ihren mächtigen Stahlschaufeln schieben sie die Trümmer beiseite. Wir erfahren von Kinderdiebstahl. Die Kinder sollen nach Amerika an adoptionswillige Eltern vermittelt werden. Berichte über ein Kinderheim, dessen Leiter der Korruption und des Kinderhandels verdächtigt wird. Anarchische Zustände drohen. Schließlich tauchen die ersten Soldaten auf und beschützen die gefährdeten Lebensmittelverteilungen.

Zwischen 250 000 und 300 000 Menschen sollen bei dem Beben ums Leben gekommen sein. Port-au-Prince muß im Grunde vollkommen neu aufgebaut werden. Einige Wochen später ereignete sich ein noch schwereres Erdbeben in Chile. Allerdings starben dort weit weniger Menschen, also verstummte die Berichterstattung nach kurzer Zeit. Auch von Haiti ist inzwischen –

81. Jahrhundert-Ruinen, an erschreckender Grausamkeit kaum zu überbieten. Nicht nur die Attentäter selbst, sondern mit ihnen fast 3000 unschuldige Menschen haben sich in Feuer, Rauch und Staub aufgelöst.
82. Bald werden an dieser Stelle neue Wolkenkratzer in den New Yorker Himmel wachsen, und ein Denkmal soll an die Ereignisse des 11. September erinnern.

81. Ruins of the century, showing a horrific barbarity that can scarcely be exceeded. Not only the suicide attackers themselves perished in fire, smoke and dust, but 3000 innocent human beings with them.
82. New skyscrapers will shortly grow into the New York sky and a memorial is to stand as a reminder about the events of 11 September.

Then, days later, we saw the first film images. Reporters are driving Land Rovers through a mountain range of rubble, broken glass and ruins. Thousands of people camp on the streets, beg for water and food. We hear that they are afraid of aftershocks. Full of sympathy we look into the faces of hurt and orphaned children; then we are present when, days later, a virtually uninjured man is pulled from the rubble. All the inhabitants report that they are hungry and thirsty and that marauding bands of teenagers steal their last possessions at night. We learn that 20,000 American soldiers have landed on the island and are supposed to keep order. Where are they, though?

At least the television stations are at pains to make active viewers of us. This is the new trend of all the media: We are supposed to be jolted out of our voyeurism and get directly involved, or at least donate money. The rebuilding of the city will cost a lot. Millions, billions. The ruins have to be cleared away. Bulldozers appear. With their powerful steel shovels they push the ruins aside. We hear about kidnappings. They say the children will be sent to America to couples anxious to adopt. There is a report about an orphanage whose director is suspected of corruption and of selling children. There is danger of complete anarchy. Finally the first soldiers appear and supervise the jeopardized distribution of food.

Between 250,000 and 300,000 people are said to have been killed in the earthquake. Port-au-Prince must basically be rebuilt from the ground up. A few weeks later there was an even more severe earthquake in Chile. Far fewer people died there, however, and so news reports fall silent a short time later. In the meantime – two months after the quake – no more is heard from Haiti either. The reporters have moved on, to the next trouble spot, the next catastrophe.

In contrast to military conflicts, whose goal is to establish a winner and a loser, there are only losers in catastrophes. Even the survivors have often lost everything, their huts, furniture, private

zwei Monate nach dem Beben – nichts mehr zu hören. Die Reporter sind weitergezogen, zum nächsten Krisenherd, zur nächsten Katastrophe.

Im Gegensatz zu kriegerischen Auseinandersetzungen, die das Ziel haben, einen Sieger und einen Verlierer zu ermitteln, gibt es bei Katastrophen nur Verlierer. Selbst die Überlebenden haben oft alles verloren, ihre Hütten, Möbel, private Andenken, Wohnungen, Häuser, vielleicht auch ihre Angehörigen. Für die Städte sind Erdbeben tödlich, es sei denn, alle Häuser wurden erdbeben-sicher gebaut. Die Natur reagiert jedoch gelassen. Jeder Baum schüttelt sich und lebt anschlie-ßend problemlos weiter, vielleicht bricht mancher Fels entzwei, was ihn nicht weiter stört, denn er ist auf Zerfall eingestellt. Dies deutet darauf hin, daß vor allem unsere Städte völlig unnatürliche Ergänzungen der Naturlandschaft sind; der Schutz, den sie zu bieten vorgeben, entpuppt sich in solchen Momenten als das Gegenteil, jede Betondecke wird zum tödlichen Fallbeil und jeder herunterbrechende Dachstuhl zur gefährlichen Waffe. Architektur zeigt hier ihr menschenfeind-liches Antlitz, ihre tödliche Seele.

Wir anderen, wir Fernsehzuschauer betrachten die Ereignisse aus sicherer Distanz, aus war-men und trockenen Wohnungen heraus und sehen die Empfindung bestätigt, daß die bösen Zerstörungskräfte der Welt nicht ruhen, daß sie um uns herum rumoren und jede Idylle gefährden können.

Es besteht eine Verbindungskette zwischen Fenstern (Blick in eine schöne Landschaft, in einen Garten, auf eine Straße oder einen Platz), Gemälden (Blick in mythologische Landschaften und Eiswüsten, in paradiesische Zonen und apokalyptische Höllen) und Fernseh- und Compu-terbildschirmen. Sie alle formen gerahmte Ausblicke in eine schöne oder grausame, eine lang-weilige oder ereignisgetränkte Welt, die außerhalb unserer eigenen, beschützten Lebenszone liegen.

Die medialen Bilder von Katastrophen wirken auf uns ein, abrupt und brutal, bleiben aber den-noch auf Distanz, sind letztlich zahnlos, impotent und ereignen sich in einer zweiten Scheinwelt. Wir bleiben bei ihrem Anblick unverletzt, glauben uns informiert und wissen im Grunde nicht, was wir mit dem Nervenkitzel anfangen sollen. Sind wir endgültig zu perversen, abenteuerlustigen Voyeuren verkommen, zu Pornographen der Gewalt und sollen unsere Mitleidsgefühle als ent-schuldigende Ausrede dienen? Der fremde Tod, das fremde Unglück versüßt das eigene Über-leben, heute und jetzt. Morgen beginnt der Kampf aufs neue. Irgendwann sind wir selbst betrof-fen. Dieses Desaster ist an mir vorbeigegangen. Unglück, Glück, Unglück, Glück, Glück gehabt.

mementos, apartments, houses, perhaps even their families. For the cities, earthquakes are lethal unless all the houses are earthquake-proof. But nature reacts with calm. Every tree shakes, then lives on without problems. Maybe a few rocks are shattered, which doesn't really bother them, for disintegration comes naturally to them. This suggests that our cities in particular are completely unnatural additions to the natural landscape; in moments like these, the protection they claim to offer turns out to be the opposite. Every concrete ceiling becomes a deadly guillotine, and every collapsing roof framework turns into a dangerous weapon. Here architecture shows a face that is hostile to man, its lethal soul.

The rest of us, we the TV audience, observe events from a safe distance, sitting in our warm, dry homes. We see this as further confirmation that the evil, destructive forces of the world do not rest, that they are in ferment all around us and that they can imperil every idyll.

There is a chain that links windows (a view of a beautiful landscape, a garden, a street or a square), paintings (a view of mythological landscapes and icy deserts, of celestial gardens and apocalyptic infernos) and the screens of TV sets and computers. They all provide framed views into a beautiful or cruel, boring or eventful world outside our own sheltered environment.

Media images of catastrophes affect us abruptly and brutally. Still, they keep their distance. In the final analysis, they are toothless and impotent: They take place in another, illusory world. We are not hurt by the sight of them. We think we are well-informed and basically have no idea what to do with such sensational news. Have we finally become depraved – perverse, thrill-seeking voyeurs, pornographers of violence? Are our feelings of sympathy supposed to serve as an excuse? Another person's death, another's misfortune sweetens our own survival, here and now. Tomorrow the struggle will begin anew. At some point it will be our turn. I was spared this disaster. I've been lucky.

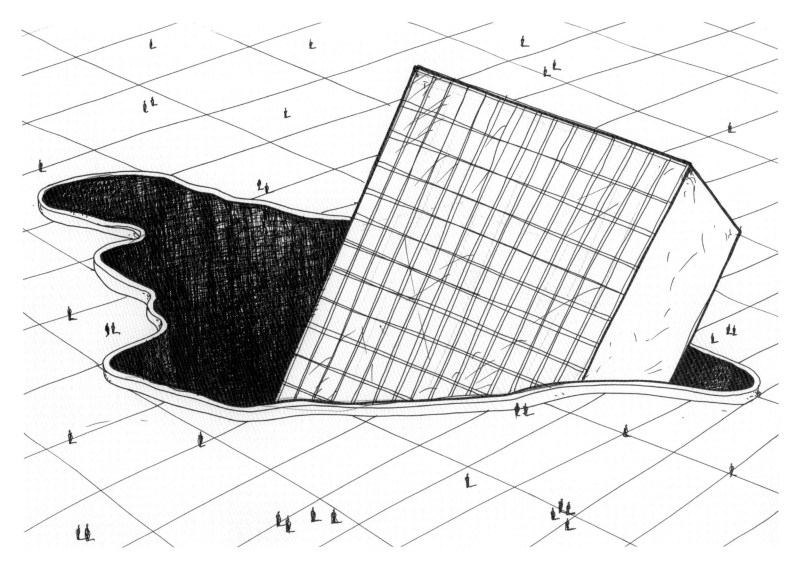

15. Vandalismus

Zerstörungen von Dingen im Alltag

»Ja, zur Übeltätigkeit,
ja, dazu ist man bereit!
Menschen necken, Tiere quälen,
Äpfel, Birnen, Zwetschgen stehlen.
Das ist freilich angenehmer
Und dazu auch viel bequemer,
Als in Kirche oder Schule
Festzusitzen auf dem Stuhle.

Aber wehe, wehe, wehe,
Wenn ich auf das Ende sehe!
Ach, das war ein schlimmes Ding,
Wie es Max und Moritz ging.
Drum ist hier, was sie getrieben,
Abgemalt und aufgeschrieben.«

So heißt es in der berühmten, grausam-komischen Bildergeschichte von Wilhelm Busch über die beiden Lausbuben Max und Moritz. Seitdem ist viel über das anarchische, oft sehr bösartige und brutale Verhalten von männlichen Kindern geschrieben worden. Pippi Langstrumpf ist der literarische Beweis dafür, daß auch Mädchen ähnlich frech und aufmüpfig sein können.

Von einem gewissen Alter an will man sich nichts mehr vorschreiben lassen, betrachtet jedes Gesetz und jedes Verbot als überflüssige Einengung. Hinzu kommt, vor allem bei männlichen Kindern, die Lust an der Zerstörung. Wände werden verschmiert, Bücher zerrissen, Käfer lustvoll zertreten, Frösche aufgeblasen und Katzen ertränkt. Aber auch eigene Werke sind vor der Vernichtung nicht sicher. Jeder Junge baut in einem bestimmten Alter Burgen und Türme, manchmal auch ganze Städte aus Holzklötzen, Dosen, Steinen, Ästen, Sand oder anderen Fundstücken, und jeder zerstört sie wieder mit großer Freude. Der Anblick eines vollendeten Werkes ist langweilig, man kann nichts mehr anbauen, die Klötze sind verbraucht, außerdem ist das Gebilde eindeutig am Rande seiner statischen Möglichkeiten angekommen. Modelleisenbahnen sind weniger wegen des glatten Ablaufs der verschiedenen Zugkreisläufe interessant. Der Unfall, das Zusammenkrachen zweier Lokomotiven, der Brand eines Bahnhofs und die mit viel Lärm und Tatütata herannahende Feuerwehr verleihen diesem Spielzeug seine eigentliche Faszination.

Werden die Knaben größer, wachsen sie zu Jugendlichen heran, steigern sich auch die Potentiale der Zerstörung. Auf Streifzügen durch die Umgebung hecken sie ihre mehr oder weniger bösartigen Max-und-Moritz-Streiche aus, werfen Fenster in den Nachbarhäusern ein, üben sich im Rauchen und Trinken; heute hat sich das Repertoire um Spray-Aktionen, Schaufensterbemalungen, Drogenkonsum, Koma-Saufen, Vandalismus an Stadtparkbänken, Litfaßsäulen, Papierkörben und Autos erweitert.

Die modernen Medien halten mit ihren Angeboten von Computerspielen zahlreiche Möglichkeiten noch brutalerer Gangarten bereit. Auftauchende Gegner werden mit Pistolen und Maschinengewehren gejagt und erschossen. Genauso ergeht es wilden Tieren oder intergalaktischen Feinden. Der Tod gehört zum Kalkül, als wäre er etwas Vorübergehendes. Lausbubenstreiche verwandeln sich spielerisch in alltägliche Morde, Blutorgien und kriegerische Auseinandersetzungen. Nebenbei werden auch noch Autos, Busse und Häuser in die Luft gejagt – echte Ruinen, mediale Ruinen.

Leben die Jugendlichen in vernachlässigten, gewaltbereiten Stadtregionen, schließen sie sich vorhandenen Gangs an, beteiligen sich an Raufereien, Schlägereien oder an Revierkämpfen, die mit Waffen und Killerhunden ausgetragen werden. Der Übergang zwischen medialer Fiktion und Realität ist fließend, man erprobt das in den Spielen erlernte Verhalten. Manche Jugendliche tauchen ganz in diese Zwischenwelt ein und mutieren, sofern sie tödliche Waffen besitzen, zu realen Killern. Sie erschießen ihre Eltern und Geschwister, sie gehen in ihre Schulen und richten Massaker an. Wir kennen die Meldungen aus Erfurt, Winnenden, Helsinki und Amerika. Meist berichten Zeugen, daß ihnen die Täter, die sie von früher her kannten, unauffällig und harmlos erschienen seien. In Wirklichkeit sind alle jungen Männer zwischen 15 und 25 auf der ganzen Welt, in allen Gesellschaften, potentiell anfällig für gewaltsame Lösungen ihrer Probleme. Es ist die Zeit

15. Vandalism

The destruction of things in everyday life

»Ah, the wickedness one sees
Or is told of such as these,
Namely Max and Moritz; there!
Look at the disgraceful pair!
... But designs of malefaction
Find them keen on instant action!
Teasing folk, tormenting beasts,
Stealing fruit for lawless feasts
Are more fun, as one can tell,
And less troublesome as well,
Than to sit through class or sermon,
Never fidgeting or squirming. –
Looking at the sequel, though:
Woe, I say, and double woe!! –
How it all at last came out
Chills the heart to think about.
That's why all the tricks they played
Are retold here and portrayed.«
[Wilhelm Busch, *Max and Moritz*, trans. Walter Arndt (New York, 1982)]

That's a quote from the famous, cruelly funny comic strip by Wilhelm Busch about the two little rascals Max and Moritz. Since then a great deal has been written about the anarchical, often very nasty and brutal behavior of male children. Pippi Longstocking is the literary proof that girls, too, can be just as impudent and rebellious.

After you reach a certain age you don't want to be dictated to anymore, and regard every rule and prohibition as unnecessary restrictions. Added to this, especially in male children, there's pleasure in destroying things. Kids scrawl on walls, tear books, squash beetles with relish, inflate frogs and drown cats. But even their own creations are not safe from annihilation. Every boy of a certain age builds castles and towers, sometimes whole towns out of wood blocks, cans, rocks, branches, sand or other finds, and they all destroy them again with great delight. Looking at a completed work is boring – there's nothing you can add on, the blocks are all used up, and besides the construction has clearly reached the limits of its static possibilities. Model railways are interesting, less because of the smooth functioning of the various loops. It is the accident, the collision of two locomotives, fire at a station and the fire engine approaching with a lot of noise and wailing sirens that make this toy so fascinating.

Once boys get older and reach their teens, potentials for destruction increase. As they roam through the neighborhood they think up their more or less mischievous Max-and-Moritz pranks, break the neighbors' windows, practice smoking and drinking; today the repertoire has expanded to include the spray-painting of graffiti, painting on store windows, drugs, binge drinking, vandalism involving park benches, advertisement pillars, trash cans and cars.

The modern media offer computer games with large numbers of even more brutal possibilities. Here adversaries are pursued and shot down with pistols and machine guns. So are wild animals or intergalactic enemies. Death is part of the game, as though it were something temporary. Mischievous pranks are playfully transformed into everyday murders, killing sprees and armed conflicts. On the side, cars, buses and houses are blown up – real ruins, media ruins.

If the teenagers live in neglected neighborhoods rife with violence, they join existing gangs and participate in brawls or turf wars carried out with weapons and killer dogs. The transition from media fiction to the real world is fluid. They try out behaviors learned in playing computer games. Some teenagers are completely submerged between the two worlds and mutate – provided they have deadly weapons – into real killers. Some shoot their parents and siblings, some go to their schools and massacre their peers. We are familiar with the reports from Erfurt, Winnenden, Helsinki and America. In most cases witnesses say that the perpetrators, whom they had known previously, seemed inconspicuous and harmless. In reality all young men between 15 and 25 all over the world, in every society, are potentially prone to solve their problems violently. It is the period when their testosterone levels peak, forcing them to act out their sexually based aggressions.

ihrer maximalen Testosteronausschüttung, die sie im Grunde dazu zwingt, ihre sexuell geprägten Aggressionen auszuleben. Ein Funke genügt, und viele von ihnen stehen in Flammen, schlagen los, unerbittlich, gewalttätig. Keine Hauswand, kein Schaufenster, kein Denkmal, keine Mauer, kein Zaun, keine Bank, kein Brunnen, keine Telephonzelle, kein Nebenbuhler und kein Feind sind dann mehr vor ihnen sicher.

Zahlreiche Psychologen, Psychiater und Philosophen haben sich mit dem Thema »Aggression« auseinandergesetzt: Sigmund Freud, Konrad Lorenz, Erich Fromm und Friedrich Hacker, alle gehen sie von einem angeborenen Trieb aus, der mit Sexualität, Rangordnungskämpfen, Revier-markierung, manchmal auch mit Nekrophilie zu tun hat. Als Naturtrieb dient er der Kontaktauf-nahme mit dem andern Geschlecht und somit der Fortpflanzung. Fehlgeleitet kann er viel Unheil anrichten.

Junge Männer sind oft bereit, sich radikalen politischen oder religiösen Gruppierungen anzu-schließen. Man kennt dies aus der Nazizeit, auch die sogenannten 68er bieten hierfür ein Beispiel, nicht zu vergessen die heutigen Neonazis sowie die islamistischen und palästinensischen Selbst-mordattentäter. Den fast noch jugendlichen japanischen Kamikazefliegern am Ende des Zweiten Weltkrieges wurde befohlen, sich mit ihren kleinen Flugzeugen auf amerikanische Kriegsschiffe zu stürzen. Es war ihnen verboten, von den Einsätzen zurückzukehren, sobald sie gestartet waren, wurden sie in die Liste der Gefallenen eingetragen. Aggression und Selbstmord als Einheit. Er-zwungene Perversionen männlicher Selbstdefinition.

Hormonbedingt gibt es in der Pubertät die größten Unterschiede zwischen Jungen und Mäd-chen, zwischen Männern und Frauen. Es heißt, Mädchen seien in diesem Alter weniger aggressiv. Ihr Wesen sei von Natur aus liebevoller und sozialer programmiert. Allerdings verwischen sich in den fortschrittlichen Industrienationen die Unterschiede zunehmend.

In vielen Filmen wurde und wird das Thema »jugendliche Aggression« im Zusammenhang mit »Vandalismus«, behandelt und bilderreich dargestellt. Wir denken an James Dean in *Denn sie wissen nicht, was sie tun*, an Marlon Brando in *Die Faust im Nacken*, an Horst Buchholz in *Die Halbstarken*, an Jean-Paul Belmondo in *Außer Atem*, an Dennis Hopper in *Easy Rider* und Matthieu Carrière in *Der junge Törleß*. Im Treiben der pubertierenden Helden spielen ruinöse Verstecke oft eine große Rolle. Der scheue James Dean fährt mit seiner Freundin in eine halbzerfallene Bergvilla über Los Angeles, die Internatsschüler in Schlöndorffs *Törleß* treffen sich auf einem abgelegenen Dachboden, um dort ihren jüdischen Mitschüler zu quälen. Törleß schaut zu, wird zum duldenden Voyeur. Am brutalsten geht es in Stanley Kubricks *Uhrwerk Orange* aus dem Jahr 1970/71 zu. Eine kostümierte Jungmänner-Gang, ausgerüstet mit Baseballschlägern, zieht eine Spur des Unheils quer durch London. Dazu erklingt die Lieblingsmusik des Helden Alex: Symphonien von Ludwig van Beethoven. Die von ihnen ausgeübten Gewaltakte sind vollkommen sinnlos, ihr Van-dalismus richtet sich gegen Dinge und Menschen. Zuerst wird ein alkoholisierter Penner zusam-mengeschlagen, dann die Frau eines Schriftstellers vergewaltigt und ermordet. Dabei geht auch das gesamte Mobiliar der schicken Villa in die Brüche. Zu Hause spielen die jungen Männer harmlose Söhne, die sich von ihren Müttern oder Stiefmüttern herumkommandieren lassen.

Nach dem erneuten Mord an einer Frau wird Alex von der Polizei festgenommen und in einem Krankenhaus behandelt. Die Behandlung hat den Charakter einer Folter: Er ist gezwungen, unun-terbrochen Gewalt- und Sexfilme anzusehen, dazu erklingt permanent die Musik Beethovens. Nach seiner Entlassung will niemand mehr etwas von ihm wissen, weder seine eigene Familie noch seine Ex-Freunde, die jetzt Polizisten geworden sind und ihn bei einer Begegnung brutal zusammenschlagen. Der Film, gedreht nach einem Roman von Anthony Burgess, zeigt, daß auch Beethovens Musik durch häufiges Abspielen zertrümmert werden kann, und ist damit selbst zynisch-vandalistisch. Außerdem bewegt sich die Koppelung von Neunter Symphonie und mörde-rischer Vergewaltigung hart an der Geschmacksgrenze und erinnert fatal an die Vorlieben der deutschen Nazis. Alle Werte werden auf den Kopf gestellt. Am Ende bleibt nur noch die Gewalt gegen Dinge, Menschen, gegen alles.

Auch in den James-Bond-Filmen endet jede Verfolgungsjagd in einer Zerstörungsorgie, nicht nur die Villen der Bösewichte werden gesprengt, sondern auch Autos, Wohnungseinrichtungen und Flugzeuge. Beim Betrachten der Vernichtung möglicher Sehnsuchtsobjekte empfinden viel-leicht manche junge männliche Zuschauer jene Lust, die ihnen sagt: Wenn ich schon so schöne Villen, Autos, Frauen, Waffen und Flugzeuge nicht bekommen kann, dann will ich sie wenigstens kaputtgehen sehen. Erst wird Gier aufgebaut, dann Wut und schließlich die Lust auf Zerstörung.

»Macht kaputt, was euch kaputt macht!« lautete ein Kampfspruch der 68er »Revolutionäre«. Eine ganze Generation lebte ihre wütende Aggression gegen die Eltern und alles Etablierte aus. Autos brannten, Schaufensterscheiben zersplitterten, Polizisten wurden mit Steinen und Molo-

204

A spark is enough for many of them to burst into flames, to strike out, pitilessly, violently. No wall, no store window, no monument, no fence, no bench, no fountain, no phone booth, no rival or enemy is safe from them then.

Many psychologists, psychiatrists and philosophers have studied aggression: Sigmund Freud, Konrad Lorenz, Erich Fromm and Friedrich Hacker all assume that there is an innate instinct that has to do with sexuality, battles over ranking order, territorial marking, sometimes even with necrophilia. As a natural instinct it serves to establish contacts with the opposite sex and thus reproduction. Misdirected it can do a great deal of damage.

Young men are often ready to join radical political or religious groups. We know what happened during the Nazi regime, but also in 1968; we have heard about neo-Nazis today, Islamist and Palestinian suicide bombers. There were similar shocking occurrences at the end of World War II when barely adult Japanese kamikaze pilots were ordered to crash their small aircraft into American warships. They were forbidden to return from the missions. As soon as they had taken off, their names were entered in the list of those killed in action. Aggression and suicide go hand in hand. These were forced perversions of male self-definition.

During puberty the biggest differences between boys and girls, men and women are hormone-related. Normally girls are less aggressive at this age. By nature they have been programmed to be more loving and socially caring. However, in the progressive industrial nations the differences are increasingly becoming blurred.

Many films have dealt with and graphically represented the topic of teenage »aggression«, in connection with »vandalism«. We think of James Dean in *Rebel Without a Cause*, Marlon Brando in *On the Waterfront*, Horst Buchholz in *Teenage Wolfpack,* Jean-Paul Belmondo in *Breathless*, Dennis Hopper in *Easy Rider* and Matthieu Carrière in *Young Toerless*. Often ruined buildings are the hideouts of the pubescent heroes. A shy James Dean drives to a half-dilapidated mansion in the mountains above Los Angeles with his girlfriend; the students at the boarding school in Schlöndorff's *Toerless* meet in a secluded attic in order to torture their Jewish fellow student there. Toerless watches, becomes the complicit voyeur. Things get especially brutal in Stanley Kubrick's 1970/71 *A Clockwork Orange*. A costumed gang of young men, equipped with baseball bats, leaves a trail of disaster across London. The soundtrack is the favorite music of the protagonist Alex: the symphonies of Ludwig van Beethoven. Completely senseless acts of violence, vandalism against things and people. At first they beat up an inebriated tramp, then rape and murder the wife of a writer. In the process all the furniture of the elegant home is smashed. At home the young men play at being harmless sons who allow their mothers or stepmothers to order them around.

After a second woman is murdered, Alex is arrested by the police and undergoes treatment in a hospital. The treatment resembles torture: He is forced to watch violent and porn movies without interruption to the constant sound of Beethoven's music. After he is discharged no one will have anything more to do with him, neither his own family nor his ex-friends, who have now joined the police force and brutally beat him up during an encounter. The film, based on a novel by Anthony Burgess, is itself cynical and vandalistic. Even Beethoven's music can be reduced to rubble by constant playing! Moreover the coupling of the Ninth Symphony and murderous rape verges on the borderline of taste and reminds one fatally of the predilections of German Nazis. In Kubrick's film all values have been turned on their head. In the end, only violence remains – against objects, against people, against everything.

In the James Bond movies, too, every pursuit ends in an orgy of destruction. It is not only the mansions of the villains that are blown up, but also cars, furnishings and airplanes. As they watch the destruction of potential objects of desire some young male spectators perhaps experience a thrill that tells them: Even though I can't get such beautiful mansions, cars, women, weapons and airplanes, then at least I want to watch them being smashed. First, the film builds up greed, then rage and finally the urge for destruction.

»Destroy what is destroying you!« was one of the mottos of the 1968 »revolutionaries«. An entire generation lived out its furious aggression against its parents and the establishment. Cars were burned, store windows were shattered, police were hurt so badly with rocks and Molotov cocktails that they had to be hospitalized. In the meantime almost all traces of this anarchist-vandalistic period have vanished. It is true that the special prison set up for the members of the RAF (Red Army Faction) in Stuttgart-Stammheim still exists, but some politicians are already thinking of razing the building. Perhaps here, too, the ruin solution would be a good idea.

The vandalism of the next younger generation produces primarily mountains of garbage. Take the »Love Parade« on the Strasse des 20. Juni and in Berlin's Tiergarten Park. To the rumbling

towcocktails krankenhausreif verletzt. Inzwischen sind fast alle Spuren dieser anarchistisch-van-dalistischen Zeit verwischt. Zwar steht das Sondergefängnis, das man für die RAF-Mitglieder in Stuttgart-Stammheim eingerichtet hatte, noch an Ort und Stelle, aber einige Politiker denken bereits über eine Entsorgung des Gebäudes nach. Vielleicht wäre auch hier die Ruinenlösung ein guter Weg.

Der Vandalismus der nachfolgenden, jüngeren Generation produziert vor allem Müllberge. Et-wa während der »Love-Parade« auf der Straße des 20. Juni und im Berliner Tiergarten. Zu wum-mernden Technoklängen tanzt man sich die überschüssigen Kräfte aus dem Leib. Die Bezeich-nung »Love-Parade« war nicht schlecht gewählt, denn bei derartigen Veranstaltungen, die von jungen Männern und Frauen besucht werden, bestand eine echte Chance, Aggressionen in sexuelle Lust umzuwandeln. Viele Paare, berichteten die Zeitungen, zogen sich während und nach der Parade ins dichte Unterholz des Tiergartens zurück, um sich dort der körperlichen Liebe hinzugeben.

Andere junge Männer, die vielleicht kein Glück bei den Frauen hatten, streiften nachts frustriert durch die Straßen Berlins und besprayten Schaufenster oder Hausfassaden. Sie waren aufge-putscht, angestachelt in ihrer erotischen Lust und in ihrem Tatendrang. Ersatzhandlungen mußten Befreiung und Erlösung bringen. Ob der Film *Die fetten Jahre sind vorbei* den Vandalismustrieb der heutigen, jungen Generation auf den Punkt bringt, vermag ich nicht mit Sicherheit zu sagen. Auf jeden Fall wirkt Daniel Brühl mit seinen Kumpanen sehr überzeugend, wenn er, wie ein Enkel Rudi Dutschkes und Daniel Cohn-Bendits, in unbewohnte, reiche Villen einbricht, das Mobiliar zu sinnlosen Türmen aufschichtet und am Ende daran jenen Text befestigt, der dem ganzen Film seinen Titel gegeben hat: »Die fetten Jahre sind vorbei!« Entsetzt und sprachlos stehen die rei-chen Besitzer nach ihrer Rückkehr aus dem Urlaub im sonnigen Süden mit ihren Familien vor dem Chaos. Die Provokation ist gelungen.

Aus Sicht der Polizei stellt der Vandalismus vor allem in Städten ein großes Problem dar. Jähr-lich müssen die Stadtverwaltungen Millionen für die Entfernung von Spraybildern in U- und S-Bahnen ausgeben. Nach manchen Wochenenden, vor allem nach Wochenenden mit wichtigen Fußballspielen oder Pop-Konzerten, sind ganze Bankreihen in den Zügen aufgeschlitzt und Fens-ter zerkratzt. Viele Verantwortliche fordern Videoüberwachung in jedem Abteil. Manche Städte sind dazu übergegangen, Polizeiabteilungen einzurichten, die auf Vandalismus spezialisiert sind. In London, Paris, New York und Los Angeles stehen ihnen Hubschrauber zur Verfügung, so kön-nen sie die Sprayergangs, die nachts über Bahnhöfe herfallen, aus der Luft verfolgen.

Ein weiteres Problem bilden die nächtlichen Vandalenüberfälle auf öffentliche Parks. In Lon-don und Paris sind inzwischen viele davon wieder eingezäunt worden, und in den größeren Grün-anlagen patrouillieren Polizisten. Ihr besonderes Augenmerk gilt den Fixern, die sich gern an Kin-derspielplätzen aufhalten, wo sie ihre Spritzen im Sand vergraben. Im Zeitalter von Aids kann dies gefährlich sein.

Neben den Wochenenden bringen gewisse Festtage mit ihren speziellen Bräuchen eine zusätz-liche Vandalismusgefahr in unsere Städte. Dazu gehört vor allem der heidnische Fasching. Bei Umzügen kommt es immer wieder zu kleineren und größeren Zerstörungen. Berühmt-berüchtigt ist auch die Walpurgisnacht, die dem 1. Mai vorausgeht. In dieser Nacht sollen »Hexen« auf den Bergen, in den Wäldern und auf den Stadtplätzen ihr Unwesen treiben. Inzwischen haben sich die »Autonomen«, die früher Hausbesetzer hießen, dieses Brauches bemächtigt. Bekanntlich schlägt ihr Herz für die Anarchie. Jedes Jahr wird in den Fernsehnachrichten und Zeitungen von erneuten Ausschreitungen in den großen Städten berichtet. Am bekanntesten sind die destruktiven Akti-onen in Berlin-Kreuzberg. Autos stehen in Flammen, Schaufenster gehen zu Bruch, Supermärkte und Tankstellen werden geplündert und Polizisten durch Steinwürfe verletzt. Früher, als es noch gläserne Telephonzellen gab, überlebte kein Zellenglas diese Nacht. Tage später kann man als in-teressierter »Ruinentourist« die Ergebnisse betrachten.

In rechtsradikalen Gegenden kommt es vor, daß jugendliche Banden über alte jüdische Fried-höfe ziehen und Grabsteine umwerfen. Gibt es keine jüdischen Friedhöfe, sind auch normale Gottesacker geeignete Opfer. Jede Stadt führt im Sommer traditionelle Feste durch, die über ihren reinen Vergnügungscharakter hinaus ein durchaus militaristisch-aggressives Potential besitzen. In Biberach an der Riß nennt sich das Ereignis »Schützenfest« und wird von Schützenvereinen getra-gen. In Ulm an der Donau heißt es »Schwörmontag«. An diesem Tag fahren junge Männer auf fla-chen Schiffen mit Lanzen aufeinander zu und versuchen, sich gegenseitig in die Donau zu stoßen. Wasserritter der seltsamen Art. Wer am längsten stehenbleibt, wird zum Sieger erklärt.

Nach Aussage vieler mit diesem Thema befaßter Autoren existiert Vandalismus, seitdem es menschliche Gesellschaften gibt. Jeder räuberische oder kriegerische Akt ist mit Vandalismus

sounds of techno, people use their excess energy to dance their hearts out. The expression »Love Parade« was not a bad choice, for at this kind of event attended by young men and women there was a genuine opportunity to transform feelings of aggression into sexual desire. Many couples, reported the newspapers, retired into the dense undergrowth of the park during and after the parade in order to make love.

Other young men, who perhaps had no luck with women, roamed through the streets of Berlin in frustration that night spray-painting store windows or house façades. They had been stirred up, their erotic desire and thirst for action had been turned on. Surrogate actions had to bring release of tension and relief. I cannot judge whether the film *The Edukators* (*Die fetten Jahre sind vorbei*) really sums up the vandalism instinct of today's young generation. In any event Daniel Brühl and his buddies are very convincing as they break into uninhabited rich villas like grandsons of Rudi Dutschke and Daniel Cohn-Bendit, pile up the furniture in senseless towers and finally attach to them the text that gave the whole film its title: »Die fetten Jahre sind vorbei! (Your days of plenty are numbered!)« Horrified and speechless, the wealthy owners, back from a vacation with their families in the sunny south, stand looking at the chaos. The provocation has succeeded.

From the perspective of the police, vandalism is a big problem, especially in the cities. Every year city councils have to spend millions of euros to remove spray-painted graffiti in subway and suburban trains. After some weekends, particularly after weekends with important soccer games or pop concerts, whole rows of seats in the trains have been slashed and windows have been scratched. Many local administrators demand video surveillance in every compartment. Some cities now have police departments that specialize in vandalism. In London, Paris, New York and Los Angeles they have helicopters at their disposal, and can pursue the gangs of spray-painters who operate in the railway stations at night from the air.

verbunden. Schon im alten Rom zogen einzelne, angetrunkene Cliquen durch die Stadt und schlugen den Götterfiguren die Gesichter, Geschlechtsteile oder Arme ab. Kriegerische Zeiten erleichterten das enthemmte Marodieren und Zerstören.

Während und nach allen Kriegen wurden Skulpturen zerstört oder von ihren Sockeln gestoßen. Es gehörte zum Siegergebaren und betonte den Unterwerfungscharakter der militärischen Aktionen. Feldherren sammelten, neben den männlichen und weiblichen Gefangenen, wertvolle künstlerische Beutestücke und führten sie bei Triumphmärschen – im antiken Rom oder in Verdis *Aida* – dem jubelnden Stadtvolk vor. Die imposantesten Kunstwerke erhielten Ehrenplätze über Tempel- oder Kirchenportalen, vor Palästen und auf öffentlichen Plätzen. Erinnert sei an die ägyptischen Obelisken im antiken Rom und an die bronzenen Pferde über dem Portal des Markusdoms in Venedig. Diese Tradition lebte über die Jahrhunderte fort. Auch Napoleon sammelte Beutestücke, Schadows »Quadriga« etwa auf dem Brandenburger Tor und ließ sie nach Paris schaffen. Später, als Napoleon niedergerungen war, kamen die Pferde samt Siegesgöttin wieder zurück nach Berlin und wurden mit großem Pomp am angestammten Ort erneut aufgestellt.

Religiös begründeten Vandalismus gab es vor allem nach der Reformation. Die Wut der protestantischen Bilderstürmer entzündete sich an dem Bibelsatz: »Du sollst dir kein Bildnis oder Gleichnis machen!« Obwohl Luther versuchte, die aufgeheizte Stimmung unter den verarmten Handwerkern und Bauern zu dämpfen, konnte er nicht verhindern, daß sie in Kirchen und Dome eindrangen und mit Sensen und Äxten wertvolle gotische Altäre und Heiligenbilder zerschlugen. Diese Auswüchse der Aggression waren natürlich auch Racheakte gegen alle Institutionen, von denen sie unterdrückt wurden, gegen Zünfte, Stadtverwaltungen und den auf seine angeblich

A special problem are the nightly vandal attacks on public parks. In London and Paris, in the meantime, many parks have again been fenced, and police patrol the larger green spaces. They direct their particular attention to the junkies who like to hang out in children's playgrounds. In the age of AIDS, syringes buried in the sand are an especially great danger.

Besides weekends, certain holidays with their special traditions bring an additional risk of vandalism into our cities. First and foremost among these is the pagan carnival. During processions, time after time, there are large and small incidents of property damage. Walpurgis Night, the night before May 1st, is also famous and notorious. On this night »witches« are supposed to be up to their mischief on the mountains, in the woods and on city squares. In the meantime the »Independents (*die Autonomen*)«, who used to be called »squatters«, have adopted this date as their own. It is a well-known fact that their hearts beat for anarchy. Every year there are TV and newspaper reports of renewed riots in the large cities. The best-known are the destructive actions in Berlin-Kreuzberg. Cars are set on fire, shop windows broken, supermarkets and gas stations looted and police pelted with rocks. In the old days, when there were still glass phone booths, not one of their glass panes survived this night. Days later, as an interested »ruin tourist«, one can inspect the results.

In radical right-wing neighborhoods it can happen that teenage gangs break into old Jewish cemeteries and overturn tombstones. If there are no Jewish cemeteries, normal cemeteries will do. In summer every town celebrates traditional festivals that over and above their pure entertainment value have a militaristic-aggressive potential. In Biberach an der Riss the event is called »*Schützenfest* (shooting festival)« and is sponsored by shooting clubs. In Ulm an der Donau it is called »*Schwörmontag*«. On this day young men in flat boats row toward each other with lances and try to push each other into the Danube. They are a strange type of water knights. The one who stays on his feet the longest is declared the winner.

According to many authors who have studied this topic, vandalism has existed ever since there have been human societies. Every act of robbery or war is linked to vandalism. Back in ancient Rome, inebriated cliques used to roam through town smashing the faces, private parts or arms of the statues of the gods. Times of war made uninhibited marauding and destruction easier.

During and after all wars sculptures were destroyed or pushed off their pedestals. This was how victors behaved; it emphasized the goal of military actions – subjugation. Besides male and female captives, commanders collected art – valuable booty – and showed it off to the cheering populace in triumphal marches – im ancient Rome or in Verdi's *Aida*. The most imposing artworks

86. Dieses Szenenbild könnte aus vielen Action-Filmen stammen. Immer wieder knallen schnelle Autos gegen Wände, explodieren Häuser und Flugzeuge. Die Freude an der Zerstörung ist die Grundmotivation aller Handlungen.
87. Einstige Helden werden gestürzt, zerstört oder musealisiert.

86. This stage set could come from a number of action films. Fast cars repeatedly crash into walls, buildings and aeroplanes explode. Enjoying destruction is the basic motif behind all these activities.
87. Former heroes are dispossessed, destroyed or exhibited in a museum.

uralten Rechte pochenden Adel. Der bereits erwähnte Sturm auf das Ulmer Münster ereignete sich am 21. Juni 1531. In einem zeitgenössischen Bericht wird er so beschrieben: »All altar abbrochen, die taflen darab abgenommen, zerschlagen, erhawen; alle bultnussen, als gemel in der Kirchen und ausserhalb als hinweg und verderbt …«

Die Wiedertäufer, die in Münster am 23. Februar 1534 die Macht in der Stadt übernommen hatten, zerstörten nicht nur alle Altäre, Kirchengemälde und Heiligenbilder, sondern auch alle Manuskripte, Urkunden und Archivalien, deren sie habhaft werden konnte. Man schichtete sämtliche Bücher der Stadt – außer den Bibeln – auf dem Markplatz zu einem Berg auf und zündete sie an. Im Gegensatz zu Luther predigten Zwingli und Calvin den radikalen Ikonoklasmus. Aus diesem Grunde wüteten die Bilderstürmer in Genf, Zürich und Bern besonders heftig. Selbst die Orgeln wurden zertrümmert und als Teufelswerk verbrannt. Auch die Hugenotten in Frankreich tobten sich mit rabiaten Destruktionsorgien aus, zerstörten sogar ganze Kirchen, zündeten 1567 die Kathedrale von Rouen an und plünderten die berühmte Bibliothek von Cluny. Der Kampf zwischen Katholiken und Hugenotten gipfelte in der berüchtigten Bartholomäusnacht – vom 23. zum 24. August 1572 –, in der es Tausende von Opfern gab, Brandruinen, Untergänge.

Auch in England und Schottland zerstörten die Calvinisten wertvolle Kirchenbilder. Erst während der Französischen Revolution kam es in Frankreich wieder zu einem ähnlichen, weltanschaulich begründeten Vandalismus. Damals versuchten die Revolutionäre, alle Kirchen zu Tempeln der Vernunft umzudeuten, vernichteten die Altäre und bauten an ihrer Stelle Freiheitsberge und Freiheitsbäume auf.

Die kommunistischen Revolutionäre in der Sowjetunion brachten die gesamte Zarenfamilie um und zerstörten alle religiösen Bilder, in freier Interpretation des Satzes von Karl Marx: »Religion ist Opium für das Volk!« Kirchen wurden zu Versammlungsstätten oder Museen umfunktioniert. In manchen gedachte man jetzt Lenins und der übrigen Helden des gewaltsamen Umsturzes. Nach der Auflösung der Sowjetunion erhielten viele Kirchen ihre alten, angestammten Funktionen zurück, die ehrwürdigen Ikonenwände wurden restauriert und die Kuppeln neu vergoldet. Heute lebt der orthodoxe Glaube in Rußland weiter, als sei er nie unterdrückt worden.

Im Zuge der Perestroika wandten sich alle Ostblockstaaten vom Kommunismus ab. Wir erinnern uns an die Bilder der überall auftauchenden Denkmalsstürmer. Stalindenkmäler und Sowjetsterne wurden umgestürzt, bespuckt, mit Füßen getreten oder gesprengt. Auch Saddam Hussein erging es später nicht besser, allerdings haben hier die USA nachgeholfen. Andere sogenannte Helden – Mao, Che Guevara, Fidel Castro – haben ihre Bedeutung in manchen Köpfen und Weltanschauungen immer noch nicht eingebüßt.

were given places of honor over the portals of temples or churches, in front of palaces and on public squares. We need only think of the Egyptian obelisks in ancient Rome and the bronze horses above the portal of St. Mark's Basilica in Venice. This tradition continued over the centuries. Napoleon also collected booty, Schadow's »Quadriga« on the Brandenburg Gate, for instance, and had it brought to Paris. Later, after the overthrow of Napoleon, the horses and the Goddess of Victory returned to Berlin once more and were put back in their traditional place with great pomp.

Vandalism that was justified on religious grounds took place mainly after the Reformation. The rage of the Protestant iconoclasts was ignited by the *Bible* quote »You must not make for yourself a carved image, or any likeness!« Although Luther tried to dampen the heated mood of the impoverished workers and peasants, he could not keep them from breaking into churches and cathedrals and smashing valuable Gothic altars and statues of saints with their scythes and axes. These products of aggression were, of course, also acts of vengeance against all the institutions that oppressed them: guilds, town councils and the nobility, which insisted on its allegedly age-old rights. The storming of the Ulm Minster mentioned above took place on 21 June 1531. In a contemporary report it is described as follows: »All altars demolished, the altarpieces taken off, smashed, hewn in pieces; all images, all paintings in the church and outside all removed and ruined …«

The Anabaptists who had taken over power in Münster on 23 February 1534 destroyed not only all the altars, church paintings and statues of the saints, but also all the manuscripts, documents and records they could get hold of. They piled up all the books in town – except for the bibles – in the marketplace and set fire to them. In contrast to Luther, Zwingli and Calvin preached radical iconoclasm. That is why the iconoclasts in Geneva, Zürich and Bern went on a particularly violent rampage. Even organs were smashed and burned as the work of the Devil. The Huguenots in France also gave full vent to their rage in violent orgies of destruction, even destroyed entire churches, set fire to the cathedral of Rouen in 1567 and looted the famous library of Cluny. The struggle between Catholics and Huguenots reached its climax in the infamous St. Bartholomew's Night – 23 to 24 August 1572 –, when there were thousands of victims, burned buildings, scenes of destruction.

In England and Scotland, too, the Calvinists destroyed valuable religious images. It was not until the French Revolution that there was another such wave of ideologically based vandalism, this time in France. At that time the revolutionaries tried to reinterpret all churches as temples of reason; after destroying the altars, they built freedom mountains and planted freedom trees in their stead.

The Communist revolutionaries in the Soviet Union killed the Czar and his entire family and destroyed all religious images, in a free interpretation of Karl Marx's statement »Religion is the opium for the people!« Churches were turned into assembly halls or museums. In some of them, people now commemorated Lenin and the other heroes of the violent coup d'état. After the collapse of the Soviet Union, many churches were given back their old traditional functions, the venerable walls of icons were restored and the onion domes were gilded again. Today the Orthodox faith is alive in Russia as though it had never been oppressed.

During the perestroika all the Eastern bloc countries turned away from Communism. We remember the pictures of the people everywhere who assaulted the monuments. Stalin monuments and Soviet stars were overturned, spat on, kicked or blown up. It was a fate later shared by Saddam Hussein's statues – although the US had a hand in this. Other so-called heroes – Mao, Che Guevara, Fidel Castro – are still alive in some minds and worldviews.

16. Industriebrachen und Fabrikruinen

Ruhrgebiet, Duisburg-Nord (Meiderich), Zeche Zollverein und neues Ruhr Museum

In Cape Canaveral, einer kleinen Halbinsel vor der Ostküste Floridas, wurden im Laufe der Jahre die ehemaligen, nicht mehr benutzten Raketenabschußrampen dem Verfall überlassen. Seeadler nisten auf ruinösen Betonblöcken, als handle es sich um Felszinnen der Rocky Mountains, und in den wilden Schilfbereichen ringsum leben giftige Schlangen, gefährliche Alligatoren und harmlose Gürteltiere. Ein Landschaftsparadies, wie man es in dieser hochtechnisierten, ganz der Raumfahrt gewidmeten Zone niemals erwarten würde. Auch in dem zwischen 1982 und 1985 geschlossenen Hüttenwerk Duisburg-Nord (Meiderich) entwickelte sich, dank der aufregenden Landschaftsplanung von Peter Latz, eine Vegetation, die wie ein fremdartiges Zitat des Paradieses wirkt. Ende und Anfang. Anfang und Ende.

Riesige, wild zerklüftete Betonmauern ähneln natürlichen Felsformationen. Kein Wunder, daß heutige Kletterer an ihnen hochsteigen, ganz so, als befänden sie sich an den drei Zinnen oder an der Eiger-Nordwand. Kegelförmige Reste des ehemaligen Erzbunkers ragen zwischen wildem Stahlgeäst auf wie die Opferstelen einer archaischen Kultstätte. Durch Mauerschlitze kann man als Besucher in Kellersysteme eindringen, deren Katakomben mit Wasser gefüllt sind. In der Tiefe entdecke ich langsam dahinziehende Taucher mit Scheinwerfern. In der unterirdischen Höhlenwelt suchen sie nach Spuren einstiger Tätigkeiten. Ihre magere Beute besteht aus groben Schraubenschlüsseln und rostigen Hämmern. Auch der Gasometer wurde zur Freude der Unterwasserforscher in ein Tauchbecken umgebaut.

Seitdem die alten Funktionen aufgegeben wurden, herrscht hier ein seltsames Treiben. Außer den Kletterern und Tauchern treffen sich abends Tanzgruppen in den leeren Hallen. Graziöse Tänzerinnen verstecken sich hinter gewaltigen Stahlstützen, drücken ihre nackten Oberkörper an die kalten, nietenübersäten Metallflächen, drehen sich langsam in den Raum, fordern die Turbinen zum Walzer auf. Aber keine Maschine rührt sich, nur die Tänzerinnen selbst drehen ihre Kreise, weich und elegant. Träumerinnen, die aus Fritz Langs Film *Metropolis* stammen könnten. Einstige, jetzt mild gewordene Maschinenstürmerinnen. Ihre Lungen atmen die Hallenluft ein, leise hört man ihr Stöhnen. Dazu die vorsichtigen Schlürfgeräusche ihrer Ballettschuhe auf den ölverschmierten Bodenplatten. Leben und Tod in den Ruinen, Erinnerungen.

Überraschend schnell erholte sich die Natur. Aus dem Dickicht wuchsen die kubischen Klinkergebäude der ehemaligen Industrieanlage, die zwischen 1928 und 1932 von den Architekten Fritz Schupp und Martin Kremmer mit bauhäuslerischer Strenge errichtet worden waren, eigensinnige, ganz auf die Schönheit klarer Geometrie setzende Skulpturen. Da die Gebäude im Zweiten Weltkrieg kaum Schaden erlitten hatten, konnten sie in den 1950er Jahren – nach wenigen Renovierungseingriffen – ihre Arbeit problemlos wiederaufnehmen. Erst 1986 erlosch ihr industrielles Leben engültig, übrigens ganz im Sinne der Architekten, die den Funktionsgebäuden eine Lebensdauer von 60 Jahren mit auf den Weg gegeben hatten, diese Zeitspanne war dem Kohleabbau bis zu seiner endgültigen Erschöpfung prognostiziert worden. Jetzt, nach dem Siegeszug des Heizöls, war die Zeit der Kohle endgültig vorbei, niemand brauchte sie mehr zum Heizen, auch nicht zum Erhitzen und Schmelzen von Stahl.

Drang man durch dichtes Gestrüpp, über halbzerfallene Treppen in die Innenräume ein, war man überwältigt von dieser Ansammlung metallischer Körper, von den Wäldern aus Stahlstämmen, den Rohrgedärmen, Mägen und Lungen aus rostenden Trichtern und löchrigen Containern. Kaum zu glauben, daß diese gigantischen Maschinen jemals funktioniert und gelebt haben. Es scheint so, als hätte sich ein ganzes Jahrhundert mit allen seinen Menschen in dieses unendlich große Stahladerngeflecht eingesponnen. Vielleicht verloren die Oberingenieure irgendwann den Überblick, stürzten sich in die schwarzen, dröhnenden Schächte und verstummten für immer. Seither versteht niemand mehr die wahren Zusammenhänge und die genauen Arbeitsabläufe. Pläne und Gebrauchsanleitungen gingen verloren. Dicke Staub- und Ölschichten haben sich auf den Rohren und Maschinenhäuten abgelagert. Schichten über Schichten. Schmieriger Dreck. Industrielle Korallenriffe. Vergangenheit. Zeit.

In den 70er und 80er Jahren des 20. Jahrhunderts hatten die meisten Industrieregionen der westlichen Welt die gleichen Strukturprobleme. Erst kam die Kohlenkrise, dann die Ölkrise und schließlich die Stahlkrise. Kokereien, Zechen und Stahlwerke wurden nicht mehr gebraucht. Aus China konnte Stahl zu Dumpingpreisen eingeführt werden. Viele Bürgermeister und Gemeinderäte standen vor dem gleichen Problem: Was sollte man mit den nicht mehr gebrauchten Industrierelikten, die auf dem Weg waren, gefährliche Ruinen zu werden, anfangen? In England und

16. Industrial wastelands and factory ruins

The Ruhr, Duisburg Nord (Meiderich), Zeche Zollverein and the new Ruhr Museum

In Cape Canaveral, a small peninsula on the east coast of Florida, the former launch pads, no longer used, have been allowed to fall into disrepair over the years. Eagles nest on the ruined blocks of concrete as though on the crags of the Rocky Mountains, and poisonous snakes, dangerous alligators and harmless armadillos live in the surrounding wild marshy areas. It's a landscape paradise you'd never expect to find in this high-tech zone devoted entirely to space travel. In the iron and steel works of Duisburg-Nord (Meiderich), which were closed between 1982 and 1985, there also developed a vegetation that feels like a strange reminder of paradise thanks to the exciting landscaping of Peter Latz. End and beginning. Beginning and end.

Gigantic, wildly fissured concrete walls look like natural rock formations. No wonder mountaineers today climb them as though they were on the Tre Cime di Lavaredo or the north face of the Eiger. Cone-shaped remnants of the former ore bunkers loom among the unruly steel branches like sacrificial steles at some archaic place of worship. Through slits in the walls a visitor can enter basement systems whose catacombs are filled with water. Down below I discover slow-moving divers with searchlights. They are looking for traces of former activities in the subterranean world of caves. The pickings are slim – crude spanners and rusty hammers. The gasometer, too, much to the delight of the underwater explorers, has been converted into a diving pool.

Ever since the steelworks no longer serve their original function, strange things have been going on here. In addition to the climbers and divers, dance groups meet at night in the empty halls. Graceful dancers hide behind massive steel pillars, press their naked upper bodies to the cold rivet-studded metal surfaces, twirl slowly into the room, invite the turbines to waltz with them. But the machines remain motionless, only the dancers themselves go round and round in circles, soft and elegant – dreamers who might have stepped out of Fritz Lang's film *Metropolis*. They could be former Luddites who have now grown gentle. Their lungs breathe the air of the halls, you can hear their soft panting. And then there are the cautious shuffling sounds of their ballet slippers on the oil-stained floor tiles. Life and death in the ruins, memories.

The natural environment recovered surprisingly quickly. From a thicket emerge the cubical clinker brick buildings of the former industrial plant, built between 1928 and 1932 by the architects Fritz Schupp and Martin Kremmer with Bauhaus stringency – willful sculptures focused entirely on the beauty of clear geometric forms. Since the buildings were scarcely damaged in World War II, they could resume work without any problems in the '50s – after slight renovations. Not until 1986 did their industrial life finally come to an end, incidentally just as the architects had intended: They had predicted a lifespan of 60 years for the industrial buildings, which was how long it would take for the coal seam to be exhausted. Now that fuel oil had superseded coal, the age of coal was over; no one needed it for heating now, or for heating and smelting steel.

88. Ruinöser Innenraum auf der Zeche Zollverein, Essen, vor dem Umbau zum Museum.

88. Ruined interior of the Zeche Zollverein, Essen, before its reconstruction as a museum.

213

Amerika entstanden die ersten Versuche, die aufgegebenen Kokereien, Stahl- und Gaswerke in neue Landmarks für zukünftige Bürgerparks zu verwandeln. Berühmt wurde der »Gas Works Park«, den die Landschaftsarchitekten Richard Haag & Associates seit 1973 in Seattle aufgebaut haben. Dabei gelang es zum ersten Mal, die bei der Bevölkerung verhaßten Gaswerkarchitekturen mit ihren rostigen Rohren und Containersilos in eine grüne Hügelumgebung mit Bäumen, großen See- und Wiesenflächen einzubetten und ihnen so eine publikumswirksame Attraktivität zu verleihen. Aus häßlichen Metallkonstruktionen wurden romantische Ruinen. Nachts, in künstliches Licht getaucht, nahm man sie als Zusammenspiel mittelalterlicher Burgruinen und Skulpturen von Jean Tinguely wahr.

In anderen Regionen fehlte es zwar nicht an markanten Industriebauten, aber an finanziellen Mitteln für die Umnutzung, in Cleveland etwa, der einst so blühenden Autostadt Amerikas. Auch in England gab es ähnliche Bestrebungen. Den Höhepunkt dieser Bewegung stellt die IBA-Emscherpark in Deutschland dar, der es zwischen 1989 und 1999 mit viel Geld gelang – insgesamt stand eine Summe von 4 Milliarden DM zur Verfügung –, unter der energischen Leitung von Karl Ganser, eine ganze Reihe von Zechen, Fördertürmen und Gasometern in neue, ökologisch ausgerichtete Landschaftsparks zu integrieren. Die wenigsten Industriebauten wurden abgerissen, aus vielen entstanden Kulturzentren, Museen, Schulen und Design-Institute, so auch aus der

89, 90. Industrieruinen. Gebäude und Maschinen werden nicht mehr gebraucht. Die Natur dringt ein und erobert sich die Räume zurück.

89, 90. Industrial ruins. Buildings and machines are no longer needed. Nature forces its way in and takes the rooms over again.

If you entered the buildings, forcing your way through thick shrubbery, up half-dilapidated stairs, you were overwhelmed by this accumulation of metallic bodies, jungles of steel trunks, intestines of pipes, stomachs and lungs that were rusty funnels and containers full of holes. It was hard to believe that these gigantic machines had ever functioned, had been alive. It seems as if a whole century and all its people were woven into this huge network of steel arteries. Perhaps somewhere back in time the chief engineers lost track of things, leapt into the black, echoing shafts and grew silent forever. Since then no one has been able to understand what the plant is really about and exactly how it operates. Plans and instructions were lost. Thick layers of dust and oil have collected on the pipes and the surfaces of machines. Layers upon layers. Grease and dirt. Industrial coral reefs. The past. Time.

In the 1970s and '80s most Western industrial regions had the same structural problems. First came the coal crisis, then the oil crisis and finally the steel crisis. Coking plants, collieries and steelworks were no longer needed. Steel could be imported from China at dumping prices. Many mayors and district councils faced the same problem: What should they do with the no longer needed industrial relics that were about to become dangerous ruins? In England and America there were initial attempts to turn abandoned coking plants, steel- and gasworks into new landmarks – future public parks. One such park to gain fame was the »Gas Works Park«, which the landscape architects Richard Haag Associates created in Seattle starting in 1973. It was the first time that gasworks buildings detested by local residents, with their rusty pipes and container silos, were embedded among green hills with trees, a large lake and meadows, features that made them attractive to the public. Ugly metal structures became romantic ruins. At night, bathed in artificial light, they were perceived as a kind of blend of medieval castle ruins and sculptures by Jean Tinguely.

Zeche Zollverein in Essen. Seit dem Jahr 2010, in dem sich Essen Kulturhauptstadt Europas nennen darf, erstrahlt die ehemalige Industrieruine in neuem Glanz. Die Kohlewäsche, ein Hauptgebäude der Zeche, dient seither als Ruhr Museum. Leider verschwand zu dieser Zeit auch der malerische Ruinencharakter in den Außenbereichen vollständig. In Duisburg-Nord (Meiderich) hat er sich besser erhalten. Vor allem nachts, wenn dort im Sommer die bunte Beleuchtung von Jonathan Park eingeschaltet wird, erhält man eine Ahnung davon, wie romantische Industrieruinen im 21. Jahrhundert aussehen könnten.

Der Eingangsbereich des Museums befindet sich im ersten Stock. Ein Museum von oben nach unten zu erschließen, ist als Idee – seit wir über Aufzüge und Rolltreppen verfügen – nicht neu, Frank Llyod Wright hatte damit beim Guggenheim-Museum in New York begonnen, und andere Institutionen weltweit folgten ihm. Die für die Renovierung des Gebäudes zuständigen Architekten – Heinrich Böll und Hans Kabel (mit dem niederländischen Büro OMA) – mußten die gesamte Klinkeraußenhaut, einschließlich aller Fenster, abreißen und neu aufbauen. Das alles war notwendig, um die vorgeschriebenen Dämmwerte zu erreichen. Ohne diese Maßnahmen wäre eine Klimatisierung des Museum, wie sie heute üblich ist, nicht möglich gewesen. Die bestehenden Stahltrichter, Rohre und Maschinen wurden hier oben noch erhalten, in den tieferen Geschossen hat man sie teilweise ausgebaut. Leider sind die Stahlkolosse so übermächtig, daß sie keine anderen Objekte neben sich dulden. Die Ausstellungsarchitekten kämpfen dagegen mit hellleuchtenden, sanft gebogenen, weißen Wänden an, auf deren Oberflächen Photos mit Motiven des heutigen Ruhrgebietes montiert sind. Mich erinnert die Installation an Röntgenbilder. Die Diagnose lautet leider: Alle Landschaften der Region sind zerstört, verbraucht, verdreckt, verkrebst; Metastasen überwuchern Kreuzungen und Fassaden, viele Gebäude wirken schwarz wie Raucherlungen, Straßen sehen aus, als stünden sie kurz vor dem Infarkt.

Hier, in diesem neuen Museumsumfeld, wird überhaupt nicht inszeniert, nur nüchtern aufgelistet und medientechnisch erläutert. Das unterste Geschoß befaßt sich mit der geologischen, pflanzlichen und tierischen Frühzeit des Ruhrgebiets. Elefanten- und Saurierskelette stehen auf engstem Raum beieinander. In den Nebenräumen jedoch gibt es immer wieder Zonen, die einen etwas erfreulicheren Eindruck machen und an das Neue Museum in Berlin von David Chipperfield denken lassen. Dies gilt vor allem für die Präsentation von römischen Fundstücken vor maroden und in ihrem Alterszustand belassenen Betonwänden der ursprünglichen Kohlebunker.

Als leeres Architekturobjekt – vielleicht auch als Industriemuseum – wäre dieses Gebäude viel interessanter gewesen als jetzt im Zustand eines modischen Ruhrpott-Heimat-Museums. Der Einführungstext im Museumskatalog beschreibt seine heutige Funktion, ohne die beiden disparaten Aspekte – Geschichte und Ort – wirklich miteinander zu verbinden: »Das Ruhr Museum ist das Schaufenster und Gedächtnis der Metropole Ruhr. Untergebracht in einem der größten und repräsentativsten Industriegebäude des Ruhrgebiets, der ehemaligen Kohlenwäsche der Zeche Zollverein, Schacht XII, ist es kein Industriemuseum im eigentlichen Sinne. Es zeigt vielmehr die Natur und Geschichte des Ruhrgebiets von den erdgeschichtlichen Voraussetzungen über die vormoderne Geschichte und die Industriezeit bis in die Gegenwart. Es ist das Regionalmuseum des Ruhrgebiets, eines der größten Ballungsräume Europas.«

Die leere, letztlich unnütze, tote Hülle der Kohlenwäsche steht für die nächsten Jahrzehnte als identitätsstiftender Alleinherrscher auf weiter Flur und wird Generationen von Bewohnern und Touristen in einer Weise beeinflussen, die mehr als einschränkend und hemmend ist. Vergangen ist vergangen. Als Ruine könnte der Bau langsam der Natur zurückgegeben werden. Als Museum fixieren die Betreiber einen Zustand, der nur transitorisch sein dürfte. Das jetzige Gebäude ist in Wirklichkeit ein Neubau, der vorgibt ursprünglich und originär zu sein. Die alte Industriearchitektur hingegen wurde ausschließlich für Maschinen errichtet, Arbeiter kamen darin nur vereinzelt vor, Besucher so gut wie nie. Jetzt hat sich das Verhältnis umgedreht, und aus der einst dünnen Wetterhülle mußte eine gesicherte, klimatisierte Festung kreiert werden. Vielleicht wäre eine Halbierung sinnvoller gewesen: Heutige Besucher wandern durch ein neues, modernes Museum und blicken aus den Raumfenstern immer wieder in die alten Maschinenhallen.

91. Industriemüll. Metall-Schrott. Abfall-Ruinen.

91. Industrial garbage. Discarded metal. Waste ruins.

In other regions, while there was no lack of striking industrial buildings, there were no funds for redevelopment, for instance in Cleveland, once the flourishing car city of America. In England, too, there were similar endeavors. The high point of this movement is the IBA-Emscher Park in Germany. Here, between 1989 and 1999, headed by the energetic Karl Ganser, a whole series of collieries, winding towers and gasometers were successfully integrated, at considerable expense – a total of 4 billion DM – in new, ecologically oriented landscape parks. A minimal number of industrial buildings were demolished, and many were turned into cultural centers, museums, schools and design institutes, including the Zeche Zollverein in Essen. In 2010, Essen can call itself the cultural capital of Europe. The former industrial ruin shines in new glory. The coal washing plant, one of the colliery's main buildings, has now become the Ruhr Museum. Unfortunately now the picturesque ruin character of the exterior has completely disappeared. In Duisburg-Nord (Meiderich) it has been preserved more successfully. Especially at night, when the colored lights by Jonathan Park are tuned on in summer, we get some idea of what romantic (industrial) ruins might look like in the 21st century.

The entrance of the museum is on the second floor. Accessing a museum from the top down is not a new idea – now that we have elevators and escalators. Frank Llyod Wright started the trend in the Guggenheim Museum in New York and other institutions worldwide followed him. The architects in charge of renovating the building – Heinrich Böll and Hans Kabel (with the Netherlands firm OMA) – had to demolish and rebuild the entire clinker brick outside shell, including all the windows. This was all necessary in order to attain prescribed insulation levels. Without these measures it would have been impossible to air-condition the museum in a way that is usual today. The existing steel funnels, pipes and machines were still preserved on the top floor; on lower floors they were removed in part. Unfortunately the steel colossi are so overwhelming they do not tolerate any other objects next to them. The exhibition architects tried to counteract this with luminous, gently curved, white walls, on whose surfaces are mounted photographs showing motifs of the Ruhr region today. As for me, the installation reminds me of X-ray images. Unfortunately the diagnosis is not promising: All the landscapes of the region are destroyed, used up, filthy, cancerous; metastases have overgrown intersections and façades, many buildings look black like smokers' lungs, while streets look like they're about to have a coronary.

Here, in this new museum environment, nothing is staged. There are sober lists and media-assisted explanations. The lowest floor deals with the geology, flora and fauna of the prehistorical period in the Ruhr region. Elefant and dinosaur skeletons stand crowded together. In the adjacent rooms, however, there are a number of zones that make a somewhat more positive impression and remind one of David Chipperfield's New Museum in Berlin. This is particularly true of the presentation of Roman artifacts in front of the ramshackle concrete walls of the original coal bunkers, which have been left in a state of disrepair.

As an empty architectural object – perhaps even as an industrial museum – this building would have been much more interesting than it is at present as a trendy Ruhr Basin local history museum. The introductory text in the museum catalogue describes its present-day function without really making a connection between the two disparate aspects – history and place: »The Ruhr Museum is the showcase and memory of the metropolis Ruhr. Housed in one of the largest and most representative industrial building of the Ruhr region, the former coal washing plant of the Zollverein Colliery, shaft XII, it is not an industrial museum in the actual sense of the word. Rather, it shows the natural world and history of the Ruhr region ranging from geological history to premodern history and the industrial age up to the present. It is the regional museum of the Ruhr region, one of the largest conurbations in Europe.«

The empty, now useless, dead shell of the coal washing plant will stand there in the open for decades to come, the sole provider of an identity, and will influence generations of local residents and tourists in a way that is more than limiting and hampering. What's past is past. As a ruin the mine could slowly be given back to nature. As a museum the authorities who operate the facility set in stone a condition that ought to be merely transitory. The present building is in reality a new building that claims to be original – the real thing. However, the old industrial building was erected exclusively for machines; workers would appear in it only sporadically, visitors virtually never. Now there is an inverse ratio, and the once thin shell of the building had to be transformed into a secure, air-conditioned fortress. Perhaps it would have been best to halve the whole thing: present-day visitors wandering through a new, modern museum and looking again and again out the windows of the exhibit rooms into the old machine halls.

17. Stadtuntergänge heute

Beispiel Kairo

Seit es Städte gibt, wecken sie die Begehrlichkeiten anderer Völker, Armeen, Könige und Feldherren. Man bedrohte sie, kreiste sie ein, belagerte sie, hungerte sie aus, griff sie an, eroberte, plünderte und zerstörte sie. Manchmal wurden die Gebäude verschont und die Bewohner versklavt oder ermordet.

»In Wirklichkeit befindet sich jede Stadt im natürlichen Kriegszustand mit jeder anderen«, schreibt Platon in den »Gesetzen«. Alexander wird der Große genannt, weil er mit seiner Armee elf Jahre lang die Welt und die Menschen östlich und südlich seines Heimatlandes Mazedonien überfiel und unterwarf. Nie verlor er eine Schlacht, und als er mit 32 Jahren 323 v. Chr. in Babylon starb, vergötterten ihn seine Zeitgenossen für seine Taten. Bei seinen Unternehmungen hatte er mehr Städte zerstört und Menschen getötet als die meisten Feldherren vor ihm. Die einzige bleibende Stadtgründung war Alexandria an der Nilmündung in Ägypten. Von hier aus wollte er einmal sein Reich regieren, das während der Diadochenkämpfe jedoch schnell wieder zerfiel. Ähnliche, später verherrlichte Spuren kriegerischer Zerstörungen hinterließen alle berühmten Feld- und Kriegsherren, ganz gleich ob es sich um Cäsar, Hannibal, Wallenstein, Napoleon, Hitler oder Rommel handeln mochte.

Wir Nachgeborenen haben dies meist nur den Berichten der Zeitgenossen entnommen oder den verklärenden Texten der Historiker und Schriftsteller späterer Generationen. Vielleicht befinden sich in den Archiven Urkunden über Friedensverträge. Die Spuren in den Landschaften und Städten sind fast alle verschwunden. Von Babylon etwa, einer der ältesten Städte der Welt, blieben nur sandüberdeckte Mauerreste übrig. Auch vom legendären Turmbau zu Babel wäre heute nichts mehr zu sehen, hätten nicht Archäologen die Fundamente freigelegt. Das einst so stolze, sich immer wieder erneuernde Troja, verschwand nach seiner endgültigen Zerstörung durch die Griechen in der Erde. Erst der deutsche Hobby-Archäologe Heinrich Schliemann fand die Ruinenmauern der verschiedenen Stadtschichten in einem harmlos aussehenden Hügel, den Generationen von Menschen nicht beachtet hatten.

Auch von Ur, Pergamon, Ephesos, Knossos, Mykene, Epidauros, Delphi und Karthago würden wir ohne die Ausgrabungen der Archäologen kaum etwas kennen. Natur und Landschaft haben sich alle architektonischen Spuren aus Stein – Mauern, Säulen, Kapitelle – einverleibt, sie unter Luftabschluß konserviert; Elemente aus Holz, Lehm, Fell oder gar Schilf waren im Laufe der Zeit zerfallen und verfault.

Außer den Kriegen gab es auch andere Ursachen für Stadtzerstörungen und – untergänge: Vulkanausbrüche, Erdbeben, Tsunamis und Meteoriteneinschläge. Manche Städte, die einer Naturkatastrophe zum Opfer gefallen waren, wie beispielsweise Pompeji, wurden nicht wieder aufgebaut. Jahrhunderte hindurch blieben sie vergessen. Die Bergstadt der Azteken Machu Picchu und die Hauptstadt des Khmer-Reiches in Kambodscha, Angkor Wat, erlitten ein ähnliches Schicksal. Andere einst bedeutende große Städte gingen zwar irgendwann fast unter, überlebten jedoch im ruinösen Zustand und erholten sich im Lauf der Jahrhunderte: Zu ihnen gehören viele der ganz alten Städte wie Jerusalem, Jericho, Kairo, Byzanz-Konstantinopel-Istanbul und Rom.

Manche Städte wie Lissabon nutzten ihre Zerstörung durch Erdbeben (1755) für eine glanzvolle Erneuerung. Dies gilt auch für Metropolen, die durch große Brände vernichtet wurden, wie London, Moskau, Brüssel und Paris. Die flächendeckende Auslöschung großer deutscher Städte im Zweiten Weltkrieg und ihr teilweise fragwürdiges Wiedererstehen habe ich in einem anderen Kapitel dieses Buches bereits erwähnt.

Seit etwa 100 Jahren hat sich ein neues Zerstörungsphänomen von Großstädten entwickelt. Die Ursachen und Wurzeln dafür liegen in ihrem rasant wuchernden, krebsgeschwürartigen Wachstum, der Umweltverschmutzung und der zunehmenden Verslumung. Noch vor 200 Jahren lebten die meisten Menschen in kleinen Dörfern auf dem Land. Um 1800 kamen auf einen Städter neun Dorfbewohner. Metropolen mit über 1 Million Einwohnern waren selten. Die Wissenschaft geht davon aus, daß zur Zeit von Christi Geburt die Erde von etwa 250 Millionen Menschen bewohnt wurde. Bis zum Jahr 1600 wuchs die Zahl auf etwa 550 Millionen an. Um 1800 lebten ungefähr 2 Milliarden Menschen auf der Erde, um 1980 waren es bereits etwa 5 Milliarden. Heute, im Jahr 2010, haben wir die 7 Milliardengrenze überschritten.

Über die Hälfte aller Menschen lebt in Städten. Da die Tendenz zur Verstädterung weiter anhält, liegt die Vermutung nahe, daß die meisten Menschen in 50 Jahren in städtischen Regionen

17. Dying cities today

Example: Cairo

As long as there have been cities, they have been a source of greed for other nations, armies, kings and military commanders. They've been threatened, encircled, besieged, starved out, attacked, captured, looted and destroyed. Sometimes the buildings were spared and the inhabitants enslaved or murdered.

»In reality every city is in a natural state of war with every other city«, writes Plato in the »Laws«. Alexander is called the Great because with his army he attacked and subjugated the world and the people east and south of his native country Macedonia for eleven years. He never lost a battle, and when, in 323 BCE, he died in Babylon at the age of 32, his contemporaries deified him for his deeds. During his campaigns he had destroyed more cities and killed more people than most commanders before him. The only city founded by him that lasted was Alexandria at the mouth of the Nile in Egypt. From here, he intended to rule his empire some day, but during the Diadoch Wars it quickly disintegrated again. All the famous commanders and warlords – regardless of whether we are speaking about Caesar, Hannibal, Wallenstein, Napoleon, Hitler or Rommel – left similar historical footprints, destructive acts of war that were subsequently glorified.

We who belong to a later age have for the most part learned this only from the reports of contemporaries or the transfiguring texts of historians and writers of subsequent generations. Perhaps there are documents about peace treaties in the archives. The marks they left on landscapes and cities have almost all vanished. For instance, all that is left of Babylon, one of the oldest cities in the world, are sand-covered fragments of masonry. Nor would there be even a trace of the legendary Tower of Babel today if archaeologists had not uncovered the foundations. Troy, once so proud, a city that had constantly renewed itself, disappeared underground after it was irrevocably destroyed by the Greeks. It was the German amateur archaeologist Heinrich Schliemann who found the ruined walls of various city layers in a harmless-looking hill that generations of people had overlooked.

Ur, Pergamon, Ephesus, Knossos, Mycenae, Epidaurus, Delphi and Carthage would also be virtually unknown to us had it not been for the excavations of archaeologists. Nature and landscape have absorbed all architectural traces made of stone – walls, columns, capitals – or preserved them when they were in airtight pockets; elements made of wood, clay, hide or reeds disintegrated and rotted over time.

Besides wars, there have also been other causes for the destruction and downfall of cities: volcanic eruptions, earthquakes, tsunamis and the impact of meteorites. Some cities that were the victims of a natural catastrophe, for instance Pompeii, were never rebuilt. For centuries they remained in oblivion. The Aztecs' mountain city of Machu Picchu and the capital of the Khmer empire in Cambodia, Angkor Wat, suffered a similar fate. Other once important large cities, while at one point they almost perished, did manage to survive in a ruined state and recovered over the centuries: They include many very old cities such as Jerusalem, Jericho, Cairo, Byzantium-Constantinople-Istanbul and Rome.

Some cities, such as Lisbon, used their destruction by an earthquake (1755) for a dazzling renewal. This is also true of metropolises that were destroyed by huge fires, such as London, Moscow, Brussels and Paris. I have already described in another chapter of this book the extensive obliteration of large German cities in World War II and their often questionable resurrection.

For the last hundred years, a new phenomenon of the destruction of large cities has developed. Its causes and roots can be found in their rapidly proliferating, cancerlike growth, environmental pollution and increasing urban decay. Just 200 years ago, most people were living in small rural villages. Around 1800 there were nine villagers to every city dweller. Metropolises with a population of over one million were rare. Scientists estimate that at the beginning of the Common Era the Earth was inhabited by roughly 250 million people. By 1600 the number grew to about 550 million. Around 1800 approximately two billion people lived on Earth; around 1980 there were already five billion. Today, in 2010, we have crossed the seven billion mark.

More than half of all people live in cities. Since the trend towards increasing urbanization is continuing, it is likely that 50 years from now most people will be living in urban regions, provided the Earth still exists then. The reason for the enormous population explosion and growth of cities can be found in the industrialization of the world. Around 1800 the center of this process was Great Britain, especially the city of London. Here the population grew to such an extent within a

leben werden, sofern es die Erde dann noch gibt. Der Grund für die enorme Bevölkerungsexplo-sion und das Anwachsen der Städte ist in der Industrialisierung der Welt zu suchen. Zentrum dieses Vorgangs war um 1800 Großbritannien, vor allem die Stadt London. Hier stieg die Bevöl-kerungszahl innerhalb weniger Jahrzehnte so stark an, daß sie um 1850 schon bei 2,6 Millionen lag und London damit vor Peking und Tokyo als die größte Stadt der Welt galt.

Trotz des enormen Elends, das die Familien in den frühindustriellen Städten erleiden mußten, waren ihre Überlebenschancen hier größer als auf dem Lande, wo sie ständig von Arbeitslosigkeit und Hungersnöten bedroht wurden. Fabrikbesitzer benötigten billige Arbeitskräfte und beuteten die Neuankömmlinge hemmungslos aus, selbst vor Kinderarbeit schreckten sie nicht zurück. Rings um die Metropolen entstanden proletarische Elendsviertel, später die berüchtigten Miets-kasernen.

Aber schon Mitte des 19. Jahrhunderts formierten sich in Europa Klassenkämpfer, allen voran Karl Marx und Friedrich Engels, und forderten einen humaneren Umgang mit den hart arbeiten-den Menschen. Aus dieser Bewegung entstanden die Gewerkschaften und die sozialdemokra-tischen Parteien. Im Laufe der Zeit milderte sich durch ihren Einfluß die brutalrücksichtslose Härte der ersten kapitalistischen Jahrzehnte. Parallel dazu erkannten die Bürgermeister und Stadtver-waltungen das Problem der Hygiene. Architektonische, technische und medizinische Fortschritte halfen, die schlimmsten Geißeln der Großstädte – Pest, Cholera und Typhus – zurückzudrängen.

Auch die Frauen wurden mit der Zeit besser behandelt. In den ersten Jahrzehnten des 20. Jahrhunderts erkämpften sie sich das bisher verweigerte Wahlrecht und konnten durchsetzen, daß sie an den Universitäten studieren durften. Nach den Katastrophen der beiden Weltkriege be-gann die moderne Zeit, wie wir sie kennen. Jedes Mitglied einer Industrienation sollte am techni-schen Fortschritt mit all seinen Möglichkeiten teilhaben. Man rüstete die Bevölkerung sowohl mit notwendigen als auch mit überflüssigen Dingen auf, die das Leben erleichtern und beglücken sollten. Konsum hieß das neue Zauberwort, das den Motor des Fortschritts antrieb. Kühlschrän-ke, Elektroherde, Staubsauger, Telephone, Radios, Fernsehgeräte, Tiefkühltruhen, Tabletten ge-gen jegliches Leiden, Autos zum schnelleren Erreichen der Ziele überschwemmten Städte, Woh-nungen und Landschaften. Für die Produktion und den Transport dieser schönen Luxusartikel benötigte man Energie. Küchengeräte lebten vom Strom, Autos von Benzin. Kraftwerke wurden gebaut, zunächst mit Wasser, Kohle und Gas betrieben, später mit Atomkraft.

Was zunächst aussah wie eine glückliche Bereicherung des Lebens und eine Demokratisie-rung des Wohlstands, entpuppte sich im Laufe der Zeit als zunehmende Umweltbelastung. Unver-rottbare Kunststoffgeräte, Verpackungsmaterialien, Flaschen und technische Ausrüstungen sam-melten sich zu neuartigen Gebirgen an. Autoabgase, Staub, Rauch aus Fabrikschloten und Haus-kaminen vergifteten die Luft, Kraftwerke erwärmten die Atmosphäre, und der Abfall von Atomkraft-werken war wegen seiner hohen Strahlenbelastung nicht mehr zu entsorgen. Da die Atmosphäre unseren Globus nur als hauchdünne, empfindliche Schicht umgibt, droht uns allen der langsame Tod durch Vergiftung und Ersticken.

Heute sind diese Probleme und Gefahren allgemein bekannt, nur fällt es schwer, global-kollek-tive Gegenmaßnahmen durchzusetzen, da viele Nationen noch immer dem alten, aggressiven Fortschrittsglauben verfallen sind und die Bereitschaft, die Entwicklungen zu verlangsamen oder in ökologisch vernünftige Bahnen zu lenken, nur spärlich vorhanden ist. Vor allem China, Indien und zahlreiche afrikanische Staaten weigern sich, an der neuen Bewegung teilzunehmen. Alle global agierenden Firmen haben Angst davor, daß sich ihre Produkte durch Umweltschutzmaß-nahmen verteuern und ihre Umsätze einbrechen. Niemand will Rückschritte in Kauf nehmen und auf die schönen Annehmlichkeiten der modernen Technik verzichten. Die meist auf der Nordhalb-kugel gelegenen reichen Industrienationen sind eher zum Handeln bereit als die vielfach unterent-wickelten Länder der Südhalbkugel, wo sich Überbevölkerung und Armut als größte Hemmnisse erweisen. Die Technisierung der südlichen Hälfte verläuft zudem weit ruppiger, schmutziger und zerstörerischer als auf der Nordhalbkugel. Wer heute Megacities in diesen Regionen besucht, hat das Gefühl, dem Endzustand einer architektonischen und zivilisatorischen Krebskrankheit gegen-überzustehen. In Abwandlung des oben zitierten Platon-Satzes könnte man sagen: »In Wirklich-lichkeit befindet sich jede Stadt in einem natürlichen Kriegszustand mit sich selbst.« Krieg und Krebs. Zerstörung und Tod.

Mexico-City, São Paolo, Kairo, Mumbay, Kalkutta, Bangkok, Peking und Jakarta, alle diese Städte sind im Grunde nicht mehr funktionsfähig und regierbar. Der Verkehr hat ein Ausmaß an-genommen, das nur noch als lärmendes, stinkendes Gift-Inferno beschrieben werden kann. Die Häuser sind längst nicht mehr in der Lage, die Bevölkerung aufzunehmen, sie weicht auf Bürger-steige, leerstehende Keller, Ruinen, Friedhöfe und Dächer aus. Die armseligen, grob zusammen-

few decades that around 1850 it had already reached 2.6 million and London was thus considered to be the biggest city in the world, outranking Peking and Tokyo.

In spite of the enormous hardships suffered by families in early industrial cities their chances of survival were better than in the country, where they were constantly at risk because of unemployment and famines. Factory owners needed cheap labor and exploited the new arrivals unscrupulously. They were not even afraid of using child labor. Encircling large cities, proletarian slums sprang up, and later the notorious tenements.

But as early as the mid-19th century, fighters in the class struggle began to organize in Europe, headed by Karl Marx and Friedrich Engels. They demanded more humane treatment of the hardworking people. This movement led to labor unions and social democratic parties. Over time, thanks to their influence, the brutal, ruthless harshness of the first capitalist decades was mitigated. Parallel to this development, mayors and town councils recognized the problem of hygiene. Architectural, technological and medical progress helped to curb the scourges of large cities – plague, cholera and typhoid fever.

Women, too, received better treatment as time went on. In the first decades of the 20th century they fought for and won the right to vote they had been denied hitherto and obtained the right to study at the universities. After the catastrophes of the two world wars began the modern age as we know it. Every member of an industrial nation was supposed to share in technical progress with all its opportunities. The population was provided with necessary and superfluous things that were supposed to make life easier and happier. The new magic formula was consumption, which powered the engine of progress. Refrigerators, electric stoves, vacuum cleaners, telephones, radios, television sets, freezers, pills for every ailment, tropical fruit and cars so that destinations could be reached faster flooded cities, homes and landscapes. In order to produce and transport these beautiful luxury goods one needed energy. Kitchen appliances had to have electricity, cars had to have gas. Power plants were built, initially driven by water, coal and gas, later by nuclear energy.

What had initially looked like a fortununate enrichment of life and democratization of wealth gradually turned out to be increasing environmental pollution. Rot-resistant plastic appliances, packaging material, bottles and technical utensils collected into a new kind of mountains. Exhaust fumes, dust, smoke from factory smokestacks and domestic fireplaces poisoned the air, power plants heated the atmosphere, and the waste from nuclear power stations could no longer be disposed of because it was too radioactive. Since atmosphere surrounds our planet only as an extremely thin, delicate layer, we are all in danger of a slow death by poisoning and suffocation.

Today these problems and dangers are generally known, only it is difficult to enforce global, collective countermeasures, since many nations are still addicted to the old aggressive belief in progress, and few are willing to slow down development or to channel it in ecologically sensible directions. Most notably China, India and a large number of African states refuse to take part in the new movement. All globally operating companies are afraid that their products will become more expensive as a result of environmental protection measures, and that sales will decline. No one wants to accept regression and give up the fine conveniences of modern technology. The rich industrial nations that are mostly situated in the northern hemisphere are more prepared to act than the mostly underdeveloped countries of the southern hemisphere, where overpopulation and poverty prove to be the most important impediments. Moreover the mechanization of the southern half has been far more reckless, dirty and destructive than that of the northern hemisphere. Those who visit megacities in these regions today have the feeling they are witnessing the final stages of a cancer affecting both architecture and civilization. To paraphrase the words of Plato quoted above we could say: »In reality every city is in a natural state of war with itself.« War and cancer. Destruction and death.

Mexico City, São Paulo, Cairo, Mumbai, Calcutta, Bangkok, Beijing and Jakarta. All these cities are basically no longer functional and governable. Traffic has reached proportions that can only be described as a noisy, stinking, poisonous inferno. For a long time, the houses have not been capable of sheltering the entire population: People live on the sidewalks, vacant basements, ruins, cemeteries and rooftops. The pitiful, crudely and haphazardly built slum zones are exploding; they have neither a decent water supply nor a sanitary system to remove human waste, dirty water and garbage. The problem is often exacerbated by densely built-up historic city centers, which are completely unsuited for a healthy lifestyle. There are no wide breezeways, people live in the same room with chickens, sheep, goats, mice, cockroaches and TV sets. Often beds are rented only for a number of hours, after which the next sleeper waits for his chance to rest. These are the types of conditions we are familiar with from 19th century London, Berlin and Vienna.

gewürfelten Slum-Zonen explodieren, sie kennen weder eine anständige Wasserversorgung noch die Entsorgung von Fäkalien, Schmutzwasser und Müll. Das Problem verschärft sich oft durch engbebaute Altstadtgebiete, die für eine gesunde Lebensführung vollkommen ungeeignet sind. Es gibt keine breiten Durchlüftungsschneisen, Menschen leben mit Hühnern, Schafen, Ziegen, Mäusen, Kakerlaken, Ratten und Fernsehern gemeinsam in einem Raum. Oft werden Betten nur für Stunden vergeben, danach wartet der nächste Schläfer auf seine Ruhezeit, Zustände, wie wir sie aus London, Berlin und Wien im 19. Jahrhundert kennen. Müllberge türmen sich vor den Eingangs- und Fensterlöchern auf, und in den Straßenpfützen lauern die alten Geißeln der Menschheit: die Seuchen Cholera, Pest und Typhus.

Noch nie in der Menschheitsgeschichte gab es so viele Millionenstädte wie heute. Noch nie war die Gefahr der Anarchie und des Umkippens ins unbeherrschbare Chaos so groß wie heute. Geringste Anlässe genügen, und Unruhen werden zu Aufständen unvorstellbaren Ausmaßes führen. Allerdings eskaliert die Gefahr erst dann wirklich, wenn skrupellos-gewaltbereite Anführer die Massen aufwiegeln und bewaffnen. Diese Mobilisierung kann aus kriminellen Motiven stattfinden – etwa durch die Drogenmafia – oder aus religiösen Motiven – etwa durch die muslimischen Hetzer im Iran oder in Ägypten –, beides ist denkbar.

Bisher kannte ich von den großen Millionenstädten der Welt nur London, Paris, Moskau, Los Angeles und New York aus eigener Anschauung. An Weihnachten 2009 entschloß ich mich dazu, nach Kairo zu fliegen und mir eine der heutigen Megacities mit eigenen Augen anzuschauen. Da es in Kairo keine Meldepflicht gibt, weiß niemand genau, wie hoch die Einwohnerzahl tatsächlich ist. Nach neuesten Schätzungen liegt sie zwischen 20 und 30 Millionen. Und mit jedem Tag erhöht sich die Zahl, da es immer mehr der 70 Millionen Ägypter in ihre Hauptstadt zieht.

Dabei begann alles einmal so hoffnungsvoll und großartig. Hier, in Ägypten, entlang des fruchtbaren Nils entwickelte sich vor 5000 Jahren die erste Hochkultur der Menschheit, mit den Hieroglyphen als Schrift und der ersten wirklichen Geschichtsschreibung auf diesem Globus. Innerhalb weniger Jahrhunderte brachten altägyptische Pharaonen, Priester, Architekten und Künstler die von uns bis heute bewunderten Tempel, Pyramiden, Kultfiguren, Skulpturen, Reliefs, Sarkophage, Möbel und Malereien hervor. Allerdings hätte sich niemals eine so große Anzahl von Kunstwerken erhalten, wäre dieses Volk nicht vom Tod und dem Leben im Jenseits besessen gewesen.

Jahrhunderte später, nachdem Ägypten als römische Provinz ausgedient hatte, stieg Kairo zur führenden arabischen Stadt des Mittelalters auf. Wissenschaftler gründeten die heute noch existierende Al-Azhar-Universität. Ihre Forschungsergebnisse waren genauso berühmt wie die prunkvollen Moscheen, Bibliotheken, Bäder, Markthallen und Bürgerhäuser der Kairoer Innenstadt. Im 16. Jahrhundert, nach der Eroberung Ägyptens durch die Osmanen, verlor Kairo seine einstige Bedeutung. Erst in der Zeit zwischen 1801 und 1805 gelang es dem aus Albanien stammenden Söldner Mohammed Ali mit viel List und Brutalität, die Macht in Ägypten zu übernehmen, sich

Mountains of garbage pile up in front of entrances and windows, and in the puddles on the streets lurk the old scourges of the human race – cholera, pestilence and typhoid fever.

Never before in human history have there been as many cities with over a million inhabitants as there are today. Never before has the danger of anarchy and of plunging into uncontrollable chaos been as great as today. The slightest reasons are sufficient for riots to turn into revolts of unimaginable scope. However, the danger does not really escalate until unscrupulous, violent leaders stir up and arm the masses. This mobilization may take place from criminal motives – for instance, by the drug mafia – or from religious motives – for instance, by Muslim agitators in Iran or in Egypt; both are conceivable.

Until recently, of the large megacities of the world, I knew only London, Paris, Moscow, Los Angeles and New York from my own experience. Christmas 2009 I decided to fly to Cairo and see one of today's megacities with my own eyes. Since Cairo residents are not required to register, no one knows the exact population figure. According to the latest estimates it is between 20 and 30 million. And the number increases with every day, since more and more of a total of 70 million Egyptians are drawn to their capital.

It all began so hopefully and splendidly in the old days. Here, in Egypt, along the fertile Nile River, the first advanced civilization of the human race developed 5,000 years ago, with hieroglyphs as their writing and the first real historiography on the planet. Within a few centuries ancient Egyptian pharaohs, priests, architects and artists created the temples, pyramids, cult figures, sculptures, reliefs, sarcophagi, furniture and paintings we still admire today. Such a large number of artworks would never have been preserved, of course, if this nation had not been obsessed with death and the afterlife.

zum Pascha wählen und das Land in neuem Glanz auferstehen zu lassen. Den heutigen Ägyptern gilt er als Gründer ihres modernen Staates.

Seit dem Feldzug Napoleons rückte das Land zunehmend in den Fokus der europäischen Archäologen. Die altägyptische Kunst beeinflußte den Klassizismus, vor allem den französischen Empire-Stil. Mit dem wirtschaftlichen Aufschwung, den der Bau des Suezkanals in der zweiten Hälfte des 19. Jahrhunderts auslöste, erblühten Ägypten, Kairo und Alexandria zum letzten Mal in orientalischem Glanz. Damals hatten die Engländer Ägypten als Kolonie annektiert und es geschafft, aus Kairo ein mondänes Ziel der europäischen High Society zu machen. Es gehörte zum guten Ton vieler reicher Familien aus England, Frankreich und Deutschland, den Winter in Kairo zu verbringen. An den Ufern des Nils entstanden damals vornehme Villen und Paläste mit orientalischen Gartenanlagen.

Diese letzte Ägypten-Romantik fand ihren Höhepunkt in den Ausgrabungen des britischen Archäologen Howard Carter. Ihm war es, zusammen mit seinem Finanzier Lord Carnarvon gelungen, das Grab des Tutanchamun zu entdecken, eine Jahrhundertsensation. Danach jedoch ging es nur noch abwärts. Kairo wurde zwar immer größer und bevölkerungsreicher, gleichzeitig aber auch immer unattraktiver, lauter und verdreckter. 1952 kam es zu Unruhen, in deren Verlauf die Innenstadt Kairos in Flammen aufging. Der korrupte König Faruk wurde durch einen Militärputsch gezwungen, ins französische Exil zu gehen. 1953 erklärte die neue Regierung Ägypten zur Republik. 1954 übernahm der Offizier Gamal Abdel Nasser die Regierungsgewalt. Da er einen rigorosen Staatssozialismus propagierte und mit der Sowjetunion zusammenarbeitete, betrachtete der Westen seine Aktivitäten – vor allem nach der Verstaatlichung des Suezkanals – mit großer Skepsis. 1967 verlor Ägypten den Krieg gegen Israel; damit sank auch der Stern Nassers. Nach seinem Tod wurde Anwar el-Sadat 1970 neuer ägyptischer Präsident. Er vollendete das von seinem Vorgänger begonnene Assuan-Staudamm-Projekt und mußte sich 1973 erneut mit Israel kriegerisch auseinandersetzen. Sadat versuchte anschließend sein Land gegenüber Amerika und den übrigen arabischen Staaten zu öffnen.

Ägypten und seine Hauptstadt Kairo kamen jedoch nicht zur Ruhe. Nach der Ankündigung von Preiserhöhungen brachen in Kairo schwere Unruhen aus. Häuser brannten. Die fundamentalistische Bewegung wurde immer stärker. 1981 ermordeten radikale Islamisten Sadat während einer öffentlichen Parade. Sein Nachfolger im Präsidentenamt, Hosni Mubarak, mußte sich weiterhin mit Unruhen und Attentaten auseinandersetzen. Im Februar 1986 meuterten wütende Polizeirekruten in Kairo, deren Dienstzeit ohne Vergünstigungen verlängert werden sollte. Bei Straßenschlachten wurden sechs große Luxushotels angezündet, drei von ihnen brannten vollständig aus, es gab über 100 Tote. Als Folge der zunehmenden Radikalisierung der Islambewegung kam es in den 1990er Jahren immer wieder zu Anschlägen auf Polizisten, christliche Kopten und aus-

Centuries later, after Egypt had had its day as a Roman province, Cairo became the leading Arab city of the Middle Ages. Scientists founded Al-Azhar University, which still exists today. The results of their research were just as famous as the magnificent mosques, libraries, baths, covered markets and town houses of Cairo's inner city. In the 16th century, after Egypt was conquered by the Ottomans, Cairo lost its former importance. It was only in the period between 1801 and 1805 that the mercenary Mohammed Ali, who came from Albania, succeeded, with much cunning and brutality, in taking over power in Egypt, getting himself elected pasha and restoring the country to new glory. Egyptians today consider him to be the founder of their modern state.

Since Napoleon's campaign, the country was increasingly becoming the focus of European archaeologists. Ancient Egyptian art influenced classicism, particularly the French Empire style. During the economic upswing triggered by the building of the Suez Canal in the latter part of the 19th century, Egypt, Cairo and Alexandria blossomed in oriental splendor for the last time. At that time the British had annexed Egypt as a colony and had managed to make Cairo into a trendy destination for European high society. It was good form for many wealthy families from England, France and Germany to spend the winter in Cairo. It was during this period that elegant villas and palaces with oriental gardens were built on the banks of the Nile.

This final romance with Egypt peaked with the excavations of the British archaeologist Howard Carter. Together with his financial backer Lord Carnarvon he had succeeded in discovering the tomb of Tutankhamun, the sensation of the century. Afterward, however, things only started going downhill. It is true that Cairo kept getting bigger and more populous, but simultaneously more and more unattractive, loud and polluted. In 1952 there were riots, in the course of which the inner city of Cairo went up in flames. The corrupt King Farouk was forced by a military coup d'état to go into exile in France. In 1953 the new government declared Egypt a republic. In 1954 the officer Gamal Abdel Nasser took over the government. Since he advocated a rigorous state socialism and collaborated with the Soviet Union, the West regarded his activities – especially after the nationalization of the Suez Canal – with a great deal of skepticism. In 1967 Egypt lost the war against Israel; because of this Nasser's star declined. After his death Anwar el-Sadat became the new Egyptian president in 1970. He completed the Aswan Dam project begun by his predecessor and had to engage in renewed military conflict with Israel in 1973. Sadat subsequently tried to open his country to America and the other Arab countries.

There was no respite for Egypt and its capital Cairo, however. After price increases were announced, violent rioting broke out in Cairo. Houses were set on fire. The fundamentalist movement became more and more powerful. In 1981 radical Islamists assassinated Sadat during a public parade. The man who succeeded him as president, Hosni Mubarak, had to continue dealing with riots and assassinations. In February 1986 furious police recruits mutinied in Cairo when

94, 95. Ruinöse Szenen im heutigen Kairo.

94, 95. Ruinous scenes in today's Cairo.

ländische Touristen. Mubarak ließ in den letzten Jahren die Polizei- und Militärpräsenz in Kairo und an allen touristischen Zielen im ganzen Land verstärken, so daß es für islamistische Kämpfer immer schwerer wird, diese Ziele anzugreifen.

Die Minarette zweier Moscheen am Nilufer ragen dünn und abgemagert wie die Finger einer Greisin in den nächtlichen Smog-Himmel. Im Dunkeln sehen die Kuppeln aus wie vergrößerte Schildkrötenpanzer. Ihre schlafende Ruhe steht in einem krassen Gegensatz zum lebhaften Verkehr davor. Künstliche Lavaglut, glühende Lunten kurz vor der Bombe, kurz vor der Detonation.

In einem Bericht über Mohammed Atta heißt es, dieser sei einer der Attentäter des 11. September 2001 gewesen. Er entstamme einer Kairoer Mittelschichtsfamilie und habe an der berühmten Universität der Stadt Architektur studiert, bevor er nach Hamburg umgezogen sei, um dort an der Technischen Universität, am Institut für Städtebau, sein Studium abzuschließen. In seiner Diplomarbeit, die später mit »sehr gut« bewertet wurde, habe er den Konflikt zwischen traditionellem islamischem Urbanismus und der westlichen Moderne untersucht. Erst nach dem Attentat in New York hätten sich seine Prüfer den vorangestellten, arabisch geschriebenen Koranspruch übersetzen lassen. Er habe gelautet: »Mein Opfer und mein Leben und mein Tod sind für Allah, den Herrn der Welt.«

Es scheint so, als wolle sich die lärmige, gesichtslose, heutige Stadt die berühmten Relikte aus ferner Vergangenheit wie Masken vor das stinkende, verwesende Alltagsgesicht halten. In Wirklichkeit wird jedem Besucher sofort klar, daß es keinen Zusammenhang zwischen der Zeit der Pharaonen und dem Staate Mubaraks gibt, weder in der Architektur noch im Erscheinungsbild der Stadt. Jahrtausende trennen die Zeiten. Menschenmassen, Automassen, ruinöse Architekturen, Dreck und Staub. Staub in der Luft, Staub in grauen Schichten auf Mauern und an Wänden, auf dem Asphalt, Staub auf den Autos, Staub auf den Gesichtern und Kleidern der Menschen. Staub auf dürren Palmwedeln.

Ich bin sicher, daß Kairo die lauteste und dreckigste Stadt ist, die ich je gesehen habe. Umweltverschmutzung, mangelnde Hygiene und Armut sind stets die Hauptgründe des Niedergangs. In amerikanischen und südamerikanischen Megacities drohen zusätzlich die Gefahren einer übermäßigen Kriminalisierung. In Rio de Janeiro oder Mexiko City gibt es Stadtteile, die vollständig von rivalisierenden Banden kontrolliert werden. Prostitution und Drogenhandel gehören zu den Hauptwirtschaftszweigen dieser anarchistischen Gegenwelt. Auch in Los Angeles, Washington und New York weigern sich Bus- und Taxifahrer, selbst manche Polizeieinheiten oft, gewisse Stadtteile zu durchqueren oder zu betreten.

Daß es möglich ist, Innenstädte zu »säubern«, zeigt das Beispiel von Manhattan. In den 1970er und 1980er Jahren war es dort lebensgefährlich, abends allein durch die Straßen der Innenstadt zu gehen. Fast jeder Passant lief Gefahr, von bewaffneten Banden überfallen zu werden. Ich selbst erinnere mich an den Zustand bei einem Besuch in der Stadt 1983. In jedem dunklen Hauseingang lagen Wohnsitzlose, kam man vorbei, streckten sie ihre Hände mehr oder weniger aggressiv ins Licht. Gab man nichts, wurde man beschimpft oder tätlich angegriffen. In Hofeinfahrten oder an Parkeingängen lungerten — wie in Kubricks *Uhrwerk Orange* – Gangs herum, die Passanten mit Messern oder Pistolen zur Herausgabe ihrer Geldbeutel zwangen. Erst, als ein neuer Oberbürgermeister dazu überging, alle Wohnsitzlosen und Kleinkriminellen aus der City zu vertreiben und an die Stadtränder zu verbannen, wurde die Lage besser. Heute kann man relativ ruhig, auch abends und nachts, durch die Straßen New Yorks wandern, allerdings sollte man nach wie vor gewisse Hafengegenden, U-Bahn-Eingänge und vor allem den Central Park meiden.

their working hours were to be extended without additional remuneration. During street battles six large luxury hotels were set on fire; three were completely gutted, and there were over 100 deaths. As a result of the increasing radicalization of the Islamic movement there were repeated attacks on the police, Christian Copts and foreign tourists in the '90s. In recent years Mubarak has had the police and military presence in Cairo and at all tourist destinations in the entire country reinforced, so that it is getting more difficult for Islamist fighters to attack these targets.

The minarets of two mosques on the banks of the Nile loom thin and emaciated like the fingers of an old woman into the smoggy night sky. In the dark the cupolas look like supersized turtle shells. Their somnolent calm is in sharp contrast with the congested traffic in front of them. Arti- ficial red-hot lava, glowing fuses, just before the bomb, moments before detonation.

In a report about Mohammed Atta he is described as one of the assassins of 11 September 2001. The report states that he comes from a middle-class Cairo family and studied architecture at the city's famous university before he moved to Hamburg to conclude his studies there at the Institute for Urban Design of the University of Technology. In his dissertation, which was later graded as »very good«, he is said to have investigated the conflict between traditional Islamic urbanism and Western modernity. It was not until after the assassination in New York that his examiners had the Koranic verse that preceded the dissertation, which was written in Arabic, translated. It said: »My sacrifice and my life and my death are for Allah, the Lord of the world.«

It seems as if the noisy, faceless city of today wanted to hold the famous relics of the distant past like masks before its stinking, decaying everyday face. In reality every visitor immediately realizes that there is no connection between the time of the pharaohs and the state of Mubarak, neither in the architecture nor in the outward appearance of the city. Millennia separate the two periods. Masses of people, masses of cars, architecture in a state of dilapidation, dirt and dust. Dust in the air, dust in gray layers on masonry and walls, on the asphalt, dust on the cars, dust on the faces and clothes of the people. Dust on the dry fans of the palm trees.

I am sure that Cairo is the worst, the noisiest and dirtiest city I have ever seen. It is always environmental pollution, lack of hygiene and poverty that are the main reasons for decline. In North and South American megacities there are added dangers: excessive crime. In Rio de Janeiro or Mexico City there are parts of town that are completely controlled by rival gangs. Prostitution and drug dealing are among the main sectors of the economy in this anarchistic counter-world. In Los Angeles, Washington and New York bus and taxi drivers, and even some police units, also often refuse to cross or enter certain neighborhoods.

The example of Manhattan shows that it is possible to »clean up« inner cities. In the 1970s and '80s people risked their lives walking through the streets of the inner city alone at night. Almost every passerby was in danger of being attacked by armed gangs. I myself remember what it was like when I visited the city in 1983. Homeless people lay in every dark building entrance. When you would walk by, they stretched out their hands toward the light more or less aggressively. If you didn't give anything, you would be verbally abused or physically attacked. Gangs hung out in the entrances of courtyards or parks — just as in Kubrick's *Clockwork Orange* – forcing passersby with knives or pistols to hand over their wallets. It was only when a new mayor began driving all the homeless and petty criminals out of the city and banishing them to the outskirts that the situation improved. Today you can wander through the streets of New York relatively peacefully even at night, though one still ought to avoid certain waterfront areas, subway entrances and especially Central Park.

18. Ruinen und Auslöschungen in der Kunst, Architektur und Literatur heute

Im 20. Jahrhundert hatte die Ruine merkwürdigerweise trotz aller Katastrophen als naheliegendes zentrales Motiv der Kunst wenig Chancen. Zwar gab es zahlreiche Künstler, die an der Zerstörung alter Ideale arbeiteten, außerdem genoß das Fragment, vor allem als Collage, großes Ansehen, aber bildhaft dargestellte Ruinen kommen selten vor. Nur bei Alfred Kubin, George Grosz, Otto Dix, Pablo Picasso, Giorgio de Chirico, Max Ernst, Salvador Dalí, Franz Radziwill, Karl Hofer und Werner Heldt tauchen sie auf. In abgewandelter Form anderer Destruktionen freilich lassen sich die Nachwirkungen brutaler Gewalt in vielen, fast möchte man sagen, in allen modernen Kunstwerken nachweisen. Städte, Landschaften, Räume, alte und neue Dinge, tierische und menschliche Körper, Köpfe und Gesichter werden zerschnitten, zerstückelt, expressiv verzerrt, eingefroren oder in abstrakte Welten aufgelöst. Verletzungs- und Zerstörungsaktionen im Mikro- und Makrobereich, allerdings meist ohne direkten Ruinenbezug, die in besonders extremer Ausprägung bei Pablo Picasso, Alberto Giacometti, Henry Moore, Francis Bacon und Lucian Freud zu finden sind.

Künstler, die in Konzentrationslager deportiert wurden, überlebten die Katastrophen meist nicht (wie etwa Felix Nussbaum). Aus diesen Todeszonen gibt es – von wenigen Ausnahmen abgesehen – nur Zeichnungen und Texte von Menschen, die weder Schriftsteller noch Maler waren. Die meisten Überlebenden schwiegen jahrzehntelang, sie konnten nicht über ihr Unglück sprechen. Manche wurden später von ihren Erinnerungen in den Selbstmord getrieben.

Vier bedeutende Gemälde der Moderne behandeln das Ruinen- und Auslöschungsthema in besonders visionärer Weise. Am Anfang steht Giorgio de Chiricos *Der große Metaphysiker* aus dem Jahr 1917. Wie jedes wichtige Kunstwerk ist auch dieses Gemälde vielschichtig und mehrdeutig lesbar: als reale Szenerie auf einem mediterranen, seltsam menschenleeren Stadtplatz, als metaphysisch-surreales Bild der Melancholie, als Bild der Bedrohung, kurz vor dem Absturz eines Meteoriten oder als Bild der tödlichen Stille nach der Explosion einer Bombe. Der zentrale Platz und damit die Bildmitte sind nicht leer, hier ragt eine rätselhafte, hieroglyphenartige Figurenkonstruktion auf, einsam und labil.

Giorgio de Chirico ist, obgleich er Italiener war, in Griechenland aufgewachsen. 1915 wurde er – damals 28 Jahre alt – zum Militär einberufen. Bis 1917 war er in Ferrara stationiert. Seine Tätigkeit im Lazarett ließ ihm genügend Zeit zum Malen. Neben der alten italienischen Stadt Ferrara mit dem berühmten Castello Estense, den Türmen, Villen und Plätzen beeinflußten ihn

96. Henry Moore, *Die Liegende*, Bronzeskulptur vor der Akademie der Künste, Hanseatenweg, Berlin.
97. Alberto Giacometti, *Bildnis Annette*, 1964, Kunsthaus Zürich.
98. Francis Bacon, *Drei Studien Muriel Belchers*, 1966, Privatsammlung.

96. Henry Moore, *Die Liegende*, bronze sculpture in front of the Akademie der Künste, Hanseatenweg, Berlin.
97. Alberto Giacometti, *Portrait of Annette*, 1964, Kunsthaus Zürich.
98. Francis Bacon, *Three Studies for a Portrait of Muriel Belcher*, 1966, private collection.

18. Ruins and extinctions in art, architecture and literature today

Strangely enough, in spite of all the catastrophes the ruin as an obvious central motif had little chance in 20th century art. It is true that there were many artists who were working on the destruction of old ideals; besides, the fragment – especially in the form of a collage – enjoyed a good reputation, but graphically represented ruins occur seldom. They appear only in the work of Alfred Kubin, George Grosz, Otto Dix, Pablo Picasso, Giorgio de Chirico, Max Ernst, Salvador Dalí, Franz Radziwill, Karl Hofer and Werner Heldt. In a somewhat altered form, as other types of destruction, the aftereffects of brutal violence can be demonstrated in many, you could almost say in all, modern works of art. Towns, landscapes, rooms, the old and the new, the bodies of animals and human beings, heads and faces are cut up into pieces, distorted, frozen or resolved into abstractions. There are minor and major scenes of injury and devastation, although generally without a direct connection to ruins, found in especially extreme form in the works of Pablo Picasso, Alberto Giacometti, Henry Moore, Francis Bacon and Lucian Freud.

Artists who were deported to concentration camps (for instance, Felix Nussbaum) generally did not survive the catastrophes. With very few exceptions, we have only drawings and texts from these zones of death by people who were neither writers nor painters. Most of the survivors kept silent for decades, unable to speak about their misfortune. Some were later driven to suicide by their memories.

Four significant paintings of the modern period treat the theme of ruins and extinction in a particularly visionary way. The first is Giorgio de Chirico's *The Great Metaphysician*, dated 1917. Like every important artwork, this painting too is multilayered and can be read in a number of ways: as real scenery on a strangely deserted square in a Mediterranean city, as a metaphysically surreal depiction of melancholy, as a symbol of menace, shortly before the impact of a meteorite, or as an image of deathly silence after the explosion of a bomb. The central place and thus the middle of the picture is not empty: Here a mysterious, hieroglyphlike structure of figures looms lonely and frail.

Though he was Italian, Giorgio de Chirico grew up in Greece. In 1915, at the age of 28, he was drafted into the military. Until 1917 he was stationed in Ferrara. His work at the military hospital left him enough free time to paint. Besides the old Italian town of Ferrara with its famous Castello Estense, towers, villas and squares, he was also influenced by the motifs of his friend, the painter Carlo Carrà, who coincidentlally also had to do his military service in Ferrara and with whom Giorgio de Chirico shared a studio for months. As if intoxicated, and at the same time seemingly paralyzed, Chirico developed his »metaphysical painting« during this period, a combination of surreal, utopian and theatrical motifs in the style of classical antiquity. He writes: »Within us we carry the sadness and the hope of far-reaching expeditions. There will be bad days, I know; days of storm and windless days ...«

It seems as though the (former) inhabitants of the town (Ferrara) – or was it only a single artist? – had cobbled together a sculpture from found objects, scraps of furniture, artists' tools, draftsman's squares, trangles, coffins, cloths, parts of shop window displays, laths and beams, had given up before it was finished and had suddenly abandoned it. Or does the structure only show the preparatory, inner supporting framework of a future sculpture? However, the composition does not feel particularly stable; rather, we think of amateurs who have crudely nailed together random spare pieces of furniture, fragments of frames, garbage, flotsam and jetsam, and an empty doll's head. Perhaps this strange creation also represents the unsuccessful memory of a classical monument, a distorted Apollo, a Venus with parts chewed off. Associations with the Trojan horse or the Statue of Liberty in New York are also conceivable. In one case, however, the animal aspect would be missing, in the other the raised arm with the torch.

Then again we are struck by the mechanical, artificial aspect of the figure, which depicts neither a real person nor another real natural form, is more reminiscent of poor design, fragments of an abandoned, uncompleted project, anatomical confusion, the failed model of a skyscraper capped by a human head, a chaotic Frankenstein doll, a lonely skeletal marionette abandoned by its strings, a ruin.

After long contemplation I suddenly seem to hear a crunching, scraping noise, the structure raises its arms and legs, though only bony, handless laths appear in the space, the cloth drops on the ground, and the shoulder triangles become detached from their bandage. The figure takes a step forward. At that moment this completely unstable construction loses its cohesion, the iffy balance of the parts finally goes out of kilter, and like a tower of building blocks playfully and cursorily piled up by children the monument pathetically collapses. Before me is nothing but a paltry

auch die Motive seines Malerfreundes Carlo Carrà, der zufällig ebenfalls in Ferrara seinen Militär-dienst ableisten mußte und mit dem Giorgio de Chirico monatelang ein Atelier teilte. Wie be-rauscht, gleichzeitig auch wie gelähmt, entwickelte Chirico in dieser Zeit seine »metaphysische Malerei«, die sich aus antikisierenden, surreal-utopischen und theaterhaften Motiven zusam-mensetzt. Er schreibt: »Wir tragen in uns die Traurigkeit und die Hoffnung weitreichender Expe-ditionen. Es wird schlimme Tage geben, das weiß ich; Sturmtage und windstille Tage.«

Man hat den Eindruck, die (einstigen) Bewohner der Stadt (Ferrara) – oder war es nur ein ein-zelner Künstler? – hätten aus Fundstücken, Möbelfragmenten, Künstlerutensilien, Winkeln, Drei-ecken, Särgen, Tüchern, Schaufensterdekorationsteilen, aus Latten und Balken eine Skulptur zusammengezimmert, sie im unfertigen Zustand aufgegeben und plötzlich verlassen. Oder zeigt die Konstruktion nur das vorbereitende, innere Tragwerk einer zukünftigen Skulptur? Die Zusam-mensetzung allerdings wirkt nicht sonderlich stabil, wir denken eher an unprofessionelle Täter, die nach dem Zufallsprinzip überflüssige Möbelstücke, Rahmenfragmente, Müll, Strandgut und einen leeren Puppenkopf grob zusammengenagelt haben. Vielleicht stellt dieses merkwürdige Gebilde auch die mißglückte Erinnerung an ein klassisches Denkmal dar, einen verzerrten Apoll, eine ab-genagte Venus. Assoziationen an das Trojanische Pferd oder an die New Yorker Freiheitsstatue sind ebenfalls denkbar. Allerdings würde in einem Fall der Tieraspekt, im anderen der erhobene Arm mit der Fackel fehlen.

Dann wieder fällt uns das Mechanisch-Künstliche der Figur auf, die weder einen wirklichen Menschen noch eine andere reale Naturform abbildet, mehr erinnert sie an eine Fehlkonstruktion, an Fragmente eines aufgegebenen, unvollendeten Projekts, an eine anatomische Verwirrung, ein verfehltes Hochhausmodell mit menschlichem Kopf als Gipfelform, eine chaotische Frankenstein-Puppe, eine von ihren Schnüren verlassene, einsame Skelett-Marionette, eine Ruine.

Nach langem Betrachten glaube ich, plötzlich ein Knirschen und Schaben zu hören, die Kon-struktion hebt Arme und Beine, dabei erscheinen nur knochig-handlose Latten im Raum, das Handtuch fällt zu Boden, und die Schulterdreiecke lösen sich aus ihrem Verband. Die Figur macht einen Schritt vorwärts, in diesem Moment verliert die völlig unsolide Konstruktion ihren Zusam-menhalt, das fragwürdige Gleichgewicht der Teile kippt endgültig aus dem Lot, und wie ein von Kindern spielerisch-flüchtig aufgeschichteter Klötzchenturm fällt das Denkmal kläglich in sich zusammen. Vor mir liegt nur noch ein kümmerlicher Sperrmüllhaufen, der darauf wartet, angezün-det zu werden. Die Gravitation hat gesiegt. Das Projekt »Kunst«, vielleicht auch das Projekt »Mensch-heit«, wurde als Fehlkonstruktion entlarvt.

Giorgio de Chirico gab dem Bild den Titel *Der große Metaphysiker* und verweist damit auf eine Welt hinter der sichtbaren Oberfläche. Das, was wir sehen, sind nur Andeutungen, Zeichen von Knochen, Trümmern und Resten, das eigentliche Dasein führt diese Ruine vielleicht in einer zwei-ten, uns verborgenen, geistigen Welt. Die »Offenbarung« der Wahrheit fand nicht statt. Oder sieht de Chirico in diesem bühnenbildhaft-oberflächlichen Scheindasein die eigentliche Wahrheit, ganz nach dem Satz Nietzsches: »Schein, wie ich es verstehe, ist die wirkliche und einzige Realität der Dinge.« (Aus: *Die Geburt der Tragödie aus dem Geist der Musik*)? Der Kunsthistoriker Wieland Schmied formuliert den Sachverhalt in seinem Buch *Giorgio de Chirico: Die beunruhigenden Musen* so: »De Chirico malt die Welt als Schein, als Traum, als Vision … Diesem Ziel dient im besonderen die Konstruktion des Bildraums als Bühne … De Chirico malt die Welt als Schein vor dem Hintergrund des Nichts so, daß sie dabei nicht banal oder bedeutungslos wirkt, sondern daß sie – ganz im Sinne Nietzsches – in ihrer offenbaren Scheinhaftigkeit alle Fragen, alle Rätsel, alle Geheimnisse, die sie uns aufgibt, zur Darstellung bringt oder, anders gesagt, daß der Schein der Kunst das Mysterium der Realität in einer Weise suggeriert, die durch nichts anderes erreicht wer-den kann als eben diesen Schein.« Wie auch immer: Trotz des gemütlichen Sonnenlichts, das von rechts vorn in den Bildraum fällt, Skulptur und Hausfragmente harte Schatten auf die Platzfläche werfen läßt, ist vor allem die Leere beängstigend. Bedrohlich schwarz wie ein verkohltes Schloß, ein Krematorium, wirkt das dunkle Haus, das links den Blick in die Ferne versperrt. Statt eines Kamins, einer klassischen Giebelfigur streckt eine dünne Antenne – oder ist es ein Blitzableiter, eine Himmelsspritze? – ihren metallischen Finger gegen die abendlich glühenden Wolken. Wenn die hellen, sonnenbestrahlten Häuser und die kleine Figur im Hintergrund des Bildes so tot und hohl sind, wie es den Anschein hat, dann könnte das Gemälde auch als eine Nachricht aus dem Jenseits gedeutet werden, das hinter Caspar David Friedrichs *Eismeer* und hinter Böcklins *Toteninsel* liegt. Die Abgeschiedenen haben sich in den Häusern zur »ewigen« Ruhe gelegt und werden erst am »Jüngsten Tag« (wenn überhaupt) wieder in Erscheinung treten.

Was bleibt ist die Beunruhigung über die Rätselhaftigkeit der Szene. Wir können die ruinösen Hieroglyphen nicht wirklich entschlüsseln, wir verstehen die Botschaft nicht genau, Ahnungen

99. Giorgio de Chirico, *Der große Metaphysiker*, 1917, The Museum of Modern Art (MoMA), New York.

99. Giorgio de Chirico, *The Great Metaphysician*, 1917, The Museum of Modern Art (MoMA), New York.

pile of refuse waiting to be set on fire. Gravity has won. The project »Art«, and perhaps the project »Humanity« as well, has been unmasked as a faulty design.

Giorgio de Chirico gave the painting the title *The Great Metaphysician* and thus draws our attention to a world beneath the visible surface. What we see are only suggestions, signs of bones, rubble and remains. Perhaps this ruin leads its true existence in a second, spiritual world concealed from us. There has been no »revelation« of the truth. Or does de Chirico see the actual truth in this surface phantom existence that looks like a stage set, in accordance with Nietzsche's statement »Appearance, as I understand it, is the real and only reality of things.« (From: *The Birth*

und Vermutungen überwiegen. Im Schweben zwischen den möglichen Bedeutungsebenen stellen wir vielleicht fest, daß unser Leben auf Sand gebaut ist, unser Ich-Verständnis und unsere Weltinterpretationen attrappenhaft, hochstaplerisch, hohl, unsolide und provisorisch sind. Wir lügen uns die Welt zurecht, wir spielen uns selbst und den anderen Menschen ein Welt- und Ichverständnis vor, das in keiner Weise der Realität entspricht. Oder wir sagen mit Nietzsche: Dieser falsche Schein ist die Realität, zumindestens: eine wesentliche Facette davon. Das Gemälde wird in jedem Fall zum Gleichnis menschlicher Hilflosigkeit. Unsere Blicke streifen die Dinge der Welt, unsere Ohren hören mögliche Sätze der Erklärung, unsere Körper halten sich zwischen anderen Körpern auf, wir bleiben Fremde und verstehen überhaupt nichts, unsere Wahrnehmung bleibt ein Stochern im Ungewissen. Als größte Illusion erweisen sich klassische Architekturen, Städte, Plätze und Skulpturen. Bei aller Perfektion und angeblicher Harmonie, die durch Symmetriesysteme suggeriert wird, stecken auch in ihnen nur lächerliche Baugerüste, die das rasende Chaos hinter der so ruhig scheinenden Wirklichkeit zu verbergen suchen. Fremden Mächten ausgesetzt, bleibt unser Gehirn eine wuchernde, hormon- und gefühlsgesteuerte Illusionsmaschine, unsere Ichs kopfunter im Weltall hängende, vom grellen Licht der Sonne beschienene Fleischsäcke, die, kaum geboren, zum Tode verurteilt sind. Die kommenden Katastrophen werden nicht mehr so bühnenbildhaft dekoriert und museal-harmlos aussehen. Uns erwarten Untergänge und Ruinenlandschaften ganz anderer Art. Am Ende werden verkohlte, blutgetränkte Scherben und Körperteile über alle Plätze zerstreut sein. Was einmal Gehirn oder Herz war, wird zum Aschefleck unter Milliarden anderer Ascheflecken geworden sein. Bomben werden kein Erbarmen kennen, feuerspeiend und strahlenverseuchend werden sie über Häuser, Dächer, Denkmäler, Museen und Menschen herfallen, auf Plätzen, in Dachstühlen, Räumen und Kellern explodieren, Städte und alles Leben endgültig auslöschen.

In den drei altarartigen Gemälden von Otto Dix *Der Krieg* (Triptychon, 1929/30) ist es bereits soweit. Die Katastrophe des Ersten Weltkriegs hat stattgefunden. Zerstörung, Tod und verbrannte Ruinenlandschaften überwiegen. Ob man es als zynische Blasphemie oder als stures Beharren auf klassischen Werten ansehen muß, daß Otto Dix seine Bilder komponierte und malte wie Matthias Grünewald, bleibt eine offene Frage. Der Bezug auf eines der berühmtesten Altarbilder des ausgehenden Mittelalters – den »Isenheimer Altar« – könnte auch als Anklage gegen die christliche Religion verstanden werden. Hier, in diesem bisher brutalsten aller Kriege, war von göttlicher Zuversicht nichts mehr zu spüren. Die Mitte, das Kreuz mit dem toten Christus, ist jetzt leer, ganz im Sinne Nietzsches und seines Postulats: »Gott ist tot!« In langen Skizzenreihen, die Otto Dix in den Schützengräben zwischen verletzten, schreienden und sterbenden Kameraden notiert hat, bereitete er sich auf den Gemäldekomplex vor.

Die linke Tafel zeigt schwerbewaffnete Soldaten, die in den Krieg ziehen. In Anspielung auf Caspar David Friedrich umwabern Bodennebel die martialischen Rückengestalten. Diese *Wanderer über dem Nebelmeer* suchen keine romantischen Naturerlebnisse, sie bringen Tod und

100. Otto Dix, *Der Krieg*, dreiteiliges Altargemälde, 1932, Staatliche Kunstsammlungen Dresden.
101. Hans Dieter Schaal, Präsentation des Groß-stadt-Triptychons von Otto Dix, 1927/28, bei der Jubiläumsausstellung zu seinem 100. Geburtstag, 1991, in der Galerie der Stadt Stuttgart. Die künstliche, schwarze Ruine als Bildhintergrund war damals heftig umstritten.

100. Otto Dix, *War*, tripartite altarpiece, 1932, Staatliche Kunstsammlungen Dresden.
101. Hans Dieter Schaal, presentation of the city triptych by Otto Dix, 1927/28, at the exhibition for his 100th anniversary in the Galerie der Stadt Stuttgart, 1991. The black artificial ruin was highly controversial at the time.

of Tragedy from the Spirit of Music*) The art historian Wieland Schmied describes the facts of the case in his book *Giorgio de Chirico: Die beunruhigenden Musen* as follows: »De Chirico paints the world as appearance, as a dream, as a vision … The fact that the space of the picture is structured like a stage serves this purpose especially well. … De Chirico paints the world as appearance against a background of the void in such a way that the effect is neither banal nor meaningless. Rather – and this is exactly what Nietzsche meant – because this is obviously a world of appearances it represents all questions, all riddles, all secrets that it poses for us; in other words, the appearance of art suggests the mystery of reality in a way that can be achieved by nothing but this very appearance.« Be that as it may: In spite of the friendly sunlight that falls into the space of the picture from the right forefront and causes the sculpture and the fragments of houses to cast hard shadows on the square, it is the emptiness that is particularly disquieting. The dark building that blocks one's view into the distance on the left feels black and menacing like a charred castle, a crematorium. Instead of a chimney or a classical pediment figure, a thin antenna – or is it a lightning rod, a hypodermic pointed at the sky? – pokes its metal finger into the glowing evening clouds. If the bright, sunlit houses and the small figure in the background of the picture are as dead and hollow as they appear to be, then the painting could also be interpreted as a message from the hereafter that is behind Caspar David Friedrich's *Sea of Ice* and Böcklin's *Isle of the Dead*. The departed have gone to their »eternal« rest in the houses and will not reappear until the »Day of Judgment« (if at all).

What remains is uneasiness about the mysteriousness of the scene. We cannot really decipher the ruin hieroglyphs, we do not understand the message exactly: Forebodings and conjectures predominate. As we vacillate between possible levels of meaning, we realize, perhaps, that our lives are built on sand, our self-understanding and our interpretations of the world are sham, fraudulent, hollow, unreliable and makeshift. We create a world of lies, we act out for ourselves and others a sham understanding of the world and of ourselves that in no way corresponds to reality. Or, with Nietzsche, we say: This false appearance is reality, or at least an essential facet of it. In any case, the painting becomes a simile of human helplessness. Our eyes glance fleetingly at the things of this world, our ears hear possible explanations, our bodies live among other bodies, we remain strangers and understand nothing at all, our perception is merely a fumbling around in uncertainty. Classical architectural objects, cities, squares and sculptures prove to be the greatest illusion of all. They may be perfect and allegedly harmonious, as symmetrical systems suggest, but inside them, too, there is only laughable scaffolding that tries to conceal the raging chaos behind a seemingly peaceable reality. Exposed to alien forces, our brain is still a teeming illusion machine controlled by hormones and emotions. Our egos are bags of flesh suspended in the cosmos, lit by the glaring light of the sun – condemned to die no sooner than we were born. The catastrophes that are yet to come will not look like stage sets, harmless, like something in a museum. The destructions and ruin landscapes that await us will be very different. In the end the square will be strewn with charred, blood-soaked shards and body parts. What was once a brain or a heart will no longer be recognizable, a smudge of ashes among billions of such smudges. Bombs have no pity, they spew their fire and contaminate houses, rooftops, monuments, museums and people with their radiation, explode on squares, in attics, living rooms and basements, efface cities and all life forever.

In the three altarlike paintings of Otto Dix, *War* (triptych, 1929/30), this future has already arrived. The catastrophe of World War I has taken place. Destruction, death and burned ruin landscapes now prevail. It is still an open question whether we should regard it as cynical blasphemy or stubborn insistence on classical values that Otto Dix composed and painted his pictures like Matthias Grünewald. The reference to one of the most famous altarpieces of the late Middle Ages – the »Isenheim Altar« – could also be understood as an accusation of the Christian religion. Here, in a war that was the most brutal ever to have taken place so far, there was no longer a trace of divine providence. The center – the cross with the dead Christ – is empty now. As Nietzsche postulated, »God is dead!« In long series of sketches that Otto Dix jotted down in the trenches surrounded by wounded, screaming and dying comrades, he was preparing to paint the triptych.

The left panel shows heavily armed soldiers going off to war. In an allusion to Caspar David Friedrich, ground mists waft around the backs of the martial figures. These *Wanderers above the Mists* are not in search of romantic experiences in nature, they bring death and disaster upon the world or are themselves ripped to shreds by grenade splinters. On the right altar wing we can recognize the painter, rescuing a wounded comrade from the burning war zone like a good Samaritan. Under the altar lthe dead lie in their graves. The large, square central picture depicts the actual fighting. When we look at it closely, however, we realize that the battle is over. There are

Verderben über die Welt oder werden selbst von Granatsplittern zerfetzt. Auf dem rechten Altar-flügel ist der Maler zu erkennen, der wie ein barmherziger Samariter einen verletzten Kameraden aus der brennenden Kriegszone rettet. Unter dem Altar liegen die Toten in ihren Gräbern. Auf dem großen, quadratischen Zentralbild ist das eigentliche Kriegsgeschehen dargestellt. Bei genauem Hinsehen allerdings stellen wir fest, daß die Schlacht schon vorüber ist. Es gibt nur noch blutig-zerfetzte Menschenleiber, verkohlte Baumstämme, Hausfragmente und im Hintergrund eine Bombentrichterlandschaft mit Ruinen. Daß auch hier der romantische Nebel zwischen den ge-stürzten Balken, einsamen Kaminfingern und Baumstammresten wabert, muß als falsch und zynisch bezeichnet werden. Grausame Ruinenschönheiten, herrlich wie am ersten oder letzten Tag. Auch der einsame Wanderer Caspar David Friedrichs taucht wieder auf, jetzt scheint er zu rasten, in eine lausige Decke gehüllt, den Kopf mit einem Stahlhelm geschützt und das Gesicht durch eine Gasmaske unkenntlich gemacht. Ist er der letzte Überlebende, oder verbirgt sich hin-ter der Tarnung ein Toter? Dort, wo bei Grünewald das Kreuz aufragt, herrscht bei Otto Dix die Leere vor. Vielleicht ist das dünne Stahlskelett, das mit einem aufgespießten, völlig zerfetzten Soldaten von links in den Bildraum hineinragt, ein Kreuzigungszitat.

Wie viele seiner Zeitgenossen hatte sich Otto Dix 1914 begeistert als Freiwilliger zum Miltär-dienst gemeldet. Damals war er 23 Jahre alt. Entsetzt über seine Kriegserlebnisse, kehrte er von den Fronten in Frankreich, Polen und Rußland nach Deutschland zurück und begann in den 1920er Jahren, seine Kunst zu entwickeln. Erst zehn Jahre nach Kriegsende glaubte er, soweit zu sein und nahm das »Kriegstriptychon« in Angriff. Seine ästhetische Mischung aus »Neuer Sach-lichkeit« und »Altmeisterlichkeit« machten ihn berühmt. 1927 wurde er zum Professor an der Kunstakademie in Dresden ernannt. Bereits 1933, kurz nach der Machtübernahme der Nazis, ver-lor er das Amt jedoch wieder. Sein Werk wurde als »entartet, wehrkraftzersetzend und pornogra-phisch« diffamiert angesehen. Von nun an mußten Soldaten wieder zu Helden aufgebaut werden, und deprimierend-destruktive Blicke auf Schlachtfelder waren verpönt. 250 seiner Arbeiten ver-schwanden aus den deutschen Museen. Dix zog sich deprimiert nach Hemmenhofen am Boden-see zurück und »emigrierte« in die Landschaftsmalerei. Er starb zwar hochgeehrt als Klassiker der Moderne 1969 in Singen am Hohentwiel, aber in Wirklichkeit konnte er mit seinen ver-söhnlich-harmlosen Bildern der Nachkriegszeit nicht mehr an die Erfolge der 1920er Jahre an-knüpfen.

Pablo Picasso wollte sich im Sommer 1937 eigentlich mit seinem geliebten Thema »Maler und Modell« befassen. Er war von der offiziellen republikanischen Regierung Spaniens um einen bild-nerischen Beitrag zum spanischen Pavillon auf der Pariser Weltausstellung gebeten worden und hatte, entgegen seiner Angewohnheit, Auftragsarbeiten abzulehnen, zugesagt. Da geschah in Spanien etwas Ungeheuerliches. Seit einem Jahr herrschte Bürgerkrieg: Unter der Führung General Francos kämpften Faschisten gegen Republikaner. Der erste Luftangriff faschistischer Bomber – mit Unterstützung der deutschen Luftwaffe (die berühmt-berüchtige Formation »Con-dor«) – traf die kleine, wehrlose, in der Nähe von Bilbao gelegene baskische Stadt Guernica so schwer, daß sie völlig zerstört wurde. Entsetzt reagierte die ganze Welt auf das Massaker an der unschuldigen Zivilbevölkerung. Sofort änderte Picasso seine Pläne und schuf in einem wahren Arbeitsrausch das größte und eindrucksvollste Antikriegsbild des 20. Jahrhunderts. Monate später hing das fertige Gemälde, das wie eine schreiende Anklage gegen den Faschismus und den totalen Krieg wirkte, im spanischen Pavillon. Nicht weit davon entfernt, standen sich, direkt an der Seine, Albert Speers klassizistisch-stolz aufragender deutscher und der ähnlich herrsch-süchtige sowjetische Pavillon gegenüber.

In einem poetisch-expressiven Text beschrieb Picasso seine Gefühle und Absichten: »… Schreie der Kinder, Schreie der Frauen, Schreie der Vögel, Schreie der Blumen, Schreie der Bäume und der Steine, Schreie der Ziegelsteine, der Möbel, der Betten, der Stühle, der Vorhänge, der Töpfe, der Katzen und des Papiers, Schreie der Gerüche, die nacheinander greifen, Schreie des Rauchs, der in die Schulter sticht, Schreie, die in dem großen Kessel schmoren, und des Regens von Vö-geln, die das Meer überschwemmen …«

Dargestellt wird auf dem riesigen Gemälde – es ist 350 x 780 cm groß – der Moment des Bom-beneinschlags in ein Haus. Alle Menschen, Tiere, Möbel, Lampen und Wände stürzen durch-einander, brüllen mit weit geöffneten Mündern und Mäulern stumme Schreie in den Raum und werden im nächsten Moment verletzt oder tot in sich zusammenbrechen. Eine grelle Blitzlichtsitu-ation, für alle überraschend, unverständlich und schmerzhaft. Durch Picassos Linien werden Kör-per, Gesichter, Gliedmaßen und Gegenstände zerteilt, verstümmelt. Abgeschlagene Köpfe, Arme, Hände und Füße liegen am Boden. Blutiges Schlachthaus. Ende. Ein Mann umklammert im Tod sein abgebrochenes Schwert. Diese Waffe hat nichts genützt gegen die Angreifer aus dem Him-

102. Albert Speer, Deutscher Pavillon auf der Pariser Weltausstellung 1937. Ihm gegenüber stand, in aggressiver Konfrontation, der sowjetische Pavillon, mit dem monumentalen Bronze-Paar *Arbeiter und Kolchosbäuerin* von Vera Muchina auf dem Dach.
103. Pablo Picasso, *Guernica*, 1937, Museo Nacional Centro de Arte Reina Sofia, Madrid.

102. Albert Speer, German Pavilion on Paris World Fair, 1937. Confronting it aggressively opposite was the USSR Pavilion with the monumental bronze sculpture group *Worker and Kolchos Farmgirl* by Vera Muchina on the roof.
103. Pablo Picasso, *Guernica*, 1937, Museo Nacional Centro de Arte Reina Sofia, Madrid.

only bloody, torn human bodies, charred tree trunks, fragments of houses and in the background a landscape dotted with bomb craters and ruins. Here, too, the romantic mist wafts between the collapsed rafters, the pointing fingers of solitary chimneys, and remains of tree trunks, a fact we cannot help describing as false and cynical. The cruel beauty of ruins, as glorious as on the first or last day of creation. Caspar David Friedrich's lonely wanderer reappears as well. Now he seems to be resting, wrapped in a lousy blanket, his head protected by a steel helmet, his face made unrecognizable by a gas mask. Is he the last survivor, or does the camouflage conceal a dead man? Where the cross looms in Grünewald's picture, there is emptiness in Otto Dix's work. Perhaps the thin steel skeleton that leans into the picture from the left with the lacerated body of a soldier impaled on it is an allusion to the crucifixion.

Like many of his contemporaries Otto Dix had enthusiastically enlisted in the military as a volunteer in 1914. He was 23 at the time. Horrified by his war experiences he returned to Germany from the front lines in France, Poland and Russia, and began developing his art in the 1920s. Only ten years after the end of the war he believed he was ready to tackle the »War Triptych«. His aesthetic mixture of »New Functionalism« and the »style of the old masters« made him famous. In 1927 he was appointed professor at the Dresden Academy of Fine Arts. As early as 1933, shortly after the Nazis took power, he lost his position again. His work was defamed for undermining military morale and being »degenerate and pornographic«. From now on soldiers had to be built up into heroes again, and depressing, destructive battlefield scenes were frowned upon. 250 of his works disappeared from German museums. Depressed, Dix retired to Hemmenhofen near Lake Constance and »emigrated« into landscape painting. It is true that he died highly honored as a modern classic in 1969 in Singen am Hohentwiel, but in reality he was no longer able to build on the successes of the 1920s with his placatory, innocuous postwar paintings.

In the summer of 1937 Pablo Picasso actually intended to work on a favorite theme, »artist and model«. He had been asked by the official republican government of Spain to contribute an artwork for the Spanish pavilion at the Paris World Fair and, contrary to his habit of refusing commissioned work, had agreed. Then something monstrous happened in Spain. For a year, Spain had been embroiled in a civil war: Under the leadership of General Franco, fascists had been fighting republicans. The first air raid by fascist bombers – with the support of the German air force (the famous-notorious »Condor« formation) – hit the small, defenseless Basque town of Guernica near Bilbao so severely that it was completely destroyed. The world reacted to the massacre of the innocent civilian population with horror. Picasso immediately changed his plans and in a veritable frenzy of work created the largest and most impressive antiwar picture of the 20th century. Months later the finished painting, a glaring accusation against fascism and total war, was hanging in the Spanish pavilion. Not far away, directly by the Seine, Albert Speer's classicis-

mel, sie stammt aus einer Zeit der Stierkämpfe, damals, als man noch die Kräfte Körper gegen Körper miteinander gemessen hat. Jetzt geht es um schnelles, maschinelles Töten, um Auslöschung von Dörfern, Kindern, Frauen und Männern mit Bomben, die von Flugzeugen abgeworfen werden.

Im Gegensatz zu Giorgio de Chirico und Otto Dix, hat Pablo Picasso ein vollkommen neues Bildsujet geschaffen. Es gibt zwar klassische Schlachtenbilder aus allen Zeiten – von Altdorfer, Bosch, Rubens, Velasquez, Ingres, Goya –, aber noch nie hat ein Künstler die Zertrümmerung und Zerstückelung von Architektur und menschlichen Körpern soweit getrieben wie Picasso in seinem *Guernica*-Gemälde. Natürlich konnte er dabei seine kubistischen Seziertechniken und Körpererkundungen nutzen, aber der ausschließliche Blick auf die Zerstörung und Vernichtung, auf die Opferwelt war neu. Der Mensch mit Dolch und Schwert ein machthungriges Raubtier, der Mensch mit maschinellen Waffen ein zynischer Killer, ein blutrünstiger Unheilbringer. Die Rückkehr zum friedlichen Leben danach war kaum vorstellbar.

Wer sich in diesem Bürgerkrieg gegen die Faschisten stellte, hatte wenig Überlebenschancen. Bekanntlich siegten die Truppen Francos und beherrschten das einst so stolze Land von 1938 bis zu Francos Tod im Jahr 1975. Erstaunlich bleibt die Tatsache, daß sich General Franco, der diktatorisch-autoritäre Staatschef, trotz Drängen seiner faschistischen Freunde in Deutschland und Italien, ganz aus dem Zweiten Weltkrieg herausgehalten hat.

Der Zweite Weltkrieg war vorüber und hatte Deutschland in eine apokalyptische Ruinenlandschaft verwandelt. Werner Heldt, der 1904 in Berlin geboren wurde, gehört zu den wenigen Künstlern des 20. Jahrhunderts, der im Ruinenmotiv sein Lebensthema fand. Von ihm stammt das Aquarell *Bombentrichter*, das 1946 entstand. Im Grunde malte er nach 1945 nur noch Ruinen. Viel Zeit blieb ihm nicht mehr. 1954 ist er gestorben.

Erhart Kästner schreibt in einem Text, der aus dem Jahr 1963 stammt, über den Künstler: »Die Stadt, die angespielt wird, kein Trümmer-Berlin und auch kein geträumtes heiles Berlin, hat allerwenigste Farben. Schöne, unsagbare Stadt, die gemeint ist. Diese Stadt. Jeder kennt sie, keiner ist sie gegangen. Jeder weiß, wenn er sie eines Tages gehen wird, wird es wie altgewohnt sein. Diese Häuser, es fehlt ihnen Körper, diese Fronten, es ist nichts dahinter. Nichthäuser, wie auf Faltbilderbogen … Und so auch die Fenster. Keine Fensterstöcke, keine Scheiben. Hinter solchen Fenstern wird doch nicht gewohnt? Diese Häuser könnten ausgebrannt sein, aber heil die Fassaden und Dächer, also keine Ruinen. Doch hat man gelernt aus Ruinen; man kennt jetzt die Kraft solcher saugender Schlitze, man kennt ihre Sehkraft. Und so auch die Straßen, die Plätze. Keine Menschenseele. Kein Leben. Leergewischt, leergeweht, lieblich … es sind überhaupt nicht die Straßen, es ist ihre Leere gemeint … Sie ist ihm nie zu vergessen, die zärtliche Leere, zu welcher es dieser Maler gebracht hat. Leere Gassen, Hohlwege. Alles ist voller Höhlung und Ansog, alles ist voller Erwartung. Alles quillt über vor Leere, alles ist voller Bedarf.«

Es scheint so, als sei der Schrecken der Stadtzerstörung in die nächste, von Ästhetik geprägte Phase übergegangen. Auch Ruinen können schön sein, wie wir wissen. Und jetzt konnte man sich mit diesem Motiv vollsaugen, sich bilderreich betrinken. Dazu passend, wehten existenzialistische Gedanken aus Paris nach Deutschland und Berlin herüber. Bombentrichter und Ziegelberge bestimmten die Hinterhöfe, aber im Grunde glichen die oft fensterlosen, grauen Berliner Brandwände schon immer leblosen Ruinen. Fließende Übergänge. Schon früher war die Stadt für Werner Heldt ein Ort der Verlassenheit und der unerfüllten Träume. Am Anfang seiner Laufbahn, vor dem Krieg, stand seine Bewunderung für die melancholischen Bilder Maurice Utrillos, jetzt, nach dem Krieg, fand er zu seinem unverwechselbaren, auch nicht vor Abstraktionen zurückschreckenden, lapidaren Stil. Seine schwarzen, kräftigen Linien umgreifen diese Häuser, die Wohngebäude, Hinterhöfe oder auch Ruinen sein konnten. Sie bestimmten das tägliche Bühnenbild, sobald die überlebenden Bewohner an ihre inzwischen reparierten Fenster traten. Man konnte die Ausblicke mit Obstschalen und Gitarren dekorieren, aber keinem Gegenstand war es möglich, der Stadt ihre Melancholie auszutreiben. Selbst die Melonen und Äpfel erinnerten an Bomben, und das runde Klangloch in der Gitarre ähnelt einem Bombenkrater.

Obwohl Werner Heldt während des »Dritten Reiches« nicht emigrierte, wurde er, ähnlich seinem älteren Kollegen Karl Hofer, der ein Jahr nach ihm starb, in den 50er Jahren hochverehrt und bewundert. Seine Bilder trafen den Zeitgeist genau. Von heute aus gesehen, wirken sie wie Bindeglieder zwischen Vorkriegs-, Kriegs- und Nachkriegszeit. Er hält mit seinen Motiven und seiner ästhetisch reduzierten Sparsamkeit eine Tradition aufrecht, die später nur noch im Ostteil Deutschlands weiterlebte.

Im befreiten und befriedeten Westen ging der Kampf avantgardistisch gewagt weiter, die Traditionen zählten nichts mehr, galten als vergiftet und tot. Ab jetzt wurden Objektkörper und Lein-

tic, proudly towering German pavilion and the equally domineering Soviet pavilion stood facing each other.

In a poetic, expressive text Picasso described his feelings and intentions: »… screams of children, screams of women, screams of birds, screams of flowers, screams of trees and stones, screams of bricks, furniture, beds, chairs, curtains, pots, cats and paper, screams of smells that cling to each other, screams of smoke stinging one's shoulder, screams that braise in the big kettle, and of the rain of birds that inundate the sea …«

Represented in the huge painting – it measures 350 x 780 centimeters – is the moment when a bomb strikes a house. All the people, animals, furniture, lamps and walls are thrown into confusion, roar with their mouths wide open, send silent screams into space and will collapse injured or dead. It is a glaring flash exposure, taking everyone unawares, incomprehensible and painful. Picasso's lines divide and mutilate bodies, faces, limbs and objects. Severed heads, arms, hands and feet lie on the ground. A bloodbath. The end. A man clutches his broken sword as he dies. This weapon was no help against the attackers from the sky, it comes from a time when there were bullfights, back in the days when strength was measured body against body. Now the killing

wände behandelt wie Schlachtfelder, wütend malträtiert, zerrissen und zerfetzt. Manche Künstler griffen gar zu den Waffen. Lucio Fontana etwa nahm ein scharfes Messer und zerschnitt damit seine Bildleinwände. Niki de Saint Phalle schoß mit einem Gewehr auf Farbbeutel, die vor Leinwänden hingen. Den Verlauf der Farbspritzer und Abflußbahnen bestimmte der Zufall. Yves Klein tauchte weibliche Nacktmodelle in blaue Farbeimer und zog sie wie geteerte Hexen über seine Riesenleinwände. Jackson Pollock bespritzte seine Bilder wie ein verrückt gewordener Bilderstürmer. Allerdings war er bei diesen Aktionen beides in einer Person: Bilderschöpfer und Bilderzerstörer. Piero Manzoni verpackte die eigenen Darmausscheidungen in Konservendosen, und Wolf Vostell goß Beton über wertvolle Limousinen. Claes Oldenburg baute ganze Tortenburg-Ruinen aus Kunststoff nach und Dieter Rot ließ Beethoven-Schokoladenköpfe verschimmeln. Günther Ücker schlug Nägel in Alltagsgegenstände und Möbel. George Segal verband seine Modelle mit Gipsbinden. Mimmo Rotella zerriß Plakatwände und machte daraus bunte Ruinen-Collagen. Gerhard Richter malte unscharfe Schwarzweißphotos und entstellte die sichtbare Welt in die unzulängliche Wahrnehmung eines Kurzsichtigen. Auch das sind Ruinen, bezogen auf die präzis begrenzten Formen der realen Dinge. Unschärfe gibt es in der Natur vor allem in Nebelzonen und in der Physik (Heisenbergs Unschärferelation!). Nam June Paik widmete sich der Destruktion der Welt durch die Medien. Hanne Darboven übersetzte die Wirklichkeit in einen völlig unverständlichen Wort-DIN-A-4-Blätter-Kosmos, der gerahmt an die Wand gehängt, aussieht wie ein abgenagtes Zeit-Skelett. Christo baute aus leeren Ölfässern Straßensperren in Paris, verpackte klar identifizierbare Dinge in Folie und entzog ihnen damit ihre sichtbaren Oberflächen. Durch Entstellungen, Störungen und Zerstörungen spielten die Künstler mit unseren Realitätswahrnehmungen. Der Aggressionsgrad war dabei sehr unterschiedlich. Gordon Matta-Clark, der später in Abbruchgebäude runde Löcher sägte und sie so in völlig neuartige Ruinen verwandelte, steigerte die Gefährlichkeit, als er 1976, einen Tag vor der Eröffnung der Ausstellung »Idea as Model« in New York, alle Fenster des Ausstellungsgebäudes mit einem Kleinkalibergewehr zerschoß. Natürlich erhielt er daraufhin Hausverbot, auch der Kurator wurde umgehend entlassen. Die Destruktion eines intakten Gebäudes gilt nach wie vor als Straftatbestand, schließlich muß der Wert eines ordentlich erworbenen Immobilienbesitzes durch den funktionierenden Rechtsstaat beschützt werden.

In den Kunstwerken des (ausgehenden) 20. Jahrhunderts wurde die akademische Vollendung im Sinne des 19. Jahrhunderts nicht mehr angestrebt. Die letzte Blüte in dieser Richtung ist den Künstlern der inzwischen untergegangenen totalitären Staaten zuzuschreiben. Arno Breker und

is done quickly by machines, and villages, children, women and men are extinguished with bombs dropped from planes.

Unlike Giorgio de Chirico and Otto Dix, Pablo Picasso chose a completely new subject for his painting. While there are classical battle pictures from all periods – by Altdorfer, Bosch, Rubens, Velasquez, Ingres, Goya – no artist has ever carried the smashing and dismembering of architecture and human bodies to the extremes Picasso did in his *Guernica* painting. Naturally he was able to use his cubist dissection and body exploration techniques, but the exclusive visual focus on destruction, on the world of the victims, was new. Man with a dagger and sword – a power-hungry beast of prey; man with mechanical wea-pons – a cynical killer, a bloodthirsty bringer of calamity. It was hard to imagine a return to a peaceful life after this.

Those who opposed the fascists in this civil war had little chance of survival. As we now know, Franco's troops were victorious and controlled the once so proud country from 1938 until Franco's death in 1975. What is amazing is the fact that General Franco, the dictatorial and authoritarian head of state, kept completely out of the Second World War in spite of the urging of his fascist friends in Germany and Italy.

World War II was over. It had transformed Germany into an apocalyptic landscape of ruins. Werner Heldt, who was born in 1904 in Berlin, is one of the few artists of the 20th century who found his lifelong subject in the motif of the ruin. He created the watercolor *Bomb Crater*, dated 1946. After 1945 he basically painted nothing but ruins. He did not have much time left. He died in 1954.

In a 1963 text, Erhart Kästner writes as follows about the artist: »The city that is alluded to, not a ruined Berlin, nor a dreamed, intact Berlin, has extremely few colors. A beautiful, unutterable city that is intentional. This city. Everyone knows it, none has walked it. Everyone knows that when they walk it one day it will feel like something old and familiar. These houses, they need body, these façades, there's nothing behind them. Non-houses, like something on folding card models … And the same goes for the windows. No windowframes, no panes. Surely no one lives behind such windows? These houses could be gutted, though the façades and roofs are intact, so they aren't ruins. But people have learned from ruins; they now know the power of such sucking slits, they know their visual power. And the same goes for the streets, the squares. Not a living soul. No life. Wiped empty, blown empty, lovely … it's not the streets that are meant at all, it's their emptiness … We must never forget it, the tender emptiness this painter has achieved. Empty streets, narrow passages. All full of hollow and suction, all full of expectation. All overflowing with emptiness, all full of need.«

It seems as though the terror engendered by the destruction of cities has entered another – aesthetic – phase. Ruins, too, can be beautiful, as we know. And now you were able to become saturated with this motif, get drunk on images. In keeping with this, existentialist ideas wafted over to Germany and Berlin from Paris. There were still bomb craters and mounds of bricks in the courtyards, but basically the often windowless, gray fireproof walls of Berlin had always resembled lifeless ruins. Fluid transitions. For Werner Heldt the city had been a place of loneliness and unfulfilled dreams even in earlier times. In the beginning of his career, before the war, he had admired the melancholy pictures of Maurice Utrillo. Now, after the war, he found his way to his unmistakable, lapidary style, which did not shy away even from abstractions. His strong, black lines encompassed these houses, which might be apartment buildings, inner courtyards or ruins. They dominated the daily scenery whenever surviving inhabitants looked out their windows, which had meanwhile been repaired. You could decorate the view with bowls of fruit and guitars, but no object was capable of exorcising the city's melancholy. Even the melons and apples reminded you of bombs, and the round sound hole in the guitar looked like a bomb crater.

Although Werner Heldt did not emigrate during the Third Reich, he was highly esteemed and admired in the '50s, like his older colleague Karl Hofer, who died a year after him. His paintings truly reflected the spirit of the times. From today's perspective they feel like links between the pre-war, war and postwar periods. With his motifs and aesthetically reductionist austerity he upholds a tradition that later survived only in the eastern part of Germany.

In the liberated and pacified West a daring avant-garde continued the battle. Traditions no longer counted, were considered to be poisoned and dead. From now on object bodies and canvases were treated like battlefields, furiously mistreated, ripped apart and slashed. Some artists even took up arms. Lucio Fontana, for instance, took a sharp knife and cut up the canvases of his paintings. Niki de Saint Phalle took a gun and shot at containers of paint hanging in front of canvases. Chance determined where the spatters of paint landed or flowed. Ives Klein ducked nude female models in buckets of blue paint and dragged them like tarred witches across his gi-

Joseph Thorak in Hitlers Deutschland, Carl Milles in Schweden, Carlo Sarrabezolles und Georges Gori in Paris, Vera Muchina in der Sowjetunion. Nach dem Zweiten Weltkrieg überwogen Experimente, Aktionen und ruinös-skizzenhafte Vorschläge, die oft an Gedanken von Künstlern der 1920er Jahre anknüpften. Joseph Beuys, die einflußreichste Künsterpersönlichkeit dieser Zeit, plädierte in seinen Werken für fragmentarisch-rätselhafte Eingriffe in das Leben. Heute sehen die Reste seiner Aktionen aus wie echte Museumsruinen, irrationale, runenhafte Anmerkungen zu Realitäten, die wir so nie gesehen und erlebt haben. Auch die gesprochenen Worte sind konserviert und jetzt, Jahre nach dem Tod des Künstlers, noch abhörbar. Tonruinen, Filmruinen, Photoruinen.

Wer heute in Wien die Untergeschoßräume des Museums Moderner Kunst Stiftung Ludwig durchwandert, begegnet einer ganzen Reihe von österreichischen Ruinenliebhabern. Fast jeder der bekanntgewordenen Wiener Aktionskünstler hat Photo- und Filmspuren hinterlassen, die unter Glasstürzen gezeigt, aussehen wie Modelle klassischer, romantischer Ruinen. Daß bei einigen Aktionskünstlern der Todestrieb manchmal größer war als der Wunsch nach einem glücklichen Leben, macht sie ebenfalls zu Verwandten der alten Romantiker. Rudolph Schwarzkogler etwa brachte sich in jungen Jahren um, nachdem er Photosequenzen seiner ziemlich widerlichen Selbstverstümmelungsaktionen aufgenommen hatte, auch die Hinterlassenschaften von Otto Mühl, Günter Brus und Hermann Nitsch sind nicht weniger blutrünstig und »sittenwidrig«.

Für einen amerikanischen Künstler war Edward Kienholz erstaunlich depressiv. Er verweigerte den positiv-verklärenden Keep-smiling-Blick auf die Realität, den Künstler wie Andy Warhol oder Roy Lichtenstein mit ihren bunten Pop-Art-Bildern bevorzugten. Kienholz war die unkritische Akzeptanz der städtischen Realität, der Kunstgeschichte und Warenwelt fremd, er suchte die düstere Gegenwelt, das Verwesende mitten in seiner Umgebung. Und er fand die Untoten in düsteren Kneipen, – seine Karriere begann er als Kneipier –, billigen Bordells und schmutzigen Abtreibungszimmern. Da saßen nun die mitten im Leben Abgestorbenen, mit Aquarien statt Köpfen, zum Skelett vertrocknet, als kämen sie direkt aus Alfred Hitchcocks Film *Psycho*. Unvergeßlich bleibt mir die Installation einer Vergewaltigungsszene auf der documenta 1972 in Kassel. Um die zentrale Gewalttat herum stand ein Kreis amerikanischer Limousinen, wie wir sie heute kaum noch auf den Straßen sehen. Alle Autos hatten das Licht eingeschaltet, so daß die Besucher genau sehen konnten, was hier geschieht. Kienholz inszenierte wie ein Theater- oder Filmregisseur: direkt, brutal und sehr realistisch. Dabei arbeitete er mit Mitteln, die wir aus Wachsfigurenkabinetten, Jahrmarktsgespensterbahnen oder Kriminalmuseen kennen. Niemand konnte sich der Wirkung dieser Gruselszene entziehen. Sie grub sich tief in das Langzeitgedächtnis ein.

Es war nicht verwunderlich, daß dieser todessüchtige amerikanische Künstler auf dem Höhepunkt seiner Karriere zusammen mit seiner Frau nach Berlin übersiedelte. In Deutschland entdeckte er auch seine Vorgänger, darunter den untergangsbegeisterten Komponisten Richard Wagner, dem er einige seiner späten Objekte widmete.

Landart-Künstler wie Walter De Maria, Michael Heizer und Robert Smithson bezogen in ihre temporäre Installationen den Verfall bewußt mit ein. Ihre Objekte existieren nur noch auf Photos und in Filmen fort. Kaum ein Besucher war Zeuge der realen Aufbausituationen. In den Galerien wurden ausschließlich die gezeichneten Konzepte und das photographische Abbildungsmaterial der Aktionen, die in abgelegen Regionen Amerikas stattfanden, gezeigt. Besonders Robert Smithson gilt heute als gern zitiertes Landart-Genie. Das liegt vor allem auch daran, daß er in jungen Jahren (1973 mit 36) den Tod fand, als er mit dem Helikopter in seine eigene, damals entstehende Landart-Arbeit *Spiral Jetty*, eine flache, in das Wasser des großen Salzsees von Utah hinausreichende Spirale, stürzte. Sein Tod ist nur vergleichbar mit dem von Mark Rothko, dem berühmtesten aller amerikanischen Farbfeldmaler, der am Morgen des 25. Februar 1970 in einer zweimal zwei Meter großen Blutlache aufgefunden wurde. Er hatte sich in der Nacht im Badezimmer seines New Yorker Ateliers die Pulsadern aufgeschnitten und lag als Leiche im geronnenen, roten Farbfeld seines eigenen Blutes.

Robert Smithson liebte das Zerstören von Gebäuden. Bereits 1970 ließ er von einem Lkw Erdmassen solange auf einen Holzschuppen karren, bis dieser unter der Last zusammenbrach. Er wollte im Zeitraffer den normalen Verfall dieses Gebäudes simulieren. Natürlich wurde die Aktion in Photos und Filmen dokumentiert. Smithson verfaßte auch interessante Texte, die seine künstlerischen Aktivitäten philosophisch reflektieren. In einem Essay über die »Sedimentierung des Bewußtseins« schrieb er: »Die Erde und das menschliche Bewußtsein werden unablässig erodiert, Gedankenströme tragen abstrakte Dämme ab, Gehirnwellen unterspülen Denkklippen, Ideen verwittern zu Steinen des Nichtwissens, und konzeptuelle Kristallisierungen zerfallen zu Ablagerungen sandiger Vernunft.«

gantic canvases. Jackson Pollock poured and dripped paint on his pictures like a crazed iconoclast. Of course, during these actions he was both the creator of pictures and their destroyer rolled into one. Piero Manzoni packed his own excreta in cans, and Wolf Vostell poured concrete over expensive limousines. Claes Oldenburg built models of entire cake fortress ruins from plastic and Dieter Rot let chocolate heads of Beethoven go moldy. Günther Ücker drove nails into everyday objects and furniture. George Segal wrapped his models in plaster bandages. Mimmo Rotella tore up advertising posters and made them into colorful ruin collages. Gerhard Richter painted blurred black-and-white photographs and distorted the visible world into one inadequately perceived by the nearsighted. These, too, are ruins, in relation to the precisely defined forms of real things. In nature lack of definition exists mainly in fog zones and in physics (Heisenberg's uncertainty principle!). Nam June Paik devoted himself to the destruction of the world through the media. Hanne Darboven translated reality into a completely incomprehensible cosmos of DIN-A4-size-sheets of paper, which, hung framed on the wall, looks like a gnawed skeleton of time. Christo built roadblocks in Paris out of empty oil barrels, and packaged clearly identifiable things in foil, thus depriving them of their visible surfaces. By means of distortions, disruptions and destructions, the artists played with our perceptions of reality. In their work, the degree of aggression varied a great deal. Gordon Matta-Clark, who later sawed round holes in buildings slated for demolition and thus transformed them into a totally new type of ruins, raised the level of danger when, in 1976, one day before the opening of the exhibition »Idea as Model« in New York, he shot out all the windows of the exhibition building with a small-bore rifle. Naturally he was then banned from the building, and the curator, too, was promptly fired. The destruction of an intact building is still considered a criminal offense – after all, the value of regularly purchased real estate must be protected by a functioning state.

Almost all the works of art of the (latter part of the) 20th century no longer strived for the kind of academic perfection that had been prevalent in the 19th century. The last upswings in this direction were undertaken by artists in now-defunct totalitarian states, Arno Breker and Joseph Thorak in Hitler's Germany, Carl Milles in Sweden, Carlo Sarrabezolles and Georges Gori in Paris, Vera Mukhina in the Soviet Union. Predominant after World War II were experiments, actions and ruinously sketchy proposals that often picked up where artists in the 1920s had left off. In his works, Joseph Beuys, the most influential artistic personality of this period, pleaded for fragmentary, enigmatic interventions in life. Today the remains of his actions look like genuine museum ruins, irrational, runelike footnotes to realities we have never seen or experienced this way. His spoken words have also been preserved and can still be listened to now, years after the artist's death. Sound ruins, film ruins, photo ruins.

Wandering through the basement rooms of the Modern Museum of Vienna today, one encounters a whole series of Austrian ruin enthusiasts. Almost every one of the Viennese Action artists who became well known left photographic and cinematic traces which, displayed under glass, look like models of classical, romantic ruins. The fact that in some Action artists the death instinct was sometimes stronger than the wish for a happy life also shows their kinship to the Romantics of old. Rudolph Schwarzkogler, for instance, killed himself while still young after taking sequences of photographs of his rather repulsive self-mutilation actions. The artistic legacies of Otto Mühl, Günter Brus and Hermann Nitsch are also no less bloodthirsty and »immoral«.

For an American artist, Edward Kienholz was amazingly depressed. He rejected the positive, transfiguring, keep-smiling view of reality preferred by artists like Andy Warhol or Roy Lichtenstein with their colorful Pop Art pictures. The uncritical acceptance of urban reality, art history and the world of consumerism was alien to Kienholz. He looked for the bleak counter-world, the decay in the world around him. And he found the undead in dingy bars – he began his career as a bar owner –, cheap bordellos and dirty abortion rooms. There they sat – numbed in the midst of life, with aquariums in lieu of heads, mummified into skeletons as though they came directly out of Alfred Hitchcock's film *Psycho*. I still cannot forget the installation of a rape scene at documenta 1972 in Kassel. Surrounding the central act of violence there was a circle of the kind of American limousines we hardly ever see on the streets today. All the headlights were switched on, so that visitors could see clearly what was going on. Kienholz staged his installations like a theater or film director, directly, brutally and very realistically. He was working with methods that are familiar to us from waxworks, tunnels of horror or crime museums. No one could help reacting to this scene of horror. It carved itself deeply into a viewer's long-term memory.

To nobody's surprise this death-obsessed American artist, together with his wife, moved to Berlin at the peak of his career. In Germany he also discovered his precursors, among them the

108. George Segal, *Cinema*, 1963, Albright-Knox Art Gallery, Buffalo, NY. Die Pompeji-Abguß-Menschen kehren zurück.
109. Arnulf Rainer, *Female*, aus der FKK-Serie, 2008. Ein Strichvorhang beginnt die körperliche Nacktheit zu verdecken und damit auszulöschen.

108. George Segal, *Cinema*, 1963, Albright-Knox Art Gallery, Buffalo, NY. The Pompeii cast figures are coming back.
109. Arnulf Rainer, *Female*, from the nudism series, 2008. A dash curtain starts to cover the physical nude, deleting it in this way.

Andere Künstler, die Spurensucher, sammelten ebenfalls in den 70er Jahren fragmentarische Dinge in der Landschaft und stellten sie in Museen aus. Am bekanntesten sind in diesem Zusammenhang die Steinkreise von Richard Long. Auch sie sind »Landschaftsruinen« mit autobiographischem Hintergrund. In Deutschland wurde Nikolaus Lang, der eine Ausbildung als Holzschnitzer in Oberammergau hinter sich hatte, mit seinen Spureninszenierungen bekannt. Dorothee von Windheim produzierte zur gleichen Zeit Abdrücke von alten Wänden mit all ihren Schrammen und Flecken. Wie gehäutete Tiere hingen die Raumfelle später an den Museumswänden. Christian Boltanski und Raffael Rheinsberg sammelten Alltagsdinge und legten damit Dingfelder und Erinnerungsarchive an.

Eine ganz andere Art von Ruinen schuf Daniel Spoerri. Er konservierte abgegessene Tische und hängte sie an Ausstellungswände, auch sie Erinnerungsruinen an fröhliche Abende, an gelebte, vergangene Zeit. Arman und Cesar dagegen gossen Gegenstände und Geräte des Alltags in Kunststoffblöcke ein, als seien sie von Bernstein umfangen. Wie leuchtende Architekturruinen sehen Dan Flavins Neonstrukturen aus. Sie kriechen durch heutige Museumsräume, als würden sie eine Welt beschreiben, die es vielleicht nie gab. Lichtarchitekturen, Lichterinnerungen, Zäune und Dome der fiktiven Art.

Ganz anders erscheinen die Kunstruinen von John Chamberlain. In fröhlicher Umdeutung der allgemeinen Meinung nimmt dieser amerikanische »Bildhauer« einfach kaputte Autokarosserien und schichtet sie zu Skulpturen auf, ganz so, als hätten sie es verdient. In Wirklichkeit waren die Autos natürlich in ihrem funktionierenden Zustand viel attraktiver und schöner. Interessant wäre eine direkte Gegenüberstellung mit klassischen Skulpturen, der *Venus von Milo* etwa, dem *Apollo von Belvedere* oder der *Laokoongruppe*. Natürlich würden hier auch naturgetreue Gipsabgüsse genügen. Daneben sind als Tonspur die blumigen Erläuterungen Winckelmanns zu hören.

Wahrscheinlich, stellen wir fest, enthalten die modernen Plastiken viel subversiven und aggressiven Humor, den wir auf diese Weise freilegen könnten. Das antike Pathos müßte nicht unbedingt als Sieger aus diesem ästhetisch-geistigen »Boxkampf« hervorgehen. Wir, die Nachgeborenen, lieben offensichtlich auch das Abseitige, das Häßliche, das Zerstörte, das Unvollkommene und damit das Ruinöse.

Die früher angestrebte Vollkommenheit ist wahrscheinlich durch den Mißbrauch der faschistischen Diktatoren endgültig zum Thema der Vergangenheit geworden. Wir leben in einer Zeit der Neudefinitionen, der Fragen und der Suche. Die hehren Ideale der von Menschen gemachten

110. Joseph Beuys, *Das Ende des 20. Jahrhunderts*, 1983, Pinakothek der Moderne, München.
111. Dan Flavin, Neon-Installation in der Pinakothek der Moderne, München.

110. Joseph Beuys, *Das Ende des 20. Jahrhunderts* (the end of the 20th century), 1983, Pinakothek der Moderne, Munich.
111. Dan Flavin, Neon-Installation in the Pinakothek der Moderne, Munich.

composer Richard Wagner, another artist who was passionate about death and destruction, to whom he dedicated a few of his late installations.

Land art exponents such as Walter De Maria, Michael Heizer and Robert Smithson deliberately included decay in their temporary installations. Their objects now exist only in photographs and films. Hardly a single visitor had witnessed the actual creation of the situations. What was displayed in the galleries were only the sketched concepts and the photographic images of the actions, which took place in remote regions of America. Robert Smithson in particular is considered to be a land art genius who is often quoted. One of the main reasons for this is that he met his death while young (in 1973 at age 36) when the helicopter he was flying crashed into his own land art work, then in progress – »Spiral Jetty«, a flat spiral that extended into the Great Salt Lake in Utah. His death can only be compared to that of Mark Rothko, the most famous of all American color-field painters, who was found on the morning of 25 February 1970 in a 6 by 6 foot pool of blood. During the night he had slashed his arteries in the bathroom of his New York studio, and his body lay in the congealed red color field of his own blood.

Robert Smithson loved destroying buildings. Back in 1970 he had truckloads of dirt dumped on a woodshed until it collapsed under the weight. By means of time-lapse photography he wanted to simulate the normal dilapidation of this building. Naturally the action was documented in photographs and films. Smithson also wrote interesting texts that reflect his artistic activities philosophically. In an essay about the »sedimentation of the mind« he said: »One's mind and the earth are in a constant state of erosion, mental rivers wear away abstract banks, brain waves undermine cliffs of thought, ideas decompose into stones of unknowing, and conceptual crystallizations break apart into deposits of gritty reason …«

Other artists, the *Spurensucher* (Seekers of Traces), also collected things in the landscape in the 1970s and exhibited them in museums. The best known of these are the stone circles of Richard Long. They too are »landscape ruins« with an autobiographical background. In Germany Nikolaus Lang, who had been trained as a wood carver in Oberammergau, became known for his installations of traces. At the same time, Dorothee von Windheim produced impressions of old walls with all their scratches and stains. Like skinned animals the space skins later hung on the walls of a museum. Christian Boltanski and Raffael Rheinsberg collected everyday objects and assembled fields of objects and memory archives with them.

Daniel Spoerri created quite a different type of ruins. He preserved tables at which a meal had been eaten and hung them from exhibition walls – they too were memory ruins recalling merry evenings, lived, past time. Arman and Cesar, on the other hand, embedded everyday objects and utensils in plastic blocks, as if they were trapped in amber. Don Flavin's neon structures look like

»Schönheit« haben wir in die Bereiche der Mode, der Werbung, des Tourismus, der Architektur und des Auto-Designs verdrängt, verlagert, ausgebürgert. Als verbindendes Medium bleibt uns die »Naturschönheit« erhalten. Der Sonnenauf- und Sonnenuntergang, Nebelstimmungen an Seen und im Gebirge, herbstliche Laubwälder und rauschende Palmenhaine, sonnige Sandstrände und sanfte Windgeräusche … So gesehen muß der Tourismus mit seinen romantisch-verklärten Zielen zu einem der Hauptsieger des Umwandlungsprozesses erklärt werden. Heute ist es möglich, paradiesische Inseln (mit romantischen Ruinen und archäologischen Verwesungszonen) tatsächlich aufzusuchen, wenn auch nur zeitlich begrenzt und in Reservaten geschützt.

Es gab in den letzten 100 Jahren auch Künstler, die noch weiter in die Kulturgeschichte zurückblickten als etwa Otto Dix. Der rumänisch-französische Bildhauer Constantin Brancusi arbeitete in seinen wichtigsten Skulpturen ähnlich reduziert-archaisierend wie frühe Steinzeitkünstler. Pablo Picasso, Georges Braque und viele expressionistische Maler interessierten sich für den Primitivismus afrikanischer Masken und Körperfetische. Paul Klee verfolgte ähnliche Spuren, zurück zum Einfachen, Kindlichen, Unverstellten, in ein vorzivilisatorisches Traumreich, ins Unterbewußtsein wie es Sigmund Freud und C. G. Jung erforscht haben. Der 1935 in Dresden geborene A. R. Penck malt und zeichnet seit 1960 Strichmännchen, die auch von steinzeitlichen Höhlenmalern stammen könnten. Ulrich Rückriem arbeitet in seinen Steinsetzungen nach dem Prinzip der Stonehenge- und Carnac-Erbauer. Auch Walter Pichler und Hannsjörg Voth spüren mit ihren Arbeiten den Gefühlswelten und Traditionen animistischer Kulturen nach.

Diese Werke, die sich der Kategorie »Ruinen« nicht eindeutig zuordnen lassen, wollen unfertig, grob und mythisch sein, nahe der Natur und ihren Zerfallsprozessen. Es gibt auch Ruinenkünstler, die beide Welten – Gegenwart und Vergangenheit – miteinander verbinden wollen: die archäologischen Spurensucher. Vor allem die beiden Franzosen Anne und Patrick Poirier sind hier zu nennen. Angeregt durch einen längeren Aufenthalt in Rom von 1967 bis 1971 in der französischen Akademie Villa Medici bauten sie aus Holzkohle, Steinen, Ton und Wasser antike Ruinenstädte nach, ganz so, als seien sie moderne, wissenschaftliche Archäologen. Aber ihre Ruinenstädte gab es nie wirklich, sie waren freie Erfindungen ihrer Phantasie. Über ihre 11 x 6 Meter große Installation *Ville construction* aus dem Jahr 1973, die aus gebranntem Ton besteht und sich mit der antiken und heutigen Stadt Ostia befaßt, haben sie den folgenden, sehr poetischen Text geschrieben.

112. Claes Oldenburg, *Houseball*, 1995–1997, place at the Mauerstraße, Berlin.
113. John Chamberlain, Automobile Scrap Sculpture, Pinakothek der Moderne, Munich.
New ruin forms: waste, garbage, machine and car scrap.

glowing architectural ruins. Inhabiting modern exhibit spaces they seem to describe a world that may never have existed. Light architecture, light memories, fences and cathedrals of a fictitious kind.

The art ruins of John Chamberlain have an altogether different appearance. Cheerfully reinterpreting public opinion, this American »sculptor« simply takes junk auto bodies and piles them up into sculptures, just as if they deserved it. In reality, of course, the cars were much more attractive and beautiful when they were functional. It would be interesting to juxtapose them directly with classical sculptures such as the *Venus de Milo*, the *Apollo Belvedere* or the *Laocoön Group*. Naturally here realistic plaster casts would be sufficient. As a background soundtrack, exhibit visitors would hear the flowery elucidations of Winckelmann ….

Probably, we realize, the modern sculptures contain a great deal of subversive and aggressive humor that we could lay bare this way. There is no reason why the pathos of classical antiquity should emerge as the winner in this aesthetic, intellectual »boxing match«. We who belong to a later generation obviously also love what is esoteric, ugly, destroyed, imperfect and thus ruinous.

The perfection for which artists strived in the old days has no doubt definitively become a thing of the past, thanks to its abuse by fascist dictators. We live in a time of redefinitions, questions and searching. We have ousted, shifted, exiled the noble ideals of man-made »beauty« to the realms of fashion, advertising, tourism, architecture and auto design. We still have »natural beauty« to connect us. Sunrise and sunset, misty moods by lakes and in the mountains, the colors of fall woods and rustling groves of palm trees, sunny beaches and the gentle sound of breezes … Seen from this perspective, tourism and its romantic, transfigured destinations must be declared one of the chief winners in this process of transformation. Today – as long as one has the financial means – an actual visit to paradisic islands (with romantic ruins and archaeological zones of decay) could not be easier, though only for a limited period of time and restricted to protected preserves.

During the last 100 years, there have also been artists who looked even further back in cultural history than, say, Otto Dix. The Romanian French sculptor Constantin Brancusi, in his most important sculptures, worked with the same kind of reductionist, archaic forms as early Stone Age artists. Pablo Picasso, Georges Braque and many expressionist painters were interested in the primitivism of African masks and fetishes. Paul Klee followed a similar trail, back to something simple, childlike, genuine, into a realm of dreams that predates civilization, into the subconscious – a realm explored by Sigmund Freud and C. G. Jung. A. R. Penck, who was born in 1935 in Dresden, has been painting and drawing little stick figures since 1960. They, too, could have

114. Anne und Patrick Poirier, *Ville construction*, 1967–1971. Künstliches Ausgrabungsmodell aus Holzkohle, Stein und Wasser.

114. Anne und Patrick Poirier, *Ville construction*, 1967–1971. Artificial excavation model made of wood charcoal, stone and water.

»Begrabenes Haus, angehaltene Zeit.
Es scheint, als hätten die Kräfte der Zerstörung niemals aufgehört, sich auszubreiten.
Ostia entvölkert sich langsam
Ostia wird zu einem brachen und wüsten Ort,
man gräbt, man wühlt, um Erinnerungen wiederzufinden; in der feuchten Erde,
die die Natur durchdrungen hat, erscheinen der Stein, Ruinen in der Stille;
zwei Stille, die Flugzeuge …
Der Lärm der Schaufeln: man versucht, das Aufgelöste wieder zusammenzufügen.
Die Stunden gehen dahin, die Zeit hält an, Schweigen.
Sie starben an Hunger, Malaria, an der Stille.
Die Zeit, diese Zeit, ist stehengeblieben.
Ein Ruinenfeld wurde fixiert, wie die Zeit, in dieser verbotenen Zone,
von Stacheldraht umgeben; privilegierte Zone, bewacht während des Tages und der Nacht;
Sie haben die Häuser mit großem Lärm zerstört, die Menschen haben sich verstreut,
die rosa Stadt löschte aus, die Stadt löst sich auf, Tod.
Die Erde steigt, die Zeit fließt vorüber.
Sie vergessen.«

Das französische Künstlerehepaar bevorzugte vollkommen abgedunkelte, schwarze Räume für die Aufstellung ihrer Ruinenlandschaften. Nur minimale Lichtquellen beleuchteten die Szene gespenstisch. Ich erinnere mich daran, wie sehr ich 1977 von ihrer Installation auf der Documenta 6 in Kassel beeindruckt war. Leider kenne ich kein Museum in Deutschland, in dem ein Werk dieser Kunstarchäologen vertreten wäre.

Auch Anselm Kiefer gehört hierher. Seine Blei-, Erd- und Strohbilder lassen sich ebenfalls als Ruinenlandschaften und Ruinenskulpturen interpretieren. Sie zitieren historische Freignisse, ohne

246

been drawn by Stone Age cave painters. Ulrich Rückriem, in his arrangements of stones, works according to the principle of the people who built Stonehenge and Carnac. Walter Pichler and Hansjörg Voth also explore the emotional worlds and traditions of animist cultures in their work.

These artworks, which cannot be unambiguously categorized as »ruins«, are intended to be unfinished, rough and mythical, close to nature and its processes of decay. There are also ruin artists who want to connect both worlds – the present and the past: the archaeological seekers of traces, represented primarily by the two French artists Anne and Patrick Poirier. Inspired by a lengthy stay in Rome from 1967 to 1971 in the French Academy in Villa Medici, they recreated ancient ruined cities with charcoal, stones, clay and water, exactly as though they were modern, scientifically trained archaeologists. But their ruined cities had never really existed: They were the free inventions of their imagination. They wrote the following, very poetic text about their 11 x 6-meter installation *Ville construction*, dated 1973, made from fired clay and concerned with the ancient and present-day town of Ostia:

»Buried house, arrested time.
It seems as if the forces of destruction had never stopped spreading.
Ostia is slowly becoming deserted.
Ostia is becoming fallow and desolate,
people dig, they burrow in the ground to recover memories; in the damp soil
that nature has penetrated, stone appears, ruins in the silence;
two silent presences, the planes …
The noise of shovels: they're trying to join together what was dispersed once more.
The hours go by, time stops, silence.
They died of hunger, malaria, of the silence.
Time, this time, stands still.
A field of ruins was immobilized, like time, in this forbidden zone,
surrounded by barbed wire; privileged zone, guarded by day and night;
they destroyed the houses with much noise, the people dispersed,
the pink town went out like a light, the town disintegrated, death.
The earth rises, time flows past.
They forget.«

The French art couple preferred totally darkened, black rooms for displaying their ruin landscapes. Only minimal light sources eerily illuminated the scene. I remember how impressed I was by their installation at Documenta 1977 in Kassel. Unfortunately I know no museum in Germany in which the work of these art archaeologists is represented.

Anselm Kiefer, too, belongs here. His lead, earth and straw images can also be interpreted as ruin landscapes and ruin sculptures. They quote historical events without directly representing them. Handwritten comments remind the viewer of what happened long ago. The true traces have long since been covered over and decayed; sometimes obscure, enigmatic allusions suffice to create a romantic atmosphere of irrational poetry. At his last large exhibition in the Grand Palais in Paris Kiefer had huge concrete towers built which he subsequently demolished. The result: a ruin landscape that is reminiscent of earthquake and war zones.

In one of Kiefer's most famous paintings, *Deutsche Geisteshelden* (*Germany's Spiritual Heroes),* one can see an old wooden attic in which the former heroes are made present as bowls containing flickering fires along the vertical beams that subdivide the space. Inscriptions in antiquated script give their names. The arrangement resembles the walls of the memorial in Klenze's Valhalla. Only here, in Kiefer's work, the noble marble of yore has disappeared. History with its dubious constructs has been relegated to the attic (the brain or a loft people rarely enter?). Wood and fire, however, make dangerous bedfellows. A mere breath of wind would be enough to make the whole lot go up in flames. The eternal lights of the myths and errors are a constant danger. In defense, Kiefer writes that it is a mistake to think that »… because the Nazis used – or rather, controlled – the myths, we must now get rid of them. But that is wrong. That's the same as the delusion that you can defeat fascism by blowing up buildings.«

The fact is that Anselm Kiefer was the first artist of the postwar period who dared to go back and mine the contaminated terrain of Germanic myths once more. That is why Werner Spies in his 2009 Paulskirche laudation – the occasion was the presentation of the »Peace Prize of the German Book Trade« – rightly called Kiefer an »incendiary«. Kiefer, he said, was »playing« with contaminated material, with toxic and enormously flammable mental images.

sie direkt darzustellen. Handschriftliche Bemerkungen erinnern an das einmal Geschehene. Die wahren Spuren sind längst verweht und verwest, manchmal genügen dunkle rätselhafte Andeutungen, und es entsteht eine romantische Atmosphäre irrationaler Poesie. Für seine letzte große Ausstellung im Pariser Grand Palais ließ Kiefer riesige Betontürme aufbauen, die er anschließend zertrümmerte. Das Ergebnis: eine Ruinenlandschaft, die an Erdbeben- und Kriegszonen erinnert.

Auf einem der berühmtesten Gemälde Kiefers, *Deutsche Geisteshelden*, ist ein alter, hölzerner Dachstuhl zu sehen, in dem die einstigen Heroen als Schalen mit flackernden Feuern entlang der senkrechten, raumgliedernden Balken zugegen sind. Dazu nennen altertümliche Schriften deren Namen. Die Anordnung gleicht den Denkmalswänden in Klenzes Walhalla. Nur hier, bei Kiefer, ist der edle Marmor von einst verschwunden, die Geschichte mit ihren fragwürdigen Gedankengebäuden wurde auf den Dachboden (in das Gehirn oder in das abseitige Depot, den selten betretenen Speicher?) verdrängt. Allerdings bilden Holz und Feuer eine gefährliche Einheit. Ein Windhauch würde genügen, um die ganze Herrlichkeit in Flammen aufgehen zu lassen. Die ewigen Lichter der Mythen und Irrtümer bilden eine ständig anwesende Gefahr. Kiefer schreibt verteidigend, es sei ein Irrtum zu glauben »… weil die Nazis die Mythen benutzt – man muß sagen bewirtschaftet – haben, müsse man sie nun verschwinden lassen. Das ist aber falsch. Das ist dasselbe wie der Irrglaube, durch Sprengen von Gebäuden den Faschismus besiegen zu können.«

Tatsache ist, daß Anselm Kiefer der erste Künstler der Nachkriegszeit war, der es wagte, im verseuchten germanischen Mythensumpf erneut zu graben. Deswegen nennt ihn Werner Spies 2009 in seiner Laudatio in der Frankfurter Paulskirche, anläßlich der Verleihung des »Friedenspreises des deutschen Buchhandels«, zu Recht einen »Brandstifter«. Kiefer »zündele« mit kontaminiertem Material, mit giftigen und enorm brandgefährdeten Gedankenbildern.

Alle zuletzt aufgeführten Künstler zeigen kein Interesse an der Zukunft, an Utopien. Manchmal scheint mir, als würden sie – neben ihren privaten Verletzungen – lediglich ruinöse Vergangenheiten aufarbeiten. Anselm Kiefer – etwas verspätet – die Nazizeit mit ihrer Vorliebe für germanische Mythen und dunkle Schlachten und Edward Kienholz die gescheiterten Träume Amerikas.

Seit der letzten Kassler Documenta hat sich in diesen Kreis ein chinesischer Künstler eingereiht, der mit den Verirrungen und antidemokratischen Unterdrückungen seines Heimatlandes hart ins Gericht geht: Ai Weiwei. Berühmt wurde er vor allem mit einem Turmgebäude aus alten chinesischen Holztüren, das er auf der letzten Documenta in Kassel im Freien errichtete und das noch in der Nacht vor der Eröffnung in sich zusammenbrach. Ai Weiwei schaute sich am Morgen danach den Trümmerhaufen an und stellte nüchtern-amüsiert fest: »So sieht mein Werk noch viel besser aus!« Die Ruinenfassung seines Turms entsprach wohl mehr seiner Welt- und Chinasicht als das aufrecht stehende Gebäude.

Im Münchner Haus der Kunst war diese Tür-Turm-Ruine im Dezember und Januar 2009/10 ausgestellt. Ich habe das Werk dort gesehen und war beeindruckt von seiner destruktiven Naturhaftigkeit. Besonders hier, im monumentalen Nazibau von Paul Ludwig Troost, entfaltete es eine subversive Wirkung, die jeden Betrachter in ihren Bann zog. In Wandtexten gab Ai Weiwei seine Liebe zur Natur bekannt und sprach davon, daß er nicht wie die westlichen Künstler gegen die Natur, sondern mit ihr arbeiten wolle.

Im Bereich der Architektur entwickelte sich in den Jahren zwischen 1980 und 2010 der Dekonstruktivismus, eine Ruinen- und Erdbebenarchitektur, die mehrere Wurzeln besitzt: den russischen Konstruktivismus, die Befreiung aus den Zwängen der Postmoderne und damit aus dem modernen Historismus und die Revolution der neuen Medien. Hauptvertreter sind Frank Gehry, Zaha Hadid, Daniel Libeskind, Rem Koolhaas und Coop Himmelb(l)au. In ihren theoretischen Texten umkreisen diese Architekten eher die Leere, das Offene, weniger das Wild-Barocke, Expressive oder gar Zerstörte. Sie empfinden die heutigen Städte als verplant, wuchernd und (ruinös) zerfetzt.

Die Architekten der Wiener Gruppe Coop Himmelb(l)au, die bei ihrer Gründung in den 1960er Jahren bewußt an Pop-Formationen wie den »Beatles« oder den »Rolling Stones« anknüpfen wollten, formulierten in einem Vortrag aus dem Jahr 1984 ihre damaligen Gedanken folgendermaßen: »… Offene Architektur. Wer oder wie oder was ist das? Oder: wie sollen wir denken, planen, bauen in einer von Tag zu Tag zerfetzteren Welt? Sollen wir Angst haben vor dieser Zerfetztheit, sie verdrängen, und uns in die heile Welt der Architektur flüchten?

Es gibt sie nicht mehr, die heile Welt der Architektur, und es wird sie auch nie wieder geben … Es gibt keine Wahrheit und keine Schönheit in der Architektur.

Wir glauben daher nicht den Stadtrekonstrukteuren, die uns ins 19. Jahrhundert versetzen wollen, und dabei – und das ist kein Zufall – immer nur von Schließung sprechen. Von Schließung des Blocks, von Schließung des Straßenraums, von Schließung des Platzes … Komplexität ist

Neither of the artists last mentioned shows any interest in the future, in utopias. Sometimes I have the feeling that they are merely processing not just their own private traumas, but ruinous past histories. Anselm Kiefer – somewhat belatedly – deals with the Nazi period and its predilection for Germanic myths and dark battles, and Edward Kienholz processes the failed dreams of America.

Since the last documenta exhibition in Kassel a Chinese artist has joined the circle: Ai Weiwei is highly critical of the aberrations and antidemocratic oppression of his native country. He gained fame primarily for a tower building made of old Chinese wooden doors that he erected outdoors at the last documenta in Kassel and that collapsed upon itself the night before the opening. The next morning Ai Weiwei took a look at the heap of rubble and observed soberly and with amusement: »This way my work looks even better!« The ruined version of his tower was probably more in keeping with his view of the world and of China than the erect building.

This tower ruin of doors was exhibited at the Munich Haus der Kunst in December and January 2009/10. I saw the work there and was impressed by its destructive naturalness. Particularly here, in Paul Ludwig Troost's monumental Nazi building, it unfolded a subversive effect that fascinated everyone who saw it. In wall texts Ai Weiwei spoke of his love of nature and said that he did not want to work against nature, like Western artists, but with it.

In the realm of architecture, in the years between 1980 and 2010, there developed deconstructivism, an architecture of ruins and earthquakes that is rooted in several movements: Russian constructivism, the liberation from the constraints of Postmodernism and thus from modern historicism and the revolution of the new media. Its main representatives are Frank Gehry, Zaha Hadid, Daniel Libeskind, Rem Koolhaas and Coop Himmelb(l)au. In their theoretical texts these architects tend to circle emptiness, open space, rather than what is wild and baroque, expressive or even destroyed. They feel the cities of today are poorly planned, sprawling and (ruinously) dismembered.

In a 1984 lecture the architects of the Viennese group Coop Himmelb(l)au, who at their founding in the '60s wanted to deliberately continue in the tradition of pop groups such as the »Beatles« or the »Rolling Stones«, formulated their ideas at the time as follows: »… Open architecture. Who or how or what is that? Or: How are we to think, plan, build in a world that is becoming more segmented from day to day? Should we be afraid of this segmentation, repress the thought of it and escape into the unscathed world of architecture?

… The unscathed world of architecture no longer exists, and will never exist again … There is no truth and no beauty in architecture.

Therefore we do not believe in the urban reconstructors who want to put us back in the 19th century and at the same time – and this is not pure chance – always speak of closing. Of closing

unser Ziel. Architektur, wie sie im 19. Jahrhundert vorgegeben war, ist überholt. Wir haben zu einer Komplexität zu kommen, welche die Mannigfaltigkeit der Weltgesellschaft spiegelt … Es ist nur möglich, verwobene räumliche Systeme zu schaffen, indem man umgebenden Druck los wird. Um Komplexität in der Architektur zu erreichen, muß man etliche Dinge loswerden: erstens muß man architektonische, historische Gesetze loswerden, zweitens muß man aufhören über die Bauherren nachzudenken, drittens muß man aufhören, zuviel über das Geld nachzudenken, das man verdient, und letztlich muß man aufhören, über die Kosten nachzudenken.«

Rem Koolhaas umkreist die Öffnung und den (ruinösen) Zerfall noch eindeutiger: »Wichtiger als die Gestaltung der Städte ist heute und in naher Zukunft die Gestaltung ihres Zerfalls. Nur durch den revolutionären Prozeß des Ausradierens, der Errichtung von »Freiheitszonen«, in denen alle Architekturgesetze außer Kraft gesetzt sind, wird eines der unlösbaren Probleme städtischen Lebens aufgehoben sein: die Spannung zwischen Programm und Inhalt … Das Projekt für Amsterdam, aber mehr noch für La Villette und die Expo sind Versuche, die Qualität des Nichts als Herz der Metropole zu formulieren. Die Leere in der Metropole ist nicht sprachlos, sondern jeder Leerraum innerhalb einer bestehenden städtischen Struktur kann für die Programme genutzt werden, die interessante, heutige Aktivitäten ermöglichen … Die Beständigkeit, die selbst in der frivolsten Architektur steckt und die Instabilität der Metropole sind unvereinbar.«

Diffuse Statements, die zwar aggressiv-revolutionär klingen, in Wirklichkeit jedoch fast alle Möglichkeiten – mit Ausnahme vielleicht der historisierenden – offenlassen. Waren die Äußerungen der Architekten während der Postmoderne in der Zeit vor 1980 noch wesentlich harmloser, geschichtsverliebter, humaner und verspielter, kam jetzt ein neuer Ton auf. Ob er mehr mit Zerstörung und weniger mit Aufbau zu tun hat, ist schwer zu sagen. Immerhin lautete die Devise der Architektengruppe Coop-Himmelb(l)au zu Beginn ihrer Karriere: »Architektur muß brennen!« Es scheint so, als wolle eine neue Generation von Architekten die bisherigen Brutalitäten der modernen Stadtentwicklungen ihrerseits mit Aggressionen beantworten. Hier gleich von »Krieg« zu sprechen, wäre gewiß übertrieben, aber eine gewisse Kampfbereitschaft ist durchaus zu bemerken. Warum Leere, Überdruck und Chaos mit den gleichen Motiven, frei nach der biblischen Devise »Auge um Auge, Zahn um Zahn«, beantwortet werden muß, bleibt mehr als unklar. Auf jeden Fall werden zerfetzte, halbzerstörte Gebäude und dynamisierte Funktionsruinen dabei herauskommen. James Stirling begnügte sich bei der berühmten Stuttgarter Staatsgalerie noch mit einem harmlos-kleinen Ruinenwitz: Am Fenster in der Sockelzone scheinen einige Steinquader herausgebrochen zu sein und liegen locker verstreut auf der schmalen Wiese davor. Bei Gehry sind die Erdbeben schon gewaltiger, da wirken die Gebäudeteile am Guggenheim-Museum in Bilbao so durcheinandergewirbelt, als hätten alle Naturgewalten – Erdbeben, Stürme, Vulkanausbrüche und Tsunamis – auf einmal zugeschlagen, gewuchtet und geschoben. Architekten spielen in gewagter Selbstüberschätzung mit dem Feuer, sie ahmen Gott nach – sie sind, wie Daniel Libeskind es einmal formulierte, »zweimal Gott!«. Bescheidenheit wäre eine Zier, aber in Zeiten der fernsehwirksamen Marktschreier haben ruhigere, zweifelnde Zeitgenossen kaum eine Chance, wie überhaupt gesagt werden muß, daß die Architektur keinen Raum für zimperlich-zögernde Menschen mit mangelndem Selbstbewußtsein bietet. Immer noch gelten schicke Autos, blonde, junge Frauen, modisch-schwarze Anzüge und dicke Zigarren als Statussymbol. Die Revolutionen der Hippies, Müslis und selbstgestrickten, grünen Pullover haben in diesen Bereichen kaum Nachhall gefunden. Auffallend ist jedoch der große Ernst, mit dem in der Architekturszene argumentiert wird. Jedes Statement trifft uns gewichtig und bibelschwer; Humor und Ironie scheinen nicht als Waffen geeignet. Um so erstaunlicher scheint es deshalb, daß eine amerikanische Architektur-Kunst-Gruppe mit fröhlich-ironischen Entwürfen einige Jahre lang großen Erfolg hatte. Ich spreche vom Büro SITE, das in den 80er Jahren vor allem mit Entwürfen für die Kaufhauskette BEST weltberühmt wurde.

Die Inspirationsquelle der Entwerfer fand sich in der attrappenhaften Bauweise der amerikanischen Städte. Jeder Tornado hat mit diesen lausigen Hütten und Kaufhäusern, die so tun als wären sie solide aus Stein, Beton und Stahl gebaut, ein leichtes Spiel. Bei den SITE-Bauten hingen Fassaden quer und schräg über dem Eingang, da wurden Hausecken aus ihrem Verband herausgerissen, Glashäuser schoben sich verquer aus den Fassaden, Parkplätze wuchsen über Kaufhallendächer, Betonautos und falsche Automaten standen auf den wertvollen Verkehrsflächen, ganz so, als wären die Entwerfer bei ihrer Arbeit betrunken gewesen (3-Promille-Gags, Jahrmarktsattraktionen, Faschingskulissenzauber), oder als hätten sich vor kurzem kleine Naturkatastrophen ereignet. Jetzt benutzen wir die liebenswerten Ruinen wie Geschenke, gehen lächelnd in die Supermärkte zum Einkaufen und sind dankbar für die kleinen Störungen im langweiligen Städteeinerlei des amerikanischen Alltags.

the block, closing the street, closing the square. … Complexity is our goal. Architecture as it was defined in the 19th century is outdated. We have to come to a complexity that mirrors the diversity of the planet's society. … It is only possible to create interwoven spatial systems by getting rid of ambient pressure. In order to attain complexity in architecture one must get rid of a number of things: First of all, one must get rid of architectural, historical laws; second, one must stop thinking about the clients; third, one must stop thinking too much about the money one earns; and last of all, one must stop thinking about the cost.«

Rem Koolhaas circles the opening up and (ruinous) disintegration even more explicitly: »More important than designing cities, today and in the near future, is planning their disintegration. It is only by the revolutionary process of erasure, the setting up of »zones of freedom«, in which all laws of architecture are annulled, that we will do away with one of the insoluble problems of urban life: the tension between program and content … The project for Amsterdam, but even more so those for La Villette and the Expo are attempts to formulate the quality of nothingness as the heart of the metropolis. Emptiness in the metropolis is not speechless; rather, every vacuum within an existing urban structure can be used for the programs that make possible interesting, contemporary activities … The permanence that is inherent in even the most frivolous architecture and the instability of the metropolis are incompatible. …«

These are diffuse statements that, while they sound aggressive and revolutionary, in reality leave almost all possibilities – with the possible exception of historicist ones – open. While the reflections of architects during the postmodern period before 1980 were still quite a bit more harmless, more enamored of history, more humane and playful, a new tone arose now. It is hard to say whether it had more to do with destruction and less with reconstruction. At any rate the motto of the architects' group Coop-Himmelb(l)au at the beginning of their career was: »Architecture must burn!« It appears as though a new generation of architects wanted to respond to the prior brutalities of modern urban development with aggression on their part. It would definitely be an exaggeration to call this a »war«, but potential for a fight can hardly be ignored. Why emptiness, excess pressure and chaos must be countered in kind, according to the biblical motto »An eye for an eye, a tooth for a tooth« is unclear, to say the least. In any case the result will be tattered, half-destroyed buildings and dynamic functional ruins. James Stirling in the famous Stuttgart Staatsgalerie was still content with a harmless little ruin joke: In the lower-floor window a few blocks of stone seem to have been broken out – they lie loosely scattered on the narrow lawn in front of it. In Gehry's work the earthquakes are already more powerful; the parts of the building of the Guggenheim Museum in Bilbao seem to have been whirled around, as if all the forces of nature – earthquakes, storms, volcanic eruptions and tsunamis – had all struck, heaved and shoved at the same time. Architects play with fire in daring overestimation of their own abilities, they act like God – as Daniel Libeskind once put it, they are »God times two!«. Modesty would be becoming, but in an era of successful TV market criers quieter, more hesitant, doubting contemporaries barely have a chance; in any case, I need to say that architecture is not a field for oversensitive, hesitant people who lack self-esteem. Elegant cars, blond, young women, modishly black suits and fat cigars are still considered to be status symbols. The revolutions of the hippies, muesli and handmade green pullovers hardly resonated in these circles. What is striking, however, is how seriously people carry on arguments in architectural circles. Every statement hits home, heavy as a *bible*; we don't even consider humor and irony to be appropriate weapons. Therefore it seems all the more astonishing that for several years an American arts and architecture group enjoyed great success with its merry, ironic designs. I mean the firm SITE, which in the '80s became world famous especially with its designs for BEST Products Company.

The designers were inspired by the faux-façade construction style of American towns. Tornados have an easy time of it demolishing these lousy shacks and stores that act as though they were solidly built of stone, concrete and steel. In the SITE buildings façades hung at right angles and diagonally over the entrance, house corners were torn out of their masonry bond, glass houses projected askew from façades, parking lots grew above the roofs of supermarkets, cars made of concrete and faux automats stood in the valuable traffic areas, just as though the designers had been drunk on the job (bibulous gags, state fair attractions, carnival tricks), or as though there had recently been minor natural disasters. Now we regard the lovable ruins as gifts, go into the supermarkets with a smile to do our shopping and are grateful for the small disruptions in the boring urban monotony of American day-to-day existence.

In Germany and Europe there was nothing comparable, if we don't count a number of temporary architectural productions of the Viennese arts and architecture groups »Haus-Rucker-Co«, »Zündap« or »Coop-Himmelb(l)au«. Only the gigantic picture frame of »Haus-Rucker-Co« in

In Deutschland und Europa gab es kaum Vergleichbares, wenn man von manchen temporären Architekturinszenierungen der Wiener Architektur-Kunst-Gruppen »Haus-Rucker- Co«, »Zündap« oder »Coop-Himmelb(l)au« absieht. Nur der riesige Bilderrahmen von »Haus-Rucker-Co« in Kassel – einst entstanden zu einer »documenta«– hat überlebt. Ansonsten sind die deutschen Innenstädte übersät mit kläglichen, uninspirierten, humor- und geistlosen »Kunst-am-Bau-Ruinen«. Überflüssige Objekte, die das Trostlose unserer Plätze und Fußgängerzonen meist noch verstärken und betonen. Moderne Bilderstürmer wären hier gefragt. Es gäbe genügend zu tun. Aber niemand interessiert sich dafür. So bleiben die Objekte einzig im Blickfeld verirrter Plakatkleber, marodierender Sprayer und streunender Hunde.

Dauerhafte künstliche Ruinen gibt es nur in den neuen Stadtparks von Saarbrücken und Biberach an der Riß. Peter Latz rekonstruierte eine fiktive, römische Ruine in seinem zwischen 1979 und 1989 entstandenen Stadtpark »Hafeninsel Saarbrücken«. Ich selbst konnte eine künstliche Ruine zwischen 1995 und 2000 im Biberacher »Wieland-Park« realisieren. Allerdings verzichtete ich bei diesem Bau auf konkrete historische Anspielungen. Der Hausrest verhält sich zeitlich neutral. Nur das Motiv selbst versteht sich als Zitat aus romantischen (und nachromantischen) Zeiten.

Den Wiener Künstler Arnulf Rainer könnte man als einen professionellen »Auslöscher« bezeichnen, der sich zwischen alle Fronten und Disziplinen begeben hat. Seit Jahrzehnten benutzt er eigene und fremde Photos (leider keine bestehenden Architekturen und Fassaden), um sie teilweise oder vollständig zu übermalen. Am Ende beherrschen seine energischen Schraffuren und Schwärzungen die Bildfläche. Nur noch an den Rändern sind Spuren und Reste der einstigen Bilder zu erkennen. Früher zerstörte er mit seinen Kritzeleien auch die Gemälde berühmter Maler (oder deren Reproduktionen). Im Grunde ist sein Ansatz vandalistisch, vielleicht sogar aggressiv-kriegerisch, ähnlich den Werken anarchistischer Großstadtsprayer. Zuviel Kunstgeschichte macht eben wütend.

In einem Gespräch, das die Schriftstellerin Brigitte Schwaiger 1979 mit dem Künstler führte und das 1980 unter dem Titel *Arnulf Rainer. Malstunde* im Rowohlt Verlag erschien, bestätigt Arnulf Rainer meine Vermutung: »Es ist nur so:«, sagt er und fährt fort »Ich kann am besten arbeiten, wenn ich verärgert bin und einen Zorn hab. Je mehr Ärger und Zorn ich hab, umso mehr Wut kratz ich zusammen, und da kann ich hinhauen, und um so besser kann ich das Duell mit Pinsel und Bürste gegen das Bild führen, kann ich das Bild besiegen, erledigen. Verstehen Sie? Aber leider hat man ja nicht immer die Zorneskraft.«

Mich interessiert der Vorgang, weil er etwas von der wütenden Frustration eines am Ende-in-der-Reihe-Stehenden vermittelt. Er, der allerletzte, hat eigentlich keine Chance mehr und kann sich nur noch mit terroristischen Ausdrucksmitteln zur Wehr setzen. Arnulf Rainers Zumalungen wirken unter diesem Aspekt wie ein Aufschrei an sein Publikum: Starrt nicht immer auf das tausendste Renaissancegemälde, auf diese *Mona Lisa*, auf diesen Rembrandt oder jenen Rubens, verstellt die Welt nicht mit Abbildern der Welt, schaut hierher, an den Anfang! Ich nehme meinen ganzen Mut und Haß zusammen, male die bedeutendsten Bilder der Kunstgeschichte einfach zu, verurteile sie zum Schweigen. Sie sollen von nun an stumm sein, sich mit einem Platz im Archiv des Unsichtbaren zufriedengeben. Ab heute gilt mein – Arnulf Rainers – Prinzip. Mag sein, daß diese neue Schicht nur ein vorübergehender Kommentar ist, vielleicht jedoch liegt in ihr und ihrer

Kassel – once created for a »documenta« exhibition – has survived. Other than that, German inner cities are strewn with pathetic, uninspired, humorless and unimaginative »art-in-public-spaces ruins«. Superfluous objects that generally even reinforce and emphasize the dreariness of our squares and pedestrian zones. We need modern iconoclasts. There would be plenty to do. But nobody is interested. Thus the only ones that pay attention to the objects are straggling guys who put up posters, marauding graffiti artists and stray dogs.

The only places where there are permanent artificial ruins are the new city parks of Saarbrücken and Biberach an der Riss. Peter Latz reconstructed a fake Roman ruin in his urban park »Hafeninsel Saarbrücken«, developed between 1979 and 1989. I myself was able to create an artificial ruin between 1995 and 2000 in the »Wieland Park« of Biberach. However, I used no concrete historical allusions in this structure. The house remnant is chronologically neutral. Only the motif itself serves as a quotation from romantic (and postromantic) times.

The Viennese artist Arnulf Rainer could be called a professional »extinguisher« who has taken up his position between all the camps and disciplines. For decades he has been using his own and other people's photographs (though unfortunately no existing architectural objects and façades), overpainting them in part or in toto. At the end his energetic cross-hatching and blackening dominates the surface of the picture. Traces and remnants of the former pictures are only recognizable at the edges. At one time he also used to destroy the paintings of famous artists (or reproductions thereof) with his scrawls. Basically his approach is »vandalistic«, maybe even »aggressive and belligerent«, like the works of anarchist graffiti artists in large cities. Obviously too much art history is infuriating.

In a conversation that writer Brigitte Schwaiger had with the artist in 1979, published in 1980 under the title *Arnulf Rainer. Malstunde* by Rowohlt-Verlag, Arnulf Rainer confirms my suspicion: »That's just the way it is«, he says and continues, »I do my best work when I'm annoyed and furious. The more annoyed and furious I am, the more rage I scrape together, and then I can hit hard, and the better I can fight the duel against the picture with my brush, defeat the picture,

117, 118. Künstliche Ruinen der amerikanischen Architektengruppe SITE, die sie für die Kaufhauskette BEST entwarfen und realisierten. Katastrophenandeutungen als reklamewirksame Blickfänge.

117, 118. Artificial ruins by the American group of architects SITE, designed for Best stores. Hints of disaster, effectively catching the eye as advertising.

Ruinenhaftigkeit auch eine tiefere Wahrheit und eine neue Form der Schönheit. Moses gegen Aron. Diese Wahrheit könnte vom alttestamentarischen Gesetz: »Du sollst dir kein Bild machen!« abstammen. Wir, die Kinder Arons, tanzen süchtig-berauscht um das flimmernde »Goldene Kalb«, das heute ausschließlich aus Abbildern der Welt besteht.

Thomas Mann schrieb in *Doktor Faustus* folgende Textpassage, in der die ständige Jagd nach Schönheit der Bilder in Frage gestellt wird: »Doch das ist Vorspiegelung. Nie ist ein Werk so hervorgegangen. Es ist ja Arbeit, Kunstarbeit zum Zweck des Scheins – und nun fragt es sich, ob bei dem heutigen Stande des Bewußtseins, unserer Erkenntnis, unseres Wahrheitssinnes dieses Spiel noch erlaubt, geistig noch möglich, noch ernstzunehmen ist, ob das Werk als solches, das selbstgenügsam und harmonisch in sich geschlossene Gebilde, noch in irgendeiner legitimen Relation steht zu der völligen Unsicherheit, Problematik und Harmonielosigkeit unserer gesellschaftlichen Zustände, ob nicht aller Schein, auch der schönste, und gerade der schönste, heute zur Lüge geworden ist.«

Arnulf Rainers Bilder der Übermalung relativieren diese potentiellen Lügen, schaffen durch ihre Doppelbödigkeit ein irritierendes Klima des »Vielleicht … es könnte auch anders sein«. Jede Behauptung wird sofort zurückgenommen. Jedes Bild stellt sich vor ein anderes, verdeckt und zerstört es. Die Ruine liegt nahe und der Tod auch.

Viele österreichische Schriftsteller liebten die Nachtseiten des Lebens, die dunkle Melancholie, das Scheitern, die Lebensruinen und den tragischen Tod. Wir denken an Adalbert Stifter und seinen makabren Selbstmord mit einem Rasiermesser in Linz, an das Ende Joseph Roths im Pariser Exil, an Konrad Bayers Selbstmord in Wien und Ingeborg Bachmanns rätselhaftes Ende in Rom. Wir denken an Karl Kraus und sein Monumentalstück *Die letzten Tage der Menschheit*.

Auch in Elias Canettis Roman *Die Blendung* geht eine Welt unter, allerdings nur die des schrulligen Gelehrten Peter Kien, der am Ende seine letzte Zufluchtsstätte, die auch sein Ausgangsraum war, in Brand steckt. Der Schlußabsatz des Romans paßt gut in unseren Zusammenhang: »Von den Regalen stürzen sich Bücher zu Boden. Er fängt sie mit langen Armen auf, sehr leise, damit man ihn von außen nicht höre, trägt er Stoß um Stoß in den Vorraum hinüber. An der eisernen Tür schichtet er sie hoch. Und noch während der wüste Lärm sein Hirn zerfetzt, baut er aus Büchern eine mächtige Schanze. Der Vorraum füllt sich mit Bänden und Bänden. Er holt sich die Leiter zu Hilfe. Bald hat er die Decke erreicht. Er kehrt in sein Zimmer zurück. Regale gähnen ihn an. Vor dem Schreibtisch der Teppich brennt lichterloh. Er geht in die Kammer neben der Küche und schleppt die alten Zeitungen sämtlich heraus. Er blättert sie auf und zerknüllt sie, ballt sie und wirft sie in alle Ecken. Er stellt die Leiter in die Mitte des Zimmers, wo sie früher stand. Er steigt auf die sechste Stufe, bewacht das Feuer und wartet. Als ihn die Flammen endlich erreichen, lacht er so laut, wie er in seinem Leben nie gelacht hat.«

Von 1920 bis zu seinem Tod 1942 im Schweizer Exil arbeitete Robert Musil, der Maschinenbauingenieur und promovierte Philosoph, an seinem Hauptwerk *Der Mann ohne Eigenschaften*. Doch am Ende blieb es unvollendet und ist bis heute mit seinen über 1600 Seiten das größte Fragment der modernen Literatur. Ulrich, der Held des Romans, versucht sich in verschiedenen Berufen, denkt im Laufe des Lebens immer wieder ausführlich über seine Zeit und die Welt nach. Aber seine Suche nach der »Ordnung des Ganzen« scheitert, muß scheitern. »Kein Ding, kein Ich, keine Form, kein Grundsatz sind sicher, alles ist in einer unsichtbaren, aber niemals ruhenden Wandlung begriffen, im Unfesten liegt mehr von der Zukunft als im Festen, und die Gegenwart ist nichts als eine Hypothese, über die man noch nicht hinausgekommen ist.«

In der Nachkriegszeit entstand Ingeborg Bachmanns *Todesarten*-Projekt, das, obwohl auch unvollendet und damit fragmentarisch, inzwischen in vier Bänden herausgekommen ist. Ich zitiere einen Abschnitt aus der »Arbeitsphase 1962/63, Todesangst-Entwürfe«: »Eines Nachts träumte er, daß er sich durch ein enges Fenster zwänge und hinausspringe, er träumte also. Er stürzte hinunter, vielleicht sieben oder acht Stockwerke, und schlug auf. Das Entsetzliche beim Aufschlagen war, daß er so genau spürte, wie das Blut ihm durch die Nasenlöcher schoß, durch die Augäpfel drängte, es drängte richtig durch die Augäpfel an allen Rändern ringsum, es quoll, gestockt, mit dicken Brocken, wie Blut bei Schlächtereien, durch seinen Mund, es riß ihm die Haut durch an den Handgelenken, und das Blut stürzte auch da heraus, es zischte, es sprang ins Freie, und er, obwohl alles Blut herauswollte aus ihm, er war doch im Begriff, dran zu ersticken, an diesem hellen, schießenden Blut, an den Brocken Blut, dem gestockten Blut, das er durch seinen Mund erbrach. Es hatte ihm geträumt, daß er aus dem Fenster gesprungen war.«

Thomas Bernhard war zweifellos der bedeutendste dieser Untergangsfanatiker aus Österreich. In einer atemlosen Sprache, die wie ein Sturzbach über den Leser oder Hörer hereinbricht, beschreibt dieser Misanthrop, nicht zuletzt durch eigene Krankheitserlebnisse ausgelöst, das Schei-

119. Arnulf Rainer, aus der Serie *Female*, 1976.

119. Arnulf Rainer, from the *Female* series, 1976.

finish it off. D'you understand? But unfortunately one doesn't always have the energy of anger.«

I am interested in the process because it conveys some of the fierce frustration of a man who stands at the end of a line. He, the very last in the line, actually doesn't stand a chance and can only defend himself with terrorist means of expression. Looked at from this perspective Arnulf Rainer's overpaintings feel like an outcry addressed to his public: Don't keep staring at the thousandth Renaissance painting, at this Mona Lisa, at this Rembrandt or that Rubens, don't obstruct the world with representations of the world, look here, look at the beginning! I muster up all my courage and hatred, simply paint over the most important pictures in art history, condemn them to silence. From now on they must be mute, content themselves with a place in the archive of the invisible. As of today my principle – the principle of Arnulf Rainer – is in effect. Maybe this new layer is only a passing commentary, but perhaps there is a deeper truth and a new form of beauty in it and its ruinlike manifestation. Moses against Aaron. This truth could be derived from the Old Testament law »You shall not make for yourself an idol!«. We, the children of Aaron, dance crazed and intoxicated around the shimmering »golden calf«, which today consists exclusively of images of the world.

In *Doctor Faustus* Thomas Mann wrote the following passage, in which the constant hunt for beauty of images is called into question: »But that is only a pretense. No work has ever come into being that way. It is indeed work, artistic labor for the purpose of illusion – and now the question arises whether, given the current state of our consciousness, our comprehension, and our sense of truth, the game is still permissible, can still be taken seriously; whether the work as such, as a self-sufficient and harmonically self-contained structure, still stands in a legitimate relation to our problematical social condition, with its total insecurity and lack of harmony; whether all illusion, even the most beautiful, and especially the most beautiful, has not become a lie today.« [Thomas Mann, *Doctor Faustus*, trans. John E. Woods (New York, 1997)]

Arnulf Rainer's overpainted pictures put these potential lies into perspective. By their ambiguity they create a confusing climate of »Maybe … it could be different, too«. Every assertion is immediately revoked. Every image stands in front of another, conceals and destroys it. There is a suggestion of ruin and death.

Many Austrian writers loved the night sides of life, dark melancholy, failure, ruined lives and tragic death. We think of Adalbert Stifter and his macabre suicide with a razor in Linz, of Joseph Roth's death in Parisian exile, Konrad Bayer's suicide in Vienna and Ingeborg Bachmann's mysterious end in Rome. We think of Karl Kraus and his monumental play *Die letzten Tage der Menschheit* (*The Last Days of Mankind*).

In Elias Canetti's novel *Die Blendung* (*Auto-da Fé*) a world is also destroyed, though only that of the excentric scholar Peter Kien, who at the end sets his last refuge, which was also the place from which he had started, on fire. The final paragraph of the novel fits our discussion perfectly: »From the shelves, books crash to the floor. He catches them with his long arms, very quietly, so that he cannot be heard from the outside, he carries them stack by stack into the anteroom. By the iron door he makes a pile of them. And while the wild noise still shreds his brain, he builds a mighty redoubt out of books. The anteroom is filled with volumes upon volumes. He needs the ladder. Soon he has reached the ceiling. He returns to his room. Shelves yawn at him. In front of the desk, the carpet is ablaze. He goes into the pantry off the kitchen and schleps out all the old newspapers. He opens them, crumples them into balls and tosses them into all the corners. He places the ladder in the middle of the room where it stood before. He climbs up on the sixth step, guards the fire and waits. When the flames finally reach him, he laughs louder than he has ever laughed in his life.«

From 1920 until his death in 1942 in Swiss exile Robert Musil, the mechanical engineer and PhD in philosophy, worked on his principal work, *Der Mann ohne Eigenschaften* (*The Man without Qualities*). Yet the work remained unfinished and with its more than 1,600 pages is still the largest fragment in modern literature to date. Ulrich, the novel's main protagonist, tries his hand at various professions, and during his lifetime keeps thinking in great detail about his life and the world. But his search for the »order of the whole« fails, is doomed to fail. »No thing, no I, no form, no principle is certain, it is all in the process of invisible but never ceasing transformation; there is more of the future in the unstable than in the stable, and the present is nothing but a hypothesis that no one has gotten past yet.«

It was in the postwar period that Ingeborg Bachmann created her »*Todesarten* project«, which, although also unfinished and thus fragmentary, has meanwhile been published in four volumes. I quote a section from »Work phase 1962/63, Todesangst-Entwürfe (drafts for Mortal Fear)«: »One

tern von Künstlern, wie er selber einer ist. Es gibt für ihn nur ein Ziel: den Tod. Der Weg dorthin ist gepflastert mit Qualen und Schmerzen. Merkwürdigerweise mischt sich in seine fast barocke Prosa, wahrscheinlich durch die permanenten Übertreibungen, ein skurriler Humor, den man in diesen depressiven Bereichen nicht erwartet hätte. Der Bernhardsche Galgenhumor treibt die unendlichen Sprachkapriolen und Satzwürmer manchmal in die Nähe von Rossinis heiterer Musikmaschine. Bei beiden Künstlern hetzen und jagen sich Klänge und Worte, als gälte es eine Wette oder wilde Jagd zu gewinnen. Dabei ist eine fast verzweifelte Selbstironie nicht zu überhören.

In seinem autobiographischen Bericht *Der Atem* schreibt Thomas Bernhard über die Krankheit als Inspirationsquelle des Künstlers: »Der Künstler, insbesondere der Schriftsteller, hatte ich von ihm gehört, sei geradezu verpflichtet, von Zeit zu Zeit ein Krankenhaus aufzusuchen, gleich, ob dieses Krankenhaus nun ein Krankenhaus sei oder ein Gefängnis oder ein Kloster. Es sei das eine unbedingte Voraussetzung. Der Künstler, insbesondere der Schriftsteller, der nicht von Zeit zu Zeit ein Krankenhaus aufsuche, also einen solchen lebensentscheidenden existenznotwendigen Denkbezirk aufsuche, verliere sich mit der Zeit in die Wertlosigkeit, weil er sich in der Oberflächlichkeit verheddere. Dieses Krankenhaus, so mein Großvater, kann ein künstlich geschaffenes Krankenhaus sein, und die Krankheit oder die Krankheiten, die diesen Krankenhausaufenthalt ermöglichen, können durchaus künstliche Krankheiten sein, aber sie müssen da sein oder müssen erzeugt und müssen immer unter allen Umständen in gewissen Abständen erzeugt werden.«

Thomas Bernhards letzter 1986 veröffentlichter Roman trägt den Titel: *Auslöschung*! Natürlich sind moderne Ruinen- und Untergangstexte nicht auf Österreich beschränkt, sie wurden und werden auf der ganzen Welt verfaßt. An erster Stelle steht Samuel Beckett mit seinen Theaterstücken *Warten auf Godot* und *Endspiel*. Außerdem gehören Jean-Paul Sartres *Ekel* und *Der Fremde* von Albert Camus in diesen Themenkreis. Auch die berühmten Selbstmörder und -innen aus dem Literaturbereich dürfen nicht unerwähnt bleiben: Virginia Woolf füllte ihre Manteltaschen mit Steinen und ging ins Wasser, Walter Benjamin nahm Morphium an der Pyrenäengrenze nach Spanien, Ernest Hemingway erschoß sich mit seinem Jagdgewehr, Paul Celan schluckte Schlaftabletten und ertränkte sich in der Seine, Sylvia Plath steckte ihren Kopf in den Gasherd, Uwe Johnson trank sich zu Tode …

Samuel Becketts Roman *Molloy* endet übrigens mit den folgenden Sätzen: »Soll das bedeuten, daß ich jetzt freier bin? Ich weiß es nicht. Es wird sich zeigen. Dann ging ich in das Haus zurück und schrieb: ›Es ist Mitternacht. Der Regen peitscht gegen die Scheiben.‹
Es war nicht Mitternacht. Es regnete nicht.«

Samuel Becketts berühmtes Theaterstück *Warten auf Godot* endet ähnlich witzig: »»Wladimir: Also? Gehen wir? Estragon: Gehen wir!‹ Sie gehen nicht von der Stelle.«

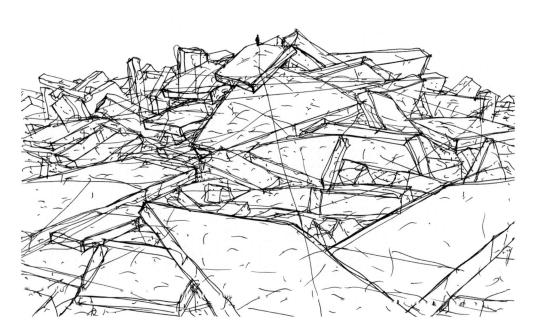

120. Hans Dieter Schaal, Zeichnung zum Thema Ruinenlandschaft, als Hommage an Caspar David Friedrich, 2009.

120. Hans Dieter Schaal, Drawing on the subject of Ruin Landscape, as a tribute to Caspar David Friedrich, 2009.

night he dreamed that he squeezed through a narrow window and jumped out – so, he was dreaming. He fell, maybe seven or eight floors down, and struck the ground. The most dreadful thing about the impact was that he felt so accurately how the blood shot through his nostrils, forced its way through his eyeballs, it actually forced its way through the eyeballs, the rims all around them, it poured, thickened, with large clots, like blood in butcher's shops, through his mouth, it tore apart the skin on his wrists, and the blood came rushing out there as well, it hissed, it leapt into the open, and he – although all the blood wanted to get out of him – he was about to be suffocated by it, by this bright, shooting blood, by the clots of blood, the thickened blood he vomited through his mouth. He had dreamed that he had jumped out the window.«

Thomas Bernhard was without doubt the most important of these fanatics of destruction from Austria. In breathless language that gushes over the reader or listener like a torrent, this misanthropist – a condition triggered by his own experiences while ill, if nothing else – describes the failure of artists such as himself. For him there is only one goal: death. The way to it is paved with torment and pain. Oddly enough, a bizarre sense of humor that one might not have expected in these depressed surroundings is intermingled in his almost baroque prose, probably because of the constant exaggerations. Bernhard's gallows humor with its endless linguistic capers and wormlike sentences sometimes comes close to Rossini's cheery music machine. In the work of both artists, sounds and words chase each other as though they had to win a wager or a wild chase. It is impossible to miss an almost desperate note of self-mockery here.

In his autobiographical report *Der Atem* (*The Breath*) Thomas Bernhard writes about disease as the artist's source of inspiration: »An artist, and especially a writer, I had heard him say, was virtually obliged to go to a hospital from time to time, regardless whether this hospital was a hospital or a prison or a monastery. This, he said, was an unconditional requirement. An artist, and especially a writer who from time to time did not go to a hospital, a crucial realm of thought necessary for existence, would gradually get lost in worthlessness, because he would get entangled in superficiality. This hospital, said my grandfather, can be an artificially created hospital, and the disease or diseases that make the hospital stay possible can be totally artificial diseases, but they have to be there or be produced and must always under all circumstances be produced at certain intervals …«

Thomas Bernhard's last novel, published in 1986, is entitled *Auslöschung* (*Extinction*)! Naturally modern texts about ruins and destruction are not limited to Austria – they have been and are being written all over the world. First and foremost there is Samuel Beckett with his plays *Waiting for Godot* and *Endgame*. Jean-Paul Sartre's *Nausea* and *The Stranger* of Albert Camus also deal with this topic. We must also not forget to mention the famous literary suicides: Virginia Woolf filled her overcoat pockets with stones and walked into the water, Walter Benjamin took morphine near the Franco-Spanish border in the Pyrenees, Ernest Hemingway shot himself with his hunting rifle, Paul Celan swallowed sleeping pills and drowned himself in the River Seine, Sylvia Plath died with her head in the oven, Uwe Johnson drank himself to death ….

Incidentally, Samuel Beckett's novel *Molloy* ends with the following sentences: »…Does this mean that I'm freer now than I was? I do not know. I shall learn. Then I went back into the house and wrote: ›It is midnight. The rain is beating on the windows.‹ It was not midnight. It was not raining.« (Samuel Beckett, *Molloy*, *Malone Dies*, *The Unnamable*, New York, 1997)

Samuel Beckett's famous play *Waiting for Godot* ends on a similar humorous note: »›Vladimir: Well? Shall we go? Estragon: Yes, let's go.‹ They do not move.« [Samuel Beckett, *Waiting for Godot* (New York, 1954)]

19. Ruinen, Fragmente, Untergänge, Katastrophen und Apokalypsen als Weltanschauung

Schriftgelehrte, Priester, Pfarrer, Philosophen, Historiker und einfache Leser denken seit Jahrhunderten über die wahre Interpretation der rätselhaften apokalyptischen Offenbarungsvisionen des Johannes nach. Ihr grandioser Bilderreichtum hat stets auch diejenigen fasziniert, die außerhalb der Kirche stehen, natürlich auch wegen der berühmten Holzschnitte Albrecht Dürers, der Darstellungen des Jüngsten Gerichts von Hieronymus Bosch, Michelangelo und James Ensor. Manche Kritiker hielten diese Bibeltexte für Fälschungen, andere, wie Martin Luther etwa, lehnten sie als zu fremdartig und unverständlich ab. Viele Künstler, Maler, Zeichner, Schriftsteller und Komponisten jedoch waren davon fasziniert. In der Dichtung und Literatur gibt es unzählige Anspielungen, Zitate und direkte Bezüge auf die »Apokalypse«, sie reichen von mittelalterlichen Bildbeschreibungen bis zu Karl Kraus, der sein sarkastisches Drama *Die letzten Tage der Menschheit* als ironisch-satirische k.-und-k.-Apokalypse verstand und schrieb:

»Lasse stehen die Zeit! Sonne, vollende du!
Mache das Ende groß! Künde die Ewigkeit!
Recke dich drohend auf, Donner dröhne dein Licht,
daß unser schallender Tod verstummt!«

D. H. Lawrence, Albert Camus, Samuel Beckett, Gabriel Garcia Marquez, Kurt Vonnegut, Thomas Pynchon, Doris Lessing, E. M. Cioran, Hans Magnus Enzensberger, Günter Kunert, Heiner Müller, Friedrich Dürrenmatt, Anthony Burgess und Cormac McCarthy griffen ebenfalls apokalyptische Untergangsthemen auf. Günter Grass sang ihr hohes Lied in seinem Roman *Die Rättin*: »Wahrlich, ihr seid nicht mehr! höre ich sie verkünden. Wie einst der tote Christus vom Weltgebäude herab, spricht weithallend die Rättin vom Müllberge: Nichts spräche von euch, gäbe es uns nicht. Was vom Menschengeschlecht geblieben, zählen wir zum Gedächtnis auf. Vom Müll befallen, breiten sich Ebenen, strändelang Müll, Täler, in denen der Müll sich staut. Synthetische Masse wandert in Flocken, Tuben, die ihren Ketchup vergaßen, verrotten nicht …«

Die biblischen Texte des Johannes haben viele Interpreten gefunden: nüchtern historisch-philologische, religionsphilosophische, theologische, esoterische und politisch-eschatologische (etwa Ernst Bloch in seinem Hauptwerk *Das Prinzip Hoffnung*). Die rätselhaften Visionen können als Beschreibungen eines real bevorstehenden Weltuntergangs interpretiert werden oder als Katastrophendrohungen, die Ungläubige erschrecken und auf den »richtigen Weg« bringen sollen.

Allein die Vorstellung, daß die Welt sich uns im Grunde nur als verschlossene Oberfläche zeigt und ihr wahres Wesen, ihren inneren Funktionsaufbau verschweigt, ist befremdlich, beängstigend und bedrohlich. Wir leben, ohne das Leben zu verstehen. Wir sterben, ohne zu wissen, was der Tod ist. Immer stehen wir vor einer Wand, einem geschlossenen Vorhang. Im Moment der Wahrheit wird – nach der Beschreibung des Johannes – das letzte, verhüllende Himmelstuch heruntergerissen, und geblendet stehen wir vor einem neuen, noch viel größeren Rätsel, einer Rätselinvasion. Das kosmisch-epochal-finale Theater entpuppt sich als ernüchternder, todbringender Striptease: Reiter und Sterne stürzen herab, Licht kämpft mit Finsternis, Gott mit dem Satan, das Gute mit dem Bösen. Wir verstehen genauso wenig wie zuvor. Was bleibt ist eine Ahnung: Die letzte Wahrheit könnte fürchterlich sein, eine Katastrophe, ein »Jüngstes Gericht«.

Schon früh erkannte Gott, der biblische Schöpfer, daß sein Werk – vor allem das Menschengeschlecht – unvollkommen ist. Deswegen werden in der *Bibel* immer wieder Weltuntergänge beschrieben, die allerdings kurz vor dem endgültigen Kollaps abgebrochen werden. Der erste Untergang findet kurz nach den Schöpfungstagen statt, die Gott zu vorschnell jeden Abend mit, »... und es war sehr gut so!« kommentierte: die Sintflut. Weder das erste Menschenpaar noch die nachfolgenden menschlichen Geschöpfe verhielten sich folgsam und gottesfürchtig. Bereits im Paradies kommt es zum sündig-prometheischen Ungehorsam, es folgen Vertreibung, Neid und Totschlag. Die Programmierung der neuen, angeblich vernunftbegabten Wesen stimmte nicht. Das Böse überstimmte das Gute. Gott dachte betrübt an die Zerstörung seiner entarteten Schöpfung und sagte: »Ich will den Menschen, den ich erschaffen habe, vom Erdboden vertilgen, mit ihm auch das Vieh, die Kriechtiere und die Vögel des Himmels, denn es reut mich, sie gemacht zu haben.«

Nur der 600jährige Noah mit seiner Familie und einzelne Tierpaare, die er in seinem Schiff aufnehmen sollte, waren zum Überleben bestimmt. »Mach dir eine Arche aus Zypressenholz! Statte

19. Ruins, fragments, scenes of destruction, catastrophes and apocalypses as a Weltanschauung

For centuries biblical scholars, priests and ministers, philosophers, historians and simple readers have been puzzling over the true interpretation of the enigmatic apocalyptic visions in the Revelation to John. Its superb wealth of imagery has also always fascinated those who are outside the Church, naturally partly because of the famous woodcuts of Albrecht Dürer, and the representations of the Last Judgment of Hieronymus Bosch, Michelangelo and James Ensor. Some critics considered these biblical texts to be forgeries, others – such as Martin Luther – rejected them, feeling they were too strange and incomprehensible. Many artists, painters, writers and composers, however, were drawn to them. In literature there are countless allusions, quotations and direct references to the »Apocalypse«; they range from medieval descriptions to Karl Kraus, who regarded his sarcastic drama *The Last Days of Mankind* as an ironic, satirical apocalypse of the Austro-Hungarian Empire and wrote:

> »Let time stand still! Sun, come to an end!
> Make the end great! Herald eternity!
> Rear your meancing head, thunder roar your light,
> That our resounding death may fall silent!«

D. H. Lawrence, Albert Camus, Samuel Beckett, Gabriel Garcia Marquez, Kurt Vonnegut, Thomas Pynchon, Doris Lessing, E. M. Cioran, Hans Magnus Enzensberger, Günter Kunert, Heiner Müller, Friedrich Dürrenmatt, Anthony Burgess and Cormac McCarthy also addressed themes of apocalyptic destruction. Günter Grass celebrated them in his novel *The Rat*: »Yea, verily, ye have ceased to be! I hear her proclaim. As resoundingly as the dead Christ speaking from the top of the world, the She-rat speaks from atop the garbage mountain: If it were not for us, nothing would bear witness to you humans. It's we who inventory what the human race has left behind. Vast plains infested with garbage, beaches strewn with garbage, valleys clogged with garbage. Synthetic flakes on the move. Tubes that have forgotten their ketchup and never rot …« [Günter Grass, *The Rat*, trans. Ralph Manheim (New York, 1987)]

The biblical texts of John have found many interpreters: soberly historical-philological, religious-philosophical, theological, esoteric and political-eschatological (for instance, Ernst Bloch in his major work *The Principle of Hope*). The enigmatic visions may be interpreted as descriptions of a real, imminent end of the world or as threats of catastrophes meant to frighten unbelievers and to lead them back on the »right path«.

The idea alone that the world basically reveals itself to us only as a closed surface and withholds its true essence, its inner functional structure, is disconcerting, alarming and threatening. We live without understanding life. We die without knowing what death is. We are always confronted with a wall, a closed curtain. At the moment of truth – according to John's description – the final, concealing cloth of heaven is torn away, and we stand blinded in the face of a new, even greater mystery, an invasion of mysteries. The cosmic, epochal, final theater turns out to be a sobering, deadly striptease: Horsemen and stars fall to the earth, light battles against darkness, God against Satan, good against evil. We understand no more than we did before. What remains is a foreboding: The ultimate truth might be terrible, a catastrophe, a »Last Judgment«.

Back at the very beginning God, the biblical creator, realized that his work – particularly the human race – was imperfect. That is why in the *Bible* the end of the world recurs over and over again, though it is always aborted just before the final collapse. The first end of the world takes place just after the days of creation, which God too rashly judged to be »very good« every evening: It is the flood in Genesis. Neither the first human couple, nor the human creatures who succeeded them, were obedient or godfearing. Even in Paradise there is sinful, Promethean disobedience followed by expulsion, envy and homicide. There was something wrong with the programming of the new, supposedly rational creatures. Evil overruled good. Saddened, God thought he would destroy his degenerate creation and said: »I will blot out man whom I have created from the face of the ground, man and beast and creeping things and birds of the air, for I am sorry that I have made them.«

Only 600-year-old Noah with his family and individual pairs of animals whom he was to bring with him in his ship were intended to survive. »Make yourself an ark of cedarwood! Make rooms in the ark and cover it inside and outside with pitch,« was the divine command. Then it rained for 40

sie mit Kammern aus und dichte sie innen und außen mit Pech ab,« so lautete der göttliche Befehl. Dann regnete es 40 Tage und Nächte lang. »Am siebzehnten Tag des siebten Monats setzte die Arche am Gebirge Ararat auf. Das Wasser nahm immer mehr ab …« Die Bewohner der Arche konnten die Erde aufs neue bevölkern. Das Ende der Welt war demnach kein wirkliches Ende. Aber der zweite Versuch mißlang genauso wie der erste.

In der dunklen Höhle von Patmos, in der Johannes während der Jahre seiner Verbannung gelebt haben soll und in der die Visionen wahrscheinlich entstanden sind, ist eine Stelle an der Felswand mit einer vergoldeten Mulde markiert. Vielleicht hat er dort auf die Bilder gewartet, die ihm schließlich durch das Gehirn geflackert sind. »Dann sah ich: Das Lamm öffnete das erste der sieben Siegel; und ich hörte das erste der vier Lebewesen wie mit Donnerstimme rufen: Komm! Da sah ich ein weißes Pferd; und der, der auf ihm saß, hatte einen Bogen. Ein Kranz wurde ihm gegeben und als Sieger zog er aus, um zu siegen. «

Nach diesen harmlosen, wenn auch dunklen Sätzen steigern sich die nachfolgenden Beschreibungen der Bilder ins Katastrophenhafte: »Und ich sah: Das Lamm öffnete das sechste Siegel. Da entstand ein gewaltiges Beben. Die Sonne wurde schwarz wie ein Trauergewand und der ganze Mond wurde wie Blut. Die Sterne des Himmels fielen herab auf die Erde, wie wenn ein Feigenbaum seine Früchte abwirft, wenn ein heftiger Sturm ihn schüttelt. Der Himmel verschwand wie eine Buchrolle, die man zusammenrollt, und alle Berge und Inseln wurden von ihrer Stelle weggerückt.«

Dann erscheinen sieben Engel und blasen in ihre Posaunen: »Der erste Engel blies seine Posaune. Da fielen Hagel und Feuer, die mit Blut verschmiert waren, auf das Land. Es verbrannte ein Drittel des Landes, ein Drittel der Bäume und alles grüne Gras. Der zweite Engel blies seine Posaune. Da wurde etwas, das einem großen brennenden Berg glich, ins Meer geworfen. Ein Drittel des Meeres wurde zu Blut. Und ein Drittel der Geschöpfe, die im Meer leben, kam um und ein Drittel der Schiffe wurde vernichtet. Der dritte Engel blies seine Posaune. Da fiel ein großer Stern vom Himmel; er loderte wie eine Fackel und fiel auf ein Drittel der Flüsse und der Quellen …«

Es folgen die Beschreibungen der menschlichen Qualen durch Heuschreckenschwärme und Angriffe von feuerspeienden Pferden mit Löwenköpfen; der Untergang der großen Hure Babylon wird prophezeit und das Jüngste Gericht verkündet. Wir sehen: Johannes, der Dichter der Bedrohung und des Untergangs, spart nicht mit infernalisch-poetischen Katastrophenbildern. Allerdings fällt auf, daß er immer nur ein Drittel der Erde, der Tiere und der Menschen auslöschen will. Zweidrittel jeder Spezies sollen, nach seiner – oder Gottes – Vorstellung, überleben. Warum nur?

Wahrscheinlich will er das abschließende Ende, die Rückkehr zum anfänglichen Chaos nicht wirklich. Die Schöpfung birgt zwar heftige Mängel, aber Gott plädiert dafür, nach Aussage des Johannes, das Projekt – zumindest für die Rechtgläubigen – doch weiterzuführen. Damals, zu biblischen Zeiten, waren Kriege noch kleine regionale Ereignisse. Erdbeben, Vulkanausbrüche, Tsunamis und Überschwemmungen konnten weit verheerendere Folgen haben. Die von Johannes beschriebenen, apokalyptischen Vorgänge erinnern eher an kosmische Katastrophen, wie etwa Meteoriteneinschläge. Man beobachtete den Tag- und Nachthimmel genau und suchte ständig nach höheren Zeichen. Schließlich waren schon die heiligen drei Könige durch einen leuchtenden Meteoritenschweif auf die Geburt des »Messias« aufmerksam geworden.

Heute nehmen Naturwissenschaftler an, daß ein Asteroid mit zwölf Kilometern Durchmesser vor über 60 Millionen Jahren die Erdoberfläche – wahrscheinlich in der Gegend von Ostmexiko – getroffen und mit der Gewalt seines Einschlags die Energie von einer Milliarde »Hiroshima-Bomben« freigesetzt hat. Die globalen Folgen der Katastrophe bestanden in einer Serie von Vulkanausbrüchen und gewaltigen Tsunamiwellen, außerdem verfinsterten die ausgestoßenen Staubpartikel die Atmosphäre zehn Jahre lang. Dadurch sank die Welttemperatur schlagartig, Pflanzen verkümmerten. Tiere, die sich von ihnen ernährten, verhungerten und starben aus. Die berühmtesten Opfer waren die Saurier.

Auch im 21. Jahrhundert könnte ein Weltende so aussehen: Ein mondgroßer Meteorit schlägt mit voller Wucht in unseren Planeten ein, läßt ihn explodieren und in tausend Stücke zerbersten. Die alten Horrorszenarien in der *Bibel* besitzen demnach noch immer – auch für die Ungläubigen – einen real-bedrohlichen Wahrheitskern. Seitdem hat sich die Zivilisation weiterentwickelt, mit ihr die Kriegs- und Zerstörungstechniken. Auf Speere, Pfeil und Bogen, folgten das Schwarzpulver und die Gewehre, danach das Dynamit, die Maschinengewehre, Kanonen, Torpedos, Panzer, Raketen und Bombenflugzeuge. Die kämpfenden Menschen wurden immer mehr zu Bedienern von todbringenden Maschinen. Selbst Meteoriten, die auf die Erde zu stürzen drohten, ließen sich – bei rechtzeitiger Entdeckung – mit Laser-Kanonen zerstören. Was früher die visionären Gefahrenbeschreibungen der *Bibel* leisteten, haben inzwischen Hollywoodfilme und

121. Albrecht Dürer, *Apokalypse*, woodcut series dating from 1498. St. John the Divine swallows the book of Revelation, which he is receiving from heaven. All around the world is collapsing and flames leap out of falling columns.

days and nights. »And the ark rested in the seventh month, on the seventeenth day of the month, upon the mountains of Ararat. And the waters decreased continually …« The inhabitants of the ark could populate the earth once more. Accordingly the end of the world was not a real end. But the second experiment was just as unsuccessful as the first.

In the dark cave of Patmos in which John is supposed to have lived during the years of his banishment, when the visions probably came into being, one spot in the rock wall is marked with a gilded hollow. Perhaps it was there when he waited for the images that finally flickered through his brain. »Now I saw when the Lamb opened one of the seven seals, and I heard one of the four living creatures say, as with a voice of thunder: Come! And I saw a white horse; and its rider had a bow; and a crown was given to him, and he went out conquering and to conquer …«

After these harmless though obscure sentences the subsequent descriptions of the visions become catastrophic: »When he opened the sixth seal, I looked, and there was a great earthquake; and the sun became black as sackcloth, the full moon became like blood, and the stars

Computerspiele übernommen. Digital animiert, explodieren nicht mehr nur Menschen, Häuser, Landschaften, Berge und Städte, sondern auch Raumstationen, Planeten und ganze Universen. Nichts ist mehr unvorstellbar. Das Weltende wurde in allen Variationen durchgespielt, und die Beschreibungen des Johannes sind nur zu einer Facette im Bilderbuch der Weltuntergänge geworden.

Vielleicht stellt die Entdeckung der Uranspaltung am 17. Dezember 1938 durch Otto Hahn, Fritz Straßmann und Lise Meitner (in Abwesenheit, sie mußte die Versuchsanordnung verlassen und als verfolgte Jüdin nach Schweden fliehen) in Berlin so etwas wie eine moderne Offenbarung dar. Bekanntlich führte die Erkenntnis der Kernspaltung zur Entwicklung von Atomwaffen, Atomkraftwerken und damit zur realistischen Möglichkeit, unseren Heimatplaneten, ohne Asteroidenangriff, in die Luft zu sprengen. Hätte der Zweite Weltkrieg noch länger gedauert und wären auch in Europa Atomwaffen eingesetzt worden, gäbe es Deutschland heute vielleicht nicht mehr. Statt dessen würde eine menschen- und tierleere, für Jahrtausende kontaminierte Wüste an seiner Stelle die restliche Menschheit von einem Besuch des einst so schönen Landes abschrecken.

Wie wir heute wissen, befanden wir uns vor allem in der Phase des Kalten Krieges, zwischen 1950 und 1965, mehrmals am Rande einer finalen Weltkatastrophe. Amerikanische und sowjetische Bombenentwickler steigerten das Erdvernichtungspotential jedes Jahr um ein Vielfaches. Einen düsteren Höhepunkt markiert die Versuchsexplosion der größten und stärksten je gezündeten Wasserstoffbombe im Jahr 1961, die der sowjetische Physiker Andrej Dmitrijewitsch Sacharow, getrieben von dem machtbesessenen Nikita Chrustschow, der sich in einem »Zweikampf« mit John F. Kennedy befand, entwickelt hatte. Man nannte sie die »Zar-Bombe«, warum auch immer. Sie enthielt eine Sprengkraft von 50 bis 60 Megatonnen und war damit tausendmal stärker als alle Bomben des Zweiten Weltkriegs zusammen. Hundert dieser Bomben hätten ausgereicht, die Erde endgültig zu vernichten. Jahre später weigerte sich Sacharow, ähnlich wie zuvor sein amerikanischer Gegenspieler Robert Oppenheimer, weiter an dem Projekt mitzuarbeiten. Er wurde zum Friedensaktivisten und Vorkämpfer der russischen Demokratisierung. 1975 war ihm der Friedensnobelpreis zugesprochen worden, allerdings konnte er ihn nicht persönlich entgegennehmen, da ihm die sowjetische Regierung die Ausreise verweigerte. Viele Jahre hatte er in der Verbannung leben müssen, erst Michael Gorbatschow holte ihn nach Moskau zurück.

Seit 60 Jahren müssen alle Zivilisationen der Erde mit dem Bewußtsein leben, daß sie jederzeit durch gezielte oder unkontrollierte Atombombenexplosionen ausgelöscht werden können. Sechs der sieben Siegel der Apokalypse scheinen endgültig geöffnet worden zu sein, wir glauben jetzt zu wissen, was die Welt im Innersten zusammenhält, wie Universum, Materie und schwarze Löcher entstanden sind und wie die Sonne, unsere lebensspendende, aber auch tödlich gefährliche Energiequelle, arbeitet. Der Urknall ist zu unserem Bild der Schöpfung geworden. Das Universum dehnt sich aus und stürzt wahrscheinlich irgendwann, in Jahrmillionen, wieder in sich zusammen, ein neuer, zukünftiger Urknall läßt es vielleicht wieder entstehen. Das Drama der Schöpfung und der Evolution beginnt im Feuer des glühenden Sternenstaubs aufs neue, ganz so wie es uns die indischen Religionsstifter und Philosophen schon seit langem lehren. Auch Schopenhauer, Nietzsche und Wagner glaubten an die ewige Wiederkehr. Die Zeit ein Kreis, der Raum eine Kugel.

Im Chaos davor und danach bildet alles eine Einheit: Menschen, Himmel, Erde, Tiere, Wolken, Gedanken, Wasser und Steine, Tag und Nacht. Erst mit der Schöpfung wurden die Elemente voneinander getrennt und das Chaos zum Kosmos umgeformt. In dem vagen Bewußtsein dieser letztlich unvorstellbaren Horizonte erscheint unser Leben mit seinen großen und kleinen Katastrophen, seinen Erinnerungsruinen, Glücksmomenten und Krankheiten wie ein kümmerlicher Funken, unerheblich für den Gesamtablauf. Selbst die neuesten Unglücke, die Erdbeben, Attentate, Müllinvasionen, Energie-, Öl- und Finanzkrisen wirken in diesem Zusammenhang lächerlich und harmlos. Trotzdem können wir nicht immer in die Unendlichkeit des Himmels hinaufschauen, auf den Absturz der Sonne warten (wie manche weltuntergangsverliebten Sektenführer), sondern müssen uns mit den Alltagsproblemen auseinandersetzen, müssen Geld verdienen, einkaufen, Müll entsorgen, uns um die Kinder, Alten und Armen kümmern, gegen die lügengetränkte Ignoranz mancher Bankberater (und Politiker) ankämpfen, wie jene Rentner-Gang, die in der *Süddeutschen Zeitung* am Dienstag, dem 9. Februar 2010, auf der Titelseite beschrieben wurde: »Traunstein – Weil sie einen Finanzberater entführt hat, steht eine fünfköpfige Senioren-Gang seit Montag vor dem Landgericht in Traunstein. Den Angeklagten im Alter zwischen 60 und 79 Jahren wird vorgeworfen, den 56jährigen im Juni entführt und einige Tage im Chiemgau festgehalten zu haben. Der Mann soll die Rentner um mehrere Millionen Euro gebracht haben.«

In Frankreich, berichteten die Zeitungen, sei es zu ähnlichen Fällen von Selbstjustiz gekommen. Dennoch ist die Anzahl der Vorfälle erstaunlich gering, wenn man bedenkt, wie viele Mon

of the sky fell to the earth as the fig tree sheds its winter fruit when shaken by a gale; the sky vanished like a scroll that is rolled up, and every mountain and island was removed from its place.«

Then seven angels appeared and blew their trumpets: »The first angel blew his trumpet, and there followed hail and fire, mixed with blood, which fell on the earth; and a third of the earth was burnt up, and a third of the trees were burnt up, and all green grass was burnt up. The second angel blew his trumpet, and something like a great mountain, burning with fire, was thrown into the sea; and a third of the sea became blood, a third of the living creatures in the sea died, and a third of the ships were destroyed. The third angel blew his trumpet, and a great star fell from heaven, blazing like a torch, and it fell on a third of the rivers and on the fountains of water ...«

There follow descriptions of human torment caused by swarms of locusts and attacks by fire-spewing horses with lions' heads; the destruction of the great Whore of Babylon is prophesied and the Last Judgment is announced. We can see that John, the poet of threat and destruction, is lavish with images of infernal, poetic images of catastrophe. However, it is striking that he always intends to annihilate only one-third of the earth, the animals and people. Two-thirds of every species are to survive, according to his – or God's – idea. Why is that?

Probably he does not really want there to be a definitive end, a return to the initial chaos. While creation has serious flaws, God, according to John, pleads, in spite of everything, for a continuation of the project – at least for true believers. Back then, in biblical times, wars were still small regional events. Earthquakes, volcanic eruptions, tsunamis and floods could have far more devastating consequences. The apocalyptic events described by John are more reminiscent of cosmic catastrophes, such as meteorite strikes. The day and night sky were carefully observed, with astrologers constantly on the lookout for signs from above. After all, the three wise men from the East had become aware of the birth of the »messiah« as a result of the gleaming tail of a meteorite.

Today scientists assume that an asteroid with a 12-kilometer diameter struck the earth's surface over 60 million years ago – probably in the region of eastern Mexico – and unleashed the energy of a billion »Hiroshima bombs« with the force of its impact. The global consequences of the catastrophe consisted of a series of volcanic eruptions and huge tsunami waves, while the dust particles that were given off darkened the atmosphere for ten years. The temperature of the planet was abruptly lowered, and plants died. Animals that had fed on them starved and became extinct. The most famous victims were the dinosaurs.

In the 21st century, too, the end of the world might look like this: A meteorite the size of the Moon slams into our planet with all of its force, causes it to explode and burst into a thousand pieces. The old horror scenarios in the *Bible* therefore still have a very real, menacing core of truth – even for unbelievers. Since biblical times civilization has continued to develop, and with it the technologies of war and destruction. Spears, bows and arrows were followed by gunpowder and guns, then by dynamite, machine guns, cannons, torpedoes, tanks, rockets and bombers. The human beings who were fighting increasingly became operators of lethal machines. Even meteorites rushing toward the Earth – if discovered in time – could be destroyed with laser cannons. In the meantime the function of former visionary descriptions of danger in the *Bible* has been taken over by Hollywood movies and computer games. Digitally animated, space stations, planets and whole universes explode where once it was only people, houses, landscapes, mountains and cities. Nothing is unimaginable anymore. The end of the war has been played out in all its variations, and the descriptions of St. John have become just a facet in the picture book of apocalypses.

Perhaps the discovery of uranium fission on 17 December 1938 in Berlin by Otto Hahn, Fritz Straßmann and Lise Meitner (in absentia – she had to leave the experiment and flee to Sweden because she was persecuted as a Jew) represented something like a modern Revelation. As we know, the discovery of nuclear fission led to the development of nuclear weapons, nuclear power stations and thus to the realistic possibility that our home planet can be blown up without an asteroid attack. If World War II had gone on even longer and if atomic weapons had been used in Europe as well, there might not be a Germany anymore. Instead, in its place, a wasteland deserted by human beings and animals and contaminated for millennia to come would deter the rest of mankind from visiting this once so beautiful country.

As we know today, we have been on the verge of a final world catastrophe several times, particularly during the phase of the Cold War, between 1950 and 1965. American and Soviet bomb developers increased the potential of destroying the Earth many times over every year. A dismal high point is marked by the experimental detonation, in 1961, of the biggest and most powerful hydrogen bomb ever to be exploded. It was developed by the Soviet physicist Andrei Dmitrievich

schen während der aktuellen Finanzkrise ihr Vermögen verloren haben. Erinnern wir uns an das apokalyptische Spektakel, den Supergau der Finanzwelt, den sich selbst Johannes auf seiner, heute ganz vom Tourismus lebenden Insel – im kleinen Hafen ankern auch einige schneeweiße Luxusjachten – nicht hätte vorstellen können (die apokalyptischen Reiter als betrügerische Spekulanten, als geldgierige Milliardenvernichter?).

Am 15. September 2008 erklärte das Geldhaus Lehman Brothers, die viertgrößte Investmentbank der Wall Street in New York, seine Insolvenz und beantragte Gläubigerschutz. Damit trat etwas ein, was zwar viele Beobachter befürchtet und prognostiziert, aber letztlich doch für unmöglich gehalten hatten, schließlich handelte es sich bei Lehmans um eine bisher solide, über 100jährige Bank, die sogar den Crash von 1928 heil überstanden hatte. Diese Pleite zog, wie wir lesen und im Fernsehen beobachten konnten, weltweit zahlreiche andere Bankinstitute in den Untergangsstrudel und löste damit die – nach 1928 – größte Bankkatastrophe der Neuzeit aus. Manche Beobachter glaubten schon, den Hauch des Todes und des (wirtschaftlichen) Weltuntergangs zu spüren.

In Amerika verloren Tausende von Immobilienbesitzern ihre nur teilweise abbezahlten Häuser, danach auch ihre Ersparnisse und ihre Jobs. Wie global verstrickt die Geldwirtschaft inzwischen ist, zeigte sich an den nachfolgenden Bankzusammenbrüchen in der gesamten Welt. Nur durch das sofortige Eingreifen der Regierungen konnte der endgültige, damit finale (wirtschaftliche) Kollaps verhindert werden. Plötzlich nannten die Regierungschefs Geldsummen, von deren Existenz bisher niemand gewußt hatte, wobei die Frage auftauchte: Waren sie wirklich vorhanden?

Ob diese Vorgänge den Globus wirklich in seinen Grundfesten erschütterten wie neue, zeitgemäße Plagen der Apokalypse oder nur an seiner wirtschaftlichen Oberfläche kratzten, darüber gehen die Meinungen auseinander. Trotz allem bleiben ruinierte Menschen zurück, und so gesehen, kann man die Traunsteiner Rentner-Gang gut verstehen. Das Pleitebild ist und bleibt eine aktuelle Ruinenmetapher und hat sich gleichwertig neben tatsächlich zerstörte Häuser gesetzt.

Es fällt auf, daß nach der Euphorie des globalen Wirtschaftswunders, der medialen Weltrevolution und dem Zusammenbruch der kommunistischen Staaten, die Zeiten der positiven Utopien, wenn man von den ökologisch-grünen Propheten (die sich im Grunde alte, vorindustrielle Paradiese zurückwünschen) absieht, vorbei sind. Überall wird das Ende der Entwicklungen beschworen, und Weltuntergangsmodelle – beschrieben und in Bilder umgesetzt – sind in Mode gekommen, worauf auch eine Viezahl aktueller Buchtitel hindeutet, von denen einige im folgenden genannt werden:

Das Ende der Geschichte; *Das Ende der Philosophie*; *Endzeit-Architektur*; *Architektur am Ende*; *Der Crash kommt*; *Das Ende der Nationalstaaten*; *Das Ende des Individuums*; *Die Welt ohne uns*; *Der Informations-Crash*; *Das Ende der Welt, wie wir sie kannten*; *Wie aus heiterem Himmel. Naturkatastrophen und Klimawandel*; *Was zu tun ist ... Kollaps*.

Manche Autoren berauschen sich geradezu an der Vorstellung einer Welt ohne die Menschen. Alan Weismann beschreibt in seinem Bestseller *Die Welt ohne uns* eine Reise über die unbevölkerte Erde und durch menschenleere Städte: »Die Vorstellung, die Natur könnte eines Tages etwas so Gigantisches und Festgefügtes wie eine moderne Großstadt schlucken, gelingt nicht ohne weiteres. Angesichts der ungeheuren Größe von New York City, scheitern alle Bemühungen, uns das Verschwinden dieser Stadt von der Landkarte vorzustellen. Die Ereignisse vom September 2001 haben lediglich gezeigt, was Menschen mit entsprechenden Mitteln bewirken können, nicht aber, wozu natürliche Prozesse wie Erosion oder Fäulnis fähig sind. Der atemberaubend rasche Zusammenbruch der Türme des World Trade Center vermittelte uns eher einen Eindruck von den Attentätern als von der extremen Verwundbarkeit, die unsere gesamte Infrastruktur bedrohen könnte. Und selbst diese zuvor unvorstellbare Katastrophe blieb auf einige wenige Gebäude beschränkt. Trotzdem: Die Zeit, welche die Natur brauchen würde, um sich aller Errungenschaften unserer urbanen Zivilisation zu entledigen, könnte kürzer sein, als wir vermuten.«

Warum, frage ich mich, habe ich das Gefühl, daß die Ruine – als Architekturruine, Landschaftsruine, psychische Ruine, Bankrott-Ruine oder Welt-Ruine – zu einem zentralen Symbol unserer Zeit geworden ist? Vielleicht ist sie die Rückseite der Erfolgsmedaille, die Schattenzone hinter den Projekten »Aufklärung« und »Fortschritt«. Ruinen gehören wie Untergänge und Auslöschungen zur dunklen, tödlichen Seite des Lebens und der Welt. Dramaturgisch interpretiert verkörpern sie »Tragödien«, und gehören damit zu den ältesten Theaterschöpfungen der Menschheit. Lustspiele, Komödien, Schauspiele, Tragikomödien, Opern, Operetten und Musicals folgten, kulturgeschichtlich betrachtet, erst viel später.

Sakharov, driven by a power-obsessed Nikita Khrushchev, who was caught up in a duel with John F. Kennedy. It was called the »Tsar Bomb«, who knows why. It had an explosive force of 50 to 60 megatons and was thus a thousand times more powerful than all the bombs of World War II combined. A hundred of these bombs would have been enough to destroy the Earth completely. Years later Sakharov refused, as his American opponent Robert Oppenheimer had done earlier, to continue working on the project, became a peace activist and champion of Russian democratization. In 1975 he was awarded the Nobel Peace Prize, though he was unable to accept it in person since the Soviet government refused to let him travel abroad. He was forced to live in exile for many years, and only Mikhail Gorbachev brought him back to Moscow.

For the last 60 years all civilizations of the Earth have had to live with the knowledge that they could be wiped out by intentional or uncontrolled atom bomb explosions. Six of the seven seals of the Apocalypse seem to have been opened finally. We now believe we know the true essence of life, how the universe, matter and black holes came into being and how the Sun, our life-giving but also lethal source of energy, works. The big bang has become our image of creation. The universe is expanding and and will probably at some point, millions of years from now, collapse back into itself. A new, future big bang may bring it back into being again. The drama of creation and evolution will begin anew in the fire of glowing stardust, just as Indian founders of religion and philosophers have long been teaching us. Schopenhauer, Nietzsche and Wagner also believed in eternal recurrence. Time as a circle, space as a globe.

In the chaos before and after, everything forms a single whole: human beings, sky, earth, animals, clouds, thoughts, water and stones, day and night. It was only at creation that the elements were separated from each other and chaos transformed into cosmos. Vaguely aware of these unimaginable horizons, our own lives with their big and little catastrophes seem like a pitiful spark, of no significance for the overall process. Even the most recent calamities, the earthquakes, assassinations, garbage invasions, energy, oil and financial crises seem ludicrous and harmless in this context. Still, we cannot always gaze at the infinite sky, waiting for the Sun to fall (like the leaders of certain sects who are enamored of the apocalypse), but have to deal with everyday problems, earn money, go shopping, take out the garbage, look after the children, the elderly and the poor, fight the mendacious ignorance of certain financial advisers (and politicians), like the gang of senior citizens who were described in a lead article by the *Süddeutsche Zeitung* on Tuesday, 9 February 2010: »Traunstein – Because they kidnapped a financial adviser, a five-member gang of seniors has been on trial since Monday at the Traunstein district court. The accused, ranging in age from 60 to 79, are accused of having kidnapped the 56-year-old man in June and of having detained him for several days in Chiemgau. The man allegedly cheated the pensioners of several million euros.«

In France, the papers reported, there have been similar cases where people take justice into their own hands. Nevertheless the number of incidents is amazingly small considering how many people have lost their assets during the current financial crisis. Let's remember the apocalyptic spectacle, the total meltdown of the financial world that even Saint John on his island, which today lives entirely on tourism – there are even a few snow-white luxury yachts anchored in the small harbor – couldn't have imagined (the Horsemen of the Apocalypse as fraudulent speculators, as greedy annihilators of billions?).

On 15 September 2008 the financial institution Lehman Brothers, the fourth largest Wall Street investment bank, declared insolvency and filed for bankruptcy protection. It was an event many observers had feared and predicted, but in the final analysis had considered to be impossible: After all, Lehman Brothers were a hundred-year-old bank that had hitherto been sound, and had even survived the crash of 1928 in good shape. As we could read and observe on TV, this bankruptcy dragged many other banking institutions all over the world into the maelstrom of ruin and thus triggered the greatest – since 1928 – bank catastrophe of modern times. Some observers already believed they could feel a whiff of death and of a (financial) apocalypse.

In America thousands of homeowners lost their mortgaged homes, and subsequently their savings and jobs. The subsequent collapses of banks all over the world showed how globally entangled the money economy has become in the meantime. Only the immediate intervention of the governments was able to prevent the final (economic) collapse. Suddenly heads of government were mentioning sums of money whose existence no one had suspected until then (and people wondered whether the sums really existed).

Opinions differ as to whether these happenings really shook the planet to the core like new, contemporary plagues of the Apocalypse, or only scratched its economic surface. In either case ruined people have been left in their wake, and looking at things from the perspective of the vic-

Noch immer gilt die These von Aristoteles, der behauptete, daß es für die Zuschauer gut und wichtig sei, Tragödien anzuschauen. Durch den dabei empfundenen Schauder träte die berühmte »Katharsis«, eine seelische Reinigung, in Aktion (Ruinen und Tragödien als mentale und psychische Waschanlagen?). Anschließend, nachdem sie die (fiktiven) Qualen und das (fiktive) Sterben des Helden – frei nach dem Grundsatz »Quäle deinen Helden!« – miterlebt haben, würde sich bei den Zuschauern das Daseinsgefühl intensivieren und die Erkenntnis einstellen, daß der einzelne ein lebendiger Teil des umfassenden, geordneten Kosmos sei. Jede vorhandene Hybris würde zerfallen und am unerbittlichen Schicksal, das durch Götter oder Gene vorbestimmt ist, abprallen. Es gibt keine wirkliche Freiheit – so die Erkenntnis –, und die Natur bestimmt uns, ob wir es wollen oder nicht. Niemand entrinnt seinem Körper, seinem Geist, seinem Schicksal, niemand seinem Tod.

Friedrich Hölderlin dichtete in *Hyperions Schicksalslied*:

»Doch uns ist gegeben,
Auf keiner Stätte zu ruhn,
Es schwinden, es fallen
Die leidenden Menschen
Blindlings von einer
Stunde zur andern,
Wie Wasser von Klippe
Zu Klippe geworfen,
Jahr lang ins Ungewisse hinab.«

tims, we can understand only too well the pensioners' gang in Traunstein. The image of bankruptcy continues to be a topical metaphor of ruin, an image as powerful as actually demolished houses.

It is striking that after the euphoria of the global financial boom, the worldwide media revolution and the collapse of Communist states, the days of positive utopias – apart from the ecologically green prophets (who basically wish they were back in a preindustrial paradise) – are over. Everywhere the end of developments is conjured up, and apocalyptic models – described in books and animated in pictures – have become fashionable. This is also evident when we look at a host of current book titles:

The End of History; The End of Philosophy; End Time Architecture; Architecture at the End; The Crash Is Underway; The End of the Nation States; The End of the Individual; The World without Us; The Information Crash; The End of the World as We Knew It; Like a Bolt from the Blue. Natural Catastrophes and Climate Change; Hot, Flat and Crowded.

Some authors are almost intoxicated by the idea of a world without human beings. In his bestseller *The World without Us* Alan Weismann describes a journey across an unpopulated Earth and through deserted cities: »The notion that someday nature could swallow whole something so colossal and concrete as a modern city doesn't slide easily into our imaginations. The sheer titanic presence of a New York City resists efforts to picture it wasting away. The events of September 2001 showed only what human beings with explosive hardware can do, not crude processes like erosion or rot. The breathtaking, swift collapse of the World Trade Center towers suggested more to us about their attackers than about mortal vulnerabilities that could doom our entire infrastructure. And even that once-inconceivable calamity was confined to just a few buildings. Nevertheless, the time it would take nature to rid itself of what urbanity has wrought may be less than we might expect.« [Alan Weisman, *The World without Us* (New York: St. Martin's Press, 2007)]

Why, I wonder, do I have the feeling that the ruin – in the form of an architectural ruin, landscape ruin, psychic ruin, bankruptcy ruin or world ruin – has become a central symbol of our times? Perhaps it is the reverse side of the medal of success, the zone of shadows behind the projects »enlightenment« and »progress«. Ruins, like scenes of destruction and extinction, belong to the dark, lethal side of life and of the world. Interpreted by a dramaturg they embody »tragedies«, and are thus the oldest theatrical creations of humankind. Farces, comedies, dramas, tragicomedies, operas, operettas and musicals follow much later in cultural history.

Aristotle's thesis still holds true: He claimed that it was good and important for spectators to watch tragedies. The shudder of dread they feel, he believed, caused the famous »catharsis«, psychic cleansing (ruins and tragedies as mental and psychological laundries?). Subsequently, after they had shared the experience of the antagonist's (fictitious) torment and (fictitious) death – along the lines of »Torture your hero!« – the spectators' sense of being alive would be intensified and they would realize that the individual was a living part of the all-encompassing, ordered cosmos. Any hybris that existed in them would disintegrate and have no effect on a relentless fate, predetermined by gods or genes. They would realize that there is no real freedom, and that nature has us in its firm grasp, whether we like it or not. No one escapes his body, his mind, his fate, and none escapes his death.

Friedrich Hölderlin wrote the following in »Hyperion's Song of Fate«:

»But on us it has been laid
Never to rest in any place;
Suffering human beings
Dwindle and fall
Headlong from one
Hour to the next,
Hurled like water
From precipice to precipice,
Down through the years into uncertainty.«
[*The Penguin Book of German Verse*, introd., ed. and trans. by Leonard Foster (Baltimore, 1957)]

122. Hans Dieter Schaal, Gekippte Bunkerruinen in schwarzer Aschelandschaft, 2009.

122. Hans Dieter Schaal, Tilting bunker ruins in a landscape of black ash, 2009.

Today we do not always need to take the detour via theater, literature, opera, the graphic arts or cinema in order to be deeply shaken: Newspapers and TV programs supply enough news of catastrophes daily to set in motion psychic cleansing in any of us. Every time we hear the news – un-

Heute brauchen wir nicht immer den Umweg über das Theater, die Literatur, die Oper, die bildende Kunst oder das Kino zu machen, um seelisch aufgewühlt zu werden, Zeitungen und Fernsehprogramme liefern uns jeden Tag genügend Nachrichten von Katastrophen, um die seelische Reinigung des einzelnen zu aktivieren. Bei jeder Nachricht empfinden wir – sofern uns die Masse der Meldungen nicht zu boshaften Zynikern gemacht hat – die archaischen Schauder- und Schauerwellen, die Aristoteles prognostiziert hat.

Wir haben überlebt, wir liegen nicht zerschmettert am Boden, wir wurden nicht verschüttet von Betondecken oder Lawinen, wir stürzten nicht ab, wir ertranken nicht, wir wurden nicht überfahren oder von Maschinengewehrsalven und Bomben getroffen, wir können im warmen Zimmer weiter essen, uns zurücklehnen, Mitleid empfinden oder die nächste Reise planen. Immer bleiben wir, die Zuschauer der künstlichen oder echten Ruinentragödien, die entscheidenden Empfangsstationen. In unseren Augen und Seelen spiegelt sich die Welt. So gesehen gelten auch heute noch die melodramatischen Vanitas-Sätze des französischen Philosophen und Schriftstellers Denis Diderot, die er im 18. Jahrhundert über den Ruinenmaler Hubert Robert geschrieben hat: »Wir betrachten die Reste eines Triumphbogens, einer Säulenhalle, einer Pyramide, eines Tempels, eines Palastes, und wir kommen auf uns selbst zurück. Wir ahnen voraus die Verheerungen der Zeit und unsere Vorstellung verstreut auf der Erde die Gebäude, die wir selbst bewohnen … Die Ideen, die Ruinen in mir wecken, sind groß. Alles wird zunichte gemacht, alles verfällt, alles vergeht. Allein die Erde bleibt übrig. Allein die Zeit dauert an. Wie die Welt doch alt ist!«

Während vor meinen Augen das apokalyptische Feuerwerk der grausam-schönen Bilder explodiert und abbrennt, die Hure Babylon endgültig am Horizont dem Feuer zum Opfer fällt, die Reiter und Engel des Johannes ihre tödlichen Bewegungen ausführen, schwenkt mein Blick über den unendlich großen Friedhof, den man in unserer Erdkugel auch sehen kann, dazu höre ich als pathetische Filmmusik »Siegfrieds Tod« aus Richard Wagners *Götterdämmerung*, danach die Requien von Wolfgang Amadeus Mozart, Franz Schubert, Giacomo Rossini, Giuseppe Verdi, Giacomo Puccini und Antonin Dvorak.

Zum Schluß erklingen die stampfenden Bluesgesänge von B. B. King und Fadolieder aus Lissabon. Traurig-melancholische Melodien, die von Gefühlsruinen, Zerfall, Verlust und von der Unmöglichkeit handeln, das Glück auf Dauer halten zu können.

123. Ein vom Fernsehen übertragenes Feuerwerk. Apokalypse als ästhetisch-unterhaltsames Ereignis.

123. Fireworks shown on television. Apocalypse as aesthetic entertainment.

less the myriad news reports have turned us into vicious cynics – we shudder with awe and dread as Aristotle predicted.

We have survived, we are not crushed, we have not been buried under concrete ceilings or avalanches, we have not fallen to our death, we did not drown, we were not run over or hit by machine guns volleys and bombs, we can finish our meal in a warm room, lean back, feel compassion or plan the next trip. We are the receivers, the spectators of artificial or genuine tragedies, of ruin. The world is mirrored in our eyes and souls. And thus the melodramatic passage about vanitas that the 18th century French philosopher and writer Denis Diderot wrote about Hubert Robert, the painter of ruins, is still true: »We contemplate the remains of a triumphal arch, a columned hall, a pyramid, a temple, a palace, and we return to ourselves. We have forebodings about the ravages of time and our imagination scatters on the earth the buildings we inhabit ourselves … The ideas that ruins awake in me are grand. Everything will go to ruin, everything will decay, everything will perish. The Earth alone remains. Time alone endures. How ancient the world is!«

While before my eyes the apocalyptic fireworks of cruelly beautiful images explode and fizzle out, while the Whore of Babylon is destroyed by fire on the horizon, and St. John's horsemen and angels go through their deadly motions, I gaze across our planet which some regard as a vast cemetery, hearing, as a dramatic soundtrack, »Siegfried's Death« from Richard Wagner's *Götterdämmerung* (*Twilight of the Gods*), followed by the requiems of Wolfgang Amadeus Mozart, Franz Schubert, Giacomo Rossini, Giuseppe Verdi, Giacomo Puccini and Antonin Dvorak.

Finally, here come the stomping blues of B. B. King and fado songs from Lisbon. Sad and melancholy melodies that speak of emotional ruins, decay and loss, which remind us that it is impossible to hold on to happiness indefinitely.

Bibliographie

Bernhard Andrae, *Laokoon und die Kunst von Pergamon*, Frankfurt am Main 1991.

Achim von Arnim und Clemens Brentano, *Des Knaben Wunderhorn – Alte deutsche Lieder*, München 1963.

Dietmar Arnold, *Die Reichskanzlei und der »Führerbunker«*, Berlin 2005.

Dieter Bartetzko, *Illusionen in Stein*, Reinbek bei Hamburg 1985.

Jürgen Becker, *Production Design: Ken Adam*, München 1994.

Samuel Beckett, *Warten auf Godot*, Fankfurt am Main 1959.

Samuel Beckett, *Das Gleiche nochmals anders*, Frankfurt am Main 2000.

Friedrich Beissner (Hrsg.), *Hölderlin. Sämtliche Werke*, 8. Bde., Stuttgart 1946–1985.

Hans Belting, *Hieronymus Bosch. Garten der Lüste*, München, Berlin, London, New York 2002.

Thomas Bernhard, *Der Atem*, Salzburg und Wien 1978.

Thomas Bernhard, *Der Untergeher*, Frankfurt am Main 1985.

Thomas Bernhard, *Die Auslöschung. Ein Zerfall*, Frankfurt am Main 1986.

Gerhard Berz, *Wie aus heiterem Himmel*, München 2010.

Hartwig Beseler und Niels Gutschow, *Kriegsschicksale Deutscher Architektur*, 2 Bde., Neumünster 1988.

Die Bibel, Einheitsübersetzung der Heiligen Schrift, Stuttgart 1980.

Christiane Borgelt und Regina Jost, *Welterbe Zollverein Essen*, Berlin 2009.

Walter Bosing, *Hieronymus Bosch (um 1450–1516) – Zwischen Himmel und Hölle*, Köln 1994.

Deena Boyer, *Die 200 Tage von Achteinhalb*, Reinbek bei Hamburg 1963.

Oksana Bulgakowa, *Leni Riefenstahl*, Berlin 1999.

René Burri, *Ein amerikanischer Traum*, Nördlingen 1986.

Albert Camus, *Die Pest*, Düsseldorf 1950.

Gertrude Cepl-Kaufmann und Hella Sabrina Lange, *Der Rhein. Ein literarischer Reiseführer*, Darmstadt 2006.

Michel Ciment, *Kubrick*, München 1980.

Emile Michel Cioran, *Die verfehlte Schöpfung*, Frankfurt am Main 1981.

Arthur Cross und Fred Tibbs, *The London Blitz*, London 1987.

Hans-Joerg Czech und Nikola Doll, *Kunst und Propaganda*, Dresden 2007.

Dante Alighieri, *Die Göttliche Komödie*, Zürich 1963.

Alexander Demandt, *Vandalismus. Gewalt gegen Kultur*, Berlin 1997.

Jared Diamond, *Kollaps. Warum Gesellschaften überleben oder untergehen*, Frankfurt am Main 2009.

Eckart Dietzfelbinger und Gerhard Liedtke, *Nürnberg – Ort der Massen*, Berlin 2004.

Alastair Dougall, *James Bond. Geheimagent 007*, München 2000.

Werner Durth und Niels Gutschow, *Träume in Trümmern*, München 1000.

Gerhard Eimer, *Caspar David Friedrich*, Frankfurt am Main 1980.

T. S. Eliot, *Gesammelte Gedichte*, Frankfurt am Main 1988.

Rolf Engelsing, *Wie Sodom und Gomorrha … Die Zerstörung der Städte*, Berlin 1979.

A. A. Evans und David Gibbons, *Der Zweite Weltkrieg*, München 2009.

Michael Foedrowitz, *Bunkerwelten*, Berlin 1998.

Gregory Fuller, *Endzeitstimmung*, Köln 1994.

Vilém Flusser, *Medienkultur*, Frankfurt am Main 1997.

Joachim Ganzert, *Der Turmbau zu Babel*, Biberach 1997.

Richard W. Gassen und Bernhard Holeczek (Hrsg.), *Apokalypse. Ein Prinzip Hoffnung?*, Heidelberg 1985.

Josef Geiß, *Obersalzberg*, Berchtesgaden 1977.

Günter Grass, *Die Rättin*, Göttingen 1993.

Gunter E. Grimm, Werner Faulstich und Peter Kuon, *Apokalypse*, Frankfurt am Main 1986.

Karoline von Günderode, *Der Schatten eines Traums*, Darmstadt und Neuwied 1979.

Günter Hartmann, *Die Ruine im Landschaftsgarten*, Worms am Rhein 1981.

Miranda Harvey, *Piranesi. The Imaginary Views*, London 1979.

Eberhard Haufe, *Deutsche Briefe aus Italien*, Leipzig 1965.

Werner Hofmann, *Caspar David Friedrich und die deutsche Nachwelt*, Frankfurt am Main 1974.

Magdalena Holzhey, *De Chirico*, Köln 2005.

Samuel P. Huntington, *Kampf der Kulturen*, Hamburg 2007.

Andreas Kasprzak, Stephen King und seine Filme, München 1996.

Keith Kittle, *The Winchester Mystery House*, San José (CA) 1997.

Evelyn Klengel-Brandt, *Der Turm von Babylon*, Leipzig 1982.

Gottfried Knapp, *Neuschwanstein*, Stuttgart und London 1999.

Karl-Adolf Knappe, *Dürer. Das graphische Werk*, Wien und München 1964.

Gerhard Köpf, *Piranesis Traum*, Hamburg und Zürich 1992.

Karl Kraus, *Die letzten Tage der Menschheit*, Frankfurt am Main 2005.

Hanspeter Krellmann, *Babel ist überall*, München 1989.

Dieter Krusche, *Reclams Filmführer*, Stuttgart 2003.

Alexander Kupfer, *Piranesis Carceri*, Stuttgart und Zürich 1992.

Lars Olof Larsson, *Albert Speer*, Brüssel 1978.

D. H. Lawrence, *Die Apokalypse*, Düsseldorf 2000.

Claus Leggewie und Harald Welzer, *Das Ende der Welt, wie wir sie kannten*, Frankfurt am Main 2009.

Rainer Lewandowski, *Die Filme von Alexander Kluge*, Hildesheim und New York 1980.

Daniel Libeskind, *Breaking Ground*, Köln 2004.

Maren Lorenz, *Vandalismus als Alltagsphänomen*, Hamburg 2009.

Nagib Machfus, *Die Midaq-Gasse*, Zürich 2007.

Michel Makarius, *Ruins*, Paris 2004.

Thomas Mann, *Tonio Kröger*, in: *Frühe Erzählungen*, Berlin 1967.

Cormac McCarthy, *Die Straße*, Reinbek bei Hamburg 2007.

Alexander Mitscherlich, *Die Unwirtlichkeit unserer Städte*, Frankfurt am Main 1966.

Hilmar Mund, *Endzeit-Architektur*, München und New York 1994.

Peter Noever, *Architektur am Ende?*, München 1993.

Novalis, *Hymnen an die Nacht*, Köln 2006.

Max Otte, *Der Crash kommt*, Berlin 2008.

Max Otte, *Der Informationscrash*, Berlin 2009.

Robert Polidori, *Sperrzonen. Pripjat and Tschernobyl*, Göttingen 2004.

Stephan Poromba und Hilmar Schmundt, *Böse Orte*, Berlin 2005.

Arnulf Rainer, *Female*, Salzburg 2009.

Peter Rautmann, *Caspar David Friedrich. Das Eismeer. Durch Tod zu neuem Leben*, Frankfurt am Main 1991.

Roland Recht, *Der Rhein. Kunstlandschaft Europas*, München 2001.

Pierre Restany und Bruno Zevi, *SITE. Architecture as Art*, London 1980.

Nelly Sachs, *Fahrt ins Staublose*, Frankfurt am Main 1961.

Rüdiger Safranski, *Romantik*, München 2007.

Rüdiger Safranski, *Goethe und Schiller*, München 2009.

Hans Sarkowicz, *Hitlers Künstler*, Frankfurt am Main und Leipzig 2004.

Wolfgang Schepers, *Hirschfelds Theorie der Gartenkunst*, Worms am Rhein 1980.

Wieland Schmied, *Giorgio de Chirico. Die beunruhigenden Musen*, Frankfurt am Main und Leipzig 1993.

Eva Schmidt und Kai Vöckler (Hrsg.) *Robert Smithson. Gesammelte Schriften*, Köln 2000.

Brigitte Schwaiger, Arnulf Rainer, *Malstunde*, Reinbek bei Hamburg 1984.

Hans-Peter Schwarz, Medien, Kunst, Geschichte, München, New York 1997.

Gerhard Schweizer, *Zeitbombe Stadt*, Stuttgart 1987.

Lee Seldes, *Das Vermächtnis Mark Rothkos*, Berlin 2008.

Deyan Sudjic, *Der Architekturkomplex. Monumente der Macht*, Düsseldorf 2006.

Teresa und Henryk Swiebocki, *Auschwitz: Residenz des Todes*, Oswiecim (Polen) 2007.

Paul Virilio, *Bunker Archeology*, New York 1994.

Paul Virilio, *Die Universität des Desasters*, Wien 2007.

Paul Virilio, *Der eigentliche Unfall*, Wien 2009.

Kai Vöckler, *Die Architektur der Abwesenheit*, Berlin 2009.

Ingo F. Walter, *Picasso*, Köln 2007.

Alan Weisman, *Die Welt ohne uns*, München und Zürich 2009.

Werner Heldt. Zeichnungen aus 25 Jahren, Hannover 1973.

Christa Wolf, *Kein Ort. Nirgends*, Darmstadt und Neuwied 1979.

Bibliography

Bernhard Andrae, *Laokoon und die Kunst von Pergamon*, Frankfurt am Main, 1991.

Achim von Arnim and Clemens Brentano, *Des Knaben Wunderhorn – Alte deutsche Lieder*, Munich, 1963.

Dietmar Arnold, *Die Reichskanzlei und der »Führerbunker«*, Berlin, 2005.

Dieter Bartetzko, *Illusionen in Stein*, Reinbek bei Hamburg, 1985.

Samuel Beckett, *Waiting for Godot*, New York, 1954.

Samuel Beckett, *Das Gleiche nochmals anders*, Frankfurt am Main, 2000.

Friedrich Beissner, *Hölderlin: Gesamtausgabe*, Stuttgart, 1961.

Hans Belting, *Hieronymus Bosch – Garten der Lüste*, Munich, Berlin, London, New York, 2002.

Thomas Bernhard, *Der Atem*, Salzburg and Vienna, 1978.

Thomas Bernhard, *Der Untergeher*, Frankfurt am Main, 1985.

Thomas Bernhard, *Die Auslöschung – ein Zerfall*, Frankfurt am Main, 1986.

Gerhard Berz, *Wie aus heiterem Himmel*, Munich, 2010.

Hartwig Beseler and Niels Gutschow, *Kriegsschicksale Deutscher Architektur*, 4 vols., Neumünster, 1988.

Christiane Borgelt and Regina Jost, *Welterbe Zollverein Essen*, Berlin, 2009.

Walter Bosing, *Hieronymus Bosch (um 1450–1516) – Between Heaven and Hell*, Cologne, 1999.

Deena Boyer, *The two hundred days of 8 1/2,* New York, 1977.

Oksana Bulgakowa, *Leni Riefenstahl*, Berlin, 1999.

René Burri, *Ein amerikanischer Traum*, Nördlingen, 1986.

Wilhelm Busch, *Max and Moritz*, New York, 1982.

Albert Camus, *The Plague*, New York, 1977.

Gertrude Cepl-Kaufmann and Hella Sabrina Lange, *Der Rhein – Ein literarischer Führer*, Darmstadt, 2006.

Michel Ciment, *Kubrick*, Munich, 1980.

Emile Michel Cioran, *Die verfehlte Schöpfung*, Frankfurt am Main, 1981.

Arthur Cross and Fred Tibbs, *The London Blitz*, London, 1987.

Hans-Joerg Czech and Nikola Doll, *Kunst und Propaganda*, Dresden, 2007.

Dante Alighieri, *Divina commedia / The Divine Comedy;* text with translation in the metre of the original by Geoffrey L. Bickerstedt, Oxford, 1972.

Alexander Demandt, *Vandalismus – Gewalt gegen Kultur*, Berlin, 1997.

Jared Diamond, *Kollaps – warum Gesellschaften überleben oder untergehen*, Frankfurt am Main, 2009.

Eckart Dietzfelbinger and Gerhard Liedtke, *Nürnberg – Ort der Massen*, Berlin, 2004.

Alastair Dougall, *James Bond, Geheimagent 007*, Munich, 2000.

Werner Durth and Niels Gutschow, *Träume in Trümmern*, Munich, 1993.

Gerhard Eimer, *Caspar David Friedrich*, Frankfurt am Main, 1980.

T. S. Eliot, *Complete Poems and Plays,* New York, 1952.

Rolf Engelsing, *Wie Sodom und Gomorrha … Die Zerstörung der Städte*, Berlin, 1979.

A. A. Evans and David Gibbons, *Der Zweite Weltkrieg*, Munich, 2009.

Michael Foedrowitz, *Bunkerwelten*, Berlin, 1998.

Leonard Foster (ed. and trans.) *The Penguin Book of German Verse*, Baltimore, 1957.

Gregory Fuller, *Endzeitstimmung*, Cologne, 1994.

Vilém Flusser, *Medienkultur*, Frankfurt am Main, 1997.

Joachim Ganzert, *Der Turmbau zu Babel*, Biberach, 1997.

Richard W. Gassen and Bernhard Holeczek, (eds.) *Apokalypse. Ein Prinzip Hoffnung*, Heidelberg, 1985.

Josef Geiß, *Obersalzberg*, Berchtesgaden, 1977.

Günter Grass, *The Rat*, New York, 1987.

Gunter E. Grimm, Werner Faulstich and Peter Kuon, *Apokalypse*, Frankfurt am Main, 1986.

Karoline von Günderode, *Der Schatten eines Traums*, Darmstadt and Neuwied, 1979.

Günter Hartmann, *Die Ruine im Landschaftsgarten*, Worms am Rhein, 1981

Miranda Harvey, *Piranesi. The Imaginary Views*, London, 1979.

Eberhard Haufe, *Deutsche Briefe aus Italien*, Leipzig, 1965.

Werner Hofmann, *Caspar David Friedrich und die deutsche Nachwelt*, Frankfurt am Main, 1974.

The Holy Bible, New York, 1989.

Magdalena Holzhey, *De Chirico*, Cologne, 2005.

Samuel P. Huntington, *The Clash of Civilizations and the Remaking of World Order*, New York, 1996.

Andreas Kasprzak, Stephen King und seine Filme, Munich, 1996.

Keith Kittle, *The Winchester Mystery House*, San José (CA), 1997.

Evelyn Klengel-Brandt, *Der Turm von Babylon*, Leipzig, 1982.

Gottfried Knapp, *Neuschwanstein*, Stuttgart and London, 1999.

Karl-Adolf Knappe, *Dürer. Das graphische Werk*, Vienna and Munich, 1964.

Gerhard Köpf, *Piranesis Traum*, Hamburg and Zurich, 1992.

Karl Kraus, *Die letzten Tage der Menschheit*, Frankfurt am Main, 2005.

Hanspeter Krellmann, *Babel ist überall*, Munich, 1989.

Dieter Krusche, *Reclams Filmführer*, Stuttgart, 2003.

Alexander Kupfer, *Piranesis Carceri*, Stuttgart and Zurich, 1992.

Lars Olof Larsson, *Albert Speer*, Bruxelles, 1978.

D. H. Lawrence, *Apocalypse*, Harmondsworth, 1974.

Claus Leggewie and Harald Welzer, *Das Ende der Welt, wie wir sie kannten*, Frankfurt am Main, 2009.

Rainer Lewandowski, *Die Filme von Alexander Kluge*, Hildesheim and New York, 1980.

Daniel Libeskind, *Breaking Ground*, Cologne, 2004.

Maren Lorenz, *Vandalismus als Alltagsphänomen*, Hamburg, 2009.

Nagib Machfus, *Die Midaq-Gasse*, Zurich, 2007.

Michel Makarius, *Ruins*, Paris, 2004.

Thomas Mann, *Tonio Kröger*, in: *Frühe Erzählungen*, Berlin, 1967.

Thomas Mann, *Death in Venice and other Stories*, New York, 1988.

Thomas Mann, *Buddenbrooks. The Decline of a Family*, New York, 1993.

Thomas Mann, *Doctor Faustus*, New York, 1997.

Cormac McCarthy, *The Road*, New York, 2009.

Alexander Mitscherlich, *Die Unwirtlichkeit unserer Städte*, Frankfurt am Main, 1966.

Hilmar Mund, *Endzeit-Architektur*, Munich and New York, 1994.

Peter Noever, *Architektur am Ende?*, Munich, 1993.

Novalis, *Hymnen an die Nacht*, Cologne, 2006.

Max Otte, *Der Crash kommt*, Berlin, 2008.

Max Otte, *Der Informationscrash*, Berlin, 2009.

Robert Polidori, *Sperrzonen. Pripjat and Tschernobyl*, Göttingen, 2004.

Stephan Poromba and Hilmar Schmundt, *Böse Orte*, Berlin, 2005.

Arnulf Rainer, *Female*, Salzburg, 2009.

Peter Rautmann, *Caspar David Friedrich. Das Eismeer. Durch Tod zu neuem Leben*, Frankfurt am Main, 1991.

Roland Recht, *Der Rhein. Kunstlandschaft Europas*, Munich, 2001.

Pierre Restany and Bruno Zevi, *SITE. Architecture as Art*, London, 1980.

Rainer Maria Rilke, *The Notebooks of Malte Laurids Brigge*, New York, 1983.

Nelly Sachs, *O the Chimneys: Selected Poems*, New York, 1968.

Rüdiger Safranski, *Romantik*, Munich, 2007.

Rüdiger Safranski, *Goethe und Schiller*, Munich, 2009.

Hans Sarkowicz, *Hitlers Künstler*, Frankfurt am Main and Leipzig, 2004.

Wolfgang Schepers, *Hirschfelds Theorie der Gartenkunst*, Worms am Rhein, 1980.

Wieland Schmied, *Giorgio de Chirico. Die beunruhigenden Musen*, Frankfurt am Main and Leipzig, 1993.

Eva Schmidt and Kai Vöckler (eds.) *Robert Smithson. Gesammelte Schriften*, Cologne, 2000.

Brigitte Schwaiger, Arnulf Rainer, *Malstunde*, Reinbek bei Hamburg, 1984.

Hans-Peter Schwarz, Medien, Kunst, Geschichte, Munich, New York, 1997.

Gerhard Schweizer, *Zeitbombe Stadt*, Stuttgart, 1987.

Lee Seldes, *The Legacy of Mark Rothko*, New York, 1996.

Deyan Sudjic, *Der Architekturkomplex. Monumente der Macht*, Düsseldorf, 2006.

Teresa and Henryk Swiebocki, *Auschwitz: Residenz des Todes*, Oswiecim (Polen), 2007.

Paul Virilio, *Bunker Archeology*, New York, 1994.

Paul Virilio, *The University of Disaster*, Malden (MA), 2007.

Paul Virilio, *The Original Accident*, Cambridge (MA), 2009.

Kai Vöckler, *Die Architektur der Abwesenheit*, Berlin, 2009.

Ingo F. Walter, *Picasso*, Cologne, 2007.

Alan Weisman, *The World without us*, New York, 2007

Werner Heldt. Zeichnungen aus 25 Jahren, Hanover, 1973.

Christa Wolf, *Kein Ort. Nirgends*, Darmstadt and Neuwied, 1979.

Bildnachweis / Photo credits

akg-images, Berlin   18.6, 47.21
Mario Amaya, *Pop as Art*, London 1965   240.108
Archiv Hans Dieter Schaal   9.1, 17.4, 19.7, 21.8,
    27.10, 37.15, 38.16, 41.17, 55.24, 58.25, 60.26,
    60.27, 61.28, 62.29, 63.30, 65.31, 100.39, 114.43,
    118.44, 119.45, 120.46, 121.47, 122.48, 122.49,
    123.50, 123.51, 127.52, 136.53, 137.54, 142.55,
    144.56, 145.57, 148.58, 148.59, 149.60, 150.61,
    151.62, 151.63, 153.64, 156.65, 161.67, 180.76,
    181.77, 182.78, 183.79, 197.80, 204.84, 209.87,
    213.88, 216.9, 222.92, 223.93, 224.94, 225.95,
    228.96, 233.101, 242.110, 243.111, 244.112,
    245.113, 246.114, 249.116
Arnulf Rainer. Female, Salzburg 2009   241.109,
    254.119
Fritz Barth   22.9
Bertha Benz Memorial Club e.V. (Reinhard Wolf)
    86.37
Bildarchiv Foto Marburg   17.5, 27.11
The Bridgeman Art Library   74.33, 75.34, 232.100,
    235.103
A. Burger, Zürich   248.115
Michel Ciment, *Kubrick*, München 1982   207.85
Arthur Cross, Fred Tibbs, *The London Blitz*, London
    1987   113.42
Deutsche Kinemathek, Berlin   165.69, 166.70,
    167.71, 175.72, 177.73
Alastair Dougall, *James Bond – Geheimagent 007*,
    München 2007   208.86
Günther Feuerstein, *Urban Space*, Stuttgart / Lon-
    don 2008   15.2
Luigi Ficacci, *Giovanni Battista Piranesi, The Com-
    plete Etchings*, Köln 2000   33.12, 34.13
Ders., *Bacon*, Köln 2006   229.98
Dennis Gilbert Cover, Neues Museum, Berlin
Peter Horn   54.23
Wolgang Jacobsen, Werner Sudendorf, *Metropolis*,
    Stuttgart / London, 2000   164.68
Stefan Koppelkamm   159.66
Robert Lebeck, 2008   239.107
Gérard Legrand, *Giorgio de Chirico*, Berlin 1976
    231.99
Bertrand Lemoine*, Cinquantenaire de l'exposition
    internationale des arts et des techniques dans
    la vie moderne*, Paris 1987   234.102
George-Louis Le Rouge, *Détail des nouveaux jar-
    dins à la mode,* Paris 1775–1790   51.22
Steve McCurry   198.81, 199.82
Hans Meyer-Veden   214.89, 214.90
Pfaueninsel, Berlin, Tübingen 1993   67.32
Piranesi, Faszination und Ausstrahlung, Leipzig 1994
    36.14
ProLitteris, Zürich   229.97
Roland Recht, *Der Rhein — Kunstlandschaft Euro-
    pas*, München 2001   81.35, 85.36
Roxanna Salceda   180.75
SITE   252.117, 253.118
Werner Heldt, *Zeichnungen aus 25 Jahren*, Aus-
    stellungskatalog, Hannover 1973   236.104,
    237.105
www.Kunstmuseumsg.ch   238.106
www.schuetzenstube-liestal.com/uploaded/images/
    1257781572_Feuerwerk   268.123